JOHN BENSON'S

A to Z

BASEBALL
PLAYER GUIDE 1994

**DIAMOND
LIBRARY**

Executive Editors: Alan Boodman and Marc Bowman
Associate Editors: Lary Bump and Bill Gray
Layout and Design: Stephen Lunsford and Brian Weaver

Library of Congress Catalog Data: Benson, John, *Baseball Player Guide A to Z 1994*
1. Baseball -- United States -- History
2. Baseball -- United States -- Records
I. Title

ISBN 1-880876-51-5

Published by Diamond Library Publishers, a division of Diamond Analytics Corporation, with offices at 196 Danbury Road and 28 Sugarloaf Drive, Wilton, Connecticut, 06897. Telephone 203-834-1231.

PRINTED IN THE UNITED STATES OF AMERICA

Cover design by Stephen Lunsford, Joe Palys and Rob Pawlak

Statistics are provided by STATS, Inc., 7366 N. Lincoln Avenue, Lincolnwood, IL 60646.
Telephone 708-676-3322.

Rotisserie League Baseball is a registered trademark of The Rotisserie League Baseball Association, Inc. For information, contact RLBA at 370 Seventh Avenue, Suite 312, New York, NY 10001.

Table of Contents

Contributing Writers:

Tony Blengino
Alan Boodman
Marc Bowman
Lary Bump
Jim Callis
Mike Cassin
Greg Gajus
Bill Gilbert
Peter Graves
Bill Gray
Bob Hazlewood
Dic Humphrey
David Luciani
Fred Matos
Steve Moyer, STATS, Inc.
Bart Pachino
John Perrotto
Steven Rubio
Ross Schaufelberger, STATS, Inc.
Dave Smith
Adam Stein
Brian Weaver

Acknowledgments

It feels a little funny to tell people, "I wrote this book," because there were so many other people who did so much of the writing. Actually, what I did was to manage a project that produced this book. The writers whose names appear on the facing page are the core of a team of which I am just one guy on the field, if you know what I mean -- fairly useless without the others.

To all of the writers, I offer a hearty "thank-you" with a special appreciation for the splendid attention to timing, by everyone. In a book of this type, the pieces must fit together in the right place at exactly the right moment, or the team can't move along. Like the daylight play at second base, the run-and-hit, and the rotation play when executed perfectly, this year's teamwork was just right. Thanks and congratulations to the writing crew.

Everyone does such an outstanding job that I have always been reluctant to single out any one writer from our team, but I think if I begin a "writer of the year" accolade in this book, all the writers will understand and appreciate and will look forward to getting similar recognition of their own in the future. This year's winner is John Perrotto, a nationally-known analyst and sportswriter for the Beaver County Times. John covers the Pirates, knows the whole National League from top to bottom, and is a master craftsman in the art of the English language. It's a real pleasure seeing your work, John.

Alan Boodman and Marc Bowman delivered their usual outstanding editorial efforts, with outstanding results. Because they always come in late in the game and get me out of trouble, I think of them as the team's co-closers. Like a good right/left tandem out of the bullpen, they complement each other nicely, with intense yet diverse talents. Both are extremely hard workers, and highly effective in what they set out to do. Thank you, Marc and Alan.

Lary Bump is a true wonder, both for his knowledge of the minor league population, and for his prolific output, year-round and especially when it's time to do this book. Lary is the 162-game player on this team, always there and always producing. My thanks and appreciation are yours, Lary. Keep up the good work.

The publishing crew, led by Stephen Lunsford and Brian Weaver, worked long hours with enthusiasm and professional excellence. Often, Steve and Brian kept me motivated by their own fine examples. Thank you, Steve, and thank you, Brian. It's been fun and rewarding to go down this road with you and reach the end successfully. The quality of your work, as reflected in this book, is self-evident. On our team, Brian and Steve are the 100-RBI guys, the ones who drive home those who bat before them. We have terrific one-two punch there in the heart of the order.

Special thanks to John Dewan of STATS, Inc. for the many helpful and light-shedding statistics. Whenever anyone asks (and sometimes before they ask) I recommend STATS as the best source for baseball information, and the fastest production of that information, and the sharpest presentation, and the most useful state-of-the-art media including their amazing on-line service. On my team, John Dewan is the number one advance scout and, of course, the team statistician.

Last but not least, a few personal notes. Bill Gray remains my top policy advisor, a true friend willing to roll up his sleeves and fix whatever's broke, on a moment's notice. On my team, Bill fulfills the roles of third base coach, director of stadium security, and vice president of baseball marketing. James Benson took on increased responsibilities this year. He has, in my opinion, a bright future in the field of baseball research and analysis. He's a smart guy and a great deal of fun. He's currently the team's financial controller and director of travel. Finally, my wife Carmelita Benson handles so many duties (always with a cheerful outlook) that it's hard to give her any job title other than General Manager. Oh, yes, I almost forgot: she's the corporate treasurer, too. Thanks for helping me through another book; we made it together.

John

INTRODUCTION

Hi. My name is John Benson, and I write about baseball. More specifically, I write annual previews of individual baseball player performance before each season starts. I also spend a lot of time, year-round, keeping my predictions up-to-date, talking to players, managers, coaches and scouts, and watching who comes and goes from the major league player population, and thinking about how my predictions can be improved by taking more into consideration.

The best source of information and insight is, of course, talking to people, baseball people -- the ones who make the decisions about who is going to play and how they are going to be used. But I'll get back to that subject. First I want to say a few words about books and references, so you can understand why this book -- the one you have in your hands now -- came into being.

THE PURPOSE OF THIS BOOK

Like most baseball writers, I have a fairly substantial reference library in my office. It's not particularly large or impressive, as a collection of books -- but it's a large enough library that I have something fairly definitive in writing about everyone who has ever played major league baseball, and many players who never reached the majors.

My focus tends to be on current information, so (when I'm not talking to people) I frequently turn to newspapers such as Baseball America, The Sporting News, and Baseball Weekly as reference sources. Also I keep a large number of lists at my fingertips, some on paper and some in computers. And speaking of computers, I also have occasion to use the STATS On Line service (a remarkable database) rather frequently. And of course I have the team media guides at my fingertips.

The more reference material I accumulated over the years, the more it struck me that there was no single book that had all of today's players between its covers. Finding a major league regular is usually easy, of course. The annual Scouting Report, for example, has excellent material covering 95% or more of the players who will have any impact in the major leagues in 1994. But the deeper you go into the player population, the more books you need, and the harder it is to find anything beyond birth dates and raw stats.

Looking at just a table of statistics for any player, of course, you can't tell if he's dead or alive, much less see if the player is injured or healthy, retired or active. Sometimes when searching for a player who had simply disappeared, it might take me half an hour to find if that player had gone to Japan, missed an entire year because of injury, retired, or simply taken a year off. And soon I learned that I was not alone in lacking information. My next step when I can't find a player after looking in every publication and database, is to call the front office of the team that last had him in their information guide, and ask, "What ever happened to Joe Bimbleman?" Usually the team media or minor league officer will know what happened, but often the answer at the other end was, "Gee, I don't know."

This book -- the one that you have in your hands now -- is my effort to get "everybody" in or near the major leagues into one book. My purpose is to have one volume at my fingertips all the time, so that I can quickly find ANY player and see immediately who he is, what he can do, and whether he is rising or falling in his career. Wanting that book for myself, I figured other people would want it too.

To make the "one book" idea reasonable to accomplish, and to make the end result something that would fit inside a briefcase without cramming, I decide to be (1) brief and (2) selective.

Being brief is easy. There are minor problems, of course, when you try to write something clever and insightful, in 50 words or less, about any established star who has already been the subject of thousands and thousands of words in print; but being brief was not the hardest part of producing this book.

WHO'S IN THIS BOOK

Being selective is quite a bit more difficult than being brief. I needed a method to choose about one third from the 5000 or so players now getting paid to play baseball and/or performing as college stars. My method was to include the following:

1. Players who were in the major leagues last year. In general, I left in the players who had retired, with a note about their retirement. There were a few exceptions, such as Nolan Ryan. I believe that anyone who is unaware that Nolan Ryan is retired could not possibly have any interest in buying or reading this book. A few obscure players who should have retired years ago, and just barely made an appearance in 1993, are deliberately omitted; but most of those players about whom you may be wondering, "Is he, or isn't he?" are in this book. Also excluded: future Hall-of-Famers George Brett, Carlton Fisk, the well-known Dale Murphy (considering the quality of his classmates at the Hall, he probably won't make it on the first try), and some guys who were in the major leagues but really shouldn't have been in 1993, like Steve Balboni (again, if you need a scouting report on Balboni, this book is probably beyond your interests.

2. Players who have been in the major leagues and might return. Last year, for example, we gave you Bob Geren and Mike Aldrete. Not many of the 1993 preseason books had Aldrete in them, but this book did. So when Aldrete emerged during spring training and people wanted to know if it was that same guy from the past, the answer was here in these pages. That's one reason for this book's existence. We also had Rich Aldrete, Mike's younger brother, in last year's book (to help avoid confusion) but this year Rich is gone.

3. Minor leaguers who are close to a major league roster. This group includes many of those Triple-A players who probably won't be in the major leagues in 1994, or ever, but are close enough to the major league depth charts that one or two serious injuries on the major league roster could elevate them. Wayne Kirby was in this group last year (near the top of the group, but still in it).

4. Minor leaguers who will probably reach the major leagues some day on the basis of their talent. We have tried to include every top prospect, every can't-miss phenom, every first round draft pick (two thirds of them reach the majors), and every minor leaguer who has been touted, publicized, recommended, or who won a prize, award, or batting title, etc.

Some players are both close to a major league roster, as in (3) above, and likely to reach the major leagues some day as in (4) above -- and these players are the best of the minor league population, at least for 1994. Many of them have major league projections, and values, for 1994.

WHO'S NOT IN THIS BOOK

Having told you who's in, now I will tell you who's not in this book. We have ruled out all the players who have no hope of ever reaching the major leagues. You would be surprised how many players fit this description, if you are not in the baseball business yourself. The minor leagues are simply jammed full of players who don't have the potential to move up. Most of them got into baseball when they were young and developing, and then they stopped developing. Why would a baseball team keep them around? Many of them can perform OK at their minor league level, and they provide a useful service by filling out the rosters of enough teams for the true prospects to play enough games against enough other players so that their skills can be developed.

There are, of course, many players not in this book, who will nonetheless reach the major leagues some day, maybe even in 1994. The reason they are not in is that they have not shown yet, to me or anyone who gives me information, enough evidence that they are probably bound for the majors. "Enough evidence" is of course a matter of opinion.

We have many players in this book, and many excluded, who are in that middle ground; they have some but not all of the tools necessary to reach the majors, for example:

- pitchers with 90 MPH fastballs and poor control, and control artists who can't throw 80; pitchers with a fastball and no breaking stuff, pitchers who need another pitch and may or may not ever find one, pitchers who need another five miles per hour on their fastball and probably won't ever find it, etc. When dealing with pitchers, we have (like most major league organizations) tended to emphasize the hard throwers, because it's easier for a hard thrower to find another pitch, than it is for a soft thrower to find a 93 MPH fastball.

- hitters who can't field and fielders who can't hit. Obviously, a star-quality hitter doesn't need a good glove, and some defensive specialists reach the major leagues before they can get a sniff off of major league pitching. Those players are exceptional, and if we think we see one (especially of the good-hit, no-field type) we included them.

PLAYER VALUES

Some baseball traditionalists using this book will be turned off when they find Rotisserie dollar values and related Rotisserie-oriented material. There is one very good reason why those dollar values are in here: people pay me to put them here.

There is a very particular type of audience that cares about my work. Obviously, some people in the business of baseball have an interest in what I have to say. I don't know the extent to which they value my observations or trust my predictions; but I do know that a few people who make baseball personnel decisions get my annual books and my monthly updates. Some of them may even call my 900 number; it's a little eerie when an unfamiliar voice asks me about a player, and I say, well, the guy hasn't drawn a walk in his last 40 plate appearances, and his minor league roommate says he never could hit a slider, and one pitcher just told me it's easy to make a guy look bad when he's so eager to swing ... and the next day, I see on the AP wire that this player got sent down or released. Sometimes I have no idea who's calling me. There are, of course, not nearly enough people in the baseball business -- even if you include the whole media horde and all the loosely affiliated types -- to support the publication of any books of the type you find in bookstores.

By far the largest audience for my work is in the baseball fan population -- but a narrow segment of that population. Most of my readers are competitors in contests to see who can pick the best players before the season starts. The so-called Rotisserie phenomenon has revolutionized the way America watches baseball, and in my opinion very much for the better. Baseball is show business, and the object of the game off-the-field is to sell tickets and video access and to maintain fan interest. Rotisserie has done more for that purpose than any development since television. And didn't the traditionalists say that television was going to ruin baseball?

But getting back to subject of dollar values, there are other good reasons why these numbers are useful. The elegant design of roster sizes and stat categories selected by Glen Waggoner and his colleagues back in 1981 are remarkably accurate measures of who's a worthwhile major leaguer and who isn't. Their methods create a population of 552 major leaguers with a positive value of $1 or more. That's 80% of the active player population at any moment. Are the other players in the major leagues really zero value or even negative impact? Probably there are, indeed, five players (most of them pitchers) on the average major league 25-man roster, who are no better than the alternatives that could be found by looking into the farm system. There are distortions of course. I am not saying that Rotisserie values are precise measures of real player value, but I am saying that these numbers are relevant (generally more relevant than real contractual salaries as a measure of worth).

On the subject of Rotisserie, I would like to say "bunk" to a couple of common misunderstandings. Too often, sitting in the press box, I hear someone speaking with an air of authority about how those damn Rotisserie people have ruined baseball, with all their home/road, grass/turf, day/night, left/right stats that now appear everywhere. Fact is: split stats and breakdowns and all those "meaningless" numbers that weren't around 20 years ago have nothing to do with Rotisserie, or any other player selection contests. Rotisserians and most other such competitions use only the simplest, widely-accepted baseball measures, namely: batting average, home runs, runs batted in, and stolen bases for hitters; and ERA, wins, saves, and opponents' on-base percentage (baserunners per inning, or BPI) for pitchers. That stuff about what a player does at home, on grass, in night games, against lefties, comes from broadcast booths, not from Rotisserie leagues.

Another false myth about Rotisserie enthusiasts is that they don't know much about baseball. Of the million or so people who annually get into some kind of contest to see who can pick the best players, there are probably a few thousand dullards (I once saw one with the word "zero" written his forehead). But what group of a million people, selected on any basis, doesn't have a few like that?

In my experience, the people who enjoy matching their knowledge against others, in any field, tend to have superior knowledge, or they would not enjoy the competition. The people who read my annual books and my monthly updates, and the people who call me on the phone, are a very knowledgeable group. There may not be a million people who care about my work, but there are many thousands of them, and their interest is intense. Very often, friends who don't really understand my work, try to make helpful suggestions for me to reach a wider audience. What they do not understand is that my work is not intended to appeal to everyone.

How many baseball fans buy books? It often amuses me to see someone trying to design a book for people who don't like books. "This is such a great book about baseball," the conversation goes, "all the people who like baseball should buy it." Well, maybe they should buy it, but if they don't buy any books, ever, they're not going to buy your book just because it's a book about something they like. When you walk into the home of someone who buys lots of baseball books, you know what you see? No, not baseball pennants and paraphernalia. You see books. Bookshelves and bookcases full of books. People who buy books about baseball like books. And many of them, well-read, intelligent people, like to compete in baseball player selection contests.

Anyway, most of the people who plan to use this book in a player selection contest (that's why most people buy it) will be using the Rotisserie standard to measure value in 1994. To those who don't like this scale, I can say only that there is no other common language. (You may, of course, buy my player valuation software and use whatever measures you like.) Other methods may yield more precise and more accurate answers about what a player is really worth, but these other methods are not widely discussed. When you speak Rotisserie, on the other hand, a million people understand you. To say a player is a $10 starting pitcher, or a $15 outfielder, or a $1 pinch hitter, or a $25 ace reliever means something, and communicates that meaning to more people than any other language could accomplish. If you are one the sabermetric types who wishes that these values gave more consideration to on base percentage, slugging average, or any other measure, my advice is that you stop complaining, stop trying to establish your own language, and start writing to the RLBA in New York (see the copyright page). If the official Rotisserie rulemakers ever change their categories, my dollar values will reflect it, and the world will then be speaking a language that you like.

To wrap up the subject of values, I should explain that my methods (all simple arithmetic, honest) are fully explained in the book Rotisserie Baseball - Playing for Blood, which is listed on the back page order form. One of the reasons I do more than one book every year (last year I did four) is that you can't keep printing the same stuff over and over without putting off your regular readers. Anyway, there is everything you might ever want to know about sources and methods in that other book. One comment I will make here, for those who don't want to buy another book, is that value is always determined within context. The 1993 season was a huge feast for major league hitters. That trend will continue in 1994, but I expect it to be somewhat diminished as the pitchers begin to catch up a little. For that reason, the same hitting stats are going to be worth a little more in 1994. You may see a few players where my 1994 projection is down a bit in every offensive category, and yet the player's value holds the same for 1994, or even goes up a dollar. That's because that hitter is expected to look better in comparison to his peers.

THE IMPORTANCE OF CONTEXT -- AND NEWS

Anyone looking at this book should be aware that it's not intended to be a self-contained volume, but to be used along with other books. If you are a baseball fan, and you want one book to get you through the season, this isn't it. That would be somewhat like choosing a dictionary as the one book to take along on vacation.

During the winter before each baseball season, I produce two books (of which this one in your hands is the smaller, less intense, and less expensive edition). My other annual book is advertised prominently in the back of this volume, so I won't say a lot about it here, except to explain briefly how the two books fit together. This book, the Baseball Player Guide, takes each player out of context and tells you about his strengths his weakness. In general, the other players on his team are not the main factors affecting my evaluation of him. The other book, The Annual, does not focus on individual players, but rather focuses on each major league job, e.g. Yankees first base. The story of Yankees first base includes many dimensions. The relative strengths and weakness of several players, including Don Mattingly, Jim Leyritz, Kevin Maas, Joe DeBerry, Don Sparks (maybe he's gone -- read my other book to find out) and Tate Seefried if we are talking about 1996. In looking at these players and the depth chart and platoon possibilities for each position on each team, there are many variables. The manager's disposition is the most important variable. But anyway, one book (this one) could be characterized as a snapshot of each player as an individual, while the other book could be described as a year-long elapsed time videotape of everyone coming and going from one position in a major league lineup.

One key point that "numbers people" often miss is that managers get to decide what a player's stats will be. Over the course of season, managers choose who will play. No one can hit a home run while sitting on the bench. Managers decide the batting order, too. The leadoff man will draw walks and scores runs. He will probably steal bases. The cleanup hitter will hit homers and produce RBI.

Any mathematical model of a player's future performance, based solely on past events as a prologue to the future, is too limited, because the past cannot tell you how a player is going to be used in the future. To use any mathematical model to get answers, you must assume that the player is going to be used the same in the future as he was in the past. And of course roles really do change.

Saves, in particular, are the most extreme example of management discretion affecting stats. People call me all the time, asking about minor league pitchers who have been getting 25 to 30 saves a year for four years, and ask me how many saves this guy will get when he arrives in the majors; and when I tell them "zero" they don't believe me. Players who hit lots of home runs in the minors will usually proceed to hit lots of home runs in the majors -- not always, but usually. You can't say "usually" about saves, however. Pitchers who get lots of saves in the high minors might get some saves in the major leagues, but probably won't. Before getting saves in the major leagues, most pitchers work for two or three years or longer as setup men, proving their worth and winning their manager's confidence. If you want one more proof that saves are entirely based on the manager's preference, picture a team that had Lee Smith, John Wetteland, Rod Beck, and Rick Aguilera all in the same bullpen. Do you think they would have gotten 160 saves among them in 1993, if they were all working for the same manager? No way.

Management discretion affects all statistics, beginning with the question of playing time (yes or no, a little or a lot), including the question of role, and ending with the questions of tactical usage in game situations. If you do not understand these management decisions, you cannot understand baseball stats as they relate to a player's ability. And if you don't look for changes in a manager's discretionary decisions about individual players, then you cannot predict accurately what a player is going to do in the coming season.

Following the news is just one method of getting information about a manager's discretionary disposition toward any player. My advice is to watch the manager does, not just listen to what he says. Sparky Anderson is notorious for announcing that can't-miss prospects (like Torey Lovullo) are not only going to play every day, but will also become stars. Anderson also likes to make promises of playing time that, if you add them all up, couldn't possibly fit into the confines of a 162-game season.

When a manager says, "Bimbleman is my ace reliever, my closer, my number one go-to guy in the pen when the game is on the line," that's a positive sign for Bimbleman's chance to get saves; but it doesn't guarantee anything. I like to keep a file of managers' announcements, to see how many of them come true, and how long they last if and when they do come true. Managers have a right to change their minds. Stat fans often forget that every manager gets 162 lineup cards each season, and he doesn't have to fill them all out before the season starts. Managers have a duty to change their minds when player performance suggests a need for a change, and sometimes they just like to experiment.

After talking to managers in person for a few years, you also begin to learn how to read them a little better. It isn't easy, because most of them are masters of being watched all the time in the dugout by opposing managers and coaches, but certainly from talking to managers extensively, you can begin to understand their choice of words and use of a metaphor within a more definitive context. You learn to discern when they are really optimistic and committed to a player, and when they're just talking a company line. Again, it isn't easy, but experience helps.

Sometimes player roles become the subject of outright deception. It is a fairly common ploy for a major league team, usually through the front office, to spread rumors during spring training that certain youngsters are making strong bids to take jobs away from certain veterans. Often these rumors include an actual announcement that the younger player is "currently winning the job" or words to that effect. And very often these announcements are nothing more than attempts to motivate the established veteran to work harder, get in shape, lose some weight, take extra batting practice or infield practice, and generally cooperate better. Whenever you hear an announcement about a change in player's role, ask yourself: why would the team make such an announcement, and who is going to react to it, and how? Consider, for example, that when a team is really planning to replace a fading veteran, they will usually want to shop that player around and see if they can get anything in trade. Telling the public that guy has just lost his job to a 23-year-old during spring training is not exactly going to enhance his trade value, so you have to wonder if such announcements really mean what they say. They are not always blowing smoke, of course. When Steve Sax lost his job as the White Sox second baseman last year, his contract was so big that he wasn't exactly prime trade bait, anyway, so telling the truth about him didn't do any harm. And there are of course real cases where major league teams say bad things about their players and then try to trade them away -- and actually wonder why there are no takers. Go figure.

Knowing a team's roster, depth chart, manager's and GM's dispositions and recent history all help you separate fact from fiction. To get a deeper discussion of each player's role, within the context of other players' abilities and the manager's preferences, I strongly recommend that you get my other book, the Rotisserie Baseball Annual 1994, and try the Benson Baseball Monthly. Or for today's news, call me at 900-773-7526; it's just $2.49/minute. Following this introduction, I am including several pages of late-breaking news that affects players' outlooks for 1994. One purpose of this inclusion is to keep this book current, but another purpose is to show what you can expect in terms of year-round updates from my monthly. Call 800-707-9090 for information (203-834-1231 from Canada).

STATISTICS

This book is not intended to provide a statistics reference manual. There are plenty of good books that cover stats far beyond my ability to add or detract, including the long-respected OFFICIAL BASEBALL REGISTER from THE SPORTING NEWS, and STATS, Inc. trio, the MAJOR LEAGUE HANDBOOK, MINOR LEAGUE HANDBOOK, and PLAYER PROFILES.

Statistics are included in this book for one simple purpose: to give you an idea what each player did last year and the year before, and what he's likely to do in the major leagues (if anything) in 1994. Sometimes this purpose leads to odd-looking or disproportionate presentations of numbers.

Taking a quick look, it appears to me that the player with the most space dedicated to statistics is Montreal prospect Rondell White. Cliff Floyd and a number of other hot rookies also get several lines of numbers, while most of the established major leaguers get only two lines (which may deliberately exclude some minor league lines from 1992 or 1993). Why? Because players like White and Floyd have appeared so many places in the last two years, and because their numbers from all those leagues and teams are necessary to give an accurate picture, we include everything from 1992 and 1993.

In the case of an established major leaguer with a clear role and a recent history in the majors, what he did in 120 minor league at bats in early 1992 simply doesn't matter much any more, so we have removed his minor league numbers while leaving his major league stats.

Many players, including everyone we expect to have a major league impact in 1994, has a Projection line, italicized to help you find the 1994 regulars while perusing these pages. In the case of players likely to appear in the major leagues this year, but not likely to have much impact (say, only 50 to

100 at bats or less, or fewer than 30 innings pitched) we generally did not include a projection. Telling you that a player is going to score six runs while driving in nine, or vice versa, doesn't accomplish any more than simply telling you that he is more of a power hitter than a speedy type, or vice versa. If you really want to see numbers for every player, no matter how small, just order my 1994 draft software which is prominently described in the back pages of this book. There are thousands and thousands of stats in that program, if you like numbers.

WORDS OF THANKS AND ADVICE

Paraphrasing the great Yogi Berra, I want to thank all my readers for making this book necessary. Gradually, more and more people have come to care what I think about baseball players, and the whole experience has taken a little getting used to.

When I went into business for myself in the late 80's, time and money became rather directly interchangeable, so I started asking higher prices for my work. Amazingly, the editors kept buying, and that phenomenon continues to this day. My 900 number was originally an idea to get people to leave me alone so I could do my work; but again it became obvious that people are willing to pay to find out what I think about this player or that player. So be it. I hired myself, and went into the baseball business full time, and now I am happy to chat baseball.

Often people ask me for advice about how to get into the baseball writing business, or they want to know how I ended up doing what I'm doing -- and that's a very long story that I may write someday, if I ever have time. People often tell me that I have the best job in the world; some of these people are wealthy and successful, with names you would recognize, and they say they wish they had my job -- which is nice to hear -- but I tell them that if they tried it, they wouldn't like it as much as they might imagine, and I say that many would quit within a week if they had to live up to the pressures and deadlines that I impose on myself to do what I think is a good job in this tiny profession.

Just for example, having a live 900 number and getting paid to chat about baseball sounds like a dreamy existence, until you realize that every time that phone rings, you have to stop what you're doing immediately, because it's your boss on the line, and you have to answer right away, "Hello, this is John," yourself, not a secretary, and you never know what the boss will want. You have to do an imposing amount of homework every day before taking that first call. Sometimes that aspect of my work reminds me of the bell ringing in the servants hall of an old manor house, where the butler has to jump. But hey, I'm not complaining; I'm just saying you cannot imagine how much work it is, if you've never tried it, for ten hours a day, seven days a week.

For those people who want advice about how to be writer, any kind of writer, I do have some practical advice: write. Jot notes, make outlines, scribble on a pad, but most important: sit down at your keyboard and start typing, and keep printing your work on paper, and send your writing to everyone who might care and be in a position to help you get published. In the beginning, give it away. I sold my first essays for $10 apiece, and thus got my name into books in bookstores, showing people what I could do. In other words, don't hide your light under a bushel. And don't sit around waiting for some big publisher to offer you a fat advance for your first work, because it isn't going to happen, ever.

Whenever I work at a ballgame, as I do 20 or 30 times a year, it always impresses me to see the wide disparity in level of activity put forth by the various writers in attendance. The daily beat writers are under obvious pressure to crank out their game stories, often facing two or three deadlines for the same game, while others seem to have nothing to do and no apparent reason for being at the game. My own work, as a columnist, requires a definite sense of urgency and some careful planning. In a typical game visit there may be half a dozen player situations that I want to discuss -- injuries, slumps, streaks, and promotions, etc., and when I arrive at the ballpark I will have a clear list of people I want to see before leaving. This work often requires long periods of waiting, mixed with rushing around when two or three of the people I want to see appear simultaneously in the clubhouse or dugout. In the press box during a game I am usually typing as fast as anyone, working on my current column or essay or book, or just getting my notes into my laptop Toshiba for editing and compilation later. When I run out of work and find myself just sort of sitting there and watching the game, and I'm not involved in conversation with a beat writer or front office person, if I realize that I have covered just about everyone I wanted to see, often I will decide not to sit through the game for three hours just to get one more five-minute interview. Looking around the press box, I can see a few others working about as hard as I do (most of the beat writers of course) but many have the luxury to just sit and watch the game, leaving me a little jealous. And yet many of them wish they had my job, or think they wish they had it, if you see what I mean.

Finally, I want to say a word of appreciation for all the would-be competitors who keep comparing themselves to me, especially to those who have to compare their best stuff against my lesser efforts in order to make themselves look good. Someone, for example, may later take this Player Guide which contains my most preliminary projections for 1994 (nowhere near as current and accurate as what you get from my annual draft day forecasts in the monthly publication) and will try to compare their best and most current predictions for 1994 versus this first pass at what I can do in the way of forecasts. (Actually, my 1994 numbers here are called projections, not forecasts, for reasons which trained professionals know very well). It is also amusing to see people take my worst predictions out of context (if you tell the future for 1700 players, a few dozen of those predictions are going to be dead wrong every year) and use those as a basis for proving the quality of their own work. That's really quite a compliment if you think about it. And in any context or method, it's always nice to be recognized as a standard to which anyone else aspires in any field, and to see this recognition in print from time to time.

John Benson
December, 1993

WHAT'S NEW -- PLAYER VALUES UPDATE

After a few years of writing books like this one, especially those that go to press fairly early, you learn to leave a page or two blank so you can slip in a few updates when the so-called blue line text is ready to go at the printer. Following is about a month of news that didn't get into the original text. In addition to making this book more current, the following is a rough example of the type of material that gets into my monthly publication -- although when you get the monthly it will come to you hot off the presses, whereas the following "news" has been sitting around for quite a while before you got this book into your hands.

Watching player values during the winter is a lot like guessing at stock prices while the market is closed. When there are no numbers going into the record books, every valuation is theoretical and hypothetical. It's worth recalling a few examples from recent history whenever you get that urge to claim discovery of a winter "sleeper." Right after the NL expansion draft last year, for example, Steve Decker suddenly looked like a $10 catcher as the Marlins' starting backstop and hitter with a strong minor league track record. But then the Marlins signed free agent Benito Santiago, and Decker never got to play. Rod Brewer suddenly looked valuable as the Cardinals first baseman right after Andres Galarraga was let go (major league teams' front offices always have a plan to fill any vacancy in the lineup; but over the course of a winter these plans often become unnecessary). In the Rod Brewer case, the acquisition of Gregg Jefferies put Brewer back on the bench, and instantly made Brian Jordan look like an everyday player with the departure of Felix Jose to get Jefferies. Jordan's everyday status, of course, lasted only until the Cards traded for Mark Whiten, and Jordan would have remained a bench player all year if not for the injuries and slumps suffered by Ray Lankford. It goes on and on.

The point is, nobody has any value until they begin putting stats into box scores, and that doesn't happen during the winter.

With that one caution in mind, it's still a great deal of fun, and a good use of time, to watch player values rise and fall during the winter, as teams shift their rosters and lineups to get ready for the coming season. Following are some of the more recent and more significant examples of changing roles and values due to winter transactions.

BALTIMORE Rafael Palmeiro's arrival is a big downer for David Segui, and for aging prospect Paul Carey. Segui now figures to become a fifth outfielder and spot backup at first base, or to be traded, and Carey now figures to start the season in the minors. Backup catcher Mark Parent going to the Cubs solidifies Jeff Tackett as the O's backup to Chris Hoiles, and also raises the possibilities that young talent Greg Zaun will be on the major league roster on opening day. Zaun is Rick Dempsey's nephew, a 22-year-old switch hitter, and a defensive whiz who hit .306 at AA Bowie last year and just needs to keep hitting to get into the lineup. The signing of Rafael Palmeiro of course puts an end to speculation that catcher Chris Hoiles might have been moved to first base in 1994, but increased appearances at DH remain a possibility for Hoiles in '94 and a likelihood and 1995 and beyond. The signing of Mark Eichhorn to a minor league contract puts this soft tosser into the cloudy saves picture, all of which depends on Gregg Olson's return to health and being re-signed, of course. Olson was initially not offered a contract for 1994 and became a free agent. Eichhorn could easily end up being worthless in 1994, but if we were having an auction, I would be bidding a dollar or two and be happy to get him. The cloud around Olson also adds value to Alan Mills and Jim Poole as the top righty/lefty tandem, and helps the outlook for wild flamethrower Brad Pennington as well. If Olson isn't on the O's roster coming out of spring training, I would take anybody from this pen for one dollar. The departure of Mike Pagliarulo for Japan enhances Leo Gomez' chance to regain the starting third base job in 1994. Gomez is of course just age 26 and still at the beginning of his career. And yet -- in that musical chairs win/lose that I just described in the introduction to these notes -- the O's were rumored to be going after Chris Sabo to meet their third base needs, and that would really put the kabosh on Gomez' everyday player chances if he stays within the Baltimore organization.

CLEVELAND The move of Eddie Murray to the Indians was bad news for Reggie Jefferson, who then got traded to Seattle. The Indians say publicly that Murray is going to be an everyday DH, which was one hope for Jefferson's playing time. The other hope was first base. Murray is still a very strong defensive player who would be wasted if he didn't get some time at first, which was already very crowded. Randy

Milligan and Paul Sorrento provided a solid platoon pair late last year, with Jefferson completely out of the picture. Right after Milligan was gone to Montreal, you could have figured that the switch hitter Jefferson could take the lefty pitchers and platoon at first base, but Jefferson hit only .196 against southpaws last year, notably worse than what Sorrento did against lefties, so the Milligan departure didn't help Jefferson that much; if anything it raises the possibility that Sorrento could play more than a strict platoon role. When he was age 22 and knocking on the door of the major leagues, Jefferson looked very exciting, but he really hasn't matured much in the last three years and had to move on to another organization to keep alive any hope of ever getting to play full-time. In Seattle he will have a shot at DH duty but isn't likely to gain everyday status there, either.

SEATTLE As noted above, Reggie Jefferson joins the pool of DH hopefuls. Felix Fermin, also over from Cleveland, will pick up the shortstop chores left behind by Omar Vizquel who goes to the Indians to help ease in the arrival of Mark Lewis. The acquisition of Eric Anthony raises his value due to change of scenery. I am not a big believer in huge impacts from ballpark effects, but it will certainly help Anthony to have Seattle for a home and to play all his games in the AL. I liked him already for his combination of youth and major league experience, and he is a three-time minor league home run champion. At this point, among all players who have never had 20 homers in a major league season, Anthony is the most likely to jump all the way to 30 in 1994, with impressive RBI totals.

CINCINNATI Chris Sabo being let go by the Reds, as expected, only confirms the likelihood that Willie Greene will be given every chance to take over at third base. I like Greene as a sleeper for 1994. Last year at this time, he was a hot prospect on everybody's list after hitting 29 home runs at three levels in 1992. But Greene hit just .160 for the Reds last year, and even his minor league numbers are deceptive because he started the year in a deep slump and then became white hot in mid June. And he still got 22 home runs in what many people consider a disappointing season.

HOUSTON The departure of Eric Anthony creates at least a temporary lift for Kevin Bass, who was signed on December 9. Also helped are the Astros younger outfielders, most notably prospect Brian Hunter, who was at AA Jackson last year hitting .294 with 10 homers and 35 steals. This is of course not the first baseman Brian Hunter who just went from Atlanta to Pittsburgh. The Astros were talking about Mike Hampton, the young lefty acquired from Seattle for Anthony, as if Hampton could move into their starting rotation in 1994. Don't look for that to happen. It was a case of duress that Hampton got pressed into service by the Mariners in 1993; he really wasn't ready for the majors and won't be a good major league pitcher until 1995 or '96. The combined trades of Xavier Hernandez and Doug Jones really raised the stock of Todd Jones, one of those hard-throwing closer-of-the-future type of pitchers who just need a chance to become a major league ace. Unless you believe that Mitch Williams is going to get better at age 29, which I don't believe, then Williams is at best a temporary closer or left co-closer who can help usher Todd Jones' arrival in 1994. Right now I figure Jones is good for 10 saves in 1994, and that number will go up quickly if Williams bombs as I expect him to.

LOS ANGELES The acquisition of Jeff Treadway has almost no impact on Treadway's value, except to verify that he can remain a major leaguer in 1994. It is however a slight negative for third baseman Tim Wallach, who was already sliding into obsolescence, as Treadway provides a veteran backup at third, which is one reason Wallach could have retained some value even if Dave Hansen takes over during spring training, as I expect him to.

MONTREAL The Expos acquisition of Randy Milligan, who has been simply crushing lefty pitching in recent years, e.g. a .383 batting average to lead all major leaguers in 1993, changes Cliff Floyd's outlook from an all-or-nothing choice coming out of spring training, to a platoon type of role as he gets used to major league pitching. Floyd's biggest question of course is not hitting but fielding, and again Milligan offers the possibility of help and support in the form of a good late-inning defensive replacement, especially if the opposition has brought in a lefty reliever. Milligan's arrival therefore signals enhanced attention to starting the 1994 season with Floyd as a major league regular, even if not as a seven-day-a-week player.

The Expos have a speedy second base prospect in Mike Hardge, who has helped himself with good play in the Arizona Fall League, but Hardge is not the beneficiary of Delino Deshields' departure, at least not immediately. The big winner is Mike Lansing, who now figure to play second base every day. And a secondary winner is Sean Berry, who won't have to contend with Lansing for playing time at third base.

PLAYER VALUE INDEX -- GAINS AND LOSSES SINCE WE WENT TO PRESS

Key:
+ or - means gain or loss of $1 to $4.
+ + or - - means gain or loss of $5 to $9
+ + + or - - - means gain or loss of $10 or more

Abbott, Kurt + +
Acre, Mark +
Anthony, Eric +
Ayala, Bobby +
Barfield, Jesse +
Bass, Kevin +
Bates, Jason +
Benzinger, Todd +
Berry, Sean +
Bolick, Frank +
Boone, Bret +
Bottalico, Ricky + +
Brantley, Jeff -
Burks, Ellis + +
Cabrera, Fran - - -
Carey, Paul -
Carter, Mike +
Charlton, Norm -
Cirillo, Jeff +
Clark, Jerald -
Clark, Will +
Cora, Joey -
Curtis, Randy + +
Cuyler, Milt +
Davis, Eric +
Deer, Rob - - -
Deshields, Delino +
Destrade, Oreste -
Eichhorn, Mark +
Elster, Kevin +
Farr, Steve - -
Fernandez, Sid -
Franco, John -
Franco, Julio +
Frye, Jeff - -
Gallagher, Dave -
Gardner, Mark -
Gladden, Dan - - -
Gooden, Dwight -
Grebeck, Craig -
Greene, Willie + +
Greer, Rusty +

Hammonds, Jeffrey +
Hanson, Erik +
Hardge, Mike +
Harris, Lenny -
Henderson, Rickey +
Henry, Dwayne -
Honeycutt, Rick +
Hunter, Brian L +
Hunter, Brian R +
Hurst, Bruce +
James, Dion - - -
Javier, Stan -
Jean, Domingo +
Jefferson, Reggie -
Johnson, Howard + +
Jones, Todd + +
Juden, Jeff +
Kingery, Mike +
Koelling, Brian -
Lansing, Mike +
Leonard, Mark -
Lindeman, Jim +
Magadan, Dave +
Martinez, Chito +
McDowell, Oddibe +
McElroy, Chuck +
McNeely, Jeff -
Menendez, Tony +
Meulens, Hensley - - -
Milligan, Randy +
Mills, Alan +
Montgomery, Ray +
Newfield, Marc -
Nixon, Otis - -
Novoa, Rafael - -
Olson, Gregg -
Owen, Spike +
Pagliarulo, Mike - - -
Palmeiro, Orlando +
Parent, Mark +
Parks, Derek +
Pemberton, Rudy +

Pena, Tony -
Perez, Robert +
Perez, Yorkis +
Phillips, JR +
Poole, Jim +
Portugal, Mark -
Quintana, Carlos +
Reed, Jody -
Rendina, Mike +
Rivera, David +
Segui, David - -
Seitzer, Kevin +
Sharperson, Mike -
Sharperson -
Shelton, Ben +
Sherman, Darrell +
Smith, Lee -
Stairs, Matt +
Surhoff, BJ -
Veras, Quilvio +
Walbeck, Matt + +
Wallach, Tim -
Wegmann, Tom + +
Wilson, Dan ++
Zaun, Greg +

ABBE, CHRIS - C - BR - Age 23
Power hitter (13 homers at AA San Antonio in just 254 at bats). Needs to make better contact to move up.

ABBOTT, KURT - SS - BR - Age 24
Check out this progression: 1992, Tacoma, .154; 1992, Huntsville, .254; 1993, Tacoma, .319. The '93 average was 48 points higher than his previous high, in Rookie ball in '89. With outfield vacancies, the A's tried him in left field last September. Abbott showed little offense through four minor league seasons, before erupting in 1993 to hit .319 with 12 homers and 19 steals at Triple-A and adding three homers in 61 at bats for Oakland at the end of the season. He is 24 years old, and may only qualify at outfield in many leagues. He might be worth a gamble if he qualifies at shortstop, but should probably not be counted on to deliver quality "outfielder" production.

	AB	R	HR	RBI	SB	BA	$
1993 Tacoma AAA	480	75	12	79	19	.319	
1993 Oakland AL	61	11	3	9	2	.248	0

ABNER, SHAWN - OF - BR - Age 27
A former first pick in entire draft (1984) who never blossomed.

	AB	R	HR	RBI	SB	BA	$
1992 Chicago AL	208	21	1	16	1	.279	1
1993 Omaha AAA	133	14	2	16	2	.246	

AFENIR, TROY - C - BR - Age 30
In four visits to the major leagues, Afenir has amassed only 79 career at bats. If he comes up again in 1994, it will be for insurance purposes, sitting on the bench.

	AB	R	HR	RBI	SB	BA	$
1993 Indianapolis AAA	254	29	8	35	2	.240	

ALDRETE, MIKE - 1B/OF - BL - Age 33
The ten homers in 1993 are a statistical blip; for his career, Aldrete now has 27 homers in 713 games. He doesn't hit lefties, so at best he is a platoon player. He is 33 years old, as recently as 1992 he spent the entire year in Triple-A, and he rarely steals. 1993 was the year for recycled veterans.

	AB	R	HR	RBI	SB	BA	$
1992 Colorado Springs AAA	463	69	8	84	1	.322	
1993 Oakland AL	255	40	10	33	1	.267	5
1994 *Projection* >>>	161	24	4	20	1	.262	1

ALEXANDER, MANNY - DH - BR - Age 23
Manny Alexander is a typical shortstop from San Pedro de Macoris. His defense is excellent, and it may bring him to the majors before he can hit major league pitching. Alexander has good base running speed. He is still considered the heir to the Ripken shortstop legacy in Baltimore.

	AB	R	HR	RBI	SB	BA	$
1992 Hagerstown AA	499	70	2	41	43	.259	
1992 Rochester AAA	24	3	0	3	2	.292	
1993 Rochester AAA	471	55	6	51	19	.244	

ALICEA, LUIS - 2B - BB - Age 28
Alicea has been the Cardinals' second baseman of the future seemingly forever. However, he missed his chance to take the job last season because of frequent injuries and mental lapses. He's a decent offensive player but doesn't seem capable of holding down a full-time spot in the lineup.

	AB	H	HR	RBI	SB	BA	$
1992 Louisville AAA	71	11	0	6	0	.282	
1992 St. Louis NL	265	26	2	32	2	.245	2
1993 St. Louis NL	362	50	3	46	11	.279	9
1994 *Projection* >>>	280	34	2	34	6	.265	5

ALLANSON, ANDY - C - BR - Age 32
Allanson got just 24 at bats in 1993, one fewer than in 1992; he hasn't been valuable since 1988.

	AB	R	HR	RBI	SB	BA	$
1993 San Fransisco NL	24	3	0	2	0	.167	-

ALLENSWORTH, JERMAINE - OF - BR - 22
Until a late-season slump at Purdue, Allensworth was considered a definite first-round pick in last year's draft. The Pirates feel that they got a steal by grabbing him with a "sandwich" pick at the end of the first round. At Single-A short-season Welland, he displayed outstanding all-around play and could get to the majors fast.

	AB	R	HR	RBI	SB	BA	$
1993 Welland A	263	44	1	32	18	.308	-

ALLRED, BEAU - OF - BL - Age 28
The Indians keep their old players at Triple-A and their young players in Cleveland. Allred isn't likely to make it back. If he does, he will hit about .240 with one home run per 40 at bats.

	AB	R	HR	RBI	SB	BA	$
1993 Charlotte AAA	347	59	20	61	4	.245	

ALOMAR, ROBERTO - 2B - BB - Age 26
Now that Ryne Sandberg has begun to fade, Alomar is the best all-around second baseman in baseball. His defense gets better each year and he continues to improve his home run totals while reducing the strikeouts. In a career year Alomar could drive in 100 runs while stealing sixty bases and batting .330.

	AB	R	HR	RBI	SB	BA	$
1992 Toronto AL	571	105	8	76	49	.310	39
1993 Toronto AL	589	109	17	93	55	.326	49
1994 *Projection* >>>	591	104	13	83	53	.315	48

ALOMAR, SANDY - C - BR - Age 27
Probably the worst player ever to start three consecutive All-Star Games, he hasn't accumulated 300 at bats in any of the last three seasons. On the rare occasions when he has been healthy, he has proven himself as one of the least productive 6'5", 200 lb. offensive players in history. He is a great defensive catcher though, and the job is clearly his when healthy.

	AB	R	HR	RBI	SB	BA	$
1992 Cleveland AL	299	22	2	26	3	.251	2
1993 Cleveland AL	215	24	6	32	3	.270	4
1994 *Projection* >>>	377	33	6	41	3	.255	5

ALOU, MOISES - OF - BR - Age 27
The Expos big payoff from their 1990 trade of Zane Smith to Pittsburgh, Alou came into his own in 1993 and became one of the bright young run producers in the National League. He severely fractured his leg and dislocated his ankle last September. The Expos believe he will be ready for the start of the season; however, his ability to steal bases may be gone after such a serious injury. A streaky hitter, Alou can play all three outfield positions and hits for power and average.

	AB	R	HR	RBI	SB	BA	$
1992 Montreal NL	341	53	9	56	16	.282	16
1993 Montreal NL	482	70	18	85	17	.286	22
1994 *Projection* >>>	494	73	16	85	12	.285	20

AMARAL, RICH - 2B - BR - Age 32
Converted his minor league credentials into major league success in 1993. However, he had only 100 at bats and three stolen bases in the second half because of injuries and the play of Bret Boone. The departure of Boone to Cincinnati certainly helps Amaral.

	AB	R	HR	RBI	SB	BA	$
1992 Calgary AAA	403	79	0	21	53	.318	
1992 Seattle AL	100	9	1	7	4	.240	0
1993 Seatle AL	373	53	1	44	19	.290	14
1994 *Projection* >>>	350	49	1	39	14	.280	10

AMARO, RUBEN - OF - BB - Age 29

He has absolutely nothing left to prove as a minor leaguer, but has only shown brief flashes in the majors. A switch hitter in name only, Amaro was 14 for 28 against lefties in the majors but otherwise hit just .200. At age 29, he has a very limited upside.

	AB	R	HR	RBI	SB	BA	$
1992 Philadelphia NL	374	43	7	34	11	.219	5
1993 Scranton AAA	412	76	9	37	25	.291	
1993 Philadelphia NL	48	7	1	6	0	.333	0
1994 Projection >>>	151	18	3	15	4	.237	0

ANDERSON, BRADY - OF - BL - Age 30

Anderson returned to Earth in 1993. The signs were there for the observant as Anderson hit only .246 after July of 1992. Chicken pox and nagging injuries slowed Anderson from his 53 stolen base total in 1992. Anderson may move to center field or right field in 1994 depending on the health of Hammonds and the status of Devereaux, but should remain the O's leadoff hitter, improving the stolen base total and holding steady in the average and home run departments.

	AB	R	HR	RBI	SB	BA	$
1992 Baltimore AL	623	100	21	80	53	.271	39
1993 Baltimore AL	560	87	13	66	24	.263	20
1994 Projection >>>	529	83	14	64	32	.263	25

ANDERSON, GARRET - OF - BL - Age 21

After a decent minor league season with Vancouver, Anderson is a long shot to win the left field spot should Polonia move to another team. Probably destined for another year in Vancouver.

	AB	R	HR	RBI	SB	BA	$
1992 Palm Springs A	322	46	1	62	1	.323	
1992 Midland AA	146	16	2	19	2	.274	
1993 Vancouver AAA	467	57	4	71	3	.293	

ANDREWS, SHANE - 3B - BR - Age 22

A first round pick in 1990, Andrews was plagued by weight problems at the start of his professional career. He has trimmed down and made the conversion from catcher to third base. He has good raw power and had a decent batting average for the first time in his career in 1993, but he needs better pitch selection and is at least one more full season away.

	AB	R	HR	RBI	SB	BA	$
1992 Albany A	453	76	25	87	8	.230	
1993 Harrisburg AA	442	77	18	70	10	.260	

ANSLEY, WILLIE - OF - BR - Age 24

Houston's number one draft pick in January, 1989, Ansley made a comeback last season after back and shoulder injuries limited him to 45 games in 1992. He had a solid Triple-A season before suffering torn ligaments in his thumb. Excellent at getting on base and stealing bases, but he hasn't developed the power potential he showed in high school. Given an opportunity, he still could help the Astros.

ANTHONY, ERIC - OF - BL - Age 26

Anthony failed to match his 1992 power production in 1993, a hitters' year. He appeared to lose confidence as the season progressed before a sore throwing shoulder caused him to miss most of September. His prime years are in front of him.

	AB	R	HR	RBI	SB	BA	$
1992 Houston NL	440	45	19	80	5	.239	15
1993 Houston NL	486	70	15	66	3	.249	9
1994 Projection >>>	408	55	15	64	4	.253	11

ARIAS, ALEX - 3B/2B - BR - Age 26

Arias has proven himself defensively at the major league level at three different positions and is in line for the starting shortstop job should free agent Walt Weiss move on. Arias is an unexciting offensive player.

	AB	R	HR	RBI	SB	BA	$
1992 Iowa AAA	409	52	5	40	14	.279	
1992 Chicago NL	99	14	0	7	0	.293	-
1993 Florida NL	249	27	2	20	1	.269	2
1994 *Projection* >>>	157	18	1	12	1	.264	0

ARMAS, MARCOS - 1B - BR - Age 24

Posted fair numbers in his first Triple-A season. Armas has 10-15 per year home run power, not 20-30. He is Tony's much younger brother.

	AB	R	HR	RBI	SB	BA	$
1993 Tacoma AAA	434	69	15	89	4	.290	
1993 Oakland AL	31	7	1	1	1	.194	-
1994 *Projection* >>>	100	11	2	13	1	.235	-

ASHLEY, BILLY - 0F - BR - Age 23

A huge, 6' 7", 227 lb. outfielder, Ashley had another impressive power year in 1993, leading the Pacific Coast League in RBI (100) and finishing second in home runs, total bases, and slugging. However, his strikeout totals rival Dave Kingman's (143 in 482 at bats) and his .297 average at AAA Albuquerque translates to about .220 in Dodger Stadium. He can't play the outfield either. When the uninformed say minor league stats don't mean anything, it is players like Ashley who provide their evidence. Ashley is not a prospect until his strike zone judgement improves.

	AB	R	HR	RBI	SB	BA	$
1992 Los Angeles NL	95	6	2	6	0	.221	-
1993 Albuquerque AAA	482	88	26	100	6	.297	
1993 Los Angeles NL	37	0	0	0	0	.243	-

AUDE, RICH - 1B - BR - Age 22

Aude was the Pirates' second-round draft pick in 1989 and spun his wheels into last season. In 1993, he had a breakthrough Double-A season and got a September callup. He showed he's not yet ready for prime time and needs Triple-A seasoning. Aude is a good power prospect, although he needs to improve his defense. The Pirates handed him an outfielder's glove when he reached the majors, in an attempt to add versatility.

	AB	R	HR	RBI	SB	BA	$
1993 Carolina AA	422	66	18	73	8	.289	
1993 Buffalo AAA	64	17	4	16	0	.375	
1993 Pittsburgh NL	26	1	0	4	0	.115	-
1994 *Projection* >>>	200	24	5	28	2	.249	2

AUSMUS, BRAD - C - BR - Age 24

The key to the Greg W. Harris/Bruce Hurst trade with Colorado, Ausmus took over the starting catcher duties as 1993 came to a close. Of the prospects obtained in their fire sale trades, Ausmus had the biggest immediate impact. A top defensive prospect with a good head and great arm, Ausmus exceeded expectations in a 160 at bats major league trial; he'll be the starter in 1994. For a catcher, Ausmus has good base stealing abilities and while he may hit for some power, a decent batting average is unlikely.

	AB	R	HR	RBI	SB	BA	$
1993 San Diego NL	160	18	5	12	2	.256	2
1994 *Projection* >>>	310	30	8	23	3	.246	4

BAAR, BRYAN - C - BR - Age 25

In four minor league seasons in hitters' ballparks, he's produced a .244 career average with moderate power stats. Not a threat to Mike Piazza.

BACKMAN, WALLY - 3B - BL - Age 34

For a guy who's generally available every winter, Wally has managed to land on his feet with unusual regularity. Backman might turn up with any club which could use a decent lefthanded hitting middle infielder. Or he might not.

	AB	R	HR	RBI	SB	BA	$
1992 Philadelphia NL	48	6	0	6	1	.271	-
1993 Seattle AL	29	2	0	0	0	.138	-
1994 *Projection* >>>	62	6	0	5	1	.226	-

BAERGA, CARLOS - 2B - BB - Age 25
Would be a great offensive player no matter what position he played, but for a second baseman, he's a potential all-time great. At his tender age, he has already stamped himself as a future 3000-hit candidate (using Bill James' method, he has established a 31% chance). Unfortunately for him, he always has been (as far back as their minor league days in the Padres' system), and probably always will be overshadowed by Roberto Alomar. He's only going to get better; he has 30 home run potential.

	AB	R	HR	RBI	SB	BA	$
1992 Cleveland AL	657	92	20	105	10	.312	33
1993 Cleveland AL	624	105	21	114	15	.321	33
1994 *Projection* >>>	630	101	20	108	11	.313	35

BAEZ, KEVIN - SS - BR - Age 27
Baez isn't the Mets' shortstop of the future. He has proven he can't hit any sort of pitching at any level. He has a gun for an arm, but won't end up in the majors in 1994 unless there's desperation somewhere.

	AB	R	HR	RBI	SB	BA	$
1992 New York NL	13	0	0	0	0	.154	-
1993 Norfolk AAA	209	23	2	21	0	.258	
1993 New York NL	126	10	0	7	0	.183	-
1994 *Projection* >>>	67	5	0	5	0	.190	-

BAGWELL, JEFF - 1B - BR - Age 25
A talented and hard-working player who hits for power and average and also gets a few steals, Bagwell missed the last 20 games of 1993 with a broken bone in his hand, costing him a shot at 100 RBI. Count on .300-20-100-10 for the next 10 years.

	AB	R	HR	RBI	SB	BA	$
1992 Houston NL	586	87	18	96	10	.273	24
1993 Houston NL	535	76	20	88	13	.320	27
1994 *Projection* >>>	555	88	20	100	12	.310	32

BAINES, HAROLD - DH - BL - Age 35
The Orioles were very happy with Harold Baines at designated hitter last year, particularly with his clutch hitting. He had a knee operation after the season, but should be healthy for '94. He still has a nice swing and some power.

	AB	R	HR	RBI	SB	BA	$
1992 Oakland AL	478	58	16	76	1	.253	11
1993 Baltimore AL	416	64	20	78	0	.313	18
1994 *Projection* >>>	448	61	17	71	1	.283	16

BARBARA, DON - 1B - BL - Age 25
Went from being stuck behind Wally Joyner to being stuck behind John Jaha. That's an improvement.

	AB	R	HR	RBI	SB	BA	$
1992 Edmonton AAA	396	70	4	63	9	.298	
1993 New Orleans AAA	255	34	4	38	1	.294	

BARBERIE, BRET - 2B - BB - Age 26
He produced when healthy in 1993 and has shown flashes of power and speed throughout most of his career. Look for him to establish himself as solid major leaguer in 1994.

	AB	R	HR	RBI	SB	BA	$
1992 Montreal NL	285	26	1	24	9	.232	2
1993 Florida NL	375	45	5	33	2	.277	6
1994 *Projection* >>>	305	34	3	27	5	.269	5

BARFIELD, JESSE - OF - BR - Age 34
Absolutely plagued by injuries. Just playing out the string in Japan.

	AB	R	HR	RBI	SB	BA	$
1992 New York AL	95	8	2	7	1	.137	-
1993 Japan	344	52	26	53	---	.215	

BARKER, TIM - SS - BR - Age 25
Obtained from the Dodgers, he was a key cog in the Harrisburg machine before his promotion to AAA Ottawa. He struggled both at bat and in the field. Before last year he had stolen at least 25 bases in each of his four pro seasons.

BARNES, SKEETER - 1B - BR - Age 37
Barnes is a hustler whose primary role is off the bench. He can hit for average and steal a few bases.

	AB	R	HR	RBI	SB	BA	$
1992 Detroit AL	165	27	3	25	3	.273	4
1993 Detroit AL	160	24	2	27	5	.281	4
1994 *Projection* >>>	161	25	3	24	5	.272	4

BASS, KEVIN - OF - BB - Age 34
Bass has adjusted well as a part time player and pinch hitter, but isn't likely to regain a position as a regular. He should continue to be productive in a reserve role.

	AB	R	HR	RBI	SB	BA	$
1992 San Francisco-NY NL	402	40	9	39	14	.269	14
1993 Houston NL	229	31	3	37	7	.284	7
1994 *Projection* >>>	309	35	6	37	8	.259	7

BATES, JASON - SS - BB - Age 23
Made the jump from Single-A to Triple-A in the Rockies system with ease in 1993; offers power and speed.

BATISTE, KIM - 3B/SS - BR - Age 26
Everybody's favorite defensive replacement, Batiste finally found his major league niche in 1993. After proving beyond a shadow of a doubt that he didn't have the range or consistency to be an everyday major league shortstop, he found a home as a backup third baseman and valuable bat off the bench. He shredded lefties at a .349 clip.

	AB	R	HR	RBI	SB	BA	$
1992 Philadelphia NL	136	9	1	10	0	.206	-
1993 Philadelphia NL	156	14	5	29	0	.282	3
1994 *Projection* >>>	127	10	3	18	0	.253	0

BATTLE, HOWARD - 3B - BR - Age 22
Toronto's fourth-round pick in '90, Battle has a strong arm and decent power as shown in the Florida State League in 1992.

	AB	R	HR	RBI	SB	BA	$
1992 Dunedin A	520	76	17	85	6	.254	
1993 Knoxville AA	521	66	7	70	12	.278	

BAUTISTA, DANNY - OF- BR - Age 22
Speed and defense are rookie Danny Bautista's strengths who impressed the Tigers after his late season callup. But he has never shown any power and only a moderate average in the minors. Do not expect more than a few steals even if he makes the Tigers out of spring training. He was rated as the fastest baserunner in the Double-A Eastern League last year.

	AB	R	HR	RBI	SB	BA	$
1993 Detroit AL	61	6	1	9	3	.331	1
1994 *Projection* >>>	100	12	1	10	4	.247	0

BEAMON, TREY - OF - BL - Age 19
A second-round pick in 1992, Beamon is one of the best athletes in the Pirates' system. He did not hit a home run last season with Single-A Augusta, but the Pirates feel his power will come. He has good speed and a very mature approach to the game. His estimated time of arrival is 1996.

	AB	R	HR	RBI	SB	BA	$
1992 Bradenton R	39	9	1	6	0	.308	
1992 Welland A	69	15	3	9	4	.290	
1993 Augusta A	373	64	0	45	19	.271	

BEAN, BILLY - OF - BL - Age 29
Bean is a fourth outfielder and career minor leaguer. He has only modest power and speed. With such a jumble of spare outfielders on the Padre roster, Billy is not worth Beans in the 1994 Rotisserie world.

	AB	R	HR	RBI	SB	BA	$
1993 San Diego NL	177	19	5	32	2	.260	3
1994 *Projection* >>>	89	10	2	11	1	.240	-

BECKER, RICH - 0F - BB - Age 22
Becker has power, hits for a good average, and has base-stealing speed, a triple-threat combination. He is also a very good fielder with a good arm. He was called up to the Twins in September but hurt his knee. With a full recovery, he will soon be a starter in the Twins outfield.

	AB	R	HR	RBI	SB	BA	$
1993 Nashville AA	516	93	15	66	29	.287	
1993 Minnesota AL	7	3	0	0	1	.286	-
1994 *Projection* >>>	327	43	9	45	9	.255	9

BELCHER, KEVIN - OF - BR - Age 26
No longer considered a prospect, Belcher didn't even merit a September callup. Likely a career minor leaguer.

	AB	R	HR	RBI	SB	BA	$
1992 Tulsa AA	381	55	18	60	6	.244	
1993 Birmingham AA	360	38	13	50	11	.222	

BELL, DAVID - 3B - BR - Age 21
One of the youngest players in the Eastern League in 1993, his offensive performance made a quantum leap. Smallish for a third baseman (5'10", 170 lbs.) and quite slow afoot, he doesn't have any one quality that stands out. His youth gives the Indians hope for the future. A 1990 seventh round pick out of noted football juggernaut, Moeller High.

	AB	R	HR	RBI	SB	BA	$
1993 Canton-Akron AAA	483	69	9	60	3	.292	

BELL, DEREK - OF - BR - Age 25
In one of several trades that appear to have greatly helped the Padres despite a lot of fan consternation, Bell was acquired from Toronto for Darrin Jackson. Bell is just 25 years old and his 41 extra base hits are evidence that he's an excellent hitting prospect despite his 122 strikeouts. Only the Padres third 20-20 player, Bell also stole 26 bases in 31 attempts. His biggest problem is poor fielding. Bell looks lost in center field at times and was miserable during a late summer trial at third base. With Plantier in left, Bell may be forced to first base or right field.

	AB	R	HR	RBI	SB	BA	$
1992 Toronto AL	161	23	2	15	7	.242	2
1993 San Diego NL	542	73	21	72	26	.262	22
1994 *Projection* >>>	500	71	18	66	26	.270	24

BELL, GEORGE - DH - BR - Age 34
Like teammates Sax and Calderon, the bottom fell out for Bell in 1993 and he found himself teamless by the end of the season. He's now 34 and his main asset has been power with tons of on base percentage (Raines, Thomas, Ventura) in front of him. He can't play defense and won't be plunked into the middle of an order anymore.

	AB	R	HR	RBI	SB	BA	$
1992 Chicago AL	627	74	25	112	5	.255	20
1993 Chicago AL	410	36	13	64	1	.217	3
1994 *Projection* >>>	507	53	19	84	2	.255	13

BELL, JAY - SS - BR - Age 28
Bell had his finest season yet in 1993, hitting .300 for the first time, scoring 100 runs, and ending Ozzie Smith's reign as the National League's Gold Glove shortstop. Bell has moderate power but his homer and RBI totals suffer from batting second; the Pirates have no plans to move him down in the order.

	AB	R	HR	RBI	SB	BA	$
1992 Pittsburgh NL	632	87	9	55	7	.264	13
1993 Pittsburgh NL	604	102	9	51	16	.310	21
1994 *Projection* >>>	614	96	10	55	12	.288	21

BELL, JUAN - 2B/SS - BR - Age 26

When the Orioles got Juan Bell and a couple of pitching prospects from the Dodgers in trade for Eddie Murray back in 1989, the PR machinery started projecting Bell as a future star, which he obviously isn't. He is however a talented infielder from San Pedro de Macoris; he can hit a little; and he is still young enough to be improving.

	AB	R	HR	RBI	SB	BA	$
1992 Philadelphia NL	147	12	1	8	5	.204	-
1993 Philadelphia NL	65	5	0	7	0	.200	-
1993 Milwaukee AL	286	42	5	29	6	.234	2
1994 *Projection* >>>	260	32	3	23	5	.216	0

BELL, MIKE - 1B - BL - Age 25

Fair hitter, but he's in an organization overloaded with outfielders and first basemen. Most likely his future role is helping other prospects develop, by playing alongside them in the minors.

	AB	R	HR	RBI	SB	BA	$
1993 Buffalo AAA	97	12	4	13	0	.155	

BELLE, ALBERT - OF - BR - Age 27

Belle is still improving, and along with Griffey, Gonzalez, Thomas and the like, is creating a new golden age for young power hitters in the American League. His power hitting has been well documented over the years, but in 1993 he added a new dimension, speed. He stole more bases in 1993 than he had previously stolen in his major league career. Now that he appears to have overcome his off-field problems (which sometimes surfaced on-field), he has established himself as a genuine superstar.

	AB	R	HR	RBI	SB	BA	$
1992 Cleveland AL	585	81	34	112	8	.260	26
1993 Cleveland AL	594	93	38	129	23	.290	38
1994 *Projection* >>>	568	83	35	118	15	.279	34

BELLIARD, RAFAEL - 2B/SS - BR - Age 32

Jeff Blauser took nearly the whole pie at shortstop and left Belliard with the crumbs. Blauser's improved defense and marvelous offense bought him the full time job and Belliard served as a defensive substitute. Belliard's .228 average in 1993 matched his career batting average and he has 20 RBI in the last two years combined. He'll remain in the majors as a late inning defensive specialist only.

	AB	R	HR	RBI	SB	BA	$
1992 Atlanta NL	285	20	0	14	0	.211	-
1993 Atlanta NL	79	6	0	6	0	.228	-
1994 *Projection* >>>	194	16	0	12	1	.226	-

BELTRE, ESTEBAN - SS - BR - Age 26

Once considered the heir to Ozzie Guillen, Beltre long ago proved that he was never going to be a hitter. He was disappointing in his role as emergency replacement in 1992.

	AB	R	HR	RBI	SB	BA	$
1992 Vancouver AAA	161	17	0	16	4	.267	
1992 Chicago AL	110	21	1	10	1	.191	-
1993 Nashville AAA	489	67	8	52	18	.292	

BENAVIDES, FREDDIE - SS - BR - Age 27

He came back strong after a stint on the Disabled List, hitting .319 between July 2 and Sept. 7, but an ankle injury ended his season. His best bet to make the team in 1994 is as a utility infielder. His thirteen errors in 74 games didn't help, either.

	AB	R	HR	RBI	SB	BA	$
1992 Cincinnati NL	173	14	1	17	0	.231	-
1993 Colorado NL	213	20	3	26	3	.286	4
1994 *Projection* >>>	174	15	2	18	2	.255	1

BENITEZ, YAMIL - OF - BR - Age 21

In a prospect-laden organization, he doesn't rank high but he has big power for a young man. If he becomes more selective, and possibly goes to another organization, he could have a future. Benitez is a good power/speed combination.

	AB	R	HR	RBI	SB	BA	$
1992 Albany A	79	6	1	6	0	.165	
1992 Jamestown A	162	24	3	23	19	.272	
1993 Burlington A	411	70	15	61	18	.273	

BENJAMIN, MIKE - 2B/SS - BR - Age 28

Benjamin's value is entirely defensive. He has hit below .200 in four of his five major league seasons; his glove and his occasional homers mean he might get 100 at bats in a season, but the .199 batting average offsets the homers he might hit. He won't play much with Clayton around, and wouldn't hit even if he did play regularly.

	AB	R	HR	RBI	SB	BA	$
1992 San Francisco NL	75	4	1	3	1	.173	-
1993 San Francisco NL	146	22	4	16	0	.199	-
1994 *Projection* >>>	116	14	3	10	1	.182	-

BENZINGER, TODD - 1B - BB - Age 31

Benzinger served well as a substitute for Will Clark in 1993; his .452 slugging percentage was the highest of his career, albeit only 177 at bats. Don't be fooled; Benzinger was never much good in his heyday, and now he's merely a 31-year-old backup first baseman with no speed, little power and an anemic on base percentage. Everyone says he's a nice guy, though.

	AB	R	HR	RBI	SB	BA	$
1992 Los Angeles NL	293	24	4	31	2	.239	2
1993 San Francisco NL	177	25	6	26	0	.288	4
1994 *Projection* >>>	256	27	5	32	1	.262	3

BERBLINGER, JEFF - 2B - BR - Age 23

A seventh-round draft pick out of the University of Kansas, Berblinger showed enough in just 38 games to be voted the New York-Penn League's All-Star second baseman; Glen Falls suffered when it's team leader advanced to the Florida State League. A solid fundamental player, Berblinger's season ended early because of a back injury.

BERROA, GERONIMO - OF - BR - Age 29

At this point, it has become crystal clear that Geronimo Berroa can hit anywhere at the minor league level. He's never been given a real chance to prove that he can hit in the majors, however, and that chance will not take place with the Marlins, given their glut of outfielders who are six or seven years younger.

	AB	R	HR	RBI	SB	BA	$
1992 Cincinnati NL	15	2	0	0	0	.267	-
1993 Edmonton AAA	327	64	16	68	1	.327	
1993 Florida NL	34	3	0	0	0	.118	-
1994 *Projection* >>>	50	6	24	4	0	.275	-

BERRY, SEAN - 3B - BR - Age 28

A long time prospect with Kansas City, Berry played well with the Expos last year, his first full season in the majors. He showed some pop (.465 slugging average) and hit for a decent batting average. However, the Expos aren't fully convinced that he can play everyday and are considering moving Wil Cordero from shortstop to third base.

	AB	R	HR	RBI	SB	BA	$
1992 Omaha AAA	439	61	21	77	6	.287	
1992 Montreal NL	57	5	1	4	2	.333	1
1993 Montreal NL	299	50	14	49	12	.261	12
1994 *Projection* >>>	414	62	15	58	13	.261	15

BERRYHILL, DAMON - C - BB - Age 30

His power was down from 1992, but he still had a respectable season. Berryhill isn't likely to be threatened immediately for playing time by the inevitable arrival of Javy Lopez; he'll probably continue in a platoon role for awhile. Still, the warning signs are showing; his below average defense, poor batting average and on base percentage, and lack of other skills will contribute to a quicker loss in playing time. Berryhill is likely to be reduced to a backup role by late 1994.

	AB	R	HR	RBI	SB	BA	$
1992 Atlanta NL	307	21	10	43	0	.228	4
1993 Atlanta NL	335	24	8	43	0	.245	3
1994 *Projection* >>>	296	21	7	37	0	.229	1

BIASUCCI, JOE - SS - BR - Age 24
A classic overachiever, Biasucci had a monster season in the Class A Midwest League for Springfield. He has outstanding pop for a middle infielder and has emerged as a prospect.

	AB	R	HR	RBI	SB	BA	$
1993 Springfield A	398	76	26	86	15	.289	

BICHETTE, DANTE - OF - BR - Age 30
1993 was a dream year; he had career highs in average, doubles, home runs, runs, RBI, and assists. Comfortable in the number three batting spot, Bichette has a gun for an arm and covered the cavernous right field at Mile High Stadium with no problems. Bichette also led the team with 99 strikeouts.

	AB	R	HR	RBI	SB	BA	$
1992 Milwaukee AL	387	37	5	41	18	.287	16
1993 Colorado NL	538	93	21	89	14	.310	26
1994 *Projection* >>>	502	72	16	72	16	.292	23

BIESER, STEVE - OF - BB - Age 26
The ultimate underdog, this 32nd round pick in 1989 managed just his second pro home run in five seasons last year, but had scrapped his way to Triple-A by late 1993. His ability to catch makes him a possibility as a third catcher/backup outfielder, but don't count on it.

BIGGIO, CRAIG - 2B - BR - Age 28
A durable player who became a different type of hitter last year, Biggio increased his homers from 6 to 21 in 1993 while his steals decreased from 38 to 15 (with 17 caught stealing). He is committed to improving his baserunning in 1994. Now in his prime, he should continue as one of top two or three National League second basemen for several more years.

	AB	R	HR	RBI	SB	BA	$
1992 Houston NL	613	96	6	39	38	.277	25
1993 Houston NL	610	98	21	64	15	.287	22
1994 *Projection* >>>	600	94	13	53	23	.285	25

BILARDELLO, DANN - C - BR - Age 34
Hasn't had over 80 at bats in a season since 1986. Career batting average is .204. Look elsewhere.

BLANKENSHIP, LANCE - OF - BR - Age 30
The Oakland Athletics might be the only team in baseball that would give regular playing time to a .190-hitting utility player. Blankenship will look at pitches all day long, which is why his career on base percentage went up in 1993 even as he hit .190. He can steal a base, and he is coming off successive seasons at .393 and .363 on base percentage. He was hurt most of the second half of '93 and he is 30 years old. Among other negatives, if Lance ever gets traded from the A's, he will probably be out of a job in a month, since no one else will put up with the low batting average.

	AB	R	HR	RBI	SB	BA	$
1992 Oakland AL	349	59	3	34	21	.241	10
1993 Oakland AL	252	43	2	23	13	.190	1
1994 *Projection* >>>	273	42	3	26	15	.218	3

BLAUSER, JEFF - SS - BR - Age 28
At age 27, Blauser blossomed into a fine hitter who was often used in the number two spot in the order. In 1993 he provided four category offense from a traditionally weak hitting position. Chipper Jones is ready to hit the big time in 1994 and Blauser is standing in his way. The challenge for the Braves in 1994 will be to get them both into the lineup, perhaps by moving one or the other to second base or third base. Blauser came up as a second baseman and has played there at times in the majors and may again be asked to shift positions since his defense isn't his strong suit.

	AB	R	HR	RBI	SB	BA	$
1992 Atlanta NL	343	61	14	46	5	.262	12
1993 Atlanta NL	597	110	15	73	16	.305	24
1994 *Projection* >>>	502	86	15	64	12	.283	19

BLOSSER, GREG OF - BL - Age 22
Boston's top pick in 1989. Blosser's performance made the record books. He's ready to spend a summer in Boston in 1994.

	AB	R	HR	RBI	SB	BA	$
1993 Pawtucket AAA	478	66	23	66	3	.228	
1993 Boston AL	28	1	0	1	1	.071	-
1994 *Projection* >>>	202	20	5	22	2	.221	-

BLOWERS, MIKE - 3B - BR - Age 28
Finally got a chance to play on a regular basis and showed the potential he was thought to have lost. He was a unanimous choice of the local BBWAA of the Mariners "unsung hero." Like teammate Amaral, even though his performance far exceeded his previous major league numbers, it was in line with his minor league track record.

	AB	R	HR	RBI	SB	BA	$
1992 Seattle AL	73	7	1	2	0	.192	-
1993 Seattle AL	379	55	15	57	1	.280	10
1994 *Projection* >>>	226	28	7	28	1	.255	3

BOGAR, TIM - SS - BR - Age 27
A classic good-glove, no-hit infielder who was in the right place at the right time in 1993 when Tony Fernandez was shipped out.

	AB	R	HR	RBI	SB	BA	$
1993 New York NL	205	19	3	25	0	.244	0
1994 *Projection* >>>	103	10	1	9	2	.234	-

BOGGS, WADE - 3B - BL - Age 35
Boggs worked hard all year to try and regain his past skills. From the first day of spring to season's end, he has shown what it takes to stay competitive on the majors. While he doesn't steal bases, he is still impressive on defense. He has improved positioning and a strong throw.

	AB	R	HR	RBI	SB	BA	$
1992 Boston AL	514	62	7	50	1	.259	7
1993 New York AL	560	83	2	59	0	.302	11
1994 *Projection* >>>	542	80	5	57	1	.303	16

BOLICK, FRANK - 1B/3B - BB - Age 27
After a big Double-A season in 1992 for Seattle, Bolick had the chance to win the Expos' starting first base or third base job last season. He didn't hit or field well and became a scapegoat for the Expos inconsistent play. Despite his regular power hitting in the minors, Bolick looks like he will be nothing more than a backup first baseman/third baseman in the majors.

	AB	R	HR	RBI	SB	BA	$
1993 Montreal NL	213	25	4	24	1	.211	-
1994 *Projection* >>>	107	13	2	12	1	.222	-

BONDS, BARRY - OF - BL - Age 29
The best player in baseball, Bonds was also a hit with the local fans, who saw little of the supposed disruption Barry was reputed to have caused in Pittsburgh. Attitude counts for nothing, anyway, so you can just enjoy his awesome four category contributions and let someone else complain about what a jerk Bonds is supposed to be.

	AB	R	HR	RBI	SB	BA	$
1992 Pittsburgh NL	473	109	34	103	39	.311	49
1993 San Francisco NL	539	129	46	123	29	.336	47
1994 *Projection* >>>	512	103	34	103	30	.307	44

BONILLA, BOBBY - OF/3B - BB - Age 31
While Bonilla's PR face has gone sour in New York, his on-field performance is coming along fine.

	AB	R	HR	RBI	SB	BA	$
1992 New York NL	438	62	19	70	4	.249	15
1993 New York NL	502	81	34	87	3	.265	19
1994 *Projection* >>>	536	83	22	89	3	.262	17

BOONE, BRET - 2B - BR - Age 24
Both his father and grandfather were successful major leaguers. He set a season record for Mariner second baseman with 12 home runs, despite playing only a half season. Lou Pinella sent him to the minors three times, once out of spring training, to work on the finer points such as following instructions, but Lou played him every day after a late July recall. The new scenery in Cincinnati will help.

	AB	R	HR	RBI	SB	BA	$
1992 Seattle AL	129	15	4	15	1	.194	-
1993 Calgary AAA	274	48	8	56	3	.332	
1993 Seattle AL	271	31	12	38	2	.251	5
1994 *Projection* >>>	441	53	14	64	5	.273	14

BORDERS, PAT - C - BR - Age 30
He's an above-average hitter as far as catchers go, but is increasingly becoming prone to chasing bad pitches. Word is spreading around the league not to pitch him strikes. He rarely walks and had the lowest on-base-percentage of any regular American League catcher. It is unlikely Borders will ever play 138 games in a season again.

	AB	R	HR	RBI	SB	BA	$
1992 Toronto AL	480	47	13	53	1	.242	7
1993 Toronto AL	488	38	9	55	2	.254	6
1994 *Projection* >>>	452	38	10	51	1	.249	6

BORDICK, MIKE - SS - BR - Age 28
Bordick returned to earth after his startling 1992 season. In 1991 he hit .238 with no power and little speed; in 1993 he hit .249 with no power and little speed (he did steal ten bases but was also caught ten times). The A's like his glove.

	AB	R	HR	RBI	SB	BA	$
1992 Oakland AL	504	62	3	48	12	.300	17
1993 Oakland AL	546	60	3	48	10	.249	7
1994 *Projection* >>>	479	54	2	43	9	.266	9

BOSTON, DARYL - OF- BL - Age 31
Boston started very slowly as a part-time outfielder in 1993. Eventually he started hitting home runs in bunches, and he ended the season strong, hitting .337 after August 3rd.

	AB	R	HR	RBI	SB	BA	$
1992 New York NL	289	37	11	35	12	.249	11
1993 Colorado NL	291	46	14	40	1	.261	7
1994 *Projection* >>>	284	38	9	33	8	.252	7

BOSTON, D.J. - OF - BR - Age 22
Daryl's brother does not have tremendous power, but can pick up a single or a double to cash in baserunners. He looks two or three years away from the majors still, but might make an impact earlier should there be an injury that creates a midseason vacancy.

	AB	R	HR	RBI	SB	BA	$
1993 Hagerstown A	464	76	13	92	31	.315	

BOURNIGAL, RAFAEL - 2B/SS - BR - Age 27
Jose Offerman's fielding problems provide Bournigal with a small opportunity for a reserve infield role. He has no chance to beat Offerman out, as Lasorda has always played the better offensive players at the expense of defense.

	AB	R	HR	RBI	SB	BA	$
1992 Los Angeles NL	20	1	0	0	0	.150	-
1993 Albuquerque AAA	465	75	4	55	3	.277	
1993 Los Angeles NL	18	0	0	3	0	.500	0

BOWERS, BRENT - OF - BL - Age 23
Bowers stole lots of bases at AA Knoxville in 1993, but he finished the season in a terrible slump and was moved from the leadoff spot to the bottom of the order. He may be stuck where he is.

	AB	R	HR	RBI	SB	BA	$
1993 Knoxville AA	577	63	5	43	36	.248	

BRAGG, DARREN - OF - BL - Age 24
Some power, lots of speed, and a great batting eye. Blue chip Mariners' prospect out of Georgia Tech and Team USA.

BRAGGS, GLENN - OF - BR - Age 31
A one time minor league sensation (with batting averages like .390 and .360) Braggs never fulfilled his promise and settled into a backup role. Now gone to Japan.

	AB	R	HR	RBI	SB	BA	$
1993 Japan	264	61	19	41	---	.345	

BRANSON, JEFF - SS/2B - BR - Age 27
Injuries to Barry Larkin and Bip Roberts gave Branson a chance to establish himself, but he didn't measure up, hitting .211 with no power or speed after the break while playing almost every day. Branson's range is limited (he suffered a career threatening knee injury in 1992) and is inadequate at shortstop, but he should still have a role as a utility player.

	AB	R	HR	RBI	SB	BA	$
1992 Nashville AAA	123	18	4	12	0	.325	
1992 Cincinnati NL	115	12	0	15	0	.296	1
1993 Cincinnati NL	381	40	3	22	4	.241	1
1994 *Projection* >>>	228	22	2	16	2	.250	0

BREAM, SID - 1B - BL - Age 33
The acquisition of McGriff hurt Bream the most, virtually wiping out his playing time. Bream took it like a professional, though, and became a useful pinch hitter down the stretch. With McGriff in the way and Klesko on the way, Bream's only hope of much playing time is with another club.

	AB	R	HR	RBI	SB	BA	$
1992 Atlanta NL	372	30	10	61	6	.261	12
1993 Atlanta NL	277	33	9	35	4	.260	6
1994 *Projection* >>>	198	19	5	26	3	.254	3

BREWER, ROD - OF/1B - BL - Age 28
Once considered a top prospect, Brewer will likely never be more than a reserve first baseman-outfielder with the Cardinals. He's a decent player, but doesn't figure to ever be a regular in the major leagues.

	AB	R	HR	RBI	SB	BA	$
1992 St. Louis NL	103	11	0	10	0	.301	0
1993 St. Louis NL	147	15	2	20	1	.286	2
1994 *Projection* >>>	110	11	1	13	1	.240	-

BRILEY, GREG - OF - BL - Age 28
Briley continued his gradual decline in 1993. He has decent speed, a little power, and might linger as an extra outfielder if he finds the right situation. He was waived by the Marlins in September 1993.

	AB	R	HR	RBI	SB	AVG	$
1992 Seattle AL	200	18	5	12	9	.275	6
1993 Florida NL	170	17	3	12	6	.194	-
1994 *Projection* >>>	216	21	3	14	10	.239	3

BRITO, BERNARDO - OF - BR - Age 30
Bernardo Brito's minor league home run totals look like he is approaching the record of Crash Davis. Brito is a career minor leaguer, called up last year as a reward for years of good service.

	AB	R	HR	RBI	SB	BA	$
1992 Minnesota AL	14	1	0	2	0	.143	-
1993 Portland AAA	319	64	20	72	0	.339	
1993 Minnesota AL	54	8	4	9	0	.241	-

BROGNA, RICO - 1B - BL - Age 23
Brogna was once considered one of the top Tigers prospects. But he has struggled in the high minors, and the Tigers are deep in first basemen. He doesn't have much of a future with Detroit. Furthermore, he wasn't protected in the expansion draft, and no one took him.

	AB	R	HR	RBI	SB	BA	$
1992 Toledo AAA	387	45	10	58	1	.261	
1992 Detroit AL	26	3	1	3	0	.192	-
1993 Toledo AAA	483	55	11	59	7	.273	

BROOKS, HUBIE - OF - BR - Age 37
Just hanging on. Good pinch hitter, but not much else. Won't last more than another year.

	AB	R	HR	RBI	SB	BA	$
1992 California AL	306	28	8	36	3	.216	2
1993 Kansas City AL	168	14	1	24	0	.286	1
1994 *Projection* >>>	163	12	3	16	1	.245	1

BROOKS, JERRY - OF - BR - Age 27
A 27-year-old outfielder/converted catcher, Brooks hit .344 with some speed at AAA Albuquerque and received a September callup. He isn't a great prospect at age 27, but the Dodger outfield is wide open.

BROSIUS, SCOTT - OF - BR - Age 27
Brosius is a low-average hitter who plays many positions. He hit 23 homers in Double-A in 1990 and has 12 homers in 368 major league at bats playing his home games in a pitcher's park. Could surprise with a big power year, especially if he is traded to a hitter's park.

	AB	R	HR	RBI	SB	BA	$
1992 Oakland AL	87	13	4	13	3	.218	1
1993 Tacoma AAA	209	38	8	41	8	.297	
1993 Oakland AL	213	26	6	25	6	.249	4
1994 *Projection* >>>	227	29	7	25	7	.242	4

BROWN, BRANT - 1B - BL - Age 22
Brown posted big time batting averages and is set to start 1994 as the AA Orlando first baseman. He hasn't shown much patience or big home run capability, but otherwise looks fairly good. Brown has only Matt Franco ahead of him if Grace departs, but anyone who thinks he's the next Mark Grace is dreaming.

BROWN, JARVIS - OF - BR - Age 27
Late in the year, Brown was starting most of the Padres games in center field. He has great speed (72 stolen bases in 1988), and he's a capable defensive player. Because defense is a needed commodity in the San Diego outfield, Brown may get even more chances in 1994. A move of Derek Bell back to center field would return Brown to the same status he had with the Twins; a pinch running and defensive outfield substitute.

	AB	R	HR	RBI	SB	BA	$
1992 Minnesota AL	15	8	0	0	2	.067	-
1993 Las Vegas AAA	402	74	3	47	22	.308	
1993 San Diego NL	133	21	0	8	3	.233	-
1994 *Projection* >>>	230	34	0	11	8	.248	2

BROWNE, JERRY - OF - BB - Age 28
Browne played well late in the season after suffering from injuries earlier. He is only 28 years old, and could easily get his batting average back into the .280s in 1994. Browne is valuable to his team, for his versatility and willingness to take a walk.

	AB	R	HR	RBI	SB	BA	$
1992 Oakland AL	324	43	3	40	3	.287	8
1993 Oakland AL	260	27	2	19	4	.250	1
1994 *Projection* >>>	286	32	2	28	3	.260	3

BRUETT, J.T. - OF - BL - Age 26
Like Jarvis Brown before him, Bruett is a speedy outfielder whose role is pinch running and occasional outfield defensive support.

	AB	R	HR	RBI	SB	BA	$
1992 Minnesota AL	76	7	0	2	6	.250	1
1993 Portland AAA	320	70	2	40	12	.322	
1993 Minnesota AL	20	2	0	1	0	.250	-
1994 *Projection* >>>	100	14	0	9	3	.261	-

BRUMFIELD, JACOB - OF - BR - Age 28
Brumfield was a solid reserve outfielder in 1993, and the Reds tried him out at second base near the end of the season. Despite eight years in the minors, he is only 28 and his role could expand in 1994.

	AB	R	HR	RBI	SB	BA	$
1992 Cincinnati NL	30	6	0	2	6	.133	-
1993 Indianapolis AAA	126	23	4	19	11	.325	
1993 Cincinnati NL	272	40	6	23	20	.268	11
1994 *Projection* >>>	216	29	3	18	16	.259	7

BRUMLEY, MIKE - 3B/SS/OF - BB - Age 30
A veteran outfielder-infielder, Brumley has never hit well in the majors, but had a big year at AAA Tucson in 1993. Claimed on waivers by Angels after the season, he could be a productive utility player.

	AB	R	HR	RBI	SB	BA	$
1992 Pawtucket AAA	365	50	4	41	14	.263	
1993 Tuscon AAA	346	65	0	46	24	.353	
1993 Houston NL	10	1	0	2	0	.300	-

BRUNANSKY, TOM - OF - BR - Age 33
The Brewers acquired Brunansky because they figured they would need outfield help some time during the 1993 season as a result of slumps and injuries, and because they figured Brunansky could still hit well. They were right on the first count and wrong on the second. Color him faded.

	AB	R	HR	RBI	SB	BA	$
1992 Boston AL	458	47	15	74	2	.266	13
1993 Milwaukee AL	224	20	6	29	3	.183	-
1994 *Projection* >>>	221	20	7	30	2	.230	2

BRYANT, PAT - OF - BR - Age 21
A very wild swinger who has averaged about one strikeout for every four at bats, this 1990 second round pick is raw, but talented. Hit for good power in 1993, and has surpassed 40 steals in both of his minor league seasons. In this organization, however, he's just another solid minor league outfield prospect.

BUECHELE, STEVE - 3B - BR - Age 32
He's about as exciting as Luis Salazar, but vastly better. Last year showed that his 1992 season was an injury induced fluke. Buechele is Gold Glove steady.

	AB	R	HR	RBI	SB	BA	$
1992 Pittsburgh-Chicago NL	524	52	9	64	1	.261	11
1993 Chicago NL	460	53	15	65	1	.272	11
1994 *Projection* >>>	493	54	13	65	1	.255	9

BUFORD, DAMON - OF - BR - Age 23
Buford hit like Ty Cobb when first called up, as he saw many fastballs, then the pitchers caught up with him, and he struggled mightily. He's a speedy guy without much power, and needs more time in Triple-A. The Orioles rushed him to the majors when Devereaux had shoulder miseries.

	AB	R	HR	RBI	SB	BA	$
1993 Rochester AAA	116	24	1	4	10	.284	
1993 Baltimore AL	79	18	2	9	2	.228	-
1994 *Projection* >>>	100	14	1	9	5	.238	0

BUHNER, JAY - OF - BR - Age 29
Hit for much better average than ever before, nearly .300 before the break, which led to an increased RBI total. He batted behind Ken Griffey who led the league in intentional walks.

	AB	R	HR	RBI	SB	BA	$
1992 Seattle AL	543	69	25	79	0	.243	13
1993 Seattle AL	563	91	27	98	2	.272	19
1994 *Projection* >>>	530	79	26	88	1	.259	17

BULLETT, SCOTT - OF - BL - Age 25
Bullett has a little power and a lot of speed. He will challenge for outfield time in Pittsburgh and could hit .265 with 10 or 12 steals, even as a platooner or off-the-bench player. Long range, he's a .280 average, 20 steals type of player.

BURKS, ELLIS - OF - BR - Age 29
After two years of complaints about unfulfilled promise in Boston, Burks had his healthiest season since 1990 for the White Sox last year. If the Chicago outfield hadn't been so crowded, Burks would have played even more. His speed is on the wane, but Burks still has fine power, and he will love hitting for the Rockies in 1994.

	AB	R	HR	RBI	SB	BA	$
1993 Chicago AL	499	75	17	74	6	.275	15
1994 Projection >>>	505	81	20	83	8	.290	17

BURNITZ, JEROMY - OF - BL - Age 24
Burnitz showed more speed than power at Tidewater last year, but he's got the power (31 homers at AA Williamsport in 1991). Jeromy is a great all-around athlete who has improved his defense and is learning to cut down his swing when behind in the count.

	AB	R	HR	RBI	SB	BA	$
1993 Norfolk AAA	255	33	8	44	10	.227	
1993 New York NL	263	49	13	38	3	.243	6
1994 *Projection* >>>	424	70	19	60	11	.239	12

BURTON, DARREN - SS - BB - Age 21
Switch hitting speedster, showed a little power at Single-A . Envisioned as leadoff hitter if he can reduce strikeouts (111 in 549 at bats in 1993). At least two years from majors.

BUSCH, MIKE - 3B - BR - Age 25
One question about Busch is how his Triple-A power numbers will translate in Dodger Stadium. At 6'5", 243 lbs., he should be big enough to hit the ball out. Busch answered another question by reducing his strikeout rate last year.

BUSH, RANDY - DH - BL - Age 35
Formerly one of Manager Tom Kelly's favorites, Bush was in only 35 games in 1993. He should retire.

	AB	R	HR	RBI	SB	BA	$
1992 Minnesota AL	182	14	2	22	1	.214	-
1993 Minnesota AL	45	1	0	3	0	.156	-
1994 *Projection* >>>	111	9	2	13	0	.225	-

BUTLER, BRETT - OF - BL - Age 36
Butler's gradual decline was hidden by the increase in league offensive totals. He scored only 80 runs despite a .387 on base percentage and 39 steals. Players of this type can play forever (or at least another year or two).

	AB	R	HR	RBI	SB	BA	$
1992 Los Angeles NL	553	86	3	39	41	.309	30
1993 Los Angeles NL	607	80	1	42	39	.298	25
1994 *Projection* >>>	591	84	2	38	37	.289	27

BUTLER, ROB - OF - BL - Age 24
Butler may inherit the left field spot in Toronto this year. He is the only Canadian on the roster, but isn't there by the virtue of his nationality. He can hit for average and is a throwback player in his effort and determination on the field. Butler has a great eye, good speed and has the potential to be a major league .300 hitter.

	AB	R	HR	RBI	SB	BA	$
1993 Syracuse AAA	208	30	1	14	7	.284	
1993 Toronto AL	48	8	0	2	2	.271	-
1994 *Projection* >>>	220	28	2	16	5	.257	3

BYRD, ANTHONY - OF - BR - Age 23
Byrd took a while to get used to professional pitching and wooden bats in 1992, but he did fine at Class A Ft. Wayne in 1993: a .292 average with 16 homers and 24 steals. The basic issue was patience for this speed/power prospect.

CABRERA, FRANCISCO - 1B - BR - Age 27
Cabrera was the man the Braves went to for a late-inning long ball. He has fine power, but was just a pinch hitter. Now he'll get to play more -- in Japan.

CALDERON, IVAN - OF/DH - BR - Age 32
Two lost seasons in a row don't paint a rosy picture for Calderon. However, he can probably still contribute as a part timer if given a chance. A season like he put together in 1991 (.300, 75 RBI, 31 steals) won't ever happen again, but Calderon could still be a 10/10 man with luck.

	AB	R	HR	RBI	SB	BA	$
1992 Montreal NL	170	19	3	24	1	.265	3
1993 Chicago AL	239	26	1	22	4	.209	-
1994 *Projection* >>>	256	31	5	32	8	.250	5

CAMERON, STANTON - 1B - BL - Age 24
Cameron appears to be the best power prospect in the Baltimore organization. Expected to reach Triple-A in 1994. Needs to reduce his strikeouts (103 in 384 at bats).

	AB	R	HR	RBI	SB	BA	$
1992 Frederick A	409	76	29	92	2	.247	
1993 Bowie AA	384	65	21	64	6	.276	

CAMINITI, KEN - 3B - BB - Age 30
This hard-nosed player has established an exceptionally consistent level of performance; he has hit 13 homers in each of the past three years, averaging 72 RBI. Caminiti should produce at this level for a few more years. His batting average dropped back to normal level in 1993. His strong defense makes him hard to replace.

	AB	R	HR	RBI	SB	BA	$
1992 Houston NL	506	68	13	62	10	.294	21
1993 Houston NL	543	75	13	75	8	.262	12
1994 *Projection* >>>	536	71	13	72	8	.270	16

CANATE, WILLIAM - OF - BR - Age 22
Canate was a Rule Five draftee. The Blue Jays couldn't demote him and had to keep him on the roster. He is almost certainly headed to the minor leagues this year. He has good speed and might hit .280-.300 one day. That day isn't in the very near future.

	AB	R	HR	RBI	SB	BA	$
1993 Toronto AL	47	12	1	3	1	.213	-
1994 *Projection* >>>	50	7	1	6	1	.236	-

CANDAELE, CASEY - - 2B - BB - Age 33
A popular and versatile utilityman who could stick around another year or two in a limited role.

	AB	R	HR	RBI	SB	BA	$
1992 Houston NL	320	19	1	18	7	.213	-
1993 Houston NL	121	18	1	7	2	.240	-
1994 *Projection* >>>	164	16	1	13	3	.235	-

CANGELOSI, JOHN - OF - BB - Age 31
Veteran John Cangelosi had a nice year in Triple-A last year in the Tigers system. He swiped 39 bases indicating that he still has some legs left. He has over 1000 major league at bats with a .235 batting average.

CANSECO, JOSE - OF - BR - Age 29

A disastrous pitching outing in Boston ended his season, and possibly his career in the field. A torn ligament in his elbow required "Tommy John" surgery. Canseco told the Rangers late in the '93 season that he would learn to play first base if the team was unable to re-sign Palmeiro.

	AB	R	HR	RBI	SB	BA	$
1992 Oakland-Texas AL	439	74	26	87	6	.244	17
1993 Texas AL	231	30	10	46	6	.255	7
1994 Projection >>>	210	35	12	42	5	.254	8

CANSECO, OZZIE - OF - BR - Age 29

Ozzie never escaped the long shadow cast by his twin brother Jose. He was sent to the minors by the Cardinals despite a big spring training performance in 1993 and never recovered from the disappointment. At the end of May, he retired from AAA Louisville to sell automobiles.

CARABALLO, GARY - 3B - BR - Age 22

He lost the third base battle with Joe Randa, then spent season at Single-A Wilmington and on the DL. He has a good batting eye and hit .303, but has little power or speed. Caraballo would have to overtake Randa to move into crowded Royals third base picture; he may move up to AA Memphis in 1994.

CARABALLO, RAMON - 2B - BB - Age 24

He still needs work defensively, but Caraballo can run and he can hit. He only seems less of a prospect when compared to his Triple-A teammates. Lemke is far from entrenched at second base in Atlanta and could be challenged by Caraballo as early as 1994. The most likely scenario is yet another year at Richmond for Caraballo while he works out the remaining defensive kinks. He won't be a big star in the majors, but he'll be a steady offensive second baseman someday.

	AB	R	HR	RBI	SB	BA	$
1992 Greenville AA	93	15	1	8	10	.312	
1992 Richmond AAA	405	42	2	40	19	.281	
1993 Richmond AAA	470	73	3	41	20	.272	

CAREY, PAUL - 1B - BR - Age 26

Paul Carey had some outstanding years with Stanford, a top college team, and the Orioles hoped that he would develop into a major league power hitter. He struggled for a few years, finally having a nice year last year in Triple-A, but the big power hasn't developed. At age 26, he will soon run out of chances. Segui could be dealt, opening a spot for the less expensive Carey as a reserve. More than likely, however, Carey will return to Rochester.

	AB	R	H	RBI	SB	BA	$
1993 Rochester AAA	325	63	12	50	0	.311	
1993 Baltimore AL	47	1	0	3	0	.213	-
1994 Projection >>>	100	11	3	10	0	.267	0

CARMONA, GREG - SS - BB - Age 25

Gets to everything with his glove, gets to nothing with his bat. Look elsewhere.

CARR, CHUCK - OF - BB - Age 25

The last National League stolen base champ who didn't repeat was Ron LeFlore in 1980. Carr is still not an accomplished hitter; he draws few walks and has little power. As recently as 1991, he hit .195 in Triple-A. He reminds me of Alex Cole; it shouldn't be long before the Marlins get Carr sick. Draft him for the steals, but if he hits the wall offensively, Carl Everett's waiting.

	AB	R	H	RBI	SB	BA	$
1992 Louisville AAA	377	68	3	28	53	.308	
1992 St. Louis NL	64	8	0	3	10	.219	1
1993 Florida NL	551	75	4	41	58	.267	27
1994 Projection >>>	388	52	3	29	42	.263	15

CARREON, MARK - OF - BR - Age 30

Carreon is a terrific pinch hitter, which should keep him in the majors for many years as a bench player. He can help with the occasional homer, but his chances of getting 400 at bats in a season are long gone.

	AB	R	HR	RBI	SB	BA	$
1992 Detroit AL	336	34	10	41	3	.232	4
1993 San Francisco NL	150	22	7	33	1	.327	7
1994 *Projection* >>>	229	25	7	34	2	.268	5

CARRILLO, MATIAS - OF -BL - Age 30

Carrillo decimated Mexican League pitching in 1992 & 1993, hitting .350 and averaging 32 home runs, 118 RBI, and 28 stolen bases - but, as Tigers fans will remember, Barbaro Garbey also ripped up Mexican League pitching.

	AB	R	HR	RBI	SB	BA	$
1993 Florida NL	55	4	0	3	0	.255	-
1994 *Projection* >>>-	60	7	1	7	0	.262	-

CARTER, JEFF - OF - BB - Age 30

Carter had a nice season last year, but it was his fourth year in Triple-A. He sure looks like a career minor leaguer.

CARTER, JOE - OF - BR - Age 34

Every year, his doubters say he drives in runs because he's always a cleanup hitter. He doesn't take a lot of walks and doesn't hit .300. However, he is the most consistent run producer over the last eight years. Every season, you can pencil him in for thirty home runs and 100 RBI. Carter has passed the threshold that says unless he proves he no longer can do it, then he will continue to do it.

	AB	R	HR	RBI	SB	BA	$
1992 Toronto AL	622	97	34	119	12	.264	29
1993 Toronto AL	603	92	33	121	8	.254	22
1994 *Projection* >>>	615	92	31	110	11	.258	25

CARTER, MIKE - SS - BR - Age 24

Third round pick in 1990. Carter has received two consecutive midseason promotions -- reminiscent of Pat Listach.

CARTER, STEVE - OF - BL - Age 29

Once one of Pittsburgh's brightest prospects, Carter was obtained by the Astros in a minor league trade with the Reds. He has topped out at Triple-A.

CASE, MIKE - OF - BR - Age 25

Case's .276-11-80-21 season for Single-A Central Valley earned him a late season promotion to AAA Colorado Springs, but he's too old to be considered a serious prospect. Besides, he strikes out way too much (120 strikeouts in 452 at bats).

CASILLAS, ADAM - OF - BL - Age 28

Good singles hitter, but little power and no speed. Your basic minor league extension of the major league bench.

	AB	R	HR	RBI	SB	BA	$
1992 Memphis AA	168	25	2	23	1	.327	
1992 Omaha AAA	362	41	0	27	3	.307	
1993 Memphis AA	450	53	4	49	3	.304	

CASTELLANO, PEDRO - 3B - BR - Age 24

Castellano hit three home runs in only 71 at bats in 1993, but he'll spend another year in Triple-A, behind some better prospects.

	AB	R	HR	RBI	SB	BA	$
1993 Colorado NL	71	12	3	7	1	.183	-
1994 *Projection* >>>	100	12	2	11	1	.242	-

CASTILLA, VINNY - 3B - BR - Age 26

He started strong as a backup, but pitchers figured him out and he hit only .193 in the second half. Look for a similar performance in 1994 with Castilla splitting time between Denver and the minors. His good glove will help him get playing time.

	AB	R	HR	RBI	SB	BA	$
1992 Richmond AAA	449	49	7	44	1	.252	
1992 Atlanta NL	16	1	0	1	0	.250	-
1993 Colorado NL	337	36	9	30	2	.255	4
1994 *Projection* >>>	255	19	6	22	2	.255	2

CASTILLO, BRAULIO - OF - BR - Age 25

Castillo was once a hot prospect in the Dodgers' organization, showing both speed and power, but then he had a bad year in 1990, which, combined with some off-field problems, led to his arrival with the Phillies and subsequent exposure in the expansion draft. Castillo had a good spring training but still couldn't make the Rockies in 1993.

	AB	R	HR	RBI	SB	BA	$
1992 Scranton AAA	386	59	13	47	8	.246	
1992 Philadelphia NL	76	12	2	7	1	.197	-
1993 Colorado Springs AAA	156	34	2	22	8	.359	

CASTRO, JUAN - SS - BR - Age 21

He has made steady progress in two and a half pro seasons, Castro is a steady hitter in the .270 range, and barely a 50 percent base stealer. Expect the same at AAA Albuquerque this season.

CEDENO, ANDUJAR - SS - BR - Age 24

Cedeno experienced a breakthrough year in 1993 both offensively and defensively. The key was cutting down on his long looping swing (which still reappears occasionally). He should continue to improve with his prime years ahead of him.

	AB	R	HR	RBI	SB	BA	$
1992 Tucson AAA	280	27	6	56	6	.293	
1992 Houston NL	220	15	2	13	2	.173	-
1993 Houston NL	505	69	11	56	9	.283	14
1994 *Projection* >>>	548	72	13	60	10	.270	15

CEDENO, DOMINGO - SS - BB - Age 25

Andujar's brother was the stop gap between Dick Schofield getting hurt and Tony Fernandez being acquired. He has great potential defensively, but his hitting is in question. Toronto without Fernandez might go with Cedeno, but only if Schofield isn't around.

	AB	R	HR	RBI	SB	BA	$
1993 Syracuse AAA	382	58	2	28	15	.272	
1993 Toronto AL	46	5	0	7	1	.174	-
1994 *Projection* >>>	50	4	0	5	3	.241	-

CEDENO, ROGER - OF - BB - Age 19

The number six prospect in the Texas League according to Baseball America, Cedeno is a high average, speedy outfielder and could move up to the Dodgers in a hurry. Cedeno hit .288-4-30-28 at AA San Antonio.

CHAMBERLAIN, WES - OF - BR - Age 27

At this point, it's become pretty clear that he will never be the star that the Phils, and before them the Pirates, envisioned. Still, he was a darn good platoon player for the Phils in 1993, mashing lefties at a .328 clip. He slugged .492, and threw out 10 baserunners from right field despite limited playing time. He still needs to become a more disciplined hitter if he is to fulfill his potential.

	AB	R	HR	RBI	SB	BA	$
1992 Philadelphia NL	275	26	9	41	4	.258	8
1993 Philadelphia NL	284	34	12	45	2	.282	9
1994 *Projection* >>>	298	34	11	45	4	.266	9

CHEMELIS, JOEL - 3B - BR - Age 26

Chemelis didn't hit in Double-A, but for the second time in two partial Triple-A seasons, he batted better than .300 at Phoenix. In five previous minor league seasons, he has never hit more than ten homers. His hope for major league service is an emergency callup.

CHRISTOPHERSON, ERIC - C - BR - Age 24
San Francisco's top pick in 1990 out of San Diego State, Christopherson is the latest in the line of Giants catching hopefuls. A good defensive catcher who hasn't proven he can hit, Christopherson lost most of the '93 season to injury.

	AB	R	HR	RBI	SB	BA	$
1992 Shreveport AA	270	36	6	34	1	.252	
1993 Shreveport AA	46	5	0	2	1	.152	

CIANFROCCO, ARCHI - 3B/1B - BR - Age 27
A pleasant surprise for a cheap midseason acquisition, Cianfrocco generated good power and was part of the reason the Padres scored more runs per game after McGriff and Sheffield were dealt. Despite the power, he has had a high strikeout rate throughout his professional career. Cianfrocco is not a guaranteed starter even with San Diego.

	AB	R	HR	RBI	SB	BA	$
1992 Montreal NL	232	25	6	30	3	.241	4
1993 Ottawa AAA	188	21	4	27	4	.298	
1993 Montreal-San Diego NL	296	30	12	48	2	.243	6
1994 *Projection* >>>	225	23	3	27	2	.242	1

CIRILLO, JEFF - 3B - BR - Age 24
A .341 start at AA El Paso earned Cirillo a job at AAA New Orleans where he did fine. Now he's a .319 career hitter.

CLARK, DAVE - OF - BL - Age 31
After spending most of the previous two seasons in Triple-A, Clark got another major league shot as a role player with the Pirates in 1993. He made the most of the opportunity and had his finest season. He isn't good enough to play everyday but can be productive if utilized correctly as a platoon player or fourth outfielder.

	AB	R	HR	RBI	SB	BA	$
1992 Buffalo AAA	253	43	11	56	6	.304	
1992 Pittsburgh NL	33	3	2	7	0	.212	-
1993 Pittsburgh NL	277	43	11	46	1	.271	7
1994 *Projection* >>>	226	33	8	36	1	.261	4

CLARK, JACK - DH - BR - Age 38
Showed up at spring training 1993 for a trial with the Expos. Obviously he didn't make it.

CLARK, JERALD - OF/1B - BR - Age 30
A 13-game hitting streak helped Clark reach career highs in homers and RBI. Don Baylor would love to have him keep the starting left field job in spring training, but he needs to hit for more power; 13 home runs for a team playing half of its games in Mile High Stadium just isn't going to cut it. Clark also filled in ably at first base in Galarraga's absence.

	AB	R	HR	RBI	SB	BA	$
1992 San Diego NL	496	45	12	58	3	.242	9
1993 Colorado NL	478	65	13	67	9	.282	15
1994 *Projection* >>>	487	49	14	62	5	.285	15

CLARK, PHIL - OF/1B - BR - Age 25
Clark played 37 games in the outfield, 24 at first base and 11 behind the plate. The kid brother of Jerald Clark and a former first round draft pick (Tigers), he's unlikely to be an everyday player and is an emergency catcher only.

	AB	R	HR	RBI	SB	BA	$
1992 Toledo AAA	271	29	10	39	4	.280	
1992 Detroit AL	54	3	1	5	1	.407	1
1993 San Diego NL	240	33	9	33	2	.313	9
1994 *Projection* >>>	138	16	4	15	1	.255	1

CLARK, TIM - OF - BL - Age 25
Clark led the minors in RBI in 1993 and led a bunch of 24-year-olds to the Single-A California League title. Clark led the California League in batting average and extra-base hits, too. However, he has no significant likelihood of making the majors, especially with all of the younger (and better) outfield prospects in the Marlins' system.

	AB	R	HR	RBI	SB	BA	$
1993 High Desert A	510	109	17	126	2	.363	

CLARK, WILL - 1B - BL - Age 30

Clark has had injuries the last couple of years, which have brought his production down. A late season surge shows Clark is still capable of very good numbers when he is healthy, and in perhaps his worst season he still hit .283. Though his career numbers are more balanced, in 1993 Clark hit .321 on the road, worth considering as he heads to Texas.

	AB	R	HR	RBI	SB	BA	$
1992 San Francisco NL	513	69	16	73	12	.300	26
1993 San Francisco NL	491	82	14	73	2	.283	13
1994 *Projection* >>>	511	90	20	93	6	.295	24

CLAYTON, ROYCE - SS - BR - Age 24

From Steven Rubio, who sees Clayton more than I do: John Benson has been saying that Clayton seems more like the next Mariano Duncan than the next Barry Larkin. After 1993, perhaps somewhere in the middle, but closer to Larkin, is the right spot to place Royce. At age 23, Clayton had a better season than any Duncan had had before he was 27, and many of his stats are better than Larkin's at the same age. However, Clayton still strikes out too much and he needs to work on his basestealing. His 70 RBI are somewhat deceiving; he hit only .253 with runners in scoring position, his high RBI total was a result of the league's leader in on base percentage batting two spots ahead of Clayton in the Giants lineup.

	AB	R	HR	RBI	SB	BA	$
1992 Phoenix AAA	192	30	3	18	15	.240	
1992 San Francisco NL	321	31	4	24	8	.224	2
1993 San Francisco NL	549	54	6	70	11	.282	14
1994 *Projection* >>>	385	37	4	43	8	.264	8

CLYBURN, DANNY - OF - BR - Age 20

Taken in the second round of the 1992 draft from a rural South Carolina high school, Clyburn has shown power and speed in the minors. He's still very raw but some members of the Pirates' front office feel he may be the best player in the system. Clyburn won't reach the majors for a while, though, as the Pirates must polish his rough edges.

	AB	R	HR	RBI	SB	BA	$
1992 Bradenton R	149	26	4	25	7	.342	
1993 Augusta A	457	55	9	66	5	.265	

COLBERT, CRAIG - C - BR - Age 29

Colbert plays the infield in addition to serving as a third catcher; he can't hit.

	AB	R	HR	RBI	SB	BA	$
1992 Phoenix AAA	140	16	1	12	0	.321	
1992 San Francisco NL	126	10	1	16	1	.230	-
1993 San Francisco NL	37	2	1	5	0	.162	-
1994 *Projection* >>>	60	4	1	8	0	.209	-

COLBRUNN, GREG - 1B - BR - Age 24

Claimed by the Marlins from the Expos on waivers just after the end of the 1993 season, Colbrunn was once a premier catching prospect. 1991 elbow surgery necessitated his move to first base and he missed the second half of the 1993 season due to recurring elbow problems. He has a live bat with decent power, but is totally impatient, a major drawback. If healthy, he'll get to battle Destrade for a platoon first base job in 1994.

	AB	R	HR	RBI	SB	BA	$
1992 Indianapolis AAA	216	32	11	48	1	.306	
1992 Montreal NL	168	12	2	18	3	.268	2
1993 Montreal NL	153	15	4	23	4	.255	3
1994 *Projection* >>>	132	11	3	17	3	.260	1

COLE, ALEX - OF - BL - Age 28

Don Baylor wanted a center fielder/leadoff hitter who could get innings started. Cole didn't pan out despite stealing 30 bases. He finished badly with just two RBI in his final 93 at bats and no extra base hits after August 21. Cole's job is far from guaranteed. What is guaranteed is the three year contract given to Ellis Burks.

	AB	R	HR	RBI	SB	BA	$
1992 Cleveland AL	97	11	0	5	9	.206	
1992 Pittsburgh NL	205	33	0	10	7	.278	4
1993 Colorado NL	348	50	0	24	30	.256	12
1994 *Projection* >>>	339	49	0	21	25	.263	12

COLEMAN, VINCE - OF - BB - Age 32

Coleman has actually played very well when on the field in a Mets uniform. He just hasn't been on the field enough, due to physical and personal problems (he was, by the way, NOT implicated in the World Trade Center bombing). Somewhere there is a team that wants, or needs, his speed in 1994.

	AB	R	HR	RBI	SB	BA	$
1992 New York NL	229	37	2	21	24	.275	12
1993 New York NL	373	64	2	25	38	.279	18
1994 *Projection* >>>	309	51	2	22	33	.270	16

COLES, DARNELL - OF - BR - Age 31

Coles has become a reserve infielder-outfielder. He works hard and serves his team well. His big swing is capable of producing occasional pinch hit home runs, and he is more selective at the plate than he had been in his National League years. He appears to have grown comfortable at both third base and in left field. He will continue to pick up plate appearances coming off the bench.

	AB	R	HR	RBI	SB	BA	$
1992 Nashville AAA	81	19	6	16	1	.296	
1992 Cincinnati NL	141	16	3	18	1	.312	4
1993 Toronto AL	194	26	4	26	1	.253	1
1994 *Projection* >>>	146	17	3	18	1	.257	1

COLON, CRIS - SS - BB - Age 25

Good glove, no bat. No room for him on the Rangers roster; dropped from the 40-man roster, with the team citing his "lack of confidence".

	AB	R	HR	RBI	SB	BA	$
1992 Tulsa AA	415	35	1	44	7	.263	
1992 Texas AL	36	5	0	1	0	.167	-
1993 Tulsa AA	490	63	11	47	6	.300	

CONINE, JEFF - OF - BR - Age 27

Conine surprised some people in 1993. He'll move to first base if both Nigel Wilson and Darrell Whitmore win outfield jobs; otherwise, he'll remain in left field. He has below average power for either a first baseman or outfielder, and future development is doubtful at the age of 27. Conine led the National League in games played; he didn't miss a single contest.

	AB	R	HR	RBI	SB	BA	$
1992 Omaha AAA	397	69	20	72	4	.302	
1992 Kansas City AL	91	10	0	9	0	.253	-
1993 Florida NL	595	75	12	79	2	.292	15
1994 *Projection* >>>	508	63	9	65	2	.288	15

COOLBAUGH, SCOTT - 3B - BR - Age 27

It is significant that the Orioles did not call up veteran Scott Coolbaugh from Rochester when they needed a third baseman. But he did hit 18 dingers last year, so he may get another shot somewhere in 1994.

	AB	R	HR	RBI	SB	BA	$
1993 Rochester AAA	421	52	18	67	0	.245	

COOMER, RON - 3B - BR - Age 27

Third baseman who went absolutely bonkers at two stops last year after no previous history of success. He's old for a guy who has yet to debut in the majors and doesn't walk much. Almost a year older than Ventura and probably a one year wonder.

	AB	R	HR	RBI	SB	BA	$
1993 Birmingham AA	262	44	13	50	1	.324	
1993 Nashville AAA	211	34	13	51	1	.313	

COOPER, GARY - 3B - BR - Age 29

Just a career minor leaguer, but a good one. With a few lucky breaks he could get some major league time in 1993. Hit over .300 with fair power both of the last two years at Triple-A.

	AB	R	HR	RBI	SB	BA	$
1993 Buffalo AAA	349	66	16	63	2	.269	

COOPER, SCOTT - 3B - BL - Age 26

Is there life in Boston after Wade Boggs? Sure. Cooper is no star, but he can play. Has better power than what he showed so far. Cooper is, of course, the guy who made Boston willing to trade Jeff Bagwell.

	AB	R	HR	RBI	SB	BA	$
1992 Boston AL	337	34	5	33	1	.276	6
1993 Boston AL	526	67	9	63	5	.279	12
1994 Projection >>>	526	64	10	61	4	.281	13

CORA, JOEY - 2B - BB - Age 28

Who'da thunk it? 579 at bat's for Joey Cora. He will take a walk, and therefore score some runs and steal some bases. Also he led the American League in sac bunts. Is supposed to be fantastic on defense, but is overrated. Give Cora some slump time or an injury, and Grebeck will be back.

	AB	R	HR	RBI	SB	BA	$
1992 Chicago AL	122	27	0	9	10	.246	3
1993 Chicago AL	579	95	2	51	20	.268	14
1994 Projection >>>	369	63	1	32	15	.263	9

CORDERO, WILFREDO - SS - BR - Age 22

Though he's still very young, Cordero has been described as a disappointment to the Expos. The criticism is bunk. Cordero is already a competent major leaguer, at an age when many players are in college or Class A. This guy is a future star, big time.

	AB	R	HR	RBI	SB	BA	$
1992 Indianapolis AAA	204	32	6	27	6	.314	
1992 Montreal NL	126	17	2	8	0	.302	2
1993 Montreal NL	475	56	10	58	12	.248	10
1994 Projection >>>	509	62	11	58	11	.256	15

CORDOVA, MARTY - OF - BR - Age 24

Talented top prospect Marty Cordova had some difficulty adjusting to Class Double-A pitching last year. He started strong, but tailed off later in the season. He has some power and speed, but needs to cut down on the strikeouts.

	AB	R	HR	RBI	SB	BA	$
1992 Visalia A	513	103	28	131	13	.341	
1993 Nashville AA	508	83	19	77	10	.250	

CORREIA, ROD - SS - BR - Age 26

Will back up DiSarcina. Worth watching as he is a better hitter than DiSarcina, and fields well.

	AB	R	HR	RBI	SB	BA	$
1993 Vancouver AAA	207	43	4	28	11	.271	
1993 California AL	128	12	0	9	2	.266	-
1994 Projection >>>	64	6	0	5	1	.225	-

COSTO, TIM - OF - BR - Age 25

Previously a free swinging power hitter, Costo made significant progress in 1993, cutting his strikeouts in half and hitting .326 at Triple-A . His power totals were down but his versatility (he has played first base, third base and outfield) gives him a good chance to make the team out of spring training in 1994.

	AB	R	HR	RBI	SB	BA	$
1992 Chattanooga AA	424	63	28	71	4	.241	
1992 Cincinnati NL	36	3	0	2	0	.222	-
1993 Cincinnati NL	98	13	3	12	0	.224	-

COTTO, HENRY - OF - BR - Age 33

A useful spare outfielder, he toasted lefthanded pitching at about a .400 clip in 1993. It was noted here last year that his 1992 base-stealing performance raised his all-time success rate to 84.4 percent - well, the percentage went up again in 1993 to an even 85 percent, as he was thrown out only once in twelve tries. He's been essentially the same player for six years - very consistent. Cotto became a free agent at the end of 1993 season; the Marlins wanted him back as an insurance policy on their kids.

	AB	R	HR	RBI	SB	BA	$
1992 Seattle AL	294	42	5	27	23	.259	12
1993 Seattle AL	105	10	2	7	5	.190	-
1993 Florida NL	135	15	3	14	11	.296	6
1994 Projection >>>	247	32	5	23	18	.260	10

COTTON, JOHN - 2B - BL - Age 23

A 1989 10th-round pick, this converted second baseman has an interesting array of skills. Until 1993, his minor league averages were around .200, but he has always hit for decent power, with high walk totals. He has consistently stolen over 20 bases. His biggest negative is that he has spent two seasons at Class A Kinston, with lots of strikeouts. Another drawback is the abundance of outfield prospects in line ahead of him.

	AB	R	HR	RBI	SB	BA	$
1993 Kinston A	454	81	13	51	28	.264	

CRAWFORD, CARLOS - OF - BR - Age 22

Made great strides at Single-A Kinston in 1993, cutting his walks in half without sacrificing power. One more year of similar development will give him a chance to reach the major leagues.

CROMER, TRIPP - SS - BR - Age 26

The slick fielding Cromer had a breakthrough offensive season at AAA Louisville last year; he's the Cardinals' shortstop of the future. Of course, with Ozzie Smith still around, that's kind of like being the Maytag repairman.

	AB	R	HR	RBI	SB	BA	$
1993 Louisville AAA	309	39	11	33	1	.275	

CRON, CHRIS - 1B - BR - Age 30

Will only see playing time in the event of an injury to Frank Thomas.

	AB	R	HR	RBI	SB	BA	$
1992 Vancouver AAA	500	76	16	81	12	.278	
1992 Chicago AL	10	0	0	0	0	.000	-
1993 Nashville AAA	460	69	22	68	2	.257	

CRUZ, IVAN - 1B - BL - Age 25

Cruz was once rated highly in the Detroit farm system, but he had a bad year at Triple-A last year, setting him back.

	AB	R	HR	RBI	SB	BA	$
1993 Toledo AAA	402	44	13	50	1	.226	

CUMMINGS, MIDRE - OF - BB - Age 22

The Pirates' most-hyped prospect since Barry Bonds, the sweet-swinging Cummings has hit well throughout his minor league career, and the consensus is that he should become a superstar. However, during his September callup to Pittsburgh, Cummings showed he needs at least another half season in the minors. His only drawback might be a questionable work ethic.

	AB	R	HR	RBI	SB	BA	$
1992 Salem A	420	55	14	75	23	.305	
1993 Buffalo AAA	232	36	9	21	5	.276	
1993 Pittsburgh NL	36	5	0	3	0	.111	-
1994 Projection >>>	100	11	2	8	2	.246	-

CURTIS, CHAD - OF - BR - Age 25

Will start again in center. Steals a lot of bases, but gets caught 50 percent of the time.

	AB	R	HR	RBI	SB	BA	$
1992 California AL	441	59	10	46	43	.259	25
1993 California AL	583	94	6	59	48	.285	33
1994 *Projection* >>>	437	66	6	45	38	.276	24

CURTIS, RANDY - OF - BL - Age 23

The Mets farm has lost a few prospects over the years, but it still has Curtis, the franchise hope for it's first exciting home-grown leadoff hitter since Len Dykstra. Last year at Class A St, Lucie he hit .319 with 52 stolen bases.

CUYLER, MILT - OF - BB - Age 25

Several years ago, Milt Cuyler said that his game is centered around his legs. Last year he was injured for the second year in a row. He is a singles hitter, and there is big upward potential, though. He won't have much value if he doesn't return at full speed.

	AB	R	HR	RBI	SB	BA	$
1992 Detroit AL	291	39	3	28	8	.241	4
1993 Detroit AL	249	46	0	19	13	.213	2
1994 *Projection* >>>	301	49	2	24	16	.234	5

DALESANDRO, MARK - 3B - BR - Age 25
Hit better after he moved up from the California League to the Texas League. Doesn't have the power you'd associate with a cornerman. It's a good thing for his career that he also has done some catching. Could reach the majors as a utilityman in '95.

	AB	R	HR	RBI	SB	BA	$
1993 Vancouver AAA	107	16	2	15	1	.299	

DAMON, JOHNNY - OF - BL - Age 20
Sandwich pick in 1992 between first and second rounds. Rated Royals best prospect by Baseball America and compared to George Brett. Has excellent speed and good batting average (59 stolen bases, .290). Will move up rapidly through the thin Royals farm system. An excellent athlete.

DANIELS, KAL - OF - BL - Age 30
Daniels was rumored to be at spring training with the Expos in 1993. Knee injuries ruined what looked to be a promising career. He hit .296 with 27 home runs and 94 RBI in 1990, but fell off sharply.

	AB	R	HR	RBI	SB	BA	$
1992 LA-Chicago NL	212	21	6	25	0	.241	2

DASCENZO, DOUG - OF - BB - Age 29
Injuries to Rangers outfielders created playing time for Dascenzo in 1993. This year he should see playing time mainly as a late inning defensive replacement or pinch-runner.

	AB	R	HR	RBI	SB	BA	$
1992 Chicago NL	376	37	0	20	6	.255	3
1993 Oklahoma City AAA	157	21	1	13	6	.248	
1993 Texas AL	146	20	2	10	2	.199	-
1994 Projection >>>	238	29	1	15	5	.238	0

DAUGHERTY, JACK - OF - BB - Age 33
The past season was likely the end of the line for Daugherty, as he was released by the Reds. Daugherty has no power, speed, or defense.

	AB	R	HR	RBI	SB	BA	$
1992 Texas AL	127	13	0	9	2	.205	-
1993 Tuscon AAA	141	23	2	29	1	.390	
1993 Cincinnati NL	62	7	2	9	0	.226	-
1994 Projection >>>	97	9	1	9	1	.209	-

DAULTON, DARREN - C - BL - Age 32
Daulton enjoyed his second straight stellar offensive season. He has slugged .502 with 51 home runs, 214 RBI, and 205 walks over the past two seasons. He now has competition from Wilkins and Piazza for offense among National League catchers, and while they are on the upswing, Daulton has likely peaked. Still only a career .237 hitter.

	AB	R	HR	RBI	SB	BA	$
1992 Philadelphia NL	485	80	27	109	11	.270	29
1993 Philadelphia NL	510	90	24	105	5	.257	16
1994 Projection >>>	454	69	20	80	6	.244	13

DAVIS, ALVIN - 1B - BL - Age 33
In the middle of 1992, Davis went to Japan hoping to re-discover his power stroke. He won't likely come back without it.

DAVIS, BUTCH - OF - BR - Age 35
Another Ranger outfielder who benefitted from the injuries to Canseco and Hulse in 1993. Davis was dropped from the 40-man roster after the season, but will get a shot at making the team in the spring.

	AB	R	HR	RBI	SB	BA	$
1992 Syracuse AAA	550	67	9	74	19	.280	
1993 Texas AL	159	24	3	20	3	.245	1
1994 Projection >>>	80	12	2	10	2	.244	-

DAVIS, CHILI - DH - BB - Age 34

In 1993 Chili was happy to be back in sunny southern California, and happy to see expansion's effect on the pitcher population.

	AB	R	HR	RBI	SB	BA	$
1992 Minnesota AL	444	63	12	66	4	.288	
1993 California AL	573	74	27	112	4	.243	16
1994 *Projection* >>>	524	67	20	87	4	.253	15

DAVIS, ERIC - OF- BR - Age 31

The Tigers were very pleased with Eric Davis last year, and planned to make a strong effort to sign him for 1994. He is a very talented multi-dimensional player who can be very valuable to a Rotisserie team, but he has a history of major injuries.

	AB	R	HR	RBI	SB	BA	$
1992 Los Angeles NL	267	21	5	32	19	.228	9
1993 Los Angeles NL	376	57	14	53	33	.234	18
1993 Detroit AL	75	14	6	15	2	.253	1
1994 *Projection* >>>	402	56	16	57	30	.242	20

DAVIS, GLENN - 1B - BR - Age 33

Another injury-plagued season solidifed the view that his acquisition was the worst trade in club history. Oriole fans know that with Curt Schilling, Pete Harnisch and Steve Finley in the lineup during the last two seasons instead of Davis, Baltimore would have won at least one division title. Meanwhile, Davis' future looks gloomy.

	AB	R	HR	RBI	SB	BA	$
1992 Baltimore AL	398	46	13	48	1	.276	11
1993 Baltimore AL	113	8	1	9	0	.177	-
1994 *Projection* >>>	218	24	6	25	1	.244	1

DAVIS, RUSSELL - 3B - BR - Age 24

Could this guy be the reason the Yankees gave up Charlie Hayes? Not for 1994. In the Eastern League in 1992, Davis was voted both the league's best batting prospect and its best defensive third baseman in the Baseball America poll. He helped himself in the Arizona Fall League.

	AB	R	HR	RBI	SB	BA	$
1992 Albany AA	491	77	22	71	3	.285	
1993 Columbus AAA	424	63	26	83	1	.255	

DAWSON, ANDRE - DH/OF - BR - Age 39

Dawson is on the downside of a Hall of Fame career. He's had problems with his knees, which cut into his playing time, for several years now. Dawson is not as good as his stats appear; he was helped by playing in Wrigley Field all those years and his RBI totals are high only because he refuses to take a walk. He can't run well anymore and is prone to slumps, but when he's hot, he's in a zone alone.

	AB	R	HR	RBI	SB	BA	$
1992 Chicago NL	542	60	22	90	6	.277	24
1993 Boston AL	461	44	13	67	2	.273	11
1994 *Projection* >>>	505	52	18	78	4	.263	15

DEAK, BRIAN - C - BR - Age 26

Deak is a former Braves farmhand who has shown good power at Triple-A. In two seasons combined, he has 20 home runs and 77 RBI in only 473 at bats. Should get his first taste of the majors in 1994.

	AB	R	HR	RBI	SB	BA	$
1993 Calgary AAA	235	43	11	41	5	.247	

DEAK, DARREL - 2B - BB - Age 24

A power-hitting middle infielder is an anomaly in the St. Louis organization. Deak may need to cut down his swing, sacrificing power for more frequent contact. A good start in Triple-A could get him to the bigs in 1994.

DECKER, STEVE - C - BR - Age 28

This one time Giants' catcher of the future will soon become Marlins' catcher of the past. The Giants misjudged him a future superstar on the strength of one big month at the major league level (September, 1990). He missed the entire 1993 season with a back injury. If healthy, he could battle Rob Natal for backup job in 1994.

	AB	R	HR	RBI	SB	BA	$
1992 San Francisco NL	43	3	0	1	0	.163	-
1993 Florida NL	15	0	0	1	0	.000	-
1994 *Projection* >>>	100	6	2	10	0	.215	-

DEER, ROB - OF - BR - Age 33
Deer is paid to swing hard and hit homers. He has a terrible batting average, but a relatively good on base percentage. 20-30 homers is always a reasonable expectation.

	AB	R	HR	RBI	SB	BA	$
1992 Detroit AL	393	66	32	64	4	.247	17
1993 Detroit-Boston AL	466	66	21	55	5	.210	5
1994 *Projection* >>>	439	66	25	60	4	.216	8

DELANUEZ, REX - OF - BR - Age 26
His average dropped 32 points in his second season at AA Orlando, but he increased his stolen base total from 13 to 23, and his walks from 69 to 93. Younger outfielders who are better prospects are starting to pass him by.

DELGADO, CARLOS - C - BL - Age 21
The catcher of the future/present. Delgado has tremendous power and a good eye at the plate. He's a lefthanded power hitter, with a smooth but quick swing. His defense is in question, but he should make his full time major league arrival in the very near future.

	AB	R	HR	RBI	SB	BA	$
1992 Dunedin A	485	83	30	100	2	.324	
1993 Knoxville AA	468	91	25	102	10	.303	
1994 *Projection* >>>	100	13	3	15	1	.270	1

DENSON, DREW - 1B - BB - Age 28
If the White Sox were looking for righthanded power instead of lefthanded pop, they might give a shot to this retread, out of baseball in 1991 after being released by the Braves. Formerly a switch hitter, Denson may be able to catch on somewhere as an extra bat.

DESHIELDS, DELINO - 2B - BL - Age 25
DeShields is a catalyst with the ability to hit for average and steal bases. Now playing between Eric Karros and Jose Offerman, he seems to have matured in past couple of years and has developed into a leader on a young team. He set career highs in batting average and on base percentage in 1993 and reduced his errors to a career low 11.

	AB	R	HR	RBI	SB	BA	$
1992 Montreal NL	530	82	7	56	46	.292	32
1993 Montreal NL	481	75	2	29	43	.295	24
1994 *Projection* >>>	511	79	5	42	46	.283	29

DESTRADE, ORESTES - 1B - BL - Age 31
Although he wasn't nearly the Cecil Fielder clone that the Marlins envisioned, his strong second half gave him respectable power numbers, and probably saved his job for 1994. At age 32, don't expect further development.

	AB	R	HR	RBI	SB	BA	$
1992 Japan	448	87	41	87	---	.266	
1993 Florida NL	569	61	20	87	0	.255	11
1994 *Projection* >>>	525	55	16	78	1	.248	10

DEVEREAUX, MIKE - OF - BR - Age 30
Devereaux played hurt for parts of last year, limiting his offensive production. Even if he is healthy all year, a 100-plus RBI year like his career-year 1992 is too much to expect. Devereaux was on the trading block after plummeting from 1992. Manager Johnny Oates gave Devereaux every opportunity to succeed, batting him third in the lineup even through prolonged slumps; after his 32-RBI dropoff, he won't get the same consideration in 1994.

	AB	R	HR	RBI	SB	BA	$
1992 Baltimore AL	653	76	24	107	10	.276	26
1993 Baltimore AL	527	72	14	75	3	.250	9
1994 *Projection* >>>	582	75	18	83	8	.261	17

DIAZ, ALEX - OF - BB - Age 25

Speedy, spray type switch hitter who never produced a high batting average before 1993, hitting under .269 in all six of his minor league seasons. Still improving. He feasted on optimistic lefties who guessed he was an automatic out last year (.382 batting average).

	AB	R	HR	RBI	SB	BA	$
1993 Milwaukee AL	69	9	0	1	5	.319	1

DIAZ, MARIO - SS - BR - Age 32

Performed better than expected when called up in midseason. Will try to hold a platoon situation in 1994, at least until the team determines that Benji Gil is ready for the majors.

	AB	R	HR	RBI	SB	BA	$
1992 Texas AL	31	2	0	1	0	.226	-
1993 Oklahoma City AAA	177	24	3	20	3	.328	
1993 Texas AL	205	24	2	24	1	.273	1
1994 *Projection* >>>	144	17	1	16	1	.258	0

DiSARCINA, GARY - SS - BR - Age 26

Will start at short. Offers little help at the plate, however.

	AB	R	HR	RBI	SB	BA	$
1992 California AL	518	48	3	42	9	.247	6
1993 California AL	416	44	3	45	5	.238	2
1994 *Projection* >>>	389	39	2	37	5	.241	2

DISMUKE, JAMIE - 1B - BL - Age 24

Dismuke followed a good year at Single-A Charleston with .306-20-91 hitting at AA Chattanooga in 1993, displaying good strike zone judgement.

	AB	R	HR	RBI	SB	BA	$
1993 Chattanooga AA	497	69	20	91	4	.306	

DODSON, BO - 1B - BL - Age 23

His average improved 64 points in his second try at AA El Paso, but he still hasn't shown adequate power for a first baseman.

	AB	R	HR	RBI	SB	BA	$
1993 El Paso AA	330	58	9	59	1	.312	

DONNELS, CHRIS - 3B/1B - BL - Age 27

Donnels established himself as a productive major league utility player in 1993, but did not play well enough to challenge for a starting position. He should continue in same role in 1994.

	AB	R	HR	RBI	SB	BA	$
1992 Tidewater AAA	279	35	5	32	12	.301	-
1992 New York NL	121	8	0	6	1	.174	
1993 Houston NL	179	18	2	24	2	.257	
1994 *Projection* >>>	145	13	1	15	2	.231	-

DORAN, BILL - 2B - BB - Age 35

In the All-Star ranks during the 1980's, Doran has since been slowed by a bad shoulder and various other ailments. He didn't play after July last year and retired after the season ended.

	AB	R	HR	RBI	SB	BA	$
1992 Cincinnati NL	387	48	8	47	7	.235	7
1993 Milwaukee AL	60	7	0	6	1	.217	-

DORSETT, BRIAN - 1B/C - BR - Age 32
A terrific half season at AAA Indianapolis (.299-18-57) got Dorsett back into the majors where he sat and watched Joe Oliver catch most of the games. He could make an offensive contribution if given the chance. He has too many holes in his game to be a regular, though.

	AB	R	HR	RBI	SB	BA	$
1993 Indianapolis AAA	278	38	18	57	2	.299	
1993 Cincinnati NL	63	7	2	12	0	.254	0

DOZIER, D.J. - OF - BR - Age 28
His football career was going nowhere, so he switched to baseball, but probably too late. Even his speed seems to be deserting him now. They say the legs are the first to go.

	AB	R	HR	RBI	SB	BA	$
1992 Tidewater AAA	197	32	7	25	6	.234	
1992 New York NL	47	4	0	2	4	.191	-
1993 Las Vegas AAA	122	25	2	13	6	.270	
1993 Louisville AAA	139	24	6	15	0	.230	

DUCEY, ROB - OF - BL - Age 28
Ducey has put up nice minor league numbers, but has never really gotten a chance in the majors. Performed well in a late season callup, and will be given a chance to earn the everyday rightfield job. Decent speed, little power.

	AB	R	HR	RBI	SB	BA	$
1992 California-Toronto AL	80	7	0	2	2	.188	-
1993 Oklahoma City AAA	389	68	17	56	17	.303	
1993 Texas AL	85	15	2	9	2	.282	0
1994 Projection >>>	80	11	1	6	3	.244	-

DUNCAN, MARIANO - 2B/SS - BR - Age 31
Duncan has played second base, shortstop, third base, and outfield in his two year tenure with the Phils. His offensive numbers are deceptive. He has good power for a middle infielder, but is among the least disciplined offensive players in baseball. In 1099 plate appearances as a Phil, he has only 29 walks, but 196 strikeouts.

	AB	R	HR	RBI	SB	BA	$
1992 Philadelphia NL	574	71	8	50	23	.267	19
1993 Philadelphia NL	496	68	11	73	6	.282	14
1994 Projection >>>	494	65	10	60	11	.273	16

DUNN, STEVE - 1B - BL - Age 23
Dunn is a prospect who has been overshadowed by David McCarty. He has some power, but needs to be a more consistent hitter as .262 in Double-A is nothing to write home about. Watch to see if he has a big season in Triple-A. If he does, the Twins will have an interesting decision to make in 1995.

	AB	R	HR	RBI	SB	BA	$
1993 Nashville AA	366	48	14	60	1	.262	

DUNN, TODD - OF - BR - Age 23
The third of Milwaukee's four first-round draft picks in '93, and the most successful to date. Drafted out of the University of North Florida, where he had transfered after first attending Georgia Tech on a football scholarship. Played center field at Helena.

DUNSTON, SHAWON - SS - BR - Age 31
Dunston returned after almost a two year rehab from back surgery to run around just long enough to pull a hamstring. Playing shortstop for the Cubs is out of the question, unless his back dramatically improves over the winter. If he becomes a part-time outfielder as anticipated, he has little value as a power/speed bargain. Moreover, there's an even better chance that Dunston will be in out and of the lineup too much to be worth drafting.

	AB	R	HR	RBI	SB	BA	$
1992 Chicago NL	73	8	0	2	2	.315	0
1993 Chicago NL	10	3	0	2	0	.400	
1994 Projection >>>	226	28	4	20	7	.272	3

DURHAM, RAY - 2B - BB - Age 22

As a switch hitter who can run and play the middle infield, he has a lot going for him. He'll have to work on his strikeouts, which ballooned to 100 last season. The Sox need help at second. A strong start in Triple-A could merit some consideration for Durham to move up.

	AB	R	HR	RBI	SB	BA	$
1993 Birmingham AA	528	83	3	37	39	.271	

DYKSTRA, LENNY - OF- BL - Age 31

In 1993 Dykstra put together one of the best seasons ever by a leadoff man. His 143 runs scored was the most by an NL player since 1932. Looking for weaknesses? Well, his throwing arm is meat, but that's about it.

	AB	R	HR	RBI	SB	BA	$
1992 Philadelphia NL	345	53	6	39	30	.301	22
1993 Philadelphia NL	637	143	19	66	37	.305	33
1994 *Projection* >>>	474	94	12	47	31	.294	28

EASLEY, DAMION - 2B - BR - Age 24

Easley never hit .300 in his minor league career. If he is healthy he can steal 20 bases or more. Has been disabled by an acute shin splints condition.

	AB	R	HR	RBI	SB	BA	$
1992 California AL	151	14	1	12	9	.258	3
1993 California AL	230	33	2	22	6	.313	7
1994 *Projection* >>>	295	38	2	27	11	.269	3

EDMONDS, JIM - OF- BL - Age 23

Expected to challenge for Polonia's spot in left. Fine future prospect, but could be overmatched this year.

	AB	R	HR	RBI	SB	BA	$
1993 Vancouver AAA	356	59	9	74	6	.315	
1993 California AL	61	5	0	4	0	.246	-
1994 *Projection* >>>	250	28	4	34	2	.270	3

EENHOORN, ROBERT - SS - BR - Age 26

One of the top athletes in the Netherlands, Eenhoorn chose baseball over a soccer career. Despite a lot of hype, he hasn't advanced past Double-A. His '93 season was injury shortened. If he gets to the majors, it more likely will be because of his defense than his offense.

	AB	R	HR	RBI	SB	BA	$
1993 Albany AA	314	48	6	46	3	.280	

EISENREICH, JIM - OF - BL - Age 34

A valuable cog of the improbable 1993 Phillies' success, Eisenreich managed to wedge his way into 153 games despite being a platoon player. He was second only to Dykstra in games played for the Phils. Unfortunately, there is no chance that he'll duplicate his 1993 success. Fregosi will continue to use him impeccably well, maximizing his production. At this stage, he can be expected to hit .270-.280, with little power or speed. It's a darn shame that this guy's career was short circuited by Tourette's Syndrome; he could have been a perennial .300 hitter.

	AB	R	HR	RBI	SB	BA	$
1992 Kansas City AL	353	31	2	28	11	.269	8
1993 Philadelphia NL	362	51	7	54	5	.318	13
1994 *Projection* >>>	361	41	5	41	7	.278	10

ELSTER, KEVIN - SS - BR - Age 29

Elster went to spring training with the Dodgers in 1993, but he still can't make the long throw.

ENCARNACION, ANGELO - C - BR - Age 20

He catches with flair, a la Tony Pena, and has already played two and a half pro seasons at age 20. How will he hit? His A-ball averages have improved each year, from .254 to .255 to .256. A guess for 1994 would be .257.

ESPINOZA, ALVARO - 3B/SS - BR - Age 32

Got significant playing time at shortstop and third base in 1993 as the Indians concluded that both Jim Thome and Mark Lewis would benefit from another year at Triple-A. All things considered, the Indians got more than their money's worth out of Espinoza, as he played solid defense, and wasn't a total zero offensively. With Lewis and Thome expected to play regularly in 1994, he'll have to battle for a roster spot in 1994.

	AB	R	HR	RBI	SB	BA	$
1992 Colorado Springs AAA	483	64	9	79	2	.300	
1993 Cleveland AL	263	34	4	27	2	.278	4
1994 *Projection* >>>	213	25	2	18	2	.262	1

ESPY, CECIL - OF - BB - Age 31

Espy might have had a windfall of playing time when the whole Reds outfield went on the DL, but he wasn't around long enough to benefit.

	AB	R	HR	RBI	SB	BA	$
1992 Pittsburgh NL	194	21	1	20	6	.258	3
1993 Cincinnati NL	60	6	0	5	2	.233	-
1994 *Projection* >>>	108	11	1	11	4	.249	0

EUSEBIO, TONY - C - BR - Age 26

Eusebio hit well at AAA Tucson in 1993, as usual, but remains a marginal prospect. He's behind Taubensee, Servais and Tucker in the Astros catching depth charts.

	AB	R	HR	RBI	SB	BA	$
1992 Jackson AA	339	33	5	44	1	.307	
1993 Tuscon AAA	281	39	1	43	1	.324	

EVERETT, CARL - OF - BB - Age 24

People love to talk about Wilson and Whitmore, but this guy's the real prospect. A switch hitter with blazing speed and otherworldly defensive abilities, he also showed flashes of extra-base power in a late season Triple-A trial. Kind of a switch-hitting Marquis Grissom. He'll pressure Chuck Carr for the starting center field job in the spring, but will most likely start 1994 at Triple-A. Everett was the Yankees' first round pick in 1990.

	AB	R	HR	RBI	SB	BA	$
1993 Edmonton AAA	136	28	6	16	12	.309	
1993 Florida NL	19	0	0	0	1	.105	-
1994 *Projection* >>>	150	15	2	13	5	.260	2

FABREGAS, JORGE - C - BL - Age 24

Chosen in the first round of the '91 draft. Had a solid '93 season with the bat. The Angels are in need of catching, and by mid-1994, the battle may be between Fabregas and Chris Turner.

	AB	R	HR	RBI	SB	BA	$
1993 Midland AA	409	63	6	56	1	.289	

FANEYTE, RIKKERT - OF - BR - Age 25

A better hitter than Darren Lewis, but probably not good enough to build a career. Faneyte's moderate combination of a little power and a little speed speed might earn him a season similar to Dwight Smith's once before he disappears from the majors.

	AB	R	HR	RBI	SB	BA	$
1993 Phoenix AAA	426	71	11	71	15	.312	

FARIES, PAUL - 2B - BR - Age 29

Has had a decent minor league career, but Faries has shown little in four major league stints. Faries is not the next Rich Amaral.

	AB	R	HR	RBI	SB	BA	$
1992 San Diego NL	11	3	0	1	0	.455	-
1993 Phoenix AAA	327	56	2	32	18	.303	-
1993 San Francisco NL	36	6	0	4	2	.222	-
1994 *Projection* >>>	44	6	0	4	2	.219	-

FARISS, MONTY - OF - BR - Age 26

Fariss is a former Rangers' number one pick who has stagnated. Last season was supposed to be the big chance for this former hitting star from Oklahoma State (a teammate of Robin Ventura). At 26, he's still young enough to rate a few more chances, but they probably won't be with the Marlins, who are committed to their younger prospects.

	AB	R	HR	RBI	SB	BA	$
1992 Texas AL	166	13	3	21	0	.217	-
1993 Edmonton AAA	254	32	6	37	1	.256	
1993 Florida NL	29	3	0	2	0	.172	-
1994 *Projection* >>>	75	7	1	9	0	.225	-

FARNER, MATT - OF - BR - Age 20

Toronto's second first-round pick in the '93 draft. Has good speed, which he wasn't able to showcase in pro ball because he rarely got on base.

FARRELL, JON - OF - BR - Age 22

The Pirates' first round pick in 1991, Farrell had his best pro season in 1993. However, he was aided by playing in Class A Salem's tiny ballpark. He hasn't devloped as fast as the Pirates had hoped and they are curious how he will fare at Double-A this season. This could be a telling year for Farrell.

	AB	R	HR	RBI	SB	BA	$
1992 Augusta A	320	44	8	48	8	.222	
1993 Salem A	386	58	20	51	5	.238	

FELDER, KENNY - OF - BL - Age 23

A number one pick in the 1992 draft. Several years away, but he's the Brewers' best power prospect. Big and strong.

	AB	R	HR	RBI	SB	BA	$
1992 Helena R	276	58	15	48	11	.217	
1993 Beloit A	99	12	3	8	1	.182	

FELDER, MIKE - OF - BB - Age 31

Felder spent six frustrating years in the Milwaukee organization before finding his game in the faster National League. Strictly a part-timer, and fading for the second time.

	AB	R	HR	RBI	SB	BA	$
1992 San Francisco NL	322	44	4	23	14	.286	11
1993 Seattle AL	342	31	1	20	15	.211	2
1994 *Projection* >>>	336	39	2	21	16	.244	6

FELIX, JUNIOR - OF - BB - Age 26

Despite the talents, Felix has now worn out his welcome with three teams. His defense is poor, and he has a reputation as a malcontent. Furthermore, it's been written that he's really over 30 years old.

	AB	R	HR	RBI	SB	BA	$
1992 California AL	509	63	9	72	8	.246	10
1993 Florida NL	214	25	7	22	2	.238	2
1994 *Projection* >>>	150	19	3	19	2	.248	1

FERMIN, FELIX - SS - BR - Age 30

Has done a serviceable job holding the fort at shortstop for Mark Lewis. Lewis appears ready now, and Fermin likely will battle for a utility infield job, or be traded elsewhere for pitching.

	AB	R	HR	RBI	SB	BA	$
1992 Cleveland AL	215	27	0	13	0	.270	1
1993 Cleveland AL	480	48	2	45	4	.263	5
1994 *Projection* >>>	383	38	1	32	3	.264	4

FERNANDEZ, TONY - SS - BB - Age 31

Fernandez still has trouble with low pitches, especially forkballs, but he has developed his contact skills from both sides of the plate. His performance for 1994 will depend on how his manager uses him. If he bats at the top of the lineup, look for a repeat of last year. If he bats eighth, watch for a return to the level of happiness (and performance) that he enjoyed in New York.

	AB	R	HR	RBI	SB	BA	$
1992 San Diego NL	622	84	4	37	20	.275	17
1993 New York NL	173	20	1	14	6	.225	0
1993 Toronto AL	353	45	4	50	15	.306	15
1994 *Projection* >>>	563	74	5	51	21	.276	19

FIELDER, CECIL - 1B/DH - BR - Age 30

In the second half last year, Cecil Fielder was affected by a sore ankle. It was the third consecutive year his home runs declined. But you can still expect 30+ home runs and 100+ RBI from Fielder in 1994.

	AB	R	HR	RBI	SB	BA	$
1992 Detroit AL	594	80	35	124	0	.244	20
1993 Detroit AL	573	80	30	117	0	.267	19
1994 *Projection* >>>	589	84	34	122	0	.258	22

FINLEY, STEVE - OF - BL - Age 29

Hampered by a wrist injury and muscle strains for the first half of the season, Finley fell short of the performance level he'd established in his first two years with the Astros; his steals dropped from 44 to 19. He should rebound in 1994 but needs to improve his strike zone discipline to move to the next level.

	AB	R	HR	RBI	SB	BA	$
1992 Houston NL	607	84	5	55	44	.292	31
1993 Houston NL	545	69	8	44	19	.266	13
1994 *Projection* >>>	574	77	7	49	30	.278	24

FINN, JOHN - 2B - BR - Age 26

Like teammate John Byington, Finn is 5'8". He replaces Byington's power with speed. He can also play second base. If a prospect at all, it's as a utilityman who can pinch run.

	AB	R	HR	RBI	SB	BA	$
1993 New Orleans AAA	335	47	1	37	27	.281	

FITZGERALD, MIKE - C - BR - Age 33

Veteran catcher, has been in the majors for nine years with a career .235 batting average. His role is backup.

	AB	R	HR	RBI	SB	BA	$
1992 California AL	189	19	6	17	2	.212	0
1993 New Orleans AAA	297	35	7	35	3	.259	

FLAHERTY, JOHN - C - BR - Age 26

A possible replacement for Tony Pena. Flaherty's .271 average last season represents the high water mark for his six minor league seasons. Almost anything would be an improvement over Pena's offense. Flaherty is a solid defensive catcher.

	AB	R	HR	RBI	SB	BA	$
1992 Boston AL	66	3	0	2	0	.197	-
1993 Pawtucket AAA	365	29	6	35	0	.271	
1993 Boston AL	25	3	0	2	0	.120	-
1994 *Projection* >>>	100	7	1	7	0	.238	-

FLETCHER, DARRIN - C - BL - Age 27

Fletcher's solid lefthanded hitting helped him overcome obvious defensive deficiencies to win the Expos' starting catcher job in 1993. He threw out only 26 of the 125 opponents who tried to run against him, but the Expos were willing to overlook his poor arm to get his bat into the lineup. Fletcher hit .321 with runners in scoring position in 1993. Catcher is the only position where the Expos lack prospects, so the job could be his for a long while.

	AB	R	HR	RBI	SB	BA	$
1992 Indianapolis AAA	51	2	1	9	0	.255	
1992 Montreal NL	222	13	2	26	0	.243	1
1993 Montreal NL	396	33	9	60	0	.255	6
1994 *Projection* >>>	294	22	5	41	0	.250	2

FLETCHER, SCOTT - 2B - BR - Age 35

Fletcher has made a career of filling in for injured regulars and becoming the regular himself. His 1994 outlook is the flipside of what happens with Tim Naehring, who has the second base job to lose.

	AB	R	HR	RBI	SB	BA	$
1992 Milwaukee AL	386	53	3	51	17	.275	1
1993 Boston AL	480	81	5	45	16	.285	15
1994 Projection >>>	410	59	4	43	14	.269	12

FLORA, KEVIN - 2B - BR - Age 24

Flora swiped 40 bases in 1991 at Class AA Midland, but only nine in 1992 while playing with an injured ankle that finally put him on the disabled list. Hit .324 at AAA Edmonton in 1992 and .330 at AAA Vancouver in 1993.

FLORES, MIGUEL - 2B - BR - Age 23

Speedy, spray-hitting second baseman was returned to AA Canton-Akron for a second year in 1993 despite a fine year there in 1992. Baseball America chose him as the best defensive second baseman in the Eastern League in 1992. Should rate a look as a major league utility infield prospect in 1994.

	AB	R	HR	RBI	SB	BA	$
1993 Canton-Akron AA	435	73	3	54	36	.292	

FLOYD, CLIFF - 1B - BL - Age 21

The most heralded minor league player of 1993, Floyd tore up the AA Eastern League, but slowed some in Triple-A then held his own in a short September stint in the majors. A great power/speed combination, his comparison to Willie McCovey is well founded. Floyd was drafted as a firstbaseman but also played in the outfield in the minors; he has the speed and athletic ability to play centerfield. The Expos project him to play firstbase in the majors, but he may be a little too raw to start the season with the big club in 1994; he needs some work on his defense and some polish against lefty pitchers. He may start the year at Triple-A, but his great offensive potential could force the Expos to install him in the lineup on Opening Day.

	AB	R	HR	RBI	SB	BA	$
1993 Harrisburgh AA	380	82	26	101	31	.329	
1993 Ottawa AAA	125	12	2	18	2	.240	
1993 Montreal NL	31	3	1	2	0	.226	-
1994 Projection >>>	409	54	14	66	16	.252	15

FOLEY, TOM - 2B - BL - Age 34

His career seemed to be grinding to a halt in Montreal, but the Pirates signed Foley as a free agent following the 1992 season and he had a decent year off the bench.

	AB	R	HR	RBI	SB	BA	$
1992 Montreal NL	115	7	0	5	3	.174	-
1993 Pittsburgh NL	194	18	3	22	0	.253	1
1994 Projection >>>	164	13	2	15	1	.227	-

FORBES, P. J. - 2B - BR - Age 26

Exciting young prospect. Second in hitting (.319) at AA Midland. Good power for a middle infielder. After hitting four home runs in his first three pro seasons, he broke out as a power hitter last season. Jumped from the Midwest League to the Double-A All-Star Game. At his age, it will be a stretch for him to make it as a major league regular, but he will be at Triple-A, waiting.

FORDYCE, BROOK - C - BR - Age 23

Brook is the next Mets' catching prospect. He has been working at first base too.

	AB	R	HR	RBI	SB	BA	$
1992 Binghamton AA	425	59	11	61	1	.278	
1993 Norfolk AAA	409	33	2	40	2	.259	

FOSTER, JIM - C - BR - Age 22

Hits with power, but his most dangerous weapon is his throwing arm. In the Appalachian League, where runners often steal at will, Foster gunned down four of four Johnson City base-stealers in one game. A 22nd round pick in last year's draft, out of Providence College.

FOX, ERIC - OF - BB - Age 30

Fox mouthed off at A's management for overlooking him during the 1993 season. This outburst and his .143 batting average should ensure that he has seen the last of the majors.

	AB	R	HR	RBI	SB	BA	$
1992 Oakland AL	143	24	3	13	3	.238	1
1993 Tacoma AAA	317	49	11	52	18	.312	
1993 Oakland AL	56	5	1	5	0	.143	-
1994 *Projection >>>*	75	10	1	7	2	.245	-

FRANCO, JULIO - DH - BR - Age 32

Bad knees limited him to being a designated hitter. Franco is still a fine hitter, though. He announced that he would play winter ball to prove to everyone he can still play second base. A free agent following the 1993 season, his chances of returning to the Rangers were diminished when Texas signed Will Clark.

	AB	R	HR	RBI	SB	BA	$
1992 Texas AL	107	19	2	8	1	.234	-
1993 Texas AL	532	85	14	84	9	.289	19
1994 *Projection >>>*	401	64	10	55	10	.282	15

FRANCO, MATT - 1B - BL - Age 24

Moving up the ladder as the Cubs first baseman at Double-A, then Triple-A, Franco is likely to spend 1994 at Triple-A; his advancement beyond there depends on where Mark Grace is. Franco is a longshot major league possibility in 1994 and has a better chance in 1995.

	AB	R	HR	RBI	SB	BA	$
1993 Orlando AA	237	31	7	37	3	.316	
1993 Iowa AAA	199	24	5	29	4	.291	

FRAZIER, LOU - OF - BB - Age 29

Frazier had never played above Double-A before making the Expos out of spring training last season, primarily because Felipe Alou wanted speed on his bench; Frazier stole 17 bases in 19 tries. He's a good contact hitter and can fly, evoking memories of another late bloomer (Otis Nixon.) Frazier's batting average has improved noticeably since he began wearing glasses in 1992. The Expos always seem to have good luck with castoffs and Frazier looks the latest one that will become a productive player in Quebec.

	AB	R	HR	RBI	SB	BA	$
1993 Montreal NL	189	27	1	16	17	.286	8
1994 *Projection >>>*	95	10	0	7	7	.244	0

FRYE, JEFF - 2B - BR - Age 27

Injuries caused him to miss the entire 1993 season. Will have to perform very well in spring training to regain a spot on the major league team, especially given the Rangers' crowded middle infield situation.

	AB	R	HR	RBI	SB	BA	$
1992 Oklahoma City AAA	337	64	2	28	11	.300	
1992 Texas AL	199	24	1	12	1	.256	0
1993 Texas AL			(Did Not Play)				
1994 *Projection >>>*	225	25	1	16	2	.257	0

FRYMAN, TRAVIS - SS/2B - BR - Age 25

Fryman is the best offensive shortstop in the American League, a genuine blue chip player. He's young, but has four years of major league experience. A big career can be expected.

	AB	R	HR	RBI	SB	BA	$
1992 Detroit AL	659	87	20	96	8	.266	21
1993 Detroit AL	607	98	22	97	9	.300	25
1994 *Projection >>>*	616	89	21	96	9	.282	25

FRYMAN, TROY - 2B - BL - Age 22

Travis's younger brother almost doubled his average in his second season at South Bend, then struggled a bit after being promoted to a higher Class A Florida State league. A hot spring, or a start similar to 1993's, would put him in Double-A this season.

GAETTI, GARY - 3B/1B - BR - Age 35
Gaetti was playing full-time only because Royals other third basemen were all hurt or struggling in 1993. Otherwise, the stop gap Gaetti continues as Royals third baseman. Released early in 1993 by California, actually did well for KC, driving in runs and becoming offensive leader. Still, all indications are down for Gaetti, so don't expect more than .235-10-40-2.

	AB	R	HR	RBI	SB	BA	$
1992 California AL	456	41	12	48	3	.226	4
1993 California-Kansas City	331	40	14	50	1	.245	6
1994 *Projection* >>>	216	22	7	27	1	.235	2

GAGNE, GREG - SS - BR - Age 32
Had his best offensive season in 1993. Among the better "second tier" shortstops in the AL, but not in the same class with Ripken, Fryman, etc. Marvelous fielder, will play every day, even if hitting declines. Won't continue this level of hitting, but still has value.

	AB	R	HR	RBI	SB	BA	$
1992 Minnesota AL	439	53	7	39	6	.246	6
1993 Kansas City AL	540	66	10	57	10	.280	14
1994 *Projection* >>>	484	59	9	49	9	.268	12

GAINER, JAY - 1B - BL - Age 27
Gainer was stuck behind Fred McGriff in the Padre organization and got new life with the expansion Rockies only to get stuck behind Andres Galarraga. Gainer homered on his first big league pitch in a short September callup; he's probably a year away from the majors, but batting lefthanded always helps.

	AB	R	HR	RBI	SB	BA	$
1992 Wichita AA	376	57	23	67	4	.261	
1993 Colorado Springs AAA	293	51	10	74	4	.294	-
1993 Colorado NL	41	4	3	6	1	.171	-
1994 *Projection* >>>	100	7	2	14	1	.240	-

GALARRAGA, ANDRES - 1B - BR - Age 32
He was the steal of the century for the Rockies, who paid him less than $1 million, including incentives in 1993. Galarraga had a career high in RBI and won the NL batting crown. The Big Cat is a free swinger and spanked the ball all over spacious Mile High Stadium. A good clutch hitter who responded to Don Baylor's confidence, Galarraga came back from two Disabled List stints batting even stronger than before.

	AB	R	HR	RBI	SB	BA	$
1992 Louisville AAA	34	3	2	3	1	.176	
1992 St. Louis NL	325	38	10	39	5	.243	8
1993 Colorado NL	470	71	22	98	2	370	30
1994 *Projection* >>>	442	54	14	64	5	.290	17

GALLAGHER, DAVE - OF - BR - Age 33
Gallagher thrived as the righty-hitting half of a platoon with Joe Orsulak in 1993. His playing time in 1994 will depend on other players' slumps and injuries. Now in the Braves organization, his future is more unclear than ever.

	AB	R	HR	RBI	SB	BA	$
1992 New York NL	175	20	1	21	4	.240	1
1993 New York NL	201	34	6	28	1	.274	4
1994 *Projection* >>>	204	29	2	26	2	.269	2

GALLEGO, MIKE - SS/2B/3B - BR - Age 33
Had a career year in 1993, playing all three of the infield skill positions and batting .283 with double digit home runs. He is, by age, past his prime and with an abundance of infield talent, management will have a tough decision on the extent of his playing time in 1994.

	AB	R	HR	RBI	SB	BA	$
1992 New York AL	173	24	3	14	0	.254	1
1993 New York AL	403	63	10	54	3	.283	10
1994 *Projection* >>>	341	46	8	40	3	.259	6

GANT, RON - OF - BR - Age 29

The reports of Gant's demise as a hitter were exaggerated. He continues to be one of the most productive players in baseball. His batting average was up in 1993, and he set career highs in HRs and RBI, finished in the NLs top ten in several hitting categories, all without losing his above average speed. Sure, he swings at too many bad pitches, but Gant has always been a bad ball hitter; several of his HRs in 1993 came on pitches out of the strike zone. Gant will remain a productive offensive player and one of the surest bets for 1994 and beyond.

	AB	R	HR	RBI	SB	BA	$
1992 Atlanta NL	544	74	17	80	32	.259	28
1993 Atlanta NL	606	113	36	117	26	.274	33
1993 Projection >>>	578	98	29	103	29	.266	33

GARCIA, CARLOS - 2B - BR - Age 26

By June last year, no one in Pittsburgh missed Jose Lind. A standout minor league shortstop, Garcia quickly made the transition to second base last season and had a fine rookie year. He was moved to leadoff in June and could solve that long standing Pirates' problem. He doesn't walk a lot but he can hit for average and power and he steals bases. Garcia has the ingredients to be a big star.

	AB	R	HR	RBI	SB	BA	$
1992 Pittsburgh NL	39	4	0	4	0	.205	-
1993 Pittsburgh NL	546	77	12	47	18	.269	15
1994 Projection >>>	510	70	11	44	16	.266	7

GARCIA, CHEO - 3B - BR - Age 25

Good prospect, on a team that needs help at third base. He is ready now to hit for fair average and show good speed.

	AB	R	HR	RBI	SB	BA	$
1992 Orlando AA	488	54	4	44	32	.258	
1993 Pawtucket AAA	373	48	4	32	3	.260	

GARDNER, JEFF - 2B - BL - Age 30

Gardner was the Padres' regular second baseman in 1993, playing 140 games (second highest on the team). But, it's very questionable that he'll get another 400 ABs in 1994 due to the emergence of switch hitting Luis Lopez. Also note Gardner's 100 point platoon differential. A former Mets farmhand, Gardner will become a utility player.

	AB	R	HR	RBI	SB	BA	$
1992 Las Vegas AAA	439	82	1	51	7	.335	
1992 San Diego NL	19	0	0	0	0	.105	-
1993 San Diego NL	404	53	1	24	2	.262	2
1994 Projection >>>	215	27	1	12	1	.254	-

GARRISON, WEBSTER - SS - BR - Age 28

Garrison hit .303 with 17 steals at Triple-A in 1993, but it was his tenth season in the minors and one of the only good seasons in his career. The little guy (5'10", 160 pounds) hadn't batted higher than .283 in any of his first nine pro seasons. As a middle infielder, he'd be trying to break into one of Oakland's strongest positions. He became a minor league free agent during the offseason.

GATES, BRENT - 2B - BB - Age 24

Gates has fashioned a couple of long hitting streaks already in his career, which suggests a consistency that bodes well for his future. Young enough to improve, he will approach double figures in homers and steals while maintaining a .290 average. Was 0-for-3 in steal attempts in the first half of 1993, 7-for-7 in the second half.

	AB	R	HR	RBI	SB	BA	$
1993 Oakland AL	535	64	7	69	7	.290	14
1993 Projection >>>	505	61	7	66	7	.290	16

GEDMAN, RICH - C - BL - Age 34

Though he is one of the game's good people, Gedman hasn't been a productive player for five years. He can still pop an occasional home run.

	AB	R	HR	RBI	SB	BA	$
1992 St. Louis NL	105	5	1	8	0	.219	-
1993 Columbus AAA	275	30	12	35	0	.262	-

GEISLER, PHIL - 1B - BL - Age 24

A big lefty (6'3", 200 lbs.), Geisler moved from first base in 1992 to the outfield in 1993 for Single-A Clearwater and Double-A Reading. He showed power potential, slugging .526 in the pitcher dominated Florida State League. At his age, the Phils envision him as a major league bat off of the bench, assuming continued development.

GEREN, BOB - C - BR - Age 32

Geren never could hit a slider, but kept getting to the majors due to the shortage of catching talent. Now he's a roving instructor for the Red Sox.

GIANELLI, RAY - 3B - BL - Age 28

Surfaced with the Blue Jays in 1991, but now he's just a Triple-A extension of the major league bench.

	AB	R	HR	RBI	SB	BA	$
1992 Syracuse AAA	249	23	5	22	2	.229	
1993 Syracuse AAA	411	51	11	42	1	.253	

GIBRALTER, STEVE - OF - BR - Age 21

The Midwest League MVP in 1992, the "Rock" showed some cracks last year at Double-A Chattanooga (.237, 11 HRs, 47 RBI). He has a strong arm and is still young enough to improve, but he'll have to get his offense back on track and get his strikeout/walk rate under control (108/20 in 1993).

	AB	R	HR	RBI	SB	BA	$
1992 Cedar Rapids A	529	92	19	99	12	.306	
1993 Chattanooga AA	477	65	11	47	7	.237	-

GIBSON, KIRK - DH/OF - BL - Age 36

Gibson began last season with a bang, but slowed down considerably later on. The Tigers are looking to Eric Davis for centerfield, and Milt Cuyler is also in the picture. If Gibson doesn't retire and remains with the Tigers, he will have difficulty getting 300 AB's.

	AB	R	HR	RBI	SB	BA	$
1993 Detroit AL	403	62	13	62	15	.261	15
1994 *Projection* >>>	225	30	6	27	8	.238	4

GIL, BENJI - SS - BR - Age 21

Gil was handed the starting shortstop job at the beginning of 1993 when Manny Lee was injured. He proved he wasn't yet ready for the majors. Returned to AA Tulsa where he put up good numbers. May get a midseason callup, but will probably spend most of 1994 at Triple-A. Have no doubt about it though, he is the Rangers' shortstop of the future.

	AB	R	HR	RBI	SB	BA	$
1992 Gastonia A	482	75	9	55	26	.274	
1993 Tulsa AA	342	45	17	59	20	.275	-
1993 Texas AL	57	3	0	2	1	.123	-
1994 *Projection* >>>	228	25	7	23	8	.240	4

GILBERT, SHAWN - OF - BR - Age 29

Chances for major league play in 1994 are slim; hasn't yet had a ML at bat. May appear if injuries are rampant, and give you one SB; otherwise not worth a look.

	AB	R	HR	RBI	SB	BA	$
1992 Portland AAA	444	60	3	52	31	.245	
1993 Nashville AAA	278	28	0	17	6	.227	-

GILES, BRIAN - OF - BL - Age 23

A 17th-round pick in 1989, Giles made a giant leap forward in 1993, finishing second in the Eastern League batting race to teammate Manny Ramirez. His extra-base power is negligible, though, and his speed is good, but not great. Could emerge as a major league extra outfielder candidate by 1995.

GILKEY, BERNARD - OF - BR - Age 27

After showing flashes of promise in previous seasons, Gilkey blossomed into one of the National League's top leadoff hitters in 1993. He has a good bat, above average power and speed and is at an age where he is just reaching his prime. The Cardinals are well stocked with outfielders, but they cannot afford not to play Gilkey every day in 1994.

	AB	R	HR	RBI	SB	BA	$
1992 St. Louis NL	384	56	7	43	18	.302	19
1993 St. Louis NL	557	99	16	70	15	.305	23
1994 *Projection* >>>	491	76	11	54	17	.290	20

GIRARDI, JOE - C - BR - Age 29

His maturity behind the plate and strong arm are assets the Rockies needed last year. He hit .300-plus late in the season when moved into the #2 spot in the order. Girardi hasn't much power but is good at advancing runners.

	AB	R	HR	RBI	SB	BA	$
1992 Chicago NL	270	19	1	12	0	.270	1
1993 Colorado NL	310	35	3	31	6	.290	7
1994 *Projection* >>>	402	38	3	32	5	.280	8

GLADDEN, DAN - OF - BR - Age 36

Gladden will be 37 in July, and despite the slight improvement in his statistics last year, his skills continue to slip. The 13 dingers last year were a surprise. He will get less playing time this year, and will be more of a role player.

	AB	R	HR	RBI	SB	BA	$
1992 Detroit AL	417	57	7	42	4	.254	6
1993 Detroit AL	356	52	13	56	8	.267	11
1994 *Projection* >>>	284	40	7	37	6	.258	6

GLANVILLE, DOUG - OF - BR - Age 23

Jim Frey's legacy as the Cubs first round pick in 1991, Glanville made a few strides last year at Double-A. He shows fine speed and smooth centerfield defense, and a little pop is developing in his bat.

	AB	R	HR	RBI	SB	BA	$
1992 Winston-Salem A	485	72	4	36	32	.258	
1993 Orlando AA	295	42	9	40	15	.264	-

GOFF, JERRY - C - BL - Age 29

Goff has some serious defensive deficiencies behind the plate; however, he's a lefthanded hitter with pop so he keeps getting chances. He played fairly well in an extended September trial with the Pirates last year and should wind up as Don Slaught's caddy in 1994.

	AB	R	HR	RBI	SB	BA	$
1992 Indianapolis AAA	314	37	14	39	0	.239	
1992 Montreal NL	3	0	0	0	0	.000	-
1993 Buffalo AAA	362	52	14	69	1	.251	-
1993 Pittsburgh NL	37	5	2	6	0	.297	0

GOMEZ, CHRIS - SS - BR - Age 22

Gomez fits the mold of a typical good-field no-hit shortstop. A .250 BA is about the highest you can expect, and he doesn't hit any dingers.

	AB	R	HR	RBI	SB	BA	$
1993 Toledo AAA	277	29	0	20	6	.245	
1993 Detroit AL	128	11	0	11	2	.250	-
1994 *Projection* >>>	64	7	0	6	1	.240	-

GOMEZ, LEO - 3B - BR - Age 27

Except for the 10 homers, Leo Gomez would like to forget 1992. He had a cyst removed from his wrist and missed much of the season. Gomez has a good work ethic, so watch him in winter ball and spring training to see if he is back on track to regain his starting third base job. Gomez' awful 1993 has clearly jeopardized his career in Baltimore.

	AB	R	HR	RBI	SB	BA	$
1992 Baltimore AL	468	62	17	64	2	.265	13
1993 Baltimore AL	244	30	10	25	0	.197	-
1994 *Projection* >>>	343	42	13	41	1	.235	4

GONZALES, LARRY - C - BR - Age 27

An OK defensive catcher and not a bad hitter. Could bat .240 with no power if he gets to play.

GONZALES, RENE - 3B/1B - BR - Age 32
Good utility infielder. Can steal a base.

	AB	R	HR	RBI	SB	BA	$
1992 California AL	329	47	7	38	7	.277	9
1993 California AL	335	34	2	31	5	.251	3
1994 *Projection* >>>	296	35	3	29	5	.257	4

GONZALEZ, ALEX - SS - BR - Age 20
The shortstop of the future north of the border. Tony Fernandez has the job for one more year, tops. The future could come this year for Gonzalez. There's no need to rush him, though the Jays may anyway. Great power/speed combination.

	AB	R	HR	RBI	SB	BA	$
1993 Knoxville AA	561	93	16	69	38	.289	

GONZALEZ, JUAN - OF - BR - Age 24
Gonzalez took his second consecutive AL home run crown in 1994, and he's still getting better as a hitter. Learned to go the opposite way instead of trying to pull everything. Becoming more disciplined as a hitter, cutting his strikeouts down. Has a chronic back problem, however, that can act up at any time.

	AB	R	HR	RBI	SB	BA	$
1992 Texas AL	584	77	43	109	0	.260	26
1993 Texas AL	536	105	46	118	4	.310	34
1994 *Projection* >>>	553	91	42	112	3	.285	32

GONZALEZ, LUIS - C - BL - Age 26
Now entering his prime, Gonzalez reached a new level of consistency in 1993 with a .300 average and a team leading 20 steals. A conscientious, hard-working player who will get the most out of his ability, Gonzalez will produce solid, but not spectacular, .275-15-75-15 numbers for many years.

	AB	R	HR	RBI	SB	BA	$
1992 Houston NL	387	40	10	55	7	.243	10
1993 Houston NL	540	82	15	72	20	.300	24
1994 *Projection* >>>	530	70	14	73	16	.277	19

GONZALEZ, RAUL - OF - BR - Age 20
Has made steady minor league progress, showing power and speed at Single-A Wilmington in 1993 (11 HR, 13 SB). Has good batting eye for a youngster. Should see majority of playing time at AA Memphis next year; at least two seasons from majors.

GOODWIN, TOM - OF - BL - Age 25
Strictly a stolen base specialist who wouldn't hit enought to hold a regular job (a .260 at hitter haven AAA Albuquerque). With Goodwin, Hammonds, Ochoa, Smith and Voigt, it is easy to see why Devereaux is considered expendable.

	AB	R	HR	RBI	SB	BA	$
1992 Los Angeles NL	73	15	0	3	7	.233	0
1993 Albuquerque AAA	289	48	1	28	21	.260	-
1993 Los Angeles NL	17	6	0	1	1	.294	-
1994 *Projection* >>>	100	13	0	8	9	.240	1

GORDON, KEITH - OF - BR - Age 25
The Reds second round draft pick in 1990, Gordon had a good year at AA Chattanooga, but strike zone judgement is a problem for him: 132 strikeouts and only 19 walks in 419 at-bats.

	AB	R	HR	RBI	SB	BA	$
1993 Chattanooga AA	419	69	14	59	13	.291	-

GRABLE, ROB - 3B - BR - Age 24
The Tigers' 23rd round pick in 1991 out of St. John's, Grable keyed the Class A Clearwater Phils championship run in 1993. A high average hitter with doubles power, Grable has no single quality which separates him from the pack. The fact that he has never played above Single-A at his age also works against him.

GRACE, MARK - 1B - BL - Age 29

Grace had a career season in 1993; he's a winning player whose actions on and off field enable him to impress both Larry Himes and Janine Turner. He's unlikely to duplicate his numbers across the board, but his power figures are apt to remain in the same neighborhood.

	AB	R	HR	RBI	SB	BA	$
1992 Chicago NL	603	72	9	79	6	.307	23
1993 Chicago NL	594	86	14	98	8	.325	26
1994 *Projection* >>>	601	82	11	85	6	.310	26

GRAFFAGNINO, TONY - 2B - BR - Age 22

Showing fine all around skills for Single-A Macon, Graffanino got off to a terrific start and is another good infield prospect for the Braves. He'll move up to AA Greenville in 1994. He's behind Caraballo in the minor league pecking order, but moving up fast.

GREBECK, BRIAN - SS - BR - Age 26

Decent hitter at AA level. Not ready for prime time yet.

GREBECK, CRAIG - SS - BR - Age 29

A sad little season for the "Little Hurt". Since he's a half year older than Cora, Grebeck will probably need some bad fortune on Cora's part to get the second base job back. His '92 broken foot may have ruined his opportunity for a full career. Can hit if he plays.

	AB	R	HR	RBI	SB	BA	$
1992 Chicago AL	287	24	3	35	0	.268	4
1993 Chicago AL	190	25	1	12	1	.226	-
1994 *Projection* >>>	228	27	3	23	1	.253	1

GREEN, GARY - SS - BR - Age 32

Your typical ex-prospect, Green has surfaced in the major leagues five times, with three different organizations, never getting more than 88 at bats in a season. Career .222 hitter.

	AB	R	HR	RBI	SB	BA	$
1992 Cincinnati NL	12	3	0	0	0	.333	-
1993 Indianapolis AAA	218	15	2	14	1	.188	-

GREEN, SHAWN - OF - BL - Age 21

Green made his debut in September with Toronto, and went hitless in six at bats. However, he does have a great swing in the tradition of John Olerud. He is a year away from developing into the .300 hitter he will one day be.

	AB	R	HR	RBI	SB	BA	$
1992 Dunedin A	417	44	1	49	22	.273	
1993 Knoxville AA	360	40	4	34	4	.283	-
1994 *Projection* >>>	100	8	0	7	0	.236	-

GREENE, TODD - OF - BR - Age 22

Made a big splash after being drafted in the 12th round last year out of Georgia Southern. Led the Northwest League in home runs and RBI, driving in almost a run a game. Also hit two homers in Boise's playoff-clinching win. Ranks high defensively.

GREENE, WILLIE - SS - BL - Age 22

The Reds most hyped prospect hit only .160 in a 50 AB trial before breaking his wrist in a collision with Chris Sabo. At AAA Indianapolis, a slow start limited Greene to a .267 average but he hit 22 homers in 341 ABs. His good strike zone judgement and his age indicate that he is still a very good prospect. Greene had great second half stats; by the time he was promoted to the majors, American Association pitchers could barely get him out.

	AB	R	HR	RBI	SB	BA	$
1992 Cincinnati NL	93	10	2	13	2	.269	
1993 Indianapolis AAA	341	62	22	58	2	.267	-
1993 Cincinnati NL	50	7	2	5	0	.160	-
1994 *Projection* >>>	255	32	13	34	5	.248	7

GREENWELL, MIKE - OF - BL - Age 30

One of the few career .300 hitters anywhere, Greenwell has come back strong from the injuries (knee, wrist, elbow) that ruined his 1992 season.

	AB	R	HR	RBI	SB	BA	$
1992 Boston AL	180	16	2	18	2	.233	0
1993 Boston AL	540	77	13	72	5	.315	20
1994 *Projection* >>>	512	69	11	68	7	.300	17

GREER, RUSTY - 1B - BL - Age 25

Improved across the board in his second Double-A season. Has enough speed to play the outfield, but is usually seen at first base.

GREGG, TOMMY - OF - BL - Age 30

Good pinch hitter and backup. The one time he was given a regular job (1989) he immediately broke a leg and never made it back into the lineup.

	AB	R	HR	RBI	SB	BA	$
1992 Atlanta NL	19	1	1	1	1	.263	-
1993 Indianapolis AAA	198	34	7	30	3	.318	-
1993 Cincinnati NL	12	1	0	1	0	.167	-
1994 *Projection* >>>	80	7	1	8	1	.242	-

GRIFFEY, KEN JR - OF - BL - Age 24

He has hit .300 with at least 20 homers in each of his four full seasons, and has knocked in 100 runs, despite the Mariners poor offense, in consecutive seasons. Offers the best combination of high potential and minimal risk of any player for 1994.

	AB	R	HR	RBI	SB	BA	$
1992 Seattle AL	565	83	27	103	10	.308	32
1993 Seattle AL	582	113	45	109	17	.309	40
1994 *Projection* >>>	571	97	35	105	15	.312	40

GRIFFIN, ALFREDO - SS - BB - Age 37

Griffin continued to fill in as a middle infielder, but his contribution has diminished. He doesn't run anymore, never has hit for power, and has seen his range all but disappear. It will be surprising to see him hang on much longer.

	AB	R	HR	RBI	SB	BA	$
1992 Toronto AL	150	21	0	10	3	.233	-
1993 Toronto AL	95	15	0	3	0	.211	-
1994 *Projection* >>>	78	9	0	5	1	.230	-

GRISSOM, MARQUIS - OF - BR - Age 26

Grissom is clearly one of the rising stars in the game. He hits for both average and power, steal bases and plays great defense. His RBI and steal counts will depend upon how he's used; he could swipe 70 bases and score over 100 runs in a leadoff role, or drive in 100 from the third spot in the lineup. Either way, he'll be an offensive force.

	AB	R	HR	RBI	SB	BA	$
1992 Montreal NL	653	99	14	66	78	.276	48
1993 Montreal NL	630	104	19	95	53	.298	40
1994 *Projection* >>>	625	97	15	76	65	.286	47

GROTEWOLD, JEFF - 1B - BL - Age 28

Just another ex-prospect. Twice he hit 15 home runs, but never above the Double-A level.

	AB	R	HR	RBI	SB	BA	$
1992 Scranton AAA	51	8	1	8	0	.294	
1992 Philadelphia NL	65	7	3	5	0	.200	-
1993 Portland AAA	151	27	6	30	2	.252	-

GRUBER, KELLY - 3B - BR - Age 32
Coming off a year of inactivity, he appears to be washed up. Don't look for the good old days.

	AB	R	HR	RBI	SB	BA	$
1992 Toronto AL	446	42	11	43	7	.229	6
1993 California AL	65	10	3	9	0	.277	-
1994 *Projection* >>>	193	22	5	23	3	.242	1

GUERRERO, JUAN - IF - BR - Age 27
Guerrero spent the entire 1993 season on the restricted list after being charged with marijuana possession in the Dominican Republic. He was reinstated in October and sent outright to AAA Tucson. His current status is unkown.

	AB	R	HR	RBI	SB	BA	$
1992 Houston NL	125	8	1	14	1	.200	
1993	did not play						

GUILLEN, OZZIE - SS - BL - Age 30
Still superb defensively, he now hits like Mike LaValliere with about half the walks. Ozzie's knee injury thankfully put an end to his caught-stealing adventures.

	AB	R	HR	RBI	SB	BA	$
1992 Chicago AL	40	5	0	7	1	.200	-
1993 Chicago AL	457	44	4	50	5	.280	9
1994 *Projection* >>>	431	42	4	47	8	.275	7

GULAN, MIKE - OF - BR - Age 23
The Cards second round pick in 1992, Gulan made an immediate professional impact. Although he faced weak competition as a collegian, he easily made the adjustment to the pros. Watch the power numbers carefully; four Springfield players hit 20-plus home runs in 1993.

	AB	R	HR	RBI	SB	BA	$
1992 Hamilton A	242	33	7	36	12	.273	
1993 Springfield A	455	81	23	76	8	.259	

GUTIERREZ, RICKY - SS - BR - Age 23
Gutierrez came to the Padres in the late 1992 Lefferts trade with Baltimore and became the regular shortstop when Tony Fernandez was dealt. He kept his average over .270 for much of the year before a late slump. Gutierrez had one of the best fielding percentages in the league; his good glove coupled with his limited speed and power provide evidence of why Gutierrez is a better player in real life than in Rotisserie baseball.

	AB	R	HR	RBI	SB	BA	$
1992 Rochester AAA	431	54	0	41	14	.253	
1993 San Diego NL	438	76	5	26	4	.251	3
1994 *Projection* >>>	219	38	3	13	2	.251	0

GWYNN, CHRIS - OF - BL - Age 29
Got a chance to prove himself; hit well enough in platoon role (first .300 season) but couldn't drive in runs regularly and ended up as pinch hitter. Little power, no speed, mediocre glove; his value is all in his batting average. Don't expect more than 200 AB in any season.

	AB	R	HR	RBI	SB	BA	$
1992 Kansas City AL	84	10	1	7	0	.286	0
1993 Kansas City AL	287	36	1	25	0	.300	4
1994 *Projection* >>>	195	21	2	18	0	.283	2

GWYNN, TONY - OF - BL - Age 33
Although Andres Galarraga won the National League batting crown, Gwynn's .358 second-place batting average was his highest since 1987. Weight-related knee problems are still a concern and contributed to a third consecutive season-ending injury; Gwynn played in just 122 games last year. Reversing several years of decline in base running numbers, Gwynn stole 14 bases (and was caught just once); he was more than a one-category player. Gwynn rarely had the green light with McGriff batting behind him; when McGriff was dealt, Gwynn was turned loose more often. He told me he would steal more bases after McGriff departed, and he did.

	AB	R	HR	RBI	SB	BA	$
1992 San Diego NL	520	77	6	41	3	.317	17
1993 San Diego NL	489	70	7	59	14	.358	25
1994 *Projection* >>>	506	72	6	54	9	.319	22

HACOPIAN, DEREK - OF - BR - Age 24

A 23rd-round pick in 1992 out of Maryland, he ravaged South Atlantic League pitching in 1993, slugging well over .500. But hey, at age 23, he probably should have. Has limited defensive skills, but was named as one of the "Best of the Rest" outfield prospects by USA Today Baseball Weekly. At his age, and with the Indians' stable of outfield prospects, the pressure's on him to have another monster year in 1994 at a higher level.

	AB	R	HR	RBI	SB	BA	$
1993 Columbus A	454	81	24	82	4	.315	

HALE, CHIP - 2B - BL - Age 29

Looked like he had the Twins' second base job in 1990, but manager Kelly changed his mind at the last minute. Hale is still a credible prospect, obviously on the old side. Hale had a good year in '93, hitting over his head. Tom Kelly told me Hale is reasonably assured of a utility role for 1994.

	AB	R	HR	RBI	SB	BA	$
1993 Minnesota AL	186	25	3	27	2	.333	6
1994 *Projection* >>>	156	20	2	21	1	.246	1

HALL, BILLY - 2B - BB - Age 25

Hall is a very fast, 5'9" dynamo who led the California League in batting and SB in 1992 and then hit respectably in 1993 after a promotion to Double-A Wichita. Hall and Jason Hardtke are two of the reasons that the Padres feel they are well stocked at the middle infield spots.

	AB	R	HR	RBI	SB	BA	$
1992 High Desert A	495	92	2	39	49	.356	
1993 Witchita AA	486	80	4	46	29	.270	

HALL, JOE - OF - BR - Age 28

A sparkplug of Nashville's division-winning team. Gets on base, runs a bit, has some power, plays some defense. He hasn't been to the majors yet, and like many of Nashville's overaged stars, he's not very likely to get there in '94.

HALL, MEL - OF - BL - Age 33

For years, Hall said that he could play every day, but people looked at his .151 career BA against lefty pitchers and guessed he was wrong. When Hall finally did get to play, he showed it was the stat-watchers who were wrong. For two years he clobbered lefty and righty pitchers alike. The only problem was that he then wanted $3 million, which had already been given to Danny Tartabull. Now biding his time in Japan.

	AB	R	HR	RBI	SB	BA	$
1992 New York AL	583	67	15	81	4	.280	18
1993 Japan	480	71	30	92	---	.296	

HAMELIN, BOB - 1B - BL - Age 26

First full-year in 1993 after losing parts of four years to back problems. He looks like a lefty Steve Balboni. Lots of power, no speed, marginal BA. He'll probably be the biggest beneficiary of Brett's retirement, moving into at least a platoon designated hitter role in 1994. The Royals need power and if Hamelin hits a few early season dingers, he'll get a full-time opportunity. A good place to find some cheap HRs in 1994.

	AB	R	HR	RBI	SB	BA	$
1993 Omaha AAA	479	77	29	84	8	.259	
1993 Kansas City AL	49	2	2	5	0	.224	-
1994 *Projection* >>>	302	28	9	35	2	.229	3

HAMILTON, DARRYL - OF - BL - Age 29

Long one of the most underrated players in the AL, Hamilton has good speed and has been a consistent .300 hitter since mid 1990. One negative: he stole only 6 of his 21 bases in the second half of 1993.

	AB	R	HR	RBI	SB	BA	$
1992 Milwaukee AL	470	67	5	62	41	.298	30
1993 Milwaukee AL	520	74	9	48	21	.310	23
1994 *Projection* >>>	503	73	6	56	28	.306	27

HAMMONDS, JEFFREY - OF - BL - Age 23

Hammonds has multi-dimensional power and speed talents, and an extremely quick bat. However, he had a herniated disk in his neck and could miss 8-10 months. If he plays, he'll be great.

	AB	R	HR	RBI	SB	BA	$
1993 Baltimore AL	105	10	3	19	4	.305	3
1994 *Projection* >>>	253	32	9	44	6	.265	8

HANEY, TODD - 2B - BR - Age 28

Haney has proven to be a high average hitter at Triple-A (.339 at Calgary in 1990), but has little power and just average speed. His tools aren't likely to take him any higher than Triple-A.

	AB	R	HR	RBI	SB	BA	$
1992 Indianapolis AAA	200	30	6	33	1	.265	
1992 Montreal NL	10	0	0	1	0	.300	-

HANSEN, DAVE - 3B - BL - Age 25

A strong season in a part-time role makes Hansen the likely starter at third base in 1994, sending Tim Wallach to the bench. Beginning the season as a PH, he started nearly every day in September. He won't hit .362 again, but .275 with a little power is within reach. He's young enough to improve.

	AB	R	HR	RBI	SB	BA	$
1992 Los Angeles NL	341	30	6	22	0	.214	-
1993 Los Angelas NL	105	13	4	30	0	.362	5
1994 *Projection* >>>	323	33	8	41	0	.270	4

HANSEN, TERREL - 1B/OF - BR - Age 27

Too slow for extended outfield duty, Hansen has hit only 34 homers in the last three years, fewer than you would want from a firstbaseman. The former prospect had a horrendous 103/18 strikeout to walk rate in 1993.

	AB	R	HR	RBI	SB	BA	$
1992 Tidewater AAA	395	43	12	47	4	.248	
1993 Ottawa AAA	352	45	10	39	1	.230	

HARDGE, MIKE - 2B/SS - BR - Age 22

Excellent long-term prospect with good speed. Hardge was helped by good Arizona play and by DeShields' departure.

HARE, SHAWN - OF - BL - Age 27

Tiger farmhand Shawn Hare just spent his fourth year in Triple-A. He has a nice swing and some power, but has been unable to get very much major league playing time. If and when he gets to play, he will have a decent batting average.

	AB	R	HR	RBI	SB	BA	$
1992 Toledo AAA	203	31	5	34	6	.330	
1992 Detroit AL	26	0	0	5	0	.115	-
1993 Toledo AAA	470	81	20	76	8	.264	

HARPER, BRIAN - C - BR - Age 34

Harper is one of the better hitting catchers in the AL. Last year, he hit .362 with runners in scoring position. He's not getting any younger though.

	AB	R	HR	RBI	SB	BA	$
1992 Minnesota AL	502	58	9	73	0	.307	17
1993 Minnesota AL	530	52	12	73	1	.304	16
1994 *Projection* >>>	506	52	11	69	1	.294	16

HARRIS, DONALD - OF - BR - Age 26

After failing to make the Dallas Cowboys' roster, he returned to baseball, but after three years at Double-A, Harris has yet to hit well. He doesn't walk, strikes out too much, has little power, can't hit for average. Good speed and defense, didn't show in his late season callup. Not a factor for '94.

	AB	R	HR	RBI	SB	BA	$
1992 Texas AL	33	3	0	1	1	.182	-
1993 Oklahoma City AAA	367	48	6	40	4	.253	-
1993 Texas AL	76	10	1	8	0	.197	-

HARRIS, LENNY - 3B - BL - Age 29
After four straight years getting 300 or more at bats in a utility/platoon role, his playing time was slashed following the acquisitions of Jody Reed and Tim Wallach. Harris can still hit, but he is a defensive liability and is unlikely to regain his playing time in Cincinnati.

	AB	R	HR	RBI	SB	BA	$
1992 Los Angeles NL	347	28	0	30	19	.271	11
1993 Los Angelas NL	160	20	2	11	3	.238	0
1994 *Projection >>>*	267	29	2	22	10	.265	6

HASELMAN, BILL - C - BR - Age 27
M's picked him up on waivers. He showed power and speed at Triple-A in 1991 and showed even more power last year. He is not a good defensive catcher, which led Seattle to try him in the outfield to get his bat into the line-up. Like Hector Villanueva, if he hits enough, someone will let him play. Dan Wilson has the catcher job in Seattle.

	AB	R	HR	RBI	SB	BA	$
1992 Two Teams AAA	302	49	19	53	3	.255	
1992 Seattle AL	19	1	0	0	0	.263	-
1993 Seattle AL	137	21	5	16	2	.255	1
1994 *Projection >>>*	75	11	2	8	1	.256	-

HATCHER, BILLY - OF - BR - Age 33
Hatcher's major value has been his speed. With the lead-foot BoSox, he still runs, but is at the age when he'll pop a string or pull something and miss games.

	AB	R	HR	RBI	SB	BA	$
1992 Cincinnati-Boston	409	47	3	33	4	.249	1
1993 Boston AL	508	71	9	57	14	.287	17
1994 *Projection >>>*	464	58	6	45	9	.267	11

HATCHER, CHRIS - OF - BR - Age 25
A powerhitting outfielder who was slowed by injuries in 1993, Hatcher needs to cut down on his strikeouts. He should play at Triple-A in 1994 and needs a big year to merit major league consideration.

HATTEBERG, SCOTT - C - BL - Age 24
Aaron Sele's battery mate at Washington State is bidding to rejoin him in Boston. Hatteberg had a very poor start with the bat at Pawtucket last season, indicating he'll need to prove himself at the Triple-A level this year.

HAYES, CHARLIE - 3B - BR - Age 28
The NL leader in doubles, Hayes had career highs in average, home runs, runs, RBI and steals. His only disappointment was defense, where he led the team with 20 errors. The Rockies built the team around him and hope his hitting will continue.

	AB	R	HR	RBI	SB	BA	$
1992 New York AL	509	52	18	66	3	.257	13
1993 Colorado NL	573	89	25	98	11	.305	27
1994 *Projection >>>*	533	67	20	80	7	.279	21

HELFAND, ERIC - C - BL - Age 25
The guy drafted by Florida and then traded back to Oakland, for Walt Weiss. A .270 career hitter in three low minor league seasons, with fair power. Catchers with lefty bats and workmanlike defense have a way of getting to the majors. Helfand could use a year at Triple-A though.

	AB	R	HR	RBI	SB	BA	$
1993 Huntsville AA	302	38	10	48	1	.228	
1993 Oakland AL	13	1	0	1	0	.231	-

HEMOND, SCOTT - IF/C - BR - Age 28
Solidified his role as a backup catcher who can steal bases. Hit .299 against lefties and he can play six different positions.

	AB	R	HR	RBI	SB	BA	$
1992 Chicago AL	40	8	0	2	1	.225	-
1993 Oakland AL	215	31	6	26	14	.256	8
1994 *Projection* >>>	125	16	3	14	5	.251	2

HENDERSON, DAVE - OF - BR - Age 35
Hendu is one of the most delightful players for a fan to watch, and he has come back from adversity before. He closed 1993 with a rush. He is also 35 years old, coming off successive injury-prone seasons where he hit .143 and .220, and his defense has deteriorated.

	AB	R	HR	RBI	SB	BA	$
1992 Oakland AL	63	1	0	2	0	.143	-
1993 Oakland AL	382	37	20	53	0	.220	5
1994 *Projection* >>>	309	33	14	42	1	.232	4

HENDERSON, RICKEY - OF - BR - Age 35
The best leadoff hitter in history became one of the few disappointing acquisitions Pat Gillick has ever made. He's still an offensive catalyst, but was an almost certain departure from Toronto after his non-impact stretch run. When Rickey's healthy, he's one of the best players in baseball. His speed is not what it once was, but he takes walks and hits for power better than any leadoff batter in baseball. By asking for more money and bothering his front office incessantly, Henderson actually cost himself plenty, by reducing the number of teams interested in bidding for him. When his agent called the A's to ask for an offer, the answer was: nothing.

	AB	R	HR	RBI	SB	BA	$
1992 Oakland AL	396	77	15	46	48	.283	32
1993 Oakland-Toronto AL	481	114	21	59	53	.289	40
1994 *Projection* >>>	451	97	18	54	51	.280	35

HERNANDEZ, CARLOS - C - BR - Age 26
Two years ago, Hernandez was considered a decent offensive catching prospect. But with Piazza solidly entrenched as a star, he won't see more than about 100 at bats with the Dodgers. There is a lot of untapped talent here, including a good bat and strong throwing arm. Hernandez will suddenly become valuable if he is traded or if Piazza gets hurt.

	AB	R	HR	RBI	SB	BA	$
1992 Los Angeles NL	173	11	3	17	0	.260	1
1993 Los Angeles NL	99	6	2	7	0	.253	-
1994 *Projection* >>>	109	7	2	9	0	.256	-

HERNANDEZ, CESAR - OF - BR - Age 27
Signed as a six year minor league free agent, Hernandez put together a solid year at Nashville and impressed the Reds with his defensive abilities. But when Hernandez started losing games with his glove instead of winning them, his major league days became numbered.

	AB	R	HR	RBI	SB	BA	$
1992 Cincinnati NL	51	6	0	4	3	.275	0
1993 Indianapolis AAA	272	30	5	22	5	.257-	
1993 Cincinnati NL	24	3	0	1	1	.083	-
1994 *Projection* >>>	50	5	1	5	1	.240	-

HERNANDEZ, JOSE M - SS - BR - Age 20
Ask yourself why a shrewd GM like Himes would trade a pitcher (Heath Slocumb) for another minor league shortstop. Coming over from Cleveland, Hernandez hit .304 with 8 home runs in 263 at bats including a 22-game hitting streak for AA Orlando. Hernandez previously appeared briefly in the majors for both Texas and Cleveland. He's the best shortstop in the organization not already in the majors and has a good glove.

	AB	R	HR	RBI	SB	BA	$
1992 Canton AA	404	56	3	46	7	.255	
1993 Orlando AA	263	42	8	33	8	.304	

HERRERA, JOSE - OF - BL - Age 21
Traded by the Blue Jays with Steve Karsay for Rickey Henderson last summer. With Hagerstown, D.J. Boston and Herrera formed a devastating 1-2 punch. It's a long way from the Sally League to the majors, so time will tell.

HIATT, PHIL - 3B/OF - BR - Age 24
Third in line at third base last winter, Hiatt became the starting third baseman after Jefferies was traded and Miller got hurt. He started strong, led Royals in home runs and RBI into June; but reverted to old strikeout habits, fanning once per three at bats. Went to the fall league to cut down his swing. If he learns to cut down the strikeouts and stops making bushels of errors, he'll get the third base job. Otherwise, he'll play little at the major league level. Watch his spring closely to see which way he'll go in 1994.

	AB	R	HR	RBI	SB	BA	$
1993 Kansas City AL	238	30	7	36	6	.218	3
1994 *Projection* >>>	119	15	4	17	3	.222	0

HIGGINS, KEVIN - 3B/C - BL - Age 27
Higgins is a weak-hitting prospect whose only value is his ability to play all infield and outfield positions except shortstop and centerfield. He may have a reserve role in San Diego behind Brad Ausmus and Dan Walters.

	AB	R	HR	RBI	SB	BA	$
1993 San Diego NL	181	17	0	13	0	.221	-
1994 *Projection* >>>	91	9	0	8	0	.245	-

HILL, GLENALLEN - OF - BR - Age 29
A .562 slugging percentage versus lefties made Chicago fans realize he was a player, not a new ski resort. Hill's retention by the Cubs at the end of last season was made difficult by an incredible finish with the Cubs. He can productively fill a platoon role, and if it's in Wrigley, so much the better for his power totals.

	AB	R	HR	RBI	SB	BA	$
1992 Cleveland AL	369	38	18	49	9	.241	12
1993 Cleveland AL	174	19	5	25	7	.224	3
1993 Chicago NL	87	14	10	22	1	.345	6
1994 *Projection* >>>	290	31	8	40	7	.254	7

HILL, LEW - OF - BB - Age 24
A raw power-speed source. Moving slowly up the Yankees farm ladder. All of his numbers tailed off when he advanced to high A ball last season. To make it, he'll have to improve his K/W ratio (124/29 in '93).

HINZO, TOMMY - 2B - BB - Age 30
A former Cleveland Indian, Hinzo returned from Japan to have an All-Star year in the Triple-A International League. A switch-hitter with excellent speed, Hinzo could earn a promotion to Baltimore as a utility player, but will have a tough time finding a spot if both Hulett and Reynolds are re-signed.

	AB	R	HR	RBI	SB	BA	$
1993 Rochester AAA	560	83	6	69	29	.271	

HOCKING, DENNY - SS - BB - Age 23
Top prospect Denny Hocking is a talent worth watching because he is the rare shortstop who can hit and steal bases and has all the defensive tools including a great arm. He was slowed by an injury last year, but is a strong candidate for the Twins shortstop job this year.

	AB	R	HR	RBI	SB	BA	$
1993 Nashville AAA	409	54	8	50	15	.267	-
1993 Minnesota AL	36	7	0	0	1	.139	-
1994 *Projection* >>>	150	16	3	17	4	.252	1

HOILES, CHRIS - C - BR - Age 29
Chris Hoiles has emerged as one of the best hitting catchers ever. An improved receiver, he led AL catchers in slugging percentage (.585) by a large margin and can repeat that feat in 1994. Hoiles hit 20 home runs in only 310 at bats in 1992 and 29 home runs in just 419 at bats in 1993. Look out if he gets 500 at-bats. Don't be surprised if Hoiles hits clean-up for Baltimore. He may also get designated hitter time when Baines rests.

	AB	R	HR	RBI	SB	BA	$
1992 Baltimore AL	310	49	20	40	0	.274	12
1993 Baltimore AL	419	80	29	82	1	.310	22
1994 *Projection* >>>	439	84	33	81	1	.282	19

HOLBERT, AARON - SS - BR - Age 21

The Cardinals seem to have a slick-fielding shortstop at every level of the minor leagues. Holbert, a number one pick in 1990, doesn't have much power but has good speed (45 stolen bases at Single-A St. Petersburg, 107 stolen bases in the last two years) and figures to hit for average. He probably won't be ready before 1995.

HOLBERT, RAY - SS - BR - Age 23

After starting slowly (four years at Rookie and A-ball), Holbert has now had two solid seasons at Double-A; he will ultimately contend with Gutierrez for the Padres shortstop job. A year in waiting at AAA Las Vegas would help Holbert whose base-running abilities will fit nicely with Jim Riggleman's aggressive approach.

	AB	R	HR	RBI	SB	BA	$
1992 Witchita AA	304	46	2	23	26	.283	
1993 Witchita AA	388	56	5	48	30	.260	

HOLIFIELD, RICK - OF - BL - Age 24

After struggling for four years to cross the Mendoza Line, Holifield put it together last season. In addition to his power and speed, he's a good outfielder with enough arm to play right field. He also has played center.

	AB	R	HR	RBI	SB	BA	$
1993 Dunedin A	407	84	20	68	30	.275	

HOLLANDSWORTH, TODD - OF - BL - Age 21

Combining power and speed at AA San Antonio (.251-17-63-23), Hollandsworth was tabbed as the Texas League's ninth best prospect by Baseball America. He needs to work on his strike zone judgement. He helped himself in the 1993 Arizona Fall League with clutch hitting and inspired defense, and could reach Los Angeles later in 1994.

HOLLINS, DAVE - 3B/1B - BB - Age 27

A switch hitter, Hollins struggled mightily from the left side after a midseason wrist injury. There has been talk about making him purely a righthanded hitter (.323 in 1993). Like most of the Phils, Hollins will take a walk, and has scored 104 runs in consecutive years. Entering his prime, Hollins could become a perennial 100 runs scored/100 RBI man. Defensively, he has a wild throwing arm and limited range.

	AB	R	HR	RBI	SB	BA	$
1992 Philadelphia NL	586	104	27	93	9	.270	27
1993 Philadelphia NL	543	104	18	93	2	.273	15
1994 *Projection* >>>	533	99	21	90	4	.273	18

HORN, SAM - DH/1B - BL - Age 30

Horn has had prolific minor league home run campaigns since 1987. Picked up where he left off in a September callup to the Indians. Treads into a very crowded situation with the Indians, as Sorrento and Milligan have similar skills, but are younger. Strictly a platoon player, his 1993 feats guarantee a shot at a major league job somewhere in 1994.

	AB	R	HR	RBI	SB	BA	$
1992 Baltimore AL	162	13	5	19	0	.235	1
1993 Charlotte AAA	402	62	38	96	1	.269	
1993 Cleveland AL	33	8	4	8	0	.455	1
1994 *Projection* >>>	124	14	6	18	0	.244	1

HORNE, TYRONE - OF - BL - Age 23

Horne is one of many Expos' outfield prospects. He played better for AA Harrisburg last season after being promoted from Single-A West Palm Beach late in the season. He has good power but hasn't shown any above A-ball; he could move up the ladder fast if he continues the power display at higher levels.

HOSEY, STEVE - OF - BR - Age 24

A former first round draft pick (1989), Hosey been remarkably consistent as he has moved up the minor league ladder, averaging 14 home runs and 17 stolen bases each year; this could be the year he gets a real chance in the majors, particularly if he can cut down on his strikeouts (130 in 457 at bats in 1993).

	AB	R	HR	RBI	SB	BA	$
1992 San Francisco NL	56	6	1	6	1	.250	-
1993 Phoenix AAA	455	70	16	85	16	.292	
1993 San Francisco NL	2	0	0	1	0	.500	-
1994 *Projection* >>>	150	16	4	18	3	.253	2

HOUSIE, WAYNE - OF - BB - Age 28
Appeared with the Red Sox briefly in 1991, but now he's just a career .252 hitter with fair speed after seven years in the minor leagues.

	AB	R	HR	RBI	SB	BA	$
1992 Pawtucket AAA	456	53	2	28	20	.221	
1993 New York NL	16	2	0	1	0	.188	-

HOUSTON, TYLER - C - BL - Age 23
The top hitter picked in June 1989 (ahead of Frank Thomas). Houston showed far more maturity in 1993 and hit well enough for AA Greenville to get a late promotion to AAA Richmond. Houston went to the instructional league after the 1993 season. He's still at least a year away from the majors, but his remarkable progress last season makes him a prospect again.

	AB	R	HR	RBI	SB	BA	$
1993 Greenville AA	262	27	5	33	5	.279	
1993 Richmond AAA	36	4	1	3	0	.139	

HOWARD, CHRIS - C - BR - Age 28
Not to be confused with White Sox farm pitcher Chris Howard who was at Nashville in 1993. He raised his average 82 points in his second season at Triple-A and got a September call up (one at bat). Now he's stuck behind Dan Wilson.

	AB	R	HR	RBI	SB	BA	$
1992 Calgary AAA	319	29	8	45	3	.238	
1993 Calgary AAA	331	40	6	55	1	.320	-
1993 Seattle AL	1	0	0	0	0	.000	-

HOWARD, DAVID - SS/2B - BB - Age 27
Royals offseason acquisitions of Gagne and Lind meant an end of major league playing time for good field/no-hit Howard. Hit a little at AAA Omaha (for the first time) but will never be a good major league hitter. Lacks power and speed.

	AB	R	HR	RBI	SB	BA	$
1992 Kansas City AL	219	19	1	18	3	.224	-
1993 Omaha AAA	157	15	0	18	3	.255	-
1993 Kansas City AL	24	5	0	2	1	.333	-
1994 *Projection* >>>	124	12	1	10	2	.223	-

HOWARD, THOMAS - OF - BB - Age 29
Howard came over to the Reds in exchange for Randy Milligan and performed very well. He has always had good speed and is now developing power. In line for the fourth outfield job, Howard should get about 300 at bats for the Reds in 1994.

	AB	R	HR	RBI	SB	BA	$
1992 Cleveland AL	358	36	2	32	15	.277	11
1993 Cleveland AL	178	26	3	23	5	.236	1
1993 Cincinnati NL	141	22	4	13	5	.277	3
1994 *Projection* >>>	326	41	5	32	11	.262	8

HOWELL, JACK - 3B - BL - Age 32
Howell was once on track to be the Angels third baseman of the future, but he figured his odds were better overseas.

	AB	R	HR	RBI	SB	BA	$
1992 Japan	321	55	30	69	---	.331	
1993 Japan	396	72	28	88	---	.295	

HOWELL, PAT - OF - BB - Age 25
Given a chance to play center field for a team that really needed a center fielder and leadoff hitter in 1992, Howell had one exciting game for the Mets and then faded rapidly.

	AB	R	HR	RBI	SB	BA	$
1992 New York NL	75	9	0	1	4	.187	-
1993 Portland AAA	369	57	2	29	36	.209	

HOWITT, DANN - 1B/OF - BL - Age 30
Had the last hit ever off Nolan Ryan -- an opposite field grand slam home run. Unfortunately that was a reflection of how bad Ryan's stuff was not Howitt's skill. He has good power, but his low average will keep him from being more than a fifth outfielder. Released after the season.

	AB	R	HR	RBI	SB	BA	$
1992 Oakland-Seattle AL	85	7	2	10	1	.188	-
1993 Seattle AL	76	6	2	8	0	.211	-
1994 *Projection* >>>	73	6	2	8	0	.198	-

HRBEK, KENT - 1B - BL - Age 33
1993 was Hrbek's second injury plagued year in a row. The 25 dingers were a nice surprise, but the batting average below .250 for the second consecutive year is a concern. Hrbek is assured of a starting job because of manager Kelly's confidence, but David McCarty and Steve Dunn are coming fast.

	AB	R	HR	RBI	SB	BA	$
1992 Minnesota AL	394	52	15	58	5	.244	10
1993 Minnesota AL	392	60	25	83	4	.242	13
1994 *Projection* >>>	405	59	21	76	4	.251	13

HUBBARD, TRENT - 2B - BR - Age 29
Hubbard had essentially the same kind of season for AAA Colorado Springs in 1993 that he did for AAA Tucson in 1992 and AA Jackson in 1991, hitting .314 with 33 SBs. The fleet-footed Hubbard is a marginal player at best and would get significant playing time only if several Rockies outfielders were out at the same time.

	AB	R	HR	RBI	SB	BA	$
1992 Tucson AAA	420	69	2	33	34	.310	-
1993 Colorado Springs AAA	439	83	7	56	33	.314	

HUDLER, REX - OF/IF -BR - Age 33
He is a good guy to have on a club with his intensity and ability to play anywhere in the infield or outfield. He was a standout wide receiver in high school and nearly wound up accepting a scholarship to Notre Dame.

	AB	R	HR	RBI	SB	BA	$
1992 St. Louis NL	98	17	3	5	2	.245	0
1993 Japan	410	48	14	64	---	.300	

HUFF, MIKE - OF - BR - Age 30
Huff spent most of last year at Nashville and was eventually let go by the Sox. If he manages to stay in the bigs all year for someone, he could get 10-15 steals. That's a big if, though.

	AB	R	HR	RBI	SB	BA	$
1992 Chicago AL	115	13	0	8	1	.209	-
1993 Nashville AAA	344	65	8	32	18	.294	-
1993 Chicago AL	44	4	1	6	1	.182	-
1994 *Projection* >>>	101	13	1	10	3	.220	-

HUGHES, KEITH - OF - BL - Age 30
A career minor leaguer, Hughes battled the Mendoza line in his rare major league cameos. Considering how little he played in the Reds' injury ravaged outfield, he probably has little chance to get major league meal money again.

HULETT, TIM - 3B/2B - BR - Age 34
After Leo Gomez' injury and before the acquisition of Mike Pagliarulo, Hulett was Baltimore's every day third baseman

for six weeks and performed admirably. Hulett can also contribute at second base and backs up Ripken in the late innings of blowouts.

	AB	R	HR	RBI	SB	BA	$
1992 Baltimore AL	142	11	2	21	0	.289	2
1993 Baltimore AL	260	40	2	23	1	.300	4
1994 *Projection* >>>	212	27	3	19	1	.271	2

HULSE, DAVID - OF - BL - Age 26
A speedy defensive whiz, Hulse started the season platooning in center field, but won the job full-time by midseason. A very streaky player. Good speed and defense.

	AB	R	HR	RBI	SB	BA	$
1992 Texas AL	92	14	0	2	3	.304	1
1993 Texas AL	407	71	1	29	29	.290	18
1994 *Projection* >>>	434	80	1	30	30	.270	17

HUMPHREYS, MIKE - OF - BR - Age 26
Good talent, but the Yankees outfield has been more crowded than a New York subway during rush hour.

	AB	R	HR	RBI	SB	BA	$
1992 Columbus AAA	408	83	6	46	37	.282	
1993 Columbus AAA	330	59	6	42	18	.288	
1993 New York AL	35	6	1	6	2	.171	-
1994 *Projection* >>>	60	6	1	6	2	.255	-

HUNDLEY, TODD - C - BB - Age 24
Hundley's a fine receiver who throws well, but it's going to take a while for the batting average to become respectable. There is big upward possibility. He could turn into a .250 hitter with good power any time.

	AB	R	HR	RBI	SB	BA	$
1992 New York NL	358	32	7	32	3	.209	1
1993 New York NL	417	40	11	53	1	.228	3
1994 *Projection* >>>	407	40	11	50	1	.235	4

HUNTER, BRIAN L - OF - BR - Age 23
After three years in Rookie/A-ball, speedy Hunter finally hit for average in 1992-93. The trade of Eric Anthony helps.

HUNTER, BRIAN R - 1B - BR - Age 26
The McGriff acquisition cost Hunter his major league job. He had an awful time in the majors in 1993 and didn't hit much in Richmond, but he's still young and will get another chance in Pittsburgh.

	AB	R	HR	RBI	SB	BA	$
1992 Atlanta NL	238	34	14	41	1	.239	8
1993 Richmond AAA	99	16	6	26	4	.242	-
1993 Atlanta NL	80	4	0	8	0	.138	-
1994 *Projection* >>>	165	19	7	26	0	.218	0

HUNTER, TORII - OF - BB - Age 18
The first of Minnesota's four first-round draft picks in '93. Projected as a power-speed package and center fielder.

HURST, JIMMY - OF - BR - Age 22
Has power and speed, but need polishing. He has to refine a swing that produced 141 Midwest League whiffs.

HUSKEY, BUTCH - 3B - BR - Age 22
Huskey is a good long-range prospect with outstanding power. He was scheduled to start the year at AAA Norfolk but could emerge anytime and become a much-needed team leader.

	AB	R	HR	RBI	SB	BA	$
1992 St. Lucie A	493	65	18	75	7	.254	
1993 Binghamton AA	526	72	25	98	11	.251	
1993 New York NL	41	2	0	3	0	.146	-
1994 *Projection* >>>	150	15	6	23	2	.233	1

HUSON, JEFF - SS/2B - BL - Age 29

Suffered through an injury-filled year. A versatile player who can back up at any infield position except first base. May get a chance at a platoon second base job.

	AB	R	HR	RBI	SB	BA	$
1992 Texas AL	318	49	4	24	18	.261	10
1993 Texas AL	45	3	0	2	0	.133	-
1994 *Projection* >>>	173	24	2	13	7	.232	1

HYERS, TIM - SS - BI - Age 22

A hot start put him into the Double-A All-Star Game, and his average held up for the remainder of the season. Good strike zone judgment and some speed, but nowhere near the power you'd like to see in a first baseman. A second-round draft pick in 1990.

HYZDU, ADAM - OF - BR - Age 22

A first round pick in 1990, Hyzdu is a good power/speed combination and is still maturing. After one and a half strong seasons at Single-A San Jose, he put together numbers that were poor for the Texas League.

INCAVIGLIA, PETE - OF - BR - Age 29

One of the keys to the Phils miracle season in 1993, Incaviglia had an unbelievable 89 RBI as a platoon player; his .88 RBI per hit and .24 RBI per at bat were both major league bests. Incaviglia will never improve upon 1993. However, there is the potential for increased playing time in 1994. He hit a respectable .272 against righties in 1993.

	AB	R	HR	RBI	SB	BA	$
1992 Houston NL	349	31	11	44	2	.266	10
1993 Philadelphia NL	368	60	24	89	1	.274	15
1994 *Projection* >>>	356	45	16	59	1	.262	10

JACKSON, BO - OF/DH - BR - Age 31

The box office hype and 16 dingers in 1993 give Jackson a deceptive appearance of value. He's past whatever prime he might have had. He can't run, and can barely pull the ball. His 106 whiffs in 284 at bats is historic.

	AB	R	HR	RBI	SB	BA	$
1993 Chicago AL	284	32	16	45	0	.232	5
1994 *Projection* >>>	154	15	7	23	0	.231	1

JACKSON, DAMIAN - SS - BR - Age 20

Speedy shortstop who was one of the youngest players competing in the South Atlantic League in 1993. Has shown decent doubles power and has scored a high number of runs in both minor league seasons. Lack of shortstop prospects in Indians' organization will give him an opportunity to move quickly through the ranks.

JACKSON, DARRIN - OF - BR - Age 30

Before last year, Jackson appeared to be settling in as a predictable, mid-.200s, 15-20 home run type with a glove steady enough to keep him in center field every day. Slowed by a thyroid condition in 1993, Jackson had a lost season. The condition was treatable, but by the time Jackson was ready to play, the Mets were busy looking at Ryan Thompson and Jeremy Burnitz in the outfield, with no place for Jackson to play.

	AB	R	HR	RBI	SB	BA	$
1992 San Diego NL	587	72	17	70	14	.249	18
1993 Toronto AL	176	15	5	19	0	.216	-
1993 New York NL	87	4	1	7	0	.195	-
1994 *Projection* >>>	386	43	12	45	5	.240	6

JACKSON, JEFF - 1B - BR - Age 22

OK, hindsight is 20-20, but let's say you've got the fourth overall pick in the 1989 draft. Do you take this guy, a raw 17-year-old, or Big Frank Thomas? Well, the Phils figured that since they had a big slugger in Ricky Jordan entrenched at first base, they had no need for Thomas. In Jackson's five pro seasons, he has batted no higher than .242 and struck out about once every three at bats. He was exposed, but not selected, in the expansion draft. He's just a kid, so they'll hang onto him.

	AB	R	HR	RBI	SB	BA	$
1992 Clearwater A	297	35	6	36	6	.242	
1992 Reading AA	108	12	0	6	9	.185	
1993 Reading AA	374	45	9	51	20	.238	

JACOBY, BROOK - OF - BR - Age 34

Veteran Jacoby was signed by the Indians as a free agent after his release by Oakland following a very poor '91 season, and played one more year in Cleveland before moving on to Japan.

	AB	R	HR	RBI	SB	BA	$
1992 Cleveland AL	291	30	4	36	0	.261	4
1993 Japan	60	4	2	6	---	183	

JAHA, JOHN - 1B - BR - Age 27

Big numbers at AA El Paso often mean nothing. Jaha hit .344 there and led the Texas League in home runs (30) and RBI (134) two years ago. Still, he reached age 26 before he reached the major leagues even for a brief look. After a slow start in 1993, Jaha finally showed something. He got 14 of his 19 jacks after the All-Star break.

	AB	R	HR	RBI	SB	BA	$
1992 Denver AAA	274	61	18	69	6	.321	
1992 Milwaukee AL	133	17	2	10	10	.226	3
1993 Milwaukee AL	515	78	19	70	13	.264	17
1994 *Projection* >>>	491	73	20	75	16	.270	18

JAMES, CHRIS - OF - BR - Age 31

Journeyman outfielder with occasional power. Acquired in a late-season deal with Houston, James made an immediate splash by homering in his first Ranger AB. He should stick with the team as the fourth or fifth outfielder, and righthanded pinch hitter.

	AB	R	HR	RBI	SB	BA	$
1992 San Francisco NL	248	25	5	32	2	.242	3
1993 Houston NL	129	19	6	19	2	.256	3
1993 Texas AL	31	5	3	7	0	.355	0
1994 *Projection* >>>	236	26	6	31	2	.252	3

JAMES, DION - OF - BL - Age 31

Career looked finished in 1991, but he resurfaced with the Yankees in 1992, and in 1993 he produced a surprising (to some) season, batting .332 in a part-time role. Has a good lefty swing, and is a solid contact hitter who hits line drives. Scouts have always liked that sweet swing.

	AB	R	HR	RBI	SB	BA	$
1992 New York AL	145	24	3	17	1	.262	2
1993 New York AL	343	62	7	36	0	.332	11
1994 *Projection* >>>	219	39	4	24	0	.290	4

JAVIER, STAN - OF - BB - Age 30

Javier's reached the point where he's about as good as he's going to get. He won't start, but can hit, steal bases, and play a little outfield.

	AB	R	HR	RBI	SB	BA	$
1992 L.A.-Philadelphia NL	334	42	1	29	18	.249	8
1993 California AL	237	33	3	28	12	.291	9
1994 *Projection* >>>	248	34	3	27	11	.264	7

JEFFERIES, GREGG - 1B - BB - Age 26

Jefferies has been one of my favorite players for years, because he reached the major leagues so early and was "disappointing" only because of excessive hype and New York impatience. For comparison, he's the same age as Tino Martinez. Which one would you rather have? Now Jefferies is clearly a budding superstar with batting champion potential. Could hit .300 every year with 50 extra base hits. (PS -- that was the comment I wrote last year, before his big season in St. Louis. And yes, it was that obvious.)

	AB	R	HR	RBI	SB	BA	$
1992 Kansas City AL	604	66	10	75	19	.285	23
1993 St. Louis NL	544	89	16	83	46	.342	42
1994 *Projection* >>>	554	76	13	77	34	.311	37

JEFFERSON, REGGIE - DH - BB - Age 25

Jefferson was the top prospect in the Cincinnati organization, coming to the Indians in '91 via a trade forced when the Reds found themselves in a trade-or-lose waiver snafu. He was slated to start '92 as the Indians first baseman but came down with an injury and then had a very disappointing 1993 season, now he finds himself in a real struggle for playing time. The Indians will be forced to make room in the lineup for Manny Ramirez, possibly as a designated hitter and Paul Sorrento gets all the first base time against righty pitchers. Subpar defense and inability to hit lefties doesn't help Jefferson's chances.

	AB	R	HR	RBI	SB	BA	$
1992 Cleveland AL	89	8	1	6	0	.337	2
1993 Cleveland AL	366	35	10	34	1	.249	3
1994 *Projection* >>>	331	33	9	31	1	.256	3

JENNINGS, DOUG - 1B - BL - Age 29

Just a journeyman. Jennings appeared with Oakland every year from 1988-1991 but hit only .193 in total. As the Cubs Triple-A first sacker, Jennings played a little when Mark Grace was hurt. Jennings is no more than a lefty pinch hitter; there are so many other players just like him, and a year or two younger.

	AB	R	HR	RBI	SB	BA	$
1992 Rochester AAA	396	70	14	76	11	.275	
1993 Iowa AAA	228	38	7	37	3	.294	-
1993 Chicago NL	52	8	2	8	0	.250	-

JENNINGS, LANCE - C - BR - Age 22

A hot prospect after 1992, took a step back in 1993. Hasn't proven he can hit at Double-A yet. One of Royals top prospects, still. Will be given every opportunity to develop. Has some power potential, but no speed and questionable strike zone judgement. At least two years away at this point.

JENSEN, MARCUS - C - BB - Age 21

A great athlete, Jensen can also pitch. He showed marked improvement in his second Midwest League season. He's the best catching prospect in the Giants organization.

	AB	R	HR	RBI	SB	BA	$
1992 Clinton A	264	35	4	33	4	.239	
1993 Clinton A	324	53	11	56	1	.262	

JETER, DEREK - SS - BR - Age 20

How far is it from high school to the Gulf Coast rookie league? Oh, about 270 points. Jeter hit .471 for Central High in Kalamazoo, Michigan, and then did the following in the GCL. Still, he was the top high school pick of 1992 and has about six years to improve.

	AB	R	HR	RBI	SB	BA	$
1992 Tampa R	173	19	3	25	2	.202	
1993 Greensboro A	515	85	5	71	18	.295	

JETER, SHAWN - OF - BL - Age 27

Good runner and a good outfielder, Jeter surfaced with the White Sox in 1992 but hit just .199 at Triple-A with the White Sox and Mariners farms last year.

JOHNS, KEITH - SS - BR - Age 22

Some scouts say his fielding is good enough to play in the majors now. Johns is a decent hitter who makes consistent contact and has a good eye, though he lacks power. His calling card is defense with good range, soft hands and an above-average arm. What else would you expect from a Cardinals' shortstop? He's probably still three years away from the big leagues.

	AB	R	HR	RBI	SB	BA	$
1992 Hamilton A	275	36	1	28	15	.284	-

JOHNSON, BRIAN D. - C - BR - Age 26

Johnson's good Triple-A numbers (.339 with 10 home runs at Las Vegas in '93) have been inflated by the PCL's hitter-friendly parks. He's not really much of a prospect, but could help the Padres if there is an injury.

JOHNSON, CHARLES - C - BR - Age 22

A star with the Miami Hurricanes, Johnson is clearly the Marlins' catcher of the not-too-distant future. He showed good power and excellent defense at Single-A Kane County in 1993, throwing out 47.6% of runners trying to steal. Ticketed for Double-A in 1994, the Marlins' number one pick in 1992 should be the major league starter by early to mid-1995. In spring training 1993, even Benito Santiago was surprised by Johnson's throwing exploits.

JOHNSON, ERIK - IF - BR - Age 28

Johnson can't hit for average or power and is really just a spare part. He got five at bats with the Giants in 1993 but is not a prospect. .

JOHNSON, HOWARD - 3B - BB - Age 33

First base is the only place he should play. Playing in Denver can't hurt Johnson's comeback attempt. He still has speed and power but has now suffered through two consecutive injury-plagued seasons. Speed is often wasted at first base, but HoJo's still-good legs are of no use to him defensively anyway.

	AB	R	HR	RBI	SB	BA	$
1992 New York NL	350	48	7	43	22	.223	11
1993 New York NL	235	32	7	26	6	.238	4
1994 Projection >>>	387	59	14	55	18	.239	11

JOHNSON, LANCE - OF - BL - Age 30
A defensive master, he's now developed into a decent offensive player as well. Johnson continues to improve his stolen base percentage, won't hit less than .270, and can be counted on for 70 runs scored and almost 50 ribbies. He adds a few walks each year and rarely strikes out.

	AB	R	HR	RBI	SB	BA	$
1992 Chicago AL	567	67	3	47	41	.279	26
1993 Chicago AL	540	75	0	47	35	.311	27
1994 *Projection* >>>	557	71	1	46	34	.288	25

JONES, CHIPPER - SS - BB - Age 21
Just 21 as this season starts, Jones was rated by Baseball America as the second best Triple-A prospect in 1993, one of four Richmond Braves to rank in the top six. He hits for power (173 extra-base hits in 1679 minor league ABs), hits for average (.313 career batting average), runs well (91 minor league stolen bases), plays a difficult defensive position adequately and has recently shown a better batting eye. Jones got his cup of coffee in the majors last September, now he's thirsty for a permanent spot in Atlanta. The Braves are loaded with talent, but they'll find somewhere for Jones to play in 1994, by midsummer if not immediately.

	AB	R	HR	RBI	SB	BA	$
1992 Durham A	264	43	4	31	10	.277	
1992 Greenville AA	266	43	9	42	14	.346	
1993 Richmond AAA	536	97	13	89	23	.325	
1994 *Projection* >>>	308	36	11	35	10	.282	13

JONES, CHRIS - OF - BR - Age 28
Don Baylor gave Jones a chance to win the starting center field job. He did well enough after his June recall to stick with the team, but not enough to play every day. Baylor liked him as a late-inning substitution. Jones averaged a strikeout every four at bats.

	AB	R	HR	RBI	SB	BA	$
1992 Houston NL	63	7	1	4	3	.190	-
1993 Colorado NL	209	29	6	31	9	.273	7
1994 *Projection* >>>	140	17	4	16	5	.237	1

JONES, DAX - OF - BR - Age 23
A .294 career hitter in two and a half minor league seasons, Jones has some speed but little power. He made the Double-A All-Star game in 1993. Speed and defense are more likely to get him to the majors than hitting.

JONES, MOTORBOAT- OF - BR - Age 25
A great name, but not a great ballplayer; he finally reached Double-A in his seventh season and wasn't successful there. He equaled his career home run total last season, but his stolen bases fell off from 37 to 11.

JONES, RON - OF - BL - Age 29
The Phillies' former can't-miss prospect. There is nobody now stuck in the minors with better major league production on a per-at-bat basis: .272 career average, 13 home runs and 40 RBI in 239 at bats. In an organization with less talent, he might have surfaced again by now.

	AB	R	HR	RBI	SB	BA	$
1992 Shreveport AA	198	20	4	25	3	.242	
1993 Richmond AAA	203	25	10	41	0	.291	

JONES, TIM - SS - BL - Age 31
Jones' strength lies in his versatility. He can play all four infield positions and the outfield and he bats lefthanded. He's a fringe player, however, never able to get off the shuttle between St. Louis and AAA Louisville.

	AB	R	HR	RBI	SB	BA	$
1992 St. Louis NL	145	9	0	3	5	.200	-
1993 Louisville AAA	408	72	5	46	13	.289	-
1993 St. Louis NL	61	13	0	1	2	.262	-
1994 *Projection* >>>	82	10	0	2	3	.221	-

JORDAN, BRIAN - OF - BR - Age 27

The former standout safety with the NFL's Atlanta Falcons finally blossomed in 1993 after being sent to the minors early in the season. He has incredible athletic ability and is now translating that into baseball skills. His tools are so good that the Class Triple-A American Association selected him as the best prospect in the league in a Baseball America poll although he had played in just 38 games for Louisville; Jordan hit .375 with 35 RBI in just 144 at bats for Louisville. The Cardinals' outfield picture is crowded but they'll make room for Jordan somewhere.

	AB	R	HR	RBI	SB	BA	$
1992 St. Louis NL	193	17	5	22	7	.207	2
1993 St. Louis NL	223	33	10	44	6	.309	11
1994 *Projection* >>>	388	49	14	58	12	.272	16

JORDAN, KEVIN - 2B - BR - Age 24

Had a great start and was an excellent run producer last season, getting 87 RBI for AA Albany. He's a career .296 hitter as a pro, but the fans at Albany's Heritage Park will tell you he's a butcher in the field.

JORDAN, RICKY - 1B - BR - Age 28

Jordan was heralded as a rising superstar after his fine rookie season in 1988, but pitchers found his holes quickly thereafter. Put simply, he frequently takes strike one then swings at every subsequent pitch, no matter how bad. He has drawn 70 walks in 1938 career plate appearances. Also, he can't throw; Jordan had an amazingly low four assists in 225 innings at first base in 1993. A decent bench player, he will never get 500 at bats.

	AB	R	HR	RBI	SB	BA	$
1992 Philadelphia NL	276	33	4	34	3	.304	9
1993 Philadelphia NL	159	21	5	18	0	.289	3
1994 *Projection* >>>	222	28	5	29	1	.291	6

JORGENSEN, TERRY - 3B - BR - Age 27

Terry Jorgensen has had opportunities to be the Twins starting third baseman, but he has trouble hitting major league pitching. At age 27, he may have run out of opportunities. Scott Stahoviak has better tools and is three years younger.

	AB	R	HR	RBI	SB	BA	$
1992 Minnesota AL	58	5	0	5	1	.310	0
1993 Minnesota AL	152	15	1	12	1	.244	-
1994 *Projection* >>>	95	9	1	10	0	.251	-

JOSE, FELIX - OF - BB - Age 28

Jose was held back all through the 1993 season with a shoulder injury that forced him to bat lefthanded against all pitchers. He hit .094 versus southpaws. He had corrective surgery right after the season and should be a whole new player now. When healthy he is one of the best physical specimens in the game; he just looks like a player. With above-average power and speed, his potential is unlimited.

	AB	R	HR	RBI	SB	BA	$
1992 St. Louis NL	509	62	14	75	28	.295	30
1993 Kansas City AL	499	64	6	43	31	.253	18
1994 *Projection* >>>	514	64	10	65	28	.276	25

JOYNER, WALLY - 1B - BL - Age 31

In 1992 the Royals pushed aside their best prospect (Jeff Conine) to sign Joyner to a multi-year contract. He had his worst full season in 1992, and did only a little better in 1993. Showed some signs of return to early-Angels days, but still disappointed with only 65 RBI out of a power spot in the batting order. This is as good as it gets?

	AB	R	HR	RBI	SB	BA	$
1992 Kansas City AL	572	66	9	66	11	.269	15
1993 Kansas City AL	497	83	15	65	5	.292	16
1994 *Projection* >>>	531	77	14	71	6	.285	19

JUSTICE, DAVID - OF - BL - Age 27

In 1993, Justice silenced his critics with a marvelous power season consistent with his promising 1990 rookie season. He finished second only to the remarkable Barry Bonds in home runs and RBI. Justice has always had a good batting eye; it helped him get better pitches to hit in 1993 and he drove many of them over the fence. A back injury two years ago diminished his power somewhat, but now he's himself again.

	AB	R	HR	RBI	SB	BA	$
1992 Atlanta NL	484	78	21	72	2	.256	17
1993 Atlanta NL	585	90	40	120	3	.270	24
1994 *Projection* >>>	520	82	31	99	4	.266	23

KAPANO, COREY- OF/3B - BR - Age 23
After bouncing all over the Cubs minor league system in 1992, Kapano spent most of 1993 at AA Orlando and had a marginal year. He has a little power and some speed, but he'll need to improve soon if he's to play in the majors.

KARKOVICE, RON - C - BR - Age 30
Although he looks about 50, Karko probably has at least a couple more twenty homer seasons left. His superb defense will keep him in the lineup, and, barring injury, he should get more at bats in 1994 with Fisk no longer around. I still think he's a .240 hitter.

	AB	R	HR	RBI	SB	BA	$
1992 Chicago AL	342	39	13	50	10	.237	10
1993 Chicago AL	403	60	20	54	2	.228	6
1994 *Projection* >>>	343	47	15	47	4	.240	6

KARROS, ERIC - 1B - BR - Age 26
1993 was a strange season for the 1992 Rookie of the Year. Karros cut his strikeouts but matched his 1992 performance in every category. Given the league's increase in offense, the season had to be considered a disappointment. Entering his prime, he should improve in 1994 if he's ever going to improve.

	AB	R	HR	RBI	SB	BA	$
1992 Los Angeles NL	545	63	20	88	2	.257	18
1993 Los Angeles NL	619	74	23	80	0	.247	11
1994 *Projection* >>>	522	62	19	73	1	.250	10

KATZAROFF, ROBBIE - OF - BL - Age 25
A singles hitter with some speed and a great arm, Katzaroff is an interesting prospect, but he's already 25 years old and has spent most of the last three seasons at Double-A. He looks like a bench player at best, if and when he gets to the majors.

KELLY, MIKE - OF - BR - Age 23
Kelly was the Braves top draft choice in 1991 out of Arizona State, but is making slow minor league progress. He got off to a bad start at AAA Richmond in 1993, then rebounded slightly to hit .243 with 19 home runs. He still strikes out too much, but reduced his strikeouts to "only" 109 after 161 whiffs in 1992. Kelly is a good defensive player with some speed, so only two things stand in his way to the majors: his own strikeouts and the Braves outfield depth.

	AB	R	HR	RBI	SB	BA	$
1992 Greenville AA	471	83	25	71	22	.229	
1993 Richmond AAA	424	63	19	58	11	.243	

KELLY, PAT - 2B - BR - Age 26
More relaxed at the plate, Kelly improved his average in 1993 by waiting for his pitch. He needs to stay healthy. He had the starting second base job won until bothered by different injuries. 1994 could be the year Kelly takes control.

	AB	R	HR	RBI	SB	BA	$
1992 New York AL	318	38	7	27	8	.226	4
1993 New York AL	406	49	7	51	14	.273	13
1994 *Projection* >>>	416	50	7	44	14	.255	9

KELLY, ROBERTO - OF - BR - Age 29
Kelly was leading the league in hits when he sprained his shoulder attempting a diving catch in July. A four category player if he hits in the middle of the lineup, Kelly will likely get a leadoff role in 1994.

	AB	R	HR	RBI	SB	BA	$
1992 New York AL	580	81	10	66	28	.272	23
1993 Cincinnati NL	320	44	9	35	21	.319	18
1994 *Projection* >>>	514	71	13	60	30	.288	23

KENDALL, JASON - C - BR - Age 19
Defensively, Kendall could play in the major leagues right now. The Pirates want their top pick from the 1992 draft to improve his offensive production, particularly his power. He draws comparisons to his father, former major league catcher Fred Kendall. Because of his defense, he could be in the majors by late 1995.

	AB	R	HR	RBI	SB	BA	$
1992 Bradenton R	111	7	0	10	2	.252	

KENT, JEFF - 2B - BR - Age 26
The Mets may turn out to win the David Cone trade after all. Kent was one-half of the Blue Jays payment for Cone, and is the Mets second baseman now and for the future. His talents are all-around power for a middle infielder, above-average speed (25 steals in 1991), and adequate defense still improving. Kent is also becoming a team leader among the younger generation.

	AB	R	HR	RBI	SB	BA	$
1992 Toronto AL	192	36	8	35	2	.240	
1992 New York NL	113	16	3	15	0	.239	0
1993 New York NL	496	65	21	80	4	.270	15
1994 Projection >>>	499	71	20	81	4	.261	14

KESSINGER, KEITH - SS - BB - Age 27
Too old to be considered a serious prospect, Don's son hit .299 in 281 at bats at Double-A and Triple-A combined. Kessinger's glove is good enough to land him a reserve infielder role for the Reds in 1994.

	AB	R	HR	RBI	SB	BA	$
1993 Indianapolis AAA	120	17	2	15	0	.283	
1993 Cincinnati NL	27	4	1	3	0	.259	-
1994 Projection >>>	120	10	1	14	0	.242	-

KIESCHNICK, BROOKS - OF - BL - Age 21
A two-way player at the University of Texas, selected by the Cubs as the number ten amateur player in the nation, Kieschnick was another Larry Himes/Al Goldis "character" choice. That duo has had a good track record with such players in the past. Expected to develop into a decent slugger with a smooth stroke, Kieschnick is learning third base in the Arizona Fall League.

KIMBERLIN, KEITH - SS - BB - Age 25
Formerly a Tigers prospect, Kimberlin is a speedy spray hitter who gets the most out of his ability. In the event of an injury to Kevin Stocker, Kimberlin and Kim Batiste are about the only alternatives.

KING, ANDRE - OF - BR - Age 20
The Braves lacked a first-round draft pick in 1993, but struck it rich in the second round by signing King away from the University of Michigan which wanted him to play football. For now he's a center fielder and though he didn't show much power in the Appalachian League, he had a .415 OBP.

KING, JEFF - SS - BR - Age 29
After occasional offensive flashes in the second halves of 1990 and 1992, King finally broke through with his best year in 1993. He drove in a career-high 98 runs despite hitting just nine homers; he narrowly missed becoming only the third player since 1950 to drive in 100 without 10 home runs. While he still has the strength to add to his homer total, King was concentrating on hitting to all fields in 1993. Most importantly, the Pirates 1986 top draft pick finally seems to have found the confidence necessary to hit major league pitching consistently.

	AB	R	HR	RBI	SB	BA	$
1992 Pittsburgh NL	480	56	14	65	4	.231	9
1993 Pittsburgh NL	611	82	9	98	8	.295	19
1994 Projection >>>	522	65	11	77	6	.261	12

KIRBY, WAYNE - OF - BL - Age 30
Kirby came out of nowhere to have a fairly productive season. He's 30 now, and his chief attribute, speed, is beginning to fade. A solid defensive outfielder, he will likely make way for Manny Ramirez in right field, but will continue to be valuable to the Indians as a fourth outfielder, caddying for the less-than-graceful Ramirez and Albert Belle.

	AB	R	HR	RBI	SB	BA	$
1993 Cleveland AL	18	9	1	1	0	.167	-
1993 Cleveland AL	458	71	6	60	17	.269	14
1994 Projection >>>	242	39	3	31	9	.265	6

KLESKO, RYAN - 1B - BL - Age 22

Another of the Braves quantum quartet (with Chipper Jones, Javy Lopez and Tony Tarasco), Klesko rated as the fourth best Triple-A prospect according to Baseball America. He continued to increase his power totals for Richmond last year, while also increasing his batting average and OBP. The obstacle for Klesko is the ominous Fred McGriff. Klesko has nothing left to prove in the minors, so the only real question is when he will arrive. Look for the Braves to find some way to get Klesko to Atlanta during 1994.

	AB	R	HR	RBI	SB	BA	$
1992 Richmond AAA	418	63	17	59	3	.251	
1992 Atlanta NL	14	0	0	1	0	.000	-
1993 Richmond AAA	343	59	22	74	4	.274	
1993 Atlanta NL	17	3	2	5	0	.353	0
1994 Projection >>>	150	18	5	23	1	.255	2

KMAK, JOE - C - BR - Age 30

Looking like a CML (career minor leaguer) at the beginning of spring training in 1993, Kmak got an opportunity to play in the majors when Dave Nilsson got hurt. Kmak is nothing special, but he has graduated from CML to FML (fringe major leaguer) and is obviously just as good as all those other catchers who have been FML's for many years.

	AB	R	HR	RBI	SB	BA	$
1992 Denver AAA	225	27	3	31	6	.311	
1993 New Orleans AAA	76	9	1	13	1	.303	
1993 Milwaukee AL	110	9	0	7	6	.218	-
1994 Projection >>>	55	5	0	4	3	.225	-

KNOBLAUCH, CHUCK - 2B - BR - Age 25

Knoblauch is the best hit-and-run man in the AL. He now has three years of solid major league experience and will be just age 26 in July, two facts that indicate that a career-best year can be expected in 1994. A .300-plus year with 200-plus hits and 40 stolen bases are very possible.

	AB	R	HR	RBI	SB	BA	$
1992 Minnesota AL	600	104	2	56	34	.297	27
1993 Minnesota AL	602	82	2	41	29	.277	20
1994 Projection >>>	595	89	2	47	30	.284	23

KNORR, RANDY - C - BR - Age 25

Chances are, Knorr will always be a backup catcher. His defensive skills continue to improve, and he has excellent power, but he will never hit for average and makes a lot of unnecessary outs. Look for more at bats, however, over the next few years.

	AB	R	HR	RBI	SB	BA	$
1992 Toronto AL	19	1	1	2	0	.263	-
1993 Toronto AL	101	11	4	20	0	.248	0
1994 Projection >>>	114	12	2	15	0	.249	-

KOELLING, BRIAN - 2B - BR - Age 24

A no hit, good speed (34 steals at Double-A) middle infield prospect, Koelling got a brief look in 1993. He will become a regular in 1994 only if someone gets hurt.

	AB	R	HR	RBI	SB	BA	$
1993 Chattanooga AA	430	64	4	47	34	.277	
1993 Cincinnati NL	15	2	0	0	0	.067	-

KOMMINSK, BRAD - OF - BR - Age 32

The perpetual prospect. Coulda been a contenduh. Now he's just a .218 career hitter in cameo appearances spread over eight major league seasons.

KOSCO, BRYN - 3B - BL - Age 27

Do not be fooled by his gaudy 1993 power numbers. This is a 27-year-old who dropped a level to Single-A in 1993 after three forgettable Double-A seasons, (the Marlins didn't have a Double-A team in 1993). Despite getting 55 extra-base hits and finishing third in the minor leagues with 121 RBI, he's not a prospect.

	AB	R	HR	RBI	SB	BA	$
1993 High Desert A	450	96	27	121	1	.307	

KOSLOFSKI, KEVIN - OF - BL - Age 27

Spent six years in Rookie and Class A before rapidly percolating to the top of the farm system. Good speed, good defense, spark-plug kind of player. Koz put up marginal numbers at Omaha (.276-7-45-15) and won't be a major league factor in Kansas City unless someone gets hurt.

	AB	R	HR	RBI	SB	BA	$
1992 Kansas City AL	133	20	3	13	2	.248	1
1993 Kansas City AL	26	4	1	2	0	.269	-
1994 Projection >>>	77	8	1	8	1	.253	-

KREUTER, CHAD - C - BB - Age 29

Kreuter had his career year last year, after not playing winter ball for a change. His offensive production and his good defense caused Sparky Anderson to play Tettleton in the outfield and first. The same situation will continue in 1994, but the pitchers around the league will be a little more careful with Kreuter.

	AB	R	HR	RBI	SB	BA	$
1992 Detroit AL	190	22	2	16	0	.253	0
1993 Detroit AL	374	59	15	51	2	.286	11
1994 Projection >>>	301	41	8	35	1	.252	4

KRUK, JOHN - 1B - BL - Age 33

Kruk really shouldn't be playing the outfield anymore, but may find himself there if the Phillies choose to have Ricky Jordan in the lineup more. Although he hit 21 homers in 1991, Kruk is an opposite-field singles and doubles hitter who's not likely to produce many homers unless he drops 30 or 40 points off his average. Until injuries wore him down, Kruk was in the hunt for a 1992 batting title. He has played out of shape for a number of years, partly explaining his various nagging injuries, (most recently recurring back pain). Kruk intended to work out with fitness guru Mackie Shilstone during the winter. At age 33, Kruk is likely to begin to decline, possibly accelerating if he doesn't get into better shape.

	AB	R	HR	RBI	SB	BA	$
1992 Philadelphia NL	507	86	10	70	3	.323	23
1993 Philadelphia NL	535	100	14	85	6	.316	21
1994 Projection >>>	526	88	13	77	5	.298	21

KUNKEL, JEFF - SS/OF - BR - Age 32

Kunkel has an amazing seven to one strikeout/walk ratio as a major leaguer, and he managed to do even worse at Triple-A in 1993. If the majors suddenly expand to 56 teams, he's got a chance.

	AB	R	HR	RBI	SB	BA	$
1992 Chicago NL	29	0	0	1	0	.138	-
1993 Charlotte AAA	430	65	11	46	12	.281	

LADELL, CLEVELAND - OF - BR - Age 23

On a team with Chad Mottola, Motorboat Jones and Bubba Smith, Ladell was the MVP. Ladell is a power/speed player who needs to show more patience at the plate (95 Ks, 16 BBs).

LAKE, STEVE - C - BR - Age 37

Lake continues to survive because he throws well and can hit against lefties, a little. Regardless, he's probably about through after 11 seasons in the bigs.

	AB	R	HR	RBI	SB	BA	$
1992 Philadelphia NL	53	3	1	2	0	.245	-
1993 Chicago NL	120	11	5	13	0	.225	0
1994 Projection >>>	104	9	3	9	0	.229	-

LAKER, TIM - C - BR - Age 24

An outstanding defensive catcher. The Expos have been waiting for Laker to become their starter. However, anemic hitting keeps killing his chances. Until Laker proves he can hit major league pitching he'll have a hard time unseating Darrin Fletcher. It might also help if Laker would throw out a few baserunners, as he has done in the minors.

	AB	R	HR	RBI	SB	BA	$
1992 Montreal NL	46	8	0	4	1	.217	-
1993 Ottawa AAA	204	26	4	23	3	.230	-
1993 Montreal NL	86	3	0	7	2	.198	-
1994 *Projection* >>>	58	5	1	6	1	.225	-

LAMPKIN, TOM - C - BL - Age 30

A career .203 hitter, Lampkin offers defensive skill and a lefty bat with a little pop, and he can even run a bit; but 1993 was probably his career year.

	AB	R	HR	RBI	SB	BA	$
1992 San Diego NL	17	3	0	0	2	.235	-
1993 Milwaukee AL	162	22	4	25	7	.198	1
1994 *Projection* >>>	95	12	2	13	4	.205	-

LANDRUM, CEDRIC - OF - BL - Age 30

Landrum is a good case for stat freaks to see why you should not project stolen bases on a per-at-bat basis. In 1991 with the Cubs, he got 27 steals in 86 at bats. Over a full season with 550 at bats, that would project to a season total of 173 stolen bases. The lesson is that you have to back out pinch running stats when you want to analyze a hitter. (The "Cedric Landrum" principle.) Won't play in the majors in 1994 unless he gets lucky. If he does appear, he would be a ... right, a pinch runner.

	AB	R	HR	RBI	SB	BA	$
1993 Norfolk AAA	275	39	5	29	16	.291	-
1993 New York NL	19	2	0	1	0	.263	-

LANE, BRIAN - 3B/SS - BR - Age 24

The acquisition of Willie Greene put a wet blanket on Lane's career in Cincinnati. A one-time prospect who has faded, Lane struck out 134 times in 425 at bats for AA Chattanooga, and will need a great deal of luck to reach the majors.

LANKFORD, RAY - OF - BL - Age 26

After a big 1992 season, Lankford appeared on the brink of superstardom, only to take a big step backwards. Injuries were part of the reason. Suddenly, Lankford has gone from being potentially the Cardinals' best player, to being prime trade bait as the odd man out in a crowded outfield picture.

	AB	R	HR	RBI	SB	BA	$
1992 St. Louis NL	598	87	20	86	42	.293	41
1993 St. Louis NL	407	64	7	45	14	.238	7
1994 *Projection* >>>	497	79	13	66	28	.270	24

LANSING, MIKE - SS - BR - Age 25

After being purchased from independent Miami of the Class A Florida State League, Lansing blossomed in the Expos' organization. He does not have great tools, but has good baseball savvy and works hard. The departure of Delino DeShields left second base wide open for Lansing.

	AB	R	HR	RBI	SB	BA	$
1993 Montreal NL	491	64	3	45	23	.287	16
1994 *Projection* >>>	366	45	3	33	17	.273	10

LARKIN, BARRY - SS - BR - Age 29

Thumb problems hampered and finally ended Larkin's season. The best shortstop in baseball when healthy, he has a durability record that is starting to resemble Eric Davis'. Larkin is an MVP candidate if he stays healthy for an entire year. Last time he had a full, healthy year, the Reds won the World Series.

	AB	R	HR	RBI	SB	BA	$
1992 Cincinnati NL	533	76	12	78	15	.304	26
1993 Cincinnati NL	384	57	8	51	14	.315	17
1994 *Projection* >>>	444	67	11	61	16	.299	22

LARKIN, GENE - OF - BB - Age 31

Veteran Gene Larkin injured his achilles tendon and missed several weeks last year. Promising rookies and younger players with more potential will challenge for Larkin's playing time in '94.

	AB	R	HR	RBI	SB	BA	$
1992 Minnesota AL	337	38	6	42	7	.246	6
1993 Minnesota AL	144	17	1	19	0	.264	-
1994 *Projection* >>>	227	27	3	27	3	.259	3

LAVALLIERE, MIKE - C - BL - Age 33

Appeared to be a player in decline in 1992 and 1993. LaValliere has no power and may be the slowest player in the game. He must hit for a high average and be a good defensive catcher to be a productive player. He slipped in both areas last year. We give him the benefit of the doubt, because of injuries.Went from the '92 playoffs to the unemployment line and back to the '93 playoffs. His best days are definitely behind him, though the Sox gave him a good bit of playing time. He always seems to hit OK, for a catcher.

	AB	R	HR	RBI	SB	BA	$
1992 Pittsburgh NL	293	22	2	29	0	.256	2
1993 Pittsburgh NL	5	0	0	0	0	.200	-
1993 Chicago AL	97	6	0	8	0	.258	-
1994 *Projection* >>>	205	15	1	21	0	.260	0

LEACH, JALAL - OF - BL - Age 25

He has been a leadoff hitter, but with some power, he might be better suited for the lower part of the batting order. Needs to cut down his swing (113 strikeouts in '93).

LEDESMA, AARON - SS - BR - Age 22

His future depends on whether he can recover from tendinitis and regain enough arm strength to play shortstop. He was a designated hitter most of last season. His minor league numbers to date place him squarely in the .260 range, with only fair power.

LEE, DEREK - OF - BL - Age 27

Lee hit .325 at Birmingham in 1991, but just spent his third year in Triple-A. He has some power and base-stealing speed, but is future is mostly behind him now.

	AB	R	HR	RBI	SB	BA	$
1993 Portland AAA	381	79	10	80	16	.315	-
1993 Minnesota AL	33	3	0	4	0	.152	-
1994 *Projection* >>>	100	12	1	12	1	.246	-

LEE, MANUEL - SS - BB - Age 28

An injury-plagued season limited Lee's effectiveness and his playing time. Some teamates questioned his desire to play. He has better range and a better throwing arm than the other Texas shortstop candidates, but will likely be platooned or rotated.

	AB	R	HR	RBI	SB	BA	$
1992 Toronto AL	396	49	3	39	6	.263	7
1993 Texas AL	205	31	1	12	2	.220	-
1994 *Projection* >>>	309	39	1	24	4	.242	0

LEIUS, SCOTT - SS - BR - Age 28

Leius was penciled in as the Twins starting shortstop last year, but a rotator cuff injury caused him to miss almost all of the season. He may come back this year, but he has trouble hitting righthanded pitching and wasn't penciled in for anything definite when the year ended.

	AB	R	HR	RBI	SB	BA	$
1992 Minnesota AL	409	50	2	35	6	.249	4
1993 Minnesota AL	18	4	0	2	0	.167	-
1994 *Projection* >>>	178	24	2	16	3	.252	1

LEMKE, MARK - 2B - BB - Age 28

Just can't quite make that big step forward to claim second base permanently. He played full-time but couldn't contribute much offense. His power increased and Lemke showed good plate discipline (65 walks were fourth on the team). Despite his best offensive season ever, Lemke has to worry about his job. With Chipper Jones ready to play, the Braves have to move Blauser or Jones somewhere and second base is a distinct possibility. Also, Ramon Caraballo is almost ready at AAA Richmond. Nevertheless, Lemke's defense will keep him in the lineup frequently in 1994. He's a good bunter, a smart baserunner and his strikeout to walk ratio was the best on the team. Don't count Lemke out yet.

	AB	R	HR	RBI	SB	BA	$
1992 Atlanta NL	427	38	6	26	0	.227	0
1993 Atlanta NL	493	52	7	49	1	.252	4
1994 Projection >>>	393	41	5	33	1	.242	1

LENNON, PATRICK - OF - BR - Age 25

Perennial Mariners' prospect who has now found his way into the farm system with the least opportunity for a 25 year-old outfield prospect. He has been plagued by injuries, but is still a high average hitter with decent power and marginal speed. He needs another change of scenery.

	AB	R	HR	RBI	SB	BA	$
1992 Calgary AAA	48	8	1	9	4	.354	
1993 Canton-Akron AA	152	24	4	22	4	.257	

LEONARD, MARK - OF - BL - Age 29

The Orioles acquired Leonard from the Giants last year. He has had some good years in the minors, but fared poorly in trials with the Giants. Leonard continued to prove that he is a solid minor league hitter, but did nothing in 15 at bats in Baltimore. Reserve duty at the major league level is the best Leonard can legitimately hope for in 1994.

	AB	R	HR	RBI	SB	BA	$
1992 San Francisco NL	128	13	4	16	0	.234	0
1993 Rochester AAA	330	57	17	58	0	.276	-
1993 Baltimore AL	15	1	0	3	0	.067	-
1994 Projection >>>	72	7	2	9	0	.238	-

LEVIS, JESSE - C - BL - Age 25

Levis has bounced back and forth between Cleveland and Triple-A the last two seasons. The best indicator of his status was the Indians' decision to use Junior Ortiz during the prolonged absences of Sandy Alomar. A good hitter at the minor league level, Levis' time is running out as a major league prospect. Size (5'-9", 180 lbs.) also works against this 1989 4th-round pick.

	AB	R	HR	RBI	SB	BA	$
1992 Cleveland AL	43	2	1	3	0	.279	-
1993 Charlotte AAA	129	10	2	20	0	.248	-
1993 Cleveland AL	63	7	0	4	0	.175	-

LEWIS, DARREN - OF - BR - Age 26

Fomerly with Oakland. Great defensive center fielder with good speed. Right field, fly ball hitter. Has a noticeable dip in his swing, causing his bat to slow through the hitting zone. One little adjustment could produce a big change in results. Miscast as a leadoff hitter, Lewis set records for defense in the outfield while stealing 46 bases, so he looks like he will be around for a while. His horrible OBP (last two seasons: .295 and .302) and complete lack of power (his .324 SLG in 1993 was a career high) will eventually result in his losing his job as a regular. However, that probably won't happen in 1994 and Lewis is still young enough to improve. Lewis scored only 84 runs at the top of one of the best offenses in baseball; if he drops down in the batting order, as he should, his runs scored will drop significantly.

	AB	R	HR	RBI	SB	BA	$
1992 San Francisco NL	320	38	1	18	28	.231	9
1992 Phoenix AAA	158	22	0	6	9	.228	
1993 San Francisco NL	522	84	2	48	46	.253	20
1994 Projection >>>	514	80	3	42	45	.259	21

LEWIS, MARK - SS - BR - Age 24

Lewis was returned to Triple-A for the full season in 1993, and put together a fine season, finally convincing the Indians' brass that he's ready to settle in at shortstop in Cleveland. A number one pick in 1988, he has already had extended major league trials, with mixed success. But heck, at his age most good players are just settling in at Double-A.

	AB	R	HR	RBI	SB	BA	$
1992 Cleveland AL	413	44	5	30	4	.264	6
1993 Charlotte AAA	507	93	17	67	9	.284	-
1993 Cleveland AL	52	6	1	5	3	.250	-
1994 Projection >>>	316	32	3	26	4	.262	2

LEWIS, T.R. - 1B/DH - BR - Age 22

T.R. Lewis has been rated as the best pure hitter in the Oriole farm system. He has also shown some speed on the bases. Lewis was brought along slowly after an arm injury, but may reach Baltimore this year.

	AB	R	HR	RBI	SB	BA	$
1993 Bowie AA	480	73	5	64	22	.304	

LEYRITZ, JIM - 1B/OF/DH - BR - Age 30

Held back by misunderstandings with the New York front office during his formative years, Leyritz has recovered to become a decent utility player. In 1993 his confidence rose along with his batting average. He never had an everyday role, but he showed he could play a variety of positions while keeping his offense sharp. He hit .346 with runners in scoring position and two outs.

	AB	R	HR	RBI	SB	BA	$
1992 New York AL	144	17	7	26	0	.257	3
1993 New York AL	259	43	14	53	0	.309	11
1994 Projection >>>	210	15	8	30	0	.270	4

LIEBERTHAL, MIKE - C - BR - Age 22

Drafted ahead of Alex Fernandez in 1990, Lieberthal has progressed rapidly on defense, being named the best defensive catcher in the AA Eastern League in 1992. Offensively, he has made consistent contact (just 32 whiffs in 1993) but has no power. He has grown slightly (6'0", 170 lbs.), but there are still concerns about his size and durability. In 1994 Lieberthal will challenge Todd Pratt to be Darren Daulton's backup. In future years, Jason Moler will be a factor.

	AB	R	HR	RBI	SB	BA	$
1992 Reading AA	309	30	2	37	4	.285	
1992 Scranton AAA	45	4	0	4	0	.200	
1993 Scranton AAA	382	35	7	40	2	.262	

LIND, JOSE - 2B - BR - Age 29

Never a big offensive threat, Lind had his worst season in 1992 and had another just like it in 1993. Lind was everything the Royals bargained for with his glove, but his offensive numbers were disappointing, with career lows in several offensive categories. Expect more of the same since the Royals play him for defensive purposes.

	AB	R	HR	RBI	SB	BA	$
1992 Pittsburgh NL	468	38	0	39	3	.235	0
1993 Kansas City AL	431	33	0	37	3	.248	1
1994 Projection >>>	455	38	1	41	4	.247	2

LINDEMAN, JIM - OF - BR - Age 32

This veteran first baseman led the Pacific Coast League in hitting despite recurring back problems. A former number one pick by the Cardinals, he has been a productive major league pinch hitter and can fill that role again in 1994.

	AB	R	HR	RBI	SB	BA	$
1992 Scranton AAA	53	5	0	8	0	.302	
1992 Philadelphia NL	39	6	1	6	0	.256	-
1993 Tucson AAA	390	72	12	88	5	.362	
1993 Houston NL	23	2	0	0	0	.348	-

LINDSEY, DOUG - C - BR - Age 26

Lindsey will never hit enough to be a major league asset. He has a career .220 batting average after seven minor league seasons. Lindsey was a 3-for-3 strikeout victim in David Cone's 18-K performance in 1991 and he has only three more major league at bats since then.

LINK, BRIAN - 1B - BL - Age 23
A 1993 32nd-round pick out of Austin Peay, Link outplayed many higher draft picks to earn the Appalachian League Player of the Year award. He ranked in the league's top three in all three Triple Crown stats and walked more than he struck out.

LIRIANO, NELSON - SS - BB - Age 29
Liriano seemed doomed to the minors until Freddy Benavides got injured in September. Liriano responded with a .346 average, six doubles and 22 runs. Baylor liked him as a leadoff hitter, and he'll get a long look as Rockies' starting shortstop in the spring. His .379 OBP was second only to Galarraga's .403 OBP among Rockies hitters.

	AB	R	HR	RBI	SB	BA	$
1992 Colorado Springs AAA	362	73	5	50	20	.304	
1993 Colorado Springs AAA	293	48	6	46	9	.358	
1993 Colorado NL	151	28	2	15	6	.305	5
1994 Projection >>>	241	33	3	28	9	.270	4

LIS, JOE - 2B - BR - Age 25
The son of the former major leaguer with the same name, Lis is a heady, scrappy player who is an offensive contributor and a steady defensive infielder. At his age, the best he can hope for is a good AAA season, then utility duty in the majors.

LISTACH, PAT - SS - BR - Age 26
We expected a drop-off after the stunning rookie season in 1992, but Listach was disappointing even to those who tried to be most realistic about his rise from minor league obscurity to major league stardom. Slowed by injuries, Listach did finally come to life in the second half, getting 25 of his 30 RBI after the All-Star break. Speed will be his one big strength in 1994.

	AB	R	HR	RBI	SB	BA	$
1992 Milwaukee AL	579	93	1	47	54	.290	33
1993 Milwaukee AL	356	50	3	30	18	.244	8
1994 Projection >>>	369	56	2	31	27	.268	15

LITTON, GREG - OF - BR - Age 29
Litton had career highs in batting average and RBI while filling in at first base for Tino Martinez. He won't get any better, and won't even repeat those modest accomplishments.

	AB	R	HR	RBI	SB	BA	$
1992 San Francisco NL	140	9	4	15	0	.229	0
1993 Seattle AL	174	25	3	25	0	.299	3
1994 Projection >>>	155	18	3	20	0	.262	1

LIVINGSTONE, SCOTT - 3B/DH - BL - Age 28
Sparky Anderson's nominee for most-improved Tiger of 1992, Livingstone lost playing time in 1993 with the return of Alan Trammell. Livingstone is a light singles hitter. Anderson likes to have a rotating lineup, so Livingstone can expect to get about 300 at bats.

	AB	R	HR	RBI	SB	BA	$
1992 Detroit AL	354	43	4	46	1	.282	8
1993 Detroit AL	304	39	2	39	1	.293	5
1994 Projection >>>	290	37	3	37	1	.288	6

LOCKETT, RON - 1B - BL - Age 24
This lefty first basemen has struggled for two consecutive seasons at AA Reading. He hit only .242 in 1993, but 40% of his hits were for extra bases. Lockett must improve his selectivity at the plate. He has drawn only 44 walks in 812 plate appearances over the past two seasons.

LOFTON, KENNY - OF - BL - Age 26

Lofton followed a spectacular rookie season with an even better sophomore year. An amazing athlete who was a point guard at the University of Arizona, he matured as a leadoff hitter in 1993, raising his on base percentage to the .400 range. He can basically steal as many bases as he desires, and could put up some eye-popping runs totals with the heavy artillery hitting behind him.

	AB	R	HR	RBI	SB	BA	$
1992 Cleveland AL	576	96	5	42	66	.285	38
1993 Cleveland AL	569	116	1	42	70	.325	47
1994 *Projection* >>>	557	110	3	40	65	.310	40

LONGMIRE, TONY - OF- BL - Age 25

An oft-injured prospect who missed the entire 1992 season due to shin splints, Longmire had a solid year at AAA Scranton in 1993, hitting .304 with 36 doubles and 12 steals before a late season callup. He projects as a platoon outfielder at best for the Phils, if he wins a spring training battle with Milt Thompson.

	AB	R	HR	RBI	SB	BA	$
1993 Philadelphia NL	13	1	0	1	0	.231	-

LOPEZ, JAVIER - C - BR - Age 23

One of the best catchers in the minors, he was ranked as Triple-A's fifth best prospect. An aggressive hitter, Lopez hits for power and average; his defense is already solid. A righthanded hitter, Lopez will likely be worked into a platoon catching role to start 1994 before eventually getting the job outright. After two September stints in Atlanta, Lopez is ready for The Show.

	AB	R	HR	RBI	SB	BA	$
1992 Atlanta NL	16	3	0	2	0	.375	-
1993 Richmond AAA	380	56	17	74	1	.305	-
1993 Atlanta NL	16	1	1	2	0	.375	-
1994 *Projection* >>>	241	25	7	28	1	.270	4

LOPEZ, LUIS - 2B - BB - Age 23

Switch hitting Lopez improved from .233 to .305 at AAA Las Vegas but will probably struggle at the plate in his 1994 rookie season. The Padres are very high on Lopez, and he will be given every opportunity to become the regular second baseman in 1994. Although he's considered an outstanding gloveman, Lopez does not figure to be of much of a hitter.

	AB	R	HR	RBI	SB	BA	$
1993 Las Vegas AAA	491	52	6	58	8	.305	-
1993 San Diego NL	43	1	0	1	0	.116	-

LOPEZ, LUIS - OF - BR - Age 29

A great conversation piece on the subject of why Dodgers' farm batting averages don't mean anything. Lopez hit .353 at Albuquerque in 1990 to lead the PCL, when he was still young enough to be a prospect (age 26), and Los Angeles let him go as a minor league free agent.

LOVULLO, TOREY - 2B - BB - Age 28

Sparky Anderson's most famous hyperbole: "The best prospect I've ever seen; will play second base every day." Lovullo is a perpetual prospect who was in the right place at the right time in 1993. If he sticks with the club in 1994, he's strictly a reserve.

	AB	R	HR	RBI	SB	BA	$
1992 Columbus AAA	468	69	19	89	9	.295	
1993 California AL	367	42	6	30	7	.251	5
1994 *Projection* >>>	192	21	3	15	4	.248	1

LOWERY, TERRELL - OF - BR - Age 23

A former basketball scoring machine at Loyola Marymount, he found the going just a bit too tough in the Texas League. Back in the Florida State League, he really got going. A good batting eye and speed are his greatest assets.

LUZINSKI, RYAN - OF - BR - Age 20

Son of Greg Luzinski. Hit .251 in Rookie league. Too early to get excited, but the Dodgers will give every opportunity, because they paid a big bonus to get him.

	AB	R	HR	RBI	SB	BA	$
1993 Bakersfield A	147	18	3	9	2	.279	
1993 Yakima A	237	32	4	46	6	.257	

LYDEN, MITCH - C - BR - Age 29

Lyden has nothing left to prove offensively as a minor leaguer, but he's 29 now, and it's obvious that the Marlins like Natal (and probably Decker) better as major league backups. A real life "Crash" Davis, he has 133 career minor league homers, and is beginning his 11th pro season. Anyway, the Charles Johnson countdown has already begun in South Florida. Maybe there will be an opening for a manager in Visalia...

	AB	R	HR	RBI	SB	BA	$
1993 Edmonton AAA	160	34	8	31	1	.306	-
1993 Florida NL	10	2	1	1	0	.300	-

LYDY, SCOTT - OF - BR - Age 25

Lydy made a big leap forward in 1992, but went in reverse last year. He can steal a base, and at 25 he is too young to be considered a lost cause, but faces a crowded situation in 1994.

	AB	R	HR	RBI	SB	BA	$
1993 Oakland AL	102	11	2	7	2	.225	-
1994 *Projection* >>>	155	20	3	18	3	.245	1

LYONS, STEVE - OF - BL - Age 33

"Psycho" to his friends. Staged a minor comeback in 1991, but is now thoroughly faded.

	AB	R	HR	RBI	SB	BA	$
1992 Three Teams	55	5	0	4	1	.200	-
1993 Boston AL	23	4	0	0	1	.130	-
1994 *Projection* >>>	66	6	1	4	3	.210	-

MAAS, KEVIN - DH/1B - BL - Age 29

Hit ten home runs faster than any other rookie in history (in 1990) but since then, pitchers won't throw him a fastball when they fall behind in the count. Maas has been unable to make the adjustment to look for the breaking ball and the fastball. His home run per at bat ratio has been half what it was in 1990, making him just another power hitter.

	AB	R	HR	RBI	SB	BA	$
1992 New York AL	286	35	11	35	3	.248	6
1993 New York AL	151	20	9	25	1	.205	1
1994 Projection >>>	255	33	12	35	2	.226	3

MABRY, JOHN - OF - BL - Age 23

Mabry is a gap hitter who showed some potential at AA Arkansas last year. Unlike most Cardinals' outfield prospects, he isn't a burner. Mabry is in a tough spot with so many good outfielders ahead of him in the St. Louis organization.

MACFARLANE, MIKE - C - BR - Age 29

The Royals leading power threat with 20 dingers, 67 RBI (career bests). Still stands on top of the plate to pull everything, tied his own club record with 15 HBP; has led Royals in HBP four years running - Ron Hunt would be proud. Has little value for anything except power; .273 batting average is too much to normally expect. No speed; 2 stolen bases are career high and he needed 7 tries to get that many. Has survived frequent trade rumors and platoons; is still starting catcher. Expect continued power, less batting average in 1994.

	AB	R	HR	RBI	SB	BA	$
1992 Kansas City AL	402	51	17	48	1	.234	7
1993 Kansas City AL	388	55	20	67	2	.273	13
1994 Projection >>>	372	50	18	56	2	.260	11

MACK, SHANE - OF - BR - Age 30

Mack offers everything: speed, power, high average, and good baserunning. Shoulder problems slowed Mack last year. He should bounce back in 1994 with another outstanding season.

	AB	R	HR	RBI	SB	BA	$
1992 Minnesota AL	600	101	16	75	26	.315	35
1993 Minnesota AL	503	66	10	61	15	.276	16
1994 Projection >>>	525	84	14	71	19	.305	29

MACLIN, LONNIE - OF - BL - Age 27

A typical Cardinals' outfield prospect, Maclin is a slap hitter with good speed. However, with the Cardinals overstocked in the outfield, his chance of ever seeing significant playing time in St. Louis is slim.

	AB	R	HR	RBI	SB	BA	$
1992 Louisville AAA	290	29	1	38	4	.324	
1993 Louisville AAA	220	29	4	18	4	.277	
1993 St. Louis NL	13	2	0	1	1	.077	-

MAGADAN, DAVE - 3B/1B - BL - Age 31

Magadan is a slow singles/doubles hitter, with a very good eye. He gets on base a lot but has no power and no speed. The Mariners borrowed Magadan to help at third base while Edgar Martinez was injured last year. Now that Edgar is back, Magadan has been returned to the Marlins.

	AB	R	HR	RBI	SB	BA	$
1992 New York NL	321	33	3	28	1	.283	6
1993 Florida NL	227	22	4	29	0	.286	4
1993 Seattle AL	228	27	1	21	2	.259	0
1994 Projection >>>	404	45	4	43	2	.273	7

MAGALLANES, EVER - 2B/SS - BL - Age 28

If the White Sox didn't need Magallanes in 1992 with every shortstop hurt, they sure won't need Magallenes in the majors in 1994. A longtime minor league middle infielder with a good glove, Magallanes is a career minor leaguer.

	AB	R	HR	RBI	SB	BA	$
1992 Vancouver AAA	243	32	3	23	2	.230	
1993 Oklahoma City AAA	116	16	1	14	0	.326	-

MAKSUDIAN, MIKE - C - BL - Age 27

Maksudian never showed power before 1992, and only hit for high average occasionally. If he gets to the major leagues at all, he will be a backup or pinch hitter. The Twins are Maksudian's third major league organization.

	AB	R	HR	RBI	SB	BA	$
1992 Syracuse AAA	339	38	13	58	4	.280	
1992 Toronto AL	3	0	0	0	0	.000	-
1993 Portland AAA	264	57	10	49	5	.314	
1993 Minnesota AL	12	2	0	2	0	.167	-

MALAVE, JOSE - OF - BR - Age 22

A broken hand cut short Malave's 1993 season. He was continuing the kind of hitting he produced in 1992, his third year as a pro. He and Luis Ortiz are the Boston organization's best batting prospects. Malave's defense is suspect.

	AB	R	HR	RBI	SB	BA	$
1993 Lynchburg A	312	42	8	54	2	.301	

MALDONADO, CANDY - OF - BR - Age 33

Maldonado has always been a good hitter, now best suited to the American League. He is strictly a part-time role player now. In a way, the Indians hope that he doesn't play a prominent role for them in 1994, as that would reflect failure of the Manny Ramirez project.

	AB	R	HR	RBI	SB	BA	$
1992 Toronto AL	489	64	20	66	2	.272	16
1993 Chicago NL	140	8	3	15	0	.186	-
1993 Cleveland AL	81	11	5	20	0	.247	0
1994 *Projection* >>>	321	37	13	47	1	.247	6

MANAHAN, TONY - 3B - BR - Age 25

Manahan is a rarity; a third baseman with speed. That doesn't mean much unless he gets to play. Don't be fooled by his .302 average at AAA Calgary. Everybody hits at AAA Calgary; he hit .257 the previous year.

	AB	R	HR	RBI	SB	BA	$
1993 Calgary AAA	451	70	3	62	19	.302	

MANTO, JEFF - 3B/1B - BR - Age 29

A journeyman who once again excelled in the minors, Manto flopped in a short major league stint. Strictly Triple-A insurance, his return to the majors can't be ruled out, mainly due to his ability to catch in an emergency. Most likely he'll spend 1994 working his way up the all-time Triple-A batting leader lists.

	AB	R	HR	RBI	SB	BA	$
1992 Richmond AAA	450	65	13	68	1	.291	
1993 Scranton/WB AAA	388	62	17	88	4	.289	
1993 Philadelphia NL	18	0	0	0	0	.056	-

MANWARING, KIRT - C - BR - Age 28

Manwaring is one of the best at throwing out baserunners, and the Giants love both his defense and his overall contributions. He's also an offensive millstone who has never hit more than five home runs in a season at any level or had a higher batting average than .282. He will play a lot, helping the Giants, but he's a good example of a player worth more on the field than he is on the stat sheet.

	AB	R	HR	RBI	SB	BA	$
1992 San Francisco NL	349	24	4	26	2	.244	2
1993 San Francisco NL	432	48	5	49	1	.275	6
1994 *Projection* >>>	361	35	4	36	1	.261	4

MARRERO, ELIESER - C - BR - Age 20

Marrero showed decent power in the Appalacian League last year. He's a long-range prospect, though, as his catching skills are very rudimentary.

MARRERO, ORESTE - 1B - BL - Age 24

Desperate for a first baseman who could catch the ball, the Expos gave him a brief try in 1993. Marrero had just 54 at bats above the Single-A level in six minor league seasons before last year. His .333 batting average for AA

Harrisburg was the best of his career. In his 81 at bat trial with Montreal, Marrero was just killing time until Cliff Floyd was ready.

	AB	R	HR	RBI	SB	BA	$
1993 Harrisburg AA	255	39	10	49	3	.333	
1993 Montreal NL	81	10	1	4	1	.210	-

MARSH, TOM - OF - BR - Age 28
Marsh is a decent defensive outfielder who has proven that he can hit in the minors and that he can't hit in the majors. He has never seen a pitch he didn't like, walking only 14 times in 329 plate appearances in 1993. After he got to the majors in 1992, the Phillies imported a number of outfielders from other organizations; that should tell you something about his future. He did slug .502 at Triple-A in 1993, but at age 28, he's running out of time.

	AB	R	HR	RBI	SB	BA	$
1992 Scranton AAA	158	26	8	25	5	.241	
1992 Philadelphia NL	125	7	2	16	0	.200	-
1993 Scranton AAA	315	45	12	57	10	.286	

MARSHALL, MIKE - 1B/OF - BR - Age 34
Guess what? Marshall managed to get hurt in Japan too. He surfaced again in spring training 1993, but we have probably seen the last of him.

MARTIN, AL - OF - BL - Age 26
Martin had a fine rookie season and is still learning the game. He didn't play organized baseball until his senior year of high school, then accepted a scholarship to play tailback at USC. Yet another talented player developed by the Braves organization, but was let go via the six-year free agent route. Martin has outstanding power and speed; he could develop into a 20-20 player.

	AB	R	HR	RBI	SB	BA	$
1992 Buffalo AAA	420	85	20	59	20	.305	
1992 Pittsburgh NL	12	1	0	2	0	.167	-
1993 Pittsburgh NL	480	85	18	64	16	.281	19
1994 Projection >>>	374	53	12	43	11	.265	12

MARTIN, CHRIS - SS/2B - BR - Age 26
Martin's star began to fade when he hit .227 for AA Harrisburg in 1992. However, he bounced back with the same club last year and became a prospect again. He has decent speed and can play both middle infield positions; he may wind up as a utility player in the majors.

MARTIN, NORBERTO - 2B/SS - BB - Age 27
Martin converted to shortstop to play alongside Esteban Beltre. Has the talents to play on the major league level, but he's been at Triple-A for three years now with no big visible progress.

	AB	R	HR	RBI	SB	BA	$
1992 Vancouver AAA	497	72	0	29	29	.288	
1993 Nashville AAA	580	87	9	74	31	.309	
1993 Chicago AL	14	3	0	2	0	.357	-

MARTINEZ, CARLOS - 1B/DH - BR - Age 28
Martinez had a good year with the White Sox in '89 after which he slumped and was released. Picked up by Cleveland on a minor league contract, he earned another shot with his good minor league record. The Indians finally tired of his unwillingness to take a pitch, his lack of power, and his questionable attitude, sending him to the minors in August. He's 28 now, and could be a good bench player in the right situation. His only hope as an Indian is to caddy for Jim Thome.

	AB	R	HR	RBI	SB	BA	$
1992 Cleveland AL	228	23	5	35	1	.263	4
1993 Cleveland AL	262	26	5	31	1	.244	1
1994 Projection >>>	130	14	3	18	1	.257	1

MARTINEZ, CHITO - OF - BL - Age 28

Chito was slated to be the lefty-hitting platooner in right field for 1993, but he went hitless in his first few games and got benched and then demoted. Martinez has longball potential, but got into the Orioles doghouse. Being the third baserunner on third base greatly embarrassed him in one situation. He was released in November.

	AB	R	HR	RBI	SB	BA	$
1992 Baltimore AL	198	26	5	25	0	.268	3
1993 Rochester AAA	145	14	5	23	0	.262	-
1993 Baltimore AL	15	0	0	0	0	.000	-
1994 *Projection* >>>	110	14	4	14	0	.250	0

MARTINEZ, DAVE - OF - BL - Age 29

Martinez was a mild disappointment for the Giants, with his worst offensive year since 1988. His defensive skills make him a decent backup but nothing more. He has a good glove, occasional power and some speed, but he's now a player with ever-decreasing playing time. He could still turn his career around, but would be lucky just to get a chance to do that.

	AB	R	HR	RBI	SB	BA	$
1992 Cincinnati NL	393	47	3	31	12	.254	8
1993 San Francisco NL	241	28	5	27	6	.241	3
1994 *Projection* >>>	318	38	5	31	10	.258	7

MARTINEZ, DOMINGO - 1B - BR - Age 26

Domingo's been blocked in Toronto by John Olerud. How many remember that he was the opening day first baseman against the Mariners last year? At the end of the 1993 season the Jays were trying to deal him to a club in need of a first baseman. He has an enormous power swing. Given a chance, he could put up some great power numbers ... and could also threaten Rob Deer for the strikeout title.

	AB	R	HR	RBI	SB	BA	$
1992 Toronto AL	8	2	1	3	0	.625	0
1993 Syracuse AAA	465	50	24	79	4	.273	-
1993 Toronto AL	14	2	1	3	0	.286	-

MARTINEZ, EDGAR - 3B - BR - Age 31

Martinez continued to blossom as he led the major leagues in batting average in 1992, but then in 1993 he injured his hamstring in the final spring training game and missed much of the 1993 season. He was playing at only 75%.

	AB	R	HR	RBI	SB	BA	$
1992 Seattle AL	528	100	18	73	14	.343	34
1993 Seattle AL	135	20	4	13	0	.237	-
1994 *Projection* >>>	514	92	15	62	6	.310	22

MARTINEZ, RAMON - SS - BB - Age 24

A speedy free-swinger who has yet to rise above A-ball at age 24, Martinez has a chance if he rapidly develops, only because of a lack of Marlins minor league middle infield prospects (Al Pedrique was their Triple-A shortstop in 1993).

MARTINEZ, TINO - 1B - BL - Age 26

After disappointing trials in 1990 and 1991, Martinez is maturing nicely. He nearly matched his 1992 season numbers despite missing the last eight weeks of the 1993 season after tearing a ligament in his left knee. After a slow start, he hit .289 in his final 325 at bats. His season projects to 25 homers and 90 RBI, levels which he could attain in 1994.

	AB	R	HR	RBI	SB	BA	$
1992 Seattle AL	460	53	16	66	2	.257	12
1993 Seattle AL	408	48	17	60	0	.265	9
1994 *Projection* >>>	505	60	19	73	1	.264	13

MASSE, BILLY - OF - BR - Age 27

An exceptional minor league hitter who hasn't had a chance in the majors. He led the International League with 82 walks in '93. Could be a role player for some team. If so, he'd be good for some extra homers and steals.

MATOS, FRANCISCO - 2B - BR - Age 23
In his fourth tour of duty at Huntsville, he showed considerable improvement, batting 47 points higher than in any previous visit. Can he hold a similar offensive level as he goes higher?

MATTINGLY, DON - 1B - BL - Age 32
Mattingly has had two more good years in 1992-93 but isn't anywhere near approaching his peak years of 1985-1987. What we just saw is about as good as it's going to get. His back may flare up any time.

	AB	R	HR	RBI	SB	BA	$
1992 New York AL	640	89	14	86	3	.288	20
1993 New York AL	530	78	17	86	0	.291	16
1994 Projection >>>	576	79	15	83	1	.289	20

MAURER, ROB - 1B - BL - Age 27
Missed the entire 1993 season due to injury. Nice hitter, but he'll probably spend another season at Triple-A, and by that time he'll be 28 years old. Also, the Rangers don't exactly need another first baseman after signing Will Clark.

	AB	R	HR	RBI	SB	BA	$
1992 Oklahoma City AAA	493	76	10	82	1	.288	
1992 Texas AL	9	1	0	1	0	.222	-

MAY, DERRICK - OF - BL - Age 25
The son of Dave May has shown good power which should increase as he develops. He has hit well enough to force his way into the lineup but his season-long shoulder problem affected his swing. A legitimate sleeper as a power hitter for 1994, May's .295 batting average is probably not his peak, either.

	AB	R	HR	RBI	SB	BA	$
1992 Chicago NL	351	33	8	45	5	.274	11
1993 Chicago NL	465	62	10	77	10	.295	17
1994 Projection >>>	508	71	12	78	10	.294	22

MAYNARD, TOW - OF - BR - Age 28
A base-stealing machine, with 332 steals in six pro seasons. He made good progress, even started to hit, in '91 and '92. Last year he ended up back in A-ball. Until the majors adopt a designated-runner rule, he won't make it.

MAYNE, BRENT - C - BL - Age 25
Started season in platoon, but hit poorly and defensive skills diminished. BA was OK, but has no power or speed. Former number one pick (1989), got to the majors rapidly but has stalled since with part-time play. Still young enough to win regular catching job and succeed as a hitter. For 1994, he'll be Macfarlane's backup; expect slightly more pop in bat as Mayne learns to pull pitches, BA won't hurt you.

	AB	R	HR	RBI	SB	BA	$
1992 Kansas City AL	213	16	0	18	0	.225	-
1993 Kansas City AL	205	22	2	22	3	.254	1
1994 Projection >>>	212	20	3	26	2	.244	1

McCARTY, DAVID - OF/1B - BR - Age 24
McCarty was on everyone's top prospect list last year, but he had a rough year and struggled with major league curveballs. He lacked aggressiveness, and hit many weak ground balls, especially when he was attempting to make contact with the elusive curves. He has all the tools to be a strong offensive force, and he could break out this year. He was the third overall pick in 1991.

	AB	R	HR	RBI	SB	BA	$
1993 Minnesota AL	350	36	2	21	2	.214	-
1994 Projection >>>	377	43	6	49	4	.244	4

McCLENDON, LLOYD - OF/1B - BR - Age 35
Once one of the top bench players in the National League, McClendon has had two straight poor seasons. Pirates manager Jim Leyland keeps putting him in the lineup against lefthanders, though, and McClendon still has one year left on his contract.

	AB	R	HR	RBI	SB	BA	$
1992 Pittsburgh NL	190	26	3	20	1	.253	2
1993 Pittsburgh NL	181	21	2	19	0	.221	-
1994 *Projection* >>>	181	23	3	20	1	.242	0

McCONNELL, CHAD - OF - BR - Age 22

He was plagued by recurring shoulder injuries in 1993; his shoulder would sometimes become dislocated in mid-swing. A 1992 Olympian from Creighton University and the Phils' first round pick, he's expected to be fully healed by 1994. He has not yet proven anything in pro ball (particularly with his lack of expected power hitting) and the Phils will likely start him at Double-A in 1994.

McCOY, TREY - 1B/DH - BR - Age 27

Last season, he finally stopped retiring and unretiring long enough to put together the kind of monster offensive season the Rangers always had envisioned from him. Most likely McCoy will replace Steve Balboni as Oklahoma City's designated hitter in '94.

McCRACKEN, QUINTON - OF - BR - Age 23

Speedy McCracken has the kind of quirky name you'd expect to see in a movie, but he's a viable Rockies prospect. His 60 stolen bases were third best in the minors and he hit .292 for Single-A Central Valley with a good batting eye, too. The California League is a hitter's haven, so the real test for McCracken will be at the next level.

McDAVID, RAY - OF - BL - Age 23

After being voted the California League's best prospect in 1992 (Baseball America) and showing reasonable progress at AA Wichita last year, McDavid remains a great prospect with 30/30 potential. He reduced his strikeout totals and again stole more than 30 bases. He's viewed as a cornerstone of the Padres' future and will not be rushed to the majors as San Diego management is apparently more than willing to let the big league team take its lumps.

	AB	R	HR	RBI	SB	BA	$
1992 High Desert A	428	94	24	94	43	.276	
1993 Wichita AA	441	65	11	55	33	.270	

McGEE, WILLIE - OF - BB - Age 35

McGee has had the same season so many times now that you should know what to expect. Despite his age, he should hit around .300 with little power; his value to a real baseball team is not exactly clear, but he does what he does with consistency. Though he doesn't steal much anymore, he seems to retain his speed, so he could surprise in stolen bases. McGee's skills are very narrow: his glove is erratic, and he doesn't walk very often. He's also 35 years old, so when the batting average finally does start to drop, McGee's career will probably end abruptly. It's worth noting that McGee hit .266 with only two steals after July 4 last year.

	AB	R	HR	RBI	SB	BA	$
1992 San Francisco NL	474	56	1	36	13	.297	14
1993 San Francisco NL	475	53	4	46	10	.301	13
1994 *Projection* >>>	478	56	3	41	12	.299	17

McGRIFF, FRED - 1B - BL - Age 30

McGriff was just what the doctor ordered to restore life to a flagging Braves offense. After his acquisition, Braves hitters throughout the order began to produce and the Atlanta offensive output went up by almost 50%. McGriff has at least 30 home runs in each of the last six seasons and has a good batting eye, too, although his strikeout to walk ratio was worse in 1993. What will the Braves do to get Klesko in the lineup, but keep the potent McGriff in there also?

	AB	R	HR	RBI	SB	BA	$
1992 San Diego NL	531	79	35	104	8	.286	34
1993 San Diego-Atlanta NL	557	111	37	101	5	.291	26
1994 *Projection* >>>	543	96	35	103	6	.287	30

McGRIFF, TERRY - C - BR - Age 30

A journeyman who scalded Pacific Coast League pitching in 1993, McGriff has just 212 major league at bats in ten professional seasons. He formerly played for the Reds and Astros. Has an outside shot as a backup backstop in 1994.

McGWIRE, MARK - 1B - BR - Age 30
An incredibly prolific slugger when he is in the lineup, McGwire also walks as often as anyone. What you really want to know is whether or not Mac is healthy. Pay attention to the spring reports; if McGwire can play, he will hit homers (he even hit 22 in his off year, and has hit 40+ twice.)

	AB	R	HR	RBI	SB	BA	$
1992 Oakland AL	467	87	42	104	0	.268	26
1993 Oakland AL	84	16	9	24	0	.333	4
1994 *Projection* >>>	408	66	27	84	0	.258	15

McINTOSH, TIM - C - BR - Age 29
Once a highly rated catching prospect with Milwaukee, McIntosh went to the Expos on a waiver claim last year. He has never been able to make the jump to the majors and is no longer considered a prospect. He has no chance of beating out Spehr, Laker or others for the backup job behind Fletcher. McIntosh couldn't make it in the majors with two teams that really needed catchers.

	AB	R	HR	RBI	SB	BA	$
1992 Milwaukee AL	77	7	0	6	1	.182	-
1993 Ottawa AAA	106	15	6	21	1	.292	-
1993 Montreal NL	21	2	0	2	0	.095	-

McKNIGHT, JEFF - SS - BB - Age 31
Tidewater's leading hitter (.307) in 1992, McKnight was an aging journeyman who had surfaced briefly with Baltimore in 1990 and 1991. His stints with the Mets in 1992 and 1993 were due to their running out of healthy major leaguers.

	AB	R	HR	RBI	SB	BA	$
1992 New York NL	85	10	2	13	0	.271	0
1993 New York NL	164	19	2	13	0	.256	0
1994 *Projection* >>>	117	13	2	11	0	.255	-

McLEMORE, MARK - OF - BB - Age 29
A career middle infielder, McLemore became the O's first half MVP as he surprisingly answered their right field woes, batting over .300 with 43 RBI, 15 stolen bases and fielding like a Gold Glover. Although he cooled in the second half, due to Baltimore's bonanza of minor league outfield prospects and a weakness at second base, Mac is likely to see regular duty at his original (and more natural) position in 1994. Expect him to challenge Harold Reynolds for the starting spot. A Tony Phillips-type role is also a possibility, according to manager Johnny Oates.

	AB	R	HR	RBI	SB	BA	$
1992 Baltimore AL	228	40	0	27	11	.246	4
1993 Baltimore AL	581	81	4	72	21	.284	20
1994 *Projection* >>>	376	55	2	45	14	.273	11

McNAMARA, JIM - C - BL - Age 28
McNamara made the news in 1993 only by bouncing back and forth between the Giants and Marlins. He has no role for 1994.

	AB	R	HR	RBI	SB	BA	$
1992 San Francisco NL	74	6	1	9	0	.216	-
1993 Phoenix AAA	158	10	1	23	1	.196	-
1993 San Francisco NL	7	0	0	1	0	.143	-

McNEELY, JEFF - OF - BR - Age 24
The fastest man in a slow organization, McNeely is rapidly approaching the major league skill level.

	AB	R	HR	RBI	SB	BA	$
1993 Pawtucket AAA	498	65	2	35	40	.261	
1993 Boston AL	37	10	0	1	6	.297	1
1994 *Projection* >>>	344	47	1	24	13	.228	2

McRAE, BRIAN - OF - BB - Age 26
Rebounded much more than expected, but beware - his last two months were significantly down from the first four. McRae still doesn't take a pitch, so his good batting average may be illusory. The power should be for real, though.

A dozen homers and 70 RBI are annually within reach for McRae. He has good speed but doesn't steal well. As he matures his success rate will increase, but he may not run as much. Players like McRae tend to add power and lose speed as they grow into major league jobs. Expect more power and less SBs for 1994 and beyond. A good fielder, will play almost every day.

	AB	R	HR	RBI	SB	BA	$
1992 Kansas City AL	533	63	4	52	18	.223	6
1993 Kansas City AL	627	78	12	69	23	.282	24
1994 *Projection* >>>	596	74	9	63	21	.261	18

McREYNOLDS, KEVIN - OF - BR - Age 34
Still playing major league ball, sort of. Power declined again, batting average and speed continue downward. His value is fading right before your eyes. "Earned" full-time role due to RBI ability, but careless play and lack of hustle will cost him playing time. McReynolds disappearing act will continue in 1994.

	AB	R	HR	RBI	SB	BA	$
1992 Kansas City AL	373	45	13	49	7	.247	10
1993 Kansas City AL	351	44	11	42	2	.245	4
1994 *Projection* >>>	301	37	9	39	3	.249	4

MEARES, PAT - SS - BR - Age 25
Meares came through with a nice season when he got the opportunity to start following injuries to others. However, a .250 batting average with six dingers is about the most you can expect.

	AB	R	HR	RBI	SB	BA	$
1993 Minnesota AL	346	33	0	33	4	.251	2
1994 *Projection* >>>	173	17	0	17	2	.251	-

MEJIA, ROBERTO - 2B - BR - Age 22
The Rockies stole him from the Dodgers in the expansion draft. Baylor wanted to break camp with Mejia but GM Bob Gebhart didn't want the youngster to make the jump from Single-A. After tearing up the Pacific Coast League, Baylor got his way at the All-Star break, and Mejia played adequately, though not spectacularly. He made 12 errors in 65 games and struck out 63 times, but Baylor thinks this guy is the top position prospect. Mejia has good speed.

	AB	R	HR	RBI	SB	BA	$
1993 Colorado NL	229	31	5	20	4	.231	1
1994 *Projection* >>>	440	60	12	41	9	.241	8

MELVIN, BOB - C - BR - Age 32
He's a .235 career hitter. In 1994 he will be very hard pressed for playing time.

	AB	R	HR	RBI	SB	BA	$
1992 Kansas City AL	70	5	0	6	0	.314	0
1993 Boston AL	176	13	3	23	0	.222	-
1994 *Projection* >>>	150	10	2	17	0	.243	-

MENDENHALL, KIRK - SS - BR - Age 26
When Chris Gomez arrived at AA London in '92, Mendenhall took a seat on the bench. Defensively, he takes a back seat to very few shortstops. His offense will keep him from ever playing regularly in the majors, but with another organization he could have a shot as a utilityman. Needs a solid season in Triple-A.

MERCED, ORLANDO - 1B/OF - BL - Age 27
Merced abandoned switch-hitting in mid-May, deciding to bat from the left side only, and had the best season of his career. Merced is hard to figure; he was runner-up to Jeff Bagwell for National League Rookie of the Year in 1991, then struggled horribly in 1992. Merced also didn't make a smooth conversion to right field last season and wound up splitting time between first base and right field by the end of the season. With the Pirates looking for pitching and a righthanded hitter, Merced could be used as trade bait.

	AB	R	HR	RBI	SB	BA	$
1992 Pittsburgh NL	405	50	6	60	5	.247	8
1993 Pittsburgh NL	447	68	8	70	3	.313	15
1994 *Projection* >>>	427	59	8	63	5	.272	12

MERCEDES, HENRY - C - BR - Age 24
Can't hit: in three different seasons in the hit-happy Pacific Coast League, Mercedes has hit .194, .232 and .238 with a total of four homers.

	AB	R	HR	RBI	SB	BA	$
1992 Oakland AL	5	1	0	1	0	.800	-
1993 Tacoma AAA	256	37	4	32	1	.238	-
1993 Oakland AL	47	5	0	3	1	.213	-

MERCEDES, LUIS - OF - BR - Age 26
Formerly an Orioles problem child, Mercedes once again hit for a good average with plenty of steals in the minors, and once again failed to make a splash in the majors. Some think Mercedes could be the leadoff hitter the Giants have needed since Brett Butler left, but his continuing failures in the majors, his weak glove and even weaker "character" suggest he'll never be given the opportunity to strut his stuff. He's been stuck at Triple-A for three years; his star is fading.

	AB	R	HR	RBI	SB	BA	$
1992 Baltimore AL	50	7	0	4	0	.140	-
1993 Baltimore AL	24	1	0	0	1	.292	-
1993 Phoenix AAA	244	28	0	15	14	.291	-
1993 San Francisco NL	25	1	0	3	0	.160	-

MERULLO, MATT - DH - BL - Age 28
Defensive problems, particularly throwing, and age prevent him from being considered a prospect.

	AB	R	HR	RBI	SB	BA	$
1992 Chicago AL	50	3	0	3	0	.180	-
1993 Nashville AAA	352	50	12	65	0	.332	-
1993 Chicago AL	20	1	0	0	0	.050	-

MEULENS, HENSLEY - OF - BR - Age 26
By escaping to Japan, Meulens finally got out of the Yankees farm. In late 1992 "Bam Bam" told me he would be happy if taken by an expansion team. "It's time to move on." He's a good power hitter who needs an opportunity to show what he can do. He speakes four languages (English, Dutch, Spanish, and Papiemento) and he's going for five.

	AB	R	HR	RBI	SB	BA	$
1992 New York AL	5	1	1	1	0	.600	-
1993 Columbus AAA	279	39	14	45	6	.204	
1993 New York AL	53	8	2	5	0	.170	-

MIESKE, MATT - OF - BR - Age 26
A fast start last year earned him a brief promotion to the bigs. Then tendinitis in his left wrist wiped out much of the remainder of the season. The Brewers would like him to succeed, because he came over in the unpopular Gary Sheffield trade. Mieske has a right field arm, and is quick enough to play center in a pinch.

	AB	R	HR	RBI	SB	BA	$
1993 New Orleans AAA	219	36	8	22	6	.260	-
1993 Milwaukee AL	58	9	3	7	0	.241	-
1994 *Projection* >>>	250	35	6	30	5	.241	3

MILLER, BARRY - 1B - BL - Age 25
Miller hit .281 with ten homers in A-ball in 1992, then .286 with 12 home runs in Double-A in 1993. He'll be 25 years old in 1994 and still hasn't seen Triple-A, much less the majors, but with Will Clark gone, the Giants were taking another long look at their first base depth chart.

MILLER, KEITH - 3B - BR - Age 30
Still can't stay healthy all year; lost most of 1993 to various injuries. Will get reasonable chance at regular 3B play in 1994. Could be decent 2nd place hitter in lineup with his multiple offensive talents. If healthy (big if), Miller can give you .270-6-45-12; just don't count on him for the entire year.

	AB	R	HR	RBI	SB	BA	$
1992 Kansas City AL	416	57	4	38	16	.284	14
1993 Kansas City AL	108	9	0	3	3	.167	-
1994 *Projection* >>>	238	30	2	18	9	.257	4

MILLER, ORLANDO - SS - BR - Age 25
A talented defensive player who became an offensive force in his first full year at AAA Tucson, Miller has had temper problems which have impeded his progress. He appears to have major league tools but may not get the opportunity in 1994.

MILLETTE, JOE - SS - BR - Age 27
Competent defensively, Millette has neither power nor speed nor the ability to get on base. The handful of major league games he played in 1993 may be the zenith of his career.

MILLIGAN, RANDY - 1B - BR - Age 32
Milligan suffers from the conventional baseball wisdom which expects 235 pound first basemen to swing from the heels and accumulate fat home run and RBI totals. Has one of the best eyes in the game, consistently racking up almost as many walks as hits. Deadly against lefties.

	AB	R	HR	RBI	SB	BA	$
1992 Baltimore AL	462	71	11	53	0	.240	5
1993 Cincinnati NL	234	30	6	29	0	.274	4
1993 Cleveland AL	47	7	0	7	0	.426	0
1994 *Projection* >>>	185	24	4	23	0	.267	3

MITCHELL, KEITH - OF - BR - Age 24
Mitchell was released early in 1993 but still has major league potential. Kevin's cousin Keith has a good batting eye and some speed.

	AB	R	HR	RBI	SB	BA	$
1992 Richmond AAA	403	45	4	50	14	.226	
1993 Richmond AAA	353	59	4	44	9	.232	

MITCHELL, KEVIN - OF - BR - Age 32
On a per at-bat basis, Mitchell was one of the most productive hitters in the league despite playing the entire season on a broken foot. A shoulder injury that required off-season surgery ended his season. Talented veterans with something to prove in the final year of their contracts often make good Rotisserie picks.

	AB	R	HR	RBI	SB	BA	$
1992 Seattle AL	360	48	9	67	0	.286	11
1993 Cincinnati NL	323	56	19	64	1	.341	18
1994 *Projection* >>>	339	47	17	62	2	.286	15

MOLER, JASON - C - BR - Age 23
The Phils' fourth round pick in 1992, Moler stepped up in a big way in 1993. After being sidelined by a knee injury during Olympic trials in 1992, he slugged .477 in the Single-A Florida State League, a pitcher's league. He followed that with a credible performance at Double-A, batting .283. Chosen the sixth best prospect in the Florida State League by Baseball America, he also threw out 46% of opposing baserunners, despite an unconventional throwing motion. Moler may have passed Mike Lieberthal as Phils' catcher of the future and has by far the better offensive upside of the two.

MOLITOR, PAUL - DH - BR - Age 37
Molitor's almost impossible to figure out. How many players have reached career-lows in their mid twenties and peaked in their mid to late thirties? This one has. He had his finest year in 1993 and he's destined to spend the next two in this powerful Blue Jays lineup. His performance last year was testimony to how valuable he could have been had the Brewers not wasted him in the leadoff spot for so many years.

	AB	R	HR	RBI	SB	BA	$
1992 Milwaukee AL	609	89	12	89	31	.320	37
1993 Toronto AL	636	121	22	111	22	.332	39
1994 *Projection* >>>	582	91	15	81	20	.307	32

MONDESI, RAUL - OF - BR - Age 23

A hot prospect in 1992, Mondesi stalled a bit at AAA Albuquerque, hitting only .280 with 12 home runs and 13 stolen bases in 425 at bats. A .280 average in the PCL translates to about .220 in Dodger Stadium. Nonetheless he hit well enough in his September trial to get a fair shot at the open left field job for 1994.

	AB	R	HR	RBI	SB	BA	$
1993 Los Angeles NL	86	13	4	10	4	.291	3
1994 *Projection* >>>	413	58	7	48	8	.262	9

MONTGOMERY, RAY - OF - BR - Age 24

Hit .429 with a stolen base per game at Fordham University in 1990; blossomed rather suddenly with speed and power in his second year at AA Jackson in 1993.

MONTOYO, CHARLIE - 3B - BR - Age 28

A journeyman from Milwaukee's farm system, Montoyo came up with some big hits for the Expos down the stretch last year. He's a bench player at best, though, and will only make it in the majors as the 24th or 25th man on the roster.

	AB	R	HR	RBI	SB	BA	$
1993 Ottawa AAA	319	43	1	43	0	.279	
1993 Montreal NL	5	1	0	3	0	.400	-

MOORE, KERWIN - OF - BB - Age 23

The lack of a Double-A Marlins affiliate caused Moore to drop back a level in 1993. He has great speed (71 stolen bases in 1993), a great batting eye (114 walks) and fine defensive skills, but the presence of more highly touted young outfielders in the Marlins system will force him to wait his turn.

	AB	R	HR	RBI	SB	BA	$
1993 High Desert A	510	120	6	52	71	.269	

MOORE, MIKE - OF - BR - Age 23

Moore was a first round draft pick in 1992 and a former UCLA football player. Still a little rough around the edges, Moore struck out 103 times last season. He has been bothered by injuries to his left (non-throwing) shoulder.

MOORE, VINCE - OF - BB - Age 22

Moore is a switch-hitting speedster acquired in the McGriff trade. At two Single-A stops in 1993, he hit a combined .280 with 20 home runs and 30 stolen bases. Given the Padres expressed desire to add speed to the major league roster, Moore is a candidate to see time in the San Diego outfield eventually.

MORANDINI, MICKEY - 2B - BL - Age 27

The Phils have tried to hand him the second base job for three years now, but he hasn't been able to hold it. A spray hitter with above average speed, he's overmatched by lefties (.212 in 1993 after hitting .198 in 1992 and .185 in 1991). Defensively, he is surehanded (he committed just 5 errors in 1993) with average range. The Phils have picked up Mariano Duncan's option for 1994, so Morandini seems slated for part-time duty.

	AB	R	HR	RBI	SB	BA	$
1992 Philadelphia NL	422	47	3	30	8	.265	7
1993 Philadelphia NL	425	57	3	33	13	.247	6
1994 *Projection* >>>	407	50	3	30	11	.253	6

MORMAN, RUSS - 1B/OF - BR - Age 31

The journeyman first baseman had a great season at Triple-A last year, but the Pirates never recalled him because they felt he might get in the way of their youth movement.

MORRIS, HAL - 1B - BL - Age 28

Injuries hampered Morris in 1992 and 1993. Last year he was supposed to be given a full-time job (finally) but he suffered a separated shoulder in a spring training brawl. He's one of the few active career .300 hitters.

	AB	R	HR	RBI	SB	BA	$
1992 Cincinnati NL	395	41	6	53	6	.271	11
1993 Cincinnati NL	379	48	7	49	2	.317	12
1994 *Projection* >>>	401	50	8	52	5	.302	15

MOSEBY, LLOYD - OF - BL - Age 34
Moseby passed up a shot at signing with the Oakland A's after the '91 season, and had given up baseball when the Yomiuri Giants contacted him. Lloyd put together a good season in Japan, and seems to have found a home there, so he's therefore not very likely to return to the U.S., but you never know.

MOTA, ANDY - 2B - BR - Age 28
Mota, who can still hit for average, surfaced briefly with the Astros in 1991, but is no longer a prospect.

MOTA, GARY - OF - BR - Age 23
After an MVP season in 1992 at Single-A Asheville, Mota missed most of 1993 with an injury and didn't play well when he returned. Manny's fourth son needs a big year in 1994 to regain his status as a top prospect.

	AB	R	HR	RBI	SB	BA	$
1992 Ashville A	484	92	24	90	22	.291	
1993 Jackson AA	90	7	3	8	1	.144	

MOTTOLA, CHAD - OF - BR - Age 22
The Reds first round pick in 1992, Mottola was picked as the sixth best prospect in the Carolina League by Baseball America in 1993 after hitting .280 with 21 homers, 91 RBI and 13 stolen bases. He's a good power/speed combo.

MOUTON, JAMES - 2B - BR - Age 25
A fast-rising prospect who skipped Double-A, Mouton was named MVP in the Pacific Coast League after leading the league in runs, hits, doubles, total bases and extra base hits. He also led all minor league second basemen in errors (43), but improved in the second half. Mouton may be converted back to the outfield where he played in college. He has been compared to Joe Morgan, Lou Whitaker and Rickey Henderson. Mouton should reach the majors in 1994 and could be a four-category player immediately.

MUCKER, KELCEY - OF/DH - BL - Age 18
Turned down offers to play football, basketball or baseball at Indiana and accepted $300,000 to sign with the Twins, who made him their fourth pick in the first round of last year's draft. Showed some speed in his brief pro debut.

MUNOZ, PEDRO - OF - BR - Age 25
Munoz hurt his knee in September 1992 but didn't have surgery until he found he was unable to play in 1993. It was a lost year. He can easily rebound with an excellent year in '94. There is plenty of talent here: good power and some speed. And he's still young.

	AB	R	HR	RBI	SB	BA	$
1992 Minnesota AL	418	44	12	71	4	.270	13
1993 Minnesota AL	326	34	13	38	1	.233	3
1994 Projection >>>	394	59	15	57	4	.270	13

MURPHY, MIKE - OF - BR - Age 22
A 1990 sixth round pick, Murphy abandoned switch hitting in 1992, with positive results. He has excellent speed (33 steals in 1993) and hit 29 doubles at Single-A Spartanburg, but he needs to improve his discipline at the plate (only 35 walks in 544 plate appearances). He's come a long way over the past two seasons, and another quantum leap could propel him into the Phils' future plans.

MURRAY, CALVIN - OF - BR - Age 22
The best hitting prospect in the Giants organization, Murray stole 55 bases at three minor league levels in 1993, his first pro season. He was overmatched above A-ball, but has plenty of time to improve. A first round pick in 1992, he needs more time in the high minors; look for him in 1995.

MURRAY, EDDIE - 1B - BB - Age 38
One of the smartest hitters ever, Murray took advantage of depleted pitching in 1993. There is no reason why he can't have another similar year in '94, back in the American League with Cleveland.

	AB	R	HR	RBI	SB	BA	$
1992 New York NL	551	64	16	93	4	.261	18
1993 New York NL	610	77	27	100	2	.285	21
1994 Projection >>>	585	68	21	93	4	.262	18

MURRAY, GLENN - OF - BR - Age 23

Of the Expos' multitude of outfield prospects, Murray has the best raw power. He had a breakthrough year at Double-A last season but probably needs a full year at Triple-A before he's ready for the majors. He'd be a low average, high strikeout, high power kind of hitter in the bigs.

MYERS, GREG - C - BL - Age 27

Getting virtually no playing time in Toronto behind Pat Borders, Myers was traded to California in midseason 1992, immediately becoming the Angels top catcher. Unfortunately, he broke his hamate bone and had to miss a large part of the 1992 season but he was healthy in 1993. Still young enough to reach new high levels in 1994.

	AB	R	HR	RBI	SB	BA	$
1992 Toronto-California AL	78	4	1	13	0	.231	-
1993 California AL	290	27	7	40	3	.255	4
1994 *Projection* >>>	223	19	5	30	2	.254	3

NAEHRING, TIM - SS/2B - BR - Age 27

Naehring's whole career has been a battle against injuries. Management wants him to play, but he keeps having problems. In 1993 it was shoulder surgery.

	AB	R	HR	RBI	SB	BA	$
1992 Boston AL	186	12	3	14	0	.231	-
1993 Boston AL	127	14	1	17	1	.331	2
1994 *Projection* >>>	236	18	2	18	1	.266	2

NATAL, BOB - C - BR - Age 28

Natal wasted away on the bench in 1993 and will likely do the same in 1994. He showed decent pop as a minor leaguer, but now he's looking an awful lot like Steve Lake.

	AB	R	HR	RBI	SB	BA	$
1992 Montreal NL	6	0	0	0	0	.000	-
1993 Florida NL	117	3	1	6	1	.214	-
1994 *Projection* >>>	59	6	1	5	1	.232	-

NAVARRO, TITO - SS - BR - Age 23

Navarro is the Mets' great shortstop hope for the future: their hope to bring an end to the string of Rafael Santanas, Kevin Elsters, Dick Schofields and Tim Bogars. Navarro is a slick fielder with good speed.

	AB	R	HR	RBI	SB	BA	$
1992 Tidewater AAA	(Did not play - Injured)						
1993 Norfolk AAA	273	35	0	16	19	.282	
1993 New York NL	17	1	0	1	0	.059	-
1994 *Projection* >>>	100	11	0	7	3	.248	-

NEAL, MIKE - SS - BR - Age 22

From Benson Baseball Monthly, September 1993: "Be on the lookout in a couple of years for Watertown shortstop Mike Neal." Drafted in the 16th round after helping Louisiana State to the College World Series title. Defensive shortcomings could move him to third base. His bat is strong enough to make the switch.

NEEL, TROY - 1B - BL - Age 28

His two partial seasons with Oakland create a useful line: 147 games, 22 home runs, 72 RBI, .288 average playing his home games in a pitcher's park. He's 28 years old, so don't look for improvement, but he should be able to maintain the above stats for a few more years.

	AB	R	HR	RBI	SB	BA	$
1992 Oakland AL	53	8	3	9	0	.264	0
1993 Oakland AL	427	59	19	63	3	.290	15
1994 *Projection* >>>	421	58	15	59	4	.273	14

NEVERS, TOM - SS - BR - Age 22

The Astros number one draft choice in 1990 has progressed through four levels, but has failed to put up impressive numbers. He missed much of 1993 with injuries. Still only 22, he has a chance, but must establish himself as an impact player at Double-A or Triple-A in 1994 to get back on track.

NEVIN, PHIL - 3B - BR - Age 22
The top overall draft choice and 1992 Baseball America College Player of the Year, Nevin had a successful professional debut in the Pacific Coast League. His defensive skills may need some work, but he will be ready to start a long major league career in 1994. He should hit for both power and average after he adjusts to major league pitching.

	AB	R	HR	RBI	SB	BA	$
1993 Tucson AAA	448	67	10	93	8	.286	

NEWFIELD, MARC - OF - BR - Age 21
Look at his numbers, then consider this number: 20, the age at which he reached the majors. That's a year younger than Dave Winfield and Eddie Murray, to name two. Playing in the outfield has been an adventure for Newfield, so he may be contending for a first base/designated hitter role.

	AB	R	HR	RBI	SB	BA	$
1993 Jackson AA	336	48	19	51	1	.307	
1993 Seattle AL	66	5	1	7	0	.227	-
1994 *Projection* >>>	321	32	11	37	0	.247	4

NEWSON, WARREN - OF - BL - Age 29
A walk machine, Newson could pile up runs scored if given the chance. He'd be a superb platoon player and many teams could do worse than Newson in their every day lineup.

	AB	R	HR	RBI	SB	BA	$
1992 Chicago AL	136	19	1	11	3	.221	-
1993 Nashville AAA	176	40	4	21	5	.341	-
1993 Chicago AL	40	9	2	6	0	.300	-
1994 *Projection* >>>	87	14	2	11	1	.258	-

NEWSTROM, DOUG - 3B - BL - Age 22
The Dodgers moved their seventh-round draft pick from Arizona State across the diamond from firstbase. He has gap power and a good batting eye; his average ranked seventh in a down hitting year in the Northwest League.

NIEVES, MELVIN - OF - BB - Age 22
Nieves will carry the burden of being a key part of the trade that sent Fred McGriff to Atlanta. He was considered a good but not great Braves' prospect (behind Klesko, Jones, Kelly and Lopez). A switch hitter with power, Nieves has been compared to Bonilla and Sierra; he hit 26 home runs with 108 RBI in two minor league stops in 1992, then collected 17 Triple-A home runs in 1993. Although Nieves performed weakly in a short September trial in San Diego, he'll get every opportunity to win a regular outfield spot in spring training; he may also get a chance at first base.

	AB	R	HR	RBI	SB	BA	$
1993 Richmond AAA	273	38	10	36	4	.278	
1993 Las Vegas AAA	159	31	7	24	2	.308	
1993 San Diego NL	47	4	2	3	0	.191	-
1994 *Projection* >>>	205	22	4	24	2	.233	1

NILSSON, DAVE - C - BL - Age 24
Amazingly, expectations for Nilsson seem lower now than they were a year ago. But of course we are one year farther removed from that .418 batting average at El Paso in 1991. Nilsson suffered a wrist injury that ruined his spring training last year and slowed him throughout the first half of the season. When he finally got going, he quickly became one of the best-hitting catchers in the major leagues.

	AB	R	HR	RBI	SB	BA	$
1992 Milwaukee AL	164	15	4	25	2	.232	1
1993 Milwaukee AL	296	35	7	40	3	.257	5
1994 *Projection* >>>	302	33	7	42	3	.270	7

NIXON, OTIS - OF - BB - Age 35
Nixon showed little sign of aging in 1993, besting career norms in virtually every offensive category. His stolen base success rate returned to its usual 75% or better (47 stolen bases in 60 tries - 78%) and he got his strikeout to walk ratio back to 1-to-1; even with a 25 point batting average drop, Nixon had a better on base percentage in 1993. On the flip side, two things are working against Nixon, and both are only going to get more serious: Nixon's now 35 and

he won't be able to steal a lot of bases for very much longer. Also, the Braves are overstocked with outfielders, so Nixon's playing time is likely to decrease over the next few years. For now the Braves need him to spark the offense, but his days are numbered.

	AB	R	HR	RBI	SB	BA	$
1992 Atlanta NL	456	79	2	22	41	.294	24
1993 Atlanta NL	461	77	1	24	47	.269	21
1994 Projection >>>	447	75	1	23	46	.274	24

NIXON, TROT - OF - BL - Age 19
Selected by Boston in the first round (seventh pick overall) in last June's draft. He didn't sign in time to play in '93, but agreed to terms in time to go to the Instructional League instead of staying at North Carolina State as a quarterback. Considered an excellent power prospect who can play center field. His father caught Catfish Hunter in high school.

NOKES, MATT - C - BL - Age 30
A good power hitter with adequate defense, Nokes sat and watched most of the time in 1993 while Mike Stanley had his unbelievable season. Catching Jim Abbott's no-hitter was the one highlight.

	AB	R	HR	RBI	SB	BA	$
1992 New York AL	384	42	22	59	0	.224	8
1993 New York AL	217	25	10	35	0	.249	3
1994 Projection >>>	313	35	16	50	1	.244	7

NORMAN, LES - OF - BR - Age 25
Developed both home run power and some stolen-base speed in his third pro season. Now considered a prospect the Royals will be watching closely this season at AAA Omaha.

NUNEVILLER, TOM - OF - BR - Age 24
This 1990 fifth round pick had caught the eye of the Phils' brass by 1992, but then had a major knee injury. Unfortunately, he was not nearly the same player in 1993, batting only .230 in 226 at bats at AA Reading. At this point, he appears to have no major league future.

NUNNALLY JON - 2B - BL - Age 22
A third round pick in 1992, he was converted from outfield to second base in 1993. Was selected by Baseball America as the 10th best prospect in the New York-Penn league in 1992. Not a high average hitter, he has decent speed and good power for a middle infielder, but has struck out about once in every four at bats in his two minor league seasons. Has major league ability, but no one besides Carlos Baerga will play second base for the Indians for the foreseeable future.

OBANDO, SHERMAN - DH - BR - Age 24
Obando was kept with the parent Orioles club because he was a Rule Five draftee from the Yankees. The Birds love how Obando crushes the ball. After less than 100 plate appearances in 1993, Obando will likely get a full season at AAA Rochester to develop; he is a fine prospect for a designated hitter/first base role in 1995 and beyond.

	AB	R	HR	RBI	SB	BA	$
1993 Bowie AA	58	8	3	12	1	.241	
1993 Baltimore AL	92	8	3	15	0	.272	0
1994 Projection >>>	175	16	2	19	0	.262	-

O'BRIEN, CHARLIE - C - BR - Age 32
He can't hit now and never could, but O'Brien does throw well and the pitchers love throwing to him. It's not much to put on a resume, but it keeps him in the league. 1993 was one of his better years, possibly his best.

	AB	R	HR	RBI	SB	BA	$
1992 New York NL	156	15	2	13	0	.212	-
1993 New York NL	188	15	4	23	1	.255	2
1994 Projection >>>	174	15	3	18	1	.231	-

O'BRIEN, PETE - 1B - BL - Age 36

Six or seven years ago, O'Brien was a clear (though distant) second best first basemen in the American League. In 1993 he was just barely in the American League until he retired in mid-season..

	AB	R	HR	RBI	SB	BA	$
1992 Seattle AL	396	40	14	52	2	.222	5
1993 Seattle AL	210	30	7	27	0	.257	2
1994 *Projection* >>>	182	21	5	25	1	.241	2

OCHOA, ALEX - OF - BL - Age 22

The O's third-round pick in 1991, Ochoa is one of the many good outfield prospects in the organization. Ochoa is one of the Birds' top long-range prospects, rated number two in the Carolina League (behind teammate Curtis Goodwin). Minor league managers alternately have compared him to Ron Gant, Ellis Valentine and Barry Bonds. Ochoa is respected first and foremost for his cannon-like arm. He is potentially a four-category type. Earliest ETA is 1995. Power and speed. Lots of speed, a commodity in short supply in the Baltimore organization.

	AB	R	HR	RBI	SB	BA	$
1992 Kane County A	499	65	1	59	31	.295	
1993 Frederick A	532	84	13	90	34	.276	

OFFERMAN, JOSE - SS - BB - Age 25

Over-emphasis on his defense hid an offensive improvement in almost every area in 1993. His 62 RBI were a nice bonus from a middle infielder. Lasorda has a long history of favoring bats over gloves at shortstop, so look for more playing time and more improvement in 1994.

	AB	R	HR	RBI	SB	BA	$
1992 Los Angeles NL	534	67	1	30	23	.260	12
1993 Los Angeles NL	590	77	1	62	30	.269	17
1994 *Projection* >>>	534	68	1	45	25	.263	14

O'HALLORAN, GREG - C - BL - Age 25

Could become a lefthanded-hitting platoon catcher for the Jays. He has had a decline in power and an increase in strikeouts the last two seasons, but his average has been consistent (.254-.284) in his five pro seasons.

O'LEARY, TROY - OF - BL - Age 24

Like many Brewers prospects, O'Leary had huge numbers in their farm system (.338 for Helena and .334 for AA El Paso). He was the Texas League MVP in 1992. Used strictly against righty pitchers in his '93 callup, O'Leary is making good progress toward being an everyday major leaguer.

	AB	R	HR	RBI	SB	BA	$
1993 New Orleans AAA	388	65	7	59	6	.273	-
1993 Milwaukee AL	41	3	0	3	0	.293	-
1994 *Projection* >>>	100	12	1	11	1	.263	-

OLERUD, JOHN - 1B - BL - Age 25

Olerud's sweet swing finally produced a .300 (.363 to be exact) season and a batting title to boot. This is the Wade Boggs of the 1990's. He has extraordinary patience at the plate, but last year started laying into first-pitch fastballs rather than end up behind in the count. His prime years are ahead of him and there's no reason why he can't continue to put up more seasons like his last one.

	AB	R	HR	RBI	SB	BA	$
1992 Toronto AL	458	68	16	66	1	.284	15
1993 Toronto AL	551	109	24	107	0	.363	32
1994 *Projection* >>>	504	86	25	86	0	.318	28

OLIVA, JOSE - 3B - BR - Age 23

Obtained from Texas in exchange for Charlie Leibrandt (just what the Braves need, another prospect), Oliva showed (as expected) power and a low batting average for AAA Richmond. As a hitter, he's comparable to Terry Pendleton. Oliva is too much of a free swinger at this point (134 strikeouts in 1993 after 136 strikeouts in 1992) and his defense isn't up to Pendleton's standard yet, so he's going to get another year at Triple-A. The Braves are clearly grooming this youngster to replace Pendleton within two years.

	AB	R	HR	RBI	SB	BA	$
1992 Tulsa AA	445	57	16	75	3	.270	
1993 Richmond AAA	412	63	21	65	1	.235	

OLIVER, JOE - C - BR - Age 28

Oliver set career highs in doubles, homers and RBI, and played 139 games (only Piazza and Daulton played more) behind the plate. His job is safe for the foreseeable future due to the trade of Dan Wilson.

	AB	R	HR	RBI	SB	BA	$
1992 Cincinnati NL	485	42	10	57	2	.270	12
1993 Cincinnati NL	482	40	14	75	0	.239	6
1994 Projection >>>	443	37	12	62	1	.248	7

OLSON, GREG - C - BR - Age 33

A career minor leaguer before 1990, Olson showed his roots with another sub-par season in 1993. His defense is still good, but it's slipping. Javy Lopez will be on the scene to stay in 1994 and Olson's playing days in Atlanta are all over. Charlie O'Brien will become the mentor for Lopez in 1994.

	AB	R	HR	RBI	SB	BA	$
1992 Atlanta NL	302	27	3	27	2	.238	1
1993 Atlanta NL	262	23	4	24	1	.225	-
1994 Projection >>>	301	28	4	28	1	.233	-

O'NEILL, PAUL - OF - BL - Age 31

With his good swing for the short right field line at Yankee Stadium, O'Neill had a career year in 1993. He made the transition to the American League and hit well. Still has trouble with lefty pitchers, so he didn't see many of them. With no injuries, he will be a major part of the Yankees power offense in 1994.

	AB	R	HR	RBI	SB	BA	$
1992 Cincinnati NL	496	59	14	66	6	.246	13
1993 New York AL	498	71	20	75	2	.311	20
1994 Projection >>>	503	64	18	71	5	.270	16

OQUENDO, JOSE - SS - BB - Age 30

The slick-fielding Oquendo has seen his playing time reduced dramatically by injuries each of the past two seasons; Oquendo has managed just 108 major league at bats in the last two years. He's a weak offensive player but could regain his starting second base job this season as the Cardinals look to improve upon 1993's woeful defense.

	AB	R	HR	RBI	SB	BA	$
1992 St. Louis NL	35	3	0	3	0	.257	-
1993 St. Louis NL	73	7	0	4	0	.205	-
1994 Projection >>>	110	11	0	7	0	.230	-

ORIE, KEVIN - SS - BR - Age 21

Orie was the Cubs' third pick in the first round of the 1993 draft, out of Indiana University. A big shortstop (6'4", 205 lbs.), he made an impressive power showing in his half-season debut in the Midwest League.

ORSULAK, JOE - OF - BL - Age 31

Orsulak delivered his usual steady season in 1993. He can hit righty pitching and play all three outfield positions. He also has the mental makeup for pinch-hitting.

	AB	R	HR	RBI	SB	BA	$
1992 Baltimore AL	391	45	4	39	5	.289	10
1993 New York NL	409	59	8	35	5	.284	9
1994 Projection >>>	416	54	6	38	5	.284	11

ORTIZ, JUNIOR - C - BR - Age 34

Ortiz has now completed 11 consecutive full seasons as a backup catcher, which must be some kind of record. Again he had much more playing time than expected due to repeated injuries to Sandy Alomar. Ortiz actually did a pretty darn good job defensively, throwing out close to 50% of opposing baserunners. Offensively, well, he hasn't homered this decade. He was a free agent at the end of the 1993 season; don't expect a bidding war.

	AB	R	HR	RBI	SB	BA	$
1992 Cleveland AL	244	20	0	24	1	.250	0
1993 Cleveland AL	249	19	0	20	1	.221	-
1994 *Projection* >>>	228	18	0	20	1	.230	-

ORTIZ, LUIS - 3B - BR - Age 23

When Buddy Bailey moved up from managing Class A Lynchburg to managing AAA Pawtucket, he stuck his neck out and asked for Ortiz to make the jump with him. Bailey said he expected Ortiz could bat .280 with 15-18 homers and 70-80 RBI. Only an injury kept Ortiz, a pure hitter, from posting even better stats. He will play in Boston in '94. His defense is suspect, so he could move to the outfield or DH.

	AB	R	HR	RBI	SB	BA	$
1993 Pawtucket AAA	402	45	18	81	1	.294	
1993 Boston AL	12	0	0	1	0	.250	-
1994 *Projection* >>>	100	11	3	15	0	.255	0

ORTON, JOHN - C - BR - Age 28

Once thought to be the Angels catcher of the future, Orton has struggled at the plate in every year he's been in the majors. The Angels finally ran out of patience.

	AB	R	HR	RBI	SB	BA	$
1992 California AL	114	11	2	12	1	.219	-
1993 California AL	95	5	1	4	1	.189	-
1994 *Projection* >>>	97	7	2	6	1	.202	-

OSIK, KEITH - C/3B - BR - Age 25

Osik is the Pittsburgh catching prospect closest to being ready for the majors; he's stronger offensively than defensively.

OTERO, RICKY - OF - BB - Age 21

A little guy (5'7", 150 lbs.) with base-stealing speed, Otero was a .300 hitter before reaching Double-A. He can play right field.

OWEN, SPIKE - SS - BB - Age 32

1993 was not much of a year for Owen. With Mike Gallego playing well, Owen took to the bench. He has a big contract and will probably stay with the Yankees for that reason, but will have no real role in 1994.

	AB	R	HR	RBI	SB	BA	$
1992 Montreal NL	386	52	7	40	9	.269	11
1993 New York AL	334	41	2	20	3	.234	-
1994 *Projection* >>>	266	30	3	19	4	.240	2

OWENS, JAYHAWK - C - BR - Age 25

Yes, Jayhawk is his real name. And yes, he still needs some experience, but he showed a great arm behind the plate and could emerge as a strong contender down the road, or if Girardi gets hurt or traded. Owens collected 43 RBI in just 174 at bats for AAA Colorado Springs.

	AB	R	HR	RBI	SB	BA	$
1993 Colorado Springs AAA	174	24	6	43	5	.310	-
1993 Colorado NL	86	12	3	6	1	.209	-
1994 *Projection* >>>	155	18	2	15	2	.240	1

PAGLIARULO, MIKE - 3B - BL - Age 34

Gone to Japan. Pagliarulo simply could not get an offer that he thought fair after his surprisingly strong performance in 1993.The Oriole coaches got him to pull the ball more, and Pags found his long-lost power stroke.

	AB	R	HR	RBI	SB	BA	$
1992 Minnesota AL	105	10	0	9	1	.200	-
1993 Minnesota-Baltimore	370	55	9	44	6	.303	12
1994 *Projection* >>>	282	30	5	28	3	.257	4

PAGNOZZI, TOM - C - BR - Age 31

Pagnozzi continued to be a solid offensive catcher in 1993, his third full season as a starter. He loves catching and says his goal is to catch all 162 games some season. Pagnozzi's strengths include good defense and clubhouse leadership. Expect performance similar to 1992-93 for several more years.

	AB	R	HR	RBI	SB	BA	$
1992 St. Louis NL	485	33	7	44	2	.249	6
1993 St. Louis NL	330	31	7	41	1	.258	4
1994 *Projection* >>>	403	33	6	45	3	.256	6

PALMEIRO, ORLANDO - OF - BL - Age 25

A speedy center fielder moving steadily toward Houston. Palmeiro hit .305 with 18 steals at AA Midland in '93.

PALMEIRO, RAFAEL - 1B - BL - Age 29

Palmeiro set career highs in runs scored, RBI, home runs, and stolen bases in 1993. He continues to grow as a power hitter. The stolen bases were probably an aberration, but the other numbers give true indications of what to expect in the future. Palmeiro can play outfield as well as first base, maybe better.

	AB	R	HR	RBI	SB	BA	$
1992 Texas AL	608	84	22	85	2	.268	18
1993 Texas AL	597	124	37	105	22	.295	37
1994 *Projection* >>>	606	109	30	96	12	.291	32

PALMER, DEAN - 3B - BR - Age 25

Ever since I first saw him put on a week-long power display during spring training 1989, I have believed he was a hitter of destiny. A streaky, free-swinging young power hitter, he reminds some of a young Mike Schmidt. Palmer continues to develop as a power hitter, and improved on his batting average somewhat. He's also a "special project" of hitting coach Willie Upshaw, who is trying to get Palmer to relax more at the plate, for better patience.

	AB	R	HR	RBI	SB	BA	$
1992 Texas AL	541	74	26	72	10	.229	14
1993 Texas AL	519	88	33	96	11	.245	20
1994 *Projection* >>>	504	78	29	88	9	.244	18

PAPPAS, ERIK - C/OF - BR - Age 27

After bouncing around the minor leagues with California, Kansas City and both Chicago organizations, Pappas found a home in St. Louis last season. He provided better offense than expected (.276 batting average, .368 on base percentage) when starting catcher Tom Pagnozzi went down with a knee injury early in the year. Once Pagnozzi returned, Pappas stuck as a backup catcher. He figures to return in that role in 1994.

	AB	R	HR	RBI	SB	BA	$
1993 St. Louis NL	228	25	1	28	1	.276	2
1994 *Projection* >>>	117	13	1	14	1	.251	-

PAQUETTE, CRAIG - 3B - BR - Age 25

Paquette, who was the regular Oakland third baseman for much of 1993 and managed to club 12 homers in 105 games, is a weak overall hitter thus far in his career. Paquette's 1993 statline is a match for any of Cory Snyder's worst years with the Indians: .219 average, 108 strikeouts, 14 walks. Paquette has had terrible strike zone judgment throughout his career. His ultra-low on base percentage (.245) should guarantee that he loses his job with Oakland if he doesn't improve quickly. (No team appreciates OBP as much as the A's). He hit under .200 in second half.

	AB	R	HR	RBI	SB	BA	$
1993 Oakland AL	393	35	12	46	4	.219	3
1994 *Projection* >>>	197	19	6	24	2	.230	1

PAREDES, JOHNNY - 2B - BR - Age 31
Back in 1987 he was a good prospect with the Expos: high average, high speed. Now over the hill, Paredes is a career minor leaguer. He steals a few bases, but that's about it.

PARENT, MARK - C - BR - Age 32
Parent figures to replace light-hitting Jeff Tackett as the O's reserve catcher in 1994. He was among the International League's home run leaders until his impressive August callup when he produced four home runs in 54 at bats and a .364 average against lefthanders. Parent's defensive skills nearly match Tackett's and his offense is better.

	AB	R	HR	RBI	SB	BA	$
1992 Baltimore AL	34	4	2	4	0	.235	-
1993 Rochester AAA	332	47	14	56	0	.247	-
1993 Baltimore AL	54	7	4	12	0	.259	-

PARKER, RICK - OF - BR - Age 31
Parker split time between the Astros and AAA Tucson in 1993. He hits for average with some speed but no power and isn't likely to get an opportunity for significant playing time in the majors.

	AB	R	HR	RBI	SB	BA	$
1993 Houston NL	45	11	0	4	1	.333	0

PARKS, DEREK - C - BR - Age 25
Once a top prospect, catcher Derek Parks struggled for a few years, finally regaining his skills last year with a nice year in Triple-A earning playing time with the Twins. He has some power, and he could be the number one catcher if Matt Walbeck doesn't work out as the regular.

	AB	R	HR	RBI	SB	BA	$
1992 Minnesota AL	6	1	0	0	0	.333	-
1993 Portland AAA	363	63	17	71	0	.311	-
1993 Minnesota AL	20	3	0	1	0	.200	-

PARRISH, LANCE - C - BR - Age 37
At the end of his major league career. Parrish isn't very effective behind the plate and no longer hits well enough to take up a roster spot for his bat.

	AB	R	HR	RBI	SB	BA	$
1992 California-Seattle AL	275	26	12	32	1	.233	4
1993 Cleveland AL	20	2	1	2	1	.200	-
1994 *Projection* >>>	169	16	8	20	1	.224	1

PASQUA, DAN - OF - BL - Age 32
Pasqua took a big step toward retirement in 1993. As a weak platoon hitter, his value is just an occasional longball.

	AB	R	HR	RBI	SB	BA	$
1992 Chicago AL	265	26	6	33	0	.211	-
1993 Chicago AL	176	22	5	20	2	.205	-
1994 *Projection* >>>	246	32	8	32	1	.223	1

PATTERSON, JOHN - 2B - BB - Age 27
Patterson missed virtually the entire season due to rotator cuff surgery, then hit a spectacular pinch-hit homer for the Giants in his first at bat of the season at any level, beating the Braves in a pennant race game. Once a top prospect with speed, defense and a decent bat, his future is problematic.

	AB	R	HR	RBI	SB	BA	$
1992 San Francisco NL	103	10	0	4	5	.184	-
1993 San Jose A	68	8	1	14	6	.235	-
1993 San Francisco NL	16	1	1	2	0	.188	-

PECORILLI, ALDO - DH/OF/C - BR - Age 23
Pecorilli was the number two catcher at Single-A Savannah last year and also saw action as an outfielder and designated hitter. If he can develop his catching skills, his powerful bat could get him to the big leagues.

PECOTA, BILL - IF - BR - Age 34

The Braves Jack-of-all-trades, Pecota was a frequent late-inning defensive replacement, but also served well as a table-setting pinch hitter. Because he doesn't get to the plate very often, Pecota isn't of much use for Rotisserie purposes. Nevertheless, Pecota was one of the most valuable "spare parts" in the NL in 1993.

	AB	R	HR	RBI	SB	BA	$
1992 New York NL	269	28	2	26	9	.227	3
1993 Atlanta NL	62	17	0	5	1	.323	0
1994 *Projection* >>>	187	27	2	19	6	.264	3

PEDRE, JORGE - C - BR - Age 27

Injuries have hampered Pedre's career and he has become a journeyman player. He bashed 13 home runs in 233 at bats in 1987, but hasn't shown that kind of power since. He can catch and is available in case of emergency.

PEGUES, STEVE - OF - BR - Age 25

Pegues nearly won a major league job in the spring of '93 after capturing the inaugrual Arizona Fall League batting title. Sent to Las Vegas, he hit .352 in 270 at bats with some power and speed, earning a promotion to the 40-man roster in October. A broken hand limited his playing time in 1993; he's one of many candidates for outfield duty in 1994.

	AB	R	HR	RBI	SB	BA	$
1992 Las Vegas AAA	376	51	9	56	12	.263	
1993 Las Vegas AAA	270	52	9	50	12	.352	

PELTIER, DAN - OF - BL - Age 25

Peltier has been one of the Rangers' better prospects for several years. He made the jump from rookie ball to Double-A in 1990 at the age of 21, after hitting .402 in 1989. Peltier spent most of 1993 at Oklahoma City, learning to play first base. Then he was called up to the majors and put back in the outfield. His defense was weak, and his offense suffered because of it. One of several candidates for the everyday rightfield job, he likely to win at least a platoon spot if the Rangers don't find another big-name veteran hitter.

	AB	R	HR	RBI	SB	BA	$
1992 Texas AL	24	1	0	2	0	.167	-
1993 Texas AL	160	23	1	17	0	.269	0
1994 *Projection* >>>	288	36	3	29	2	.260	3

PEMBERTORN, RUDY - OF - BR - Age 24

Pemberton has power and speed and is making slow but steady progress up the Tigers farm ladder. This San Pedro de Macoris native is still a prospect.

PENA, GERONIMO - 2B - BB - Age 27

The Cardinals feel Pena has vast potential but are tired of waiting for him to fulfill it. He can hit with some pop and has decent speed, but mental lapses in all phases of his game prevent him from becoming a regular. Pena did almost all of his worthwhile hitting early in the year, then had a seriously down second half. He'll get another chance to win the second base job this spring, but isn't a lock to claim it. He's was on the trade block during the winter and could really benefit from a change of scenery.

	AB	R	HR	RBI	SB	BA	$
1992 St. Louis NL	203	31	7	31	13	.305	13
1993 St. Louis NL	254	34	5	30	13	.256	7
1994 *Projection* >>>	225	34	6	28	13	.269	9

PENA, TONY - C - BR - Age 36

Since he went to Boston, Pena has experienced a pronounced offensive downturn and is now at or near the end.

	AB	R	HR	RBI	SB	BA	$
1992 Boston AL	410	39	1	38	3	.241	2
1993 Boston AL	304	20	4	19	1	.181	-
1994 *Projection* >>>	366	31	3	30	3	.214	-

PENDLETON, TERRY - 3B - BB - Age 33

His offense continues to erode since his 1991 MVP season, but gradually; Pendleton's 1993 results only look bad when compared to the previous two years. Still, his strikeout/walk ratio and his defense have both slipped and he lost 39 points off of his batting average last year. Despite his bad knees, Pendleton played in all but one of his team's games last year. He's a good hitting NL third baseman, but is likely to be overvalued by people looking at his past.

	AB	R	HR	RBI	SB	BA	$
1992 Atlanta NL	640	98	21	105	5	.311	33
1993 Atlanta NL	633	81	17	84	5	.272	15
1994 Projection >>>	627	80	18	82	6	.281	22

PENN, SHANNON - 2B - BB - Age 24
Tiger farmhand Penn swiped 53 bases in Double-A last year. But he hit just .260 with only 18 extra base hits. The higher he goes in the system, the more relevant the question becomes: Can he steal first base?

PENNYFEATHER, WILLIAM - OF - BR - Age 25
A great athlete who once was a wide receiver at Syracuse, Pennyfeather hasn't been able to transfer all that ability to the baseball field. He can run and catch but cannot hit breaking junk. He went hitless in spring training and wasn't equal to the challenge of a platoon role while Van Slyke was injured. He's a fifth outfielder at best.

	AB	R	HR	RBI	SB	BA	$
1992 Pittsburgh NL	9	2	0	0	0	.222	-
1993 Buffalo AAA	457	54	14	41	10	.249	-
1993 Pittsburgh NL	34	4	0	2	0	.206	-
1994 Projection >>>	100	12	2	8	1	.228	-

PEREZ, EDUARDO - 3B - BR - Age 24
Son of Tony Perez, Eduardo will be handed the third base job. At his best he's capable of hitting 10-12 home runs and can steal 20 bases. All rookies are risky, but Perez is a good bet.

	AB	R	HR	RBI	SB	BA	$
1993 California AL	180	16	4	30	5	.250	3
1994 Projection >>>	388	43	9	49	12	.252	10

PEREZ, ROBERT - OF - BR - Age 24
A good speed/power combination, Perez just had his best year at his highest level, .294-12-64-13 for AAA Syracuse.

PERRY, GERALD - 1B - BL - Age 33
After washing out as an everyday player, Perry has become an effective pinch hitter. However, he is an expensive luxury to carry on a payroll and St. Louis had no plans of bringing him back in 1994.

	AB	R	HR	RBI	SB	BA	$
1992 St. Louis NL	143	13	1	18	3	.238	0
1993 St. Louis NL	98	21	4	16	1	.337	4
1994 Projection >>>	137	20	3	20	4	.274	3

PERRY, HERBERT - 1B/3B - BR - Age 24
A former University of Florida footballer, he was leading the AA Canton-Akron Indians farm team in RBI when shoulder surgery ended his '93 season. A good power prospect, he has also played left field.

PETAGINE, ROBERTO - 1B - BL - Age 22
This young Venezuelan had a big year at Double-A Jackson, winning the league's MVP award. He should continue to progress but his path to the majors is blocked by Jeff Bagwell and first base is his only position. Petagine is projected to play at Triple-A in 1994 with a potential late season callup.

PETERSON, CHARLES - OF - BR - Age 20
The Pirates' top pick in 1993, Peterson was a high school legend in South Carolina as a center fielder and quarterback. He chose baseball and has a high ceiling with his outstanding athletic ability. He adapted well to wooden bats, but his skills are raw. The Pirates will not rush him, so his arrival in the majors could take a while. Peterson hit .303 with eight steals in 188 at bats for the Pirates Rookie League entry.

PETRALLI, GENO - C - BL - Age 34
After several years of providing a decent lefthanded bat off the bench, Petralli's performance has declined markedly. Defense and calling a game have never been his claim to fame, so his career is fading.

	AB	R	HR	RBI	SB	BA	$
1992 Texas AL	192	11	1	18	0	.198	-
1993 Texas AL	133	16	1	13	2	.241	-
1994 *Projection* >>>	130	12	1	13	1	.231	-

PHILLIPS, J.R. - 1B - BL - Age 23
Phillips hurt his progress in 1992 by hitting only .237 for Class AA Midland where nearly everyone hits over .300. He hit 20 home runs and stole 15 bases in 1991. He rebounded from this off year to earn a major league trial in 1993. He led all Giants minor leaguers in homers and RBI. With Will Clark gone, Phillips immediately became a factor in the major league first base picture, but he will have to earn whatever role he gets. Unfortunately, Phillips' glove is made of stone, he only hit .263 in the Pacific Coast League, and he strikes out with alarming regularity (127 strikeouts in 506 at bats). He'll be 24 years old later in 1994; when Dave Kingman was 24, he hit .203 with 24 homers.

	AB	R	HR	RBI	SB	BA	$
1993 San Francisco NL	16	1	1	4	0	.313	-
1994 *Projection* >>>	188	23	6	26	1	.222	1

PHILLIPS, TONY - IF/OF - BB - Age 34
It is very unusual to see a hitter have his career-best season at age 34 like Tony Phillips did last year. When he was younger, Phillips kept getting hurt every year before he could put up big numbers. He should continue to set the table for the Tiger power hitters, and have another fine year in 1994.

	AB	R	HR	RBI	SB	BA	$
1992 Detroit AL	606	114	10	64	12	.276	18
1993 Detroit AL	566	113	7	57	16	.313	22
1994 *Projection* >>>	579	104	10	59	12	.280	18

PIAZZA, MIKE - C - BR - Age 25
Piazza had one of the four or five best rookie seasons in history and is one of the best stories of the 1993 season. If his season was a fluke, it sure didn't show in his second half stats (.319, 17-54). One cannot expect a repeat of any exceptional season, but a season 80% as good would still make Piazza the best-hitting catcher in the NL by a comfortable margin, and his defense is already well beyond what most scouts had projected for him.

	AB	R	HR	RBI	SB	BA	$
1992 Los Angeles NL	69	5	1	7	0	.232	-
1993 Los Angeles NL	547	81	35	112	3	.318	30
1994 *Projection* >>>	502	62	20	79	3	.288	21

PIRKL, GREG - 1B - BR - Age 23
Has received midseason promotions in three consecutive years. The best factor a player can have going for him, other than pure talent, is someone in the front office watching his career with interest.

	AB	R	HR	RBI	SB	BA	$
1993 Calgary AAA	445	67	21	94	3	.308	-
1993 Seattle AL	23	1	1	4	0	.174	-
1994 *Projection* >>>	100	9	2	13	0	.242	-

PLANTIER, PHIL - OF - BL - Age 25
Plantier's weak 1992 season was explained by a nerve injury. At the end of 1991, when he was hitting 11 home runs in 148 at bats for Boston, Plantier looked and talked like one of the great sluggers of the 1990's. He told me, "I have a goal of hitting one home run a week, and put some streaks on top of that." Plantier may not have surprised himself in 1993, but he ranked as one of the top surprises of 1993 among those who didn't notice him earlier. Plantier got even better in the second half, hitting 20 home runs with 60 RBI to pick up the slack left by trades of McGriff and Sheffield. Plantier will bat fourth or fifth in the Padres lineup every day in 1994, barring injury.

	AB	R	HR	RBI	SB	BA	$
1992 Boston AL	349	46	7	30	2	.246	4
1993 San Diego NL	462	67	34	100	4	.240	17
1994 *Projection* >>>	371	67	27	84	4	.250	16

POLIDOR, GUS - 2B - BR - Age 32

A career .207 hitter after reaching the majors seven times in obscure fill-in roles, Polidor was a classic example of expansion's impacts. He had last been up in 1990.

POLONIA, LUIS - OF - BL - Age 29

Last year's batting average was 28 points below Polonia's career average. He should regain his form in 1994, always good for 40 to 60 stolen bases.

	AB	R	HR	RBI	SB	BA	$
1992 California AL	577	83	0	35	51	.286	29
1993 California AL	576	75	1	32	55	.271	30
1994 *Projection* >>>	581	81	1	36	52	.280	30

POSADA, JORGE - C - BB - Age 22

How many catchers had 17 home runs and 17 stolen bases last year? Posada has been known as a power-hitting catcher, but he surprised people with his speed. He did not seem overwhelmed in his short stay in Double-A. Expect him to reach Triple-A by season's end in 1994.

POSE, SCOTT - OF - BL - Age 27

Pose committed the cardinal sin of having a monster spring training, and then hitting the wall once the season started. Now he's buried deeper than Jimmy Hoffa in the minds of the Marlins' architects. He's fast and he's solid defensively, but his only hope of playing a prominent major league role is another round of expansion. He did hit .342 at AA Chattanooga in 1992, and helped himself in the 1993 Arizona Fall League. The only question was: who noticed?

	AB	R	HR	RBI	SB	BA	$
1993 Edmonton AAA	398	61	0	27	19	.284	-
1993 Florida NL	41	0	0	3	0	.195	-
1994 *Projection* >>>	75	9	0	5	2	.254	-

PRATT, TODD - C/1B - BR - Age 27

Pratt was a seldom used, but heavy hitting backup catcher for the Phils. He hit 5 home runs in only 87 at bats, slugged .529, and hit .400 against lefties. His playing time should increase somewhat in 1994, as Daulton will need more frequent rest. Pratt's defense is adequate at best, reducing his chances of ever becoming a full time catcher. He could generate as much production in 200 at bats as some catchers do in 500.

	AB	R	HR	RBI	SB	BA	$
1992 Philadelphia NL	46	6	2	10	0	.283	0
1993 Philadelphia NL	87	8	5	13	0	.287	2
1994 *Projection* >>>	150	13	5	23	0	.272	2

PRIDE, CURTIS - OF - BL - Age 25

Pride was one of last season's inspirational stories, making the major leagues despite being 95 percent deaf. Signed as a six year free agent from the New York Mets' organization, Pride split the minor league season between Double-A and Triple-A and continued his production in a September callup to the majors. Pride knocked in five runs with nine at bats and hit for the cycle with his only four major league hits, slugging 1.111 and hitting well under pressure. He has a good chance of sticking with the Expos as a reserve outfielder this season and has the talent to eventually become a starter.

	AB	R	HR	RBI	SB	BA	$
1993 Harrisburg AA	180	51	15	39	21	.356	
1993 Ottawa AAA	262	55	6	22	29	.302	
1993 Montreal NL	9	3	1	5	1	.444	0
1994 *Projection* >>>	128	15	2	14	7	.242	2

PRIDY, TODD - 1B - BL - Age 23

A 23rd-round pick in 1992, Pridy has hit for power and average in two Single-A pitchers' leagues in his first two professional seasons. He needs a big year at a higher level in 1994 to move into the Marlins' long-term plans.

PRINCE, TOM - C - BR - Age 29

After bouncing back and forth between the minors and Pittsburgh for six seasons, Prince finally spent a full season in the majors last year; the results were disappointing. Two weeks after the season ended, he was dropped from the 40-man roster. He's not much of a hitter and his highly touted defensive ability has never shown in the majors. At age 29, it's hard to imagine him getting any better or getting a serious major league role.

	AB	R	HR	RBI	SB	BA	$
1992 Pittsburgh NL	44	1	0	5	1	.091	-
1993 Pittsburgh NL	179	14	2	24	1	.196	-
1994 Projection >>>	110	8	1	14	1	.186	-

PUCKETT, KIRBY - OF - BR - Age 33

Puckett remains one of the best hitters in the game. He can do it all, and is aging gracefully.

	AB	R	HR	RBI	SB	BA	$
1992 Minnesota AL	639	104	19	110	17	.329	39
1993 Minnesota AL	622	89	22	89	8	.296	25
1994 Projection >>>	606	89	19	91	10	.302	26

PULLIAM, HARVEY - OF - BR - Age 26

Pulliam showed little in his short major league trial after some mediocre hitting at AAA Omaha (.264-5-26 in about half a season). No longer a prospect, he has become a longball bat off the bench.

	AB	R	HR	RBI	SB	BA	$
1992 Kansas City AL	5	2	0	0	0	.200	-
1993 Omaha AAA	208	28	5	26	1	.264	-
1993 Kansas City AL	62	7	1	6	0	.258	-

PYE, EDDIE - 2B - BR - Age 27

Pye hit .329-7-66-5 at AAA Albuquerque. If the Dodgers clean out the older veterans, he could get a shot at a utility role. Otherwise, he has little chance of major league play.

QUINLAN, TOM - 3B - BR - Age 26

Quinlan's career has been characterized by terrific fielding and lots of strikeouts, with a few home runs. Quinlan has put in three years at Syracuse, so it's now time to use him or lose him.

QUINTANA, CARLOS - OF - BR - Age 28

Major injuries prior to the 1992 season kept him out the whole year. When he came back, Mo Vaughn had taken over the first base job, full-time and for good. You may read some spring training previews saying that Quintana can challenge to reclaim the first base role, and how his big winter ball stats have helped him, but it's all bunk. The talent is fine, but the playing time is lacking unless someone gets hurt.

	AB	R	HR	RBI	SB	BA	$
1993 Boston AL	303	31	1	19	1	.244	-
1994 Projection >>>	233	27	2	22	1	.262	1

RADZIEWICZ, DOUG - 1B/OF - BL - Age 25

An undistinguished minor leaguer until last season, Radziewicz came out of nowhere to win the Class A Florida State League batting title. His power may be a little short for him to become a regular major league first baseman; Radziewicz had just four homers in 439 at bats. He has also played in the outfield but lacks the speed that the Cardinals crave.

RAINES, TIM - OF - BB - Age 34

Last year, we predicted that Raines would hit for more power once he got used to seeing all that breaking junk in the American League, and that's exactly what happened. Raines' homers doubled last year while his steals halved, a reminder that he's now 34. He can still easily steal 30 bases in a full season.

	AB	R	HR	RBI	SB	BA	$
1992 Chicago AL	551	102	7	54	45	.294	32
1993 Chicago AL	415	75	16	54	21	.306	24
1994 Projection >>>	526	93	12	55	34	.288	27

RAMIREZ, MANNY - OF - BR - Age 21
Cleveland's number one draft pick in 1991, Ramirez has dominated everywhere he's played, except for the brief trial in Cleveland late last year. He's going to be a great power hitter, with the added dimension of speed. The most likely career path leads through right field in 1994. The DH slot was already crowded before the acquisition of Eddie Murray.

	AB	R	HR	RBI	SB	BA	$
1993 Cleveland AL	53	5	2	5	0	.170	-
1993 Canton-Akron AA	344	67	17	79	2	.340	
1993 Charlotte AAA	145	38	14	36	1	.317	
1994 *Projection* >>>	324	45	10	47	3	.270	9

RAMIREZ, OMAR - OF - BR - Age 23
The smaller (5'9") of the Indians outfield prospects named Ramirez, Omar continued to mature in 1993, developing into a solid line-drive hitter with good speed. He had outplayed the more widely-known Darrell Whitmore when they were teammates before last year. Then in 1993 he hit .314 with 24 steals for AA Canton-Akron. He could arrive in the majors in late 1994 with a good season at Triple-A.

RAMOS, KEN - OF - BL - Age 26
Won a batting title in 1992, hitting .339 in the pitching-rich Eastern League. He's a line drive hitter with speed, and will be good for a few stolen bases if he ever gets to the majors. There are just too many Tribe outfielders, as you can see from the above entries, for example.

RAMSEY, FERNANDO - OF - BR - Age 28
With good speed (89 stolen bases in three years) Ramsey has risen from Class A to Double-A to Triple-A with hardly a ripple in his stats. But then Ramsey's greatest strength, stealing bases, fell off by two thirds in his second year at AAA Iowa. A good defensive centerfielder, Ramsey hasn't shown enough offense to stay in the majors. There are just too many Cubbie outfielders; sometimes you can see that major league teams keep these guys around, just so developing pitchers have somebody to practice on.

RANDA, JOE - 3B - BR - Age 24
Won third base battle with Caraballo, showed power and speed, good batting average and RBI bat. Will start at AAA Omaha in 1994. Won't be immediate factor in crowded Royals third base picture for next year, but watch his minor league numbers for an indication of his progress to the bigs by 1995. If he makes it, he'll hit for a decent average with marginal power.

RATLIFF, DARYL - OF - BR - Age 24
The speedy Ratliff was considered a top prospect until he hit .240 for Double-A Carolina in 1992. He bounced back with a decent year at Double-A in 1993, though, to remind the front office he's still alive.

READY, RANDY - IF - BR - Age 34
Veteran Randy Ready was not called up by the Orioles when they needed a third baseman. He has a career .259 batting average over 10 seasons, once hitting .309 for San Diego. His bat speed has slowed. Stuck in Triple-A most of the season, Ready resurfaced in the majors with the Expos late last year when Delino Deshields got hurt. Ready can play anywhere and can hit, making him a valuable addition. The Expos want him back as their jack-of-all-trades in 1994, and to provide backup for Mike Lansing who inherited the second base job during the winter.

	AB	R	HR	RBI	SB	BA	$
1992 Oakland AL	125	17	3	17	1	.200	-
1993 Montreal NL	134	22	1	10	2	.254	0
1994 *Projection* >>>	143	22	2	14	2	.237	-

REBOULET, JEFF - SS/3B - BR - Age 29
Reboulet is a typical good-field no-hit utility infielder. The .258 last year was over his head, and he faces more competition for playing time in 1994.

	AB	R	HR	RBI	SB	BA	$
1992 Minnesota AL	137	15	1	16	3	.190	
1993 Minnesota AL	240	33	1	15	5	.258	1
1994 *Projection* >>>	165	21	1	13	3	.239	-

REDINGTON, TOM - 3B - BR - Age 25
At his young age, Redington has already been a prospect and then a suspect with three organizations. The Braves made him a third round pick in 1987 but waived him in 1990. Padres picked him up and got a good year from him at AA Wichita in 1991 but then obtained Gary Sheffield for their third base needs. Redington has a cloudy future.

REDUS, GARY - 1B/OF - BR - Age 37
Looked like he was over the hill through most of the 1992 season. However, he came on late in the regular season and starred in the National League Championship Series, keeping alive hopes for 1993. Redus provided the leadership and clubhouse experience the Rangers had been sorely lacking, and provided an offensive spark when he was able to play. Arthritic knees and bad hamstrings cut into that, especially at the end of the season.

	AB	R	HR	RBI	SB	BA	$
1992 Pittsburgh NL	176	26	3	12	11	.256	5
1993 Texas AL	222	28	6	31	4	.288	6
1994 Projection >>>	212	29	5	23	8	.265	6

REED, JEFF - C - BL - Age 31
Reed's collapse coincided with Joe Oliver's comeback. Don't expect much for 1994. Reed has the skills of an aging backup catcher. Over ten seasons in the majors he has averaged around 150 at bats per year with a low batting average. Don't be fooled by his six homers in 1993; for his career Reed is averaging five homers per 400 at bats.

	AB	R	HR	RBI	SB	BA	$
1992 Cincinnati NL	25	2	0	2	0	.160	-
1993 San Francisco NL	119	10	6	12	0	.261	1
1994 Projection >>>	114	9	2	12	2	.239	-

REED, JODY - 2B - BR - Age 31
A one category player, Reed's only offensive contribution is batting average. A free agent after the 1993 season, Reed is the type of marginal veteran most likely to be squeezed out of the market.

	AB	R	HR	RBI	SB	BA	$
1992 Boston AL	550	64	3	40	7	.247	5
1993 Los Angeles NL	445	48	2	31	1	.276	4
1994 Projection >>>	509	60	3	39	4	.267	7

REESE, CALVIN - SS - BR - Age 20
Cincinnati's number one draft pick in '91, out of high school. Voted the Sally League's best defensive shortstop. He's the type of player who has to bring his skills up to the level of his talent (makes spectacular plays, blows routine grounders). Reese is a good-field, no-hit shortstop who batted .212 at Double-A Chattanooga. He won't make it on defensive ability alone; Reese must hit more and show sparkling defense consistently to have a good chance.

REIMER, KEVIN - OF/DH - BL - Age 29
Scouts and outfield coaches will tell you that Reimer is a natural DH. He is however not a good enough hitter to keep that role forever. Reimer hit just .219 after the All-Star break last year.

	AB	R	HR	RBI	SB	BA	$
1992 Texas AL	494	56	16	58	2	.267	13
1993 Milwaukee AL	437	53	13	60	5	.249	8
1994 Projection >>>	446	53	15	61	3	.259	11

RENDINA, MIKE - 1B - BL - Age 23
A good hitter who took five years to reach Double-A, now maturing more rapidly. The Tigers farm has a lot like him.

RENTERIA, RICH - 2B/3B - BR - Age 32
In the Mexican League in 1992, he hit .442, slugged .741, and had an on-base percentage of .507 -- that speaks volumes about the level of play in the Mexican League. A solid defensive player, Renteria could stick and see spot duty behind Sheffield and Barberie in 1994.

	AB	R	HR	RBI	SB	BA	$
1993 Florida NL	263	27	2	30	0	.255	1
1994 Projection >>>	132	13	1	14	0	.245	-

REYNOLDS, HAROLD - 2B - BB - Age 33

Although Harold Reynolds came to Baltimore with many years of experience, the Orioles were disappointed with his baserunning blunders. After a good start last year hitting .267 in the first half, he hit only .228 in the second half. The offensive production can decline even more this year, and the years of 20-plus stolen bases are over. Don't expect 485 at bats again in 1994.

	AB	R	HR	RBI	SB	BA	$
1992 Seattle AL	458	55	3	33	15	.247	8
1993 Baltimore AL	485	64	4	47	12	.252	8
1994 *Projection* >>>	399	54	3	36	11	.251	6

REYNOLDS, R.J. - OF - BB - Age 33

Playing in Japan (.298-18-50 for Kinetsu in 1993).

RHODES, KARL - OF - BL - Age 25

Rhodes began the 1991 season as the Astros starting right fielder but couldn't hold the job. He spent most of 1991 and 1992 at AAA Tucson with limited success. Then Rhodes, who had slugged a scholarly .305 in 226 major league at bats suddenly got the bright idea to hit 30 home runs and 43 doubles for two Triple-A teams last year. GM Larry Hines acquired him in midseason from Kansas City for Paul Assenmacher, a trade that many thought made little sense at the time; by the end of the year, he was viewed as the Cubs top prospect. Rhodes was the winter frontrunner for the biggest share of the Cubs' leadoff job in 1994; he shows patience, speed and power. By the time March 30th rolls around he won't be a sleeper anymore.

	AB	R	HR	RBI	SB	BA	$
1992 Houston NL	4	0	0	0	0	.000	-
1993 Omaha AAA	365	81	23	64	10	.318	-
1993 Houston-Chicago NL	54	12	3	7	2	.278	1
1994 *Projection* >>>	202	26	4	24	4	.242	3

RICHARDSON, JEFF - IF - BR - Age 28

Richardson is just a marginal utility type player.

	AB	R	HR	RBI	SB	BA	$
1993 Pawtucket AAA	28	2	0	1	0	.321	-
1993 Boston AL	24	3	0	2	0	.208	-

RIESGO, NIKCO - 1B/3B/OF - BR - Age 27

Appeared with Montreal in 1991, and played at Double-A Memphis in 1992. Stole 104 bases in 1988-1990, but now appears to be finished.

RILES, ERNEST - IF - BL - Age 33

Veteran utilityman played all four infield positions in limited stint with Boston in 1993. His best chance is to hook up somewhere as a lefthanded pinch hitter and utility infielder. Has shown some power, especially in 1990 with the Giants, when he hit 8 homers in only 155 at bats.

	AB	R	HR	RBI	SB	BA	$
1992 Houston NL	61	5	1	4	1	.262	-
1993 Boston AL	143	15	5	20	1	.189	-
1994 *Projection* >>>	139	14	4	17	1	.208	-

RIPKEN, BILLY - 2B - BR - Age 29

Ripken provided a defensive spark to the team early in the season, but is an offensive liability. He was released after the season, but he'll be invited to spring training to try winning a job.

	AB	R	HR	RBI	SB	BA	$
1992 Baltimore AL	330	35	4	36	2	.230	1
1993 Texas AL	132	12	0	11	0	.189	-
1994 *Projection* >>>	224	22	1	20	1	.215	-

RIPKEN, CAL - SS - BR - Age 33
Ripken spent the first half of 1993 continuing to utilize an awkward stance carried over from his poor second half (.239-4-32) in 1992. He returned to a more upright approach in the second half of 1993 and appeared to return to his more powerful "old" self, batting .294-13-47 after the All-Star break.

	AB	R	HR	RBI	SB	BA	$
1992 Baltimore AL	637	73	14	72	4	.251	12
1993 Baltimore AL	641	87	24	90	1	.257	15
1994 *Projection* >>>	600	80	19	83	2	.260	15

RIVERA, DAVID - SS - BB - Age 24
Rivera has good speed but is a career .252 hitter in the low minors. The Twins have better players ahead of him.

RIVERA, LUIS - 2B/SS - BR - Age 30
John Valentin should get the lion's share of time at short. Rivera is a good late inning defensive replacement who will add nothing else. Away from Fenway, he will hit even worse.

	AB	R	HR	RBI	SB	BA	$
1992 Boston AL	288	17	0	29	4	.215	-
1993 Boston AL	130	13	1	7	1	.208	-
1994 *Projection* >>>	230	23	2	20	3	.226	-

ROBERSON, KEVIN - OF - BB - Age 26
A powerful, speedy switch hitter, Roberson blasted seven home runs in 116 at bats but looked overmatched against offspeed stuff. He rebounded from injury to earn a major league promotion in September. A swing first, ask questions later kind of hitter, he projects as no more than a fourth man in the Cubs outfield jumble.

	AB	R	HR	RBI	SB	BA	$
1992 Iowa AAA	197	25	6	34	0	.305	
1993 Chicago NL	180	23	9	27	0	.189	0
1993 Iowa AAA	263	48	16	50	3	.304	
1994 *Projection* >>>	189	25	6	28	0	.234	0

ROBERTS, BIP - 2B - BB - Age 30
A variety of injuries and clashes with teammates and management destroyed Roberts' season. Bip is a good comeback candidate in the right situation. The right situation for Roberts is a team with Astroturf. He is expected to play the outfield in 1994, because he gets so beat up playing second base.

	AB	R	HR	RBI	SB	BA	$
1992 Cincinnati NL	532	92	4	45	44	.323	34
1993 Cincinnati NL	292	46	1	18	26	.240	9
1994 *Projection* >>>	394	65	2	29	32	.285	20

ROBERTSON, MIKE - 1B - BL - Age 23
Decent prospect moving up the Chisox farm, Robertson has fair power and some speed. His main problem is that young Frank Thomas is in the way at the top of the ladder.

RODRIGUEZ, HENRY - OF - BL - Age 26
After the trade of Eric Davis, Rodriguez received an extended look in left field. Although he hit only .222, his eight home runs in 176 at bats give him the inside track for at least a platoon role in 1994.

	AB	R	HR	RBI	SB	BA	$
1992 Los Angeles NL	146	11	3	14	0	.219	-
1993 Los Angeles NL	176	20	8	23	1	.222	1
1994 *Projection* >>>	136	14	3	16	1	.221	-

RODRIGUEZ, IVAN - C - BR - Age 22
Rodriguez has the talent to have a long major league career, and his hitting improves every year. Still one of the youngest regulars in the majors, he showed some real toughness by playing with a broken cheekbone in August. Back problems still are a concern, and he appeared to have a high opinion of himself after being named to the All-Star team.

	AB	R	HR	RBI	SB	BA	$
1992 Texas AL	420	39	8	37	0	.260	
1993 Texas AL	473	56	10	66	8	.273	13
1994 *Projection* >>>	423	46	9	52	4	.276	11

RODRIGUEZ, VICTOR - 3B - BR - Age 32
OK, so this guy's got little chance to make it back to the majors, but anyone who has toiled in the minors for 17 years with only 28 major league at bats to show for it deserves a mention. Rodriguez began his pro career in 1977 and has 3786 Triple-A at bats. He hit a solid .305 and slugged .455 at AAA Scranton. He's a career .428 major league hitter, for what it's worth.

ROHDE, DAVE - IF - BB - Age 29
If he makes the Pirates' parent club, Rohde's role is utility infielder. He's hit for high averages in Triple-A, and can steal a few bases.The one place the Bucs are set is the middle infield and Rohde hasn't yet proven that he can hit anywhere but in the Pacific Coast League.

ROHRMEIER, DAN - OF/DH - BR - Age 28
Steady progress in minors, displayed some power for AAA Omaha. Best chance at majors is in 1994 with Brett's retirement. Could be part of designated hitter platoon with part-time out field play, too. In 300 at bats, Rohrmeier might get 10 homeruns, 35 RBI for Kansas City. Watch spring reports to see if he'll get that chance in 1994. He's done as much as he's going to do in minors, so it's now or never for Rohrmeier.

ROMERO, MANDY - C - BB - Age 26
Romero spent his second year at AA Carolina in 1992, hitting just .216, and then hit .228 at AAA Buffalo in 1993. He hasn't looked like a good prospect since 1990; he backed up Jerry Goff last year.

RONAN, MARC - C - BL - Age 24
Ronan is a good-field, no-hit catcher who got a September callup because the Cardinals wanted to rest Tom Pagnozzi and his surgically repaired knees. In a best-case scenario, he will be a number two catcher in the majors, but most likely he won't get more than 50 at bats. In 1993 he got one hit in 12 at bats for St. Louis.

ROSE, BOBBY - IF/OF - BR - Age 27
Rose hit .325-19-94 in Japan in 1993. He had been the Angels' starting second baseman until he was injured in the bus accident between New York and Baltimore in 1992.

ROSSY, RICO - 2B - BR - Age 30
Backup infielder capable of little with bat or glove. Won't play regularly unless most of Royals Infielders are hurt. Won't contribute offensively even if he does play regularly. Dave Howard is a better prospect on this team. Don't waste a roster spot on Rossy.

	AB	R	HR	RBI	SB	BA	$
1992 Kansas City AL	149	21	1	12	0	.215	-
1993 Kansas City AL	86	10	2	12	0	.221	-
1994 *Projection* >>>	92	12	1	10	0	.217	-

ROWLAND, RICH - C - BR - Age 27
Rowland began swinging harder at Toledo in 1992 and produced 25 home runs (his previous career high was 13). He could be starting in the majors with the right team. Detroit has too many good catchers, so there is no room for this power hitter. He would be a very valuable Rotisserie player if he lands with a team like Boston.

	AB	R	HR	RBI	SB	BA	$
1992 Detroit AL	14	2	0	0	0	.214	
1993 Toledo AAA	325	58	21	59	1	.268	-
1993 Detroit AL	46	2	0	4	0	.217	-
1994 *Projection* >>>	204	26	8	30	1	.260	4

ROYER, STAN - 3B - BR - Age 26

Royer puts up good numbers in the minors and has some ability, but the Cardinals consider him primarily a backup. He figures to stick as a reserve in 1994, but won't get a lot of playing time unless he goes to another organization.

	AB	R	HR	RBI	SB	BA	$
1992 St. Louis NL	31	6	2	9	0	.323	0
1993 Louisville AAA	368	46	16	54	2	.280	-
1993 St. Louis NL	46	4	1	8	0	.304	0

RUPP, BRIAN - SS - BR - Age 22

Drafted in the 43rd round of the 1992 draft from the University of Missouri as a roster filler, Rupp proved to be much more than that, leading the Arizona Rookie League in six offensive categories. He was ranked the league's second best prospect by Baseball America. In 1993, he produced similarly impressive numbers in the South Atlantic League. At 6'4", 190 lbs., Rupp may be too big to play shortstop in the majors, though.

	AB	R	HR	RBI	SB	BA	$
1992 Chandler R	207	34	0	40	10	.386	
1993 Savannah A	472	80	4	81	3	.320	

RUSSELL, JOHN - OF - BR - Age 33

Russell has hung on, largely because he hasn't minded being stashed on the disabled list whenever the Rangers have needed a roster spot. He hasn't been anything but a spare part since 1986, and is at, or near, the end of his career. He was bullpen coach for much of 1993, likely to have the same job in 1994.

RUSSO, PAUL - 3B - BR - Age 24

After hitting over 20 homers each year in the lower minors, Russo's 10 dingers last year at Portland in the hitting-rich PCL were disappointing. He is not regarded as a top prospect, and he has to show more to earn a good shot at a major league job.

SABO, CHRIS - 3B - BR - Age 32

Sabo has lost some speed, but his power totals are still fine and he was the only Reds player to see action in more than 140 games. Sabo was a free agent at the end of 1993; Jim Bowden's toughest decision was whether to bring Sabo back and ease Willie Greene into the big leagues or let Sabo walk and play Greene full time.

	AB	R	HR	RBI	SB	BA	$
1992 Cincinnati NL	344	42	12	43	4	.244	9
1993 Cincinnati NL	552	86	21	82	6	.259	14
1994 *Projection* >>>	488	68	18	67	8	.259	15

SALMON, TIM - OF - BR - Age 25

A great young power hitter at the beginning of a great career. Young players are prone to slumps in the sophomore year, but Salmon is a unique talent and a great long term prospect. His right field defense is a big plus.

	AB	R	HR	RBI	SB	BA	$
1992 California AL	79	8	2	6	1	.177	-
1993 California AL	515	93	31	95	5	.283	23
1994 *Projection* >>>	504	85	21	79	6	.262	17

SAMUEL, JUAN - 2B - BR - Age 33

Samuel can't hit, field, throw, or run and had the gall to complain about his lack of playing time in 1993. He'll be struggling to find a job in 1994.

	AB	R	HR	RBI	SB	BA	$
1992 Los Angeles NL	122	7	0	15	2	.262	-
1992 Kansas City AL	102	15	0	8	6	.284	2
1993 Cincinnati NL	261	31	4	26	9	.230	3
1994 *Projection* >>>	255	28	3	24	8	.254	3

SANCHEZ, REY - SS - BR - Age 26

A pesky hitter who shows signs of consistently good play but usually ends up injured, Sanchez is now behind Vizcaino as a shortstop. He may be used as trade bait but more likely he'll hang around the Cubs as a reserve. He has zero power or speed, so there's not much of an upside even if he plays regularly.

	AB	R	HR	RBI	SB	BA	$
1992 Chicago NL	255	24	1	19	2	.251	1
1993 Chicago NL	344	35	0	28	1	.282	3
1994 *Projection* >>>	260	26	0	21	1	.272	2

SANDBERG, RYNE - 2B - BR - Age 34

It would be a big mistake to discount Sandberg due to his age. His worst year in over a decade was caused almost exclusively by injuries. A prime candidate for a big rebound and a key figure in the NL Central Division, Sandberg is changing his hitting style as he gets older.

	AB	R	HR	RBI	SB	BA	$
1992 Chicago NL	612	100	26	87	17	.304	37
1993 Chicago NL	456	67	9	45	9	.309	15
1994 *Projection* >>>	529	81	17	66	13	.295	25

SANDERS, DEION - OF - BL - Age 26

Sanders could only manage a part time role in the deep Braves outfield, getting fewer at bats, hits, home runs and stolen bases than in 1992. It doesn't get any easier, as Tony Tarasco is ready for the majors. Sanders midseason complaining didn't sit well with the Braves brass and may cost him playing time in 1994. He'd play full time for most any other team, but with the Braves, Sanders again won't get more than a part time role.

	AB	R	HR	RBI	SB	BA	$
1992 Atlanta NL	303	54	8	28	26	.304	20
1993 Atlanta NL	272	42	6	28	19	.276	11
1994 *Projection* >>>	393	64	10	43	31	.281	23

SANDERS, REGGIE - OF - BR - Age 26

Lost in the disastrous 1993 season for the Reds was Reggie Sanders' very good year. There is no reason to not expect continued improvement in 1994. A 30 home run, 30 stolen base year is not out of the question.

	AB	R	HR	RBI	SB	BA	$
1992 Cincinnati NL	385	62	12	36	16	.270	16
1993 Cincinnati NL	496	90	20	83	27	.274	25
1994 *Projection* >>>	504	91	21	75	25	.280	26

SANDERS, TRACY - OF - BL - Age 24
A power hitter who has socked 34 homers in the last two years, Sanders' numbers improved dramatically when he moved from the pitching rich Eastern League to the hitter dominated Texas League.

SANTANGELO, F.P. - SS/OF - BB - Age 26
A prototypical utility player, the scrappy Santangelo moved from shortstop to the outfield. His bat is a little weak for an outfielder and he doesn't quite field well enough to keep him at shortstop.

SANTANA, RUBEN - 2B - BR - Age 24
Trading Bret Boone was made easier by Santana's emergence in '93. He progressed from the Carolina League to the Double-A All-Star Game, and could make another jump to the majors by the end of this season. Power plus speed, a good combination in the Kingdome.

	AB	R	HR	RBI	SB	BA	$
1993 Jacksonville AA	499	79	21	84	13	.301	
1994 *Projection* >>>	100	12	2	12	2	.251	0

SANTIAGO, BENITO - C - BR - Age 29
What a waste of talent. Despite decent power and speed for a catcher, he continues to insist upon swinging at every pitch thrown to him. He'll probably remain in Florida in 1994, as no suitable replacement is ready.

	AB	R	HR	RBI	SB	BA	$
1992 San Diego NL	386	37	10	42	2	.251	8
1993 Florida NL	469	49	13	50	10	.230	7
1994 *Projection* >>>	460	47	13	54	7	.244	9

SANTOVENIA, NELSON - C - BR - Age 32
Got to the majors again due to decent power at AAA Omaha, but is still just a minor league talent. Released at the end of 1993. Little or no major league future.

	AB	R	HR	RBI	SB	BA	$
1992 Vancouver AAA	281	24	6	42	0	.263	
1992 Chicago AL	3	1	1	2	0	.333	-
1993 Omaha AAA	274	33	11	42	0	.237	-
1993 Kansas City AL	8	0	0	0	0	.125	-

SASSER, MACKEY - OF - BL - Age 31
Sasser never got started and never got a chance to play regularly. He can't throw well enough to catch and doesn't hit well enough to play anywhere else.

	AB	R	HR	RBI	SB	BA	$
1992 New York NL	141	7	2	18	0	.241	0
1993 Seattle AL	188	18	1	21	1	.218	-
1994 *Projection* >>>	179	15	2	23	1	.246	0

SAUNDERS, DOUG - 2B - BR - Age 24
A little glove and a little speed, but no bat. Saunders exemplifes the Mets farm system in the mid-1990's.

SAX, STEVE - OF/DH - BR - Age 34
Had exactly the same number of at bats (119) in his rookie year. Hadn't had less than 488 since. Can he really be that bad all of a sudden? He is 34 and his lack of defense and power hurts him as a part-timer, although he can still run. May escape the Sox and steal 20 bases somewhere else.

	AB	R	HR	RBI	SB	BA	$
1992 Chicago AL	567	74	4	47	30	.236	13
1993 Chicago AL	119	20	1	8	7	.235	1
1994 *Projection* >>>	357	51	3	30	18	.267	9

SCARSONE, STEVE - 2B - BR - Age 28
Scarsone has spent parts of eight seasons in the minors with an average in the .250's. He has two homers in 133 major league at bats and will be 28 years old in 1994.

	AB	R	HR	RBI	SB	BA	$
1992 Baltimore AL	17	2	0	0	0	.176	-
1993 San Francisco NL	103	16	2	15	0	.252	0
1994 *Projection* >>>	61	8	1	7	1	.238	-

SCHALL, GENE - 1B - BR - Age 24
A fourth round pick in 1991, Schall had a solid half season at Double-A Reading (.326 batting average, .554 slugging percentage), but struggled at Triple-A. In 1992, he similarly split his season into good and bad halves at different levels. Not a star prospect, he projects as a potential replacement for Ricky Jordan as a backup firstbase/pinch hitter.

SCHOFIELD, DICK - SS - BR - Age 31
Schofield's season ended when he went down with an injury, and Tony Fernandez was acquired. Schofield never will hit for average, and he has little speed. He is one of the best defensive shortstops in the league when he's healthy, and he has surer hands than just about anyone in baseball. He may end up as a regular shortstop this year.

	AB	R	HR	RBI	SB	BA	$
1992 California-NewYork NL	423	52	4	36	11	.206	1
1993 Toronto AL	110	11	0	5	3	.191	-
1994 *Projection* >>>	267	30	1	20	6	.208	-

SCHU, RICK - 3B - BR - Age 32
Hit .270-24-79 for the Nippon Ham fighters in 1993.

SCHWAB, CHRIS - OF - BL - Age 19
Montreal's first draft pick in 1993 was compared to Harmon Killebrew as a Minnesota high school player. He signed for a $425,000 bonus, then went homerless in his pro debut. Considered a rightfield prospect, Schwab plays with the intensity expected from a former hockey player.

SCIOSCIA, MIKE - C - BL - Age 35
All those plate-blocking collisions finally caught up to Scioscia missing '92 and '93 with injuries. A comeback is unlikely.

SCOTT, GARY - 3B - BR - Age 25
After various disappointments with the Cubs, Marlins, and Reds, Scott was swapped to the Twins. He will be 26 in August, and his opportunities for a major league career are running short. He has been overmatched in major league trials.

SEGUI, DAVID - 1B - BB - Age 27
1993 was the year David Segui proved he could do a major league job. He's a hard working slick fielder who flirted with .300 for much of the season before a late slump. Not blessed with great power, Segui could produce Wally Joyner/ Mark Grace numbers in the right situation.

	AB	R	HR	RBI	SB	BA	$
1992 Baltimore AL	189	21	1	17	1	.233	-
1993 Baltimore AL	450	54	10	60	2	.273	9
1994 *Projection* >>>	323	36	6	39	2	.270	6

SEITZER, KEVIN - 1B/3B - BR - Age 32
In any business, it pays to have friends. Seitzer was let go by the Royals because of weak defense, and the Athletics wanted to use younger players, but Milwaukee GM Sal Bando always liked Seitzer and gave him a job. Seitzer can still hit; he rewarded Bando with a .316 batting average in September and hit .287 in the second half last year.

	AB	R	HR	RBI	SB	BA	$
1992 Milwaukee AL	540	74	5	71	13	.270	15
1993 Milwaukee-Oakland AL	417	45	11	57	7	.269	11
1994 *Projection* >>>	426	52	7	56	8	.269	11

SERVAIS, SCOTT - C - BR - Age 26

Servais' improvement in 1993 was not a fluke. He worked hard in the offseason to build his strength, and it paid off with 11 homers. He's best suited for a platoon role.

	AB	R	HR	RBI	SB	BA	$
1992 Houston NL	205	12	0	15	0	.239	-
1993 Houston NL	258	24	11	32	0	.244	4
1994 *Projection* >>>	203	16	6	22	2	.240	1

SHABAZZ, BASIL - OF - BR - Age 22

One of the most gifted athletes in professional baseball with one of the most interesting names, Shabazz is a marketing campaign waiting to happen. He had major college scholarship offers in baseball, football, basketball and track as a high school senior in 1991. Knee surgery cut short his 1993 season. He has great speed, but must learn to make better contact.

	AB	R	HR	RBI	SB	BA	$
1993 Springfield A	239	44	4	18	29	.297	

SHARPERSON, MIKE - 2B - BR - Age 32

Sharperson's playing time was eliminated by the arrival of Wallach and Reed, and the Dodgers will look at younger options in the infield in 1994. The Dodgers lone 1992 All-Star representative, Sharperson was a free agent at the end of 1993.

	AB	R	HR	RBI	SB	BA	$
1992 Los Angeles NL	317	48	3	36	2	.300	9
1993 Los Angeles NL	90	13	2	10	2	.256	0
1994 *Projection* >>>	186	26	2	20	2	.285	3

SHAVE, JON - 2B - BR - Age 26

A solid but unspectacular player, also a victim of the crowded middle infield situation in Arlington. Ticketed for Triple-A unless he has a tremendous spring training.

	AB	R	HR	RBI	SB	BA	$
1993 Oklahoma City AAA	399	58	4	41	4	.263	
1993 Texas AL	47	3	0	7	1	.319	-

SHEAFFER, DANNY - C - BR - Age 32

Thank goodness for expansion, otherwise the 13 years he spent in the minors would have been wasted. When he stepped in for an injured Girardi, he earned praise from everyone.

SHEFFIELD, GARY - 3B - BR - Age 25

He's only three months older than Darrell Whitmore, nine months younger than Alex Arias and a full year younger than Bret Barberie. Those guys remain "young prospects" while the "veteran" third basemen has flirted with superstardom. The only possible drawback is his fragile psyche.

	AB	R	HR	RBI	SB	BA	$
1992 San Diego NL	557	87	33	100	5	.330	40
1993 San Diego-Florida NL	494	67	20	73	17	.294	23
1994 *Projection* >>>	520	74	24	82	13	.302	30

SHELTON, BEN - OF - BR - Age 24

The Pirates' number two pick in 1987, Shelton has never lived up to expectations in the minors. However, he played pretty well in a couple of brief shots with the Pirates last season and seemed more confident against major league pitching. He doesn't seem to be in the Pirates' plans, though, and could be helped by a change of scenery. Shelton is a good defensive firstbaseman, but shaky in the outfield and struck out 100-plus times in five consecutive minor league seasons.

	AB	R	HR	RBI	SB	BA	$
1992 Carolina AA	368	57	10	51	4	.234	
1993 Buffalo AAA	173	25	5	22	0	.277	
1993 Pittsburgh NL	24	3	2	7	0	.250	-
1994 *Projection* >>>	100	10	3	11	1	.230	-

SHERMAN, DARRELL - OF - BL - Age 26

After three minor league seasons with a collective batting average near .300, Sherman was projected as the Padres' leadoff hitter in 1993. But he batted just .222 in 63 at bats and brooded when he was sent packing for Las Vegas; Sherman finished a disappointing season with a .265 batting average and just 11 extra base hits all year (no home runs). Still, San Diego is desperate for a good fielding centerfielder and for a leadoff hitter. Slap hitting Sherman is in the running for both jobs, but it's hard to project him handling the roles on an every day basis. If he didn't stick last year with a manager who supported him (Riggleman), his chances can't be any better in 1994. A platoon role is a more likely possibility.

SHIELDS, TOMMY - 2B/3B - BR - Age 29

Shields was still hanging around in case a few Cubs infielders got hurt. Sandberg and Buechele missed 74 games last year; Shields got 34 at bats.

SHIPLEY, CRAIG - 3B/SS - BR - Age 31

Other than his 12 stolen bases in 15 attempts, Shipley has little to offer. With Gutierrez, Gardner and Lopez ahead of Shipley, he has limited opportunities. His 1993 on base percentage was only .275 and his slugging percentage .326. Even with another organization, this Aussie is pegged for a reserve role at best.

	AB	R	HR	RBI	SB	BA	$
1992 San Diego NL	105	7	0	7	1	.248	-
1993 San Diego NL	230	25	4	22	12	.235	5
1994 *Projection* >>>	165	16	2	14	6	.241	1

SHUMPERT, TERRY - 2B - BR - Age 27

He could have laid down and died after the Royals acquired Gagne and Lind, but instead had his best professional season for AAA Omaha (.300-14-59-36). His power isn't transferable to the majors, but his batting average and speed may be. He'll have difficulty getting playing time for KC, but could help another major league team, particularly in a platoon role. Look for 20 stolen bases in part-time play.

	AB	R	HR	RBI	SB	BA	$
1992 Kansas City AL	94	6	1	11	2	.149	-
1993 Omaha AAA	413	70	14	59	36	.300	-
1993 Kansas City AL	10	0	0	0	1	.100	-
1994 *Projection* >>>	99	10	1	9	4	.230	-

SIDDALL, JOE - C - BL - Age 26

A non-prospect, Siddall got a brief chance with the Expos last season. He doesn't appear capable of hitting major league pitcing. Despite his decent arm, he's a third string catcher in the majors at best.

SIERRA, RUBEN - OF/DH - BB - Age 28

Even Ruben's biggest fans have to admit 1993 was disappointment. On the bright side, even in his worst season ever, he had 101 RBI and 25 steals. On the bad side, during a season in which he should have been in his prime, Sierra posted career lows in batting average, on base percentage and slugging percentage. Often the best rotisserie bargains are superstars coming back, and they don't get much more super than Sierra, often touted as Hall of Fame material.

	AB	R	HR	RBI	SB	BA	$
1992 Texas-Oakland AL	601	83	17	87	14	.278	23
1993 Oakland AL	630	77	22	101	25	.233	21
1994 *Projection* >>>	626	88	22	103	19	.271	28

SILVESTRI, DAVE - SS - BR - Age 26

Played shortstop for the gold medal-winning U.S. Olympic team in '88, the year he was drafted in the second round by Houston. May not have enough glove to make it in the majors at shortstop.

	AB	R	HR	RBI	SB	BA	$
1992 Columbus AAA	420	83	13	73	19	.279	
1992 New York AL	13	3	0	1	0	.308	-
1993 Columbus AAA	428	76	20	65	6	.269	
1993 New York AL	21	4	1	4	0	.286	-

SIMMS, MIKE - 1B - BR - Age 27

A strong minor league player, Simms has failed to impress in three major league trials. He strikes out too much (114 Ks in 414 at bats in 1993) and fields too poorly to play regularly in the majors. Still, there is an opening at first base in San Diego.

	AB	R	HR	RBI	SB	BA	$
1992 Tucson AAA	404	73	11	75	7	.282	
1992 Houston NL	24	1	1	3	0	.250	-
1993 Las Vegas AAA	414	74	24	80	1	.268	

SKEELS, MARK - OF - BB - Age 24

An 18th-round pick in 1992, Skeels hasn't hit much in two years of A-ball, but he's from Stanford, is a switch-hitter and draws an awful lot of walks. Skeels is a hard worker who will probably advance farther than his raw skills would normally allow.

SKINNER, JOEL - C - BR - Age 33

Spent the better part of last two seasons rehabbing a surgically repaired rotator cuff before returning to Double-A Canton-Akron late in 1993. 33 year-old catchers with bad throwing arms generally aren't good investments.

	AB	R	HR	RBI	SB	BA	$
1993 Canton-Akron AA	46	6	6	5	0	.239	

SLAUGHT, DON - C - BR - Age 35

Slaught is really a marvel. At an age where most catchers are retiring or being released, he keeps getting better. He has hit .300 in three of four seasons with the Pirates and his power numbers improved last season. Logic says Slaught should start slowing down but with no viable alternative in sight, the Pirates are committed to him through 1995.

	AB	R	HR	RBI	SB	BA	$
1992 Pittsburgh NL	255	26	4	37	2	.345	12
1993 Pittsburgh NL	377	34	10	55	2	.300	11
1994 Projection >>>	310	30	6	43	2	.280	8

SMILEY, RUEBEN - OF - BL - Age 25

Smiley has made slow progress through the Giants organization. He could eventually get a bench job and has some speed; just don't look for any useful hitting. He hit .300 with 24 stolen bases at AAA Phoenix in 1993, his best year ever.

SMITH, BUBBA - 1B - BR - Age 24

Acquired in a trade for Travis Buckley, Smith was the Carolina League MVP with 27 home runs and 81 RBI. Too old for Class A, he is not considered a prospect. He's a one dimensional player who struck out 109 times last year.

	AB	R	HR	RBI	SB	BA	$
1992 Peninsula A	482	70	32	93	4	.261	
1993 Winston-Salem A	342	55	27	81	2	.301	

SMITH, DWIGHT - OF - BL - Age 30

Smith took time out from his pinch hitting/part time singer role to prove he can play every day against righthanded pitching. Part of a jumbled Cubs outfield situation, his defensive shortcomings make him at best a regular platoon batter against righties. A likely candidate for a new environment in 1994, Smith will continue to flick the stick wherever he plays.

	AB	R	HR	RBI	SB	BA	$
1992 Chicago NL	217	28	3	24	9	.276	7
1993 Chicago NL	310	51	11	35	8	.300	12
1994 Projection >>>	305	44	8	35	8	.285	11

SMITH, GREG - 2B - BB - Age 26

In his second time around with the Cubs, Smith showed he can still run and hit in Triple-A. He had a peek in the majors in 1989-91 and looks like a utility player at best.

SMITH, LONNIE - OF/DH - BR - Age 38

The Orioles acquired Lonnie Smith from Pittsburgh for the stretch drive, which didn't work out as they had hoped. It appeared highly unlikely that the Orioles will resign him, and he may have difficulty finding a job. His age is now working against him, and if he does sign with someone, he will be a role player as a pinch hitter and sub outfielder.

	AB	R	HR	RBI	SB	BA	$
1992 Atlanta NL	158	23	6	33	4	.247	5
1993 Pittsburgh NL	199	35	6	24	9	.286	7
1993 Baltimore AL	24	8	2	3	0	.208	-
1994 *Projection* >>>	224	36	5	29	5	.262	5

SMITH, MARK - OF - BR - Age 23

Smith was the O's first round draft pick in 1991 and has posted solid, if not spectacular, numbers at the Double-A and Triple-A levels during the last two years. With below-average speed and defensive skills, Smith's modest home run totals are a concern, but Smith improved from just four home runs in a tough Double-A park in 1992 to 12 home runs last year. His final .280 average could have been even better but for a 8-for-66 late season slump related to an injured right shoulder. Another year at Rochester to develop a power stroke is likely.

	AB	R	HR	RBI	SB	BA	$
1992 Hagerstown AA	472	51	4	62	15	.288	
1993 Rochester AAA	485	69	12	68	4	.280	

SMITH, OZZIE - SS - BB - Age 39

Ozzie told me he had one of his finest seasons ever in 1993, but he is slipping a tad by his standards. That still makes him better than most shortstops in the game. He still hits for average and can steal bases. The starting job is his for as long as he wants it.

	AB	R	HR	RBI	SB	BA	$
1992 St. Louis NL	518	73	0	31	43	.295	26
1993 St. Louis NL	545	75	1	53	21	.288	16
1994 *Projection* >>>	537	70	1	43	20	.270	15

SNOW, J.T. - 1B - BB - Age 26

A roller coaster 1993 rookie season took Snow from the top of "who's hot" to the bottom of "who's not." He should be able to hit 20 home runs. Not in the Rafael Palmeiro, Frank Thomas, Will Clark category, however.

	AB	R	HR	RBI	SB	BA	$
1992 New York AL	14	1	0	2	0	.143	-
1993 California AL	419	60	16	57	3	.241	7
1994 *Projection* >>>	214	32	8	31	2	.253	4

SNYDER, CORY - 3B/OF - BR - Age 31

Snyder picked up 516 at bats filling in for various Dodgers who were injured, but faded badly in the second half (.246-5-25). If you are going to have someone strike out 147 times, it may as well be someone with a future like Ashley or Mondesi as opposed to a 31-year-old journeyman. If the numerous Dodger prospects flop, Snyder could retain his playing time in 1994.

	AB	R	HR	RBI	SB	BA	$
1992 San Francisco NL	390	48	14	57	4	.269	14
1993 Los Angeles NL	516	61	11	56	4	.266	9
1994 *Projection* >>>	315	37	8	36	2	.240	4

SOJO, LUIS - 2B/SS - BR - Age 28

Sojo is confined to spending his career as a backup infielder. He's a great contact hitter, but swings too weakly and doesn't place the ball well enough to be a valuable contribution. He has no speed and is average defensively.

	AB	R	HR	RBI	SB	BA	$
1992 California AL	368	37	7	43	7	.272	9
1993 Toronto AL	47	5	0	6	0	.170	-
1994 *Projection* >>>	207	21	3	21	3	.256	2

SORRENTO, PAUL - 1B - BL - Age 28

His 1992 & 1993 stats were virtually identical. In both seasons, he was practically useless against lefties, prompting the Indians to acquire Randy Milligan who hit .380 versus lefties last year. The Indians solved this right/left dilemma by aquiring switch-hitting future Hall-of-Famer Eddie Murray.

	AB	R	HR	RBI	SB	BA	$
1992 Cleveland AL	458	52	18	60	0	.269	13
1993 Cleveland AL	463	75	18	65	3	.257	11
1994 *Projection* >>>	291	42	12	43	2	.262	7

SOSA, SAMMY - OF - BR - Age 25

Sosa is the electric guitar in the Cubs orchestra, full of vibrancy and pizazz but lacking subtlety. He walks and whiffs about as much as Juan Samuel did when he was Sosa's age, not the best model when considering the chances for a long, outstanding career. But for at least the next four years or so, Sosa might be the number one candidate in baseball to make the 40/40 club. His home park and new running-oriented manager could make that happen in 1994.

	AB	R	HR	RBI	SB	BA	$
1992 Chicago NL	262	41	8	25	15	.260	11
1993 Chicago NL	598	92	33	93	36	.261	32
1994 *Projection* >>>	526	87	27	80	31	.272	31

SPEARMAN, VERN - OF - BL - Age 24

A leadoff prospect who now has 131 steals in three pro years, Spearman needs to bring the rest of his game up near the level of his speed.

	AB	R	HR	RBI	SB	BA	$
1992 Vero Beach A	276	50	0	16	33	.304	
1992 San Antonio AA	185	24	0	11	18	.281	
1993 Albuquerque AAA	185	31	0	15	11	.254	

SPEHR, TIM - C - BR - Age 27

Spehr had a chance to become the Expos' starting catcher last season after being acquired in a trade from Kansas City the previous winter. However, he didn't turn out to be the answer. Spehr has only shown power in one Triple-A season (1992 at Omaha) and won't hit major league pitching for a good average. A good defensive catcher, he looks like the Expos backup catcher going into 1994.

	AB	R	HR	RBI	SB	BA	$
1993 Ottawa AAA	141	15	4	13	2	.199	-
1993 Montreal NL	87	14	2	10	2	.230	0
1994 *Projection* >>>	100	11	2	13	2	.231	-

SPIERS, BILL - 2B - BL - Age 27

Although they won't say so for the record, Brewers insiders are pessimistic about Spiers's ability to make a full comeback from his back problems. The injury was severe, and the most strenuous infield position is an unforgiving location from which to forge a recovery. Before the injury, Spiers showed the promise of becoming one of the AL's best.

	AB	R	HR	RBI	SB	BA	$
1992 Milwaukee AL	16	2	0	2	1	.313	-
1993 Milwaukee AL	340	43	2	36	9	.238	4
1994 *Projection* >>>	246	34	2	28	7	.253	3

SPRAGUE, ED - 3B - BR - Age 26

Going into last season, Sprague was asked to hit well and play an average third base. What he did was have the third-best fielding percentage of any third baseman in the American League. Sprague has a slight uppercut to his swing that pitchers have tried to exploit, but he approaches each at bat with a level mentality. He's the third baseman of the present and should only get better with more exposure to the league.

	AB	R	HR	RBI	SB	BA	$
1992 Toronto AL	47	6	1	7	0	.234	-
1993 Toronto AL	546	50	12	73	1	.260	9
1994 *Projection* >>>	316	30	7	42	1	.260	5

STAHOVIAK, SCOTT - 3B - BL - Age 24

Stahoviak is a big man who is beginning to develop some power. He is the Twins third baseman of the future, but he may struggle for a year or two as he gets on-the-job training in the majors. It helps that he bats left and that manager Tom Kelly likes him.

	AB	R	HR	RBI	SB	BA	$
1993 Nashville AAA	331	40	12	56	10	.272	-
1993 Minnesota AL	57	1	0	1	0	.193	-
1994 *Projection* >>>	176	18	3	20	2	.248	1

STAIRS, MATT - OF - BL - Age 25

Stairs won the 1991 AA Eastern League batting title but never quite made it with the Expos. He was sold to a Japanese club last season, though he has aspirations of returning to the major leagues. He hit .250 for the Chounichi Dragons in 1993.

	AB	R	HR	RBI	SB	BA	$
1992 Montreal NL	30	2	0	5	0	.167	-
1993 Montreal NL	8	1	0	2	0	.375	-
1994 *Projection* >>>	100	11	3	13	1	.260	0

STANKIEWICZ, ANDY - 2B - BR - Age 29

1992 was his career year. Don't expect another. Stankiewicz is an OK glove, but that's about it. In Houston, Stankiewicz will have a utility role if he makes the major league roster out of spring training.

	AB	R	HR	RBI	SB	BA	$
1992 New York AL	400	52	2	25	9	.268	7
1993 Columbus AAA	331	45	0	32	12	.242	-
1993 New York AL	9	5	0	0	0	.000	-
1994 *Projection* >>>	137	20	1	8	3	.259	0

STANLEY, MIKE - C - BR - Age 30

After finally seeing good pitches in 1993, Stanley caught fire. He had career numbers in almost every offensive category. It's hard to say if he will ever have another year like last year, but once a hitter gets used to seeing strikes, he usually won't go back to swinging at bad pitches.

	AB	R	HR	RBI	SB	BA	$
1992 New York AL	173	24	8	27	0	.249	3
1993 New York AL	423	70	26	84	1	.305	20
1994 *Projection* >>>	404	56	16	66	1	.270	13

STATON, DAVID - 1B - BR - Age 25

After rehabilitating from a 1992 shoulder injury at Single-A Rancho Cucamonga for much of the season, Staton showed that he is a tremendous raw power prospect and a sleeper worth watching. Staton connected for five long home runs in just 42 major league at bats after hitting 7 home runs in just 37 Triple-A at bats. Overall at three minor league levels and in the majors, Staton hit home runs at a Ruthian rate, getting 25 homeruns in 270 minor league at bats. Expected to be fully recovered in 1994, Staton is a strong candidate in the wide open battle for the Padres' first base job despite his iron glove.

	AB	R	HR	RBI	SB	BA	$
1993 Rancho Cuca A	221	37	18	58	0	.317	-
1993 San Diego NL	42	7	5	9	0	.262	1
1994 *Projection* >>>	252	30	11	40	0	.239	4

STEINBACH, TERRY - C - BR - Age 32

Steinbach is not very durable (never more than 130 games in a season, only 104 last year), though this may ultimately serve to prolong his career (he hasn't been worn down by too much catching). His power increase seems to be legitimate; his slugging percentage the last two years were .411 and .416. Should be OK for another season or five.

	AB	R	HR	RBI	SB	BA	$
1992 Oakland AL	438	48	12	53	2	.279	12
1993 Oakland AL	389	47	10	43	3	.285	9
1994 *Projection* >>>	417	47	10	49	3	.275	11

STEPHENSON, PHIL - 1B - BL - Age 33

Had surfaced every year for four years, but never did enough to stick. Now he's strictly an injury backup who will be stored at Triple-A, if he's still in baseball.

	AB	R	HR	RBI	SB	BA	$
1992 San Diego NL	71	5	0	8	0	.155	-
1993 Omaha AAA	72	12	4	8	0	.306	

STEVENS, LEE - OF - BL - Age 26

Stevens struggled in '92, and he has yet to show that he can hit major league pitching, though he had already done fine in the minors.

	AB	R	HR	RBI	SB	BA	$
1992 California AL	312	25	7	37	1	.221	1
1993 Syracuse AAA	401	61	14	66	2	.264	-

STILLWELL, KURT - 2B/SS - BB - Age 28

Released by the Angels. Last stop is at Cincinnati before fading out of the game.

	AB	R	HR	RBI	SB	BA	$
1992 San Diego NL	379	35	2	24	4	.227	0
1993 San Diego NL	121	9	1	11	4	.215	0
1993 California AL	61	2	0	3	2	.262	-
1994 Projection >>>	282	25	2	24	5	.237	1

STINNETT, KELLY - C - BR - Age 24

His '93 average and home run ratio, in his Triple-A debut, were comparable to the norms for his four year career. A dependable catcher. Stinnett now has a .267 batting average in four minor league seasons.

STOCKER, KEVIN - SS - BB - Age 24

Stocker was a major surprise offensively after his July promotion; he batted a lusty .395 righthanded, while giving the Phils some much-needed defensive stability. Nevertheless, Stocker is a prime candidate for the sophomore jinx, at least offensively. He hit .233 at Triple-A in 1993, and was a career .253 hitter in the minors. He's so valuable defensively to the Phils that no offensive slump will be enough to earn him a seat on the bench.

	AB	R	HR	RBI	SB	BA	$
1993 Philadelphia NL	259	46	2	31	5	.324	8
1994 Projection >>>	130	17	1	12	3	.254	0

STRANGE, DOUG - 2B - BB - Age 29

Strange made the opening day roster only because he was versatile enough to play both second and third base. Injuries to just about every Ranger infielder gave him a chance to play nearly every day, and he took advantage of it. Will compete for the starting second base job or a platoon in 1994.

	AB	R	HR	RBI	SB	BA	$
1992 Chicago NL	94	7	1	5	1	.160	-
1993 Texas AL	484	58	7	60	6	.256	8
1994 Projection >>>	275	31	4	32	4	.246	3

STRAWBERRY, DARRYL - OF - BL - Age 32

When he's healthy, Strawberry is an offensive force, but he has missed most of the last two years due to serious back pain. There have been no positive indications of Strawberry's healthy return for 1994, so he must be considered a doubtful player. Even if he returns, his back injuries may force him to cut down on his swing.

	AB	R	HR	RBI	SB	BA	$
1992 Los Angeles NL	156	20	5	25	3	.237	3
1993 Los Angeles NL	100	12	5	12	1	.140	-
1994 Projection >>>	187	27	9	31	3	.224	2

STUBBS, FRANKLIN - OF - BL - Age 33

Another disappointing season for Stubbs in 1993, although his power numbers show decent productivity on a per at bat basis.

	AB	R	HR	RBI	SB	BA	$
1992 Milwaukee AL	288	37	9	42	11	.229	6
1993 Pawtucket AAA	334	47	15	58	3	.237	-

SUERO, WILLIAM - 2B - BR - Age 27

The Blue Jays have a knack of trading away their less promising prospects just before they turn into suspects. Suero hit 16 home runs and stole 40 bases for Double-A Knoxville in 1990, but after a slow start at AAA Syracuse the next year, he was gone to the Brewers as part payment for Candy Maldonado, and has hardly been heard from since then. Suero got two brief callups in 1993, one in June and one in July. He is not a .286 hitter and no longer a prospect.

	AB	R	HR	RBI	SB	BA	$
1992 Denver AAA	276	42	1	25	16	.257	
1992 Milwaukee AL	16	4	0	0	1	.188	-
1993 New Orleans AAA	124	14	1	13	8	.226	-
1993 Milwaukee AL	14	0	0	0	0	.286	-
1994 Projection >>>	100	9	1	8	1	.244	-

SURHOFF, B.J. - 3B/OF - BL - Age 29

Every year for five years, Surhoff has hit down around .200 in April and May and then proceeded to bat .280 from June 1 until the end of the year. In 1993 he had his worst start ever, but made up for it by hitting .298 after the All-Star break. Moral: trade for him on May 15, as I do every year.

	AB	R	HR	RBI	SB	BA	$
1992 Milwaukee AL	480	63	4	62	14	.252	11
1993 Milwaukee AL	552	66	7	79	12	.274	15
1994 Projection >>>	558	68	6	75	12	.266	15

SUTKO, GLENN - C - BR - Age 25

Sutko surfaced with the Reds in 1990 and 1991. Although still young, he has been labeled a good defense, no offense type of catcher, a label that became even more indelible when he hit .187 for Double-A Chattanooga. Get the idea?

SVEUM, DALE - 1B - BB - Age 30

Sveum can play all four infield positions when needed. He was considered a potential star until he broke his leg in 1988. When he doesn't play regularly, he doesn't hit well; and he hasn't been playing regularly.

	AB	R	HR	RBI	SB	BA	$
1992 Chicago AL	114	15	2	12	1	.219	-
1992 Philadelphia NL	135	13	2	16	0	.178	-
1993 Calgary AAA	163	41	8	32	2	.313	-
1993 Oakland AL	79	12	2	6	0	.177	-
1994 Projection >>>	129	16	2	16	0	.200	-

SWEENEY, MARK - OF - BL - Age 24

Hit .356 at Double-A Midland with 9 home runs. Not ready for the majors, but worth watching.

TACKETT, JEFF - C - BR - Age 28

Tackett is a candidate for the Orioles backup catching job. He has never hit very much, not even in the minors. Tackett played just 39 games although he was with the Birds all season. When Hoiles was injured, Parent was recalled and given most of the playing time. Tackett's in danger of losing the backup catching job to Parent in 1994. He had just three extra base hits in 1993.

	AB	R	HR	RBI	SB	BA	$
1992 Baltimore AL	179	21	5	24	0	.240	1
1993 Baltimore AL	87	8	0	9	0	.172	-
1994 Projection >>>	104	11	2	12	0	.210	-

TALANOA, SCOTT - OF - BR - Age 24

A torn Achilles tendon cut short what could have been a minor league-leading power year (25 home runs in 258 at bats for the Brewers' Midwest League farm). At his age, a recovery and continued improvement this year are important to his career. A pure power source in an organization needing power. He also will take a walk.

TARASCO, TONY - OF - BL - Age 23

Tarasco can do it all: hit for average and power, run, field and throw. He'd be a major league regular in almost any other organization. But, the Braves are deep and Tarasco will have to fight for playing time. Baseball America's fifth best Triple-A prospect, Tarasco has time on his side and although he may have to play musical chairs with the other Braves outfielders in 1994, the future belongs to Tony.

	AB	R	HR	RBI	SB	BA	$
1992 Greenville AA	489	73	15	54	33	.286	
1993 Richmond AAA	370	73	15	53	19	.330	-
1993 Atlanta NL	35	6	0	2	0	.229	-
1994 Projection >>>	256	34	8	29	5	.275	7

TARTABULL, DANNY - OF/DH - BR - Age 31

If he would play the whole season unhurt, Tartabull would post absolutely phenomenal numbers. But it's a safe bet he'll be on the DL part of the season.

	AB	R	HR	RBI	SB	BA	$
1992 New York AL	421	72	25	85	2	.266	18
1993 New York AL	513	87	31	102	0	.250	16
1994 Projection >>>	478	81	29	96	2	.266	20

TATUM, JIM - 1B/3B - BR - Age 26

A sentimental favorite who found a great role as a pinch hitter, Tatum got 17 hits and a grand slam as a PH. A utility infielder, he's probably not long for The Show.

	AB	R	HR	RBI	SB	BA	$
1992 Milwaukee AL	8	0	0	0	0	.125	-
1993 Colorado NL	98	7	1	12	0	.204	-
1994 Projection >>>	52	5	1	7	0	.240	-

TAUBENSEE, EDDIE - C - BL - Age 25

The guy traded for Kenny Lofton, Taubensee made expected improvement in 1993 as he established himself as a major league catcher in a productive platoon with Scott Servais. His strong arm is an asset which assures playing time. At age 25, Taubensee has room for further improvement as he reaches his prime.

	AB	R	HR	RBI	SB	BA	$
1992 Tucson AAA	74	13	1	10	0	.338	
1992 Houston NL	297	23	5	28	2	.222	-
1993 Houston NL	288	26	9	42	1	.250	4
1994 Projection >>>	283	23	7	36	1	.250	3

TAVAREZ, JESUS - OF - BR - Age 23

Yet another young Marlins' outfield prospect, Tavarez took a step back to Single-A in 1993 because the Marlins had no Double-A affiliate. But, he still has clearly fallen behind Carl Everett in the race to succeed Chuck Carr. Tavarez answered any questions about his health after a leg injury with a big stolen base year. A prolific base stealer (185 stolen bases in four years). Tavarez can run, get on base and play centerfield, so there is a major league job in his future somewhere, someday.

	AB	R	HR	RBI	SB	BA	$
1992 Jacksonville AA	392	38	3	25	29	.258	
1993 High Desert A	444	104	7	71	47	.293	

TAYLOR, SAM - OF - BL - Age 25

Taylor is a .266 career hitter after five years on the Phillies farm. A 14th round pick in 1989 out of Kentucky, he has always played just well enough to move up to the next level. He has increased his home runs every year while his batting average drops. At this point, he doesn't appear to have much of a major league future.

TAYLOR, WILL - OF - BB - Age 25
Once going places as a base stealer, now just going, going - gone.

TETTLETON, MICKEY - C/1B/OF - BB - Age 33
Tettleton is gradually shifting from catcher to outfield, a move that will lengthen his career. Now settling around .240, he won't give you average, but you can expect 25 to 30 home runs and 90 to 100 RBI.

	AB	R	HR	RBI	SB	BA	$
1992 Detroit AL	525	82	32	83	0	.238	15
1993 Detroit AL	522	79	32	110	3	.245	17
1994 Projection >>>	503	72	26	90	2	.241	13

TEUFEL, TIM - 2B - BR - Age 35
Teufel is not likely to be back in 1994 as the Padres will go with cheaper and younger infield reserves. With seven home runs and 31 RBI in 200 at bats (good totals for a middle infielder), Teufel should land a job someplace. Shea Stadium became a definite possibility now that Joe McIlvaine is back with the Mets.

	AB	R	HR	RBI	SB	BA	$
1992 San Diego NL	246	23	6	25	2	.224	2
1993 San Diego NL	200	26	7	31	2	.250	3
1994 Projection >>>	139	16	5	18	2	.236	1

THOMAS, FRANK - 1B - BR - Age 25
Look out because he's just entering his prime. The best pure hitter in the game. You should know there's something special happening when the guy's breaking records held by Shoeless Joe Jackson. Junior and Frank will be the best hitters of the 90's. It does take him a month to warm up.

	AB	R	HR	RBI	SB	BA	$
1992 Chicago AL	573	108	24	115	6	.323	34
1993 Chicago AL	549	106	41	128	4	.317	34
1994 Projection >>>	559	106	34	120	4	.320	38

THOMAS, GREG - BL - Age 22
1993 ninth round pick out of Vanderbilt, he tore up the short-season New York-Penn League in 1993. Was a fourth round pick of the Red Sox out of high school in 1990, and had his best college season as a soph (.401, 16 home runs, 71 RBI) in 1991. He has big-league size (6'-3", 205), and the Indians hope he rises through the ranks quickly.

THOMAS, SKEETS - OF - BL - Age 25
In his first triple-A season, Thomas hit about the same as he has throughout his four year pro career. Thomas has a .278 lifetime batting average. He doesn't have the speed expected of a Cardinals' outfielder and lacks the power to compensate.

THOME, JIM - 3B - BL - Age 23
The Indians' non-contender status prompted them to take their time developing Thome, and it appears to have been an effective strategy. A long time top prospect, Thome put the entire package together at Charlotte in 1993, hitting for power and average with a high number of walks in a league not noted for offense. He appeared very comfortable in his late season trial, as compared to his 1992 washout. Ready to become an impact player at the major league level.

	AB	R	HR	RBI	SB	BA	$
1992 Cleveland AL	117	8	2	12	2	.205	-
1993 Cleveland AL	154	28	7	22	2	.266	3
1994 Projection >>>	432	59	13	52	7	.281	15

THOMPSON, FLETCHER - 2B - BL - Age 25
A very good offensive second baseman, Thompson has had difficulty in the field. He gets on base very well and has stolen 76 bases in two and a half pro season but at only a 67 percent success rate.

THOMPSON, MILT - OF - BL - Age 35

His outstanding World Series performance notwithstanding, his offensive skills have begun to deteriorate. He stole fewer than 10 bases for the first time since arriving in the majors for good. Still an above-average defensive player, he might last a couple more years as a reserve.

	AB	R	HR	RBI	SB	BA	$
1992 St. Louis NL	208	31	4	17	18	.293	11
1993 Philadelphia NL	340	42	4	44	9	.262	7
1994 *Projection* >>>	294	40	4	32	12	.272	9

THOMPSON, ROBBY - 2B - BR - Age 31

In 1993, Thompson set or tied career highs in batting average, slugging, on base percentage, homers and RBI. He will be 32 years old in 1994, and injuries have held him to 128 games in each of the last two seasons. This is one case where you definitely want to look at career totals rather than last year's totals: a .260 average with 15 home runs and 60 RBI is a lot more likely than another season like 1993. He stole ten bases last year, but none after June 25th.

	AB	R	HR	RBI	SB	BA	$
1992 San Francisco NL	443	54	14	49	5	.260	13
1993 San Francisco NL	494	85	19	65	10	.312	22
1994 *Projection* >>>	477	69	16	53	8	.278	17

THOMPSON, RYAN - OF - BR - Age 26

Toronto's 13th-round pick in '87, out of high school. He is fast enough to play center (which the Mets need) and has a strong enough arm to play right, and he plays so hard that he literally knocked himself out diving for a line drive last season. On the down side, before 1992 he never batted better than .273, and that was in a short-season. Thompson made progress by cutting his swing to be more compact, generating even more power than he had with his big looping swing. Another plus: the Mets are very likely to let him play frequently, to show value from the Cone deal.

	AB	R	HR	RBI	SB	BA	$
1992 New York NL	108	15	3	10	2	.222	0
1993 New York NL	288	34	11	26	2	.250	4
1994 *Projection* >>>	480	65	17	48	7	.244	10

THON, DICKIE - 2B/3B/SS - BR - Age 35

The Brewers were his sixth major league team; Thon just keeps hanging on. Once a great talent, Thon hit only .200 and got just three of his 33 RBI after the All-Star break last year.

	AB	R	HR	RBI	SB	BA	$
1992 Texas AL	275	30	4	37	12	.247	7
1993 Milwaukee AL	245	23	1	33	6	.269	4
1994 *Projection* >>>	255	24	2	30	5	.252	3

THURMAN, GARY - OF - BR - Age 29

Once a Royals can't-miss prospect, Gary Thurman's lack of offensive production keeps him from being a regular. The Royals lost patience, and his major league future is as a role player: late inning defensive substitute and occasional pinch runner.

	AB	R	HR	RBI	SB	BA	$
1992 Kansas City AL	200	25	0	20	9	.245	3
1993 Detroit AL	89	22	0	13	7	.213	0
1994 *Projection* >>>	142	23	0	15	9	.242	2

TIMMONS, OZZIE - OF - BR - Age 23

Timmons now has 51 home runs in 1080 minor league at bats. The best long range power prospect in the Cubs organization, Timmons came on strong last season at Double-A with his first full year with a decent batting average (.284-18-58 for AA Orlando). He has always shown very good power and an intriguing batting eye; his defense is marginal.

TINGLEY, RON - C - BR - Age 34

Backup to Myers, can't hit a lick. In jeopardy of losing his job.

	AB	R	HR	RBI	SB	BA	$
1992 California AL	127	15	3	8	0	.197	-
1993 California AL	90	7	0	12	1	.200	-
1994 *Projection* >>>	106	10	1	11	1	.199	-

TINSLEY, LEE - OF - BB - Age 25

Tinsley is a very fast base stealer who has struggled at the plate. The Indians released him after 1992, and he was signed by Seattle, his third organization.

	AB	R	HR	RBI	SB	BA	$
1993 Calgary AAA	450	94	10	63	34	.302	
1993 Seattle AL	19	2	1	2	0	.158	-
1994 *Projection* >>>	100	12	2	11	2	.239	-

TOALE, JOHN - DH - BL - Age 29

Forget the 125 RBI at Class A High Desert. He's too old to be in A-ball.

TOKHEIM, DAVE - BL - Age 25

A seventh-round pick in 1991 out of UCLA, Tokheim is a high average hitter with minimal power and decent speed. He'll most likely play at Triple-A in 1994, with an outside chance of a September callup. He projects as a major league bench player at best. The Pirates have better prospects.

TOLENTINO, JOSE - 1B - BL - Age 32

Went to Japan in 1993, with unimpressive results.

TOMBERLIN, ANDY - OF - BL - Age 27

Tomberlin spent the last two months with the Pirates and showed signs of becoming a capable fifth outfielder. He can hit a little and run. However, the Pirates let him go at the end of the season. He could play in the majors if he finds the right situation.

	AB	R	HR	RBI	SB	BA	$
1993 Buffalo AAA	221	41	12	45	3	.285	-
1993 Pittsburgh NL	42	4	1	5	0	.286	-

TOVAR, EDGAR - SS - BR - Age 20

His outstanding defense carried him from short-season A-ball to Double-A in less than a year. Scouts say his glove will get him to the major leagues, probably as a second baseman.

	AB	R	HR	RBI	SB	BA	$
1993 West Palm Beach A	467	52	2	32	4	.229	
1993 Harrisburg AA	42	5	0	3	0	.262	

TRAMMELL, ALAN - SS/3B - BR - Age 36

After two injury-plagued seasons, Alan Trammell rebounded very nicely last year, even winning back his shortstop job. He had a strong finish, hitting .336 in the second half.

	AB	R	HR	RBI	SB	BA	$
1992 Detroit AL	102	11	1	11	2	.275	1
1993 Detroit AL	401	72	12	60	12	.329	21
1994 *Projection* >>>	298	47	8	41	8	.288	12

TREADWAY, JEFF - 3B - BL - Age 31

Treadway was very productive as the lefty-hitting half of a platoon for much of last year, until the Indians handed the third base job to Jim Thome. Is probably one of the worst hitters against lefties in the history of the sport (.059 in 1993). Was a free agent at the end of the 1993 season. If the price is right, the Indians could bring him back as an insurance policy on Thome.

	AB	R	HR	RBI	SB	BA	$
1992 Atlanta NL	126	5	0	5	1	.222	-
1993 Cleveland AL	221	25	2	27	1	.303	4
1994 *Projection* >>>	204	20	2	20	1	.276	2

TUBBS, GREG - OF - BR - Age 31

A ten year minor leaguer, Tubbs got a brief look when the Reds ran out of outfielders in August. He's too old to be considered a prospect despite decent Triple-A stats (.305-10-45-15).

	AB	R	HR	RBI	SB	BA	$
1993 Indianapolis AAA	334	59	10	45	15	.305	
1993 Cincinnati NL	59	10	1	2	3	.186	-

TUCKER, MICHAEL - 2B - BB - Age 21

Royals first round draft pick (1992) and US Olympian. Has been unimpressive with the glove, but hit like a first round pick (.292-15-79-24) at Class A and Double-A ball. Hits for average, power and speed. Expect Tucker to start 1994 at Memphis, with a late-1995 arrival.

TUCKER, SCOOTER - C - BR - Age 27

An aggressive receiver who again hit well at Triple-A Tucson, but again failed to hit in a late season callup with the Astros, Tucker is older than Eddie Taubensee and Scott Servais. He does not appear to have a future with the team; his best chance is with another organization.

	AB	R	HR	RBI	SB	BA	$
1992 Tucson AAA	288	36	1	29	5	.302	
1992 Houston NL	50	5	0	3	1	.120	-
1993 Tucson AAA	318	54	1	37	1	.274	
1993 Houston NL	26	1	0	3	0	.192	-

TURANG, BRIAN - OF - BR - Age 26

Former second baseman was converted to the outfield. He'll never be a star, especially in the outfield, but is a solid player with good speed.

	AB	R	HR	RBI	SB	BA	$
1993 Seattle AL	140	22	0	7	6	.250	0
1994 Projection >>>	270	36	1	18	8	.243	2

TURNER, CHRIS - C - BR - Age 25

Just another catcher, Turner was a September callup; not much to offer. He hits for a better average than Tingley or Orton. Vancouver bound.

	AB	R	HR	RBI	SB	BA	$
1993 Vancouver AAA	283	50	4	57	6	.276	
1993 California AL	75	9	1	13	1	.280	0
1994 Projection >>>	62	7	1	8	1	.247	-

TWARDOSKI, MIKE - 1B - BL - Age 29

Former Indians farmhand, about what you would expect from a minor league first baseman: can hit .280 with 10+ home runs in a good, full season.

	AB	R	HR	RBI	SB	BA	$
1993 Norfolk AAA	427	66	9	38	9	.281	

URIBE, JOSE - SS - BB - Age 35

Uribe was signed as shortstop insurance for Andujar Cedeno in 1993, but wasn't needed. His playing time has decreased in each of the last five years and he appears to be at the end of the line.

	AB	R	HR	RBI	SB	BA	$
1992 San Francisco NL	162	24	2	13	2	.241	0
1993 Houston NL	53	4	0	3	1	.245	-

VALENTIN, JOHN - SS - BR - Age 27

He is highly touted, and did pretty well in 58 games for Boston in 1992 and even better in 1993, but he is a late arrival who never hit above .270 at any level before 1992. Caveat City.

	AB	R	HR	RBI	SB	BA	$
1992 Boston AL	185	21	5	25	1	.276	4
1993 Boston AL	468	50	11	66	3	.278	11
1994 *Projection* >>>	425	50	9	53	3	.265	9

VALENTIN, JOSE - SS - BB - Age 24

A decent all-around prospect who will challenge for playing time as the older middle infield wears out, but not likely in 1994. He hit .240 with 3 home runs and 9 stolen bases for AAA Denver in 1992. With maturity he could hit .270 with 5-10 home runs and 5-10 steals in the majors, but he isn't there yet.

	AB	R	HR	RBI	SB	BA	$
1993 New Orleans AAA	389	56	9	53	9	.247	
1993 Milwaukee AL	53	10	1	7	1	.245	-

VALLE, DAVE - C - BR - Age 33

Valle turned his career around in 1993. He was a free agent at the end of the season, which might have inspired his performance. He is well-respected for his defense which will keep him in the lineup even if his 1993 hitting was an anomaly. He can still cut down runners. With Dan Wilson over in Seattle, Valle will have to find a new team to reach my projection for him.

	AB	R	HR	RBI	SB	BA	$
1992 Seattle AL	367	39	9	30	0	.240	3
1993 Seattle AL	423	48	13	63	1	.258	8
1994 *Projection* >>>	388	40	9	44	1	.238	3

VANDERWAL, JOHN - 1B/OF - BL - Age 27

VanderWal looked like a potential star with a live lefthanded bat when he came up to the majors in 1991. However, he has settled into a reserve role at first base and in the outfield. The Expos are loaded with young talent at both spots; he'll need a change of scenery to become a regular. His .118 batting average against lefties will keep him a platoon player at best.

	AB	R	HR	RBI	SB	BA	$
1992 Montreal NL	213	21	4	20	3	.239	2
1993 Montreal NL	215	34	5	30	6	.233	3
1994 *Projection* >>>	188	28	4	25	4	.246	2

VAN BURKLEO, TY - 1B - BL - Age 30

Below average first base prospect, who will remain in the minors.

	AB	R	HR	RBI	SB	BA	$
1992 Edmonton AAA	458	83	19	88	20	.273	
1993 Vancouver AAA	361	47	6	56	7	.274	
1993 California AL	33	2	1	1	1	.152	-

VAN SLYKE, ANDY - OF - BL - Age 33

Van Slyke was on his way to another fine offensive season in 1993 when he suffered a broken collarbone in mid-June. Van Slyke has suffered a succession of knee and back injuries in recent seasons, a signal that age is catching up to him;. Until some young players develop further, Van Slyke will be counted on to be the Pirates' top offensive threat.

	AB	R	HR	RBI	SB	BA	$
1992 Pittsburgh NL	614	103	14	89	12	.324	33
1993 Pittsburgh NL	323	42	8	50	11	.310	14
1994 *Projection* >>>	445	70	12	67	11	.288	19

VARSHO, GARY - OF - BL - Age 32

Strictly a pinch hitter in 1993, Varsho was released at the end of the year.

	AB	R	HR	RBI	SB	BA	$
1992 Pittsburgh NL	162	22	4	22	5	.222	2
1993 Cincinnati NL	95	8	2	11	1	.232	-
1994 *Projection* >>>	65	7	1	8	2	.238	-

VATCHER, JIM - OF - BR - Age 27

He has hit for average and power, showed on base ability and at times stolen bases, without really getting a major league shot. He may not get another.

	AB	R	HR	RBI	SB	BA	$
1992 Las Vegas AAA	280	41	8	35	2	.275	
1992 San Diego NL	16	1	0	2	0	.250	-
1993 Las Vegas AAA	293	36	7	45	3	.317	-

VAUGHN, GREG - OF/DH - BR - Age 28

We've seen the best of Greg Vaughn: solid power, but still streaky. When he's on a tear, he can hit .350 for a month, but then he always follows up by hitting .180 for a month. Vaughn did reach a new high level in 1993 and is likely to stay there for a few years.

	AB	R	HR	RBI	SB	BA	$
1992 Milwaukee AL	501	77	23	78	15	.228	16
1993 Milwaukee AL	569	97	30	97	10	.267	23
1994 *Projection* >>>	542	88	27	91	10	.251	20

VAUGHN, MO - 1B - BL - Age 26

Hitting coach Mike Easler really lifted Vaughn from prospect to star. Vaughn is one of the great hitters of the 1990's.

	AB	R	HR	RBI	SB	BA	$
1992 Boston AL	355	42	13	57	3	.234	7
1993 Boston AL	539	86	29	101	4	.297	24
1994 *Projection* >>>	540	84	28	102	4	.286	26

VELARDE, RANDY - OF/SS - BR - Age 31

Velarde, with no set position, fits the Yankee roster perfectly. A "jack of all trades" player, he will find a role in 1994.

	AB	R	HR	RBI	SB	BA	$
1992 New York AL	412	57	7	46	7	.272	11
1993 New York AL	226	28	7	24	2	.301	6
1994 *Projection* >>>	280	35	6	29	4	.275	6

VELASQUEZ, GUILLERMO - 1B - BL - Age 25

Velasquez was given an opportunity to play first (getting nearly 150 at bats after the McGriff trade) but hit just .210 with a slugging average and on base percentage under .300. With all the uncertainty involving the outfield and first base roles in San Diego, Velasquez will get another chance, but it's a crowded situation.

	AB	R	HR	RBI	SB	BA	$
1992 San Diego NL	23	1	1	5	0	.304	-
1993 San Diego NL	143	7	3	20	0	.210	-
1994 *Projection* >>>	160	14	4	22	0	.249	-

VENTURA, ROBIN - 3B - BL - Age 26

While it seems that Ventura is a mature veteran, he is in fact still young and improving. Primo defensively and durable too. The 20-point batting average drop was not a sign of things to come.

	AB	R	HR	RBI	SB	BA	$
1992 Chicago AL	592	85	16	93	2	.282	19
1993 Chicago AL	554	85	22	94	1	.262	14
1994 *Projection* >>>	575	86	20	95	2	.273	19

VERAS, QUILVIO - 2B - BB - Age 23

Veras led the minor leagues in stolen bases, and the Sally League in batting average. Named the league's best baserunner and best defensive second basemen in the Baseball America poll in 1992. And the Mets need help, though not at second base.

	AB	R	HR	RBI	SB	BA	$
1992 Columbia A	414	97	2	40	66	.319	
1993 Binghamton AA	444	87	2	51	52	.306	

VIDRO, JOSE - OF - BR - Age 19

Vidro showed a quick bat with power and good defense in R-ball after his selection from a high school in the 1992 draft. A sprained wrist slowed his development in 1993.

	AB	R	HR	RBI	SB	BA	$
1993 Burlington A	287	39	2	34	3	.240	

VILLANUEVA, HECTOR - C - BR - Age 29

The big man lost his backup catching job to Erik Pappas last season. He went to AAA Louisville and sulked. When he failed to return phone calls from Cardinals manager Joe Torre while in the minors he was released.

	AB	R	HR	RBI	SB	BA	$
1992 Chicago NL	112	9	2	13	0	.152	-
1993 St. Louis NL	55	7	3	9	0	.145	-
1994 Projection >>>	97	10	4	14	0	.192	-

VINA, FERNANDO - 2B - BL - Age 24

Vina was returned to the Mets after starting 1993 in Seattle as a winter draft pick. He stole 78 bases in his first two pro seasons. Still, he doesn't run quite as well (and doesn't even come close to hitting as well) as prospect Quilvio Veras who is coming up behind him. Vina also played shortstop, which could help him earn a major league utility job.

VITIELLO, JOE - 1B - BR - Age 23

First round pick (1991). Made excellent Double-A progress in 1993. The Royals like his power and will promote him to AAA Omaha. Still strikes out too much, but getting better. Could eventually be a big power threat. May challenge for part-time first base or designated hitter job in Kansas City by 1995.

	AB	R	HR	RBI	SB	BA	$
1992 Baseball City A	400	52	8	65	0	.283	
1993 Memphis AA	413	62	15	66	2	.288	

VIZCAINO, JOSE - SS/3B/2B - BB - Age 26

Vizcaino played a little above his head in 1993, maybe a lot. The switch hitter impressed the Cubs with his stability in the field and was no slouch from the left side of the plate. He's the frontrunner for regular shortstop duty with injury prone Sanchez as his only competitor, although there is always the Shawon Dunston variable.

	AB	R	HR	RBI	SB	BA	$
1992 Chicago NL	285	25	1	17	3	.225	-
1993 Chicago NL	551	74	4	54	12	.287	13
1994 Projection >>>	394	45	2	33	7	.266	6

VIZQUEL, OMAR - SS - BB - Age 26

Barely hit .200 in the second half and had almost as many errors (11) as RBI (12). He tried to run often but had a terrible success rate. His glove will keep him in the lineup every day, which is bad for his team's overall batting average.

	AB	R	HR	RBI	SB	BA	$
1992 Seattle AL	483	49	0	21	15	.294	12
1993 Seattle AL	560	68	2	31	12	.255	7
1994 Projection >>>	512	57	1	29	12	.264	8

VOIGT, JACK - OF - BR - Age 27

Jack Voigt finished up last year very nicely, and he may have earned a job as the 4th or 5th outfielder for 1994. He is a little older, and with the Orioles preferring to go with talented rookies like Mark Smith and Jeffrey Hammonds, Voigt's best role is as the substitute man. Voigt slugged .500, with 18 extra-base hits in 152 at bats and showed he could play all the outfield and corner positions. Voigt hit .352 against lefthanded pitching, suggesting platoon possibilities.

	AB	R	HR	RBI	SB	BA	$
1993 Baltimore AL	152	32	6	23	1	.296	3
1994 Projection >>>	100	13	2	11	2	.239	-

WAKAMATSU, DON - C - BR - Age 31
Wakamatsu hung around the majors only because he has had experience handling the knuckleball; he may never return.

WALBECK, MATT - C - BB - Age 24
Trade to the Twins will open up new opportunities. Walbeck had been cast as a shadow behind Rick Wilkins as the Cubs backup catcher. He was named the best catching prospect in the American Association. Walbeck can pop a few home runs and hit for average. Also he is good defensively.

	AB	R	HR	RBI	SB	BA	$
1993 Iowa AAA	331	31	6	43	1	.281	
1993 Chicago NL	30	2	1	6	0	.200	-
1993 *Projection* >>>	298	20	5	27	0	.251	2

WALEWANDER, JIM - 2B - BB - Age 32
Bounced around the minors and majors for years. Still has a lot of speed for his age, but he'll never win a regular job, and won't have any significant role in 1994.

WALKER, CHICO - OF/3B - BB - Age 35
Formerly a versatile utilityman and top pinch hitter, Walker wasn't any kind of hitter in 1993 and may be through. He does play just about every position except catcher.

	AB	R	HR	RBI	SB	BA	$
1992 Chicago-New York NL	253	26	4	38	15	.289	12
1993 New York NL	213	18	5	19	7	.225	2
1994 *Projection* >>>	127	12	2	13	4	.230	2

WALKER, HUGH - OF - BL - Age 24
The Royals' 1988 first round draft pick, Walker has developed slowly. He has good speed, but hasn't hit sufficiently for average while striking out too much. At least a year away.

WALKER, LARRY - OF/1B - BL - Age 27
Probably the best-ever Canadian-born position player, Gold Glove outfielder Walker was hampered by injuries and slipped a little in 1993 after looking like a potential 30/30 player in 1992. He seemed to lose some desire and appeared distracted. As the Expos look to maintain some fiscal sanity in a player payroll ready to swell, Walker was being discussed as the salary that could be traded.

	AB	R	HR	RBI	SB	BA	$
1992 Montreal NL	528	85	23	93	18	.301	34
1993 Montreal NL	490	85	22	86	29	.265	25
1994 *Projection* >>>	522	86	24	90	23	.282	29

WALLACH, TIM - 3B/1B - BR - Age 36
Wallach has been in a "slump" since late 1990. Now at the end of the line at age 36, Wallach's best case for 1994 is a platoon role with Dave Hansen.

	AB	R	HR	RBI	SB	BA	$
1992 Montreal NL	537	53	9	59	2	.223	4
1993 Los Angeles NL	477	42	12	62	0	.222	2
1994 *Projection* >>>	255	25	6	33	1	.223	2

WALTERS, DAN - C - BR - Age 27
Walters failed after being given a chance to take over the catching chores following the free agent departure of Benito Santiago. He hit only .123 against righthanders, and got sent back down. He rebounded by hitting well enough at AAA Las Vegas to earn a return to San Diego as Ausmus' backup. Walters can't really be considered a serious candidate for regular playing time despite a good glove; he has only hit well in two hitters parks, Wichita and Las Vegas.

	AB	R	HR	RBI	SB	BA	$
1992 San Diego NL	179	14	4	22	1	.251	2
1993 San Diego NL	94	6	1	10	0	.202	-
1994 *Projection* >>>	106	8	2	12	0	.229	-

WALTON, JEROME - OF - BR - Age 28

The NL Rookie of the Year in 1989. Injuries and ineffective play have marked his career since then. He has never walked or stolen enough to be a lead-off man. He does not have much power but is a good defensive replacement. He hit .313 at AAA Vancouver last year.

	AB	R	HR	RBI	SB	BA	$
1992 Chicago NL	55	7	0	1	1	.127	-
1993 Vancouver AAA	176	34	2	20	5	.313	-
1993 California AL	2	2	0	0	1	.000	-
1994 *Projection* >>>	65	9	1	4	2	.220	-

WARD, TURNER - OF - BB - Age 28

Ward was surprisingly left off the post-season roster, in favor of Rob Butler. This omission confirmed Ward's low standing on the Toronto totem pole. He will always be a backup outfielder at best. He has been given brief opportunities to play, and despite his value on the bench, he just doesn't have many moments to shine. Ward's uppercut swing hasn't produced any power numbers, and unless he changes his approach, he is destined to spend his remaining days filling in for injured players.

	AB	R	HR	RBI	SB	BA	$
1992 Toronto AL	29	7	1	3	0	.345	0
1993 Toronto AL	167	20	4	28	3	.192	-
1994 *Projection* >>>	112	15	2	17	2	.226	-

WARNER, MIKE - OF - BL - Age 23

Warner showed good speed and a fine batting eye for Single-A Durham after a similarly impressive rookie season for Single-A Macon in 1992. He'll move on to AA Greenville in 1994, but the Braves superior organizational depth makes it unlikely he'll play in Atlanta soon.

WATKINS, PAT - OF - BR - Age 21

Cincinnati's first round draft pick in 1993, Watkins was a right fielder for East Carolina University. He will be tried in center field by the Reds because of his speed.

WAWRUCK, JIM - OF - BL - Age 23

Came out of the chute as if he was going to have a super season in '93, slumped badly, and then finished strong. The former U. of Vermont soccer player showed good speed, but questionable defense. Overall he hit .297-4-44 with 28 stolen bases for AA Bowie.

WEBSTER, LENNY - C - BR - Age 29

Webster's role has been strictly a backup to Brian Harper, and now he faces the prospect of being a backup to Matt Walbeck. Webster's seniority will work in his favor, within limits. Long term, Walbeck is the guy now, but Webster can be used to help ease him in. Webster hits better than the typical backup catcher, and can slam an occasional homer.

	AB	R	HR	RBI	SB	BA	$
1992 Minnesota AL	118	10	1	13	0	.280	1
1993 Minnesota AL	106	14	1	8	1	.198	-
1994 *Projection* >>>	224	24	3	22	2	.252	1

WEBSTER, MITCH - OF - BB - Age 34

Webster's playing time went to others in 1993, with Snyder, Mondesi, Ashley and Rodriguez taking his at bats. He is still okay as a reserve with a good glove, and a little power and speed, but the youngsters will continue to erode his playing time in 1994.

	AB	R	HR	RBI	SB	BA	$
1992 Los Angeles NL	262	33	6	35	11	.267	10
1993 Los Angeles NL	172	26	2	14	4	.244	1
1994 *Projection* >>>	212	27	3	21	5	.239	1

WEDGE, ERIC - 1B/C - BR - Age 26

1993 was a rehab year for Wedge, who blew out his elbow. He has a bright future, but he'll get another year in Colorado Springs, where he hit .287 in 90 at bats while playing first base. Wedge isn't a strong defensive player and may eventually surface in the majors at another position.

	AB	R	HR	RBI	SB	BA	$
1992 Boston AL	68	11	5	11	0	.250	1
1993 Colorado Springs AAA	90	17	3	13	0	.267	-
1993 Colorado NL	11	2	0	1	1	.182	-

WEGER, WES - SS - BR - Age 23

If Jose Valentin doesn't make it as Milwaukee's shortstop, Weger might. He has developed rapidly in two pro seasons. Weger hit .291-5-53 with nine stolen bases for AA El Paso last year, after starting 1992 with a .429 average in Rookie Ball before earning a promotion to Class A Stockton.

WEHNER, JOHN - 3B - BR - Age 26

That .340 batting average he compiled in 37 games as a 1991 rookie with the Pirates seems so long ago. He has fallen from third base prospect and hometown hero (he's a Pittsburgh native) to mediocre Triple-A utility infielder.

	AB	R	HR	RBI	SB	BA	$
1992 Pittsburgh NL	123	11	0	4	3	.179	-
1993 Pittsburgh NL	35	3	0	0	0	.143	-
1994 *Projection* >>>	76	8	0	4	2	.219	-

WEINKE, CHRIS - 1B - BR - Age 21

Weinke is one of several good first base prospects in the Toronto minor league system. He is a flyball hitter who can spray the ball to the gaps and pop an occasional home run. Weinke had 17 home runs and 98 RBI at Class A Dunedin last year. Watch for him no later than 1996.

WEISS, WALT - SS - BB - Age 30

Weiss had a career year at the plate in 1993, and still didn't amount to much. At his worst, he'll revert to pre-1993 offensive form, field well enough to remain in the lineup, and ruin a team batting average. Weiss was eligible for free agency following the 1993 season.

	AB	R	HR	RBI	SB	BA	$
1992 Oakland AL	316	36	0	21	6	.212	-
1993 Florida NL	500	50	1	39	7	.266	6
1994 *Projection* >>>	377	39	1	29	7	.249	3

WHITAKER, LOU - 2B - BL - Age 36

Whitaker is now being platooned exclusively. He hit just .122 against lefties last year. Although the 1993 home run output was down sharply, Whitaker still looked good at the plate, collecting 32 doubles and actually raising his career slugging percentage. Expect more taters in 1994.

	AB	R	HR	RBI	SB	BA	$
1992 Detroit AL	453	77	19	71	6	.278	12
1993 Detroit AL	383	72	9	67	3	.290	11
1994 *Projection* >>>	421	72	14	67	4	.273	14

WHITE, DERRICK - 1B - BR - Age 24

Needing a first baseman in mid-1993, the Expos promoted White from Triple-A rather than megaprospect Cliff Floyd from Double-A. That raised eyebrows in Montreal and White didn't help matters by not producing. A wrist injury hurt his 1993 production after he turned in solid seasons at Single-A and Double-A during the previous two years. He's a strong defensive player and a decent prospect but has no chance in Montreal with Floyd on the scene.

	AB	R	HR	RBI	SB	BA	$
1993 Ottawa AAA	249	32	70	29	10	.281	-
1993 Montreal NL	49	6	2	4	2	.224	0
1994 *Projection* >>>	108	12	2	11	2	.226	-

WHITE, DEVON - OF - BB - Age 31

Offensively, he will likely re-inherit the leadoff spot in the Toronto batting order. White continues his habit of chasing pitches low and inside of the strike zone, but has occasional moments of brilliance that make his presence worthwhile. Where defense is all that counts, he's an MVP. Offensively, he's an average power hitter with great speed. No one is better at picking the right spots to run. White gets thrown out stealing less frequently that once a month. That's excellent for a man who steals thirty to forty bases a season.

	AB	R	HR	RBI	SB	BA	$
1992 Toronto AL	641	98	17	60	37	.248	25
1993 Toronto AL	598	116	15	52	34	.273	27
1994 *Projection* >>>	620	109	16	56	35	.266	27

WHITE, RONDELL - OF - BR - Age 22

Another in the Expos' bevy of outstanding prospects, White can do it all, hitting for average and power while driving in runs. White has hit above .300 at three different minor league levels over the last two seasons, including a .380 mark for AAA Ottawa last year. The Expos also like his advanced instincts for a player so young. He's ready to play in the majors and will this year if the Expos clear a spot in the outfield by dealing Larry Walker or Marquis Grissom. Think Andre Dawson to get an idea of White's potential.

	AB	R	HR	RBI	SB	BA	$
1993 Harrisburg AA	372	72	12	52	21	.328	
1993 Ottawa AAA	150	28	7	32	10	.380	
1993 Montreal NL	73	9	2	15	1	.260	1
1994 *Projection* >>>	278	36	5	31	9	.267	7

WHITEN, MARK - OF - BB - Age 27

The Cardinals acquistion of Whiten from Cleveland for pitcher Mark Clark in spring training proved to be one of the steals of 1993. Long noted for having one of the strongest outfield arms in the game, Whiten finally showed his offensive potential in St. Louis. Whiten led the Cardinals in home runs last year and his four homer, 12 RBI game late last season speaks volumes about his potential.

	AB	R	HR	RBI	SB	BA	$
1992 Cleveland AL	508	73	9	43	16	.254	13
1993 St. Louis NL	562	81	25	99	15	.253	20
1994 *Projection* >>>	518	72	17	71	13	.252	16

WHITMORE, DARRELL - OF - BL - Age 25

Whitmore got off to a hot start in the PCL in 1993, then struggled mightily in an extended major league trial. This is a guy who, in 1992, as a Class A Indians' prospect, was clearly the third best (and the oldest) prospect in the starting outfield (the Ramirez boys were the other two.) Whitmore will probably be handed the starting right field job in 1994.

	AB	R	HR	RBI	SB	BA	$
1992 Kinston A	443	71	10	52	17	.280	
1993 Florida NL	250	24	4	19	4	.204	-
1994 *Projection* >>>	425	51	9	45	9	.274	12

WILKERSON, CURTIS - IF - BB - Age 32

Wilkerson couldn't repeat his 1992 mini-comeback success; he was slowed by an injury nearly all year in 1993. He won't play much behind Gagne, Lind, et al. He has better chance with another club and could get 10 or more stolen bases in a limited playing role.

	AB	R	HR	RBI	SB	BA	$
1992 Kansas City AL	296	27	2	29	18	.250	9
1993 Kansas City AL	28	1	0	0	2	.143	-
1994 *Projection* >>>	144	13	1	13	7	.226	0

WILKINS, RICK - C - BL - Age 26

Along with Sammy Sosa, Wilkins is the bedrock for any Cub assault in the next few seasons. His strength with his compact swing indicates he will detonate bombs off righties for the next several years. With a great release, Wilkins is a top notch defensive catcher and an All-Star who has the makeup to continue improving and become a team leader. Everyone will predict a decline after 1993's peak, which is just the way he likes it.

	AB	R	HR	RBI	SB	BA	$
1992 Chicago NL	244	20	8	22	0	.270	5
1993 Chicago NL	446	78	30	73	2	.303	21
1994 *Projection* >>>	428	49	20	62	3	.270	15

WILLIAMS, BERNIE - OF - BB - Age 25

The trade of Roberto Kelly showed a big vote of confidence for Williams as the everyday center fielder in 1993 and for the future. Bernie has power from both sides of the plate, with good speed and excellent strike zone judgment. He thrived when moved down from first to sixth in the batting order. With no demands on him except that he try to drive the ball in every plate appearance, Williams hit .312 in the number six slot and actually began stealing more bases.

	AB	R	HR	RBI	SB	BA	$
1992 Columbus AAA	363	68	8	50	20	.306	
1992 New York AL	261	39	5	26	7	.280	8
1993 New York AL	567	67	12	68	9	.268	14
1994 *Projection* >>>	540	69	10	61	11	.266	11

WILLIAMS, CARY - OF - BR - Age 26

Williams has a little power, a little speed and a powerful arm. He has never hit for average and took a giant step backwards in 1993, hitting just .216 for AAA Scranton on the Phillies' farm.

WILLIAMS, EDDIE - C - BR - Age 29

Williams hasn't hit much in his professional career and was hampered last season by injuries suffered in an automobile accident. However, the Cardinals still believe Williams has the offensive and defensive tools to be a decent catcher if he ever gets a chance.

WILLIAMS, GEORGE - C - BB - Age 24

A year ago, Oakland was believed to have some of the best catching prospects around -- Henry Mercedes, Izzy Molina, Eric Helfand. That guy who batted .304 at Class A Madison in '92 wasn't exactly chopped liver, and Williams followed it up by beating Helfand out of a catching job at AA Huntsville. His offense is made even more impressive by the fact that he walked more than he struck out in his Double-A debut. The A's now consider Williams a prospect and sent him to winter ball.

WILLIAMS, GERALD - OF - BR - Age 27

With the Yankees importing a big-name outfielder/DH or two every year, Williams has effectively been ruled out of the regular lineup. Manager Buck Showalter would have been happy to use Gerald as a platooner against lefty pitching, or even something bigger, but it wasn't practical to have Williams play if it meant having a big-bucks superstar sit and watch. Williams is now just a backup/reserve, not a prospect, but he still has a great combination of speed, power, and athletic presence on the field.

	AB	R	HR	RBI	SB	BA	$
1992 New York AL	27	7	3	6	2	.296	1
1993 Columbus AAA	336	53	8	38	29	.283	-
1993 New York AL	67	11	0	6	2	.149	-
1994 *Projection* >>>	100	14	2	12	5	.252	1

WILLIAMS, KEITH - OF - BR - Age 21

Drafted in the seventh round in 1993 out of Clemson, Williams finished in the top three in the Northwest League in all three Triple Crown categories, for the Giants' Everett farm. He has good speed (21 stolen bases), but may be limited to left field on defense.

WILLIAMS, MATT - 3B - BR - Age 28

One of the premier sluggers in the game today, Williams has hit 125 homers over the last four seasons. Bonds had a lot to do with Williams' 1993 resurgence: not Barry Bonds, who was supposed to "protect" Williams in the lineup, but hitting coach *Bobby* Bonds, who can count Williams as one of his top accomplishments of the year. Williams had averaged close to one strikeout for every hit over the first six years of his career; last year he had 170 hits and only 80 strikeouts.

	AB	R	HR	RBI	SB	BA	$
1992 San Francisco NL	529	58	20	66	7	.227	13
1993 San Francisco NL	579	105	38	110	1	.294	26
1994 *Projection* >>>	564	84	31	93	4	.269	23

WILLIAMS, REGGIE - OF - BB - Age 27
Williams is a good defensive outfielder with base-stealing speed. He probably won't hit enough to win a major league job, but he has tremendous speed. He stole 50 bases for Vancouver in 1993.

WILSON, BRANDON - SS - BR - Age 25
Chicago's 18th-round pick in 1990, out of the University of Kentucky. His maturity shows in his leadership and take-charge attitude. He was protected from expansion draft but didn't get a September callup. A good defensive shortstop who can hit a little and steal some bases, he would probably get a shot now if Ozzie Guillen went down, but will get a year at Triple-A if Ozzie's healthy. He hit .270-2-48 with 43 stolen bases at AA Birmingham in 1992.

WILSON, CRAIG - IF/OF - BR - Age 29
Wilson missed part of 1993 with unspecified personal problems, and was a mediocre singles hitter when he did play. He's a marginal major leaguer with some speed, no power. Unsettled Royals 3B picture gives Wilson a chance, but he's the longest shot of all candidates.

	AB	R	HR	RBI	SB	BA	$
1992 St. Louis NL	106	6	0	13	1	.311	1
1993 Kansas City AL	49	6	1	3	1	.265	-
1994 *Projection* >>>	73	6	1	8	1	.252	-

WILSON, DAN - C - BR - Age 25
Seattle will provide a fresh start and a big opportunity for this defensive wizard, Cincinnati's No. 1 draft pick in 1990. He stuck with the Reds at the end of spring training 1993, but hardly played until sent to AAA Indianapolis in June. At Indy, he hit .262 with one homer and 17 RBI in 191 at bats.

	AB	R	HR	RBI	SB	BA	$
1992 Nashville AAA	366	27	4	34	1	.251	
1992 Cincinnati NL	25	2	0	3	0	.360	-
1993 Cincinnati NL	76	6	0	8	0	.224	-
1994 *Projection* >>>	312	27	1	34	1	.238	-

WILSON, GLENN - OF - BR - Age 35
Yes, it was that same old Glenn Wilson you saw pop up in Pirates' box score for a while last summer. After retiring from Atlanta's AAA Richmond farm club and sitting out all of 1992, Wilson made the Pirates' AAA Buffalo club out of spring training. Though he had a decent 1993 as a part-time player with Buffalo, he was completely overmatched against major league pitching. His career as a big leaguer is certainly over now.

WILSON, NIGEL - OF - BL - Age 24
The first pick in the expansion draft, Wilson is ticketed for stardom by the Marlins. But wait. He didn't dominate in the hitting-rich PCL in 1993, and has had lots of trouble judging the strike zone. He struck out practically every time up in a late season major league trial, and struggled with asthma in the South Florida humidity. Only 24, he still might pull it together, but don't expect him to win the major league left field job in the spring. A torn quadricep muscle prevented him from playing winter ball, further hindering his progress.

	AB	R	HR	RBI	SB	BA	$
1992 Knoxville AA	521	85	26	69	13	.274	
1993 Edmonton AAA	370	66	17	68	8	.292	
1993 Florida NL	16	0	0	0	0	.000	-
1994 *Projection* >>>	150	20	5	19	2	.268	2

WILSON, WILLIE - OF - BB - Age 38
1993 was not exactly the disastrous season everyone in Chicago says it was. Wilson joined the Cubs to provide some leadoff hitting, leadership and defense; two out of three ain't bad. Maligned as a malcontent because he was sick of watching bad baseball, Wilson should be back as a defensive replacement for the final year of his contract.

	AB	R	HR	RBI	SB	BA	$
1992 Oakland AL	396	38	0	37	28	.270	15
1993 Chicago NL	221	29	1	11	7	.258	2
1994 *Projection* >>>	151	17	1	12	8	.260	2

WIMMER, CHRIS - 2B - BR - Age 23

Wimmer was an Olympic shortstop who switched to second base in 1993 and set a California League record for fielding percentage. He also stole 49 bases and was the MVP of the San Jose Giants.

WINFIELD, DAVE - OF - BR - Age 42

Like the Energizer bunny, Dave Winfield keeps going and going. Many people used to believe Carlton Fisk couldn't come back and have another good year, but he surprised many and came back for about ten years. Winfield is the same position. He is an athlete who stays in shape, and the conditioning enables him to continue having good years.

	AB	R	HR	RBI	SB	BA	$
1992 Toronto AL	583	92	26	108	2	.290	26
1993 Minnesota AL	547	72	21	76	2	.271	14
1994 Projection >>>	462	57	16	63	2	.252	11

WINNINGHAM, HERM - OF - BL - Age 32

Strictly a platoon player who does nothing especially well, Winningham played at AAA Pawtucket and AAA Norfolk last year, hitting .254 with 15 stolen bases overall.

WITKOWSKI, MAT - 2B - BR - Age 24

His 1993 season at AAA Las Vegas (.283-1-35-10 in a hitters' haven) typified this player -- unspectacular. He could challenge for the Padres' second base job, but he really doesn't offer anything more than Jeff Gardner.

WITMEYER, RON - 1B - BL - Age 26

Has failed to hit for average in three PCL seasons, a condemnation for a first baseman. And Witmeyer doesn't have enough power to compensate, either. Rapidly becoming a former prospect.

WOLAK, JERRY - OF - BR - Age 23

A high average, high speed outfielder at least a year away from the White Sox. Hit .305-9-64-16 at Double-A in '93.

WOLFE, JOEL - OF - BR - Age 23

Wolfe got 300 at bats in the California League last year, enough to qualify for (and win) the batting title (.350 average). He kept hitting well after he advanced to Double-A, but is still a year or two away from Oakland.

WOMACK, TONY - SS - BL - Age 24

The speedy little shortstop made an improbable rise to the majors in 1993. He began the season with Single-A Salem but ended it with a September promotion to Pittsburgh. Womack stole 49 bases in the minors last season, and two more for Pittsburgh. He's far from a polished hitter, though, and needs at least one full season in Triple-A.

WOOD, TED - OF - BL - Age 27

A 1988 U.S. Olympian, Wood never lived up to expectations in San Francisco's organization. He was dealt to Montreal last season but doesn't have much of a chance of making the majors as the Expos are overstocked with outfielders. To move from the Giants to the overloaded Expos wasn't good for Wood's career. Time is running out.

	AB	R	HR	RBI	SB	BA	$
1992 San Francisco NL	58	5	1	3	0	.207	-
1993 Ottawa AAA	231	39	1	21	12	.255	-
1993 Montreal NL	26	4	0	3	0	.192	-

WOODS, TYRONE - OF - BR - Age 24

Woods has moved up a notch each season and has shown power at every stop. The Expos' collection of good young outfielders will keep him in in Triple-A this year.

WOODSON, TRACY - 3B - BR - Age 31

Woodson resurrected his career in 1992 but didn't do much as a reserve first baseman / third baseman last season. A journeyman who will struggle to stay in the majors, he isn't in the Cardinals' plans for 1994.

	AB	R	HR	RBI	SB	BA	$
1992 St. Louis NL	114	9	1	22	0	.307	2
1993 St. Louis NL	77	4	0	2	0	.208	-
1994 Projection >>>	76	5	0	8	0	.257	-

WOOTEN, SHAWN - 1B/3B/DH - BR - Age 21

A catcher at Mount San Antonio Junior College, Wooten was drafted in last year's 18th round. Switching positions didn't affect him at the plate one bit, for he led the Appalachian League in batting. If he finds a position, he's a prospect down the road for the Tigers.

WORTHINGTON, CRAIG - 3B - BR - Age 28

Worthington's Triple-A (International League) MVP award is five years old, and two organizations removed. He can still be a steady third baseman and run producer, but it will be in the minors unless a big league club has an emergency.

WRONA, RICK - C - BR - Age 30

A perennial third string catcher. If he plays he will hit about .200 with no power. Not what you want.

	AB	R	HR	RBI	SB	BA	$
1993 Nashville AAA	184	24	3	22	0	.212	-
1993 Chicago AL	8	0	0	1	0	.125	-

YELDING, ERIC - IF/OF - BR - Age 29

A fast outfielder and former shortstop, and a Cubs pinch-runner in 1993, Yelding played second base when Sandberg was hurt mid-way through September. He's unlikely to make the Cubs roster in 1994.

	AB	R	HR	RBI	SB	BA	$
1993 Chicago NL	108	14	1	10	3	.204	-
1994 Projection >>>	104	11	1	8	3	.223	-

YOUNG, DMITRI - 3B - BB - Age 20

At the tender age of 19, Young wound up at AA Arkansas last year. He owns a powerful bat and, despite his size, good quickness and agility. Young, a first round pick in 1991, has an iron glove and moved from third base to first base as he progressed to the Double-A level. He has moved through the minors quickly and could be in the majors by 1995.

	AB	R	HR	RBI	SB	BA	$
1992 Springfield A	493	74	14	72	14	.310	
1993 St. Petersburg A	270	31	5	43	3	.315	
1993 Arkansas AA	166	13	3	21	4	.247	

YOUNG, ERIC - 2B - BR - Age 26

What can you say about a guy who is the first batter at the first home game ever and hits a home run? Nothing, except he waited 460-plus at bats to hit his next two, in the last home game. Young started the season at second base, where he committed most of his 18 errors, then moved to left field for the second half, where he'd played in college. Young led the team in steals, and stole the hearts of the fans, too. His great speed will create value somewhere in 1994.

	AB	R	HR	RBI	SB	BA	$
1992 Los Angeles NL	132	9	1	11	6	.258	2
1993 Colorado NL	490	82	3	42	42	.269	21
1994 Projection >>>	289	44	2	25	23	.267	12

YOUNG, ERNIE - OF - BR - Age 24

The complete package -- hits for average and power, runs the bases well, gets on base, plays well in center field. The only things holding him back during his first three pro seasons were injuries. Cutting down his swing also helped last year. His dropoff in Double-A ball indicates he'll need to start '94 at that level, but by the end of '95, he should be in Oakland.

YOUNG, GERALD - OF - BB - Age 29

Once valuable for his exceptional speed, Young can no longer get on base enough, and he lacks the skills in other departments to have a chance to play regularly in the majors. If his hitting somehow magically reappears, Young has value for his stolen bases, but don't count on him returning to the majors.

	AB	R	HR	RBI	SB	BA	$
1992 Houston NL	76	14	0	4	6	.184	-
1993 Indianapolis AAA	103	15	1	6	7	.301	-
1993 Colorado NL	19	5	0	1	0	.053	-
1994 Projection >>>	59	8	0	5	5	.207	-

YOUNG, KEVIN - 1B - BR - Age 24

Of the three rookies in the Pirates' regular lineup last year, Young had the biggest billing. However, his production was way behind that of Carlos Garcia and Al Martin. Young made a good transition from minor league third baseman to major league first baseman, flashing Gold Glove form. However, he'll have to shorten his swing if he's going to hit major league pitching. The talent is still there, and his confidence is still intact. Young is one of the players most likely to be underrated at the beginning of the 1994 season.

	AB	R	HR	RBI	SB	BA	$
1992 Buffalo AAA	490	91	8	65	18	.314	
1992 Pittsburgh NL	7	2	0	4	1	.571	-
1993 Pittsburgh NL	449	38	6	47	2	.236	2
1994 *Projection* >>>	457	46	6	56	2	.263	2

YOUNT, ROBIN - OF - BR - Age 38

For three consecutive years, Yount has fallen into a deep slump sometime during the season. Last year he hit just .236 in the second half. Still, he occasionally shows flashes of that old brilliance that will put him in the Hall of Fame.

	AB	R	HR	RBI	SB	BA	$
1992 Milwaukee AL	557	71	8	77	15	.264	16
1993 Milwaukee AL	454	62	8	51	9	.258	9
1994 *Projection* >>>	446	60	7	53	7	.248	8

ZAMBRANO, EDDIE - 1B/OF - BR - Age 28

A darkhorse bid for the 1994 "All-Z" team, Zambrano was a Triple-A MVP at an advanced age in 1993, producing 32 home runs and 115 RBI; he's been in the minors since 1985. He now has two consecutive seasons indicating that he could hit 15 or 20 homers in the majors. The Cubs need to cut costs and if a job opens at firstbase, Zambrano may get first shot there or in the outfield.

	AB	R	HR	RBI	SB	BA	$
1993 Iowa AAA	469	95	32	115	10	.303	-
1993 Chicago NL	17	1	0	2	0	.294	-

ZAUN, GREGG - C - BB - Age 22

Rick Dempsey's nephew is an excellent defensive catcher who ended the season on an offensive roll. The only drawback is his size; he's listed at 5'9" and 170 pounds, but looks more like a jockey. Scouts say his defensive skills are already near the major league level, and some of the long-range talk has Zaun taking over at catcher when Chris Hoiles moves to first base or DH in a few years to lengthen his career.

ZEILE, TODD - 3B - BR - Age 28

Few players had a bigger turnaround in 1993 than Zeile. He struggled so much in 1992 that he was sent back to the minors for three weeks. However, he bounced back with his biggest season and drove in 100 runs for the first time. He now seems to be over the hump and ready to live up to his big potential.

	AB	R	HR	RBI	SB	BA	$
1992 St. Louis NL	439	51	7	48	7	.257	10
1993 St. Louis NL	571	82	17	103	5	.277	17
1994 *Projection* >>>	526	71	13	81	8	.272	17

ZINTER, ALAN - C/1B - BB - Age 25

The Mets' first round draft pick in 1989 from the University of Arizona, Zinter raised his batting average 39 points in his third Double-A season and emerged as a home run threat. He has also improved his strike zone judgment, as his strikeout/walk ratio has dropped from 1.7 to 1.1. The question is whether he'll take two or three years at the Triple-A level to show he can hit enough for a major league chance. He has struggled defensively, explaining the work at first base.

	AB	R	HR	RBI	SB	BA	$
1992 Binghamton AA	431	63	16	50	0	.223	
1993 Binghamton AA	432	68	24	87	1	.262	

ZOSKY, EDDIE - SS - BR - Age 26

Toronto's first pick in 1989, out of Fresno State. In three years at Triple-A, Zosky has gone steadily downhill. He has shown nothing in his brief major league trials (34 at bats) and simply isn't making progress.

ZUBER, JON - 1B/OF - BL - Age 24

A natural hitter, Zuber has averaged .306 over his first two pro seasons. He has 56 doubles, but only nine home runs in 788 pro at bats. At his age, it's a big concern that he has yet to play above Single-A. Also, he's a man without a position, as he has been shuttled between first base, outfield and designated hitter. Zuber projects as a major league bench player.

ZUPCIC, BOB - OF - BR - Age 27

Zupcic has taken a nosedive since teasing his fans with a .328 batting average at the All-Star break in 1992. When Jeff McNeely arrives, probably in 1994, Zupcic will become a spare part.

	AB	R	HR	RBI	SB	BA	$
1992 Boston AL	392	46	3	43	2	.276	7
1993 Boston AL	286	40	2	26	5	.241	1
1994 *Projection* >>>	277	36	2	28	3	.256	2

ABBOTT, JIM - TL - Age 26
Abbott's chance to become the number one pitcher of the Yankee staff ended prematurely in 1993. By July, he'd lost confidence in himself. He has the skills to win, and it's still early enough in his career to improve.

	W	SV	ERA	IP	H	BB	SO	BPI	$
1992 California AL	7	0	2.77	211	208	68	130	1.31	11
1993 New York AL	11	0	4.37	214	221	73	95	1.37	6
1994 *Projection* >>>	12	0	3.73	216	214	69	112	1.31	10

ABBOTT, KYLE - TL - Age 26
His disastrous year in 1992 (1-14) cost him the organizations' confidence. Despite a decent year at Triple-A in 1993, he received no recall to the majors. Abbott has a solid repertoire of power and offspeed pitches, but his growth has been stunted the last two seasons. Getting out of the Phils' organization now, he's still young and talented enough to make it at the major league level, even if he has to work in Japan for a while.

	W	SV	ERA	IP	H	BB	SO	BPI	$
1992 Philadelphia NL	1	0	5.13	133	147	45	88	1.43	-
1993 Scranton AAA	12	0	3.95	173	163	62	109	1.30	

ABBOTT, PAUL - TR - Age 26
Former Twins prospect who turns into a pumpkin every time he's called up to the majors. Running out of chances; he doesn't even dominate at the minor league level anymore. Has had shoulder problems. Granted free agency at the end of 1993.

	W	SV	ERA	IP	H	BB	SO	BPI	$
1992 Minnesota AL	0	0	3.27	11	12	5	13	1.54	-
1993 Cleveland AL	0	0	6.38	18	19	11	7	1.66	-
1994 *Projection* >>>	0	0	5.44	19	18	12	10	1.60	-

ACKER, JIM - TR - Age 35
Just another ex-major leaguer playing out the string at Triple-A in 1993.

	W	SV	ERA	IP	H	BB	SO	BPI	$
1992 Seattle AL	0	0	5.28	30	45	12	11	1.86	-
1993 Oklahoma City AAA	0	0	8.31	4	7	4	2	2.75	

ACRE, MARK - TR - Age 25
The 6'8", 240-pound Acre could become one of the biggest bargains in baseball. An undrafted free agent signed for a $500 bonus, he made as much progress as any pitcher in the Oakland organization in '93. He had two saves in his first season and a half as a pro, then 30 last year. He was virtually unhittable in the Midwest League, and nearly as good in the Southern League. The Athletics have had Dave Duncan working with Acre on a forkball. Acre ran into a little trouble in the 1993 Arizona fall league but remains an exciting prospect.

	W	SV	ERA	IP	H	BB	SO	BPI	$
1993 Madison A	0	20	0.29	31	9	13	41	0.70	
1993 Huntsville AA	1	10	2.42	22	22	3	21	1.11	

ADAMS, WILLIE - TR - Age 21
The second of two pitchers drafted by Oakland in the first round last June. He signed for $240,000. Late in his career at Stanford, he was weakened by a virus. The Athletics are trying to get him to gain weight on his 6'7", 205-pound frame.

AGOSTO, JUAN - TL - Age 36
Agosto got bombed and released early. He's through.

	W	SV	ERA	IP	H	BB	SO	BPI	$
1992 St. Louis NL-Seattle AL	2	0	6.12	50	66	12	25	1.56	-
1993 Houston NL	0	0	6.00	6	8	0	3	1.33	-
1993 Tucson AAA	7	3	5.29	51	66	29	33	1.86	

AGUILERA, RICK - TR - Age 32
Aguilera is one of the top closers in baseball. His setup relievers were worse in '93 than in '92, a factor that cut down the number of saves.

	W	SV	ERA	IP	H	BB	SO	BPI	$
1992 Minnesota AL	2	41	2.84	67	60	17	52	1.16	34
1993 Minnesota AL	4	34	3.11	72	60	14	59	1.03	34
1994 Projection >>>	3	37	2.96	70	58	17	57	1.07	36

AHERN, BRIAN - TR - Age 25
Gradual minor league progress stunted at Double-A. May be better in relief role; he doesn't quite have starter stamina, or enough pitches to go through the order a second and third time. Will stay at Triple-A in '94.

	W	SV	ERA	IP	H	BB	SO	BPI	$
1993 Memphis AA	4	0	5.34	97	113	46	63	1.63	
1993 Omaha AAA	1	0	5.68	19	18	13	16	1.63	

AKERFELDS, DARREL - TR - Age 31
Pitched well for the Rangers in 1989 and the Phillies in 1990, but now he's about done.

	W	SV	ERA	IP	H	BB	SO	BPI	$
1992 Buffalo AAA	0	1	4.18	32	34	17	14	1.58	
1993 Syracuse AAA	3	0	4.36	64	68	30	34	1.53	

ALDRED, SCOTT - TL - Age 25
If this hard thrower had ever been able to find the strike zone, pitching poor Detroit and Colorado would have never given up on him. One thing in his favor is he's still young enough to turn his career around.

	W	SV	ERA	IP	H	BB	SO	BPI	$
1992 Detroit AL	3	0	6.78	65	80	33	34	1.74	-
1993 Colorado-Montreal NL	1	0	9.00	12	19	10	9	2.42	-
1994 Projection >>>	2	0	5.98	32	40	15	19	1.71	-

ALLEN, RONNIE - TR - Age 23
A third round pick in 1991, Allen has had absolutely no success above Single-A. His finesse stuff was enough for him to excel in A-ball, but higher level hitters have made a nibbler out of him. He needs to show dramatic improvement soon or he will join the Phils' long list of wasted early round draft picks. Had a 4.45 ERA at AA Reading and a 5.18 at AAA Scranton in 1993, giving up more than a hit per inning overall.

ALEXANDER, GERALD - TR - Age 26
Things have gone from bad to worse for Alexander. His failure at the major league level in 1991 impaired his confidence. Before that, he was dominant in the low minors. If he gets his curveball over for strike one, he's tough; if he misses, he's in deep fondue. Was in the Indians organization at the end of 1993.

	W	SV	ERA	IP	H	BB	SO	BPI	$
1992 Texas AL	1	0	27.00	1	5	1	1	3.59	-
1993 Oklahoma City AAA	1	0	9.25	24	40	9	13	2.04	

ALLISON, DANA - TL - Age 27
Allison surfaced in the majors in 1991, but he failed then and didn't pitch well at Triple-A in '93. A longshot.

	W	SV	ERA	IP	H	BB	SO	BPI	$
1992 Huntsville AA	4	1	2.93	61	51	5	40	0.91	
1992 Tacoma AAA	2	0	4.84	44	63	17	17	1.79	
1993 Tacoma AAA	3	0	4.48	62	75	19	30	1.51	

ALVAREZ, TAVO - TR - Age 22
If not for an expanding waistline and a ballooning ERA at Triple-A, Alvarez would have been called up to the Expos last season. He has a live fastball, a good curveball and a circle change that is getting better. Alvarez was 17-5 with a combined 1.84 ERA between Single-A and Double-A in 1992. Likely to get a callup in 1994.

	W	SV	ERA	IP	H	BB	SO	BPI	$
1992 West Palm Beach A	13	0	1.49	139	124	24	83	1.07	
1992 Harrisburg AA	4	0	2.85	47	48	9	42	1.06	
1993 Ottawa AAA	7	0	4.22	140	163	55	77	1.55	

ALVAREZ, WILSON - TL - Age 24

Alvarez "finally" arrived in 1994, despite a major league-leading 122 walks allowed. At age 24, he has oodles of time to develop, and is very likely to get better as he matures -- a scary thought for American League batters.

	W	SV	ERA	IP	H	BB	SO	BPI	$
1992 Chicago AL	5	1	5.20	100	103	65	66	1.67	-
1993 Chicago AL	15	0	2.95	207	168	122	155	1.40	14
1994 *Projection* >>>	16	0	3.30	211	170	120	153	1.39	10

ANDERSEN, LARRY - TR - Age 40

A veteran of the previous Phillies World Series team (1983), Andersen was re-united with the Phils again last year. Always ready with a quick quip, Andersen is still effective as a spot reliever against righthanders; he held them to a .199 batting average in 1993. The much travelled Andersen will probably not be back with Philadelphia in 1994; but maybe they will bring him back in 2003 for another trip to the Series.

	W	SV	ERA	IP	H	BB	SO	BPI	$
1992 San Diego NL	1	2	3.34	35	26	8	35	0.97	2
1993 Philadelphia NL	3	0	2.92	61	54	21	67	1.23	3
1994 *Projection* >>>	2	2	2.95	52	44	16	47	1.16	6

ANDERSON, ALLAN - TL - Age 30

American League ERA champ in 1988, and won 17 games in 1989, but he's lost it.

	W	SV	ERA	IP	H	BB	SO	BPI	$
1993 Oklahoma City AAA	2	1	5.32	115	137	37	52	1.51	

ANDERSON, BRIAN - TL - Age 22

Shades of Greg Swindell. The third pick overall in last year's draft, he signed for a $680,000 bonus. He could start this season in California's rotation, but unless he improves his control, he'll be in Triple-A. Pitched at Wright State, where he scored victories over Arizona and Ohio State. Good mechanics and a live arm. Pitched a few innings at AA Midland and AAA Vancouver in 1993, and then did this for the Angels:

	W	SV	ERA	IP	H	BB	SO	BPI	$
1993 California AL	0	0	3.97	11	11	2	4	1.17	-
1994 *Projection* >>>	2	0	4.08	30	29	8	12	1.23	1

ANDERSON, MIKE - TR - Age 27

A late developing righthanded starter, Anderson was moderately effective at Triple-A, going 10-6 with a 3.75 ERA. He then pitched five highly ineffective innings for the Reds, but remains in line for another chance in 1994.

APPIER, KEVIN - TR - Age 26

One of league's best young hurlers. Actually out-did his great 1992 season with league leading ERA and a career high 18 wins in 1993. A candidate for Cy Young and 20 victories in 1994 and beyond. He often starts out slowly, so try to trade for Appier in May.

	W	SV	ERA	IP	H	BB	SO	BPI	$
1992 Kansas City AL	15	0	2.46	208	167	68	150	1.13	21
1993 Kansas City AL	18	0	2.56	238	183	81	186	1.11	29
1994 *Projection* >>>	17	0	2.91	227	181	82	172	1.16	26

AQUINO, LUIS - TR - Age 28

The consummate 10th man on a pitching staff, he'll give you the occasional start, work in long relief, and generally do nothing to embarrass you. Unfortunately, he does nothing outstanding in any category, statistical or otherwise.

	W	SV	ERA	IP	H	BB	SO	BPI	$
1992 Kansas City AL	3	0	4.52	67	81	20	11	1.49	-
1993 Florida NL	6	0	3.42	110	115	40	67	1.41	3
1994 *Projection* >>>	5	0	3.63	102	108	35	52	1.40	1

ARD, JOHNNY - TR - Age 26
The guy traded for Steve Bedrosian, Ard hasn't exactly blossomed; he had a "stiff arm" last year and pitched just five innings at AA Shreveport. Still, Giants pitchers have a way of appearing from nowhere and doing well.

ARMSTRONG, JACK - TR - Age 29
Really hasn't pitched well since the first half of the 1991 season, which was capped by a start in the All-Star Game. Always putting up decent strikeout totals, he's tough on righthanded batters. His September move to the bullpen might be in his best long-term interest. Armstrong will be forced back into the rotation if Marlins' kids aren't ready.

	W	SV	ERA	IP	H	BB	SO	BPI	$
1992 Cleveland AL	6	0	4.64	167	176	67	114	1.46	-
1993 Florida NL	9	0	4.49	196	210	78	118	1.47	-
1994 *Projection* >>>	8	0	4.61	182	195	74	114	1.48	-

ARNOLD, JAMIE - TR - Age 20
LSU quarterback Jamie Arnold had a decent year at Single-A Macon, leading his team in games started and innings pitched, but he's mostly a thrower rather than a pitcher at this point. He was assigned to the Instructional League by the Braves; Arnold's an excellent athlete, so he will move up quickly as he learns how to pitch.

	W	SV	ERA	IP	H	BB	SO	BPI	$
1993 Macon A	8	0	3.12	164	142	56	124	1.20	

ARNSBERG, BRAD - TR - Age 30
Arnsberg had a good year in '90 as a setup man with Texas. Since then he's had arm problems and disappointments.

	W	SV	ERA	IP	H	BB	SO	BPI	$
1992 Colorado Springs AAA	1	0	7.56	25	34	13	11	1.88	
1992 Cleveland AL	0	0	11.81	11	13	11	5	2.25	-
1993 Louisville AAA	0	0	5.31	40	47	27	19	1.82	

AROCHA, RENE - TR - Age 28
The Cuban defector started strong in his rookie season with the Cardinals last year but tailed off towards the end. To minimize the wear and tear on his arm, St. Louis moved him to the bullpen late in the season. Arocha uses a bagful of pitches and constantly keeps hitters off balance. He looks like a solid starter with the potential to become a star.

	W	SV	ERA	IP	H	BB	SO	BPI	$
1993 St. Louis NL	11	0	3.78	188	197	31	96	1.21	10
1994 *Projection* >>>	12	0	3.67	190	196	30	88	1.18	12

ASHBY, ANDY - TR - Age 26
There aren't many major league staffs that would allow a pitcher to accumulate 123 innings with a 6.80 ERA, but that's the kind of pitching the Padres and Rockies had in 1993. Ashby was just awful. Righties hit .365 against him.

	W	SV	ERA	IP	H	BB	SO	BPI	$
1992 Philadelphia NL	1	0	7.54	37	42	21	24	1.70	-
1993 Colorado-San Diego NL	3	1	6.80	123	168	56	77	1.82	-
1994 *Projection* >>>	3	1	5.85	89	110	40	56	1.69	-

ASHWORTH, KYM - TL - Age 17
This Australian pitcher was the youngest player among the youngsters of the Pioneer League. He relied on a curve and changeup remarkable for a youngster. With maturity, he may put a few MPH on a fastball that isn't presently very strong.

ASSENMACHER, PAUL - TL - Age 33
Even though he arrived too late to make any big difference in the pennant race, Assenmacher became the key setup man for the Yankees. He was brought in to face lefty batters in clutch situations. His fastball has slowed, but he'll stay around the majors for a while with his big overhand curve.

	W	SV	ERA	IP	H	BB	SO	BPI	$
1992 Chicago NL	4	8	4.10	68	72	26	67	1.44	4
1993 Chicago NL	2	0	3.49	38	44	13	34	1.49	-
1993 New York AL	2	0	3.12	17	10	9	11	1.11	1
1994 *Projection* >>>	4	2	3.59	64	62	24	59	1.35	4

ASTACIO, PEDRO - TR - Age 24
Astacio finished strong after a weak start, leading the Dodgers in wins. His mediocre strikeout rate and past minor league performance suggest that he won't get much better.

	W	SV	ERA	IP	H	BB	SO	BPI	$
1992 Los Angeles NL	5	0	1.98	82	80	20	43	1.22	5
1993 Los Angeles NL	14	0	3.57	186	165	68	122	1.25	11
1994 Projection >>>	11	0	3.28	150	135	51	94	1.24	10

AUGUST, DON - TR - Age 30
Had one good year with the Brewers in 1988, but has been struggling ever since. Needs to get the sharp curveball over the plate more consistently.

	W	SV	ERA	IP	H	BB	SO	BPI	$
1992 Toledo AAA	0	0	8.59	14	25	7	6	2.18	
1993 Charlotte AAA	3	0	5.48	44	57	10	24	1.52	

AUSANIO, JOE - TR - Age 28
Pitched extremely well at Class A and AA in 1988-1990, and finally achieved success at Triple-A in 1992. It's not too late for him to be a major league success. Pirates released him; Expos thought there was hope. Check that SO/BB rate in 1993.

	W	SV	ERA	IP	H	BB	SO	BPI	$
1992 Buffalo AAA	6	15	2.90	83	64	40	66	1.24	
1993 Harrisburg AA	2	6	1.21	22	16	4	30	0.90	

AUSTIN, JAMES - TR - Age 30
Strong righty with effective slider, but too many walks to be a star. Still, he is a possible beneficiary of the unsettled Brewers pen situation.

	W	SV	ERA	IP	H	BB	SO	BPI	$
1992 Milwaukee AL	5	0	1.85	58	38	32	30	1.20	5
1993 Milwaukee AL	1	0	3.82	33	28	13	15	1.24	0
1994 Projection >>>	2	1	3.32	38	33	14	18	1.24	3

AVERY, STEVE - TL - Age 23
This guy's only 23 as the 1994 season starts and he's already won 50 major league games. In a year of increased offense, Avery cut his ERA and also won 18 games for the second time in his career. The main thing to pay attention to is Avery's reduced walk count; 71 in 1992, 43 in 1993 in about the same number of innings, and he did it without reducing his strikeout rate. He's got talent, youth, control, poise, and a well-defined starting role for a team that can score in bunches - what more could you possibly want from a pitcher?

	W	SV	ERA	IP	H	BB	SO	BPI	$
1992 Atlanta NL	11	0	3.20	233	216	71	129	1.23	9
1993 Atlanta NL	18	0	2.94	223	216	43	125	1.16	21
1994 Projection >>>	16	0	3.11	225	213	55	127	1.19	20

AYALA, BOBBY - TR - Age 24
Ayala pitched well in relief, picking up three quick saves when Davey Johnson took over the team from Tony Perez. But when Ayala moved to the rotation, he was bombed, usually tiring by the 4th or 5th inning. He seems best suited for a relief role and is young enough to still be considered a prospect. Has a chance to get saves in Seattle.

	W	SV	ERA	IP	H	BB	SO	BPI	$
1992 Cincinnati NL	2	0	4.34	29	33	13	23	1.59	-
1993 Cincinnati NL	7	3	5.60	98	106	45	65	1.54	-
1994 Projection >>>	5	4	4.44	68	68	28	47	1.41	3

AYRAULT, BOB - TR - Age 27
Briefly looked good in a trial with the Phillies, but since 1990 he has generally struggled in repeated shots at the majors.

	W	SV	ERA	IP	H	BB	SO	BPI	$
1992 Philadelphia NL	2	0	3.12	43	32	17	27	1.13	0
1993 Philadelphia-Seattle	3	0	5.40	30	36	16	15	1.73	0

BACKLUND, BRETT - TR - Age 24

Backlund was an incredible story in 1992; a fifth round draft pick from the University of Iowa who got all the way to Triple-A before season's end, he had every opportunity to win the fifth starter's job last spring but lost that chance due to control problems. Ironically, Backlund's strength is the ability to throw four average pitches wherever he wants. Backlund also struggled at Triple-A last season before finally settling down at Double-A. The Pirates now realize he needs some more minor league seasoning.

	W	SV	ERA	IP	H	BB	SO	BPI	$
1993 Carolina AA	7	0	4.58	106	115	28	94	1.34	
1993 Buffalo AAA	0	0	10.55	21	30	14	10	2.09	

BAILES, SCOTT - TR - Age 31

Bailes is a lefty setup reliever last up with the Angels in '92; he hasn't had a major league save since 1987.

	W	SV	ERA	IP	H	BB	SO	BPI	$
1992 California AL	3	0	7.45	39	59	28	25	2.25	-
1993 Syracuse AAA	0	2	2.21	20	19	3	22	1.10	

BAILEY, CORY - TR - Age 23

The big ace reliever in the Red Sox farm system for the last three years, Bailey twice led his league in saves and has been among the leaders in strikeouts per inning. In a less crowded bullpen he would have been promoted earlier than September in 1993.

	W	SV	ERA	IP	H	BB	SO	BPI	$
1992 Lynchburg A	5	23	2.44	66	43	30	87	1.11	
1993 Pawtucket AAA	4	20	2.88	66	48	31	59	1.20	
1993 Boston AL	0	0	3.45	15	12	12	11	1.58	-
1994 *Projection* >>>	0	1	3.74	20	19	8	14	1.35	1

BAKER, SCOTT - TL - Age 23

Acquired from the Cardinals after the '92 season. Last year he won 10 games for the second consecutive year. He has completed just two of 73 pro starts, so if he makes it to the majors, you can expect it to be as a reliever.

BALDWIN, JAMES - TR - Age 22

When Chicago traded Johnny Ruffin, they set about to trade Baldwin to the Mets for Sid Fernandez. The Sox are glad they pulled the plug on that deal and kept the hard-throwing righthander. He's a big youngster with fastball in high 80's, also throws a good curve and foshball. Won the Southern League ERA title in 1993 and has pitched well everywhere since 1991, leaving a series of sub-3.00 ERA's in the Rookie Gulf Coast League, Low A South Bend, and High A Sarasota. In 1993 he did this:

	W	SV	ERA	IP	H	BB	SO	BPI	$
1993 Birmingham AA	8	0	2.25	120	94	43	107	1.14	
1993 Nashville AAA	5	0	2.61	69	43	36	61	1.14	

BALLARD, JEFF - TL - Age 30

Ballard has fallen a long way from his 18 victory season for Baltimore in 1989. He underwent two elbow operations following his big year and has never been the same. The Pirates used him primarily in relief last season, though he looked much more comfortable in his five starts. His fastball barely reaches 80 MPH and he really relies on his curve and change. His best hope of sticking in the majors is as a lefty relief specialist.

	W	SV	ERA	IP	H	BB	SO	BPI	$
1993 Pittsburgh NL	4	0	4.86	53	70	15	16	1.60	-
1994 *Projection* >>>	2	0	5.07	45	58	12	15	1.55	-

BANKHEAD, SCOTT - TR - Age 30

Basic sinker/slider pitcher. One of the Mariners' best starters in 1989, Bankhead missed almost all of 1990 with a bad shoulder and was ineffective in 1991. Cincinnati salvaged him with a wise conversion to short relief. Now among the more reliable middle/setup relievers.

	W	SV	ERA	IP	H	BB	SO	BPI	$
1992 Cincinnati NL	10	1	2.93	70	57	29	53	1.22	5
1993 Boston AL	2	0	3.50	64	59	29	47	1.37	2
1994 *Projection* >>>	5	1	3.45	66	60	28	47	1.34	3

BANKS, JIM - TR - Age 24

As hard as it was for Midwest League batters to hit Banks's pitches in '93, it was that hard for him to throw them over the plate.

BANKS, WILLIE - TR - Age 25

All things considered, hard throwing Willie Banks had an excellent year in 1993 finally proving that he belongs in the majors. He was a little erratic, but much improved over prior years. This year, he should improve even more in the National League pitching for the Cubs.

	W	SV	ERA	IP	H	BB	SO	BPI	$
1992 Minnesota AL	4	0	5.70	71	80	37	37	1.65	-
1993 Minnesota AL	11	0	4.04	171	186	78	138	1.54	3
1994 *Projection* >>>	12	0	4.02	188	190	71	150	1.40	6

BAPTIST, TRAVIS - TL - Age 22

Went 11-2 in the Sally League in '92, then went on the disabled list much of last season because of an elbow problem. He also was the first minor leaguer to run afoul of the new tobacco ban.

BARBER, BRIAN - TR - Age 21

Barber is still very young but the Cardinals like his maturity and command of four pitches. He finished last season at Triple-A (just one game for Louisville) after a solid year at Double-A . If the Cardinals have trouble with their rotation in 1994, it's not out of the question for Barber to be in St. Louis later in the summer.

	W	SV	ERA	IP	H	BB	SO	BPI	$
1992 Springfield A	3	0	3.73	51	39	24	56	1.24	
1992 St. Petersburg A	5	0	3.26	113	99	46	102	1.28	
1993 Arkansas AA	9	0	4.02	143	154	56	126	1.46	

BARCELO, MARC - TR - Age 22

Drafted as the third of Minnesota's four first-round draft picks last June, out of Arizona State, and signed for a $235,000 bonus. Overpowering in the Florida State League, and not overmatched in the Southern League. Expect a return to Double-A in '94.

BARFIELD, JOHN - TL - Age 29

Basically a finesse/control pitcher, Barfield had some good outings with the Rangers in 1989-1991, but now his career is going the wrong way.

	W	SV	ERA	IP	H	BB	SO	BPI	$
1992 Charlotte A	0	1	7.71	7	10	1	4	1.57	
1992 Oklahoma City AAA	7	2	4.14	71	75	26	26	1.42	
1993 Birmingham AA	5	1	3.86	42	57	5	18	1.48	
1993 Nashville AAA	3	1	4.11	35	36	11	15	1.34	

BARK, BRIAN - TL - Age 25

The numbers recorded by Bark at Triple-A in 1993 don't impress immediately, but his gradual progress and steadiness have caught the attention of the Braves brass. He'll get an outside shot at the rotation in 1994 and could get a recall in case of injury to one of the Braves starters. He's not much more than a marginal major league starter right now, but he's still improving.

	W	SV	ERA	IP	H	BB	SO	BPI	$
1993 Richmond AAA	12	0	3.67	162	153	72	110	1.38	

BARNES, BRIAN - TL - Age 27

Barnes hasn't blossomed like the Expos hoped, failing to shine as either a starter or reliever. The little lefty has two above average pitches, a changeup and a curve, but struggles to be consistent with both. He doesn't have the stamina to be a starter. Barnes still has a chance to emerge but he had better do it pretty soon, before Montreal loses patience.

	W	SV	ERA	IP	H	BB	SO	BPI	$
1992 Montreal NL	6	0	2.97	100	77	46	65	1.23	3
1993 Montreal NL	2	3	4.41	100	105	48	60	1.53	-
1994 *Projection* >>>	4	2	3.97	106	100	51	65	1.42	1

BARTON, SHAWN - TL - Age 30
Long-time Phillies/Mets farmhand. Reaching the majors in 1992 was his career highlight.

	W	SV	ERA	IP	H	BB	SO	BPI	$
1992 Calgary AAA	3	4	4.25	53	57	24	31	1.53	
1992 Seattle AL	0	0	2.92	12	10	7	4	1.38	-
1993 Calgary AAA	3	4	3.56	60	64	27	29	1.51	

BATCHELOR, RICHARD - TR - Age 26
Acquired by the Cardinals in the Lee Smith trade last August, Batchelor was a rising star in the Yankees' farm system, getting 25 saves at AA Albany and AAA Columbus combined in 1993. He's not overpowering but he keeps the ball down, throws strikes and doesn't get rattled. He'll have a chance to save some games for St. Louis this year.

BATISTA, MIGUEL - TR - Age 23
Batista is an exciting hard thrower whose poor control improved last year, to show some of the results that the Pirates were anticipating when they made him a Rule Five pick in 1992. The Pirates opted not to keep Batista through the 1992 season, so he went back to the Expos farm.

	W	SV	ERA	IP	H	BB	SO	BPI	$
1992 West Palm Beach A	7	0	3.79	135	130	54	92	1.36	
1992 Pittsburgh NL	0	0	9.00	2	4	3	1	3.50	-
1993 Harrisburg AA	13	0	4.34	141	139	86	91	2.02	

BAUTISTA, JOSE - TR - Age 29
Bautista replaced Greg Maddux as the Cubs' team ERA leader; the Cubs still won 84 games. Bautista uses a two-speed forkball to get batters out and has tremendous strike zone command learned from eons spent in the minors.

	W	SV	ERA	IP	H	BB	SO	BPI	$
1993 Chicago NL	10	2	2.82	111	105	27	63	1.19	11
1994 *Projection* >>>	6	1	3.18	68	65	17	38	1.21	5

BEATTY, BLAINE - TL - Age 29
Beatty surfaced with the Mets and did OK in 1989 and 1991, but he's just a lefty journeyman. Some guys are good Triple-A pitchers, Beatty has been reduced to a good Double-A pitcher. Had a 5.50 ERA at AAA Buffalo last year.

	W	SV	ERA	IP	H	BB	SO	BPI	$
1992 Indianapolis AAA	7	0	4.31	94	109	24	54	1.41	
1993 Carolina AA	7	0	2.86	94	67	35	67	1.08	

BECK, ROD - TR - Age 25
Arguably the best reliever in the majors, Beck gets nearly all of the saves for a team expected to win 90 to 100 games in each of the next few years. His significant career stats include 211 strikeouts in 223.2 innings with just 172 hits and 41 walks - a career 0.95 ratio. In addition to his great stuff, Beck has a good stopper's attitude which he displays effectively without being a jerk about it.

	W	SV	ERA	IP	H	BB	SO	BPI	$
1992 San Francisco NL	3	17	1.76	92	62	15	87	0.84	26
1993 San Francisco NL	3	48	2.16	79	57	13	86	0.88	47
1994 *Projection* >>>	3	40	2.43	80	61	18	82	0.99	44

BECKETT, ROBBIE -TL - Age 21
Beckett is the Padres' version of Mitch Williams. He struck out 88 and walked 93 in 83 innings at Single-A Rancho Cucamonga. A 6'5" lefthander with a 90 MPH fastball, he'll keep getting chances. It's doubtful that Beckett's fastball will find the majors (much less home plate). He's not quite as advanced as Rudy Seanez.

	W	SV	ERA	IP	H	BB	SO	BPI	$
1992 Waterloo A	4	0	4.77	121	77	140	147	1.79	
1993 Rancho Cucamonga A	2	4	6.02	83	75	93	88	1.90	

BEDROSIAN, STEVE - TR - Age 36
Bedrosian "un-retired" in 1993 after sitting out in 1992 and put up fine numbers in a setup role. He no longer has the fastball velocity he once displayed, but Bedrosian is now a better pitcher; he moves the ball around in the strike zone and changes speeds.

	W	SV	ERA	IP	H	BB	SO	BPI	$
1993 Atlanta NL	5	0	1.63	49	34	14	33	0.98	6
1994 *Projection* >>>	4	1	2.80	38	34	14	24	1.21	3

BELCHER, TIM - TR - Age 32
Continued to fade in 1993, ending the season out of the Sox rotation. He still allows less than a hit per inning and puts up a good number of strikeouts.

	W	SV	ERA	IP	H	BB	SO	BPI	$
1992 Cincinnati NL	15	0	3.91	227	201	80	149	1.23	6
1993 Cincinnati NL	9	0	4.47	137	134	47	101	1.32	2
1993 Chicago AL	3	0	4.40	71	64	27	34	1.27	-
1994 *Projection* >>>	13	0	4.09	215	199	74	141	1.27	7

BELINDA, STAN - TR - Age 27
Hard-throwing, former Pirates closer. Has high velocity fastball, but nothing to go with it, and the fastball is often too straight. A particularly embarrasing blown save in 1992's NLCS Game 7, then sporadic failures in 1993 caused the cost-cutting Bucs to dump Belinda to the Royals, who needed a setup man. In Kansas City, the pressure will be off of Belinda, but his value will be much more limited in a setup role.

	W	SV	ERA	IP	H	BB	SO	BPI	$
1992 Pittsburgh NL	6	18	3.15	71	58	29	57	1.22	18
1993 Pittsburgh NL	3	19	3.61	42	35	11	30	1.09	17
1993 Kansas City AL	1	0	4.28	27	30	6	25	1.31	-
1994 *Projection* >>>	5	2	3.61	71	62	22	57	1.18	5

BELL, ERIC - TL - Age 30
The surprise winner in the competition for Houston's special situation lefty reliever job in 1993, Bell made 10 appearances before being sent to AAA Tucson in May. From then on he had a mediocre year as a starter (4-6, 4.05 ERA, 131 hits in 107 innings). Bell probably won't get another chance in the majors.

	W	SV	ERA	IP	H	BB	SO	BPI	$
1992 Cleveland AL	0	0	7.36	15	22	9	10	2.02	-
1993 Houston NL	0	0	6.14	7	10	2	2	1.69	-

BENE, BILL - TR - Age 26
A hard-throwing first round draft pick in 1988, Bene struggled mightily in his first five pro seasons, going 9-19 with 312 walks in 251 innings. In 1993 he threw the most innings and had the most success of his career and also cut his walks well below one per inning.

BENES, ALAN - TR - Age 22
The younger brother of Padres ace Andy Benes, Alan was the Cardinals' first-round draft pick from Creighton University last June. He has command of a fastball, curveball, slider and changeup. The Cardinals would like him to raise his arm angle and throw more from over the top. Though he didn't win a game for Glens Falls in seven starts in the short-season New York-Penn League, he could come to St. Louis quickly.

	W	SV	ERA	IP	H	BB	SO	BPI	$
1993 Glens Falls A	0	0	3.65	37	39	14	29	1.43	

BENES, ANDY - TR - Age 26
Benes' season caved in shortly after the Sheffield and McGriff deals were completed. After a dominating first half (9 wins, 2.57 ERA, 1.03 ratio), Benes stumbled to 6 wins, a 5.53 ERA and a 1.54 ratio after the All-Star break. His concentration seemed to wane considerably and Benes was one of the most vocal of the Padres in protesting management's cost cutting measures; Benes almost seemed like he was trying to force a trade. His skills remain set for a true breakthrough year.

	W	SV	ERA	IP	H	BB	SO	BPI	$
1992 San Diego NL	13	0	3.35	231	230	61	169	1.26	8
1993 San Diego NL	15	0	3.78	230	200	86	179	1.24	12
1994 *Projection* >>>	15	0	3.44	230	209	72	175	1.22	16

BENITEZ, ARMANDO - TR - Age 21
Held Sally League batters to a .164 average last season, then went up to the Carolina League and stepped up his strikeout rate to finish the year with better than 15 strikeouts per nine innings. The Dominican throws a 90 MPH fastball that moves. Look for him in Double-A this year.

BENNETT, ERIK - TR - Age 25
Bennett has been a success in the lower minors, but still has a lot to prove before pitching in Anaheim. He had a 6.49 ERA at AA Midland and a 6.05 at AAA Vancouver in 1993.

BENNETT, JOEL - TR - Age 24
Mr. Strikeout in the Carolina League in '93, using a sharp-breaking curve to punch out most of his victims.

BERE, JASON - TR - Age 22
A definite candidate to be the Cal Eldred of 1994. Bere is a good pitcher, for sure, with a 90-plus fastball, slurve, and a foshball changeup, but look for a little tumble in '94. His walk total in 1993 was too high. He'll most certainly be overrated by people who get excited about emerging young talent.

	W	SV	ERA	IP	H	BB	SO	BPI	$
1993 Chicago AL	12	0	3.47	142	109	81	129	1.34	9
1994 Projection	14	0	3.60	190	169	88	150	1.35	10

BERGMAN, SEAN - TR- Age 23
Detroit's best rookie pitching prospect for 1994, despite his poor showing in the majors last season. A fastball pitcher who can throw a good breaking pitch, he has to prove that he can win; in five stops during the past three seasons, he has had a winning record only in the Florida State League in '92. Bergman had a good first half with AAA Toledo last year (6-4 with a 2.61 ERA), but struggled in the second half as hitters adjusted. Tigers pitching being thin, Bergman has a good shot at the starting rotation for 1994. You can expect a typical erratic rookie if he makes the team.

	W	SV	ERA	IP	H	BB	SO	BPI	$
1993 Detroit AL	1	0	5.67	39	47	23	19	1.79	-

BERUMEN, ANDRES - TR - Age 23
Originally a Royals prospect, Berumen came to San Diego from Florida in the Sheffield trade and is another of the many prospects for a role on the Padres' staff. Well regarded by scouts, Berumen is still at least a year away from major league success.

BEVIL, BRIAN -TR - Age 22
Earned promotion to AA Memphis with 7-1, 2.30 performance at Class A Wilmington, but had less success at the higher level, with a 4.36 ERA and three wins in six starts. Bevil is a hard thrower, but needs polish and will start 1994 at Memphis. Being groomed for starter role; won't be in Kansas City until 1995.

BIELECKI, MIKE - TR - Age 34
Bielecki had arm troubles and surgery in 1992. Cleveland gave him a shot at starting, but he couldn't make it with them. The Orioles tried him at Triple-A.

	W	SV	ERA	IP	H	BB	SO	BPI	$
1992 Atlanta NL	2	0	2.57	80	77	27	62	1.29	1
1993 Cleveland AL	4	0	5.90	68	90	23	38	1.66	-
1994 Projection >>>	4	0	4.62	83	94	28	49	1.47	-

BIRKBECK, MIKE - TR - Age 33
Once considered a failed prospect, Birkbeck was awarded a spot on the Braves winter roster in recognition of his solid work at Richmond.

	W	SV	ERA	IP	H	BB	SO	BPI	$
1992 New York NL	0	0	9.00	7	12	1	2	1.86	-
1993 Richmond AAA	13	0	3.11	159	143	41	136	1.15	

BLACK, BUD - TL - Age 36
His 8-2 record was largely an illusion; the Giants scored more than six runs per game in Black's starts. For many years a solid journeyman, Black is now a 36-year-old lefty with a history of serious injuries. Black's career W-L record: 113-

112. His value to his major league teams has been far greater than it has to his Rotisserie owners.

	W	SV	ERA	IP	H	BB	SO	BPI	$
1992 San Francisco NL	10	0	3.97	177	178	59	82	1.34	0
1993 San Francisco NL	8	0	3.56	93	89	33	45	1.31	4
1994 *Projection* >>>	9	0	3.79	131	128	45	62	1.32	4

BLAIR, WILLIE - TR - Age 28
Blair moved into the starting rotation and showed promise until suffering an August arm injury.

	W	SV	ERA	IP	H	BB	SO	BPI	$
1992 Houston NL	5	0	4.00	78	74	25	48	1.26	-
1993 Colorado NL	6	0	4.75	146	184	42	84	1.55	-
1994 *Projection* >>>	5	0	4.66	115	139	34	66	1.50	-

BLAZIER, RON - TR - Age 22
After a superb year at Single-A Spartanburg in 1992 (1.08 ratio, 4.66 strikeout/walk ratio in 160 innings), Blazier disappointed at Single-A Clearwater in 1993. He didn't appear on Baseball America's Top 10 Prospect list for the South Atlantic League in 1992 despite his big year, mainly because he doesn't overpower hitters. In the small jump to a higher Single-A league, his strikeout rate dropped from 8.38 per 9 innings to 4.99. Either he's got arm troubles, or Baseball America was right from the outset. He's not a prospect at this time.

BLOMDAHL, BEN - TR - Age 23
Blomdahl had some good and some bad outings as a starter in Double-A and Triple-A last year. He is working on his pitches and could be called up to Detroit this year. He has a decent fastball but is not overpowering.

BODDICKER, MIKE - TR - Age 36
The Brewers gave Boddicker one more chance to regain his former greatness, but he is now just another old Cadillac with high mileage and in need of repairs.

	W	SV	ERA	IP	H	BB	SO	BPI	$
1992 Kansas City AL	1	3	4.98	86	92	37	47	1.49	-
1993 Milwaukee NL	3	0	5.67	54	77	15	24	1.70	-

BOEVER, JOE - TR - Age 33
National League veteran Joe Boever was signed by Oakland and later Detroit in 1993. The Tigers needed him to shore up middle relief and to close a few games. He has 41 major league saves. Success in 1992 was largely the result of a better mix of fastballs with his forkball/palmball.

	W	SV	ERA	IP	H	BB	SO	BP	$
1992 Houston NL	3	2	2.51	111	103	45	67	1.33	4
1993 Oakland-Detroit AL	6	3	3.61	102	101	44	63	1.42	6
1994 *Projection* >>>	5	2	3.28	105	101	46	67	1.40	5

BOHANON, BRIAN - TL - Age 25
The former number one pick struggled again in 1993, although by season's end the Rangers had pretty much settled on using Bohanon in a long relief role. Stayed on the major league roster because he was out of options. He had surgery in October 1992 in an attempt to locate the cause of pain in his left bicep.

	W	SV	ERA	IP	H	BB	SO	BPI	$
1992 Texas AL	1	0	6.31	45	57	25	29	1.79	-
1992 Oklahoma City AAA	4	0	2.73	56	53	15	24	1.24	
1993 Texas AL	4	0	4.76	92	107	46	45	1.66	-
1994 *Projection* >>>	3	0	4.95	76	88	35	39	1.62	

BOLTON, RODNEY - TR - Age 25
While teammate Jason Bere shined in his 1993 trial, Bolton floundered. He's a finesse pitcher and has shown fine control throughout his minor league career. Will likely spend another full year in the minors.

	W	SV	ERA	IP	H	BB	SO	BPI	$
1993 Nashville AAA	10	1	2.88	115	108	37	75	1.25	
1993 Chicago AL	2	0	7.44	42	55	16	17	1.69	

BOLTON, TOM - TL - Age 31
Lefty starter/reliever Tom Bolton is a Red Sox cast-off who caught on with the pitching-poor Tigers in 1993. He had some good outings last year, and some very bad ones. Effective lefty curveball pitcher when he throws strikes, which he does not do consistently.

	W	SV	ERA	IP	H	BB	SO	BPI	$
1992 Boston-Cincinnati	4	0	4.54	75	86	37	50	1.63	-
1993 Detroit AL	6	0	4.47	102	113	45	66	1.55	0
1994 Projection >>>	6	0	4.57	95	107	43	55	1.58	-

BONES, RICKY - TR - Age 24
Like most pitchers who live or die with their breaking stuff, Bones needs to get ahead in the count to be effective. Too often he falls behind and has to throw a fat pitch, making him one of the most generous sources of home runs in the American League. Still, Bones showed flashes of brilliance in 1993. When he's in a groove, he's terrific, and he deserves to be on your list of ten starters most likely to have a breakthrough year in 1994.

	W	SV	ERA	IP	H	BB	SO	BPI	$
1992 Milwaukee AL	9	0	4.57	163	169	48	65	1.33	2
1993 Milwaukee AL	11	0	4.86	203	222	63	63	1.40	3
1994 Projection >>>	12	0	4.68	210	225	64	77	1.38	3

BORBON, PEDRO - TL - Age 26
Pedro Jr. isn't much of a prospect despite two consecutive September callups to the Braves. He has produced good strikeout totals recently, but really doesn't have major league stuff. He could contend for a middle relief role in 1994 but has little value even if he wins the job. His famous name and being lefthanded may keep Borbon hanging around the major league fringe longer than his talent might otherwise merit.

	W	SV	ERA	IP	H	BB	SO	BPI	$
1992 Atlanta NL	0	0	6.75	1	2	1	1	2.25	-
1993 Richmond AAA	5	0	4.23	77	71	42	95	1.47	
1993 Atlanta NL	0	0	21.60	1	3	3	2	3.60	-

BORLAND, TOBY - TR - Age 24
A career reliever, Borland has developed a pattern of pitching exceedingly well at Double-A (for example a 2.52 ERA with 13 saves last year) but then bombing at Triple-A (6.47 ERA, 46 walks in 57 innings over the past two seasons). The Phils will not give up on him yet, considering his powerful repertoire and the Phils' current big league bullpen needs. He has been mentioned as one of those "closer of the future" type pitchers, but first he must get over the Triple-A hurdle.

BOSIO, CHRIS - TR - Age 30
Bosio broke his collarbone in April and spent most of the season hurt. If he's healthy, the wins will jump back to pre-1993 levels.

	W	SV	ERA	IP	H	BB	SO	BPI	$
1992 Milwaukee AL	16	0	3.62	231	223	44	120	1.15	16
1993 Seattle AL	9	1	3.45	164	138	59	119	1.20	13
1994 Projection >>>	12	0	3.49	188	168	54	119	1.18	16

BOSKIE, SHAWN - TR - Age 27
Boskie tried a cut fastball to get yet another crack at the Cubs staff in 1993. He pitched OK in long relief, which is where he'll settle for 1994. If the Cubs are saying he's a candidate for the rotation in the spring, that's a sign that they have serious pitching problems.

	W	SV	ERA	IP	H	BB	SO	BPI	$
1992 Chicago NL	5	0	5.01	91	96	36	39	1.44	-
1993 Chicago NL	5	0	3.43	65	63	21	39	1.29	2
1994 Projection >>>	4	0	4.26	80	81	29	41	1.38	-

BOTTALICO, RICKY - TR - Age 24
How much do the Phils think of this guy? Well, the Astros insistence upon his inclusion in a potential deal for Mark Portugal during the 1993 stretch run killed that trade. Bottalico was converted into a reliever in 1992, and did have a solid year split between Single-A and Double-A (24 saves, 8.22 strikeouts per 9 innings), but this one good year

doesn't justify PR announcements that Bottalico is surely the closer of the future. Just a year ago, Toby Borland was held in the same high esteem. Botallico did have a very strong showing in the 1993 Arizona Fall League.

BOTTENFIELD, KENT - TR - Age 25
After being traded from the Expos in July, Bottenfield got roughed up. He has good control but isn't overpowering. He's definitely not excited to pitch in Denver's thin air.

	W	SV	ERA	IP	H	BB	SO	BPI	$
1992 Montreal NL	1	1	2.23	32	26	11	14	1.14	1
1993 Montreal-Colorado NL	5	0	5.07	159	179	71	63	1.57	-
1994 Projection >>>	3	0	4.81	106	116	46	42	1.53	-

BOUCHER, DENIS - TL - Age 26
Montreal fans never forgave the Expos for not signing this lefty from Quebec. The Expos finally rectified the mistake last season, acquiring Boucher from the Padres. After stops in Toronto, Cleveland and San Diego, he found himself in Montreal and appears ready to live up to his huge potential. Good control helped him succeed last year. Considering he's a native and a great drawing card (attendance tripled in his five starts), the Expos will give Boucher every chance in the world to win a spot in their rotation. He needs pinpoint control to be effective, and thus far it's eluded him.

	W	SV	ERA	IP	H	BB	SO	BPI	$
1992 Cleveland AL	2	0	6.37	41	48	20	17	1.66	-
1993 Ottawa AAA	6	0	2.72	43	36	11	22	1.09	
1993 Montreal NL	3	0	1.91	28	24	3	14	0.96	3
1994 Projection >>>	6	0	4.16	70	72	20	32	1.32	2

BOVEE, MIKE - TR - Age 20
Not big (5'11", 190 pounds), but he throws hard. His arm took some wear and tear last season, when he missed time with shoulder and elbow injuries.

BOWEN, RYAN - TR - Age 26
The inconsistency that has plagued him throughout his career dogged him once again in 1993. He either dominated or was dominated in virtually every start, then suffered a broken thigh bone in September, ending his season. Although he'll be handed a spot in the rotation in 1994, based on his handful of good starts in 1993, at this point it appears that he will remain the poster child for "potential".

	W	SV	ERA	IP	H	BB	SO	BPI	$
1992 Houston NL	0	0	10.96	33	48	30	22	2.32	-
1993 Florida NL	8	0	4.42	156	156	87	98	1.56	-
1994 Projection >>>	9	0	4.29	160	162	78	105	1.50	

BOZE, MARSHALL - TR - Age 22
The leading winner in the Milwaukee organization in '93, and 30-12 the last two seasons after spending parts of '90 and '91 in Rookie ball. If he can continue his success in Triple-A this season, he'll be in Milwaukee during '94.

BRANTLEY, CLIFF - TR - Age 25
A former second-round draft choice who showed promise in 1992 but then had a lost season in '93.

	W	SV	ERA	IP	H	BB	SO	BPI	$
1992 Scranton AAA	3	0	1.76	30	19	14	26	1.08	
1992 Philadelphia NL	2	0	4.60	76	71	58	32	1.69	-
1993 Ottawa AAA	2	0	6.50	54	81	37	37	2.19	

BRANTLEY, JEFF - TR - Age 30
Brantley became the whipping boy for Candlestick fans after failing as a starting pitcher (4.86 ERA, 1.60 ratio), but he pitched well enough as a reliever (3.55 ERA, 1.12 ratio). He can be useful in a setup/long relief role, but his ERA has gone from 1.56 to 2.45 to 2.95 to 4.28 in four years.

	W	SV	ERA	IP	H	BB	SO	BPI	$
1992 San Francisco NL	7	7	2.95	91	67	45	86	1.22	10
1993 San Francisco NL	5	0	4.28	113	112	46	76	1.40	0
1994 Projection >>>	6	4	3.76	105	95	46	80	1.34	6

BRENNAN, BILL - TR - Age 31
The wily veteran of the 1993 Triple-A champion Iowa Cubs, Brennan led his league in strikeouts with 143 in 179 innings. He'll still need a miracle to get a mop-up role in the Cub pen.

	W	SV	ERA	IP	H	BB	SO	BPI	$
1993 Iowa AAA	10	0	4.42	179	180	64	143	1.36	
1993 Chicago NL	2	0	4.20	15	16	8	11	1.60	-

BREWER, BILLY - TL - Age 25
1993 was an excellent season for this Rule Five draftee. Showed good poise for a youngster, but not enough control to have extended success. Must reduce walks before he'll get a larger role. For 1994, he'll start the season in a lefty setup and mop-up role.

	W	SV	ERA	IP	H	BB	SO	BPI	$
1993 Kansas City AL	2	0	3.46	39	31	20	28	1.31	1

BRINK, BRAD - TR - Age 29
Another first round horror story in Phils' history, Brink was damaged goods when drafted, but persevered and transformed himself into a finesse pitcher, then got a taste of the majors in 1992 and 1993. Brink has excellent control, and should be in contention for one of many available spots in Phils' bullpen.

	W	SV	ERA	IP	H	BB	SO	BPI	$
1992 Philadelphia NL	0	0	4.14	41	53	13	16	1.60	-
1993 Scranton AAA	7	0	4.22	106	104	27	89	1.22	
1993 Philadelphia NL	0	0	3.00	6	3	3	8	1.00	-

BRISCOE, JOHN - TR - Age 26
Became an effective closer in the minors last season, but his major league performance gave Dennis Eckersley no reason to fear for his job. Strikeout pitcher who gets absolutely pounded by lefties (.389 batting average in '92, .405 last year). Terrible control; has walked more than he struck out in each of his three major league seasons. Did pick up 22 saves in the minors last year, and struck out 24 in 24 major league innings. An extreme longshot.

	W	SV	ERA	IP	H	BB	SO	BPI	$
1992 Oakland AL	0	0	6.43	7	12	9	4	3.00	-
1993 Huntsville AA	4	16	3.03	38	28	16	62	1.13	
1993 Oakland AL	1	0	8.03	24	26	26	24	2.15	-

BROCAIL, DOUG - TR - Age 26
A 1986 first round draft pick, Brocail got more starts than any other Padres rookie (24) and has a good fastball. One of many young hurlers with a good opportunity in the wide open Padres organization. As with most Padre pitchers, the recommendation is to stay away.

	W	SV	ERA	IP	H	BB	SO	BPI	$
1992 San Diego NL	0	0	6.43	14	17	5	15	1.57	-
1993 Las Vegas AAA	4	1	3.68	51	51	14	32	1.26	
1993 San Diego NL	4	0	4.56	128	143	42	70	1.44	-

BRONKEY, JEFF - TR - Age 28
He was the bullpen ace for a very poor Triple-A team in '93, his fourth season in Oklahoma City. Spent nearly as much time traveling between Arlington and Oklahoma City as he did actually pitching. Not tremendously effective at the major league level. His primary asset is a "take-charge" attitude on the mound that characterizes effective relievers. Got 16 saves in 1992 at AA Tulsa and AAA Oklahoma City combined.

	W	SV	ERA	IP	H	BB	SO	BPI	$
1993 Oklahoma City AAA	2	14	2.65	37	29	7	19	0.96	
1993 Texas AL	1	1	4.00	36	39	11	18	1.39	0

BROSS, TERRY- TR - Age 28
A tall drink of water (6'9"), Bross has spent seven years in the minors without distinguishing himself outside of a 28 save season at Double-A in 1990. He's been an effective Triple-A setup man and is an injury or two away from being an extra in the Giants' bullpen.

	W	SV	ERA	IP	H	BB	SO	BPI	$
1992 Las Vegas AAA	7	0	3.26	86	83	30	42	1.31	
1993 San Francisco NL	0	0	9.00	2	3	1	1	2.00	-
1993 Phoenix AAA	4	5	3.97	79	76	37	69	1.43	

BROW, SCOTT - TR - Age 25

Started 0-7 in Triple-A, then won six of his final seven decisions and returned to the majors to win the final game of the American League season. Advanced quickly in '93 after going 14-2 in the Florida State League in '92. Things got bad enough in Toronto that Brow was temporarily in the starting rotation early in 1993. That situation was quickly remedied as Jack Morris and Dave Stewart returned to health. Brow has had bouts with wildness and doesn't look like he has enough of a fastball to be a major league pitcher just yet. He has great composure on the mound, but his stuff just isn't there.

BROWN, KEITH - TR - Age 30

His sixth Triple-A season was his best since he went 13-4 in A-ball in '87. He had four brief trials with Cincinnati, but hasn't won a major league game since '88. Never has thrown hard, and gave up 25 homers last season. Non-roster invitee to spring training in 1993. Former Reds pitcher. Led AAA Omaha in wins easily; was their most reliable starter. Showed good control, but allowed too many hits. Could get into a major league rotation somewhere in 1994.

	W	SV	ERA	IP	H	BB	SO	BPI	$
1992 Nashville AAA	12	0	3.61	150	157	43	102	1.33	
1992 Cincinnati NL	0	0	4.50	8	10	5	5	1.87	-
1993 Omaha AAA	13	0	4.84	148	166	36	98	1.36	

BROWN, J. KEVIN - TR - Age 29

Pulled a ribcage muscle late in spring training, and some think the injury was never given enough time to properly heal, and that it bothered him all season long. Showed flashes of 1992 brilliance, but too often couldn't get his sinker to stay down. Should return to 1992 form, barring injury.

	W	SV	ERA	IP	H	BB	SO	BPI	$
1992 Texas AL	21	0	3.32	265	262	76	173	1.26	17
1993 Texas AL	15	0	3.59	233	228	74	142	1.30	15
1994 *Projection* >>>	16	0	3.57	241	240	76	147	1.31	15

BROWN, KEVIN D. - TL - Age 28

Still the wrong Kevin Brown.

	W	SV	ERA	IP	H	BB	SO	BPI	$
1992 Calgary AAA	6	0	4.84	151	163	64	49	1.50	
1992 Seattle AL	0	0	9.00	3	4	3	2	2.33	-
1993 Phoenix AAA	6	0	4.94	120	134	60	75	1.61	

BROWN, TIM - TR - Age 25

He pitched a seven-inning perfect game last season, his sixth as a pro, but except for that game he was far from perfect. And in the generally successful Toronto farm system, he has a 27-47 career record.

BROWNING, TOM - TL - Age 33

After a horrendous start, Browning was showing improvement under Davey Johnson, but then Browning suffered a broken hand. He needs near-perfect location to be effective. After three straight sub-par years, it's questionable whether he can ever return to form.

	W	SV	ERA	IP	H	BB	SO	BPI	$
1992 Cincinnati NL	6	0	5.07	87	108	28	33	1.56	-
1993 Cincinnati NL	7	0	4.74	114	159	20	53	1.57	-
1994 *Projection* >>>	7	0	4.85	118	152	26	53	1.59	-

BRUMLEY, DUFF - TR - Age 23

It took him three years to get past short-season leagues in the Cardinals' system, but he caught the Rangers' eye last season and was acquired for Todd Burns. Brumley's out pitch is a slider.

BRUMMETT, GREG - TR - Age 26

The former Wichita State ace had pitched just three games above A-ball before last season. Minnesota acquired him from the Giants as part of the trade for Jim Deshaies. Brummett hasn't shown he can throw the ball by major league hitters, but he impressed Twins manager Tom Kelly in September, and he has a shot to make the rotation in the spring. His breaking stuff was among the best in the Pacific Coast League.

	W	SV	ERA	IP	H	BB	SO	BPI	$
1993 Phoenix AAA	7	0	3.70	107	114	27	84	1.31	
1993 San Francisco NL	2	0	4.70	46	53	13	20	1.43	-
1993 Minnesota AL	2	0	5.74	26	29	15	10	1.68	-

BRUSKE, JIM - TR - Age 29

Signed as a strong armed outfielder by the Indians in 1986, Bruske didn't start pitching full time until 1990 and returned to a regular rotation only after joining the Houston organization during the 1992 season. He inspired the well-known tavern expression "Give me a Bruske."

BRYANT, SHAWN - TL - Age 25

Bryant has moved up only one notch in Indians' system since 1991, partially due to mediocre results (ERA consistently around 4.00), but also due to intense competition within organization. Has become more efficient hurler, cutting walks in half since 1991. Not a premier prospect at this time.

	W	SV	ERA	IP	H	BB	SO	BPI	$
1993 Canton-Akron AA	10	0	3.72	172	179	61	111	1.39	

BUCKLEY, TRAVIS - TR - Age 23

Has been in five organizations, including four since 1992. The Mariners obtained him in a trade for Bubba Smith. Then Buckley's season ended because of ligament damage to his right ankle.

BULLINGER, JIM - TR - Age 28

The Triple-A closer for the Iowa Cubs, Bullinger pitched better in 1993 than in 1992, but he wasn't effective above Triple-A and isn't even remotely a save candidate with the big club. The Cubs relief corps is so unsettled behind Myers that Bullinger might get a shot at the setup job. His control is still too suspect to give this former shortstop much hope for major league success.

	W	SV	ERA	IP	H	BB	SO	BPI	$
1992 Chicago NL	2	7	4.66	85	72	54	36	1.48	0
1993 Iowa AAA	4	20	3.42	73	64	43	74	1.45	
1993 Chicago NL	1	1	4.32	16	18	9	10	1.67	-
1994 *Projection* >>>	1	1	4.56	36	33	22	17	1.52	-

BULLINGER, KIRK - TR - Age 24

The younger brother of Chicago Cubs' reliever Jim Bullinger, Kirk topped the Class A Midwest League with 33 saves for Springfield. His fastball is just average, but he usually keeps the ball low in the strike zone.

	W	SV	ERA	IP	H	BB	SO	BPI	$
1993 Springfield A	1	33	2.28	51	26	21	72	0.92	

BUNCH, MELVIN - TR - Age 22

Successful as a closer and a starter at Rockford, he earned a promotion to the Carolina League without missing a beat. A 15th-round draft choice in '92.

BURBA, DAVE - TR - Age 27

Burba had his best season in 1993 and could emerge as a top setup man. He's vulnerable to the longball, but only 27 years old and improving.

	W	SV	ERA	IP	H	BB	SO	BPI	$
1992 San Francisco NL	2	0	4.97	70	80	31	47	1.57	-
1993 San Francisco NL	10	0	4.25	95	95	37	88	1.39	2
1994 *Projection* >>>	7	0	4.41	82	84	33	60	1.43	1

BURGOS, ENRIQUE -TL - Age 28
An interesting story. After pitching three years in Taiwan, came back and threw well enough to earn a promotion to the majors. A definite strikeout pitcher. Walks and wild pitches may keep him from becoming a reliable closer.

	W	SV	ERA	IP	H	BB	SO	BPI	
1993 Omaha AAA	2	9	3.16	62	36	37	91	1.17	
1993 Kansas City AL	0	0	9.00	5	5	6	6	2.20	-

BURKE, JOHN - TR - Age 24
Burke was the first player taken in the amateur draft by the Rockies organization. His first full Single-A season ended with 114 strikeouts in 119 innings. The Rockies didn't have a Double-A team, so the righthander made a late season jump to Triple-A and showed similar success with a 3.14 ERA. Burke is a product of a suburban Denver High School (Cherry Creek), so Rockies ownership would certainly like to see him in a Rockies uniform for the start of 1995 at the very latest.

	W	SV	ERA	IP	H	BB	SO	BPI	$
1992 Bend A	2	0	2.41	41	38	18	32	1.37	
1993 Central Valley A	7	0	3.18	119	104	64	114	1.41	

BURKETT, JOHN - TR - Age 29
Burkett has always been able to throw strikes. In 1993, with a great defense behind him, and getting excellent run support, a slightly-imporved Burkett won 22 games. Often he looks like a righthanded Jimmy Key. The 22 wins were partly luck, but Burkett is a good pitcher, able to take advantage of luck when it comes his way.

	W	SV	ERA	IP	H	BB	SO	BPI	$
1992 San Francisco NL	13	0	3.84	189	194	45	107	1.26	4
1993 San Francisco NL	22	0	3.65	231	224	40	145	1.14	19
1994 *Projection >>>*	18	0	3.75	217	215	43	128	1.19	15

BURLINGAME, DENNIS - TR - Age 24
Despite a poor start for AA Greenville, Burlingame eventually moved up to AAA Richmond and also moved to the bullpen. A finesse pitcher, Burlingame walks too many batters to succeed in the majors at this point.

	W	SV	ERA	IP	H	BB	SO	BPI	$
1992 Greenville AA	9	0	3.09	151	137	62	84	1.31	
1993 Greenville AA	4	0	5.00	66	76	37	35	1.71	
1993 Richmond AAA	2	0	4.91	14	12	14	5	1.77	

BURNS, TODD - TR - Age 30
The luster has long since faded on Burns' once bright star. He was acquired by the Cardinals from Texas in August to help a struggling bullpen, and he was awful. The Cardinals soon tired of his act and released him with two weeks left in the season. He seems to be out of chances, even though he still gets people out.

	W	SV	ERA	IP	H	BB	SO	BPI	$
1992 Texas AL	3	1	3.84	103	97	32	55	1.28	5
1993 Texas AL	0	0	4.57	65	63	32	35	1.46	-
1993 St. Louis NL	0	0	6.16	30	32	9	10	1.36	-

BURROWS, TERRY - TL - Age 25
Made 25 starts last season despite a bout with shoulder tendinitis. The Rangers need lefthanders, and he finished strong (5-4 after a 2-11 start). He led Oklahoma City in wins.

BUSBY, MIKE - TR - Age 21
After going 4-13 for Single-A Savannah in 1992, Busby made quite a turnaround for the same club in 1993. The Cardinals credit Busby's sudden success to increased maturity to go along with an above-average fastball and slider. He suffered an elbow injury last August which did not require surgery. He'll likely be ready for 1994.

	W	SV	ERA	IP	H	BB	SO	BPI	$
1993 Savannah A	12	0	2.44	143	116	31	125	1.02	

BUSHING, CHRIS - TR - Age 26
Bushing had a very impressive season as AA Chattanooga closer, collecting 29 saves and 84 strikeouts in 70 innings. He has had strong strikeout totals throughout his minor league career. In a surprise move, the Reds released him in

late November. He will likely surface somewhere in 1994, quite possibly in the major leagues on Opening Day.

	W	SV	ERA	IP	H	BB	SO	BPI	$
1993 Chattanooga AA	6	29	2.31	70	50	23	84	1.04	
1993 Cincinnati NL	0	0	12.46	4	9	4	3	3.17	-

BUTCHER, MIKE - TR - Age 28
Was the closer until his arm gave out. He had surgery in September. If healthy, Butcher is the frontrunner for the closer job with his good hard fastball. There are, however, other candidates -- and it took the Angels a long time to focus on Butcher as a credible ace.

	W	SV	ERA	IP	H	BB	SO	BPI	$
1992 California AL	2	0	3.25	28	29	13	24	1.52	-
1993 Vancouver AAA	2	3	4.44	24	21	12	12	1.35	
1993 California AL	1	8	2.86	28	21	15	24	1.28	7
1994 *Projection* >>>	1	5	2.99	25	21	13	20	1.35	5

BYRD, PAUL - TR - Age 23
A 1991 fourth round pick from LSU, Byrd has quickly moved through the Indians' ranks. Not an overpowering pitcher, he must improve his control to become a major league caliber starter. Didn't dominate at Triple A and is probably headed back there in 1994.

	W	SV	ERA	IP	H	BB	SO	BPI	$
1993 Canton-Akron AA	1	0	3.60	10	7	3	8	1.00	
1993 Charlotte AAA	7	0	3.89	81	80	30	54	1.35	

CABRERA, JOSE - TR - Age 22
Skinny righthander who was selected as the fifth best prospect in the Appalachian (Rookie) League in 1992. Power and control both dropped off in A-ball in 1993.

	W	SV	ERA	IP	H	BB	SO	BPI	$
1993 Columbus A	11	0	2.67	155	122	53	105	1.12	

CADARET, GREG - TL - Age 32
A journeyman reliever at this point in his career, he didn't fare well in 1993. With Rob Dibble collapsing, Cadaret had his first chance to do something remarkable since he saved two games in one day for the Yankees in 1990; but Cadaret was no help for the Reds' needs in 1993. Not likely to be a factor in Royals' overstuffed bullpen for 1994. May catch on elsewhere.

	W	SV	ERA	IP	H	BB	SO	BPI	$
1992 New York AL	4	1	4.25	103	104	74	73	1.71	-
1993 Cincinnati AL	2	1	4.96	32	40	23	23	1.96	-
1993 Kansas City AL	1	0	2.93	15	14	7	2	1.39	0
1994 *Projection* >>>	4	1	4.17	72	75	46	40	1.68	-

CAMPBELL, KEVIN - TR - Age 29
Picked up 12 saves in Triple-A last year, and has had other good seasons in the minors. In the majors he forgets where the strike zone is (70 walks and 63 strikeouts in 104 innings).

	W	SV	ERA	IP	H	BB	SO	BPI	$
1992 Oakland AL	2	1	5.12	65	66	45	38	1.71	-
1993 Oakland AL	0	0	7.31	16	20	11	9	1.94	-
1994 Projection >>>	1	0	5.61	31	32	22	18	1.74	-

CAMPBELL, MIKE - TR - Age 30
Failed in three trials with the Mariners, 1987-1989. Really too late now.

	W	SV	ERA	IP	H	BB	SO	BPI	$
1992 Oklahoma City AAA	2	0	5.71	41	43	12	25	1.34	
1992 Texas AL	0	0	9.82	3	3	2	2	1.32	-
1993 Las Vegas AAA	2	1	5.40	31	39	9	24	1.54	

CANDELARIA, JOHN - TL - Age 40
Candelaria signed with the Pirates as a free agent prior to last season and hoped to end his career where it started.

It ended in Pittsburgh but not the way Candelaria had hoped; he pitched poorly and was released in early July. Though many contenders were desperate for lefthanded relief help, they all passed him over. His lengthy career is almost certainly done.

	W	SV	ERA	IP	H	BB	SO	BPI	$
1992 Los Angeles AL	2	5	2.84	25	20	13	23	1.30	3
1993 Pittsburgh NL	0	1	8.24	19	25	9	17	1.77	-
1994 *Projection* >>>	1	2	5.76	23	24	11	17	1.52	1

CANDIOTTI, TOM - TR - Age 36
1993 was a typical year for Candiotti except for his win total, which was ruined by a lack of run support. One of the most reliable starters in the league, he should be good for at least five more years thanks to his knuckleball.

	W	SV	ERA	IP	H	BB	SO	BPI	$
1992 Los Angeles NL	11	0	3.00	203	177	63	152	1.18	11
1993 Los Angeles NL	8	0	3.12	213	192	71	155	1.23	13
1994 *Projection* >>>	10	0	3.09	213	189	69	155	1.21	16

CARLSON, DAN - TR - Age 24
Carlson pitched well at AA Shreveport, but got pounded at AAA Phoenix. He won 31 games at Double-A in 1991 and 1992; watch what he does with his second Triple-A chance.

	W	SV	ERA	IP	H	W	SO	BPI	$
1992 Shreveport AA	15	0	3.19	186	166	60	157	1.22	
1993 Shreveport AA	7	0	2.24	100	86	26	81	1.12	
1993 Phoenix AAA	5	0	6.56	70	86	26	81	1.60	

CARLYLE, KENNY - TR - Age 25
Carlyle has been quickly promoted up the Detroit minor league system. He is still working on developing his pitches and mechanics, and finally ran into trouble at AAA Toledo in 1993 (2-10 with a 6.42 ERA in 14 starts). He could be pitching in Detroit soon where he would be a typical erratic rookie.

CARMAN, DON - TL - Age 34
Hasn't been a good pitcher since 1986, but lefties keep getting try-outs. During the mid 1980's I had a young man working for me, who had been a lefty pitcher with the University of Connecticut. Nothing special, he had trouble reaching 70 MPH on the radar gun at a country fair. Nonetheless, every six months or so, someone would call and ask if we would come for a try-out. It went on for years. Probably still going on.

	W	SV	ERA	IP	H	BB	SO	BPI	$
1992 Texas AL	0	0	7.71	2	4	0	2	1.71	-
1993 Calgary AAA	1	0	3.55	12	12	2	6	1.16	

CARPENTER, CHRIS - TR - Age 19
The first of Toronto's four first-round draft picks last season. He didn't pitch because he signed late, for a $580,000 bonus. Then in the Instructional League, he suffered from lower back pain. When he can pitch, the 6'5" Carpenter throws a mid-90s fastball. He would arrive in the majors sometime after the mid-'90s.

CARPENTER, CRIS - TR - Age 28
Obtained in a mid season trade with Florida, Carpenter quickly established himself as the Rangers' setup man for Henke. Overwork is a concern.

	W	SV	ERA	IP	H	BB	SO	BPI	$
1992 St. Louis NL	5	1	2.97	88	69	27	46	1.09	5
1993 Florida NL	0	0	2.89	37	29	13	26	1.13	1
1993 Texas AL	4	1	4.22	32	35	12	27	1.47	1
1994 *Projection* >>>	5	1	3.38	75	65	25	50	1.20	6

CARTER, JOHN - TR - Age 22
Once a nondescript Pirates' farmhand, Carter attracted attention of Indians' brass with a big year (17 wins, 3-to-1 strikeout/walk ratio) at Single-A Columbus in 1993. This was is a pitcher's league, though, so the jury is still out.

	W	SV	ERA	IP	H	BB	SO	BPI	$
1993 Columbus A	17	0	2.79	180	147	48	134	1.08	

CARTER, LARRY - TR - Age 28
Rose to the majors in 1992, but his 1993 season was shortened by injury.

	W	SV	ERA	IP	H	BB	SO	BPI	$
1992 Phoenix AAA	11	0	4.37	185	188	62	126	1.35	
1992 San Francisco NL	1	0	4.64	33	34	18	21	1.58	-
1993 Phoenix AAA	3	0	2.88	34	28	15	31	1.26	

CARY, CHUCK - TL - Age 34
Returned for a short stay in the majors last year after pitching in Japan in 1992. He hasn't really pitched well anywhere since 1989.

	W	SV	ERA	IP	H	BB	SO	BPI	$
1993 Chicago AL	1	0	5.23	20	22	11	10	1.65	-
1994 Projection >>>	1	0	5.43	18	20	10	9	1.64	-

CASIAN, LARRY - TL - Age 28
Lefty setup man who had his career-best year last year. His role could expand if anything happens to Mark Guthrie.

	W	SV	ERA	IP	H	BB	SO	BPI	$
1992 Minnesota AL	1	0	2.70	7	7	1	2	1.20	0
1993 Minnesota AL	5	1	3.02	56	59	14	31	1.30	5
1994 Projection >>>	3	1	3.21	38	41	9	20	1.31	3

CASTILLO, FRANK - TR - Age 25
A miserable 1993 derailed what had been a steady progression of major league success. The word was that Castillo was tipping his pitches, and with his best pitch being the changeup, that could explain the carnage. He's still got fine control and strikes out his share, but he's a flyball pitcher in Wrigley.

	W	SV	ERA	IP	H	BB	SO	BPI	$
1992 Chicago NL	10	0	3.46	205	179	63	135	1.18	8
1993 Chicago NL	5	0	4.84	141	162	39	84	1.42	-
1994 Projection >>>	7	0	4.27	158	162	45	98	1.31	1

CASTILLO, JUAN - TR - Age 23
Hard worker with good stamina, making slow but steady progress up the Mets ladder.

	W	SV	ERA	IP	H	BB	SO	BPI	$
1993 Binghamton AA	7	0	4.56	166	167	55	118	1.33	

CASTILLO, TONY - TL - Age 31
Castillo turned out to be a valuable addition to the Blue Jays. With Bob MacDonald gone to Detroit, Castillo became the lefthanded setup man and responded with a solid year. He doesn't have blazing speed or pinpoint control, but the movement on his curveball is good enough to dazzle major league hitters. Look for similar contributions this year.

	W	SV	ERA	IP	H	BB	SO	BPI	$
1992 Toledo AAA	2	2	3.63	44	48	14	24	1.39	
1993 Toronto AL	3	0	3.38	50	44	22	28	1.31	
1994 Projection >>>	2	0	3.37	34	31	14	19	1.33	1

CHAPIN, DARRIN - TR - Age 28
Chapin was a closer with AAA Portland last year. He could be called up to take over a middle relief role, but he didn't look very impressive even when getting saves in 1993.

	W	SV	ERA	IP	H	BB	SO	BPI	$
1992 Philadelphia NL	0	0	9.00	2	2	0	1	1.00	-
1993 Portland AAA	5	14	4.31	56	58	24	43	1.90	

CHARLTON, NORM - TL - Age 31

Charlton tore a ligament in his pitching elbow in August, ending his season and possibly his career. He underwent "Tommy John" surgery and might not return until after the All-Star break. When he was healthy, he was very good.

	W	SV	ERA	IP	H	BB	SO	BPI	$
1992 Cincinnati NL	4	26	2.99	81	79	26	90	1.29	23
1993 Seattle AL	1	18	2.34	34	22	17	48	1.14	16

CHAVEZ, TONY - TR - Age 23

Struck out nearly 1.5 batters an inning in the Midwest League. The closer's numbers suffered in his short Double-A stint, so he'll probably have to start '94 in the Texas League.

CHIAMPARINO, SCOTT - TR - Age 27

Has now frustrated three organizations with his penchant for debilitating arm injuries. The Marlins released him the day after the season ended, but he'll probably get a minor league offer from someone in 1994. Last time he was a little healthy, he did this:

	W	SV	ERA	IP	H	BB	SO	BPI	$
1992 Texas AL	0	0	3.55	25	25	5	13	1.18	1

CHITREN, STEVE - TR - Age 25

The former "heir to Eckersley" spent the entire 1991 season with Oakland and actually got four saves before falling back into the minor league pack in 1992. An effort to convert him to starter was a disaster. Last year, this Stanford-educated relief specialist pitched well at AAA Tacoma and will make another bid for that "heir" label in 1994. Chitren still has a good fastball and is now working on finesse and location.

	W	SV	ERA	IP	H	BB	SO	BPI	$
1992 Tacoma AAA	4	0	6.82	62	64	46	37	1.77	
1993 Tacoma AAA	1	1	3.00	24	21	14	27	1.45	

CHOUINARD, BOB - TR - Age 20

Chouinard led the Midwest League in ERA and had 10 complete games in 1992. He will not be a candidate for major league time for at least a year or two.

	W	SV	ERA	IP	H	BB	SO	BPI	$
1992 Kane County A	10	0	2.08	182	152	38	112	1.04	
1993 Modesto A	8	0	4.26	145	154	56	82	1.44	

CHRISTMAN, SCOTT - TL - Age 22

Drafted in the first round last season out of Oregon State, and signed for a $450,000 bonus. Throws only in the high 80s, but is projected to reach the majors during '95 or '96.

CHRISTOPHER, MIKE - TR - Age 30

A longtime minor leaguer, this crafty righty has had cups of coffee the past three seasons. Bred to be a reliever, he's extremely tough on righties and has pinpoint control.

	W	SV	ERA	IP	H	BB	SO	BPI	$
1992 Colorado Springs AAA	4	26	2.91	59	59	13	39	1.23	
1992 Cleveland AL	0	0	3.00	18	17	10	13	1.50	-
1993 Cleveland AL	0	0	3.86	11	14	2	8	1.43	-

CLARK, DERA -TR - Age 28

Pitched at three levels during 1992. Has a 4.00 career minor league ERA.

	W	SV	ERA	IP	H	BB	SO	BPI	$
1993 Omaha AAA	4	5	4.37	82	86	30	53	1.41	

CLARK, MARK - TR - Age 25

Big righty (6'5", 225) whose style belies his size. Not a strikeout pitcher, he relies on breaking stuff and excellent control (just over two walks per nine innings in '93). Pitched great in September, but inability to get a strikeout will work against him. Major league hitters will wait for that one hittable pitch per at bat that Clark will give.

	W	SV	ERA	IP	H	BB	SO	BPI	$
1992 St. Louis NL	3	0	4.45	113	117	36	44	1.35	-
1993 Cleveland AL	7	0	4.28	109	119	25	57	1.32	4
1994 Projection >>>	8	0	4.33	135	144	32	67	1.30	4

CLEMENS, ROGER -TR - Age 31

Coming off his worst season ever, Clemens still throws well into the 90's, making his failure quite a mystery. The Red Sox worked on two theories during 1993: (1) that Clemens worked out so hard between starts (he is a fanatic about exercise) that he might have been too tired all the time, and (2) that he became over-fascinated with breaking pitches and offspeed stuff, moving away from the heater that made him dominant.

	W	SV	ERA	IP	H	BB	SO	BPI	$
1992 Boston AL	18	0	2.41	246	203	62	208	1.07	30
1993 Boston AL	11	0	4.46	191	175	67	160	1.27	8
1994 Projection >>>	15	0	3.24	201	170	65	180	1.17	21

CLEMENTS, PAT - TL - Age 32

Clements came to Baltimore on waivers from the Padres and became a garden variety lefty reliever. He was displaced from the major league roster when fellow southpaws Jim Poole returned to health and Brad Pennington earned a look.

	W	SV	ERA	IP	H	BB	SO	BPI	$
1992 San Diego NL	2	0	2.66	24	25	12	11	1.56	-
1992 Baltimore AL	2	0	3.28	24	23	11	9	1.38	-
1993 Rochester AAA	0	1	5.91	10	14	8	8	2.20	

COCHRAN, JAMIE - TR - Age 25

Cochran's 46 saves at Savannah was a single season minor league record and came on the heels of his record setting 24 save performance in the New York-Penn League with Single-A Hamilton in 1992. His fastball is just average, which prevents him from being a "can't miss" prospect. But, Cochran is aggressive and throws strikes; it'd be hard for the Cardinals to ignore his success.

	W	SV	ERA	IP	H	BB	SO	BPI	$
1993 Savannah A	4	46	1.55	64	51	22	62	1.14	

COLE, VICTOR - TR - Age 26

Cole was ineffective in the major leagues in 1992. He made four starts and tired in all of them once he got to the fifth inning. Converted to relief in 1993, he went back to Double-A to regroup. First big leaguer from Russia in 60 years.

	W	SV	ERA	IP	H	BB	SO	BPI	$
1992 Buffalo AAA	11	0	3.11	116	102	61	69	1.41	
1992 Pittsburgh NL	0	0	5.48	23	23	14	12	1.61	-
1993 Carolina AA	0	8	5.93	41	39	31	35	1.70	

COLEMAN, BILLY - TR - Age 25

In his third pro season, Coleman made great strides, overpowering Sally League batters.

COMBS, PAT - TL - Age 27

The Phils' 1988 first round pick, he had a meteoric rise through the system and looked like a future Cy Young winner in September 1989. Elbow problems in 1992 and poor control in 1993 have set him back; he was reduced to an 0-9 season at Triple-A. His only hope lies in the fact that he throws a baseball with his left hand.

	W	SV	ERA	IP	H	BB	SO	BPI	$
1992 Philadelphia NL	1	0	7.71	18	20	12	11	1.71	-
1993 Scranton AAA	0	0	4.84	83	97	27	60	1.49	

COMPRES, FIDEL - TR - Age 28

A career minor leaguer, Compres has been waiting ten years. A change in organizations (from the Cardinals to the Padres) didn't help, so he may never make it.

	W	SV	ERA	IP	H	BB	SO	BPI	$
1992 Arkansas AA	4	28	3.28	57	55	23	39	1.35	
1993 Las Vegas AAA	1	4	5.54	26	33	10	7	1.65	

CONE, DAVID - TR - Age 31

Cone would have had a winning record with reasonable run support. Again among the leaders in innings, strikeouts, ERA. Will be one of Royals top two guns in 1994 and could be a big rebound candidate.

	W	SV	ERA	IP	H	BB	SO	BPI	$
1992 New York NL	13	0	2.88	196	162	82	214	1.24	10
1992 Toronto AL	4	0	2.55	53	39	29	47	1.28	3
1993 Kansas City AL	11	0	3.33	254	205	114	191	1.26	17
1994 Projection >>>	15	0	3.30	240	201	99	220	1.25	18

CONVERSE, JIM - TR - Age 22

Converse was rushed to the majors after a good spring. He struggled there and never recovered, even after being sent back to Triple-A. At Calgary he had a 5.40 ERA in 22 starts. He's a couple years away from being a major leaguer.

	W	SV	ERA	IP	H	BB	SO	BPI	$
1992 Jacksonville AA	12	0	2.66	159	134	82	157	1.36	
1993 Seattle AL	1	0	5.31	20	23	14	10	1.84	-

COOK, ANDY - TR - Age 26

Fairly unimpressive minor league starter whose callup was mainly to see if he had anything left.

	W	SV	ERA	IP	H	BB	SO	BPI	$
1993 Columbus AAA	6	0	6.54	118	149	49	47	1.67	
1993 New York AL	0	0	5.06	5	4	7	4	2.16	-

COOK, DENNIS - TL - Age 31

A fiery competitor who will continue to get chances solely because he is lefthanded. One of the best hitting pitchers in baseball, which comes in real handy in the AL.

	W	SV	ERA	IP	H	BB	SO	BPI	$
1992 Cleveland AL	5	0	3.82	158	156	50	96	1.30	4
1993Cleveland AL	5	0	5.67	54	62	16	34	1.44	-
1994 Projection >>>	5	0	4.48	82	86	25	45	1.35	-

COOK, MIKE - TR - Age 30

Journeyman reliever Mike Cook hooked on with the Orioles in 1993, spending most of his time at AAA Rochester. He doesn't have much of a future with the Orioles. At best he is a fourth or fifth man in the bullpen.

COOKE, STEVE - TL - Age 24

Cooke had a solid rookie season, posting the most wins by a Pirates' rookie lefthander since Woodie Fryman's 12 in 1966. A big breaking curveball is Cooke's best pitch and should make him a consistent winner for many seasons.

	W	SV	ERA	IP	H	BB	SO	BPI	$
1992 Pittsburgh NL	2	1	3.52	23	22	4	10	1.13	0
1993 Pittsburgh NL	10	0	3.89	210	207	59	132	1.27	8
1994 Projection >>>	12	0	3.70	200	195	51	130	1.23	11

CORBIN, ARCHIE - TR - Age 26

He has spent three years in Rookie ball, two years in A-ball and three in Double-A. He surfaced for two innings with the Royals in 1991 and could again reappear if he can pitch like he did for Harrisburg last year.

	W	SV	ERA	IP	H	BB	SO	BPI	$
1992 Memphis AA	7	0	4.73	112	115	72	100	1.66	
1992 Harrisburg AA	0	0	0.00	3	2	1	3	1.00	
1993 Harrisburg AA	5	4	3.68	73	43	59	91	1.39	

CORMIER, RHEAL - TL - Age 26

In 1992 Cormier looked like a big winner in the making, but he was inconsistent in1993. When he's going well, he has pinpoint control and uses his sinker to induce grounders. This season will likely point the direction for Cormier's future.

	W	SV	ERA	IP	H	BB	SO	BPI	$
1992 St. Louis NL	10	0	3.68	186	194	33	117	1.20	5
1993 St. Louis NL	7	0	4.33	145	163	27	75	1.31	2
1994 *Projection* >>>	8	0	4.08	150	162	29	80	1.27	4

CORNELIUS, REID - TR - Age 23

A Team USA member in 1988, Cornelius is highly regarded but has been beset by arm problems in his professional career. 1993 was the first season in four years that Cornelius completed without serious injury, so there is hope.

CORSI, JIM - TR - Age 32

A serious shoulder injury could spell the end of this veteran reliever's career.

	W	SV	ERA	IP	H	BB	SO	BPI	$
1992 Oakland AL	4	0	1.43	44	44	18	19	1.41	2
1993 Florida NL	0	0	6.64	20	28	10	7	1.89	-
1994 *Projection* >>>	1	0	3.88	33	37	14	15	1.55	-

COSTELLO, FRED - TR - Age 27

Pitched well for championship teams at AA Jackson and AAA Tucson in 1993, his eighth minor league season. He may get a look in spring training, but rates as a long shot to reach the majors.

COURTRIGHT, JOHN - TL - Age 24

After a strong 1992 campaign, Courtright struggled some at AA Chattanooga last year, going 5-11.

	W	SV	ERA	IP	H	BB	SO	BPI	$
1992 Charleston A	10	0	2.50	173	147	55	147	1.17	
1993 Chattanooga AA	5	0	3.50	175	179	70	96	1.42	

COX, DANNY - TR - Age 34

Although his numbers make Cox look like a top setup man, he does not have the bounce-back type of arm that would make him really valuable. Still, his fastball is better now than it was when he was a starting pitcher with the Cardinals.

	W	SV	ERA	IP	H	BB	SO	BPI	$
1992 Philadelphia-Pittsburgh	5	3	4.60	62	66	27	48	1.48	-
1993 Toronto AL	7	2	3.12	83	73	29	84	1.23	8
1994 *Projection* >>>	6	2	3.66	79	73	30	60	1.30	5

CRABTREE, TIM - TR - Age 24

A second-round pick in '92 out of Michigan State, he reached Double-A at the end of that season. His second go-round in the Southern League was not a successful one. He'll have to beef up his ability to strike out batters if he's to advance to the majors.

CREEK, DOUG - TL - Age 25

Likely to start this season at AAA Louisville, Creek will work on his control. In another organization, he would have a better chance to move up quickly, but St. Louis is well stocked with lefties.

	W	SV	ERA	IP	H	BB	SO	BPI	$
1993 Arkansas AA	11	0	4.02	147	142	48	128	1.28	
1993 Loulsvllle AAA	0	0	3.21	14	10	9	9	1.35	

CRIM, CHUCK - TR - Age 32

Crim led the Angels' staff in games in 1992 but was unable to regain the form he displayed in Milwaukee through 1990. His career is on the wane.

	W	SV	ERA	IP	H	BB	SO	BPI	$
1992 California AL	7	1	5.17	87	100	29	30	1.48	-
1993 California AL	2	0	5.87	15	17	5	10	1.46	-
1994 Projection >>>	4	1	5.21	44	51	14	19	1.48	-

CROSS, JESSE - TR - Age 26

Cross was second in strikeouts at AAA Syracuse last year, and his control has improved consistently the past few seasons. He is close to earning a major league cameo.

	W	SV	ERA	IP	H	BB	SO	BPI	$
1992 Syracuse AAA	0	0	9.45	6	11	3	3	2.10	
1992 Knoxville AA	8	0	3.45	147	136	44	126	1.22	
1993 Syracuse AAA	8	0	3.16	151	137	53	127	1.25	

CUMMINGS, JOHN - TL - Age 25

One of the various minor league starters who got pressed into service by the pitching-starved Mariners in 1993, Cummings was among the least prepared. After getting sent back down to the minors, he had a losing record with a 4.13 ERA at AAA Calgary.

	W	SV	ERA	IP	H	BB	SO	BPI	$
1993 Seattle AL	0	0	6.02	46	59	16	19	1.63	-
1994 Projection >>>	0	0	5.92	28	35	10	11	1.62	-

DAAL, OMAR - TL - Age 22

Partly on the merits of a strong winter ball performance a year ago, Daal was called up after just six games at AAA Albuquerque in 1993. He was used sparingly in lefty situational relief roles. With only 108 professional innings in the record books, Daal needs seasoning but has a good career ahead.

	W	SV	ERA	IP	H	BB	SO	BPI	$
1993 Los Angeles NL	2	0	5.09	35	36	21	19	1.62	-
1994 *Projection* >>>	3	1	4.55	40	39	17	25	1.40	-

DALTON, MIKE - TL - Age 31

When he didn't get a callup at the end of a strong 1992 season, Dalton fell into the career minor leaguer stereotype.

	W	SV	ERA	IP	H	BB	SO	BPI	$
1992 Buffalo AAA	3	10	3.66	71	56	18	25	1.04	
1993 Buffalo AAA	3	2	4.11	35	37	12	16	1.40	

D'ANDREA, MIKE - TR - Age 24

For a guy who's only 5'10", D'Andrea throws hard. He's from Maine, so he hasn't pitched as much as players from warm weather states and consequently may be a late bloomer.

	W	SV	ERA	IP	H	BB	SO	BPI	$
1993 Macon A	8	0	4.03	136	129	55	156	1.34	

D'AMICO, JEFF - TR - Age 18

The first of Milwaukee's four first-round draft picks last year, he didn't play after signing late (for a $525,000 bonus) and experiencing some shoulder weakness. The youngster is 6'7" and weighs 240.

DARENSBOURG, VIC - TL - Age 23

A smallish (5'10", 165) lefty, Darensbourg has been overpowering in his first two years of pro ball, striking out well over a batter per inning. Converted to a reliever in 1993, he made USA Today's list of bullpen "Hot Prospects". He hasn't yet pitched above Single-A level; if he continues to dominate at higher levels, he'll be worth a look.

	W	SV	ERA	IP	H	BB	SO	BPI	$
1993 Kane County A	9	16	2.14	71	58	28	89	1.21	

DARLING, RON - TR - Age 33

Darling's decline was as predictable as these things get; in 1990 he struck out 99 batters in 126 innings, but by 1992 he struck out 99 in 206.1 innings. Sure enough, despite good run support, Darling went 5-9 in 1993. The league hit .281 against him, and he hasn't had a really good season since 1989.

	W	SV	ERA	IP	H	BB	SO	BPI	$
1992 Oakland AL	15	0	3.66	206	198	72	99	1.31	10
1993 Oakland AL	5	0	5.16	178	198	72	95	1.52	-
1994 *Projection* >>>	8	0	4.57	188	197	72	100	1.43	-

DARWIN, DANNY - TR - Age 38

The National League ERA leader of 1990 had a lost season in 1991, ending in shoulder surgery. He came half way back in 1992 and all the way back in 1993. His only problems now are age and the ballpark.

	W	SV	ERA	IP	H	BB	SO	BPI	$
1992 Boston AL	9	3	3.96	161	159	53	124	1.31	7
1993 Boston AL	15	0	3.26	229	196	49	130	1.07	24
1994 Projection >>>	13	1	3.60	193	173	55	119	1.18	15

DARWIN, JEFF - TR - Age 24

His claim to fame is that he was traded twice for the same player (Dave Magadan). Hasn't yet shown that he can get batters out above the AA level. A full-time reliever in '93.

DAVIS, MARK - TL - Age 33

Once again a free agent, Davis won't attract quite the attention that he did after winning the Cy Young award in 1989. His four saves in 1993 came in a quick midseason streak when Gene Harris was on the shelf. At best, Davis may turn into a useful lefty-versus-lefty matchup specialist .

	W	SV	ERA	IP	H	BB	SO	BPI	$
1992 Kansas City-Atlanta	2	0	7.13	53	55	39	47	1.77	
1993 Philadelphia NL	1	0	5.17	31	35	24	28	1.88	-
1993 San Diego NL	1	4	4.26	69	79	44	70	1.78	-
1994 Projection >>>	2	3	4.99	64	73	42	55	1.70	-

DAVIS, RAY - TR - Age 21

Only a 61st round draft pick in 1991, Davis came on strong at the end of his Arizona Rookie League season in 1992. He threw four shutouts in his last six starts and missed a fifth because of an error. Davis also made solid progress in the South Atlantic League in 1993.

	W	SV	ERA	IP	H	BB	SO	BPI	$
1992 Chandler R	5	0	2.49	76	57	22	74	1.03	
1993 Savannah A	9	0	3.63	131	141	53	120	1.48	

DAVIS, STORM - TR - Age 32

Pitched well in relief for the Tigers following his acquisition late in the 1993 season. In 1994, Davis might even get some consideration as a game finisher. If he becomes a starter again, however, he will get crushed.

	W	SV	ERA	IP	H	BB	SO	BPI	$
1992 Baltimore AL	7	4	3.43	89	79	36	53	1.28	2
1993 Detroit AL	2	4	5.05	98	93	48	73	1.44	1
1994 Projection >>>	4	4	4.59	97	94	44	60	1.42	0

DAYLEY, KEN - TL - Age 35

Former top setup man for St. Louis, still recovering from 1992 surgery.

DEJESUS, JOSE - TR - Age 29

Had a 100 MPH fastball that attracted a small crowd around the practice mound when he first arrived at Phillies camp in 1990. Now trying to come back from a sore arm.

	W	SV	ERA	IP	H	BB	SO	BPI	$
1993 Clearwater A	3	0	4.07	55	65	19	33	1.52	

DELAHOYA JAVIER - TR - Age 24

This slender righty was picked up on waivers from the Dodgers in September 1993 after he stalled at Double-A. He progressed slowly through Dodgers' system while striking out about a batter per inning each season. A fourth-round pick of the Dodgers in 1989, he was considered a superior prospect compared to Pedro Astacio. He fits into Marlins' game plan of stockpiling live arms backed up in other organizations (see Kurt Miller, Robb Nen, etc.).

	W	SV	ERA	IP	H	BB	SO	BPI	$
1993 San Antonio AA	8	0	3.66	125	122	42	107	1.31	

DELEON, JOSE - TR - Age 33

In 1993 DeLeon turned in his first winning record since 1989. After a career of inexplicable losing with good stuff, low opponents' batting averages, and lots of strikeouts, he now has the distinction of being undefeated since 1992 -- at least until opening day.

	W	SV	ERA	IP	H	BB	SO	BPI	$
1992 Philadelphia NL	2	0	4.37	117	111	48	79	1.36	-
1993 Philadelphia NL	3	0	3.26	47	39	27	34	1.40	0
1993 Chicago AL	0	0	1.74	10	5	3	6	0.79	0
1994 *Projection* >>>	3	0	3.59	86	75	38	60	1.31	3

DELUCIA, RICH - TR - Age 29

Struggled in Seattle and struggled more in Calgary. The bright side is that he struck out a batter per inning. Unlikely to be a Mariner, but could shine in the right situation.

	W	SV	ERA	IP	H	BB	SO	BPI	$
1992 Seattle AL	3	1	5.49	83	100	35	66	1.61	1
1993 Seattle AL	3	0	4.64	42	46	23	48	1.64	-
1994 *Projection* >>>	4	0	5.07	69	76	32	45	1.56	-

DESHAIES, JIM - TL - Age 33

Basically cruddy in a late season stint with the Giants, Deshaies has not had a winning record since 1989. He pitched well for the Twins -- was actually their most consistent starter for the first half of the year. You can never count out lefthanded starters, but Deshaies gave up 26 homers in 1993, about twice as many as the year before.

	W	SV	ERA	IP	H	BB	SO	BPI	$
1992 San Diego NL	4	0	3.28	96	92	33	46	1.30	0
1993 Minnesota AL	11	0	4.41	167	159	51	80	1.26	8
1993 San Francisco NL	2	0	4.24	17	24	6	5	1.76	-
1994 *Projection* >>>	10	0	4.25	156	153	51	75	1.31	3

DESILVA, JOHN - TR - Age 26

Formerly of the Tigers organization, DeSilva has a good fastball, but not much else. Although he has decent control, he can't fool batters the second or third time through the order; they time his fastball and he gets mashed. He needs another pitch.

	W	SV	ERA	IP	H	BB	SO	BPI	$
1993 Detroit AL	0	0	9.00	1	2	0	0	2.00	-
1993 Los Angeles NL	0	0	6.75	5	6	1	6	1.37	-

DETTMER, JOHN - TR - Age 24

Dettmer impressed by going 12-1 in 13 second half starts at Charlotte. He didn't allow more than two runs or two walks in any of those starts.

	W	SV	ERA	IP	H	BB	SO	BPI	$
1993 Charlotte A	16	0	2.15	163	132	33	128	1.01	

DEWEY, MARK -·TR - Age 29

Dewey, a journeyman who previously had stints with the Giants and Mets, had a chance to win the Pirates' closer job after Stan Belinda was traded to Kansas City. However, Dewey converted just seven of twelve save opportunities. He relies on a sinking fastball but doesn't get enough strikeouts with it to be an effective closer. If the Pirates fail to find a more established closer, he will get his share of 1994 save opportunities in a bullpen by committee.

	W	SV	ERA	IP	H	BB	SO	BPI	$
1992 New York NL	1	0	4.32	33	37	10	24	1.41	-
1993 Pittsburgh NL	1	7	2.36	26	14	10	14	0.92	7
1994 *Projection* >>>	2	10	3.21	52	45	15	32	1.15	11

DIBBLE, ROB - TR - Age 30

Whatever could go wrong did go wrong in 1993. The primary problem was his control; he walked more than a batter per inning. Missing a month with a broken arm did not help matters, and shoulder problems contributed to a horrible September. Dibble's strikeout and hits per innings ratios were still good, but not up to previous Dibble standards. Star relievers occasionally have bad years, but meltdowns this bad are unusual. Dibble is a major gamble for 1994.

	W	SV	ERA	IP	H	BB	SO	BPI	$
1992 Cincinnati NL	3	25	3.07	70	48	31	110	1.12	24
1993 Cincinnati NL	1	19	6.48	41	34	42	49	1.84	8
1994 *Projection* >>>	2	15	4.25	54	40	35	55	1.39	11

DICKSON, LANCE - TL - Age 24
A former first-round pick (1990) and top rated prospect, Dickson was rushed to the majors after combining for a 7-3 record and a 0.94 ERA at three minor league stops in 1990. His career was derailed by torn cartilage in his left shoulder in 1992. Dickson started his comeback last year by pitching at all three minor league levels. He began with three good starts at Class A Daytona, and finished with two horrible outings at AAA Iowa. In between, he produced the following 1993 line at Double-A. Aside from Greg Hibbard, Dickson was really the only lefty starter anywhere close to the majors in the Cubs organization at year end.

	W	SV	ERA	IP	H	BB	SO	BPI	$
1993 Orlando AA	2	0	3.83	49	37	17	46	1.10	

DIPINO, FRANK - TL - Age 37
Released by the Royals at season's end, DiPino had little command of his pitches in very short Kansas City stint and was unremarkable at AAA Omaha. May be finished, but lefties have a way of turning up on major league rosters.

	W	SV	ERA	IP	H	BB	SO	BPI	$
1992 St. Louis NL	0	0	1.64	11	9	3	8	1.09	-
1993 Omaha AAA	1	1	2.78	22	21	4	9	1.10	
1993 Kansas City AL	1	0	6.89	15	21	6	5	1.78	-

DIPOTO, JERRY - TR - Age 25
A 1989 third round pick who was converted to a reliever late in 1992, and then became the primary closer for the Indians by the end of 1993. His ERA was deceptively low, as he allowed a lot of inherited runners to score. Indians will give him first crack at the job in the spring, but he is not safe bet to hold it.

	W	SV	ERA	IP	H	BB	SO	BPI	$
1993 Cleveland AL	4	11	2.40	56	57	30	41	1.55	11
1994 *Projection* >>>	2	16	2.98	68	66	31	43	1.42	14

DIXON, STEVE - TL - Age 24
This lefthander did not pitch well in his first major league shot with the Cardinals last season. However, he is highly regarded by the organization which believes that he can become a solid lefty setup man.

DOHERTY, JOHN - TR - Age 26
Doherty was inconsistent while adjusting to his new role as a starter. Prior to 1992, he was a minor league reliever never pitching more than 65 innings in a season. He had some good outings last year, and should continue to improve.

	W	SV	ERA	IP	H	BB	SO	BPI	$
1992 Detroit AL	7	3	3.88	116	131	25	37	1.34	5
1993 Detroit AL	14	0	4.44	184	205	48	63	1.37	1
1994 *Projection* >>>	11	1	4.30	146	163	36	52	1.36	4

DOORNEWEERD, DAVID - TR - Age 21
The Pirates' second-round pick in 1991, Doorneweerd stalled last season and got demoted from Pittsburgh's high Single-A Salem farm club to low Single-A Augusta. The Pirates like the way he mixes pitches and works hitters like a veteran but his fastball is only fair.

DOPSON, JOHN - TR - Age 30
Sinker/slider pitcher with a forkball. In 1993 the sinker didn't sink enough, and the forkball didn't fork. Now has questionable value.

	W	SV	ERA	IP	H	BB	SO	BPI	$
1992 Boston AL	7	0	4.08	141	159	38	55	1.39	1
1993 Boston AL	7	0	4.97	155	170	59	89	1.48	-
1994 *Projection* >>>	6	0	4.70	136	150	47	70	1.45	-

DOUGHERTY, JIM - TR - Age 26
A sidearming reliever who has posted outstanding numbers in all three professional seasons (including an ERA below 2.00 each year). He has recorded 94 saves, with a Texas League record 36 in 1993. Without an overpowering fastball, he has not been regarded as a top prospect. However, he has to be given a chance based on his exceptional record.

DOWNS, KELLY - TR - Age 33

A terrible pitcher, 33 years old, with a history of arm trouble. Last year he was 5-10; he shouldn't get any more opportunities to lose that many games in one season.

	W	SV	ERA	IP	H	BB	SO	BPI	$
1992 San Francisco NL	1	0	3.47	62	65	24	33	1.43	-
1992 Oakland AL	5	0	3.29	82	72	46	38	1.44	0
1993 Oakland AL	5	0	5.64	119	135	60	66	1.64	-
1994 *Projection* >>>	6	0	4.73	126	132	62	67	1.54	-

DOYLE, IAN - TR - Age 22

A 31st-round pick in 1991, he has been used solely as a closer his entire minor league career. Was chosen as the top reliever in the South Atlantic League in 1992. Not a flamethrower, he will need to improve his control to become a serious major league prospect.

	W	SV	ERA	IP	H	BB	SO	BPI	$
1993 Kinston A	5	23	3.08	52	44	29	51	1.40	

DRABEK, DOUG - TR - Age 31

After five years as one of the top pitchers in baseball, Drabek slipped badly in 1993. Poor run support was part of the problem, but he repeatedly failed to make big pitches when he needed them. Never overpowering, he needs to be more effective in changing speeds. Improvement in 1994 can be expected.

	W	SV	ERA	IP	H	BB	SO	BPI	$
1992 Pittsburgh NL	15	0	2.77	256	218	54	177	1.06	22
1993 Houston NL	9	0	3.79	237	242	60	157	1.27	9
1994 *Projection* >>>	15	0	3.40	243	235	59	150	1.21	17

DRAHMAN, BRIAN - TR - Age 27

A closer-in-waiting in the ChiSox farm system for seven years, Drahman finally became a true ace for Vancouver in 1992. Has good major league possibilities, but he is blocked by Roberto Hernandez and Scott Radinsky in Chicago, and his control still poses a question.

	W	SV	ERA	IP	H	BB	SO	BPI	$
1992 Chicago AL	0	0	2.57	7	6	2	1	1.14	-
1993 Nashville AAA	9	20	2.91	55	59	19	49	1.40	
1993 Chicago AL	0	1	0.00	5	7	2	3	1.76	-

DRAPER, MIKE - TR - Age 27

Won 11 or more games three years in a row as a starter, then was moved to the bullpen. Demolished the International League saves record and set a Triple-A mark in 1992. Now Draper is most noteworthy as living proof that minor league saves do not have any major league equivalent, unless you can find meaning in this equation: 37 AAA SV = 0 NL SV.

	W	SV	ERA	IP	H	BB	SO	BPI	$
1992 Columbus AAA	5	37	3.60	80	70	28	42	1.23	
1993 New York NL	1	0	4.25	42	53	14	16	1.59	-

DREES, TOM - TL - Age 30

Long time White Sox prospect. Never made it. Not likely to reach a new high level in 1994.

	W	SV	ERA	IP	H	BB	SO	BPI	$
1992 Oklahoma City AAA	2	0	5.20	36	43	13	22	1.54	
1992 Calgary AAA	7	0	5.18	92	108	37	38	1.58	
1993 Portland AAA	15	0	6.22	153	183	62	83	1.60	

DREIFORT, DARREN - TR - Age 21

After leading Wichita State to the College World Series, Dreifort was the second player taken in the 1993 draft, but the contract negotiations dragged through the summer and he didn't pitch again until the Instructional League season. With a $1.3 million signing bonus in the bank, he showed an effective tailing fastball. There is some concern about the physical condition of his knees.

DRESSENDORFER, KIRK - TR - Age 24

First round pick in 1990. Made it to the A's in 1991, but ended his season with shoulder surgery. He was supposed to be ready for spring training 1992, but is, shall we say, behind schedule. If you want farm system picks, take some nice speedy outfielders.

DREWS, MATT - TR - Age 19
The 6'8" grandson of former Yankees lefthander Karl Drews hasn't yet pitched as a pro because he signed late (for a $620,000 bonus). His best pitch is a low-90s fastball.

DREYER, STEVE - TR - Age 24
The Rangers' eighth-round draft pick in 1990 progressed farther than anyone else in the organization last year, from Double-A to the majors. Showed near pinpoint control in the minors, but couldn't find the plate in the majors. Effectiveness will depend on finding that control. Will be given a shot at the Rangers' fourth or fifth starter spot.

	W	SV	ERA	IP	H	BB	SO	BPI	$
1993 Oklahoma City AAA	4	0	3.03	107	108	31	59	1.29	
1993 Texas AL	3	0	5.71	41	48	20	23	1.66	-

DUBOIS, BRIAN - TL - Age 27
He started his pro career in 1985, but missed virtually all of '91 and '92 after twice having elbow surgery. The Orioles have been patient with DuBois and his injuries over the years, giving him many opportunities. Last year he produced a 2.52 ERA in 75 innings at AA Bowie, and then went 0-2 with a 9.00 ERA in a brief stint with AAA Rochester. He is a finesse pitcher and if he pitches well in Triple-A in 1994, he will be considered for promotion.

DUKE, KYLE - TL - Age 23
Duke has good control and had some success in a part time closer role for Single-A Central Valley, where he struck out a batter per inning, and walked only 12 in 41 innings. He'll move up quickly as the Rockies badly need lefty pitchers (and righty pitchers).

	W	SV	ERA	IP	H	BB	SO	BPI	$
1993 Central Valley A	3	9	3.07	41	42	12	40	1.31	

DUNNE, MIKE - TR - Age 31
Remember the rookie pitcher of the year from 1987? He hasn't had a good year since, and is just hanging on in 1994. Last year he pitched in Florida with the White Sox Rookie Gulf Coast League and Class A Florida State League teams.

ECKERSLEY, DENNIS - TR - Age 39
He's 39 years old, coming off his worst season since 1986. He gave up a hit per inning for the first time in seven years, including seven homers in only 67 innings. He is no longer the premier closer in the game. However, he notched 36 saves in a bad year, he is the only apparent closer in the near future for the Oakland organization, he is still in terrific shape, and he struck out 80 batters in 67 innings with only 13 walks.

	W	SV	ERA	IP	H	BB	SO	BPI	$
1992 Oakland AL	7	51	1.91	80	62	11	93	0.91	49
1993 Oakland AL	2	36	4.16	67	67	13	80	1.19	31
1994 *Projection* >>>	4	30	3.55	72	69	17	70	1.19	28

EDDY, CHRIS - TL - Age 24
Part of a big 1992 draft for the Royals, Eddy was the lefty platoon closer for Single-A Wilmington last year. He throws hard but walks too many. Needs another pitch to go with his fastball. May get promotion to AA Memphis to start 1994. No major league impact until at least 1995.

	W	SV	ERA	IP	H	BB	SO	BPI	$
1992 Eugene A	4	5	1.59	45	25	23	63	1.06	
1993 Wilmington A	2	14	3.00	54	39	37	67	1.40	

EDENS, TOM - TR - Age 32
A curveball specialist who posted reasonably good numbers but was rarely used in critical situations, Edens now rates as a borderline major league pitcher.

	W	SV	ERA	IP	H	BB	SO	BPI	$
1992 Minnesota AL	6	3	2.83	76	65	36	57	1.32	5
1993 Houston NL	1	0	3.12	49	47	19	21	1.35	0
1994 *Projection* >>>	3	1	3.36	56	52	23	32	1.34	2

EGGERT, DAVID - TL - Age 24
The lefthanded closer for Montreal's Midwest League team, Eggert blew away the league's batters.

EGLOFF, BRUCE - TR - Age 28
Former Cleveland prospect spent 1993 trying to come back from rotator cuff operations and broken hands. Pitched 18 decent innings for the Angels AAA Vancouver team.

EICHHORN, MARK - TR - Age 33
Eichhorn's a free agent, and his future in Toronto looked cloudy after the 1993 season. His sidewinding frisbee throw continues to fool hitters into hitting the ball on the ground, but his control isn't what it once was. In crucial situations, batters now try to lay off his pitches, hoping that a sweeping breaking ball won't find the plate as it floats by.

	W	SV	ERA	IP	H	BB	SO	BPI	$
1992 California-Toronto	4	2	3.08	87	86	25	61	1.27	6
1993 Toronto AL	3	0	2.72	72	76	22	47	1.36	4
1994 *Projection* >>>	3	1	3.06	78	78	22	51	1.28	4

EILAND, DAVE - TR - Age 27
Eiland had great success in the Yankee farm system but has struggled at the big league level. He has posted ERA's over 5.00 in each of his last three major league seasons, and he allowed more walks than strikeouts in 1993.

	W	SV	ERA	IP	H	BB	SO	BPI	$
1992 San Diego NL	0	0	5.67	27	33	5	10	1.41	-
1993 San Diego NL	0	0	5.21	48	58	17	14	1.56	-
1994 *Projection* >>>	0	0	5.32	44	53	14	13	1.52	-

EISCHEN, JOEY - TL - Age 24
Stolen by the Expos from Texas in the 1991 trade for Oil Can Boyd, Eischen is another in a long line of outstanding Montreal pitching prospects. He was a Double-A All-Star for Harrisburg last year and could be in the majors before the end of this season, possibly in a bullpen role.

ELDRED, CAL - TR - Age 26
One of my favorite told-you-so cases of 1993. Eldred is a good pitcher with a great curve, but his dominance for half a season in 1992 was largely a fluke. Rookie pitchers with sharp breaking stuff often have disproportionate success when they first come up, especially in the American League. At best, Eldred will have a career similar to Mike Witt.

	W	SV	ERA	IP	H	BB	SO	BPI	$
1992 Denver AAA	10	0	3.00	141	122	42	99	1.16	
1992 Milwaukee AL	11	0	1.79	100	76	23	62	0.99	14
1993 Milwaukee AL	16	0	4.01	258	232	91	180	1.25	16
1994 *Projection* >>>	13	0	3.66	187	164	62	128	1.21	14

ELLIOTT, DON - TR - Age 25
Yet another prospect obtained from the rich Braves farm system, Elliott is a hard thrower who stumbled in a short Las Vegas stint following his trade to the Padres. Prior to 1993, his minor league stats were very impressive, including a 2.08 ERA at AA Greenville in 1993, but last year he had a 4.72 ERA with 1.42 baserunners per inning at AAA Richmond, and then went 2-5 with a 6.37 ERA at Las Vegas.

ELLIS, ROBERT - TR - Age 23
A third round pick in 1990 from Panola Junior College in Texas, Ellis delivered an impressive season at Class A South Bend in 1992 with a 2.8:1 strikeout/walk ratio and an ERA that got as low as 1.98 in midseason. Last year he moved up to AA Birmingham after a strong start at Class A Sarasota, and he didn't miss a beat at the higher level, with 77 strikeouts in 81 innings and a 3.7 strikeout/walk ratio. Scouts like Ellis because he has a full repertoire and good poise.

EMBREE, ALAN - TL - Age 23
Generally accepted as the best of a very strong lot of Indians' pitching prospects after the 1992 season, he lost the 1993 season to elbow surgery.

	W	SV	ERA	IP	H	BB	SO	BPI	$
1992 Canton-Akron AA	7	0	2.28	79	61	28	56	1.12	
1993 Canton-Akron AA	0	0	3.38	5	3	3	4	1.20	

ERICKS, JOHN - TR - Age 26
A very hard thrower who stalled in the Cardinals system. He was a first round pick in 1988 but got released after the 1992 season. Ericks was last seen working in the Pirates instructional league, trying to find that good old velocity.

ERICKSON, SCOTT - TR - Age 26
Twins manager Tom Kelly said that Scott Erickson was a very unlucky pitcher last year. Always one of the toughest competitors in baseball, Erickson needs to make some adjustments, especially in getting out lefty batters who hit .342 against him last year.

	W	SV	ERA	IP	H	BB	SO	BPI	$
1992 Minnesota AL	13	0	3.40	212	197	83	101	1.32	10
1993 Minnesota AL	8	0	5.19	218	266	71	116	1.54	-
1994 *Projection* >>>	11	0	4.47	215	238	74	111	1.45	

ESTES, SHAWN - TL - Age 21
Seattle's number one draft pick in 1991, out of high school. In his second year at Class A Bellingham in 1992, this hard thrower cut his walks considerably, from 14.6 to 5.2 per nine innings. But he struggled in 1993 with Appleton in the higher A-ball Midwest League in 1993, going 5-9 with a 7.24 ERA and 52 walks in 83 innings.

ETTLES, MARK - TR - Age 27
After spending three years in A-ball, Ettles jumped quickly from Double-A in 1992 to the majors. His inexperience showed, though, and his stay was brief. That short trial with the Padres may become the highlight of his career.

	W	SV	ERA	IP	H	BB	SO	BPI	$
1993 Las Vegas AAA	3	15	4.71	49	58	22	29	1.63	
1993 San Diego NL	1	0	6.50	18	23	4	9	1.50	-

EVANS, BART - TR - Age 21
Walked more than a batter per inning in his pro debut in '92. Still walked too many last year, but cut the ratio down significantly while striking out better than 12 per nine innings last season.

EVERGERD, BRYAN - TL - Age 25
A very effective setup man last season, he can be counted on to get a strikeout in a clutch situation. He'll try to do that for AAA Louisville in 1994.

EYRE, SCOTT - TL - Age 21
Became a big strikeout pitcher because of a curve he developed last year. Sat out some time because of a tired arm.

FAJARDO, HECTOR - TR - Age 23

Continued problems with his shoulder, including the rotator cuff, cut short Fajardo's winter ball season a year ago, and he wasn't ready for spring training in 1993. Eventually he worked 30 good innings of rehab in the Gulf Coast League, made one A-ball start, and faced two batters for Texas. Hs's a big talent, with a fastball, slider, change and splitter. If healthy, he'll start the season at Triple-A, and could get a callup any time.

FARMER, HOWARD - TR - Age 28

Six-year Expos farmhand, he surfaced in Montreal in 1990, did poorly in four starts, and has been essentially the same pitcher ever since, although he works out of the pen more now.

	W	SV	ERA	IP	H	BB	SO	BPI	$
1992 Indianapolis AAA	3	0	3.75	84	89	24	64	1.35	
1993 New Orleans AAA	4	0	5.73	75	93	24	55	1.25	

FARR, STEVE - TR - Age 37

For a pitcher without a big fastball, Farr got some amazing results as a closer in 1988-1992. Over the years he has had various problems with his back, arm and shoulder, and in late 1993 it got so he couldn't pitch day after day, and the Yankees brought in Lee Smith. Farr's days as a big ace reliever are behind him now, but he still shows flashes of brilliance.

	W	SV	ERA	IP	H	BB	SO	BPI	$
1992 New York AL	2	30	1.56	52	34	19	37	1.02	27
1993 New York AL	2	25	4.21	47	44	28	39	1.53	19
1994 *Projection* >>>	2	19	3.12	51	43	24	39	1.31	17

FARRAR, TERRY - TL - Age 24

Acquired from Baltimore in a trade for Lonnie Smith, Farrar had a typical season in 1993. In four stops in his pro career he has been a .500 or slightly better pitcher with an ERA around 3.50.

FARRELL, JOHN - TR - Age 31

Made it back after nearly 3 years away. Was once a good pitcher, but is no where near that level now.

	W	SV	ERA	IP	H	BB	SO	BPI	$
1993 California AL	3	0	7.35	90	110	44	45	1.71	-
1994 *Projection* >>>	2	0	5.19	54	61	25	27	1.60	-

FASSERO, JEFF - TL - Age 31

The Expos moved Fassero from the bullpen to the rotation and he immediately became a dominant starter. A late bloomer, Fassero has the tools to be a good starter with a forkball, hard sinking fastball, a wicked slider and an adequate changeup. He allowed more than three earned runs in only one of his 15 starts. Fassero struck out almost a batter per inning and has allowed just nine homers in over 290 major league innings. After his performance in the rotation last season, he doesn't appear to be going back to the bullpen anytime soon.

	W	SV	ERA	IP	H	BB	SO	BPI	$
1992 Montreal NL	8	1	2.84	85	81	34	63	1.34	3
1993 Montreal NL	12	1	2.29	150	119	54	140	1.16	17
1994 *Projection* >>>	10	0	3.19	160	141	53	110	1.21	12

FERNANDEZ, ALEX - TR - Age 24

With his huge fastball that had scouts pursuing him way back when he was in high school, Fernandez just needed to learn how to pitch. For years he resisted the learning process, just wanting to blow people away. In 1993 he wised up, with outstanding results. With just a little luck, he could roll out seasons similar to last year's for the next ten years.

	W	SV	ERA	IP	H	BB	SO	BPI	$
1992 Chicago AL	8	0	4.27	187	199	50	95	1.33	3
1993 Chicago AL	18	0	3.13	247	221	67	169	1.17	24
1994 *Projection* >>>	16	0	3.53	224	212	64	144	1.23	17

FERNANDEZ, SID - TL - Age 31

El Sid was hampered by knee and elbow problems in 1993. He is still one of the best pitchers anywhere because he pitches high and hides the ball well. A free agent, he signed with Orioles. He should do fine in the American League, with just one caution: Fernandez produces so many flyballs that the Mets often avoided using him in parks like Wrigley

Field; in the smaller American League confines, Sid might give up 25 to 30 homers.

	W	SV	ERA	IP	H	BB	SO	BPI	$
1992 New York NL	14	0	2.73	214	162	67	193	1.07	18
1993 New York NL	5	0	2.93	120	82	36	81	0.99	11
1994 Projection >>>	10	0	2.89	170	125	65	131	1.12	17

FERRY, MIKE - TR - Age 24
A 1990 fourh round draft pick, Ferry turned in a strong year at AA Chattanooga. Note the 3.7 strikeout/walk ratio. The Reds are desperate for pitching and Ferry will get every consideration.

	W	SV	ERA	IP	H	BB	SO	BPI	$
1993 Chattanooga AA	13	0	3.42	187	176	30	111	1.10	

FETTERS, MIKE - TR - Age 29
Fetters was on his way to taking the closer's job away from Doug Henry, but had elbow surgery after the 1992 season and simply wasn't ready when the '93 season started. Late in the summer, he finally got back on track. Good sleeper quality for 1994 source of saves.

	W	SV	ERA	IP	H	BB	SO	BPI	$
1992 Milwaukee AL	5	2	1.87	62	38	24	43	0.99	9
1993 Milwaukee AL	3	0	3.34	59	59	22	23	1.37	2
1994 Projection >>>	4	8	2.98	59	53	23	29	1.28	10

FILER, TOM - TR - Age 37
Before 1992, Filer's last major league season was 1990, when he gave the Brewers a 6.14 ERA. Filer gave the Mets 22 decent innings, but his presence was a comment on a decimated staff.

	W	SV	ERA	IP	H	BB	SO	BPI	$
1992 New York NL	0	0	2.05	22	18	6	9	1.09	
1993 Norfolk AAA	2	0	3.79	123	132	34	65	1.34	

FINLEY, CHUCK - TL - Age 31
Back in top form. One of the best starters available.

	W	SV	ERA	IP	H	BB	SO	BPI	$
1992 California AL	7	0	3.96	204	212	98	124	1.52	-
1993 California AL	16	0	3.15	251	243	82	187	1.29	19
1994 Projection >>>	14	0	3.42	235	231	89	167	1.36	12

FIREOVID, STEVE - TR - Age 35
The only interesting thing about Fireovid at this point in his career is the fairly decent book he wrote entitled "The 26th Man". It details his travels in the minors and his couple of trips to the show. As a pitcher, he makes a pretty good writer.

	W	SV	ERA	IP	H	BB	SO	BPI	$
1992 Oklahoma City AAA	7	0	3.10	105	130	28	54	1.51	
1992 Texas AL	1	0	4.05	6	10	4	0	2.10	-
1993 Oklahoma City AAA	1	0	7.59	21	35	4	14	1.85	

FISHER, BRIAN - TR - Age 32
Yankee fans remember Fisher's 14 saves in 1985. Later he bombed with the Pirates and Astros and was fortunate to get back to the major leagues in 1992. He was barely hanging on in 1993.

	W	SV	ERA	IP	H	BB	SO	BPI	$
1992 Seattle AL	4	1	4.53	91	80	47	26	1.39	0
1993 Phoenix AAA	3	0	8.08	49	75	15	25	1.83	

FLEMING, DAVE - TL - Age 24
In two minor league seasons, he had combined for a 19-9 record and a 2.56 ERA. He did it with good control, not with overpowering stuff; it was inevitable that the hitters were going to catch up to him, which they did in 1993. Fleming also had to contend with elbow tendinitis early last year. Overall he did about as well as could be expected, and should do at least that well again in 1994.

	W	SV	ERA	IP	H	BB	SO	BPI	$
1992 Seattle AL	17	0	3.39	228	225	60	112	1.25	14
1993 Seattle AL	12	0	4.36	167	189	67	75	1.53	2
1994 *Projection* >>>	12	0	3.99	171	183	58	80	1.41	3

FLENER, HUCK - TL- Age 25
Flener was rushed to the major leagues so rapidly that he made his major league debut wearing Shawn Green's jersey and Al Leiter's shoes. He's a hard thrower with better control than he showed when up with Jays.

	W	SV	ERA	IP	H	BB	SO	BPI	$
1993 Knoxville AA	13	4	3.30	136	130	39	114	1.24	
1993 Toronto AL	0	0	4.05	7	7	4	2	1.77	-
1994 *Projection* >>>	1	0	4.03	45	49	14	20	1.40	-

FLETCHER, PAUL - TR - Age 27
The Phillies best minor league pitcher in 1992, Fletcher had minor arm miseries and generally lost it in '93.

FLORIE, BRYCE - TR - Age 23
After laboring for five years to get out of A-ball, he was the organization's pitcher of the year in his Double-A debut. Control can be a problem for Florie; he'll need to cut his walk total to succeed at AAA Las Vegas in 1994.

FORTUGNO, TIMOTHY - TL - Age 31
Fortugno was a first round pick in 1984 but did not make his rookie debut until the summer of 1992 as a 30 year old. A shutout of Detroit highlighted his season if not his career. He has little chance of making anybody's rotation but could contribute as a reliever.

	W	SV	ERA	IP	H	BB	SO	BPI	$
1992 Edmonton AAA	6	1	3.56	73	69	33	82	1.40	
1992 California AL	1	1	5.18	42	37	19	31	1.34	-
1993 Ottawa AAA	2	1	3.60	40	28	31	42	1.47	

FOSSAS, TONY - TL - Age 36
Decent situational pitcher for lefty/lefty matchups, but no longer effective for whole innings.

	W	SV	ERA	IP	H	BB	SO	BPI	$
1992 Boston AL	1	2	2.43	29	31	14	19	1.52	1
1993 Boston AL	1	0	5.18	40	38	15	39	1.33	-
1994 *Projection* >>>	1	1	4.29	39	38	16	25	1.38	0

FOSTER, KEVIN - TR - Age 25
A journeyman minor leaguer (formerly in the Expos and Mariners systems) Foster was acquired by the Phils in exchange for Bob Ayrault. He has struck out over a batter per inning throughout his minor league career. If he can improve his control slightly (about 4.50 walks per 9 innings over his pro career), he could fit into the muddled Phils' bullpen picture as a middleman.

	W	SV	ERA	IP	H	BB	SO	BPI	$
1994 *Projection* >>>	2	0	4.94	66	71	25	50	1.46	-

FOSTER, STEVE - TR - Age 27
With Dibble hurt and nearly everyone else ineffective, Foster was on the verge of expanding his role when he went down for the year with a shoulder problem that required surgery. Now he is just one of a half dozen candidates for a setup role. Has a good fastball and slider.

	W	SV	ERA	IP	H	BB	SO	BPI	$
1992 Nashville AAA	5	1	2.68	50	53	22	28	1.49	
1992 Cincinnati NL	1	2	2.88	50	52	13	34	1.30	1
1993 Cincinnati NL	2	0	1.75	26	23	5	16	1.11	1
1994 *Projection* >>>	2	3	2.92	32	32	9	21	1.28	3

FRANCO, JOHN - TL - Age 33
Franco's days as the top NL reliever are over. He's been injured for the past two years. Still has great knowledge and poise which can carry him until his physical condition improves. He's a useful lefty who can still find the plate.

	W	SV	ERA	IP	H	BB	SO	BPI	$
1992 New York NL	6	15	1.64	33	24	11	20	1.06	16
1993 New York NL	4	10	5.20	36	46	19	29	1.80	4
1994 *Projection* >>>	5	13	3.92	37	40	15	28	1.49	10

FRASER, WILLIE - TR - Age 29
Veteran Willie Fraser was a closer with the AAA Mud Hens last year, trying to get back to the majors again.

	W	SV	ERA	IP	H	BB	SO	BPI	$
1992 Edmonton AAA	7	6	4.90	90	110	24	49	1.49	
1993 Toledo AAA	10	8	4.69	71	79	24	63	1.45	

FREDRICKSON, SCOTT - TR - Age 26
Fredrickson was not ready for the big leagues, and it showed. He had spotty control and will return to Triple-A (or lower) in 1994. He may eventually make it as a middle innings reliever, but his future doesn't look bright.

	W	SV	ERA	IP	H	BB	SO	BPI	$
1993 Colorado Springs AAA	1	7	5.47	26	25	19	20	1.67	
1993 Colorado NL	0	0	6.21	29	33	17	20	1.72	-

FREEMAN, MARVIN - TR - Age 30
Freeman is a good hard thrower who has been held back by strained arm and shoulder muscles and back pain. He was out of action most of the year and not very effective when he pitched. He's just barely hanging on to his major league role and was released by the Braves and signed by the Rockies.

	W	SV	ERA	IP	H	BB	SO	BPI	$
1992 Atlanta NL	7	3	3.22	64	61	29	41	1.40	3
1993 Atlanta NL	2	0	6.08	24	24	10	25	1.47	-
1994 *Projection* >>>	3	1	4.25	38	36	16	28	1.37	0

FREY, STEVE - TL - Age 30
When the entire Angels bullpen went on the DL (or so it seemed) Frey was promoted from lefty situation specialist to co-closer. Manager Buck Rogers had, of course, given Frey nine saves back in 1990 in similar circumstances in Montreal. There may not be 13 saves for Frey in 1994, but there will be plenty of work; and if none of the righthanders steps forward, Frey could get more than 13 saves.

	W	SV	ERA	IP	H	BB	SO	BPI	$
1992 California AL	4	4	3.57	45	39	22	24	1.35	4
1993 California AL	2	13	2.98	48	41	26	22	1.39	12
1994 *Projection* >>>	2	9	3.32	47	41	25	23	1.40	8

FRITZ, JOHN - TR - Age 25
Fritz became the first 20-game winner in baseball while at Quad City in 1992, capping an undefeated second half. Although the strikeouts were plentiful, Fritz is not a power pitcher and is still a year or two away from the majors.

	W	SV	ERA	IP	H	BB	SO	BPI	$
1992 Quad City A	20	0	3.03	172	129	69	143	1.15	
1993 Midland AA	9	0	3.61	130	125	42	85	1.28	

FROHWIRTH, TODD - TR - Age 31
Submariner Todd Frohwirth had a few bad outings last year, increasing his ERA and ratio. He is still one of the league's better setup men, and he can become the closer or co-closer if Gregg Olson's elbow doesn't come around.

	W	SV	ERA	IP	H	BB	SO	BPI	$
1992 Baltimore AL	4	4	2.46	106	97	41	58	1.30	9
1993 Baltimore AL	6	3	3.83	96	91	44	50	1.40	6
1994 *Projection* >>>	6	6	3.20	99	90	42	55	1.33	10

FRONIO, JASON - TR - Age 24
After being used exclusively out of the pen his first two pro seasons, he was moved into the rotation with excellent results at Class A Kinston. Over last two seasons, he has allowed only six hits per nine innings, with well over a strikeout per inning. However, he's 24 and hasn't pitched an inning above Class A. If he impresses at the next level, he could arrive in bigs in mid-1994.

	W	SV	ERA	IP	H	BB	SO	BPI	$
1993 Kinston A	7	0	2.41	138	95	66	147	1.16	

FYHRIE, MIKE - TR - Age 24

Moving rapidly through farm system. Started quickly at single-A Wilmington, pitched well all year. Finished strong at AA Memphis, winning big (11-4). Could make a September start for Royals in 1994, but look for 1995 impact. Not a big strikeout pitcher.

	W	SV	ERA	IP	H	BB	SO	BPI	$
1993 Wilmington A	3	0	3.68	29	41	19	45	1.36	
1993 Memphis AA	11	0	3.56	131	143	59	59	1.54	

GAKELER, DAN - TR - Age 29

After failing as a Tiger starter (5.74 ERA for Detroit in 1991) and spending most of 1992 on the DL, Gakeler began a comeback attempt as a short reliever in the Red Sox system.

	W	SV	ERA	IP	H	BB	SO	BPI	$
1992 London AA	0	0	0.00	2	3	1	1	2.00	
1992 Toledo AAA	0	0	7.11	12	14	4	11	1.42	
1993 Lynchburg A	3	9	1.49	42	31	11	28	1.00	

GARCES, RICH - TR - Age 22

Rich Garces, once the Twins closer of the future, struggled in Triple-A yielding 70 hits and 64 walks in 54 innings.

	W	SV	ERA	IP	H	BB	SO	BPI	$
1992 Orlando AA	3	13	4.54	73	76	39	72	1.59	
1993 Portland AAA	1	0	8.33	54	70	64	48	2.48	
1993 Minnesota AL	0	0	0.00	4	4	2	3	1.50	-

GARCIA, APOLINAR - TR - Age 26

After retreating to A-ball in 1992, Garcia bounced back with some impressive numbers as a starter/reliever at AA Canton-Akron. Had a strikeout/walk ratio of 3-to-1 in 1993, and he walked less than three batters per nine innings. He is, however, becoming an elderly prospect.

	W	SV	ERA	IP	H	BB	SO	BPI	$
1993 Canton-Akron AA	8	3	3.89	111	103	37	110	1.26	

GARCIA, RAMON - TR - Age 24

The White Sox liked Garcia so much in 1991, they brought him up before Wilson Alvarez. The enchantment wore off, however. Garcia was not recalled again and was released at the end of 1993. He's still young enough to surface somewhere in 1994.

	W	SV	ERA	IP	H	BB	SO	BPI	$
1992 Vancouver AAA	9	0	3.71	170	165	56	79	1.30	
1993 Nashville AAA	4	0	4.01	43	45	56	79	2.34	

GARCIA, VICTOR - TR - Age 27

From 1988 to 1991 Garcia could do no wrong; he swept through all five levels of the Reds farm system in just four years. In 1992 he couldn't do anything right, and in 1993 he slipped back to A-ball as a setup man.

GARDINER, MIKE - TR - Age 28

A former Eastern League pitcher of the year (1990) Gardiner is only age 28 but he has already been with Seattle, Boston, Montreal, and Detroit. He was very successful in the minors, but is still learning how to pitch in the majors. The potential to be a good pitcher is still there, and maybe the right team and pitching coach are all that is necessary.

	W	SV	ERA	IP	H	BB	SO	BPI	$
1992 Boston AL	4	0	4.75	130	126	58	79	1.41	-
1993 Montreal AL	2	0	5.21	38	40	19	21	1.55	-
1993 Detroit AL	0	0	3.97	11	12	7	4	1.67	-
1994 *Projection* >>>	3	0	4.83	82	83	38	48	1.48	-

GARDNER, CHRIS - TR - Age 25
After moving rapidly through the minors, Gardner made his major league debut in 1991, but failed to stick in 1992, then missed the entire 1993 season with arm problems. He started his comeback attempt in the Instructional League after the 1993 season and faces an uphill battle to return to majors.

	W	SV	ERA	IP	H	BB	SO	BPI	$
1992 Tucson AAA	6	0	5.69	110	141	63	49	1.84	

GARDNER, MARK - TR - Age 32
Coming off of his worst season ever, Gardner's status is unclear. The Royals fourth/fifth starter roles are unsettled, but Gardner has done little to earn the job. Surrendered gopher balls at a positively Ruthian rate, 17 in 91.2 innings. Had trouble holding leads. He needs another pitch besides a good curve. Has been a winner in the past and could do so again, but must be regarded as a distant hope at this point.

	W	SV	ERA	IP	H	BB	SO	BPI	$
1992 Montreal NL	12	0	4.36	179	179	60	132	1.33	0
1993 Kansas City AL	4	0	6.19	92	92	36	54	1.40	-
1994 Projection >>>	7	0	5.09	126	123	47	78	1.35	-

GARRELTS, SCOTT - TR - Age 32
Been on the comeback trail a long time. His last good season was 1989.

	W	SV	ERA	IP	H	BB	SO	BPI	$
1992 San Jose A	0	0	2.25	4	3	3	1	1.50	
1992 Shreveport AA	0	0	1.86	9	4	3	15	0.72	
1992 Phoenix AAA	0	0	8.49	11	14	5	7	1.63	
1993 Las Vegas AAA	0	0	21.00	3	10	2	1	4.00	

GEORGE, CHRIS - TR - Age 27
After he produced a 1.78 ERA and 13 saves at AA El Paso in 1990, the Brewers thought highly enough of George to make him one of the two players they sent to the first official major league "orientation" seminar for rookies in the spring of 1991. He made two appearances for Milwaukee in 1991, but started the 1992 season in the minors, had elbow problems leading to surgery, and didn't pitch in 1993.

GIBBS, PAUL - TR - Age 23
Flamethrowing reliever who has struck out about twelve (yes, twelve) batters per nine innings in his first three pro seasons. ERA has consistently been below 2.00. How deep is the Indians system? He wasn't even the closer at Class A Columbus (see Cesar Perez).

	W	SV	ERA	IP	H	BB	SO	BPI	$
1993 Columbus A	1	3	1.63	55	32	27	68	1.07	

GIBSON, PAUL - TL - Age 34
Developed a tired arm in May 1991 -- while on the streak of his career -- and hasn't been the same since.

	W	SV	ERA	IP	H	BB	SO	BPI	$
1992 New York NL	0	0	5.23	62	70	25	49	1.53	-
1993 New York -New York	3	0	3.48	44	45	11	37	1.27	
1994 Projection >>>	2	1	4.27	55	60	19	38	1.43	-

GLAVINE, TOM - TL - Age 28
Three consecutive twenty win seasons with an ERA almost a run better than league average each year is what you need to know about Glavine; he's 62-25 over the last three years. He's a ground ball pitcher who lets his defense work for him. If the Braves bring youngsters Chipper Jones and others into the infield mix in 1994, Glavine's success may be tested slightly. Still, Glavine's a great bet to again win 20 and be a Cy Young candidate (again). His previous Cy award will keep him expensive, though.

	W	SV	ERA	IP	H	BB	SO	BPI	$
1992 Atlanta NL	20	0	2.76	225	197	70	129	1.19	17
1993 Atlanta NL	22	0	3.20	239	236	90	120	1.36	15
1994 Projection >>>	21	0	3.14	236	221	81	130	1.28	19

GLEATON, JERRY DON -TL - Age 36

If you have a left-handed son, teach him to pitch! Only six more seasons, and this guy will have pitched in four decades. He was Ferguson Jenkins' teammate at Texas in 1979. But he's just a journeyman nearing the end of his journey.

	W	SV	ERA	IP	H	BB	SO	BPI	$
1992 Pittsburgh NL	1	0	4.26	31	34	19	18	1.67	-
1993 Edmonton AAA	3	7	3.99	65	73	26	46	1.52	

GOHR, GREG - TR - Age 26

Sparky Anderson said he is considering Gohr for a co-closer role, but of course Sparky considers a lot of different ideas every year. Gohr has a 90 MPH fastball, but he's still a long shot to make it as a reliever.

	W	SV	ERA	IP	H	BB	SO	BPI	$
1992 Toledo AAA	8	0	3.99	130	124	46	94	1.30	
1993 Detroit AL	0	0	5.96	23	26	14	23	1.80	-

GOMES, WAYNE - TR - Age 21

The Phils' first-round pick in 1993 (4th overall), Gomes is a big, flamethrowing righty who pitched relief throughout his collegiate career. He signed late, but in 15 innings as a pro, he walked 17, whiffed 24, and gave up only five hits. He also instigated a brawl and helped win a championship in Clearwater. The Phillies will fast track him, hoping to at least modestly improve his control. If all goes well, he could get a peek at the majors late in 1994. The Phils fully expect him to be a closer at the major league level by 1995 or 1996.

GOMEZ, PAT - TL - Age 26

Another former Braves farmhand, Gomez spent seven years in the minors before getting to the Padres last year only to spend most of the year on the DL. He's not a great prospect in any case, but he'll battle for a bullpen job if healthy.

	W	SV	ERA	IP	H	BB	SO	BPI	$
1993 Greenville AA	7	0	1.13	47	25	19	38	0.92	
1993 Richmond AAA	3	0	5.45	71	79	42	48	1.70	
1993 San Diego NL	1	0	5.12	32	35	19	26	1.73	-

GONZALES, FRANK - TL- Age 26

Gonzales has been tried as a starter and reliever with mediocre results. He has moved steadily up the minor league ladder, but showed only minor improvement in his second try at the Triple-A level in 1993.

	W	SV	ERA	IP	H	BB	SO	BPI	$
1993 Toledo AAA	6	0	3.95	109	116	37	71	1.40	

GOODEN, DWIGHT - TR - Age 29

If there was ever such a thing as "minor" rotator cuff surgery, Gooden had it. He looks the same now as he did before. He will of course never be the same as he was back in 1985, but chances are no pitcher will have another season like that for ten or fifteen years. Gooden is on track to be one of the winningest pitchers ever. Now, if the Mets can just help him a little ...

	W	SV	ERA	IP	H	BB	SO	BPI	$
1992 New York NL	10	0	3.67	206	197	70	145	1.30	3
1993 New York NL	12	0	3.45	208	188	61	149	1.20	14
1994 *Projection* >>>	12	0	3.53	206	190	63	148	1.23	12

GORDON, TOM - TR - Age 26

Gordon made a fine two-month transition back to the starting role. He threw more fastballs in 1993, with good results. Still, he must continue to mix pitches to be a winner. Works a lot of long counts and walks a lot of batters. Has to get ahead of batters early to succeed. Likely to start the season as third or fourth starter; would get sent back to bullpen if unsuccessful. Which Flash Gordon will show up on any particular day is anyone's guess.

	W	SV	ERA	IP	H	BB	SO	BPI	$
1992 Kansas City AL	6	0	4.59	117	116	55	98	1.45	-
1993 Kansas City AL	12	1	3.58	156	125	77	143	1.30	11
1994 *Projection* >>>	10	1	3.86	145	123	71	120	1.34	6

GORECKI, RICK - TR - Age 20
One of the younger players on a young team in the Texas League, he got off to a 6-2 start that landed him in the Double-A All-Star game. He then lost his last seven decisions. His greatest asset is a major league caliber fastball.

GOSSAGE, GOOSE - TR - Age 42
Would like to pitch another season if Oakland wants him. Struck out 40 batters in 48 innings in '93. Still has good command, and still pitches inside. Hard to imagine that he will have much value in 1994, though.

	W	SV	ERA	IP	H	BB	SO	BPI	$
1992 Oakland AL	0	0	2.84	38	32	19	26	1.34	0
1993 Oakland AL	4	1	4.53	48	49	26	40	1.59	0
1994 Projection >>>	3	1	4.00	44	42	23	33	1.48	0

GOTT, JIM - TR - Age 34
Gott regained the closer role when Todd Worrell couldn't come back from tendinitis. Gott was one of the better Rotisserie gems of 1993 with 25 unplanned saves. He has had an ERA consistently under 3.00 in Los Angeles and the only real challenge to Gott's closer role now would be the healthy return of Worrell.

	W	SV	ERA	IP	H	BB	SO	BPI	$
1992 Los Angeles NL	3	6	2.45	88	72	41	75	1.28	7
1993 Los Angeles NL	4	25	2.32	78	71	17	67	1.14	26
1994 Projection >>>	4	16	2.65	81	71	25	70	1.19	20

GOZZO, MAURO -TR - Age 28
Gozzo has been in a number of organizations. He's had some good years in the minors but usually struggles in the majors.

	W	SV	ERA	IP	H	BB	SO	BPI	$
1992 Minnesota AL	0	0	27.00	2	7	0	1	4.20	-
1993 Norfolk AAA	8	0	3.45	190	208	49	97	1.35	
1993 New York NL	0	1	2.57	14	11	5	6	1.14	0

GRAHE, JOE - TR - Age 26
Had some arm problems last year. Grahe's future as a closer will depend on health and stamina.

	W	SV	ERA	IP	H	BB	SO	BPI	$
1992 California AL	5	21	3.52	95	85	39	39	1.31	18
1993 California AL	4	11	2.86	57	54	25	31	1.41	11
1994 Projection >>>	4	11	3.33	70	67	30	34	1.38	11

GRANGER, JEFF - TL - Age 22
Royals first round pick in 1993 (fifth overall). Texas A&M star. Showed why he was high pick with 56 strikeouts in 36 innings for Eugene. Made one major league appearance; the September callup was in his contract. A raw talent, Granger is a great hope for the Royals rotation by 1996. Will probably start 1994 at Single-A Wilmington with a move to AA Memphis later in the year.

	W	SV	ERA	IP	H	BB	SO	BPI	$
1993 Eugene A	3	0	3.00	36	28	10	56	1.05	
1993 Kansas City AL	0	0	27.00	1	3	2	1	5.00	-
1994 Projection >>>	2	0	5.50	41	47	23	20	1.70	-

GRANT, MARK - TR - Age 30
Grant is a journeyman middle reliever who has now reached the end of his journey.

	W	SV	ERA	IP	H	BB	SO	BPI	$
1992 Seattle AL	2	0	3.89	81	100	22	42	1.51	-
1993 Houston-Colorado NL	0	1	7.46	25	34	11	14	1.79	-
1994 Projection >>>	1	1	5.27	40	51	13	21	1.61	-

GRATER, MARK - TR - Age 30
Grater has been a top minor league closer -- 32 saves in 1989 led the Florida State League, and he had 24 saves with a 2.13 ERA for AAA Louisville in 1992. He got three innings with St. Louis in 1991, and the Tigers gave him a brief look last year. Grater had a horrendous 8.13 at AAA Toledo in 1993, and also pitched poorly for AAA Calgary.

GRAY, JEFF - TR - Age 30
Suffered a stroke in the middle of a fine season in 1991. Very unlikely to make it back, although he keeps trying. The Red Sox finally made him a free agent at the end of 1993.

GREEN, OTIS - TL - Age 30
Minor league outfielder 1983-1990. Tried pitching in 1991 and did well at Single-A and Double-AA.

	W	SV	ERA	IP	H	BB	SO	BPI	$
1992 Denver AAA	11	0	4.61	152	148	70	114	1.43	
1993 Vancouver AAA	2	0	5.61	109	109	53	97	1.48	

GREEN, TYLER - TR - Age 24
An injury-plagued righty who was the Phils' number one pick in 1991, Green has an average fastball, but throws a devastating knuckle/curve at almost the same speed. He started 1993 as a reliever, but his arm couldn't handle the daily usage. For that reason, his future appears to be as a starter.

	W	SV	ERA	IP	H	BB	SO	BPI	$
1992 Scranton AAA	0	0	6.10	10	7	12	15	1.90	
1993 Scranton AAA	6	0	3.95	118	102	43	87	1.22	
1994 *Projection* >>>	3	1	4.96	59	67	19	30	1.46	-

GREENE, RICK - TR - Age 23
Greene has a nice moving fastball. He has been a setup reliever in the minors with a below-average record. Greene is a former U.S. Olympian who could be called up this year if the Tigers need help in middle relief.

	W	SV	ERA	IP	H	BB	SO	BPI	$
1993 Lakeland A	2	2	6.20	41	57	16	32	1.78	

GREENE, TOMMY - TR - Age 26
Greene has been a Jekyll and Hyde pitcher over the past three seasons. When he's on, he's dominant. He had a stretch of five consecutive complete games early in 1993, but only two for the rest of the season. His 16-4 record was somewhat misleading, as he received excellent run support (6.00 per start). Greene had a 1st inning ERA of 6.90 in 1993, so forget about a future as a reliever. He has a history of arm trouble, which cost him a good chunk of the 1992 season. If healthy Greene should remain a 15 game winner in the short term.

	W	SV	ERA	IP	H	BB	SO	BPI	$
1992 Philadelphia NL	3	0	5.32	64	75	34	39	1.69	-
1993 Philadelphia NL	16	0	3.42	200	175	62	167	1.19	15
1994 *Projection* >>>	11	0	3.64	160	145	55	127	1.25	9

GREER, KEN - TR - Age 26
Greer made a big move in 1992 with a 2.42 ERA as he rose from Class A to Double-A to Triple-A. He's a hard worker with a rubber arm.

	W	SV	ERA	IP	H	BB	SO	BPI	$
1993 Colubmus AAA	9	6	4.42	79	78	36	50	1.43	
1993 New York NL	1	0	0.00	1	0	0	2	0.00	

GRIFFITHS, BRIAN - TR - Age 25
Had a dominant season in A-ball in 1991, but found the going tougher in Double-A. Still a prospect.

	W	SV	ERA	IP	H	BB	SO	BPI	$
1992 Jackson AA	3	0	3.80	97	95	42	91	1.41	
1993 Shreveport AA	5	0	4.85	134	152	68	83	1.64	

GRIMSLEY, JASON - TR - Age 26
Grimsley had one of the best curves ever seen when he was first called up by the Phils in 1989. Unfortunately, no one ever taught this kid how to pitch. Has walked about seven batters per nine innings in his major league career.

	W	SV	ERA	IP	H	BB	SO	BPI	$
1993Charlotte AAA	6	0	3.39	135	138	49	102	1.38	
1993 Cleveland AL	3	0	5.31	42	52	20	27	1.71	-
1994 *Projection* >>>	2	0	5.23	32	37	16	18	1.67	-

GROOM, BUDDY - TL - Age 28

Groom had a good record as a starter at AAA Toledo last year (9-3, 2.74 ERA) but he pitched like a typical erratic rookie with the Tigers. As a promising lefty on a team that needs help, he will get another look, and another.

	W	SV	ERA	IP	H	BB	SO	BPI	$
1992 Detroit AL	0	1	5.82	38	48	22	15	1.81	-
1993 Toledo AAA	9	0	2.74	102	98	30	78	1.25	
1993 Detroit AL	0	0	6.14	37	48	13	15	1.69	-
1994 Projection >>>	0	0	5.81	34	44	14	14	1.71	-

GROSS, KEVIN - TR - Age 32

An average pitcher who benefits from Dodger Stadium, Gross capped his season by knocking the Giants out of the playoffs on the final day of the season. If you value consistency and durability, Gross is a good choice; he has made 25 or more starts in eight of the last nine years: he failed to make 25 starts only once, in 1991, when he was used primarily out of the bullpen.

	W	SV	ERA	IP	H	BB	SO	BPI	$
1992 Los Angeles NL	8	0	3.17	205	182	77	158	1.27	6
1993 Los Angeles NL	13	0	4.14	202	224	74	150	1.47	2
1994 Projection >>>	11	0	3.80	194	201	73	140	1.41	3

GROSS, KIP - TR - Age 29

Gross put together a solid performance at Triple-A, leading the team with 13 victories and a 4.05 ERA. He also saved 13 games while showing good control and his strong September in Los Angeles makes him a good bet for a return ticket to the majors in a setup role for 1994. Control pitchers frequently develop later in their careers.

	W	SV	ERA	IP	H	BB	SO	BPI	$
1992 Los Angeles NL	1	0	4.18	23	32	10	14	1.77	-
1993 Albequerque AAA	13	13	4.05	124	115	41	96	1.25	
1993 Los Angeles NL	0	0	0.60	15	13	4	12	1.13	0

GUARDADO, EDDIE - TL - Age 23

Due to a pitching shortage last year, Guardado was jumped from Double-A to the majors before he was ready. He struggled, and he needs to develop a third pitch to go along with an average fastball and curve. As a lefty with good control (just 10 walks in 65 innings at AA Nashville) he has a very promising future.

	W	SV	ERA	IP	H	BB	SO	BPI	$
1993 Minnesota AL	3	0	6.18	95	123	36	46	1.69	-
1994 Projection >>>	2	0	6.00	57	74	22	28	1.68	-

GUBICZA, MARK - TR - Age 31

The last remnant from the Royals 1985 championship. His return from debilitating shoulder surgery in 1990 stalled a bit last year. He was awful in six early 1993 starts, then rebounded to become a respectable long man in relief . For a while he was the Royals only reliable bullpen pitcher except for closer Montgomery. For Rotisserie purposes he has little value since he'll usually only pitch in blow outs. Allows too many hits to be valuable otherwise. A free agent, his future may be elsewhere.

	W	SV	ERA	IP	H	BB	SO	BPI	$
1992 Kansas City AL	7	0	3.72	111	110	36	81	1.31	3
1993 Kansas City AL	5	2	4.66	104	128	43	80	1.64	-
1994 Projection >>>	6	1	4.50	109	126	41	76	1.53	-

GUETTERMAN, LEE - TL - Age 35

Guetterman was pulled off the scrap heap by the Cardinals last season after pitching for Seattle and both New York clubs. He pitched well and likely secured a role as a left-handed relief specialist for next year. He relies on a sinkerball and gets into serious problems when he leaves his pitches high in the strike zone. Guetterman must have perfect control to succeed.

	W	SV	ERA	IP	H	BB	SO	BPI	$
1992 New York AL-New York NL	4	2	7.09	66	92	27	20	1.80	-
1993 St. Louis NL	3	1	2.93	46	41	16	19	1.24	3
1994 Projection >>>	3	2	4.52	56	61	20	21	1.44	-

GULLICKSON, BILL - TR - Age 35
Gullickson is a good example of why it is usually good policy to stay away from Tiger pitchers. He is a workhorse who may win 12-18 games, but his high ERA and ratio can kill you.

	W	SV	ERA	IP	H	BB	SO	BPI	$
1992 Detroit AL	14	0	4.34	221	228	50	64	1.25	7
1993 Detroit AL	13	0	5.37	159	186	44	70	1.45	1
1994 *Projection* >>>	14	0	4.82	185	206	46	70	1.36	0

GUNDERSON, ERIC - TL - Age 28
Gunderson has been terrific at Double-A for years, including two great seasons for Shreveport and one for Jacksonville. His fastball just isn't good enough for the better, more disciplined hitters.

	W	SV	ERA	IP	H	BB	SO	BPI	$
1992 Seattle AL	2	0	8.68	9	12	5	2	1.82	-
1993 Norfolk AAA	3	0	3.71	34	41	9	26	1.47	

GUTHRIE, MARK - TL - Age 28
The Twins strong bullpen was weakened last year when lefty Mark Guthrie came down with a blood clot in his left shoulder, limiting him to 22 games. He had been a good middle reliever and setup man.

	W	SV	ERA	IP	H	BB	SO	BPI	$
1992 Minnesota AL	2	5	2.88	75	59	23	76	1.09	8
1993 Minnesota AL	2	0	4.71	21	20	16	15	1.71	-
1994 *Projection* >>>	3	2	3.71	45	41	21	35	1.38	2

GUZMAN, JOHNNY - TL - Age 23
Guzman is always mentioned as a top Oakland prospect; he is only 23 and has had some success in the lower minors. But last year this book said "Still needs to prove himself above Double-A." With Tacoma in 1993, Guzman was 2-7, 7.32. Still a long way from the majors.

	W	SV	ERA	IP	H	BB	SO	BPI	$
1992 Oakland AL	0	0	12.00	3	8	0	0	2.67	-
1993 Tacoma AAA	2	0	7.32	87	130	44	50	1.33	

GUZMAN, JOSE - TR - Age 30
Guzman should do better in 1994 than he did in 1993. He has an improved offense behind him. His ability to get groundballs and strikeouts is well suited to Wrigley Field. At times last year he was dominant, although he did develop shoulder tendinitis in September.

	W	SV	ERA	IP	H	BB	SO	BPI	$
1992 Texas AL	16	0	3.66	224	229	73	179	1.35	9
1993 Chicago NL	12	0	4.34	191	188	74	163	1.37	3
1994 *Projection* >>>	13	0	4.00	199	197	74	155	1.36	4

GUZMAN, JUAN - TR - Age 27
1993 was not the first time Guzman has suffered from wildness; that problem was all that kept him in the minors for years. Despite the lack of control, he very rarely loses, and when his control is on, he's the best pitcher in baseball. He has the hardest slider in the American League and a fastball that occasionally reaches ninety-eight miles per hour.

	W	SV	ERA	IP	H	BB	SO	BPI	$
1992 Toronto AL	16	0	2.64	180	135	72	165	1.15	18
1993 Toronto AL	14	0	3.99	221	211	110	194	1.45	7
1994 *Projection* >>>	14	0	3.56	201	177	94	178	1.35	10

HAAS, DAVE - TR - Age 28
Haas is a tough competitor but has below-average stuff. He was decent as a starter back in '92, but has since given up a lot of hits and homers. It takes more than mental toughness to be a winning pitcher in the majors.

	W	SV	ERA	IP	H	BB	SO	BPI	$
1992 Detroit AL	5	0	3.94	61	68	16	29	1.36	1
1993 Detroit AL	1	0	6.11	28	45	8	17	1.89	-
1994 *Projection* >>>	2	0	5.02	36	47	11	20	1.62	-

HABYAN, JOHN - TR - Age 30
Once a reliable setup man with his low sinker/slider repertoire, Habyan now throws too many fastballs up in the strike zone.

	W	SV	ERA	IP	H	BB	SO	BPI	$
1992 New York AL	5	7	3.84	72	84	21	44	1.44	5
1993 New York-Kansas City AL	2	1	4.15	56	59	20	39	1.41	1
1994 *Projection* >>>	3	3	3.79	65	68	20	44	1.36	3

HALL, DARREN - TR - Age 29
Hall was the top reliever at AAA Syracuse last year, but he's aging and doesn't throw hard enough to have much of a major league impact.

	W	SV	ERA	IP	H	BB	SO	BPI	$
1993 Syracuse AAA	6	13	5.33	79	75	31	68	1.34	

HALL, DREW - TL - Age 31
A journeyman major and minor leaguer whose last big league stop was Montreal in 1990, Hall had a solid year at AAA Scranton in the Phillies farm in 1993 (2.76 ERA with 7 saves) giving him a chance to stick as a situational lefty someplace. He's a charter member of the Bob McClure Society, devoted to the advancement and elongation of the careers of mediocre lefthanded relief pitchers.

HAMILTON, JOEY - TR - Age 23
Hamilton was the eighth pick overall in the 1991 amateur draft; he could get a major league opportunity by midseason in 1994. He was promoted to AAA Las Vegas for eight starts last year and will be watched closely in the spring. Hamilton may be the best San Diego pitching prospect but is probably a year or two away from any major league success. Hamilton helped himself in the 1993 Arizona Fall League.

	W	SV	ERA	IP	H	BB	SO	BPI	$
1993 Wichita AA	4	0	3.97	91	101	36	50	1.50	
1993 Las Vegas AAA	3	0	4.40	47	49	22	33	1.51	

HAMMOND, CHRIS - TL - Age 28
Hammond had a great first half and an awful second half in 1993. His status as the only lefty in the Marlins' rotation makes his continued presence a virtual certainty. A finesse pitcher, he needs to concentrate on being direct, not wasting pitches, and working quickly enough to keep his defense in the game.

	W	SV	ERA	IP	H	BB	SO	BPI	$
1992 Cincinnati NL	7	0	4.21	147	149	55	79	1.38	-
1993 Florida NL	11	0	4.66	191	207	66	108	1.43	0
1994 *Projection* >>>	9	0	4.51	169	178	62	94	1.42	-

HAMPTON, MIKE - TL - Age 21
One of several young pitchers pressed into service by the Mariners in 1993, Hampton was the one most talented ... and least prepared. At AA Jacksonville, where he belonged, he was 7-4 with a 3.71 ERA. Just 5'10" and with an assortment of breaking pitches, Hampton has been compared to Whitey Ford. He has a good career ahead of him.

	W	SV	ERA	IP	H	BB	SO	BPI	$
1993 Seattle AL	1	1	9.53	17	28	17	8	2.65	-

HANCOCK, CHRISTOPHER - TL - Age 24
Dominated two A-ball leagues in 1990-1991 but hasn't advance far since then. Second round pick in 1988.

	W	SV	ERA	IP	H	BB	SO	BPI	$
1992 San Jose A	7	0	4.04	111	104	55	80	1.43	
1992 Shreveport AA	2	0	3.10	49	37	18	30	1.11	
1993 Shreveport AA	8	0	4.06	124	126	52	93	1.43	

HANCOCK, LEE - TL - Age 26
Acquired from the Mariners organization in 1990, Hancock's minor league career has been characterized by a low ERA, but relatively little success in the won/loss column (3.06 ERA, 41-40 record lifetime). Because he's lefthanded, he'll probably get a shot somewhere.

HANEY, CHRIS - TL - Age 25

Still a viable prospect even after the washout year in 1993. The Royals need a lefty in the rotation and Haney has the inside track. He wrecked Triple-A hitters, then pitched well in majors for a short time, but finished the year very poorly. Royals must have patience with Haney, he'll eventually pay dividends.

	W	SV	ERA	IP	H	BB	SO	BPI	$
1992 Kansas City AL	2	0	3.86	42	35	16	27	1.21	1
1993 Kansas City AL	9	0	6.02	124	141	53	65	1.56	-
1994 *Projection* >>>	7	0	4.95	107	113	42	60	1.45	-

HANSON, ERIK - TR - Age 28

After a rotten 1992 season, Hanson lost his arbitration case and came into 1993 with something to prove. Initially he did well. Hanson was 5-1 through May 25, but then 6-11 with an ERA of 4.34 the rest of the season. Overall, he lowered his ERA almost a run and a half from 1992. He looks to be returning to his form of the early '90s. Hanson should do well in the National League.

	W	SV	ERA	IP	H	BB	SO	BPI	$
1992 Seattle AL	8	0	4.82	186	209	57	112	1.42	-
1993 Seattle AL	11	0	3.47	215	215	60	163	1.28	14
1994 *Projection* >>>	10	0	3.87	203	211	61	146	1.34	6

HARKEY, MIKE - TR - Age 27

Plain and simple, Harkey's fragile arm is incapable of pitching injury-free for more than two months with any kind of effectiveness. His good control and moving fastball are the only assets in his over-hyped pitching arsenal. The Cubs apparently are still optimistic about their former top prospect.

	W	SV	ERA	IP	H	BB	SO	BPI	$
1992 Chicago NL	4	0	1.89	38	34	15	21	1.29	1
1993 Chicago NL	10	0	5.26	157	187	43	67	1.46	-
1994 *Projection* >>>	7	0	4.90	108	125	31	48	1.44	-

HARNISCH, PETE - TR - Age 27

Harnisch had his best season in 1993, ranking as one of the top ten starting pitchers in the National League. A hard thrower who has gained confidence and command of his other pitches, he held opposing batters to a .214 batting average, the second time in three years he has led the league in that category. He should begin the 1994 season as the ace of the Astros staff which was second only to Atlanta's in 1993.

	W	SV	ERA	IP	H	BB	SO	BPI	$
1992 Houston NL	9	0	3.70	206	182	64	164	1.19	6
1993 Houston NL	16	0	2.98	218	171	79	185	1.15	20
1994 *Projection* >>>	14	0	3.16	214	173	75	177	1.16	19

HARRIGER, DENNY - TR - Age 24

Finally stuck in Double-A in his seventh pro season, even though his career record in 51-29 and his ERA a low 2.78. When he's on, he can be very tough (he had three shutouts in 1993) but when he's not, he can get pounded. Harriger needs good control to win.

HARRIS, GENE - TR - Age 29

With 23 saves and six wins, he was the most valuable of the three "G. Harris" pitchers in the majors in 1993. Rumored to be on the trading block at season's end because of pending arbitration rights, Harris may have reached his peak in 1993. He had his manager's confidence through the first half, but lost it.

	W	SV	ERA	IP	H	BB	SO	BPI	$
1992 Seattle AL	0	0	7.00	9	8	6	6	1.89	-
1992 San Diego NL	0	0	2.95	21	15	9	19	1.13	-
1993 San Diego NL	6	23	3.03	59	57	37	39	1.59	19
1994 *Projection* >>>	4	20	3.29	46	42	28	32	1.53	17

HARRIS, GREG A. - TR - Age 38

Formerly an ace reliever, Harris became the bullpen workhorse with 80 appearances in 1993. Great curveball. He can still get saves when necessary.

	W	SV	ERA	IP	H	BB	SO	BPI	$
1992 Boston AL	4	4	2.51	107	82	60	73	1.32	8
1993 Boston AL	6	8	3.77	112	95	60	103	1.38	10
1994 *Projection* >>>	6	6	3.43	117	97	61	96	1.35	10

HARRIS, GREG W. - TR - Age 30

Too bad curveballs go so straight at high altitudes. Acquired during the Padres fire sale, Harris struggled with the Rockies, going 1-8 with a 6.50 ERA. The Rockies desperately need this veteran to settle down and give them 200-plus innings. The 225 innings in 1993 easily represent a career high for Harris, but his ERA and all the other numbers are going in the wrong direction.

	W	SV	ERA	IP	H	BB	SO	BPI	$
1992 San Diego NL	4	0	4.12	118	113	35	66	1.25	0
1993 San Diego-Colorado NL	11	0	4.59	225	239	69	123	1.36	-
1994 *Projection* >>>	9	0	4.33	184	189	56	103	1.33	1

HARRIS, REGGIE - TR - Age 25

A Rule Five pick in December 1989, the A's were able to keep Harris by disabling him for the first half of 1990, while he pitched rehab in the minors. The walks were a minor nuisance with Oakland in 1991, but have a become a major block in his career now. Harris is a good hard thrower but hasn't made any progress in three years.

	W	SV	ERA	IP	H	BB	SO	BPI	$
1992 Tacoma AAA	6	0	5.71	149	141	117	111	1.72	
1993 Calgary AAA	8	0	5.20	88	74	61	75	1.53	

HARTGRAVES, DEAN - TL - Age 27

Earned an invitation to the 1993 major league spring training camp based upon a strong 1992 performance at AA Jackson, then faltered at AAA Tucson in 1993 before being shut down with arm problems.

	W	SV	ERA	IP	H	BB	SO	BPI	$
1993 Tucson AAA	1	0	6.37	78	90	40	42	1.66	

HARTLEY, MIKE - TR - Age 32

Veteran ex-Phillie Hartley let a high 37 percent of inherited runners score last year. His role is strictly middle relief. He has an effective splitfinger fastball, but not much more.

	W	SV	ERA	IP	H	BB	SO	BPI	$
1992 Philadelphia NL	7	0	3.44	55	54	23	53	1.40	-
1993 Minnesota AL	1	1	4.00	81	86	36	57	1.51	0
1994 *Projection* >>>	3	1	3.90	73	75	33	56	1.48	0

HARTSOCK, JEFF - TR - Age 27

A former Dodgers farmhand acquired for Steve Wilson. In his first two years of pro ball, he was 19-7 with a 2.64 ERA. In 1991, he was 12-6 with a 3.80 ERA at Albuquerque, where Pedro Astacio had an ERA of 5.47. Hartsock had a brief trial with the Cubs in September 1992 and was ineffective.

	W	SV	ERA	IP	H	BB	SO	BPI	$
1992 Iowa AAA	5	0	4.36	173	177	61	87	1.37	
1992 Chicago NL	0	0	6.75	9	15	4	6	2.04	-
1993 Phoenix AAA	2	0	5.53	55	83	20	35	1.87	

HARVEY, BRYAN - TR - Age 30

Harvey, Rod Beck and John Wetteland stand atop the hierarchy of National League closers. During spring training 1993, Harvey told me he was completely healthy again. But could he return to 1991 performance levels? "Well, everything worked just right in 1991," he said; "That was a special year." So was 1993. In addition to the big stats, Harvey was also the 1993 leader in trade rumors.

	W	SV	ERA	IP	H	W	SO	BPI	$
1992 California AL	0	13	2.83	29	22	11	34	1.14	10
1993 Florida NL	1	45	1.70	69	45	13	73	0.84	44
1994 *Projection* >>>	1	36	2.50	58	39	20	64	1.01	36

HATHAWAY, HILLY - TL - Age 24

Highly regarded prospect who was oft-injured and ineffective last year. Not likely to suddenly move to the head of the class, but the talent is there. Keep your eye on him.

	W	SV	ERA	IP	H	BB	SO	BPI	$
1992 California AL	0	0	7.94	6	8	3	1	1.94	-
1993 Vancouver AAA	7	0	4.09	70	60	27	44	1.23	
1993 California AL	4	0	5.02	57	71	26	11	1.70	-
1994 *Projection* >>>	2	0	5.17	36	45	16	15	1.70	-

HAWBLITZ, RYAN - TL - Age 22

Hawblitzel suffered in his Triple-A debut, and was hit even harder than it might appear, for his totals include nine innings of no-hit ball against Vancouver. Improvement in 1994 still could leave him on course for a major league job.

	W	SV	ERA	IP	H	BB	SO	BPI	$
1993 Colorado Springs AAA	8	0	6.15	165	221	49	90	1.63	

HAWKINS, LATROY - TR - Age 22

A 1990 high school draftee from Gary, Indiana, Hawkins took two tries at the Gulf Coast League Rookie League before moving up. He made up for lost time in 1993 with an outstanding season at Class A Ft. Wayne: 15-5 with a 2.06 ERA and a 4.4 strikeout/walk ratio. He's a large guy, a hard thrower, and he's getting stronger as he matures.

HAYNES, HEATH - TR - Age 25

Signed as an undrafted free agent in 1991, Haynes has done nothing except get batters out. As a pro, he's 23-2 with 31 saves, a 2.20 ERA and 255 strikeouts in 184 innings. His best pitch is a curve.

HEATON, NEAL - TL - Age 34

Developed shoulder trouble after a strong first half in 1990. Hasn't been the same since.

	W	SV	ERA	IP	H	BB	SO	BPI	$
1992 Kansas City-Milwaukee	3	0	4.07	42	43	23	31	1.57	-
1993 New York AL	1	0	6.00	27	34	11	15	1.67	-
1994 *Projection* >>>	2	0	5.00	36	41	16	20	1.57	-

HELLING, RICH - TR - Age 23

Arguably the top pitching prospect in the Rangers organization, Helling will be given a spring training shot at a spot in the starting rotation in 1994.

	W	SV	ERA	IP	H	BB	SO	BPI	$
1993 Tulsa AA	12	0	3.60	177	150	46	188	1.10	
1993 Oklahoma City AAA	1	0	1.64	11	5	3	17	0.72	

HENDERSON, KENNY - TR - Age 21

Milwaukee's number one pick in 1991, Henderson rejected the Brewers offer and instead took a scholarship to play for the Hurricanes. Eligible for the draft again in '94.

HENDERSON, ROD - TR - Age 23

After his first pro season was curtailed in 1992 due to injuries suffered in an auto accident, Henderson made up for lost time last year, going 17-7 with a 2.71 ERA at Single-A and Double-A. He has a live fastball, two above average breaking pitches (slider and curveball) and great poise. He's another Expos' prospect on the fast track to the majors.

HENKE, TOM - TR - Age 36

The unquestioned stopper for Texas. Henke set a career high for saves in 1993 because, for a change, he didn't have a slow start. The team was concerned about using him for too many "long" appearances.

	W	SV	ERA	IP	H	BB	SO	BPI	$
1992 Toronto AL	4	34	2.26	55	40	22	46	1.11	29
1993 Texas AL	5	40	2.91	74	55	27	79	1.11	39
1994 *Projection* >>>	4	37	2.70	66	48	24	67	1.09	37

HENNEMAN, MIKE - TR - Age 32

Although Sparky Anderson made Mike Henneman more of a one inning closer last year, he still recorded only 24 saves. He has never reached 25. Late in the year, Sparky kept saying that Storm Davis and even Greg Gohr will be given shots as co-closers in 1994.

	W	SV	ERA	IP	H	BB	SO	BPI	$
1992 Detroit AL	2	24	3.96	77	75	20	58	1.23	19
1993 Detroit AL	5	24	2.64	72	69	32	58	1.42	23
1994 *Projection* >>>	5	24	3.08	75	72	29	58	1.35	23

HENNIS, RANDY - TR - Age 28

This righthander made a promising debut with the Astros in late 1990 before missing most of the last three years with arm problems. He pitched in the Instructional League after the 1993 season and will try to launch a comeback in 1994.

	W	SV	ERA	IP	H	BB	SO	BPI	$
1993 Osceola A	0	0	3.31	35	21	15	26	1.02	

HENRY, BUTCH - TL - Age 25

Lefthanders are always in demand, which explains why Henry has bounced from Cincinnati to Houston to Colorado to Montreal. With an outstanding changeup, some scouts have compared Henry to Tom Glavine. However, Henry's results certainly haven't resembled Glavine's. Henry's good control can't overcome the 11.8 hits he allowed per 9 innings in 1993. The Expos have a way of getting the most out of other organizations' castoffs; Henry's another reclamation project.

	W	SV	ERA	IP	H	BB	SO	BPI	$
1992 Houston NL	6	0	4.02	165	185	41	96	1.36	-
1993 Colorado-Montreal	3	0	6.12	103	135	28	47	1.57	-
1994 *Projection* >>>	4	0	5.18	112	138	28	57	1.48	-

HENRY, DOUG - TR - Age 30

When Henry was giving up hits and runs like a batting practice pitcher, manager Phil Garner made a big deal about Henry's success percentage in converting saves. "That's the only statistic I care about," said Garner. Well, in 1993 Henry started blowing saves, and he lost the closer's job even though there was no good candidate to replace him. Henry is a classic example of a pitcher with a fastball and not much else. He has experimented with a splitter and a slider but can't rely on either.

	W	SV	ERA	IP	H	BB	SO	BPI	$
1992 Milwaukee AL	1	29	4.02	65	64	24	52	1.35	21
1993 Milwaukee AL	4	17	5.56	55	67	25	38	1.67	10
1994 *Projection* >>>	3	10	4.73	56	61	23	41	1.50	5

HENRY, DWAYNE - TR - Age 32

The knock on Henry is that he can't pitch with runners on base. Last year, he couldn't pitch even with the bases empty.

	W	SV	ERA	IP	H	BB	SO	BPI	$
1992 Cincinnati NL	3	0	3.33	83	59	44	72	1.23	1
1993 Seattle AL	2	2	6.67	54	56	35	35	1.69	-
1994 *Projection* >>>	2	1	4.95	67	60	41	45	1.50	-

HENTGEN, PAT - TR - Age 25

Hentgen was the beneficiary of tremendous run support last year and he responded with a nineteen win season. He is improving at the major league level and should see his ERA continue to get better in future years. With a good fastball, hard slider and excellent poise on the mound, he is virtually assured a spot in the starting rotation.

	W	SV	ERA	IP	H	BB	SO	BPI	$
1992 Toronto AL	5	0	5.36	50	49	32	39	1.61	-
1993 Toronto AL	19	0	3.87	216	215	74	122	1.34	13
1994 *Projection* >>>	16	0	3.80	200	198	66	120	1.32	10

HEREDIA, GIL - TR - Age 28

Heredia put up good minor league numbers in San Francisco's system but has struggled in the big leagues. The Expos gave him a chance as both a starter and reliever last season and he did little to distinguish himself in either role.

Heredia has good offspeed stuff and a strange herky/jerky motion; he made the International League All-Star team in 1993 and he'll get another shot at the majors this year.

	W	SV	ERA	IP	H	BB	SO	BPI	$
1992 San Francisco-Montreal	2	0	4.23	44	44	20	22	1.43	-
1993 Ottawa AAA	8	0	2.98	102	97	26	66	1.19	
1993 Montreal NL	4	2	3.92	57	66	14	40	1.40	2
1994 Projection >>>	3	1	4.00	51	55	15	30	1.38	0

HERNANDEZ, JEREMY - TR - Age 27

Acquired from the Padres in midseason 1993, Hernandez became a key member of Indians' bullpen committee. In Cleveland he was allowed to throw his forkball extensively, while Padres management had wanted him to use it sparingly because of concern about wear and tear on his arm. The results in Cleveland were excellent, initially, with Hernandez looking like the new ace, but then he began having problems. Were the Padres right all along? More likely, the AL hitters simply learned how to lay off and wait for a fat pitch.

	W	SV	ERA	IP	H	BB	SO	BPI	$
1992 Las Vegas AAA	2	11	2.91	56	53	20	38	1.30	
1992 San Diego NL	1	1	4.17	37	39	11	25	1.36	-
1993 San Diego NL	0	0	4.72	34	41	7	26	1.46	0
1993 Cleveland AL	6	8	3.14	77	75	27	44	1.32	11
1994 Projection >>>	4	5	3.65	80	83	24	50	1.34	6

HERNANDEZ, ROBERTO - TR - Age 29

Good control, a 90+ fastball and a wicked slider and forkball make Hernandez a top-notch closer. He has no real trouble getting lefties out, either. Could get 50 saves in the right circumstances.

	W	SV	ERA	IP	H	BB	SO	BPI	$
1992 Vancouver AAA	3	2	2.61	20	13	11	23	1.16	
1992 Chicago AL	7	12	1.65	71	45	20	68	0.92	19
1993 Chicago AL	3	38	2.29	79	66	20	71	1.10	38
1994 Projection >>>	4	40	2.61	70	57	19	64	1.09	40

HERNANDEZ, XAVIER - TR - Age 28

The Astros' most effective reliever in 1993 was one of the top setup men in the league for the second straight year. He has excellent movement on his pitches with good control. He isn't overpowering, but was one of only three National League pitchers to average more than one strikeout per inning in 1993. He should continue to get more save opportunities, and could develop into a top closer if given the chance. The Yankees will use Hernandez as their righty closer initially, and if he thrives he will take the role that Steve Farr had.

	W	SV	ERA	IP	H	BB	SO	BPI	$
1992 Houston NL	9	7	2.11	111	81	42	96	1.11	16
1993 Houston NL	4	9	2.61	97	75	28	101	1.07	15
1994 Projection >>>	5	18	2.77	98	77	33	95	1.12	25

HERSHISER, OREL - TR - Age 35

He only looks bad when compared to his 1988 form. With a better than average ERA and ratio, Hershiser is one of the safer pitchers available. The infamous Dodger defense again victimized Hershiser, with 20 unearned runs in 1993.

	W	SV	ERA	IP	H	BB	SO	BPI	$
1992 Los Angeles NL	10	0	3.67	211	209	69	130	1.32	2
1993 Los Angeles NL	12	0	3.59	216	201	72	141	1.27	11
1994 Projection >>>	11	0	3.61	204	195	68	131	1.29	9

HESKETH, JOE - TL - Age 35

Had one great, happy season in 1991 after years of trying to break back into a starting rotation since Montreal had put him in the pen in 1987. Now he's just another lefty with a poor strikeout/walk ratio, probably past the point of being able to deal with Fenway Park.

	W	SV	ERA	IP	H	BB	SO	BPI	$
1992 Boston AL	8	1	4.36	148	162	58	104	1.48	0
1993 Boston AL	3	1	5.06	53	62	29	34	1.71	-
1994 Projection >>>	5	1	4.43	92	100	40	62	1.52	-

HIBBARD, GREG - TL - Age 29
The only Cub starter who met expectations in 1993. His sharp command and nice sinker made him a solid number four starter.

	W	SV	ERA	IP	H	BB	SO	BPI	$
1992 Chicago AL	10	1	4.40	176	187	57	69	1.39	1
1993 Chicago NL	15	0	3.96	191	209	47	82	1.34	7
1994 *Projection* >>>	13	0	4.12	187	201	51	77	1.35	5

HICKERSON, BRYAN - TL - Age 30
Getting up there in years, Hickerson hasn't overwhelmed major league hitters thus far, and his strikeout rate is falling. As a lefty he'll find a job, but he's nothing special at this point. He could make it as a fifth starter.

	W	SV	ERA	IP	H	BB	SO	BPI	$
1992 San Francisco NL	5	0	3.09	87	74	21	68	1.09	4
1993 San Francisco NL	7	0	4.26	120	137	39	69	1.47	0
1994 *Projection* >>>	6	0	3.93	103	109	31	60	1.36	1

HIGUERA, TEDDY - TL - Age 35
The comeback trail has included some faint sparkles of former greatness, but Higuera's physical condition remains a serious question.

	W	SV	ERA	IP	H	BB	SO	BPI	$
1993 New Orleans AAA	0	0	9.00	8	11	7	7	2.25	
1993 Milwaukee AL	1	0	7.20	30	43	16	27	1.97	-

HILJUS, ERIK - TR - Age 21
A flamethrower, Hiljus doesn't always know where the ball is going. He has some potential if he can gain control.

HILL, KEN - TR - Age 28
Bothered by a strained groin muscle and lack of support from his Expos' teammates, Hill had a disappointing 1993 season after winning 16 the previous season. Hill has some of the best stuff in the National League with a 95 MPH fastball and a devastating forkball which breaks at the last second. If healthy in 1994, there's no reason to believe Hill can't return to his 1992 form.

	W	SV	ERA	IP	H	BB	SO	BPI	$
1992 Montreal NL	16	0	2.68	218	187	75	150	1.20	15
1993 Montreal NL	9	0	3.23	184	163	74	90	1.29	10
1994 *Projection* >>>	13	0	3.18	194	169	74	111	1.25	14

HILL, MILT - TR - Age 28
Hill became the Reds top minor league closer two years ago and then pitched well in two brief major league trials in 1991 and 1992, but he was a bust last year as the Reds searched for any reliable arm in their revolving door bullpen. Hill has always had good control with his fastball/slider repertoire, and last year was no exception.

	W	SV	ERA	IP	H	BB	SO	BPI	$
1992 Cincinnati NL	0	1	3.15	20	15	5	10	1.00	0
1993 Indianapolis AAA	3	2	4.08	53	53	17	45	1.32	
1993 Cincinnati NL	3	0	5.65	29	34	9	23	1.52	-

HILL, TYRONE -TL - Age 22
Milwaukee's first round pick in 1991 and a Midwest League all-star in 1992, holding opponents to a .188 batting average. Shut down his 1992 season with a sore elbow in August. Needs to recover physically and demonstrate further progress before reaching the major leagues. When healthy, throws 88 MPH and has three usable pitches.

	W	SV	ERA	IP	H	BB	SO	BPI	$
1992 Beloit A	9	0	3.25	114	76	74	133	1.32	
1993 Stockton A	1	1	4.50	66	43	60	65	1.56	

HILLEGAS, SHAWN - TR - Age 29
Was the Indians' closer for a month when Cleveland didn't win any games (June 1991). Good forkball worked for a while, but the hitters stopped swinging at it. Oakland tried to make him a starter, with disastrous results.

	W	SV	ERA	IP	H	BB	SO	BPI	$
1992 New York-Oakland	1	0	5.23	86	104	37	49	1.64	-
1993 Oakland AL	3	0	6.97	61	78	33	29	1.84	-
1994 *Projection* >>>	2	1	5.91	71	85	36	39	1.71	-

HILLMAN, ERIC - TL - Age 27

The Randy Johnson look alike was better in 1993 than his record would indicate. He throws a sinker and a cutting slider, mixed with a fastball and changeup to keep batters guessing. He could start in the four or five spot, or work in long relief.

	W	SV	ERA	IP	H	BB	SO	BPI	$
1992 New York NL	2	0	5.33	52	67	10	16	1.48	-
1993 New York NL	2	0	3.97	145	173	24	60	1.36	1
1994 *Projection* >>>	2	0	4.18	103	124	18	41	1.38	-

HITCHCOCK, STERLING - TL - Age 22

A young prospect with a variety of pitches. He throws a good slider and a sinking fastball. He could make the starting rotation in 1994 with a soild performance in spring training.

	W	SV	ERA	IP	H	BB	SO	BPI	$
1992 New York AL	0	0	8.31	13	23	6	6	2.23	-
1993 Columbus AAA	3	0	4.81	76	80	28	85	1.40	
1993 New York AL	1	0	4.65	31	32	14	26	1.48	-

HOEME, STEVE - TR - Age 26

Hoeme spent five-plus years in Rookie ball and A-ball, mostly with the Royals organization, partly explaining why he's an old Double-A reliever. In 1993 he led Wichita with 19 saves, struck out a batter per inning and had decent control.

HOFFMAN, TREVOR - TR - Age 26

Hoffman was one of three pitchers acquired from the "deep" Marlins' staff in the Sheffield trade. After spending last year setting up Brian Harvey and Gene Harris, Hoffman may well get the opportunity to close for the Padres, especially if Harris is dealt. This converted infielder has a 95 MPH fastball.

	W	SV	ERA	IP	H	BB	SO	BPI	$
1993 San Diego NL	4	5	3.90	90	80	39	79	1.32	5
1993 Florida NL	2	2	3.28	35	24	19	26	1.21	
1994 *Projection* >>>	2	8	3.90	54	48	23	47	1.32	6

HOLLINS, JESSIE - TR - Age 24

The second coming of Lee Smith may be more like the second coming of Mike Harkey. Hollins missed the entire season with a rotator cuff problem. He was said to have thrown at 97 MPH before the injury, but wasn't ever totally dominant in the minors. The Cubs' sorry righthanded relief situation still leaves him an opportunity, though.

	W	SV	ERA	IP	H	BB	SO	BPI	$
1992 Charlotte AA	3	25	3.20	70	60	32	73	1.31	
1992 Chicago NL	0	0	13.50	4	8	5	0	2.78	-

HOLMAN, BRAD - TR - Age 26

Brian Holman's younger brother. Brad was signed by the Royals out of Auburn, but released during spring training 1991. The Mariners got steady results from Holman at Class A Eugene and AA Jacksonville (2.57 ERA and almost 4:1 strikeout/walk ratio in 1992). Holman attracted attention in the 1992 Arizona Fall League and eventually helped fill the saves void left by Norm Charlton. He should be even more prominent in 1994.

	W	SV	ERA	IP	H	BB	SO	BPI	$
1993 Seattle AL	1	3	3.72	36	27	16	17	1.19	3

HOLMAN, BRIAN - TR - Age 29

Holman missed the entire 1992 and 1993 seasons after undergoing rotator cuff surgery, but he was expected to be ready for spring training 1994. He was in double figures in wins in both 1990 and 1991 and could return to that level if he has recovered. Despite pitching in the Kingdome, his career ERA is 3.71.

HOLMAN, SHAWN - TR - Age 29

Holman split time between the rotation and the bullpen for AAA Richmond. He could serve either role for the Braves in 1993, but would probably fare better out of the bullpen since he doesn't have a wide enough repertoire to last through a batting order more than twice. He's got good control, but gives up too many hits to have a real shot at the majors anytime soon.

	W	SV	ERA	IP	H	BB	SO	BPI	$
1993 Richmond AAA	12	0	4.18	155	174	46	101	1.41	

HOLMES, DARREN - TR - Age 27

Holmes was handed the Rockies closer role after the expansion draft, and initially blew the opportunity; manager Don Baylor sent him to AAA Colorado Springs for a reality check with a 17.18 ERA. Holmes returned with a new attitude and converted 21 of his last 22 save opportunities, with glittering numbers across the board. Holmes didn't make many mistakes in the second half of the season. Because of the weak start, he is likely to be underrated by people who look only at his full year numbers.

	W	SV	ERA	IP	H	BB	SO	BPI	$
1992 Milwaukee AL	4	6	2.55	42	35	11	31	1.09	8
1993 Colorado NL	3	25	4.05	67	56	20	60	1.15	22
1994 *Projection* >>>	3	27	3.82	60	53	18	51	1.18	25

HOLT, CHRIS - TR - Age 22

The Astros' top pitching prospect in the low minors, Holt had an outstanding year at Single-A in his second professional season. A third round draft choice in 1992, he finished second in ERA in the Midwest League and is probably three years away.

	W	SV	ERA	IP	H	BB	SO	BPI	$
1993 Quad City A	11	0	2.27	186	162	54	176	1.16	

HOLZEMER, MARK - TR - Age 24

Was unimpressive in a brief stint with the Angels late in 1993. He was given the callup despite a very ordinary performance at Triple-A (4.72 ERA with more than a hit per inning). Holzemer has potential to be a decent major league starter, but he's not there yet.

	W	SV	ERA	IP	H	BB	SO	BPI	$
1993 Vancouver AAA	9	0	4.82	145	158	70	80	1.56	
1993 California AL	0	0	8.87	23	34	13	10	2.03	-

HONEYCUTT, RICK - TL - Age 39

Still effective as a one-out specialist, but he ceased being the first choice to sub for Eck in an emergency. Unlikely to see an expanded role in Texas.

	W	SV	ERA	IP	H	BB	SO	BPI	$
1992 Oakland AL	1	3	3.69	39	41	10	32	1.31	2
1993 Oakland AL	1	1	2.81	42	30	20	21	1.21	3
1994 *Projection* >>>	1	2	3.14	41	35	17	23	1.26	3

HOPE, JOHN - TR - Age 23

Hope made a quick rise through the Pirates' system last season. After having never pitched above Single-A, Hope began the season in Double-A, made four starts at Triple-A and finished the year by making seven starts for the Pirates. Though he failed to win a game in the majors, he impressed with his poise and live arm. His fastball reaches 92 MPH but he has never regained the touch on his curveball since undergoing elbow surgery in 1990. Because of his lack of a quality second pitch, the Pirates may move him to the bullpen. If he stays as a starter, he will likely need more time at Triple-A.

	W	SV	ERA	IP	H	BB	SO	BPI	$
1993 Pittsburgh NL	0	0	4.03	38	47	8	8	1.45	-
1994 *Projection* >>>	1	0	4.53	71	87	15	28	1.44	-

HORSMAN, VINCE - TL - Age 27

Horsman is supposed to be a one-batter lefty specialist, but lefties hit .304 against him last season. Has more walks than strikeouts in his major league career. No prospect; just hanging on at this point.

	W	SV	ERA	IP	H	BB	SO	BPI	$
1992 Oakland AL	2	1	2.49	43	39	21	18	1.38	1
1993 Oakland AL	2	0	5.40	25	25	15	17	1.60	-

HOSTETLER, MIKE - TR - Age 23

Hostetler had made rapid progress in the Braves farm system before 1993, but took a step backward last year with a poor Triple-A start that brought him a demotion to AA Greenville. Hostetler doesn't throw particularly hard, instead using four pitches and changing speeds well. He's young enough to overcome the setback; he'll get another Triple-A chance in 1994.

	W	SV	ERA	IP	H	BB	SO	BPI	$
1993 Greenville AA	8	0	2.72	136	122	36	105	1.60	

HOUGH, CHARLIE - TR - Age 46

Hough made his major league debut the same summer that Jim Morrison, Janis Joplin and Jimi Hendrix died. He became a free agent at the end of 1993. His teammates over the years have ranged from Maury Wills (now 61) to Nigel Wilson (24).

	W	SV	ERA	IP	H	BB	SO	BPI	$
1992 Chicago AL	7	0	3.93	176	160	66	76	1.28	5
1993 Florida NL	9	0	4.27	204	202	71	126	1.34	4
1994 Projection >>>	8	0	4.15	195	185	72	109	1.32	3

HOWARD, CHRIS - TL - Age 28

Both players named Chris Howard are non-prospects. This one has been adequate in the minors, but doesn't have the pitches to be a major league success. Howard has never started a game in his pro career.

	W	SV	ERA	IP	H	BB	SO	BPI	$
1992 Vancouver AAA	3	0	2.92	24	18	22	23	1.62	
1993 Nashville AAA	4	3	3.38	66	55	16	53	1.07	
1993 Chicago AL	1	0	0.00	2	2	3	1	2.38	-

HOWE, STEVE - TL - Age 36

Howe just never got going in 1993. He spent some time on the DL with an ankle injury, but his arm was strong all year. He had a few dominating games but was frequently hurt by bad pitch location. Howe told me that the overwhelmingly bad press in New York finally affected him, because fans would read the (often unfounded) negative stories and then scream at him when he was trying to pitch. A change of scenery would be a big help. Howe still throws 93 MPH with a sharp slider. One silver lining from his past difficulties: for a pitcher his age, he's got low mileage on his arm.

	W	SV	ERA	IP	H	BB	SO	BPI	$
1992 New York AL	3	6	2.45	22	9	3	12	0.55	7
1993 New York AL	3	4	4.97	51	58	10	19	1.35	3
1994 Projection >>>	3	5	3.64	42	41	8	26	1.17	6

HOWELL, JAY - TR - Age 38

Howell was added before the 1993 season to provide bullpen insurance in case the Braves closer(s) couldn't do the job; the insurance wasn't needed and Howell pitched setup innings all year. He's no longer the fearsome everyday closer he once was, but he is a high-quality setup man.

	W	SV	ERA	IP	H	BB	SO	BPI	$
1992 Los Angeles NL	1	4	1.54	47	41	18	36	1.26	4
1993 Atlanta NL	3	0	2.31	58	48	16	37	1.10	5
1994 Projection >>>	3	5	2.97	54	48	18	37	1.22	8

HOY, PETE - TR - Age 27

One more arm, now far down in the BoSox bullpen depth chart. Hoy was just a little behind Ken Ryan at the end of 1992, but he hasn't advanced since then.

	W	SV	ERA	IP	H	BB	SO	BPI	$
1992 Pawtucket AAA	3	5	4.81	73	83	25	38	1.48	
1992 Boston AL	0	0	7.36	3	8	2	2	2.72	-
1993 New Britain AA	9	0	3.84	80	86	41	37	1.58	

HRUSOVSKY, JOHN - TR - Age 23
A major strikeout pitcher at the Single-A level, Hruvosky will pitch at Double-A in 1994 and may have a chance to reach the majors in 1995 or 1996 if he can continue his success.

HUBER, JEFF - TL - Age 23
The bullpen ace for San Diego's California League farm club.

HUDEK, JOHN - TR - Age 27
A veteran minor league reliever who had some success at AAA Tucson after being claimed on waivers from Detroit, Hudek should get a long look in spring training.

	W	SV	ERA	IP	H	BB	SO	BPI	$
1993 Tuscon AAA	3	0	3.79	19	17	11	18	1.47	
1993 Toledo AAA	1	0	5.82	39	44	22	32	1.69	

HUISMAN, RICK - TR - Age 24
After a strong 1992 season (10 wins and a 2.37 ERA at Double-A and Triple-A), Huisman went backward in 1993 with a 5.97 ERA at AAA Phoenix. Don't confuse Rick with Mark Huismann, the elderly minor league save artist.

	W	SV	ERA	IP	H	BB	SO	BPI	$
1992 Shreveport AA	7	0	2.35	103	79	31	100	1.07	
1992 Phoenix AAA	3	0	2.41	56	45	24	44	1.23	
1993 Phoenix AAA	3	0	5.97	72	78	45	59	1.70	

HUNTER, BOBBY - TR - Age 25
The Pirates' minor league pitcher of the year in 1993, Hunter set a Southern League record by throwing 40.1 consecutive scoreless innings. Despite their pitching woes and Hunter's impressive numbers, the Pirates never gave Hunter a call. Scouts simply don't believe he has major league stuff.

	W	SV	ERA	IP	H	BB	SO	BPI	$
1993 Carolina AA	5	7	1.01	71	54	35	53	1.25	

HUNTER, JIM - TR - Age 29
Still a marginal prospect at the end of 1992, Hunter is now just a reserve arm stored on the Triple-A roster.

	W	SV	ERA	IP	H	BB	SO	BPI	$
1992 El Paso AA	1	0	3.00	18	18	3	9	1.17	
1992 Denver AAA	6	2	3.68	134	144	46	56	1.41	
1993 New Orleans AAA	5	1	4.19	69	82	25	35	1.57	

HURST, BRUCE - TL - Age 36
The Rockies picked up Hurst as part of the Greg Harris deal, hoping to get some quality innings from a lefty. After shoulder surgery and a slow comeback, the question is how much pitching he has left in his talented arm.

	W	SV	ERA	IP	H	BB	SO	BPI	$
1992 San Diego NL	14	0	3.85	217	223	51	131	1.26	5
1993 San Diego NL	0	0	12.46	4	9	6	9	3.75	-
1993 Colorado NL	0	0	7.62	13	15	6	9	1.62	-
1994 *Projection* >>>	6	0	4.43	95	96	34	50	1.37	0

HURST, JONATHAN - TR - Age 27
Hurst nearly made the Expos' rotation out of spring training in 1992. Since then he has been consistently unimpressive. In 1993 he had a 4.15 ERA with 101 hits in 87 innings at AAA Albuquerque.

HURTA, BOB - TL - Age 28
A lefthanded reliever who had a disappointing campaign in 1993, Hurta split time between AAA Tucson and AA Jackson. He averaged over a strikeout per inning in 1992 at Jackson, but failed to challenge in a wide open competition for the Astros' lefty reliever job in 1993. He may not get another chance.

	W	SV	ERA	IP	H	BB	SO	BPI	$
1993 Jackson AA	7	2	4.42	94	101	38	72	1.47	

HUTTON, MARK - TR - Age 24

Australian native ranked as the Yankees' fourth best prospect by Baseball America in 1991. Hutton was 10-4 with a 3.18 ERA at AAA Columbus in 1993 but looked unready in his late season callup.

	W	SV	ERA	IP	H	BB	SO	BPI	$
1993 New York AL	1	0	5.73	22	24	17	12	1.86	-

IGNASIAK, MIKE - TR - Age 28

Highly successful as a relief ace in the minors, Ignasiak never got a chance to help fill the void created by Doug Henry's failure in 1993. Ignasiak is a good hard thrower who often looks impressive but is plagued by wildness.

	W	SV	ERA	IP	H	BB	SO	BPI	$
1993 New Orleans AAA	6	9	1.09	57	26	20	61	0.80	
1993 Milwaukee AL	1	0	3.65	37	32	21	28	1.43	0

ILSLEY, BLAISE - TL - Age 29

Ilsley has nine years in the minors without so much as a cup of coffee in the majors. A starter/reliever with excellent control and not much else, Ilsley's presence on the Cubs 40-man winter roster is a clear symbol of the state of the organization's lefthanded pitching shortage.

INNIS, JEFF - TR - Age 31

Throws that sidearmed sinker/slider stuff to keep the ball on the ground. He'll probably be used as setup and middle relief, unless Franco can't perform. Innis could become a part-time closer.

	W	SV	ERA	IP	H	BB	SO	BPI	$
1992 New York NL	6	1	2.86	88	85	36	39	1.38	2
1993 New York NL	2	3	4.11	77	81	38	36	1.56	0
1994 *Projection* >>>	3	2	3.55	81	81	36	38	1.44	1

IRVINE, DARYL - TR - Age 29

Last appeared in the majors with Boston in 1992. Irvine is a sinker/slider pitcher whose best pitches are not quite in the strike zone, and major league hitters know it.

	W	SV	ERA	IP	H	BB	SO	BPI	$
1992 Boston AL	3	0	6.11	28	31	14	10	1.61	-
1993 Buffalo AAA	1	0	4.30	46	41	26	19	1.45	

JACKSON, DANNY - TL - Age 32

In a major surprise, Jackson had a good year in a major role for the Phils in 1993. It was his first winning season since 1988 and he hasn't given up less than a hit per inning in any year since then. Jackson got it done with lots of heart in 1993. Like many Phillies, he will have trouble repeating in 1994.

	W	SV	ERA	IP	H	BB	SO	BPI	$
1992 Chicago-Pittsburgh NL	8	0	3.84	201	211	77	97	1.43	-
1993 Philadelphia NL	12	0	3.77	210	214	80	120	1.40	6
1994 *Projection* >>>	10	0	3.90	194	201	76	104	1.43	1

JACKSON, MIKE - TR - Age 29

With an outstanding fastball and improved control, Jackson has become one of the best setup men in the National League. He won't get saves with Beck on the scene, but otherwise he's excellent.

	W	SV	ERA	IP	H	BB	SO	BPI	$
1992 San Francisco NL	6	2	3.73	82	76	33	80	1.33	1
1993 San Francisco NL	6	1	3.03	77	58	24	70	1.06	7
1994 *Projection* >>>	6	3	3.27	80	64	28	73	1.15	8

JANICKI, PETE - TR - Age 22

Janicki was California's first round pick in the June 1992 draft and was signed in October after protracted negotiations. The transaction was made more complicated by the fact that Janicki suffered a stress fracture in his arm during the Olympic Trials. He then suffered the same injury in his second inning pitching last season. Fastball/forkball pitcher was at UCLA.

JEAN, DOMINGO - TR - Age 25

When they Astros traded away Xavier Hernandez, they got this Houston prospect with a 94 MPH fastball and a world of potential. He came over from the White Sox farm in the Steve Sax trade. Came up briefly in 1993 more for experience than to help in the pennant chase. Look for him to be major league success in 1995 after more work on ball control, holding runners, and commuting to the Astrodome.

	W	SV	ERA	IP	H	BB	SO	BPI	$
1993 ColumbusAAA	2	0	2.82	44	40	13	39	1.18	
1993 New York AL	1	0	4.46	40	37	13	39	1.25	
1994 *Projection* >>>	1	0	4.47	24	22	11	12	1.39	-

JIMINEZ, MIGUEL - TR - Age 24

A strikeout pitcher with control problems, Jiminez struggled in his late-season callup in '93. If he finds his control he can be a good one; for now, he's more of a project than a prospect. Jimenez is a graduate of Fordham University.

	W	SV	ERA	IP	H	BB	SO	BPI	$
1993 Oakland AL	1	0	4.00	27	27	16	13	1.59	-
1994 *Projection* >>>	1	0	4.40	34	32	21	20	1.55	-

JOHNSON, DAVE - TR - Age 34

Ex-Oriole Johnson worked his way back to the majors with the pitching-poor Tigers. He has had shoulder surgery. Even as a healthy youngster, he usually had a high ERA.

	W	SV	ERA	IP	H	BB	SO	BPI	$
1993 Toledo AAA	1	0	0.00	17	6	5	8	0.64	
1993 Detroit AL	1	0	12.96	8	13	5	7	2.20	

JOHNSON, JEFF - TL - Age 27

Johnson was a sensation when he produced a 4-1 record with a 1.88 ERA immediately after his callup in 1991, a classic lesson why a 4-1 record doesn't mean a darn thing. When you get excited about this pitcher or that pitcher who is 4-1 in May 1994, stop and think about Jeff Johnson.

	W	SV	ERA	IP	H	BB	SO	BPI	$
1992 New York AL	2	0	6.66	52	71	23	14	1.78	-
1993 New York AL	0	0	30.38	3	12	2	0	6.36	-
1994 *Projection* >>>	1	0	6.00	30	40	10	12	1.67	-

JOHNSON, RANDY - TL - Age 30

Johnson harnessed his wildness in August 1992 and became one of the league's best pitchers in 1993. He reduced his walks per nine innings from 6.1 to 3.5. Johnson dedicated each win to his recently deceased father. He finished strong, which is always a good sign.

	W	SV	ERA	IP	H	BB	SO	BPI	$
1992 Seattle AL	12	0	3.77	210	154	144	241	1.42	3
1993 Seattle AL	19	1	3.24	255	185	99	308	1.11	27
1994 *Projection* >>>	16	0	3.44	236	172	118	280	1.23	19

JOHNSTON, JOEL - TR - Age 27

Johnston struggled so terribly with his control early last season that he was placed on the disabled list at AAA Buffalo. The official reason was a strained shoulder but the real reason was lost confidence. The hard throwing Johnston, though, bounced back and had a decent second half with the Pirates. He has closer's stuff but his control and penchant for giving up homers will likely relegate him to a setup or middle relief role.

	W	SV	ERA	IP	H	BB	SO	BPI	$
1992 Kansas City AL	0	0	13.50	2	3	2	0	1.88	-
1993 Buffalo AAA	1	1	7.76	31	30	25	26	1.75	
1993 Pittsburgh NL	2	2	3.38	53	38	19	31	1.07	4
1994 *Projection* >>>	1	1	3.64	35	33	14	21	1.34	0

JOHNSTONE, JOHN - TR - Age 25

Another in a long line of prospects to have their confidence shaken by a stint in the dreaded Pacific Coast League, Johnstone nevertheless averaged almost a strikeout per inning. Shifted to the bullpen late in the season, he seemed to thrive in the new role and he'll contend for a big league middle relief role in the spring. Overall, he was 4-15 with a 5.18 ERA at AAA Edmonton, but he did get four saves.

	W	SV	ERA	IP	H	BB	SO	BPI	$
1993 Edmonton AAA	4	4	5.18	144	167	59	126	1.56	
1993 Florida NL	0	0	5.91	11	16	7	5	2.25	-

JONES, BARRY - TR - Age 31

Jones got thrashed in the bigs for the second straight season, although he continues to impress whenever demoted to the minors. He will probably will pitch somewhere in 1994, but not well.

	W	SV	ERA	IP	H	BB	SO	BPI	$
1992 New York NL	7	1	5.68	69	85	35	30	1.72	-
1993 Nashville AAA	0	2	2.60	17	16	2	19	1.03	
1993 Chicago AL	0	0	8.59	7	14	3	7	2.39	-
1994 *Projection* >>>	3	2	5.45	34	41	14	18	1.63	-

JONES, BOBBY - TR - Age 26

Penciled in to be in the 1994 rotation, Jones brings a variety of pitches to a staff in need of help. He doesn't throw hard, but he is a smart pitcher who doesn't overthrow. He already has one of the majors' best changeups.

	W	SV	ERA	IP	H	BB	SO	BPI	$
1992 Binghamton AA	12	0	1.88	158	118	43	144	1.02	
1993 NewYork NL	2	0	3.65	61	61	22	35	1.36	0
1994 *Projection* >>>	8	0	3.95	180	177	63	90	1.33	3

JONES, CALVIN - TR - Age 30

Former Mariner who took a step back to Double A in 1993 and, of course, dominated. You see, Double A hitters, unlike major leaguers, were up there hacking at his forkballs. Jones has more trouble at the major league level, where he has to come in with his so-so fastball.

	W	SV	ERA	IP	H	BB	SO	BPI	$
1992 Seattle AL	3	0	5.69	61	50	47	49	1.57	-
1993 Canton-Akron AA	5	22	3.30	63	40	26	73	1.04	

JONES, DOUG - TR - Age 36

After a superb 1992 season, Jones was a major disappointment in 1993. Hitters learned to stay away from his changeups in the dirt and teed off when he got one up in the strike zone. He doesn't have a good enough fastball to keep hitters honest and isn't likely to regain his previous effectiveness as a closer, especially not in Philly.

	W	SV	ERA	IP	H	BB	SO	BPI	$
1992 Houston NL	11	36	1.85	111	96	17	93	1.01	45
1993 Houston NL	4	26	4.54	85	102	21	66	1.45	19
1994 *Projection* >>>	6	20	3.62	91	98	20	72	1.30	20

JONES, JIMMY - TR - Age 29

Drafted ahead of Dwight Gooden in June 1982, Jones is the hard thrower who didn't blossom. He has never lived up to his vast potential. Injuries have hampered Jones, who has never developed any consistency. He's going to have to really fight to stay in the major leagues much longer.

	W	SV	ERA	IP	H	BB	SO	BPI	$
1992 Houston NL	10	0	4.07	139	135	39	69	1.25	2
1993 Ottawa AAA	1	0	1.20	15	10	5	12	1.00	
1993 Montreal NL	4	0	6.35	40	47	9	21	1.43	-
1994 *Projections* >>>	6	0	4.81	79	83	22	42	1.33	1

JONES, STACY - TR - Age 26

Pitched well in relief in 1991, rising from Double-A to Baltimore. Released from A-ball in 1992, then started to make his way back with the Giants.

	W	SV	ERA	IP	H	BB	SO	BPI	$
1993 Shreveport AA	4	1	3.58	50	53	19	28	1.44	

JONES, TODD - TR - Age 25

Jones pitched better in Houston than he did at AAA Tucson. This hard thrower is being groomed as the successor to Doug Jones; he has a good breaking ball, but needs the confidence to throw it in tight spots. Jones appears to have the arm and makeup to be a closer and should be a strong candidate for the position in 1994.

	W	SV	ERA	IP	H	BB	SO	BPI	$
1993 Tucson AAA	4	12	4.44	48	49	31	45	1.64	
1993 Houston NL	1	2	3.13	37	28	15	25	1.16	2
1994 *Projections* >>>	1	1	3.54	48	40	21	32	1.27	1

JUDEN, JEFF - TR - Age 23

His 95 MPH fastball mysteriously slowed down after he signed as a pro. Now it's getting back up there, and he has added a slider. Ex-Astros typically do well in Philadelphia.

	W	SV	ERA	IP	H	BB	SO	BPI	$
1993 Tucson AAA	11	0	4.63	169	174	76	156	1.47	
1993 Houston NL	0	0	5.40	5	4	4	7	1.60	-

JUHL, MIKE - TL - Age 24

A smallish lefty with incredible control, Juhl has walked only 25 batters in 141 innings over his three year pro career. He has yet to pitch above Single-A, so he hasn't really been tested yet.

KAISER, JEFF - TL - Age 33

Like many veteran lefties past their prime years, Kaiser was able to find major league work in 1993. He is (to understate the case) not a prospect.

	W	SV	ERA	IP	H	BB	SO	BPI	$
1993 Norfolk AAA	1	9	5.64	22	23	6	23	1.29	
1993 New York NL	0	0	7.88	8	10	5	9	1.88	-

KAMIENIECKI, SCOTT - TR - Age 29

Two years after back surgery for a painful disc, Kamieniecki came back to post double digit wins while having only 20 starts. He won't be the top pitcher in any organization, but for someone with no clear role on Opening Day, he had a successful season in 1993.

	W	SV	ERA	IP	H	BB	SO	BPI	$
1992 New York AL	6	0	4.36	188	193	74	88	1.42	-
1993 New York AL	10	1	4.08	154	163	59	72	1.44	5
1994 *Projection* >>>	8	1	4.18	155	162	60	73	1.43	1

KARCHNER, MATT - TR - Age 26
Terrific season at A-ball in 1991; struggled some at AA Memphis in 1992 and 1993.

	W	SV	ERA	IP	H	BB	SO	BPI	$
1993 Memphis AA	3	0	4.20	30	34	4	14	1.26	

KARL, SCOTT - TL - Age 22
Drafted in the sixth round in '92, out of the University of Hawaii. Throws only a mid-80s fastball, but gets batters to beat balls into the ground with his changeup and curve. Karl was 13-8 with a 2.45 ERA at AA El Paso in 1993.

KARP, RYAN - TL - Age 23
Overpowered the South Atlantic League, and more than held his own in his first promotion of the year, to the Carolina League. Expect to see him start '94 in AA Albany.

KARSAY, STEVE - TR - Age 22
A terrific prospect, Karsay has posted great minor league numbers, and he pitched well for Oakland in 1993. He will be given every chance to succeed, since he is the tangible asset from the Rickey Henderson trade. It's tough for a young pitcher to succeed on a bad team, but Karsay is already as good as people think Todd VanPoppel will someday be, and they are the same age.

	W	SV	ERA	IP	H	BB	SO	BPI	$
1993 Oakland AL	3	0	4.04	49	49	16	33	1.33	1
1994 *Projection* >>>	2	0	4.04	29	29	10	20	1.33	0

KELLY, JOHN - TR - Age 26
A closer throughout his three and a half year career with 108 saves while finishing 169 of 188 appearances, Kelly's strikeout rate has declined with each move to a higher level, raising the question of whether it would be high enough in the majors for him to keep a closers job.

KEY, JIMMY - TL - Age 32
One of last year's best free-agent acquisitions, Key had a banner year in 1993. He kept batters off balance with his curveball, changeup, and slider. He's now the anchor of the Yankee staff.

	W	SV	ERA	IP	H	BB	SO	BPI	$
1992 Toronto AL	13	0	3.53	216	205	59	117	1.22	12
1993 New York AL	18	0	3.00	237	219	43	173	1.11	26
1994 *Projection* >>>	15	0	3.19	228	214	55	151	1.18	22

KIEFER, MARK - TR - Age 25
A top prospect being brought along carefully by the Brewers, Kiefer has a strong fastball and a good mix of breaking pitches. He has a chance to be one of the top rookie starters of 1994.

	W	SV	ERA	IP	H	BB	SO	BPI	$
1993 New Orleans AAA	3	0	5.08	28	28	17	23	1.58	
1993 Milwaukee AL	0	1	0.00	9	3	5	7	0.88	1
1994 *Projection* >>>	1	1	4.41	43	51	15	25	1.53	-

KIELY, JOHN - TR - Age 29
Following some solid minor league seasons and an excellent 1992 season with the Tigers as a middle reliever, Kiely was expected to be a solid contributor to the Tigers bullpen last year. He regressed, however, losing the strike zone even at Triple-A, and now has to prove himself all over again.

	W	SV	ERA	IP	H	BB	SO	BPI	$
1992 Detroit AL	4	0	2.13	55	44	28	18	1.31	3
1993 Toledo AAA	3	4	3.88	58	65	25	48	1.55	
1993 Detroit AL	0	0	7.71	12	13	13	5	2.32	-

KILE, DARRYL - TR - Age 25
A hard (94 MPH) thrower who became a complete pitcher in 1993, Kile's key improvement was self confidence, which was bolstered by an All-Star team selection in July and a September no-hitter. He has gained command of his curveball, among the best in baseball. Kile has the potential to become one of the top pitchers in the league.

	W	SV	ERA	IP	H	BB	SO	BPI	$
1992 Houston NL	5	0	3.95	125	124	63	90	1.49	-
1993 Houston NL	15	0	3.51	172	152	69	141	1.29	10
1994 *Projection* >>>	14	0	3.63	180	165	80	145	1.36	7

KILGUS, PAUL - TL - Age 32
The soft-throwing journeyman made his way back to the majors with the Cardinals last year, but he couldn't stay healthy. He was once a promising starter for Texas, however, at this point his best bet is to continue his major league career is as the 10th or 11th pitcher somewhere.

	W	SV	ERA	IP	H	BB	SO	BPI	$
1993 Louisville AAA	7	0	2.65	68	59	19	54	1.14	
1993 St. Louis NL	1	1	0.63	29	18	8	21	0.92	4

KING, KEVIN - TL - Age 25
Moved to the bullpen in '93, and shot from the California League to the American League. He's tall (6'4") and slight (170 pounds), and doesn't throw hard from a three-quarters motion. Major league role likely to be to get out one lefthanded batter for the Mariners.

	W	SV	ERA	IP	H	BB	SO	BPI	$
1993 Jacksonville AA	2	1	3.14	28	25	7	13	1.14	
1993 Seattle AL	0	0	6.17	12	9	4	8	1.16	-

KIPPER, BOB - TL - Age 29
Kipper was last up with the Twins in 1992, as a lefty setup man and middle reliever behind Mark Guthrie and Gary Wayne. These specialists are supposed to be safe, but Kipper wasn't. Future looks gloomy.

	W	SV	ERA	IP	H	BB	SO	BPI	$
1992 Minnesota AL	3	0	4.42	39	40	14	22	1.40	-

KIRKREIT, DARON - TR - Age 21
Cleveland drafted him in last year's first round out of Cal-Riverside, and signed him for a $600,000 bonus. The 6'6", 235-pound '92 Olympian is a sinker/slider-type pitcher who throws his fastball in the low-mid 90's.

	W	SV	ERA	IP	H	BB	SO	BPI	$
1993 Watertown A	4	0	2.23	36	33	11	44	1.38	

KISER, GARLAND - TL - Age 25
Terrific in the low minors 1989-1991. Still stuck in the minors but still young enough to make it.

	W	SV	ERA	IP	H	BB	SO	BPI	$
1993 New Orleans AAA	5	1	5.40	67	69	24	42	1.38	

KLINGENBECK, SCOTT - TR - Age 23
A fifth-round draft pick in 1992, he started last season on the disabled list because of an arm infection caused by a spider bite. He made up for lost time with an outstanding season in the Carolina League.

KLINK, JOE - TL - Age 32
A veteran lefty, Klink was used in very small doses in 1993, averaging 2/3 innings per appearance, mostly facing lefty hitters. The righties he did face wore him out, hitting well over .300 against him. If he were a righty, he would have gone on with his life's work years ago; instead, he'll probably battle Rich Rodriguez for a bullpen spot in 1994.

	W	SV	ERA	IP	H	BB	SO	BPI	$
1993 Florida NL	0	0	5.02	38	37	24	22	1.64	-

KNACKERT, BRENT - TR - Age 24
A Rule Five pick in 1989, has been stuck at Double-A since spending a year in Seattle with a 6.51 ERA.

	W	SV	ERA	IP	H	BB	SO	BPI	$
1993 Binghamton AA	1	0	5.56	44	59	13	27	1.63	

KNUDSEN, KURT - TR - Age 27
After a good first half in '92, hitters figured out Knudsen in the second half, and he was hammered. Lefty batters hit him at .392 last year. He is still adjusting.

	W	SV	ERA	IP	H	BB	SO	BPI	$
1992 Detroit AL	2	5	4.58	70	70	41	51	1.57	-
1993 Toledo AAA	2	6	3.78	33	24	11	39	1.05	
1993 Detroit AL	3	2	4.78	38	41	16	29	1.53	1
1994 *Projection* >>>	2	3	4.68	44	46	22	25	1.54	0

KNUDSON, MARK - TR - Age 33
Knudson pitched well enough at AAA Colorado Springs to earn another trip to the majors, then was roundly mashed with the Rockies. Sometimes tiny samples of numbers tell an accurate story. Behind that outrageous ERA, the details are: Knudson got 17 batters out, while allowing 21 baserunners with four home runs and three wild pitches. He will probably retire now.

	W	SV	ERA	IP	H	BB	SO	BPI	$
1993 Colorado Springs AAA	3	0	2.25	28	30	8	15	1.35	
1993 Colorado NL	0	0	22.24	6	16	5	3	4.04	-

KRAMER, TOM - TR - Age 26
Finally put in significant big league time in his seventh year in the Indians organization. Swung between rotation and pen both of the last two seasons, looking for a useful role, but righty pitchers who are touched by righty hitters at a .300+ clip often have trouble fitting in.

	W	SV	ERA	IP	H	BB	SO	BPI	$
1993 Cleveland AL	7	0	4.02	121	126	59	71	1.53	2
1994 *Projection* >>>	4	0	4.06	73	77	35	43	1.53	-

KRIVDA, RICK - TL - Age 24
Last year, Oriole prospect Rich Krivda's breaking ball was rated the best in the pitching-rich AA Eastern League. He was promoted to Triple-A and looked superb in five starts. Next stop: Oriole Park.

	W	SV	ERA	IP	H	BB	SO	BPI	$
1993 Bowie AA	7	0	3.08	125	114	50	108	1.30	
1993 Rochester AAA	3	0	1.89	33	20	16	23	1.09	

KRUEGER, BILL - TL - Age 35
Bill Krueger is a very streaky pitcher who can pitch six or seven nice games in a row, only to lose his sharpness mysteriously overnight. His career 4.19 ERA is an accurate overall summary.

	W	SV	ERA	IP	H	BB	SO	BPI	$
1992 Minnesota AL	10	0	4.30	161	166	46	86	1.31	4
1992 Montreal NL	0	0	6.75	17	23	7	13	1.73	-
1993 Detroit AL	6	0	3.40	82	90	30	60	1.46	3
1994 *Projection* >>>	8	0	3.94	120	129	40	65	1.41	2

LACY, KERRY - TR - Age 21
He has developed from a 15th-round draft pick in '91 to a relief ace in A ball. He has above-average velocity, and throws a sinker and a slurve.

LANCASTER, LES - TR - Age 31
Once a solid reliever with the Cubs, Lancaster has been bouncing around. He pitched well enough for the Cardinals last season before injuring his shoulder, but they had no plans to bring him back in 1994. Lancaster has lost most of the velocity on what used to be a good fastball. Someone may give him another shot this spring, but he is just hanging on now.

	W	SV	ERA	IP	H	BB	SO	BPI	$
1992 Detroit AL	3	0	6.33	86	101	51	35	1.75	-
1993 St. Louis NL	4	0	2.93	61	56	21	36	1.26	3
1994 *Projection* >>>	4	0	4.18	78	79	33	42	1.43	-

LANDRUM, BILL - TR - Age 35

Landrum was pitching well when shoulder problems ended his season. The Reds have plenty of inexpensive young pitchers to fill his role; he isn't likely to be back with the Reds.

	W	SV	ERA	IP	H	BB	SO	BPI	$
1992 Indianapolis AAA	1	0	3.95	27	27	4	23	1.15	
1992 Montreal NL	1	0	7.20	20	27	9	7	1.80	-
1993 Cincinnati NL	0	0	3.74	22	18	6	14	1.13	-
1994 *Projection* >>>	1	2	4.35	27	27	8	15	1.31	1

LANGSTON, MARK - TL - Age 33

In 1989, Don Mattingly told me that Langston was the best pitcher in the American League, alongside Clemens but ahead of all the rest. Langston's high-velocity fastball moves sharply and in different directions, so that a great hitter who can pick up the fastball and see it coming is still helpless much of the time.

	W	SV	ERA	IP	H	BB	SO	BPI	$
1992 California AL	13	0	3.66	229	206	74	174	1.22	12
1993 California AL	16	0	3.20	256	220	85	196	1.19	23
1994 *Projection* >>>	15	0	3.31	247	212	84	188	1.20	21

LaPOINT, DAVE - TL - Age 34

LaPoint pitched for the Twins' Triple-A franchise last year, hoping to make a comeback. He didn't.

	W	SV	ERA	IP	H	BB	SO	BPI	$
1993 Portland AAA	6	0	6.09	75	99	29	40	1.70	

LA ROSA, MARK - TL - Age 25

West Palm Beach's bullpen ace, La Rosa overpowered Florida State League batters. If He does well at Double-A in 1994, the could be in the majors in 1995.

LAYANA, TIM - TR - Age 30

Last up with the Reds in 1991 (with a 6.97 ERA), he followed with a weak performance at Rochester in 1992 and the following so-so results which lifted him to the National League for another cup of coffee:

	W	SV	ERA	IP	H	BB	SO	BPI	$
1993 Phoenix AAA	3	9	4.81	67	80	24	55	1.55	
1993 San Francisco NL	0	0	22.50	2	7	1	1	4.00	-

LEACH, TERRY - TR - Age 40

Underwent a wrist-to-elbow ligament transplant in September. Leach vows a return despite his age. As with most righty submariners, could probably make a living retiring righthanded batters almost indefinitely.

	W	SV	ERA	IP	H	BB	SO	BPI	$
1992 Chicago AL	6	0	1.95	73	57	20	22	1.05	8
1993 Chicago AL	0	1	2.81	16	15	2	3	1.06	1
1994 *Projection* >>>	2	1	3.15	38	38	9	12	1.23	3

LEAHY, PAT - TR - Age 23

Leahy was a sixth-round pick in 1992 out of Notre Dame. You would think that when batters face a 6'6", 245 lb. pitcher, they would be reluctant to dig in; but Leahy managed to hit 23 of them in 1993. His control isn't really that bad. He walked only 41 unintentionally. The results were 8-11 with a 3.22 ERA for Kane County Marlins farm in the Midwest League.

LEARY, TIM - TR - Age 35
For one half of one season (1988) Leary was a top pitcher in the National League. The Mariners acquired him partly because they felt he could give innings, and partly because the Yankees paid them to take him. Even if someone pays you, don't make the same mistake.

	W	SV	ERA	IP	H	BB	SO	BPI	$
1992 New York-Seattle AL	8	0	5.36	141	131	87	46	1.55	-
1993 Seattle AL	11	0	5.05	169	202	58	68	1.54	-
1994 *Projection* >>>	9	0	5.25	156	176	66	63	1.55	-

LEE, JEREMY - TR - Age 19
The third of four Toronto first-round draft picks in '93, and the second of three pitchers. He also was the only one who signed early enough to pitch in the minors, because he accepted a relatively meager $165,000 bonus. Another big one, at 6'7".

LEE, MARK - TL - Age 29
Hasn't appeared in the majors since 1991, when he was a promising reliever. Last year he was trying to come back with the Rangers.

	W	SV	ERA	IP	H	BB	SO	BPI	$
1993 Oklahoma City AAA	5	4	4.34	102	112	43	65	1.51	

LEFFERTS, CRAIG - TL - Age 36
Ineffective as a starter or reliever, Lefferts wasn't expected to be back with the Rangers in 1994.

	W	SV	ERA	IP	H	BB	SO	BPI	$
1992 San Diego NL	13	0	3.69	163	180	35	81	1.32	3
1992 Baltimore AL	1	0	4.09	33	34	6	23	1.21	0
1993 Texas AL	3	0	6.05	83	102	28	58	1.56	-
1994 *Projection* >>>	6	2	4.76	116	134	30	68	1.41	-

LEFTWICH, PHIL - TR - Age 24
Earned a promotion to the majors by winning five of his final six decisions at Vancouver. His secret? Throwing strikes. Likely to be in a California rotation short on righthanders in '94. A longshot for immediate success.

	W	SV	ERA	IP	H	BB	SO	BPI	$
1993 California AL	4	0	3.79	80	81	27	31	1.35	3
1994 *Projection* >>>	2	0	3.79	48	48	16	19	1.34	1

LEIBRANDT, CHARLIE - TL - Age 37
Leibrandt was the real bright spot for the Rangers early in 1993, but collapsed in the second half, and spent time on the disabled list late in the year. The fourth starter if he's healthy.

	W	SV	ERA	IP	H	BB	SO	BPI	$
1992 Atlanta NL	15	0	3.36	193	191	42	104	1.21	9
1993 Texas AL	9	0	4.55	150	169	45	89	1.43	3
1994 *Projection* >>>	11	0	4.00	171	180	46	97	1.32	5

LEITER, AL - TL - Age 28
Finally, Al Leiter found his place in the Blue Jays championship puzzle. Leiter is like Juan Guzman on a bad day. He flashes a good fastball but walks batters left and right, sometimes with the bases loaded. With a possible vacancy in Toronto this year, he may get the number five starting spot. If he could ever throw strikes, he'd be an ace pitcher. His fastball is too good to ignore.

	W	SV	ERA	IP	H	BB	SO	BPI	$
1992 Toronto AL	0	0	9.00	1	1	2	0	3.00	-
1993 Toronto AL	9	2	4.11	105	93	56	66	1.42	5
1994 *Projection* >>>	5	1	4.15	64	57	34	38	1.42	1

LEITER, MARK - TR - Age 30
Starter/reliever Mark Leiter had shoulder surgery last year, placing his future in doubt. He has a history of shoulder problems and tough battles to stay active.

	W	SV	ER	IP	H	BB	SO	BPI	$
1992 Detroit AL	8	0	4.18	112	116	43	75	1.42	1
1993 Detroit AL	6	0	4.73	107	111	44	70	1.46	0
1994 *Projection* >>>	7	0	4.49	111	114	44	70	1.42	-

LEON, DANNY - TR - Age 26
After a good season at AA Tulsa in 1992, Leon hasn't done much to impress. Poor control is holding him back.

	W	SV	ERA	IP	H	BB	SO	BPI	$
1992 Tulsa AA	5	1	0.60	30	15	8	34	0.77	
1992 Texas AL	1	0	5.89	18	18	10	15	1.53	-
1993 Oklahoma City AAA	2	0	5.52	31	28	26	33	1.74	

LESKANIC, CURT - TR - Age 25
Thanks to expansion, guys like Leskanic got a chance to pitch in The Show. Manager Don Baylor let him start eight times. A bit on the eccentric side, his teammates think he's cool. He could be back, but the best bet is to give him another year at Triple-A.

	W	SV	ERA	IP	H	BB	SO	BPI	$
1993 Colorado NL	1	0	5.37	57	59	27	30	1.51	-
1994 *Projection* >>>	1	0	5.37	34	35	16	18	1.51	-

LEWIS, JIM - TR - Age 24
A second round draft choice from Florida State in 1991, Lewis had two encouraging seasons before missing almost all of 1993 with arm problems. He's a hard thrower when healthy.

	W	SV	ERA	IP	H	BB	SO	BPI	$
1992 Osceola A	5	0	1.12	80	54	32	65	1.08	
1992 Jackson AA	3	0	4.11	70	64	30	43	1.34	
1992 Tucson AAA	0	0	0.00	1	0	2	0	2.00	

LEWIS, RICHIE -TR - Age 28
This little righty made a successful conversion to the bullpen in 1993. He'll throw his nasty curveball on any count, in any situation. In one classic example, he froze John Kruk in Philadelphia with a bases loaded, no out, bottom of the 12th, 3-2 hook. Exciting, but his spotty control makes him a little risky.

	W	SV	ERA	IP	H	BB	SO	BPI	$
1992 Rochester AAA	10	0	3.28	159	136	61	154	1.24	
1992 Baltimore AL	1	0	10.80	7	13	7	4	3.00	-
1993 Florida NL	6	0	3.26	77	68	43	65	1.44	2
1994 *Projection* >>>	4	0	3.12	48	44	26	35	1.46	0

LEWIS, SCOTT - TR - Age 28
Still hasn't reached his potential. The Angels want him to start, but they noticed his success as a closer in Vancouver (1.37 ERA, nine saves, 4:1 strikeout/walk ratio). Unsettled bullpen situation makes him an interesting speculation.

	W	SV	ERA	IP	H	BB	SO	BPI	$
1992 California AL	4	0	3.99	38	36	14	18	1.30	0
1993 California AL	1	0	4.22	32	37	12	10	1.53	-
1994 *Projection* >>>	2	0	4.48	37	41	14	15	1.49	-

LIEBER, JON - TR - Age 23
Acquired by the Pirates last season in the trade that sent Stan Belinda to Kansas City, Lieber does not throw hard but has good command of various pitches and outstanding control. He will likely start this season at Triple-A and could be in the Pirates' rotation at some point this season.

LILLIQUIST, DEREK - TL - Age 28

Has settled in nicely as a lefty bullpen committee man. Not enough of a strikeout pitcher to be a dominant closer, Lilliquist also has a problem working day after day. Nonetheless he will continue to be a valuable setup man and occasional closer.

	W	SV	ERA	IP	H	BB	SO	BPI	$
1992 Cleveland AL	5	6	1.75	62	39	18	47	0.92	12
1993 Cleveland AL	4	10	2.25	64	64	19	40	1.30	13
1994 *Projection* >>>	4	8	2.85	58	52	18	39	1.21	11

LINTON, DOUG - TR - Age 29

Long-time Jays farmhand, he wasn't very good at Syracuse in 1992 and got just a brief look with the Angels in '93.

	W	SV	ERA	IP	H	BB	SO	BPI	$
1992 Toronto AL	1	0	8.63	24	31	17	16	2.00	-
1993 Syracuse AAA	2	2	5.32	47	48	14	42	1.30	
1993 Toronto-California	2	0	7.36	37	46	23	23	1.91	-

LIRA, FELIPE - TR - Age 21

The Venezuelan doesn't throw hard, but he has a good sinker that gets him ground-ball outs. London's ace in '93; expect the same at Toledo in '94.

	W	SV	ERA	IP	H	BB	SO	BPI	$
1993 London AA	10	0	3.38	152	157	39	122	1.24	

LISTER, MARTY - TL - Age 21

In 1993, Lister improved his control considerably over his 1992 pro debut when he walked more than a batter per inning in Rookie ball.

LIVERNOIS, DEREK - TR - Age 26

For someone who's been in the minors for nine years, he's still fairly young. Running out of chances.

	W	SV	ERA	IP	H	BB	SO	BPI	$
1993 Pawtucket AAA	2	0	5.72	85	89	37	69	1.48	

LLOYD, GRAEME - TL - Age 27

A talented lefty who could have figured prominently in the Brewers' saves picture in 1993 if fellow southpaw Jesse Orosco had not delivered such a gem season, Lloyd remains a top candidate for committee work or even co-closer duty if the situation calls for his help.

	W	SV	ERA	IP	H	BB	SO	BPI	$
1993 Milwaukee AL	3	0	2.83	64	64	13	31	1.22	4
1994 *Projection* >>>	2	0	3.13	38	39	8	19	1.23	2

LONG, STEVE - TR - Age 24

Acquired last spring from Montreal in a trade for Terrel Hansen, Long wasn't as effective at Double-A as he had been in his first two and a half seasons in A-ball.

LOONEY, BRIAN - TL - Age 24

This savvy lefthander started last season in A-ball and ended in the majors. He relies on changing speeds but has a good enough heater to strike people out. Looney fanned 59 in his first 43 innings for AA Harrisburg, including a 13 strikeout complete game shutout. He made a big jump and probably needs at least a few months at Triple-A. He's a pitcher to watch, though.

	W	SV	ERA	IP	H	BB	SO	BPI	$
1993 Montreal NL	0	0	3.00	6	8	2	7	1.67	-
1993 Harrisburg AA	3	0	2.38	56	36	17	76	0.94	
1994 *Projection* >>>	1	0	3.96	31	35	10	20	1.46	-

LOPEZ, ALBIE - TR - Age 22
Made great progress in 1993, his first season above A-ball. His best pitch is a fastball. He has to watch his weight. A 20th-round 1991 pick, he exploded through the Indians' system so far, but it's a stretch to expect that he will be a major league success in 1994.

	W	SV	ERA	IP	H	BB	SO	BPI	$
1993 Canton-Akron AA	9	0	3.11	110	79	47	80	1.14	
1993 Cleveland AL	3	0	5.98	50	49	32	25	1.65	-
1994 *Projection* >>>	2	0	5.98	30	30	19	15	1.63	-

LOWE, DEREK - TR - Age 20
Seattle's eighth-round draft pick in '92 was hit hard last season. At 6'5", he may be able to add a few MPH to his fastball.

LOYND, MIKE - TR - Age 30
Loynd is a former Ranger who joined the Braves as a free agent. He's a decent pitcher but wasn't much of a threat to crack the Atlanta rotation. Signed a minor league contract with Kansas City.

LUEBBERS, LARRY - TR - Age 24
Rushed to the majors when the Reds rotation was decimated by injuries, Luebbers was simply not ready. He has made just 29 career starts above Class A. Luebbers is a control pitcher and needs more seasoning; he posted a 4.16 ERA and walked 5.5 batters per 9 innings at AAA Indianapolis.

	W	SV	ERA	IP	H	BB	SO	BPI	$
1993 Cincinnati NL	2	0	4.54	77	74	38	38	1.45	-
1994 *Projection* >>>	1	0	4.54	46	44	23	23	1.45	-

LUKASIEWICZ, MARK - TL - Age 21
The last of Toronto's four first-round draft picks in '93. He signed for a $250,000 bonus, but not in time to play last season. The big guy (6'7", 235 pounds) pitched at Brevard (Fla.) Junior College, and has a mid-90s fastball.

LYNCH, JOHN - TR - Age 22
At press time, Lynch was leading all of professional baseball in tackles, as a starting safety for the 1993 Tampa Bay Bucs. A second-round pick in 1992 out of Stanford, he throws serious gas, but has walked almost a batter per inning in his limited pro experience. He could eventually be a number one starter, but not if he keeps using that valuable right arm trying to tackle guys like Barry Sanders.

MABERRY, LOUIS - TR - Age 23
Charleston's MVP was a setup man for closer Marty Lister, Maberry is a strikeout pitcher with pretty good control.

MacDONALD, BOB - TL - Age 28
Lefty Bob MacDonald was acquired from Toronto and quickly made some valuable contributions to the Tigers bullpen. His role is situational pitching and middle relief, but he can pick up a few saves.

	W	SV	ERA	IP	H	BB	SO	BPI	$
1992 Toronto AL	1	0	4.37	47	50	16	26	1.39	-
1993 Detroit AL	3	3	5.35	66	67	33	39	1.53	0
1994 *Projection* >>>	2	2	4.88	59	60	27	34	1.48	-

MACHADO, JULIO - TR - Age 28
Big talent with big legal problems. Has been trying to get out of Venezuela for two years.

MADDUX, GREG - TR - Age 27
So much for the Cy Young jinx. Maddux again mastered National League hitters, recording a mirror image season to his 1992 Cy Young campaign. He again led the league in innings pitched and won 20 games, but this time he also led the league in ERA. He combines a miniscule opponents' batting average with a fine 4-to-1 strikeout to walk ratio by throwing four pitches with precision and timing. Batters are often puzzled by his excellent circle change and a sinking fastball with which he changes speeds well. Maddux is consistent to boot, he's thrown at least 237 innings in each of the last six years and has never been on the disabled list. Amazing. It's appropriate that baseball's best pitching staff also has the game's best pitcher.

	W	SV	ERA	IP	H	BB	SO	BPI	$
1992 Chicago NL	20	0	2.18	268	201	70	199	1.01	32
1993 Atlanta NL	20	0	2.36	267	228	52	197	1.05	33
1994 *Projection* >>>	20	0	2.77	267	220	68	198	1.08	33

MADDUX, MIKE - TR - Age 32

A good utility pitcher. Maddux can face one batter, or go for a couple of innings if needed. Will probably be used as a setup man for John Franco. Although he cannot compare to his brother Greg, this Maddux has put together two good, 5-save seasons in a row in middle relief.

	W	SV	ERA	IP	H	BB	SO	BPI	$
1992 San Diego NL	2	5	2.37	80	71	24	60	1.19	7
1993 New York NL	3	5	3.60	75	67	27	57	1.25	6
1994 *Projection* >>>	3	5	3.60	79	69	28	55	1.23	7

MAGNANTE, MIKE - TL - Age 28

Back to a starting role after pitching in relief most of 1992. Magnante had some late season success at Omaha, then for Kansas City. Still better out of the bullpen, he may end up there again in 1994. Probably the Royals' long relief lefty for next season and will get spot starts, too.

	W	SV	ERA	IP	H	BB	SO	BPI	$
1992 Kansas City AL	4	0	4.94	89	115	35	31	1.68	-
1993 Kansas City AL	1	0	4.08	35	37	11	16	1.37	0
1994 *Projection* >>>	2	0	4.34	54	63	20	23	1.53	-

MAGRANE, JOE - TL - Age 29

The Cardinals let Magrane go, because his inconsistency was maddening. Every time he had a couple of bad outings, and his role in the starting rotation was in jeopardy, he would go out and pitch a gem ... then slip back into the same old rut. The Angels were more willing to take a few roughs with the smooth.

	W	SV	ERA	IP	H	BB	SO	BPI	$
1992 St. Louis NL	1	0	4.02	31	34	15	20	1.56	-
1993 St. Louis NL	8	0	4.97	116	127	37	38	1.41	-
1993 California AL	3	0	3.94	48	48	21	24	1.44	0
1994 *Projection* >>>	7	0	4.60	108	115	39	43	1.43	-

MAHOMES, PAT - TR - Age 23

In the shambles that was Minnesota's pitching staff was Mahomes. He pitched more and better with the big league team in '92. Last year he was sent to the bullpen and then to the Pacific Coast League, where his control continued to give him trouble, although his stats were good. The Twins didn't even bring him back up in September. He is still young, and he could be a key member of the Twins rotation in '94. With better concentration, he could be one of the best in the league with his 92 MPH fastball, hard slider, and good curve.

	W	SV	ERA	IP	H	BB	SO	BPI	$
1992 Minnesota AL	3	0	5.04	70	73	37	44	1.58	-
1993 Portland AAA	11	0	3.03	115	89	54	94	1.23	
1993 Minnesota AL	1	0	7.71	37	47	16	23	1.70	-
1994 *Projection* >>>	2	0	6.00	43	50	21	27	1.64	-

MALDONADO, CARLOS - TR - Age 27

Maldonado progressed through the Royals system to become the AAA Omaha relief ace in 1992. Then he got traded to the Brewers. He's ready for the majors, but won't get a shot at saves.

	W	SV	ERA	IP	H	BB	SO	BPI	$
1992 Omaha AAA	7	16	3.60	75	61	35	60	1.28	
1993 Milwaukee AL	2	1	4.58	37	40	17	18	1.54	0

MALLICOAT, ROB - TL - Age 29
Once the brightest pitching prospect in the Astros' organization, Mallicoat missed the entire 1993 season with a rotator cuff problem. Released in October, his career appears to be over.

	W	SV	ERA	IP	H	BB	SO	BPI	$
1992 Tucson AAA	1	3	2.32	50	36	21	53	1.14	
1992 Houston NL	0	0	7.23	23	26	19	20	1.90	-

MANON, RAMON - TR - Age 26
In eight minor league seasons in three organizations he has won 10 games twice, including '93. Pitched one game with the Rangers in '90.

MANSUR, JEFF - Twins - TL - Age 23
Has made steady progress in three stops in his three pro seasons -- at least in terms of moving up to higher classifications. He has shown himself to be slightly better than a .500 pitcher with an ERA about 4. Expect about the same (most likely with a higher ERA) in the Pacific Coast League this year.

MANUEL, BARRY - TR - Age 28
Manuel went on the DL during spring training with a sore elbow. While rehabing he moved to the Orioles organization. He relies on location and change of speed; needs pinpoint control to be effective.

	W	SV	ERA	IP	H	BB	SO	BPI	$
1992 Texas AL	1	0	4.76	5	6	1	9	1.24	-
1992 Oklahoma City AAA	1	5	5.27	27	32	26	11	2.14	
1993 Rochester AAA	1	0	3.66	20	14	7	11	1.05	

MANZANILLO, JOSIAS - TR - Age 26
Former Red Sox prospect. Was 7-10 with a 4.36 ERA at Omaha in 1992.

	W	SV	ERA	IP	H	BB	SO	BPI	$
1993 Norfolk AAA	1	0	3.11	84	82	25	79	1.27	
1993 Milwaukee AL	1	1	9.53	17	22	10	10	1.88	-
1993 New York NL	0	0	3.00	12	8	9	11	1.42	-

MARTINEZ, DENNIS - TR - Age 38
What a strange season it was for Martinez. He openly lobbied for a trade in spring training, going as far as wearing a New York Yankees' cap prior to a spring game between them and the Expos. He then was traded to Atlanta in August and turned down the deal. He spent the season with the Expos and had another good year, though his ERA was higher than normal. Now he's in Cleveland. A crafty veteran, Martinez played out his option at the end of the season and apparently was headed out of Montreal, possibly to the presidency of his native Nicaragua. Martinez is the seventh pitcher in baseball history to win 100 games in both leagues.

	W	SV	ERA	IP	H	BB	SO	BPI	$
1992 Montreal NL	16	0	2.47	226	172	60	147	1.03	23
1993 Montreal NL	15	1	3.85	225	211	64	138	1.23	13
1994 *Projection* >>>	15	0	3.86	225	197	75	139	1.21	14

MARTINEZ, JOSE - TR - Age 23
Martinez struggled in 14 appearances for AAA Las Vegas after arriving from the Marlins in the Gary Sheffield trade. The fourth player picked in the expansion draft, Martinez went 40-21 with a 2.01 ERA in four years in the Mets' organization and developed a reputation for throwing strikes. San Diego is counting on Martinez or Andres Berumen, the other key figure in the Sheffield deal, to play a significant role in 1993.

	W	SV	ERA	IP	H	BB	SO	BPI	$
1993 Las Vegas AAA	2	0	9.93	35	56	15	16	2.00	
1993 Edmonton AAA	6	0	4.28	80	92	24	29	1.45	

MARTINEZ, PEDRO A - TL - Age 25

Pedro A. Martinez, no relation to Pedro J., Ramon, Jose or Dennis, was one of San Diego's most successful pitchers in a dismal 1993 season. Pitching entirely in relief, this lefty held batters to a .172 average in 32 appearances and had a ratio under 1.00. Although most of the Padre saves will go elsewhere, Martinez could pick up four to eight saves as a set up man.

	W	SV	ERA	IP	H	BB	SO	BPI	$
1993 Las Vegas AAA	11	0	4.72	87	94	40	65	1.53	
1993 San Diego NL	3	0	2.43	37	23	13	32	0.97	
1994 *Projection* >>>	3	1	4.42	60	70	20	36	1.50	-

MARTINEZ, PEDRO J - TR - Age 22

Ramon's younger brother pitched much like Ramon did when he first came up, only better. Pedro struck out 10 batters per 9 innings.The Expos will use him as a starter in 1994.

	W	SV	ERA	IP	H	BB	SO	BPI	$
1992 Albuquerque AAA	7	0	3.81	125	104	57	124	1.29	
1992 Los Angeles NL	0	0	2.25	8	6	1	8	0.88	0
1993 Los Angeles NL	10	2	2.61	107	76	57	119	1.24	11
1994 *Projection* >>>	12	0	2.98	157	114	84	100	1.26	12

MARTINEZ, RAMON - TR - Age 26

Martinez made 32 starts with a good ERA but his walks were up and his strikeout rate was down in 1993. He still hasn't recovered from the high pitch counts in 1990 and 1991.

	W	SV	ERA	IP	H	BB	SO	BPI	$
1992 Los Angeles NL	8	0	4.00	151	141	69	101	1.39	-
1993 Los Angeles NL	10	0	3.44	212	202	104	127	1.45	5
1994 *Projection* >>>	10	0	3.55	194	183	91	122	1.41	5

MASON, ROGER - TR - Age 35

A rubber armed righty who led all NL relievers in innings in 1993, Mason's stats in 1992 and 1993 were eerily identical. He has a nagging gopher ball problem, allowing 10 homers in each of the past two seasons, and in one long evening at the Vet last year, he performed the unparalleled feat of giving up consecutive homers to Steve Buechele, Steve Lake, and the powerful Willie Wilson in the space of seven pitches. His ability to gobble up innings will keep him employed for at least a couple more seasons.

	W	SV	ERA	IP	H	BB	SO	BPI	$
1992 Pittsburgh NL	5	8	4.09	88	80	33	56	1.28	6
1993 San Diego-Philadelphia	5	0	4.06	99	90	34	71	1.24	
1994 *Projection* >>>	5	3	4.03	89	79	31	62	1.24	5

MASTERS, DAVE - TR - Age 29

Long-time Giants farmhand, never made it to San Francisco and won't likely make it anywhere.

	W	SV	ERA	IP	H	BB	SO	BPI	$
1993 Shreveport AA	0	2	1.07	25	21	15	25	1.44	

MATHEWS, TERRY - TR - Age 29

Mathews followed a solid debut in 1991 with a disastrous performance in 1992. Every phase of his game deteriorated, and his future at the major league level is in doubt.

	W	SV	ERA	IP	H	BB	SO	BPI	$
1992 Texas AL	2	0	5.95	42	48	31	26	1.87	-
1992 Oklahoma City AAA	1	1	4.32	17	17	7	13	1.41	
1993 Jackson AA	6	0	3.67	103	116	29	74	1.40	

MATHILE, MIKE - TR - Age 25

Moving up steadily through the Montreal organization from short-season A-ball to Triple-A since 1990, Mathile will have to show more than he did in 1993 to make the last big step to the majors. He doesn't throw hard enough to put batters away.

MATTHEWS, MIKE - TL - Age 20
After a dominant season at Rookie and A-ball in 1992 (8-0, 1.35), this 1992 second round pick had rotator cuff surgery and missed all of 1993. He resumed throwing in August 1993, showed no ill effects and was added to the Instructional League roster. His conditioning has been subpar, a no-no for a guy who's not a flamethrower and must have pinpoint location to be effective. Watch his comeback closely.

MAUSER, TIM - TR - Age 27
Former Phillie Mauser was tough on lefthanded hitters, holding them to a .202 batting average in 1993 but was otherwise hit pretty hard. He's destined for middle relief at best.

	W	SV	ERA	IP	H	BB	SO	BPI	$
1993 San Diego NL	0	0	4.00	54	51	24	46	1.39	-
1994 *Projection* >>>	0	0	4.11	34	33	15	20	1.41	-

MAY, DARRELL - TL - Age 22
May had a great start for Single-A Macon, going 10-4 with a 2.24 ERA and striking out 111 in 104 innings. He earned a promotion to the Braves higher level Class A franchise at Durham, where he continued his torrid pace, going 5-2 with a 2.09 ERA and 47 strikeouts in 52 innings. May led the Braves minor leaguers with his 15 victories in 1993 and was sent to the Instructional League last fall. The lefthander is making rapid progress, but is at least two years away.

MAYSEY, MATT - TR - Age 27
Journeyman starter/reliever who worked his way up the Padres and Expos farm systems, Maysey doesn't have any one big pitch.

	W	SV	ERA	IP	H	BB	SO	BPI	$
1992 Indianapolis AAA	5	5	4.30	67	63	28	38	1.36	
1992 Montreal NL	0	0	3.86	2	4	0	1	1.71	-
1993 New Orleans AAA	0	2	4.13	52	48	14	40	1.19	
1993 Milwaukee AL	1	1	5.73	22	28	13	10	1.86	-

McANDREW, JAMIE - TR - Age 26
Dodgers top pick in 1989, consistently ran into trouble at AAA Albuquerque, but he's been good everywhere else. This 1993 season in the Brewers system represents progress.

	W	SV	ERA	IP	H	BB	SO	BPI	$
1993 New Orleans AAA	11	0	3.94	167	172	45	97	1.30	

McCASKILL, KIRK - TR - Age 32
McCaskill was hit hard in 1993. Now hasn't had a good season since 1990.

	W	SV	ERA	IP	H	BB	SO	BPI	$
1992 Chicago AL	12	0	4.18	209	193	95	109	1.38	4
1993 Chicago AL	4	2	5.23	114	144	36	65	1.59	-
1994 *Projection* >>>	7	1	4.67	149	164	57	79	1.48	-

McCLURE, BOB - TL - Age 40
The much-maligned lefty has lasted this long only because he can get lefthanders out. He's forty and was released by an expansion team, so color him gone.

	W	SV	ERA	IP	H	BB	SO	BPI	$
1992 St. Louis NL	2	0	3.17	54	52	25	24	1.43	-
1993 Florida NL	1	0	7.11	6	13	5	6	2.95	-

McCREADY, JIM - TR - Age 24
Though not overpowering, McCready blossomed in his first season exclusively in the bullpen; he held his own in Double-A.

	W	SV	ERA	IP	H	BB	SO	BPI	$
1993 St. Lucie A	6	16	1.76	61	51	22	40	1.18	
1993 Binghamton AA	1	0	3.44	18	18	4	12	1.20	

McCULLERS, LANCE - TR - Age 30
Once a top reliever with San Diego, McCullers has suffered through years of injuries (including blood clot surgery) and minor league obscurity but never made it back. Looks like the end.

	W	SV	ERA	IP	H	BB	SO	BPI	$
1992 Texas AL	1	0	5.40	5	1	8	3	1.80	-
1992 Albuquerque AAA	4	12	1.84	44	34	10	35	1.00	
1993 Calgary AAA	4	1	5.67	87	106	40	42	1.68	

McCURRY, JEFF - TR - Age 24
McCurry's a big, hard thrower, who emerged as a prospect in the Pirates organization last season; he'll probably start this season in Double-A. However, the Pirates aren't shy about promoting players and they certainly need relievers, so he could move up quickly.

McDONALD, BEN - TR - Age 26
Experience is a wonderful thing. The turning point for Ben McDonald was June 1 when he suddenly became a pitcher rather than the erratic thrower of the past. He had a stretch of 24 starts when his ERA was a nice 2.84. Look for a very good 1994 season.

	W	SV	ERA	IP	H	BB	SO	BPI	$
1992 Baltimore AL	13	0	4.24	227	213	74	158	1.26	7
1993 Baltimore AL	13	0	3.39	220	185	86	171	1.23	17
1994 *Projection* >>>	14	0	3.44	213	187	79	159	1.25	16

McDOWELL, JACK - TR - Age 28
McDowell's 1993 was eerily similar to Dave Stewart's 1989. Black Jack has, for all intents and purposes, become the new Stewart. It always seems dangerous to pay too much for these types, but then again, they always seem to win 20. There are, of course, very few pitchers coming off two consecutive 20 win seasons.

	W	SV	ERA	IP	H	BB	SO	BPI	$
1992 Chicago AL	20	0	3.18	260	247	75	178	1.24	19
1993 Chicago AL	22	0	3.37	257	261	69	158	1.29	21
1994 Projection >>>	21	0	3.32	258	252	73	167	1.26	21

McDOWELL, ROGER - TR - Age 33
McDowell allowed almost as many unearned (15) runs as he did earned runs(17).The reason why McDowell is kept around is to get ground balls, which he did in 1993: 145 in 60 innings. Where was the defense?

	W	SV	ERA	IP	H	BB	SO	BPI	$
1992 Los Angeles NL	6	14	4.09	84	103	42	50	1.73	5
1993 Los Angeles NL	5	2	2.25	68	76	30	27	1.56	4
1994 *Projection* >>>	6	2	3.35	76	87	35	36	1.60	1

McELROY, CHUCK - TL - Age 26
This hard throwing lefty with the slider and forkball totally lost the strike zone in 1993. He had to resort to an overabundance of hittable fastballs. He's still learning to pitch after three full seasons - not a good sign.

	W	SV	ERA	IP	H	BB	SO	BPI	$
1992 Chicago NL	4	6	3.55	83	73	51	83	1.48	2
1993 Chicago NL	2	0	4.56	47	51	25	31	1.61	-
1994 *Projection* >>>	3	2	3.75	64	61	36	50	1.51	0

McGARITY, JEREMY - TR - Age 23
After going 3-12 for Single-A St. Petersburg in 1992, he bounced back to post a 9-7 record for the same club last season. He's considered to have one of the better arms in the organization but the Cardinals don't know whether to use him as a starter or out of the bullpen. He's expected to make the jump to AA Arkansas and the Cardinals figure to get a better read on his potential at a higher level.

McGEHEE, KEVIN - TR - Age 25
Acquired during last season in a trade for Luis Mercedes. He throws only in the mid-80s, but relies on breaking pitches to fool batters. He was among the International League ERA leaders in '93, and is a candidate for the Baltimore rotation.

	W	SV	ERA	IP	H	BB	SO	BPI	$
1993 Rochester AAA	7	0	2.96	133	124	37	92	1.21	
1993 Baltimore AL	0	0	5.94	17	18	7	7	1.54	-

McMICHAEL, GREG - TR - Age 27

When Mike Stanton's adventurous outings became too much for Bobby Cox to bear, McMichael was installed as the closer and was the most pleasant surprise of the Braves' season. The Indians gave up on McMichael in 1990 after a mediocre year split between Double-A and Triple-A. With the Braves farm team, he split time between the starting rotation and the bullpen, but rose quickly to AAA Richmond in 1992. The National League hitters apparently haven't figured him out yet. He slumped slightly at season's end, but is still the incumbent closer going into spring training.

	W	SV	ERA	IP	H	BB	SO	BPI	$
1993 Atlanta NL	2	19	2.06	92	68	29	89	1.06	23
1994 Projection >>>	1	18	3.22	55	43	25	50	1.24	17

MEACHAM, RUSTY - TR - Age 26

Spent most of the season on the DL with a sore elbow. A quick worker with control of several pitches, Meacham can be effective as the righty set up man when healthy.

	W	SV	ERA	IP	H	BB	SO	BPI	$
1992 Kansas City AL	10	2	2.74	101	88	21	64	1.07	12
1993 Kansas City AL	2	0	5.57	21	31	5	13	1.71	-
1994 Projection >>>	4	1	3.67	46	47	12	27	1.28	2

MELENDEZ, JOSE - TR - Age 28

Sidelined with a sprained thumb and then a sore neck, Melendez had a lost season in 1993. The talent is still there.

	W	SV	ERA	IP	H	BB	SO	BPI	$
1992 San Diego NL	6	0	2.92	89	82	20	82	1.14	4
1993 Boston AL	2	0	2.25	16	10	5	14	0.94	1
1994 Projection >>>	4	0	3.15	46	42	14	34	1.22	3

MENDOZA, REYNOL - TR - Age 23

A 1992 seventh round pick, Mendoza dominated at the Single-A level in 1993, with a ratio barely above 1.00, and a strikeout/walk ratio of over 3 to 1. At his age, he must have another big year at a higher classification in 1994 to move into contention for a future big league spot.

MENENDEZ, TONY - TR - Age 29

The hard throwing Menendez was the American Association's top closer last season with 24 saves for AAA Buffalo. He also pitched decently in two trials with the Pirates, but he was dropped from the 40-man roster at the end of the season. He's a journeyman at best but will be in someone's camp this spring as every club looks for pitching help and he still has the tools to get people out.

	W	SV	ERA	IP	H	BB	SO	BPI	$
1992 Cincinnati NL	1	0	1.93	4	1	0	5	0.21	-
1993 Buffalo AAA	4	24	2.42	63	50	21	48	1.12	
1993 Pittsburgh NL	2	0	3.00	21	20	4	13	1.14	0

MERCKER, KENT - TL - Age 26

The Braves took the pressure off of Mercker by using him as a long reliever and spot starter, and he performed well in both roles. He's not really much as a starter; he loses his effectiveness after four or five innings, but he was enough for the Braves purposes. Mercker will continue to strikeout a batter per inning and also walk batters at a high rate, too. He just had his best year at age 25; his future is likely to get even brighter.

	W	SV	ERA	IP	H	BB	SO	BPI	$
1992 Atlanta NL	3	6	3.42	68	51	35	49	1.26	5
1993 Atlanta NL	3	0	2.86	66	52	36	59	1.33	2
1994 Projection >>>	3	2	3.00	67	51	36	56	1.30	4

MERRIMAN, BRETT - TR - Age 27

The ace of Portland's bullpen was a joker in the Twins' deck. He couldn't throw strikes in his major league debut.

Though he moved to the bullpen full time in 1990, his 15 saves last season were a career high. Obtained from Colorado in a trade last spring.

	W	SV	ERA	IP	H	BB	SO	BPI	$
1993 Portland AAA	5	15	3.00	48	46	18	29	1.32	
1993 Minnesota AL	1	0	9.67	27	36	23	14	2.19	-

MESA, JOSE - TR - Age 27
Those guys with 90+ MPH fastballs keep getting work even when they can't get people out. Has now pitched almost 600 innings in his career, and his career ERA is still over 5.00.

	W	SV	ERA	IP	H	BB	SO	BPI	$
1992 Baltimore-Cleveland	7	0	4.59	161	169	70	62	1.49	-
1993 Cleveland AL	10	0	4.92	209	232	62	118	1.41	2
1994 Projection >>>	9	0	4.90	186	206	64	96	1.45	-

MICELI, DANNY - TR - Age 23
Obtained from Kansas City last season in the trade for Stan Belinda, Miceli impressed the Pirates in a September callup from Double-A. His fastball reached 95 MPH and he showed outstanding poise. In an organization starved for a closer, Miceli has a chance to earn that role. He will be worked in slowly, though, and could start the season at AAA Buffalo.

	W	SV	ERA	IP	H	BB	SO	BPI	$
1993 Memphis AA	6	7	4.60	58	54	39	68	1.60	
1993 Pittsburgh NL	0	0	5.06	5	6	3	4	1.76	-

MILACKI, BOB - TR - Age 29
Oriole retread who was one of about sixty guys who started for the Indians in 1993, Milacki was a decent major league starter as recently as 1991, so there's still a little hope. Needs to challenge hitters to be effective, something he's never done in back to back seasons.

	W	SV	ERA	IP	H	BB	SO	BPI	$
1992 Baltimore AL	6	1	5.84	116	140	44	51	1.59	-
1992 Rochester AAA	7	0	4.57	61	57	21	35	1.28	
1993 Cleveland AL	1	0	3.38	16	19	11	7	1.88	-
1994 Projection >>>	3	0	4.93	63	71	25	30	1.53	-

MILCHIN, MIKE - TL - Age 26
After starring in the Arizona Fall League following the 1992 season, the Cardinals had Milchin penciled in as a member of their bullpen in 1993. However, Milchin didn't make the club out of spring training and spent the whole season at AAA Louisville. He split time between the rotation and the bullpen and his stock has clearly fallen after a sub-par year.

	W	SV	ERA	IP	H	BB	SO	BPI	$
1993 Louisville AAA	3	0	3.95	112	108	43	72	1.35	

MILITELLO, SAM - TR - Age 24
The Sporting News once rated him the top prospect in the minors. Baseball America named him the number one prospect in the International League. In the minors, he just toyed with the opposition, compiling a 34-8 record and a 1.44 ERA without a dominating fastball. Hitters learned to lay off his low pitches, and then he developed arm problems. He had a 5.73 ERA in 31 innings at AAA Columbus.

	W	SV	ERA	IP	H	BB	SO	BPI	$
1992 New York AL	3	0	3.45	60	43	32	42	1.25	1
1993 Columbus AAA	1	0	5.73	33	36	20	39	1.69	
1993 New York AL	1	0	6.75	9	10	7	5	1.87	-
1994 Projection >>>	2	0	4.23	24	22	11	14	1.39	-

MILLER, KURT - TL - Age 21
Hoo boy! Within a few years, this trade, Cris Carpenter for Kurt Miller and Robb Nen will be remembered as the biggest gaffe of the Rangers' 1993 season. Miller struggled with his control at AAA Edmonton, but didn't Darryl Kile once have an ERA of about 9.00 in that league? Miller doesn't turn 22 until August, which might be just about the time he arrives in the Marlins rotation to stay.

	W	SV	ERA	IP	H	BB	SO	BPI	$
1992 Charlotte A	5	0	2.39	75	51	29	58	1.07	
1992 Tulsa AA	7	0	3.68	88	82	35	73	1.33	
1993 Edmonton AAA	3	0	4.50	48	42	34	19	1.58	

MILLER, PAUL - TR - Age 28

A 53rd-round draft pick, Miller bucked the odds to reach the majors. He was a surprising addition to the Pirates' opening day roster in 1992, but had shoulder surgery following that season. Before his injury, he threw 90 MPH and he lost some velocity after the surgery. The Pirates got two poor late season major league starts from Miller before they released him at the end of last year.

	W	SV	ERA	IP	H	BB	SO	BPI	$
1992 Buffalo AAA	2	0	3.90	32	38	16	18	1.69	
1992 Pittsburgh NL	1	0	2.38	11	11	1	5	1.06	-
1993 Pittsburgh NL	0	0	5.40	10	15	2	2	1.70	
1993 Buffalo AAA	3	0	4.47	52	57	14	25	1.36	

MILLS, ALAN - TR - Age 27

If ace closer Gregg Olson's elbow isn't healed, Alan Mills may become the co-closer or even the closer. He is a decent worker who could probably handle the closer job, or give 100 innings with some wins and saves.

	W	SV	ERA	IP	H	BB	SO	BPI	$
1992 Baltimore AL	10	2	2.61	103	78	54	60	1.28	9
1993 Baltimore AL	5	4	3.23	100	80	51	68	1.31	9
1994 *Projection* >>>	6	8	3.25	93	84	42	55	1.35	11

MIMBS, MARK - TL - Age 25

The Dodgers released his twin brother, Mike, but Mark was overpowering in the Texas League. After a promotion, he struggled in the Pacific Coast League for the second straight year.

MINCHEY, NATE - TR - Age 24

Once had a problem completing games because of an undiagnosed heart problem. Now on medication, he has become a workhorse, completing eight games with Pawtucket and Boston last season. Despite his size (6'7", 210 pounds), he does not throw hard. Acquired in the trade for Jeff Reardon in '92.

	W	SV	ERA	IP	H	BB	SO	BPI	$
1993 Pawtucket AAA	7	0	4.02	194	182	50	113	1.19	
1993 Boston AL	1	0	3.55	33	35	8	18	1.30	0
1994 *Projection* >>>	1	0	4.05	20	22	5	11	1.34	-

MINOR, BLAS - TR - Age 28

Minor led the Pirates farm system with 18 saves in 1992, then moved up to help the major league club. He has a bright future. In a very unsettled pen, he is one of the best talents.

	W	SV	ERA	IP	H	BB	SO	BPI	$
1992 Buffalo AAA	5	18	2.43	96	72	26	60	1.02	
1992 Pittsburgh NL	0	0	4.50	2	3	0	0	1.50	-
1993 Pittsburgh NL	8	2	4.10	94	94	26	84	1.28	5
1994 *Projection* >>>	5	1	4.10	57	55	17	42	1.27	2

MINUTELLI, GINO - TL - Age 29

Minutelli has toiled in the minors since 1985 and has 40.2 major league innings to show for it. He'll turn 30 this year; the only reason he's still around is that he throws lefthanded.

	W	SV	ERA	IP	H	BB	SO	BPI	$
1993 Phoenix AAA	2	11	4.02	53	55	26	57	1.52	
1993 San Francisco NL	0	0	3.77	14	7	15	10	1.56	-

MIRANDA, ANGEL - TL - Age 24

Miranda came up through the Brewers system as a relief specialist, and then converted to starter at Denver in 1992. At first that change looked like a bad idea, but Miranda learned how to pace himself better in 1993. Late in the summer he had some sparkling outings and is now poised to be one of the most improved pitchers of 1994. He will surely win more than four games.

	W	SV	ERA	IP	H	BB	SO	BPI	$
1993 Milwaukee AL	4	0	3.30	120	100	52	88	1.27	7
1994 Projection >>>	6	0	3.65	144	123	60	100	1.27	8

MLICKI, DAVE - TR - Age 25
Has not been overly impressive in short major league stints during the past two seasons, but has improved his control gradually throughout his minor league career. Fully recovered from March 1993 rotator cuff surgery, and will have a clear shot at a spot in the big league rotation in 1994.

	W	SV	ERA	IP	H	BB	SO	BPI	$
1992 Cleveland AL	0	0	4.98	21	23	16	16	1.80	-
1993 Canton-Akron AA	2	0	0.39	23	15	8	21	1.00	
1993 Cleveland AL	0	0	3.38	13	11	6	7	1.30	-

MOELLER, DENNIS - TL - Age 26
Moeller pitched well in Kansas City's farm system and was selected as the starter in the 1992 Triple-A All-Star Game. Traded to the Pirates prior to last season, he made the Opening Day roster but got hammered. His fastball and breaking pitches are below average. It appears he may be just one of those pitchers who can't make the jump from Triple-A to the majors.

	W	SV	ERA	IP	H	BB	SO	BPI	$
1992 Omaha AAA	8	2	2.46	120	121	34	56	1.28	
1992 Kansas City AL	0	0	7.00	18	24	11	6	1.94	-
1993 Buffalo AAA	3	0	4.34	76	85	21	38	1.39	
1993 Pittsburgh NL	1	0	9.92	16	26	7	13	2.05	-

MOHLER, MIKE - TL - Age 25
Mohler had three decent seasons in Single-A and Double-A ball before struggling with the big club in 1993. He needs some time at Triple-A; his 42 appearances with Oakland are a sign of how poor their staff was. Mohler held lefties to a .192 average last year; could shine in a one-batter lefty role.

	W	SV	ERA	IP	H	BB	SO	BPI	$
1993 Oakland AL	1	0	5.60	64	57	44	42	1.58	-
1994 Projection >>>	1	0	5.60	39	39	22	22	1.57	-

MONTELEONE, RICH - TR - Age 31
Monteleone needs to find spots, which he didn't do in 1993. He's a smart pitcher who knows he needs to regroup soon to keep his career going.

	W	SV	ERA	IP	H	BB	SO	BPI	$
1992 New York AL	7	0	3.30	92	82	27	62	1.18	6
1993 New York AL	7	0	4.94	86	85	35	50	1.41	1
1994 Projection >>>	7	0	4.32	84	80	31	48	1.32	2

MONTGOMERY, JEFF - TR - Age 32
Has completed his climb to the absolute top of American League relief corps. Increased his save total again, this time tying for league lead and tying club record at 45. Has now raised his save rate for six straight years. Strikeouts still dropping gradually, but Montgomery is even more effective for not trying to blow away all hitters he faces. He's now more of a pitcher instead of hard thrower.

	W	SV	ERA	IP	H	BB	SO	BPI	$
1992 Kansas City AL	1	39	2.18	82	61	27	69	1.06	35
1993 Kansas City AL	7	45	2.27	87	65	23	66	1.01	47
1994 Projection >>>	4	40	2.68	86	66	28	68	1.09	41

MOODY, RITCHIE - TL - Age 23
During his two pro seasons, he has pitched solely in relief -- and very well (1.64 career ERA). As a hard-throwing lefthander, he is likely to reach the Rangers early in '94 with any success in spring training or in Triple-A.

MOORE, MARCUS - TR - Age 23
This guy's fastball sings when it hits the mitt. Now he needs to develop some other pitches. The Rockies don't really need another righthander; his role may eventually be as a middle reliever.

MOORE, MIKE - TR - Age 34
Once a star, now just a workhorse who pitches a lot of innings with a high ERA and ratio.

	W	SV	ERA	IP	H	BB	SO	BPI	$
1992 Oakland AL	17	0	4.12	223	229	103	117	1.49	3
1993 Detroit AL	13	0	5.22	214	227	89	89	1.48	-
1994 *Projection* >>>	15	0	4.66	216	223	95	104	1.47	-

MORGAN, MIKE - TR - Age 34
His disappointing 1993 stats reflect poor run support, defensive lapses, and a series of injuries. On many occasions in 1993 he took the mound with back, toe and elbow problems. In 1994 he's again capable of winning 16 games, if healthy.

	W	SV	ERA	IP	H	BB	SO	BPI	$
1992 Chicago NL	16	0	2.55	240	203	79	123	1.18	18
1993 Chicago NL	10	0	4.03	207	206	74	111	1.35	5
1994 *Projection* >>>	12	0	3.41	220	203	76	118	1.27	12

MORMAN, ALVIN - TL - Age 25
A hard throwing lefty, Morman was 8-0 with a 1.55 ERA as a reliever at Single-A Asheville in 1992. Converted to a starter, he pitched well at AA Jackson in 1993 but was slowed by arm problems. He'll be switched back to relief and projects as a solid prospect for arrival in 1995.

MORONES, GENO - TR - Age 23
Hard thrower, among the most improved pitchers in the Cubs system. Had a 2.45 ERA at Class A Peoria, 1.76 at Class A Daytona, and 4.88 in 24 innings at AA Orlando.

MORRIS, JACK - TR - Age 38
The long, uneven decline accelerated in 1993. You could see it even during his 21 win season in 1992. Morris is an intense competitor who can still get the ball up over ninety miles per hour, but his forkball doesn't fool hitters anymore and his control of breaking pitches is just about gone.

	W	SV	ERA	IP	H	BB	SO	BPI	$
1992 Toronto AL	21	0	4.04	240	222	80	132	1.25	12
1993 Toronto AL	7	0	6.19	153	189	65	103	1.67	-
1994 *Projection* >>>	12	0	5.01	189	203	71	118	1.45	-

MORTON, KEVIN - TL - Age 25
Good enough to get 15 starts with the Red Sox in 1991, Morton regressed in 1992, when his Pawtucket ERA was 5.45. In 1993 he was 3-6 with a 4.81 ERA.

MOYER, JAMIE - TL - Age 31
Moyer was a nice surprise for the Orioles last year. He was nearly out of baseball, but eventually earned a promotion to the O's after a successful Triple-A stint, and at times, pitched like Whitey Ford. He needs pinpoint control and changing speeds to be effective.

	W	SV	ERA	IP	H	BB	SO	BPI	$
1993 Baltimore AL	12	0	3.43	152	154	38	90	1.26	12
1994 *Projection* >>>	7	0	3.71	94	95	25	56	1.28	5

MULHOLLAND, TERRY - TL - Age 31
A finesse lefty who outdid himself in first half of 1993, Mulholland earned a start in the All-Star game. Nagging injuries (knee, hip) have slowed him over the past two seasons, seriously hindering his performance over short stretches. He must have precise location to be effective, as he has an offspeed repertoire. He's deadly against lefties, holding them to a .216 batting average in 1993, and against opposing baserunners as a result of his dangerous slide step pickoff

move; opponents stole just one base against Mulholland in 1993. He has peaked, and a return to good health is necessary for him to maintain his status as a reliable 200 inning starter.

	W	SV	ERA	IP	H	BB	SO	BPI	$
1992 Philadelphia NL	13	0	3.81	229	227	46	125	1.19	7
1993 Philadelphia NL	12	0	3.25	191	177	40	116	1.14	15
1994 Projection >>>	13	0	3.48	207	198	42	121	1.16	16

MUNOZ, BOBBY - TR - Age 26
Big hard thrower with control problems. A few more years at Columbus could help in developing him into a dominate closer. Throws a hard 95 MPH fastball.

	W	SV	ERA	IP	H	BB	SO	BPI	$
1993 Columbus AAA	3	10	1.44	31	24	8	16	1.02	
1993 New York AL	3	0	5.32	46	48	26	33	1.64	-
1994 Projection >>>	2	0	5.32	27	28	16	20	1.62	-

MUNOZ, J.J. - TL - Age 26
Despite putting up solid numbers in his first three pro seasons, this smallish (5'9", 170 lb.) lefty was returned to Single-A Clearwater for a second season in 1993. He responded with a strong year (9.59 whiffs per nine innings) in relief.

MUNOZ, MIKE - TL - Age 28
His late-season performance earns him a look in spring training for a setup/middle relief role. He struck out 16 in 18 innings.

	W	SV	ERA	IP	H	BB	SO	BPI	$
1992 Detroit AL	1	2	3.00	48	44	25	23	1.44	1
1993 Detroit AL	0	0	6.00	3	4	6	1	3.33	-
1993 Colorado NL	2	0	4.50	18	21	9	16	1.66	-
1994 Projection >>>	2	1	3.99	28	30	17	14	1.67	-

MUNOZ, OSCAR - TR - Age 24
The Indians traded him for Paul Sorrento. Pitched nearly as well in Triple-A as he had in Double-A. Expect him in the majors this season. Given the state of the Twins' pitching, Munoz could start the year in Minnesota.

	W	SV	ERA	IP	H	BB	SO	BPI	$
1993 Nashville AA	11	0	3.08	131	123	51	139	1.32	
1993 Portland AAA	2	0	4.31	31	29	17	29	1.47	

MURPHY, ROB - TL - Age 33
Murphy keeps landing in the majors. He's an adequate pitcher and he'll always have a job as long as he can get lefthanded hitters out in a relief role. Once a power pitcher, Murphy has relied more on his splitfinger pitch as he gets older.

	W	SV	ERA	IP	H	BB	SO	BPI	$
1992 Houston NL	3	0	4.04	55	56	21	42	1.38	-
1993 St. Louis NL	5	1	4.87	65	73	20	41	1.45	-
1994 Projection >>>	4	1	4.49	60	65	20	41	1.42	-

MUSSETT, JOSE - TL - Age 25
Noteworthy only for his 21 saves at AA Midland after being converted from outfielder to pitcher. Very wild. Little chance to make the Angels this year.

	W	SV	ERA	IP	H	BB	SO	BPI	$
1992 Quad City A	8	6	2.39	72	41	25	104	0.92	
1993 Midland AA	2	21	5.49	62	59	32	59	1.46	

MUSSINA, MIKE - TR - Age 25
Mussina is rated by some American League managers as the league's best pitcher. His changeup and control are outstanding. Mussina's problems last year stemmed from overwork caused by a 141-pitch game in June which caused bicep tendinitis; and secondly, getting hurt in a brawl with the Mariners. The problems are over and Mussina should be a Cy Young candidate in '94 and '95.

	W	SV	ERA	IP	H	BB	SO	BPI	$
1992 Baltimore AL	18	0	2.54	241	212	48	130	1.08	26
1993 Baltimore AL	14	0	4.46	168	163	44	117	1.24	10
1994 *Projection* >>>	15	0	3.61	182	170	43	114	1.17	16

MUTIS, JEFF - TL - Age 27

In 1991, this finesse lefty was 11-5, 1.80 in Double-A, but struck out 4.5 batters per nine innings. His major league exploits the past three seasons have been minimal. He's lefthanded, though, so he's probably got another ten or so chances left.

	W	SV	ERA	IP	H	BB	SO	BPI	$
1992 Colorado Springs AAA	9	0	5.08	145	177	57	77	1.61	-
1993 Cleveland AL	3	0	5.78	81	93	33	29	1.56	-
1994 *Projection* >>>	2	0	5.90	53	65	20	20	1.60	-

MYERS, JIMMY - TR - Age 24

Big season at Shreveport in 1991 with a 2.48 ERA got Myers to AAA Phoenix in 1993, but he stumbled, and then he came back for another try in 1993.

	W	SV	ERA	IP	H	BB	SO	BPI	$
1993 Phoenix AAA	2	0	3.68	59	69	22	20	1.54	

MYERS, RANDY - TL - Age 31

The Cubs MVP in 1993, Myers had one slump which lasted about a week and a half, far too long for the Wrigley fans who booed him for blowing a save; maybe they'd prefer Lee Guetterman. Myers was perfect in 14 September save chances, one of the best months in closer history. He worked inside and out in the strike zone masterfully with mid-90s MPH heat and a new breaking ball. He won't save 53 in 1994, but 40 is almost a lock.

	W	SV	ERA	IP	H	BB	SO	BPI	$
1992 San Diego NL	3	38	4.29	80	84	34	66	1.48	28
1993 Chicago NL	2	53	3.11	75	65	26	86	1.21	45
1994 *Projection* >>>	3	40	3.52	82	75	34	82	1.33	36

NABHOLZ, CHRIS - TL - Age 27

He took a step backwards in 1993, spending time in the minors and on the DL with a strained forearm muscle. He appears to have the stuff of a consistent 15 game winner with a very good sinker. However, things weren't clicking for him with the Expos and he finished the year working on a strict pitch count.

	W	SV	ERA	IP	H	BB	SO	BPI	$
1992 Montreal NL	11	0	3.32	195	176	74	130	1.28	6
1993 Montreal NL	9	0	4.09	117	100	63	74	1.40	2
1994 *Projection* >>>	10	0	3.73	144	127	65	93	1.33	5

NAGY, CHARLES - TR - Age 26

Underwent major shoulder surgery following eight generally ineffective starts in 1993, after establishing himself as one of the best young pitchers in baseball in 1992. He was not an overpowering pitcher to begin with, so a slight loss of velocity might not hurt him the way it might hurt, say, Jose DeJesus. He relies on location, and is expected to be helping the Indians' rotation again in 1994.

	W	SV	ERA	IP	H	BB	SO	BPI	$
1992 Cleveland AL	17	0	2.96	252	245	57	169	1.20	19
1993 Cleveland AL	2	0	6.29	49	66	13	30	1.64	-
1994 *Projection* >>>	7	0	3.93	126	136	32	80	1.33	4

NAVARRO, JAIME - TR - Age 27

The rap on Navarro has always been lack of stamina, both in terms of tiring during a game and wearing down over the course of a season. In 1992 it looked like he would break through by using fewer pitches per at bat, but in 1993 the opposing hitters became much more patient, and Navarro's old problems returned.

	W	SV	ERA	IP	H	BB	SO	BPI	$
1992 Milwaukee AL	17	0	3.33	246	224	64	100	1.17	18
1993 Milwaukee AL	11	0	5.33	214	254	73	114	1.53	-
1994 *Projection* >>>	13	0	4.53	226	244	70	110	1.39	0

NEAGLE, DENNY - TL - Age 25

He bombed as a starter in his two seasons with the Pirates but showed flashes of good form as a reliever. A finesse pitcher, Neagle won 20 games in Minnesota's farm system in 1990 but hasn't come close to that production in the majors. He often appears more interested in becoming a clubhouse character than a major league pitcher, although a brief demotion to the minors last season seemed to change his attitude.

	W	SV	ERA	IP	H	BB	SO	BPI	$
1992 Pittsburgh NL	4	2	4.48	86	81	43	77	1.44	-
1993 Pittsburgh NL	3	1	5.31	81	82	37	73	1.47	-
1994 *Projection* >>>	3	3	4.33	77	76	36	68	1.46	2

NEESE, JOSHUA - TR - Age 22

The Tigers' biggest surprise last year was their 30th-round draft pick, who started his rookie pro season in the bullpen. Neese pitched so well that when other Niagara Falls Rapids pitchers were promoted, he moved into the rotation. The result was that he led the New York-Pennsylvania League in wins.

NEIDLINGER, JIM - TR - Age 29

Pitched very well for the Dodgers (3.28 ERA) in 12 starts in 1990, but never got invited back, even though his performance at AAA Albuquerque was consistent for three years. He has good control and deserves another chance.

	W	SV	ERA	IP	H	BB	SO	BPI	$
1992 Albuquerque AAA	8	0	4.39	146	153	45	81	1.36	
1993 Portland AAA	9	0	5.19	158	175	54	112	1.44	

NELSON, GENE - TR - Age 33

Former A's setup man, Nelson helped fill the void in Angels' pen last year, then became a free agent.

	W	SV	ERA	IP	H	BB	SO	BPI	$
1992 Oakland AL	3	0	6.45	52	68	22	23	1.74	-
1993 California-Texas AL	0	5	3.12	61	60	24	35	1.40	5
1994 *Projection* >>>	1	3	4.34	57	63	23	30	1.51	-

NELSON, JEFF - TR - Age 27

Two years ago he looked like the Mariners closer of the future. By his own admission, he spent 1993 digging his own grave. He is still young enough to turn it around. Never give up on a pitcher who strikes out a batter per inning.

	W	SV	ERA	IP	H	BB	SO	BPI	$
1992 Seattle AL	1	6	3.44	81	71	44	46	1.42	4
1993 Seattle AL	5	1	4.35	60	57	34	61	1.52	1
1994 *Projection* >>>	3	5	3.98	60	55	34	49	1.48	3

NEN, ROBB - TR - Age 24

The palindromatic Nen would become the first double palindrome major leaguer if he went by Bob Nen. He was acquired from the Rangers with Kurt Miller for Cris Carpenter and has battled injuries and wildness throughout his career. But, when you pop the gun at 97 MPH, you're going to get a few chances. He needs a year or two of Triple-A to determine whether he has what it takes.

	W	SV	ERA	IP	H	BB	SO	BPI	$
1993 Texas AL	1	0	6.35	23	28	26	12	2.43	-
1993 Florida NL	1	0	7.02	33	35	20	27	1.66	-
1994 *Projection* >>>	1	0	4.75	34	33	20	24	1.55	-

NEWLIN, JIM - TR - Age 27

Has posted two strong performances at AA Jacksonville but hasn't passed the test at Triple-A yet.

	W	SV	ERA	IP	H	BB	SO	BPI	$
1993 Knoxville AA	0	0	8.89	26	41	13	19	2.07	
1993 Edmonton AAA	0	0	13.50	6	11	4	3	2.50	

NEWMAN, ALAN - TL - Age 24

With a 90 MPH fastball and four-pitch repertoire, Newman should have developed further by now. He was terrific at AA Orlando in 1991(2.69 ERA and a strikeout per inning) but since then his control has been erratic.

NEZELEK, ANDY - TR - Age 28
Good year in relief at AA Greenville. Longshot candidate for a save or two in 1994.

NICHOLS, ROD - TR - Age 29
Once a marginal pitcher for Cleveland, he has reached the same level for his new team. He's still messing around with different deliveries and pitches and is rapidly fading from the scene.

	W	SV	ERA	IP	H	BB	SO	BPI	$
1992 Colorado Springs AAA	3	0	5.67	54	65	16	35	1.50	
1992 Cleveland AL	4	0	4.53	105	114	31	56	1.38	-
1993 Los Angeles NL	0	0	5.68	6	9	2	3	1.80	-
1994 *Projection* >>>	1	0	4.34	49	54	14	26	1.38	-

NIED, DAVE - TR - Age 25
What a year for the 25-year-old. Plucked from the pitching-rich Braves with the number one overall expansion pick, he started opening day in New York as the ace of the staff, then hurt his elbow in a minor league exhibition game in June before returning in September. The Rockies still expect him to be their ace and the pressure to succeed will be less for Nied in 1994. If he could only get out of that ballpark...

	W	SV	ERA	IP	H	BB	SO	BPI	$
1992 Atlanta NL	3	0	1.17	23	10	5	19	0.65	2
1993 Colorado NL	5	0	5.17	87	99	42	46	1.62	-
1994 *Projection* >>>	4	0	4.70	59	62	27	33	1.51	-

NIELSEN, JERRY - TL - Age 27
Had a dismal season in the minors, but could make the Angels with a strong spring. Came over with Snow and Springer for Jim Abbott last year. Ace minor league closer in 1991.

	W	S	ERA	IP	H	BB	SO	BPI	$
1992 New York AL	1	0	4.58	19	17	18	12	1.78	-
1993 Vancouver AAA	2	0	4.20	55	70	20	45	1.62	
1993 California AL	0	0	8.03	12	18	4	8	1.82	-

NOVOA, RAFAEL - TL - Age 26
The Brewers have more than their fair share of promising young lefties. Novoa looked extremely sharp in his limited use as a starter in 1993, although he failed to win a game. With weak overall stats and little media attention last year, Novoa has the possibility of becoming one of the big pleasant surprises of 1994. He just needs to throw strikes to be successful.

	W	SV	ERA	IP	H	BB	SO	BPI	$
1993 Milwaukee AL	0	0	4.50	56	58	22	17	1.43	
1994 *Projection* >>>	6	0	4.34	120	121	47	60	1.40	1

NUNEZ, EDWIN - TR - Age 30
The league hit .298 against him in 1993. He's been around forever, and even in his best years he's only been average. Can still strike batters out.

	W	SV	ERA	IP	H	BB	SO	BPI	$
1992 Texas AL	1	3	4.85	59	63	22	49	1.43	-
1993 Oakland AL	3	1	3.81	6	89	29	58	1.57	1
1994 *Projection* >>>	2	1	4.17	66	75	26	45	1.53	-

O'DONOGHUE, JOHN - TL - Age 24
Lefty John O'Donoghue is a tall guy who doesn't throw very hard, reminding some of Lee Guetterman. He relies on finesse and changing speeds, and has a good minor league record. O'Donoghue will struggle as he adjusts to major league hitters but has the stuff to succeed.

	W	SV	ERA	IP	H	BB	SO	BPI	$
1992 Hagerstown AA	7	0	2.24	112	77	40	86	1.05	
1993 Baltimore AL	0	0	4.58	20	22	10	16	1.67	-

OGEA, CHAD - TR - Age 23
Going all the way back to college (LSU), it's been suspected that his off-speed repertoire wouldn't cut it at the next level. He continues to impress with pinpoint control and velocity power. Though he was hit slightly harder at Triple-A, he still appears to be the most polished of the stable of talented youngsters in the Indians' system. Was conspicuously absent from the list of September callups, but given the opportunity, should be ready in 1994.

	W	SV	ERA	IP	H	BB	SO	BPI	$
1992 Kinston A	13	0	3.50	139	135	29	123	1.18	
1993 Charlotte AAA	13	0	3.81	181	169	54	135	1.04	-

OJEDA, BOB - TL - Age 36
After being involved in the tragic boat accident that claimed the lives of teammates Steve Olin and Tim Crews, Ojeda courageously returned to the mound in late 1993. His career had been in decline prior to the accident. His best pitch is a change up.

	W	SV	ERA	IP	H	BB	SO	BPI	$
1992 Los Angeles NL	6	0	3.63	166	169	81	94	1.50	-
1993 Cleveland AL	2	0	4.40	43	48	21	27	1.60	-
1994 *Projection* >>>	4	0	3.75	95	99	43	56	1.49	0

OLIVARES, OMAR - TR - Age 26
Olivares confounds the Cardinals as they don't know whether to use him as a starter or reliever. He throws 90 MPH and has a devastating sinker but makes poor pitches in crucial situations. His act is wearing thin and this is a deciding year for Olivares.

	W	SV	ERA	IP	H	BB	SO	BPI	$
1992 St. Louis NL	9	0	3.84	197	189	63	124	1.28	2
1993 St. Louis NL	5	1	4.17	119	134	54	63	1.59	-
1994 *Projection* >>>	7	1	3.98	147	152	57	84	1.42	1

OLIVER, DARREN - TL - Age 23
The Rangers' third-round draft choice in '88 had his most successful season last year (7-5 with a 1.96 ERA and six saves for AA Tulsa) despite a tender elbow. The son of former major leaguer Bob Oliver is one of the Rangers' lefthanded bullpen candidates.

	W	SV	ERA	IP	H	BB	SO	BPI	$
1993 Texas AL	0	0	2.70	3	2	1	4	0.97	-
1994 *Projection* >>>	2	1	3.46	36	38	11	29	1.35	1

OLIVERAS, FRANCISCO - TR - Age 31
Crafty righty with good control and a nice mix of National League style hard junk (slider, cut fastball). Now fading.

	W	SV	ERA	IP	H	BB	SO	BPI	$
1992 San Francisco NL	0	0	3.63	44	41	10	17	1.14	-
1993 Oklahoma City AAA	4	2	5.68	124	146	52	77	1.59	

OLSEN, STEVE - TR - Age 24
One of an impressive group of young pitchers in the White Sox system, he was slightly less effective at Double-A than Single-A.

	W	SV	ERA	IP	H	BB	SO	BPI	$
1992 Sarasota A	11	0	1.94	88	68	32	85	1.14	
1992 Birmingham AA	6	0	3.03	77	68	29	46	1.26	
1993 Birmingham AA	10	0	4.75	142	156	52	92	1.46	

OLSON, GREGG - TR - Age 27

Closer Gregg Olson came down with a partially torn ligament in his elbow. Doctors can't agree on how bad it is or what to do about it. Some believe that his arm could go at any time. Others think the tear may have healed. When healthy, Olson has the best curveball in the American League.

	W	SV	ERA	IP	H	BB	SO	BPI	$
1992 Baltimore AL	1	36	2.05	61	46	24	58	1.14	31
1993 Baltimore AL	0	29	1.60	45	37	18	44	1.22	26
1994 *Projection* >>>	1	15	2.80	53	44	21	51	1.22	15

ONTIVEROS, STEVE - TR - Age 33

A marginal performer who has seen better days.

	W	SV	ERA	IP	H	BB	SO	BPI	$
1993 Seattle AL	0	0	1.00	18	18	6	13	1.33	0
1993 Portland AAA	7	0	2.87	103	90	20	73	1.06	
1994 *Projection* >>>	1	0	4.81	36	39	14	18	1.47	-

OQUIST, MIKE - TR - Age 25

Last year was his second year in Triple-A. He improved, but he still looks like he will have trouble winning in the majors.

	W	SV	ERA	IP	H	BB	SO	BPI	$
1992 Rochester AAA	10	0	4.11	153	164	45	111	1.37	
1993 Rochester AAA	9	0	3.50	149	144	41	128	1.27	
1993 Baltimore AL	0	0	3.86	12	12	4	8	1.43	-

OROSCO, JESSÉ - TL - Age 36

After years of hanging around as a lefty-lefty matchup specialist, Orosco stepped into the void created by Doug Henry's failure as the bullpen ace, and emerged with his best season since he won a world championship with the Mets in 1986. Orosco is the latest proof that lefties who can throw strikes are always on the verge of becoming valuable.

	W	SV	ERA	IP	H	BB	SO	BPI	$
1992 Milwaukee AL	3	1	3.23	39	33	13	40	1.18	2
1993 Milwaukee AL	3	8	3.18	57	47	17	67	1.14	.10
1994 *Projection* >>>	3	9	3.24	50	43	17	43	1.20	10

OSBORNE, DONOVAN - TL - Age 24

Osborne's unpredictability is a puzzle to the Cardinals. Sometimes he pitches like he's ready to emerge as one of the premier lefthanded starters in the game; other times he's very ordinary. Osborne's fastball hits 90 MPH but he tends to overthrow it in tight situations. His struggles are common to young hard throwing lefties and he'll have a bright future once he develops a little more consistency.

	W	SV	ERA	IP	H	BB	SO	BPI	$
1992 St. Louis NL	11	0	3.77	179	193	38	104	1.29	3
1993 St. Louis NL	10	0	3.76	156	153	47	83	1.29	7
1994 *Projection* >>>	11	0	3.66	170	173	40	91	1.25	9

OSTEEN, GAVIN - TL - Age 24

Has put in two good years at AA Huntsville but will need more Triple-A success before reaching Oakland.

	W	SV	ERA	IP	H	BB	SO	BPI	$
1992 Huntsville AA	5	0	3.61	102	106	27	56	1.29	
1993 Tacoma AAA	7	0	5.08	83	89	31	46	1.89	

OSUNA, AL - TL - Age 27

Osuna had good numbers in limited duty, but hasn't shown enough control. He rarely faces more than three batters per appearance and should stay in the majors as a lefty relief specialist. In the Astros unsettled pen, he is a candidate for occasional saves.

	W	SV	ERA	IP	H	BB	SO	BPI	$
1992 Houston NL	6	0	4.23	61	52	38	37	1.46	-
1993 Houston NL	1	2	3.20	25	17	13	21	1.20	1
1994 *Projection* >>>	3	6	3.70	42	32	24	31	1.33	5

OTTO, DAVE - TL - Age 29

Otto will be forever known as the Pirates' $525,000 mistake. He was unwittingly selected from Cleveland in the minor-league phase of the Rule Five Draft following the 1992 season without the Pirates knowing he had a guaranteed salary. He started last season in the rotation then was moved to the bullpen and had little success in either role. He was released in August and no one made a move to sign him. He's lefthanded, though, so there's always a chance he could resurface somewhere.

	W	SV	ERA	IP	H	BB	SO	BPI	$
1992 Cleveland AL	5	0	7.06	80	110	33	32	1.78	-
1993 Pittsburgh NL	3	0	5.03	68	85	28	30	1.66	-
1994 Projection >>>	0	0	5.58	37	47	15	16	1.66	-

PAINTER, LANCE - TL - Age 26

A prize prospect at AAA Colorado Springs, Painter got that September chance all rookies dream of and beat the Mets with a five hitter. Although the Mets were awful, his victory means a long look next spring. His being a southpaw doesn't hurt his chances either; lefties are in short supply for Colorado.

	W	SV	ERA	IP	H	BB	SO	BPI	$
1993 Colorado NL	2	0	6.00	39	52	9	16	1.56	-

PALACIOS, VINCE - TR - Age 30

Pitched in the Mexican winter league with some success. Keep an eye out for a possible comeback.

	W	SV	ERA	IP	H	BB	SO	BPI	$
1992 Pittsburgh NL	3	0	4.25	53	56	27	33	1.57	-

PALL, DONN - TR - Age 32

An innings gobbling middle reliever who was solid down the stretch for the Phils in 1993, Pall is a future trivia answer; he was on the mound when the Phils clinched the National League East. His out pitch is a forkball, which induces lots of grounders. Had the Phils acquired him 12 hours earlier, they would have been one pitcher deeper in the pen, possibly making the difference in the World Series.

	W	SV	ERA	IP	H	BB	SO	BPI	$
1992 Chicago AL	5	1	4.93	73	79	27	27	1.45	-
1993 Chicago AL	2	1	3.22	59	62	11	29	1.25	3
1993 Philadelphia NL	1	0	2.55	18	15	3	11	1.05	0
1994 Projection >>>	4	1	3.55	75	77	18	36	1.26	3

PARRETT, JEFF - TR - Age 32

Parrett started the season in the bullpen, but the Rockies starters were so awful he ended up starting six games. He blew out his elbow in July.

	W	SV	ERA	IP	H	BB	SO	BPI	$
1992 Oakland AL	9	0	3.02	98	81	42	78	1.25	6
1993 Colorado NL	3	1	5.38	74	78	45	66	1.68	-
1994 Projection >>>	2	1	4.48	76	75	41	54	1.52	-

PATTERSON, BOB - TL - Age 34

Released at the end of the season, and none too soon. Ineffective, prone to giving up home runs.

	W	SV	ERA	IP	H	BB	SO	BPI	$
1992 Pittsburgh NL	6	9	2.92	64	59	23	43	1.27	10
1993 Texas AL	2	1	4.78	53	59	11	46	1.34	0
1994 Projection >>>	3	4	4.08	58	60	16	40	1.31	4

PATTERSON, JEFF - TR - Age 25

A five year farmhand who has methodically, if unspectacularly, wended his way through the Phils organization, Patterson had his best year in 1993, achieving co-closer status by season's end. Formerly a starter, he's not a flamethrower, but still racks up decent whiff totals. He could be a midseason callup to Philly, with mediocre results to be expected.

	W	SV	ERA	IP	H	BB	SO	BPI	$
1993 Scranton AAA	7	8	2.69	93	79	42	68	1.30	

PATTERSON, KEN - TL - Age 29
Too many walks; not enough strikeouts.

	W	SV	ERA	IP	H	BB	SO	BPI	$
1992 Chicago NL	2	0	3.89	41	41	27	23	1.63	-
1993 California AL	1	1	4.58	59	54	35	36	1.51	-
1994 *Projection* >>>	2	1	4.22	54	50	32	32	1.51	-

PAVLIK, ROGER - TR - Age 26
Pavlik has a lively fastball that makes him a very effective pitcher. He had good control in most of his starts, and was near brilliant in a few of them. He was near awful in a few, too, so consistency is what the Rangers are hoping to get out of him. Solidly entrenched as the number three starter.

	W	SV	ERA	IP	H	BB	SO	BPI	$
1992 Texas AL	4	0	4.21	62	66	34	45	1.61	-
1992 Oklahoma City AAA	7	0	2.98	118	90	51	104	1.19	
1993 Texas AL	12	0	3.41	166	151	80	131	1.39	9
1994 *Projection* >>>	8	0	3.54	118	110	58	88	1.42	4

PENA, ALEJANDRO - TR - Age 34
The signing of Pena as a free agent from Atlanta left egg on the face of former Pirates General Manager Ted Simmons. Pena arrived at spring training with a bad elbow and underwent season ending surgery in mid-March. He was throwing well by September, and if he's fully recovered, he has a chance because the Pirates could use a hard throwing closer with experience.

	W	SV	ERA	IP	H	BB	SO	BPI	$
1992 Atlanta NL	1	15	4.07	42	40	13	34	1.26	10
1993 Pittsburgh NL			did not play						

PENA, JIM - TL - Age 29
His presence in the major leagues in 1992 was more a statement of San Francisco's needs than Pena's merit.

	W	SV	ERA	IP	H	BB	SO	BPI	$
1992 Phoenix AAA	7	1	4.15	39	45	20	27	1.67	
1992 San Francisco NL	1	0	3.48	44	49	20	32	1.57	-
1993 Las Vegas AAA	0	1	6.10	51	69	16	31	1.66	

PENNINGTON, BRAD - TL - Age 24
A fireballing lefty, he has the potential to become an outstanding closer, but he needs to harness his wildness. He had a shot as the Orioles closer when Gregg Olson got injured, but he didn't make it and was eventually demoted to AAA Rochester. He will get another shot as closer if Olson doesn't come back.

	W	SV	ERA	IP	H	BB	SO	BPI	$
1992 Hagerstown AA	1	7	2.54	28	20	17	32	1.32	
1992 Rochester AAA	1	5	2.08	39	12	33	56	1.15	
1993 Baltimore AL	3	3	4.55	33	30	20	39	1.50	3

PERCIVAL, TROY - TR - Age 24
A young flamethrower who is being developed into a closer. Results are poor at this point, but the Angels still are committed to the project.

	W	SV	ERA	IP	H	BB	SO	BPI	$
1992 Palm Springs A	1	2	5.06	11	6	8	16	1.31	
1992 Midland AA	3	5	2.37	19	18	11	21	1.53	
1993 Vancouver AAA	0	4	6.27	19	24	13	19	1.94	

PEREZ, CESAR - TR- Age 23
He held Sally League batters to a .133 average in '93, and set a Columbus record for saves. However, his prospect status is suspect because the Panamanian has been in pro ball six years and was demoted last year from the Florida State League, where he had pitched with the Yankees' Fort Lauderdale farm. Still, anyone who gives up three-- count 'em, three-- earned runs in an entire Class A season deserves to be noticed. Had a .87 ratio and 35 saves at Single-A Columbus in 1993.

PEREZ, MELIDO - TR - Age 28

The biggest disappointment for the Yankees. Perez was injured and when he wasn't he was inconsistent. He's got the tools to be a pitching force, now he needs to find it in himself. If he finds a rhythm he could be dangerous to other teams; if he dosen't he'll be dangerous to the Yankees.

	W	SV	ERA	IP	H	BB	SO	BPI	$
1992 New York AL	13	0	2.87	247	212	93	218	1.23	17
1993 New York AL	6	0	5.19	163	173	64	148	1.45	-
1994 *Projection* >>>	8	0	3.81	186	179	70	167	1.34	6

PEREZ, MIKE - TR - Age 29

Perez has posted impressive numbers in his professional career and inherited the closer's role when Lee Smith was traded to the Yankees last August. However, Perez is more comfortable in middle relief; it's safe to say that he doesn't have a closer's mentality. Perez doesn't have a closer's fastball either and relies on changing speeds and mixing pitches instead. He'll start off 1994 with the stopper job, but is hardly a lock to keep it.

	W	SV	ERA	IP	H	BB	SO	BPI	$
1992 St. Louis NL	9	0	1.84	93	70	32	46	1.10	10
1993 St. Louis NL	7	7	2.48	73	65	20	58	1.18	12
1994 *Projection* >>>	7	10	2.97	73	64	23	50	1.19	15

PEREZ, PASCUAL - TR - Age 36

In September 1991 Perez was just recovering from shoulder surgery and had put together a few classic Perez outings when the season ended. The shoulder got plenty of rest in 1992. It is inexplicable that Perez didn't get an invitation to spring training somewhere in 1993. He can still pitch.

PEREZ, YORKIS - TL - Age 26

Still hanging onto the fringe, Perez had marginal stats at Double-A and Triple-A in a set up role. He fanned hitters at an accelerated rate in 1993 (75 in 64 innings) and might get a shot as a situational lefty somewhere.

	W	SV	ERA	IP	H	BB	SO	BPI	$
1993 Ottawa AAA	0	5	3.60	20	14	7	17	1.05	

PERSCHKE, GREG - TR - Age 26

Showed definite improvement in his second year at Vancouver in 1992, but went backwards in 1993.

	W	SV	ERA	IP	H	BB	SO	BPI	$
1992 Vancouver AAA	12	0	3.76	165	159	44	82	1.23	
1993 Albuquerque AAA	7	0	6.36	105	146	24	63	1.16	

PETKOVSEK, MARK - TR - Age 28

Petkovsek's outstanding collegiate career at Texas hasn't translated into professional success. A finesse pitcher who relies on mixing pitches and changing speeds, he has worked as both a starter and reliever. He isn't in the Pirates' plans, though, as they dropped him from the roster following last season.

	W	SV	ERA	IP	H	BB	SO	BPI	$
1993 Buffalo AAA	3	0	4.33	70	74	16	27	1.27	
1993 Pittsburgh NL	3	0	6.96	32	43	9	14	1.62	-

PETT, JOSE - TR - Age 18

The Brazilian was shut down early because of tonsillitis, and tendinitis in his shoulder.

PETTIT, DOUG - TR - Age 24

A 41st-round draft pick in 1992, he has caught the eye of the Marlins brass by leading their minor leaguers in saves two years running, with ratios around 1.00 both years. Not a fireballer, it remains to be seen whether he can duplicate these performances above the Single-A level.

	W	SV	ERA	IP	H	BB	SO	BPI	$
1993 Kane County A	5	17	2.45	77	67	16	63	1.07	

PIATT, DOUG - TR - Age 28

Pitched well in 34 innings in 1991, but just didn't fit their plans in 1992. Last seen on the Pirates farm.

PICHARDO, HIPOLITO -TR - Age 24

Is "Pichardo" Spanish for "Pitcher"? Despite his losing record (7-8), he actually had as good a year as 1992 when he was 9-6. Kansas City bullpen didn't support Pichardo well. Delivery and build reminds you of Pascual Perez, but Pichardo has his wits about him. Will open 1994 in Royals rotation and could surprise nicely.

	W	SV	ERA	IP	H	BB	SO	BPI	$
1992 Memphis AA	0	0	0.64	14	13	1	10	1.00	
1992 Kansas City AL	9	0	3.95	143	148	49	59	1.37	3
1993 Kansas City AL	7	0	4.04	165	183	53	70	1.43	4
1994 *Projection* >>>	9	0	4.01	156	169	51	66	1.41	3

PIERCE, ED - TL - Age 25

Poised to challenge for major league role after good 1992 campaign, Pierce continued with decent AA Memphis performance, but unimpressive AAA Omaha showings. Was a starter, but ended up in bullpen for both clubs. Could get back to the majors in bullpen role, but has too much standing in his way to be considered a good prospect any longer.

	W	SV	ERA	IP	H	BB	SO	BPI	$
1992 Memphis AA	10	0	3.81	153	159	51	131	1.37	
1992 Kansas City AL	0	0	3.38	5	9	4	3	2.44	-
1993 Memphis AA	6	1	3.74	67	65	34	53	1.47	

PIERCE, JEFF - TR - Age 24

The possible sleeper in the Tim Belcher trade, Pierce has a 2.32 ERA, more than a strikeout per inning, and 52 saves after two professional seasons. The Reds bullpen jobs will be wide open in 1994 if Rob Dibble doesn't return to form, so Pierce is definitely worth watching.

PISCIOTTA, MARK - TR - Age 23

A hard-throwing A-ball closer who kept performing well when promoted to a higher level league.

	W	SV	ERA	IP	H	BB	SO	BPI	$
1993 Augusta-Salem A	5	24	2.76	62	54	30	62	1.35	

PITTSLEY, JIM - TR - Age 19

Missed time last season after having a cyst removed from his back. At 6'7", he has fired the ball past minor league hitters, particularly righthanders. One of Royals first round picks in 1992 (17th overall). Considered among Royals best prospects by some scouts. Will move up to Single-A Wilmington to start 1994. On track to arrive in Kansas City in 1996.

	W	SV	ERA	IP	H	BB	SO	BPI	$
1993 Rockford A	5	0	4.26	80	76	32	87	1.35	

PLANTENBERG, ERIK - TL - Age 25

In his first season above A-ball, he jumped from Double-A to the majors. With the Mariners, he was alternatively hit hard and unable to throw strikes. If he gets back to the majors, it will be as a one-lefthanded-batter type of reliever.

	W	SV	ERA	IP	H	BB	SO	BPI	$
1993 Jacksonville AA	2	1	2.01	44	38	14	49	1.18	
1993 Seattle AL	0	1	6.52	10	11	12	3	2.50	-

PLESAC, DAN - TL - Age 32

Plesac assumed Assenmacher's lefty setup role after Assenmacher was dealt in late July. He thought he could throw his 92 MPH fastball by hitters for the first couple of months, but it was flat as a board. He mixed his pitches better and rebounded slightly in his long relief role.

	W	SV	ERA	IP	H	BB	SO	BPI	$
1992 Milwaukee AL	5	1	2.96	79	64	35	54	1.25	5
1993 Chicago NL	2	0	4.74	63	74	21	47	1.53	-
1994 *Projection* >>>	3	1	4.08	71	74	27	45	1.42	-

PLUNK, ERIC - TR - Age 30
Poor control had always kept him from earning a closer's job, but in 1993 he posted career low walk totals en route to a fine season. Being used for only one inning at a time for the first time in his career seemed to work wonders. DiPoto will get first crack at closer role, but Plunk is a better fit.

	W	SV	ERA	IP	H	BB	SO	BPI	$
1992 Cleveland AL	9	4	3.64	72	61	38	50	1.38	5
1993 Cleveland AL	4	15	2.79	71	61	30	77	1.28	17
1994 Projection >>>	5	10	3.32	75	68	35	63	1.37	11

PLYMPTON, JEFF - TR - Age 28
Looked like a longshot closer candidate in 1991 but made no progress in 1992, and less in 1993.

	W	SV	ERA	IP	H	BB	SO	BPI	$
1992 Pawtucket AAA	6	1	3.43	81	78	34	57	1.38	
1993 Pawtucket AAA	2	1	4.44	51	54	15	47	1.35	

POOLE, JIM - TL - Age 27
Jim Poole had some nice stats last year, but he didn't pitch many innings. He is a good lefty setup man and situational pitcher. His role will expand if Gregg Olson's elbow doesn't come around.

	W	SV	ERA	IP	H	BB	SO	BPI	$
1992 Baltimore AL	0	0	0.00	3	3	1	3	1.20	-
1993 Baltimore AL	2	2	2.15	50	30	21	29	1.02	7
1994 Projection >>>	2	5	2.71	35	28	14	22	1.19	7

PORTUGAL, MARK - TR - Age 31
Portugal had a breakthrough season in his free agent year, leading the league in winning percentage and finishing with 12 straight wins. He has four good pitches and had good command in 1993. His key to success was reporting in good condition and staying free of injuries, which he hadn't done in the past. He has to be considered somewhat of a risk in spite of his strong performance in 1993. Being with a winning team in San Francisco can't hurt.

	W	SV	ERA	IP	H	BB	SO	BPI	$
1992 Houston NL	6	0	2.66	101	76	41	62	1.15	6
1993 Houston NL	18	0	2.77	208	194	77	131	1.30	17
1994 Projection >>>	14	0	3.10	172	155	65	109	1.28	13

POTE, LOU - TR - Age 22
A reliever in 1992, he moved into the rotation for Shreveport in 1993 with some success. Historically, there is upward mobility for pitchers in the Giants organization, because they wear out so fast in San Francisco.

POWELL, DENNIS - TL - Age 30
Last year was his best since 1987 and it really wasn't all that good. He was outstanding in the minors.

	W	SV	ERA	IP	H	BB	SO	BPI	$
1992 Seattle AL	4	0	4.58	57	49	29	35	1.37	0
1993 Calgary AAA	3	1	3.60	40	37	19	30	1.40	
1993 Seattle AL	0	0	4.15	48	42	24	32	1.40	-
1994 Projection >>>	1	0	4.31	46	43	21	25	1.40	-

POWELL, JAY - Orioles - TR - Age 22
Baltimore's first-round draft pick in '93 signed for a $492,000 bonus. A closer at Mississippi State, he was a starter as a pro. With his fastball in the mid-90s, he has been compared to Mark Wohlers.

POWELL, ROSS - TL - Age 26
A promising lefty with good strikeout totals in the minors, Powell impressed in his September trial with the Reds. He'll contend for the lefty setup role in 1994.

	W	SV	ERA	IP	H	BB	SO	BPI	$
1992 Chattanooga AA	4	1	1.26	57	43	18	56	1.06	
1993 IndianapolisAAA	10	0	4.11	179	159	71	133	1.28	
1993 Cincinnati NL	0	0	4.41	16	13	6	17	1.18	-

POWER, TED - TR - Age 39
His early season failure can be blamed in part upon the emotional distress caused by Steve Olin's death. Power ended 1993 as the favorite to be the closer in 1994.

	W	SV	ERA	IP	H	BB	SO	BPI	$
1992 Cleveland AL	3	6	2.54	99	88	35	51	1.25	10
1993 Cleveland-Seattle	2	13	5.36	45	57	17	27	1.64	7
1994 *Projection* >>>	3	10	3.85	66	70	24	37	1.42	8

PRESLEY, KIRK - TR - Age 19
The Mets' first draft pick in 1993 and the eighth player chosen overall, Elvis Presley's third cousin was lured away from Mississippi State by a $900,000 signing bonus. He signed too late to play pro ball last year; he throws a good curve and a 90 MPH fastball.

PRICHER, JOHN - TR - Age 23
A hard-throwing closer who finished all but four of his 49 appearances last season. His control was not as good as it had been in '92, his rookie pro year, when he walked just eight.

PUGH, TIM -TR - Age 27
Pugh is a sinkerball pitcher who relies on location and a strong defense to be effective. He benefitted from neither in 1993 but finished strong, throwing a one-hitter against San Diego in his final start.

	W	SV	ERA	IP	H	BB	SO	BPI	$
1992 Cincinnati NL	4	0	2.58	45	47	13	18	1.32	0
1993 Cincinnati NL	10	0	5.26	164	200	59	94	1.58	-
1994 *Projection* >>>	9	0	4.94	168	201	58	98	1.55	-

PULIDO, CARLOS - TL - Age 22
A strikeout pitcher in the low minors, where he worked out of the bullpen. Made a fairly successful transition to starter in 1993, though his strikeout ratio was down significantly. Will he continue to progress, or will his arm show the strain of 167 appearances between the ages of 18 and 21? If he throws strikes, works directly and gets careful watching, he should mature nicely in 1994.

	W	SV	ERA	IP	H	BB	SO	BPI	$
1993 Portland AAA	10	0	4.19	146	169	45	79	1.46	

PULSIPHER, BILL - TL - Age 20
A fastball/curveball pitcher who has pitched better as he has moved up through the organization. In fact, the Mets consider the rise of their 1991 second round draft pick the fastest of any pitcher since Dwight Gooden. His 1993 season started late after he cut his index finger in a fit of anger.

QUANTRILL, PAUL - TR - Age 25
A classic sinker/slider pitcher who needs good control to be effective, Quantrill had that good command through most of 1993. He's the type of pitcher who can be extremely effective but at the same time can be just a tiny margin away from disaster. Overall he's a good bet for 1994, because he pitches in a deeply talented pen where the underperformers will get less work.

	W	SV	ERA	IP	H	BB	SO	BPI	$
1992 Boston AL	2	1	2.19	49	55	15	24	1.42	1
1993 Boston AL	6	1	3.91	138	151	44	66	1.41	5
1994 *Projection* >>>	4	1	3.65	98	108	30	47	1.41	2

QUIRICO, RAFAEL - TL - Age 24
Good starter in low minors, still a couple of years away.

	W	SV	ERA	IP	H	BB	SO	BPI	$
1993 Albany AA	4	7	3.52	95	92	33	79	1.31	

RACZKA, MIKE - TL - Age 31
Had a good year at Tacoma in 1992 (3.51 ERA) but now just a journeyman lefty reliever.

	W	SV	ERA	IP	H	BB	SO	BPI	$
1993 Tacoma AAA	2	0	5.37	60	65	30	40	1.58	

RADINSKY, SCOTT - TL - Age 26
So intimidating, Radinsky always appears ready to take a big step forward each year. However, while 1992's problem was walks, 1993's was hits allowed. He certainly has the stuff.

	W	SV	ERA	IP	H	BB	SO	BPI	$
1992 Chicago AL	3	15	2.73	59	54	34	48	1.48	12
1993 Chicago AL	8	4	4.28	55	61	19	44	1.48	5
1994 *Projection* >>>	6	8	3.52	58	58	24	46	1.42	8

RAPP, PAT - TR - Age 26
The earliest indicator of his future major league success was in 1992, a 3.05 ERA in the treacherous Pacific Coast League. He did a credible job for the Marlins in 1993, and should eventually develop into the Marlins number one or number two starter.

	W	SV	ERA	IP	H	BB	SO	BPI	$
1992 San Francisco NL	0	0	7.20	10	8	6	3	1.40	-
1993 Florida NL	4	0	4.02	94	101	39	57	1.49	-
1994 *Projection* >>>	5	0	4.18	118	124	50	70	1.47	0

RASMUSSEN, DENNIS - TL - Age 34
His good luck in 1992 evaporated in 1993. Was terrible at Omaha, too, and got released at the end of the year. He'll probably turn up somewhere else again, but won't have any value in any case.

	W	SV	ERA	IP	H	BB	SO	BPI	$
1992 Kansas City AL	4	0	1.43	37	25	6	12	0.82	5
1992 Chicago NL	0	0	10.80	5	7	2	0	1.80	-
1993 Kansas City AL	1	0	7.45	29	40	14	12	1.86	-
1994 *Projection* >>>	2	0	4.83	45	49	16	18	1.44	2

RATLIFF, JON - TR - Age 22
Ratliff moved up fast after being drafted in the first round of 1993 out of LeMoyne College and signing for a $305,000 bonus. His pro debut was delayed because of foot surgery. Ratliff's best pitch is a sinker; he struggled with his control in 1993.

REARDON, JEFF - TR - Age 38
Reardon generally pitched well until fading in September when he started throwing a knuckleball almost exclusively, much to the chagrin of Davey Johnson. He can still be an effective setup man.

	W	SV	ERA	IP	H	BB	SO	BPI	$
1992 Boston AL	2	27	4.25	42	53	7	32	1.42	19
1992 Atlanta NL	3	3	1.15	15	14	2	7	1.02	3
1993 Cincinnati NL	4	8	4.09	62	66	10	35	1.24	8
1994 *Projection* >>>	4	8	3.78	60	65	10	35	1.25	9

REED, BOBBY - TR - Age 26
Has a 2.67 career ERA after three minor league seasons. Reed will be in the majors, this year or next.

	W	SV	ERA	IP	H	BB	SO	BPI	$
1993 Tulsa AA	5	0	4.26	76	88	22	35	1.44	

REED, RICK - TR - Age 29
Reed washed out of the Pirates system during spring training 1992 then hooked on with the Royals organization in 1993. He's got good control, so he won't kill you.

	W	SV	ERA	IP	H	BB	SO	BPI	$
1992 Kansas City AL	3	0	3.68	100	105	20	49	1.25	3
1993 Omaha AAA	11	0	3.09	128	116	14	58	1.01	
1993 Kansas City-Texas	1	0	5.87	7	12	2	5	1.82	
1994 *Projection* >>>	2	0	4.04	35	39	9	18	1.38	0

REED, STEVE - TR - Age 28
Like his bullpen successor Darren Holmes, Reed got to spend some time in Colorado Springs re-evaluating his baseball career. A 10.50 ERA can do that to you. When he returned he was the perfect setup man for Holmes, earning

three saves and six very big wins. His sidearm delivery sets up a great breaking ball. Fine control is his biggest strength.

	W	SV	ERA	IP	H	BB	SO	BPI	$
1992 San Francisco NL	1	0	2.30	15	13	3	11	1.02	0
1993 Colorado NL	9	3	4.48	84	80	30	51	1.31	5
1994 *Projection* >>>	6	2	4.29	55	51	19	34	1.28	2

REMLINGER, MIKE - TL - Age 28

A former top prospect who keeps struggling, Remlinger was thrown in to the Kevin Mitchell trade. He was ineffective at Triple-A in both 1992 and 1993, pushing back his return to the majors. Last chance: New York Mets.

	W	SV	ERA	IP	H	BB	SO	BPI	$
1992 Calgary AAA	1	0	6.65	70	97	48	24	2.06	
1992 Jacksonville AA	1	0	3.46	26	25	11	21	1.38	
1993 Calgary AAA	4	0	5.53	85	100	52	51	1.78	

REVENIG, TODD - TR - Age 24

The 1992 version of "the heir to Eckersley" -- and a very credible candidate.

REYES, ALBERTO - TR - Age 23

Reyes overcame the shoulder tendinitis that sidelined him for much of 1992. The righthanded half of Burlington's bullpen tandem, he proved hard for Midwest League batters to hit.

REYES, CARLOS - TR - Age 25

A successful season in a setup role for AA Greenville earned Reyes a promotion to AAA Richmond. Reyes throws a curve and a slider; he's not a traditional strikeout pitcher, but has good control. He could battle for a setup role in Atlanta soon. Actually he looks like Greg McMichael did a year ago....hmmmm.

	W	SV	ERA	IP	H	BB	SO	BPI	$
1993 Richmond AAA	1	2	3.77	29	30	11	30	1.41	

REYNOLDS, SHANE - TR - Age 26

Reynolds finished strong at Tucson in his second Triple-A season, then had some success in relief in a late season callup. An excellent control pitcher with 5 to 1 strikeout/walk ratio at Tucson in 1993, he should be a leading contender for the number five starter slot in 1994.

	W	SV	ERA	IP	H	BB	SO	BPI	$
1992 Houston NL	1	0	7.11	25	42	6	10	1.89	-
1993 Tucson AAA	10	1	3.62	139	147	21	106	1.20	
1993 Houston NL	0	0	0.82	11	11	6	10	1.55	-

REYNOSO, ARMANDO - TR - Age 27

Once mired in the Braves farm system, he became the Rockies staff ace, leading the club in complete games and wins. He's worst in the early innings, then combines finesse and power well once he figures out which pitch is working. Reynoso is nothing fancy; he just likes to throw the ball.

	W	SV	ERA	IP	H	BB	SO	BPI	$
1992 Richmond AAA	12	0	2.66	169	156	52	108	1.23	
1992 Atlanta NL	1	1	4.70	7	11	2	2	1.70	-
1993 Colorado NL	12	0	4.00	189	206	63	117	1.42	4
1994 *Projection* >>>	13	0	4.06	177	194	59	108	1.43	2

RHODES, ARTHUR - TL - Age 24

After a very strong finish in 1992, great things were expected from Rhodes last year. He started poorly then underwent knee surgery, and improved afterwards but remained erratic. He has a good fastball, but he loses concentration and looks like a typical erratic rookie. He can be good, but not great.

	W	SV	ERA	IP	H	BB	SO	BPI	$
1992 Baltimore AL	7	0	3.63	94	87	38	77	1.33	3
1993 Baltimore AL	5	0	6.51	86	91	49	49	1.64	-
1994 *Projection* >>>	8	0	4.52	120	116	52	80	1.40	2

RIGHETTI, DAVE - TL - Age 35
It was a mistake by the Giants to sign Righetti, who hasn't been in top form since 1986, and may be retired by the time you read this. Righetti's ERA in the second half of 1993 was over 8.00.

	W	SV	ERA	IP	H	BB	SO	BPI	$
1992 San Francisco NL	2	3	5.06	78	79	36	47	1.47	-
1993 San Francisco NL	1	1	5.70	47	58	17	31	1.59	-
1994 *Projection* >>>	1	4	5.17	59	65	24	35	1.50	-

RIJO, JOSE -TR - Age 28
Completely healthy for the first time with the Reds, Rijo turned in a brilliant year matched only by Greg Maddux. In a decimated rotation, with a weak offense, a bullpen that blew six wins, and an offense that scored six runs in seven losses, Jose still won 14 games; it would have been 20 with the Braves or Giants. Rijo has won 13 or more games in five of the last six seasons while posting an ERA of less than 3.00 in all six seasons. Rijo is just hitting his prime at age 28, but has over 1500 major league innings under his belt.

	W	SV	ERA	IP	H	BB	SO	BPI	$
1992 Cincinnati NL	15	0	2.56	211	185	44	171	1.09	19
1993 Cincinnati NL	14	0	2.48	257	218	62	227	1.09	27
1994 *Projection* >>>	15	0	2.77	238	203	59	210	1.10	27

RISLEY, BILL -TR - Age 26
This big righthanded reliever throws hard and is intimidating. Risley finally started to shed the "Wild Bill" tag last season at Triple-A. He has to keep throwing strikes to make the major leagues. Could get a major league set up role soon.

	W	SV	ERA	IP	H	BB	SO	BPI	$
1992 Indianapolis AAA	5	0	6.40	96	105	47	64	1.58	
1992 Montreal NL	1	0	1.80	5	4	1	2	1.00	-
1993 Ottawa AAA	2	1	2.54	63	51	34	74	1.34	
1993 Montreal NL	0	0	6.00	3	2	2	2	1.33	-

RITCHIE, TODD - TR - Age 22
Minnesota's first-round draft pick in 1990 recovered from shoulder tendinitis last season in time to pitch in the Arizona Fall League. Ritchie is one of the Twins' top prospects, and he could be pitching in Minnesota this year. He had a good record in Class AA last year. He isn't overpowering, but more the Kevin Tapani type.

	W	SV	ERA	IP	H	BB	SO	BPI	$
1993 Nashville AA	3	0	3.66	47	46	15	41	1.29	

RITCHIE, WALLY - TL - Age 28
Can be a safe lefty short reliever if his manager uses him wisely. Has a very good changeup.

	W	SV	ERA	IP	H	BB	SO	BPI	$
1992 Philadelphia NL	2	1	3.00	39	44	17	19	1.56	-
1993 Toledo AAA	1	4	4.76	45	44	15	29	1.28	

RITZ, KEVIN - TR - Age 28
Once the Tigers' most exciting young arm, Ritz was drafted by Colorado and penciled into the rotation, but he went out with a bad elbow.

RIVERA, BEN - TR - Age 25
The big (6'6", 210 lb.), hard throwing righty managed a deceiving won/loss record (13-9) because of enormous run support (6.43). 25-year-olds who throw hard are given every opportunity to perform, and Rivera isn't without assets. He held righties to a .211 average in 1992, and .246 in 1993, indicating that he has potential to become a solid reliever if - and this is a big if - he can dramatically cut down the walks (4.69 per 9 innings in 1993).

	W	SV	ERA	IP	H	BB	SO	BPI	$
1992 Philadelphia NL	7	0	3.07	117	99	45	77	1.23	4
1993 Philadelphia NL	13	0	5.02	163	175	85	123	1.60	-
1994 *Projection* >>>	10	0	4.50	133	135	65	97	1.50	-

ROBERTSON, RICH - TL - Age 25

After a big winter ball season in Venezuela following the 1992 season, Robertson suddenly became a prospect. He spent most of the season at AAA Buffalo and then showed some promise as a reliever with the Pirates. If the Pirates use him as a reliever, he has a chance to make the club thin 1994.

	W	SV	ERA	IP	H	BB	SO	BPI	$
1993 Buffalo AAA	9	0	4.28	132	141	52	71	1.46	
1993 Pittsburgh NL	0	0	6.00	9	15	4	5	2.11	-

ROBINSON, JEFF D - TR - Age 33

Once a top setup man with a great forkball; was just hanging on last year.

	W	SV	ERA	IP	H	BB	SO	BPI	$
1992 Chicago NL	4	1	3.00	78	76	40	46	1.49	-
1993 Tucson AAA	1	1	5.06	22	22	9	15	1.40	

ROBINSON, RON - TR - Age 32

Missed almost all of 1992 with a relapse of the arm trouble that kept him on the DL for most of 1991. He likely won't come back, and if he does, you don't want him.

	W	SV	ERA	IP	H	BB	SO	BPI	$
1992 Milwaukee AL	1	0	5.86	35	51	14	12	1.84	-
1993 Nashville AA	2	3	5.16	45	64	15	26	1.75	

RODRIGUEZ, FRANK - TR - Age 21

Boston's number two pick out of high school in '90, he played his first pro season as a shortstop. He throws very hard.

	W	SV	ERA	IP	H	BB	SO	BPI	$
1992 Lynchburg A	12	0	3.09	149	125	65	129	1.31	
1993 New Britain AA	7	0	3.74	171	147	78	151	1.31	

RODRIGUEZ, RICH - TL - Age 31

A serviceable lefty whose performance dropped off considerably in 1993, Rodriguez allowed too many home runs - 10 in 76 innings. Of most concern was his inability to get lefties out . The Marlins have exceptional bullpen depth for an expansion club; so Rodriguez will need to step up his performance if he wishes to retain his setup role.

	W	SV	ERA	IP	H	BB	SO	BPI	$
1992 San Diego NL	6	0	2.37	91	77	29	64	1.16	6
1993 San Diego-Florida	2	3	3.79	76	73	33	43	1.39	2
1994 *Projection* >>>	3	2	3.26	81	74	32	49	1.31	4

RODRIGUEZ, ROSARIO - TL - Age 24

Former top prospect with Reds and Bucs; missed almost all of 1992 and 1993.

ROESLER, MIKE - TR - Age 30

Major leaguer in 1989-1990; just hanging on three years later.

	W	SV	ERA	IP	H	BB	SO	BPI	$
1993 Memphis AA	2	0	2.38	23	11	4	16	0.65	

ROGERS, CHARLIE - TL - Age 25

A bullpen ace in the Texas League. Because that's traditionally a hitters' league, his numbers look especially good.

	W	SV	ERA	IP	H	BB	SO	BPI	$
1993 El Paso AA	4	23	1.74	72	50	23	55	1.01	

ROGERS, KENNY - TL - Age 29

After losing in arbitration again, Rogers asked to be converted to a starter since he felt that was the only way he was going to make the "big" dollars. He responded by leading the team in wins and setting a team record for wins by a lefthanded pitcher. Throws hard and has a big curve.

	W	SV	ERA	IP	H	BB	SO	BPI	$
1992 Texas AL	3	6	3.09	78	80	26	70	1.35	5
1993 Texas AL	16	0	4.10	208	210	71	140	1.35	10
1994 *Projection* >>>	12	2	4.04	160	162	57	112	1.37	6

ROGERS, KEVIN - TL - Age 25

Rogers has posted eye popping SO/BB and H/IP ratios for six years. He was a starting pitcher his entire career until 1993. As a setup man, he'll help you; if he gets a chance in someone's rotation, he could break out big time.

	W	SV	ERA	IP	H	BB	SO	BPI	$
1992 San Francisco NL	0	0	4.24	34	37	13	26	1.47	-
1993 San Francisco NL	2	0	2.68	81	71	28	62	1.23	4

ROJAS, MEL - TR - Age 27

Rojas has closer's stuff with a 94 MPH fastball and a nasty forkball. However, he has to get used to setting up John Wetteland. After a sparkling 1992 campaign, he didn't enjoy the same success last year, blowing nine saves and getting dinged for six homers. The nephew of Manager Felipe Alou, Rojas is one of the best at what he does in the National League and also gets a fair amount of save chances; he's a valuable reliever.

	W	SV	ERA	IP	H	BB	SO	BPI	$
1992 Indianapolis AAA	2	0	5.40	8	10	3	7	1.63	
1992 Montreal NL	7	10	1.43	100	71	34	70	1.04	20
1993 Montreal NL	5	10	2.95	88	80	30	48	1.25	13
1994 *Projection* >>>	5	6	2.90	88	73	33	64	1.21	12

ROPER, JOHN - TR - Age 22

The Reds most touted pitching prospect, Roper regressed in 1993. He has been accused of lacking concentration. Even if that's true, he's young enough to get over it.

	W	SV	ERA	IP	H	BB	SO	BPI	$
1993 Cincinnati NL	2	0	5.63	80	92	36	54	1.60	-
1994 *Projection* >>>	1	0	4.83	48	52	21	30	1.52	-

ROSENGREN, JOHN - TL - Age 21

Drafted out of the U. of North Carolina in '92. Made dramatic improvement last season because his control was much sharper.

ROSSELLI, JOEY - TL - Age 22

The best pitcher in the best A-ball league in 1992. He has been held back by a sore shoulder.

	W	SV	ERA	IP	H	BB	SO	BPI	$
1992 San Jose A	11	0	2.41	150	145	46	111	1.27	
1993 Shreveport AA	0	0	3.13	23	22	7	19	1.26	

RUETER, KIRK - TL - Age 23

Not a highly touted prospect before last season, Rueter jumped from Double-A to the majors and didn't lose a game in 14 starts for the Expos. He's a finesse pitcher who knows how to work the hitters and keeps the ball low. Based on his 1993 performance, he looks like he could be a big winner. One more time around the league will show if he's for real. Any pitcher who models himself after John Tudor can't be too bad.

	W	SV	ERA	IP	H	BB	SO	BPI	$
1993 Montreal NL	8	0	2.73	86	85	18	31	1.21	7
1994 *Projection* >>>	11	0	3.13	180	179	39	100	1.21	14

RUFFCORN, SCOTT - TR - Age 24

A former star at Baylor. The White Sox refused to trade him -- with good reason, judging from his '93 performance. Another Sox pitcher made more obscure by the excitement over Jason Bere, but just as worthy of attention. Let the 8.10 ERA, 10 walks, and 2 strikeouts mislead other people. His minor league ERA has been under 3.00 the last two seasons and he's whiffed lots of batters with few walks. Throws in the 90's effortlessly.

	W	SV	ERA	IP	H	BB	SO	BPI	$
1993 Birmingham AA	9	0	2.73	135	108	52	141	1.18	
1993 Nashville AAA	2	0	2.80	45	30	8	44	0.84	
1993 Chicago AL	0	0	8.10	10	9	10	2	1.90	-
1994 *Projection* >>>	4	0	4.40	89	85	35	66	1.34	4

RUFFIN, BRUCE - TL - Age 30

Ruffin started the season as the Rockies' only lefthanded starter. Twelve starts later, his role was to set up Darren Holmes. Ruffin led the club in ERA and strikeouts, averaging almost a strikeout per inning; a pretty impressive season after a miserable 1992 campaign.

	W	SV	ERA	IP	H	BB	SO	BPI	$
1992 Milwaukee AL	1	0	6.67	58	66	41	45	1.84	-
1993 Colorado NL	6	2	3.87	140	145	69	126	1.54	1
1994 *Projection* >>>	4	1	4.29	113	119	57	65	1.56	-

RUFFIN, JOHNNY - TR - Age 22

Ruffin came to the Reds in the Tim Belcher trade and was extremely impressive at AAA Indianapolis and in a major league trial with Cincinnati. Ruffin will be a closer candidate if Dibble falters at the start of the season.

	W	SV	ERA	IP	H	BB	SO	BPI	$
1993 Cincinnati NL	2	2	3.58	38	36	11	30	1.26	2

RUSKIN, SCOTT - TL - Age 30

Sent to Indianapolis in April, Ruskin registered 28 saves despite a 5.14 ERA. Ruskin was a free agent at the end of 1993.

	W	SV	ERA	IP	H	BB	SO	BPI	$
1992 Cincinnati NL	4	0	5.03	53	56	20	43	1.42	-
1993 Cincinnati NL	0	0	18.00	1	3	2	0	5.00	-

RUSSELL, JEFF - TR - Age 32

Russell has had all kinds of arm and shoulder problems, but he just keeps rolling along like an old Cadillac.

	W	SV	ERA	IP	H	BB	SO	BPI	$
1992 Texas-Oakland AL	4	30	1.63	66	55	25	48	1.21	28
1993 Boston AL	1	33	2.70	47	39	14	45	1.15	29
1994 *Projection* >>>	2	25	2.80	56	47	20	47	1.19	24

RUSSELL, LAGRANDE - TR - Age 23

Did not pitch well in his first season above A-ball. The year ended with elbow surgery.

RYAN, KEN - TR - Age 25

Good possibility for a shot at the closer's role, but completely unproven.

	W	SV	ERA	IP	H	BB	SO	BPI	$
1992 Boston AL	0	1	6.43	7	4	5	5	1.29	-
1993 Boston AL	7	1	3.60	50	43	29	49	1.44	-
1994 *Projection* >>>	4	3	3.78	32	27	19	29	1.43	3

SABERHAGEN, BRET - TR - Age 29

1993 was another disappointing year for this Cy Young quality pitcher. Saberhagen still has great stuff, featuring a high-velocity fastball that moves in different directions. He could still shine, if given the right situation and if he can stay healthy. Last year he sprained an ankle and had elbow and knee surgeries.

	W	SV	ERA	IP	H	BB	SO	BPI	$
1992 New York NL	3	0	3.50	97	84	27	81	1.14	2
1993 New York NL	7	0	3.29	139	131	17	93	1.06	11
1994 *Projection* >>>	9	0	3.31	146	137	24	95	1.10	13

SALKELD, ROGER - TR - Age 23

Returned to baseball after missing the entire 1992 season. Was outstanding in two major league starts in September after a solid year at Double-A. Will be a quality major league starter next year if not this year. Still has a big fastball.

	W	SV	ERA	IP	H	BB	SO	BPI	$
1993 Jacksonville AA	4	0	3.27	77	71	29	56	1.29	
1993 Seattle AL	0	0	2.51	14	13	4	13	1.21	0
1994 *Projection* >>>	7	0	3.87	84	89	27	70	1.38	2

SAMPEN, BILL - TR - Age 31

Sampen got his release from Royals after refusing minor league assignment. He threw harder in 1993, but with less success. Mostly a long reliever, he can spot start too, but is better in relief. He'll catch on somewhere.

	W	SV	ERA	IP	H	BB	SO	BPI	$
1992 Montreal NL	1	0	3.13	63	62	29	23	1.44	
1992 Kansas City AL	0	0	3.66	19	21	3	14	1.22	-
1993 Kansas City AL	2	0	5.89	18	25	9	9	1.88	-
1994 *Projection* >>>	2	0	4.05	45	49	20	22	1.54	-

SANDERS, SCOTT - TR - Age 25

Sanders was San Diego's compensation for Mark Davis' free agent departure several years ago and appears to be the most promising of the rookie starting pitchers who appeared in Jack Murphy Stadium last year. A hard thrower who won three of his nine major league starts, he held righthanded batters to a .207 average. Despite a 5-10 record, Sanders struck out 161 in 152 innings at AAA Las Vegas before his call-up. Pencil him in for a spot in the Padre rotation in 1994 with uncertain results.

	W	SV	ERA	IP	H	BB	SO	BPI	$
1993 San Diego NL	3	0	4.13	52	54	23	37	1.48	-
1994 *Projection* >>>	5	0	4.30	90	91	39	60	1.44	0

SANDERSON, SCOTT - TR - Age 37

Sanderson pitched fairly well for the Giants, but not so well for the Angels in 1993. He seemed to lose his stuff in the sixth . Properly used, he could still be a decent fourth starter for some team.

	W	SV	ERA	IP	H	BB	SO	BPI	$
1992 New York AL	12	0	4.93	193	220	64	104	1.47	0
1993 California AL	7	0	4.46	135	153	27	66	1.33	4
1993 San Fransisco NL	4	0	3.51	48	48	7	36	1.14	2
1994 *Projection* >>>	11	0	4.39	189	206	43	99	1.32	1

SANFORD, MO - TR - Age 27

A 95-MPH fastball will get you to the bigs in a hurry. Sanford struckout more than one batter per inning for the Rockies. Baylor gave him a shot as a starter, but he he also likes Sanford in a middle innings role where he had more success. Sanford could put up some big strikeout numbers if he gets enough innings.

	W	SV	ERA	IP	H	BB	SO	BPI	$
1992 Chattanooga AA	4	0	1.35	26	14	6	28	0.76	
1992 Nashville AAA	8	0	5.68	122	128	65	129	1.58	
1993 Colorado Springs AAA	3	0	5.23	105	103	57	104	1.55	
1993 Colorado NL	1	0	5.30	35	37	27	36	1.79	
1994 *Projection* >>>	3	0	5.12	98	95	70	80	1.68	-

SATRE, JASON - TR - Age 23
Big year at A-ball in 1991; hasn't made much progress since.

	W	SV	ERA	IP	H	BB	SO	BPI	$
1992 Chattanooga AA	3	0	5.43	58	56	26	36	1.41	
1993 Rochester AAA	4	0	5.85	80	87	45	42	1.65	

SAUNDERS, TONY - TL - Age 20
Just a kid, Saunders has already has gone past the throwing stage and into the pitching phase. As both a starter and reliever in his first two pro seasons, he has averaged about a strikeout per inning, and has maintained a strikeout/walk ratio of nearly 3 to 1. Of course, lots of guys do this in A-ball; so watch him closely at the next level.

SAUVEUR, RICH - TL - Age 30
Keeps surfacing, but will never amount to anything. The perverbial "just another lefty".

	W	SV	ERA	IP	H	BB	SO	BPI	$
1992 Kansas City AL	0	0	4.40	14	15	8	7	1.60	-
1993 Indianapolis AAA	2	0	1.80	35	41	7	21	1.37	

SCANLAN, BOB - TR - Age 27
1993 was a disappointing season for this young pitcher who had saved 14 games with a 2.89 ERA in 1992. He's always around the plate with less than outstanding stuff; his split-finger pitch was unreliable and his fastball had little movement. The big question is whether his arm is really bouncy enough for the heavy usage needed as the Cubs main reliever behind Myers.

	W	SV	ERA	IP	H	BB	SO	BPI	$
1992 Chicago NL	3	14	2.89	87	76	30	42	1.21	14
1993 Chicago NL	4	0	4.54	75	79	28	44	1.42	-
1994 *Projection* >>>	4	4	3.93	83	82	30	43	1.35	4

SCHILLING, CURT - TR - Age 27
Schilling always wanted to be a starter. His career was slowed by the Astros unsuccessful attempt to make him a short relief ace. Now he's back on track. The Phillies postseason hero, his high 1993 ERA was inflated by a handful of disastrous starts right before the All-Star break. His excellent 3.26 strikeout/walk ratio is more indicative of his true ability. Schilling throws a hard fastball and a biting slider, the kind of stuff that holds up well over time. He's going to be a top shelf starter for years to come.

	W	SV	ERA	IP	H	BB	SO	BPI	$
1992 Philadelphia NL	14	2	2.35	226	165	59	147	0.99	26
1993 Philadelphia NL	16	0	4.02	235	234	57	186	1.24	12
1994 *Projection* >>>	14	1	3.49	217	198	56	163	1.17	17

SCHMITT, TODD - TR - Age 24
An undrafted free agent who has stood out in both of his pro seasons (the Northwest League in 1992 and the Midwest League in 1993), Schmitt was voted Waterloo's MVP in 1993.

	W	SV	ERA	IP	H	BB	SO	BPI	$
1993 Waterloo A	1	25	1.99	58	41	33	76	1.26	

SCHOOLER, MIKE -TR - Age 31
Released by the Mariners because he'd lost too much velocity off his fastball. Signed to a Triple-A contract, where he was abysmal in the minors. Somehow, he still got a callup to the majors.

	W	SV	ERA	IP	H	BB	SO	BPI	$
1992 Seattle AL	2	13	4.70	51	55	24	33	1.53	7
1993 Texas AL	3	0	5.55	24	30	10	16	1.66	-
1994 *Projection*	3	5	4.97	34	38	14	20	1.53	1

SCHOUREK, PETE -TL - Age 24
Has three years in the majors, while most his age are still at Triple-A awaiting callups. Not overpowering, he had a standard repertoire and needs to mix his pitches better. Still plenty of time to develop into the pitcher he looked like he was going to be back in his rookie year.

	W	SV	ERA	IP	H	BB	SO	BPI	$
1992 New York NL	6	0	3.64	136	137	44	60	1.33	-
1993 New York NL	5	0	5.96	128	168	45	72	1.66	-
1994 *Projection* >>>	5	0	4.88	126	149	40	68	1.50	-

SCHRENK, STEVE - TR - Age 25

Bounced back from an injury in '91 to win 27 games the past two seasons. After spending five seasons below Double-A, he has moved up each of the past two seasons. A good start in Triple-A could get him his final promotion.

SCHWARZ, JEFF - TR - 31

A 29-year-old rookie, Schwarz had just one good minor league season as a starter, and that was in 1985. He began pitching out of the bullpen exclusively in 1992 and has been fine since, including a solid year of middle relief for the Sox, featuring on a great curveball.

	W	SV	ERA	IP	H	BB	SO	BPI	$
1993 Chicago AL	2	0	3.71	51	35	38	41	1.43	0
1994 *Projection* >>>	2	0	3.91	62	47	39	45	1.50	-

SCOTT, DARRYL - TR - 25

A very solid season as the Vancouver closer. Unsettled situation at closer make Scott very interesting for 1994. He made a serious bid for a major league bullpen role at spring training a year ago, but never got a chance to help fill the void in midseason.

	W	SV	ERA	IP	H	BB	SO	BPI	$
1993 Vancouver AAA	7	15	2.09	51	35	19	57	1.05	
1993 California AL	1	0	5.85	20	19	11	13	1.50	-
1994 *Projection* >>>	1	0	5.85	12	11	7	8	1.50	-

SCOTT, TIM - TR - Age 27

The Expos have historically had success salvaging other team's castoffs, and they believe Scott can be such a case. He has only average stuff and mixes his fastball, slider, changeup and forkball. However, he proved to be an effective middle and setup reliever last season. Two of Scott's seven victories came in a series against the Phillies during the stretch drive. He has been a closer in the minors but will continue in a setup relief role for the Expos.

	W	SV	ERA	IP	H	BB	SO	BPI	$
1992 San Diego NL	4	0	5.26	38	39	21	30	1.58	-
1993 San Diego NL	2	0	2.39	37	38	15	30	1.41	
1993 Montreal NL	7	1	3.01	71	69	34	65	1.45	4
1994 *Projection* >>>	5	1	3.69	54	52	27	40	1.47	1

SCUDDER, SCOTT - TR - Age 26

Once a hotshot Reds' prospect, Scudder has never been able to harness his good stuff at the major league level. In 1993, he had trouble getting people out at AAA Charlotte; most worrisome was his inability to strike out minor leaguers (4.5 strikeouts per 9 innings). His star has fallen.

	W	SV	ERA	IP	H	BB	SO	BPI	$
1992 Cleveland AL	6	0	5.28	109	134	55	66	1.73	-
1993 Charlotte AAA	7	0	5.03	136	148	52	54	1.47	
1993 Cleveland AL	0	0	9.00	4	5	4	1	2.25	-
1994 *Projection* >>>	2	0	5.27	45	52	24	26	1.68	-

SEANEZ, RUDY - TR - Age 25

Seanez's fastball still is clocked in the high 90s and he remains overpowering despite recent arm and back problems. The Padres believe they can cure his control problems despite his record of 229 walks to go with 466 strikeouts in 445 minor league innings. He's starting to run out of chances. Keep an eye on his winter league performance in Mexico; pay particular attention to his walk ratio.

	W	SV	ERA	IP	H	BB	SO	BPI	$
1993 San Diego NL	0	0	13.50	3	8	2	1	3.23	-
1994 *Projection* >>>	0	0	5.10	30	31	15	20	1.53	-

SELE, AARON - TR - Age 23

Boston's number one pick in '91, out of Washington State. Not overpowering, but he throws four pitches for strikes. Like many rookies with sharp breaking stuff, he dazzled American League hitters his first time around the league.

	W	SV	ERA	IP	H	BB	SO	BPI	$
1993 Pawtucket AAA	8	0	2.19	94	74	23	87	1.03	
1993 Boston AL	7	0	2.74	111	100	48	93	1.33	8
1994 *Projection* >>>	14	0	3.34	190	171	84	145	1.34	12

SEMINARA, FRANK - TR - Age 26

Demoted to AAA Las Vegas in the spring after a 1-2, 5.40 start, Seminara went 8-5 (albeit with a high 5.43 ERA), then pitched better in San Diego after his return. The sidearming Seminara is definitely a candidate for the rotation and he has been a winner at every level despite his high ERA; he went 9-4 the Padres in 1992.

	W	SV	ERA	IP	H	BB	SO	BPI	$
1992 San Diego NL	9	0	3.68	100	98	46	61	1.44	
1993 San Diego NL	3	0	4.47	46	53	21	22	1.61	-
1994 *Projection* >>>	7	0	4.06	99	100	49	57	1.50	0

SERVICE, SCOTT- TR - Age 26

Service bounced from Indianapolis to Cincinnati to Colorado and back to Cincinnati. A large, hard thrower, he looked good in a setup role.

	W	SV	ERA	IP	H	BB	SO	BPI	$
1992 Montreal NL	0	0	14.14	7	15	5	11	2.86	-
1993 Cincinnati NL	2	2	4.30	46	44	16	43	1.30	1
1994 *Projection* >>>	1	1	4.70	30	31	11	23	1.41	-

SHAW, CURTIS - TL - Age 24

A top reliever at the University of Kansas, Shaw has been used as a starter in the A's system, making good progress at low A and high A in 1991-1992. His key is being able to spot the fastball. If you were writing fiction about a ballplayer, you couldn't come up with a better hometown: Bartlesville, Oklahoma.

	W	SV	ERA	IP	H	BB	SO	BPI	$
1993 Huntsville AA	6	0	4.93	152	141	89	132	1.53	

SHAW, JEFF - TR - Age 27

A journeyman who bombed in Cleveland and did not pitch that well out of the Expos' bullpen in 1993, Shaw doesn't really have an out pitch. At best, he's the 10th or 11th man on someone's staff.

	W	SV	ERA	IP	H	BB	SO	BPI	$
1992 Cleveland AL	0	0	8.22	8	7	4	3	1.44	-
1993 Montreal NL	2	0	4.14	95	91	32	50	1.29	1
1994 *Projection* >>>	1	0	4.20	67	64	23	34	1.30	-

SHEPHERD, KEITH - TR - Age 26

Guys with 6.98 ERAs can only hope to get one more chance. He showed potential with a scoreless streak in June then faded fast.

	W	SV	ERA	IP	H	BB	SO	BPI	$
1992 Philadelphia NL	1	2	3.27	22	19	6	10	1.14	0
1993 Colorado NL	1	1	6.98	19	26	4	7	1.57	-
1994 *Projection* >>>	1	1	5.64	18	21	4	7	1.4	-

SHIFFLETT, STEVE - TR - Age 28

Couldn't build on decent half-season in majors in 1992; put up forgettable numbers for AAA Omaha and couldn't hold part time closer role there. At age 28, the Kansas City native is beginning to look like a career minor leaguer. A good example of the use of Triple-A as an extension of the major league bench; Shifflett is available if needed, but unlikely to have a major role.

	W	SV	ERA	IP	H	BB	SO	BPI	$
1992 Omaha AAA	3	14	1.65	43	30	15	19	1.03	
1992 Kansas City AL	1	0	2.60	52	55	17	25	1.38	1
1993 Omaha AAA	3	5	4.98	56	78	15	31	1.66	

SHINALL, ZAK -TR - Age 25

Shinnall led Dodger farmhands and the Pacific Coast League with 13 wins in 1992 without making a single start all season. In 1993 he got a long look as a game finisher, with mixed results.

	W	SV	ERA	IP	H	BB	SO	BPI	$
1992 Albuquerque AAA	13	6	3.29	82	91	37	46	1.56	
1993 Calgary AAA	2	5	5.01	46	55	18	25	1.58	
1993 Seattle AL	0	0	3.38	2	4	2	0	2.73	-
1994 *Projection* >>>	0	0	4.91	10	12	5	6	1.67	-

SHOUSE, BRIAN - TL - Age 25

The Pirates thought enough of Shouse to protect him in the expansion draft following the 1992 season. However, the little lefthanded reliever failed miserably in an August stint with the Pirates and was subsequently dropped from the 40-man roster. Shouse cleared waivers and accepted an assignment to the Pirates' Triple-A club but he figures to have no chance of making the big league club this year.

	W	SV	ERA	IP	H	BB	SO	BPI	$
1993 Buffalo AAA	1	2	3.83	51	54	17	25	1.39	
1993 Pittsburgh NL	0	0	9.00	4	7	2	3	2.25	-

SHUEY, PAUL - TR - Age 22

Indians first round pick in 1992, Shuey took major steps backward in 1993. After being trounced at AA Canton-Akron, he was placed in the bullpen at Single-A Kinston to work through his problems. Indians will give him all the time he needs; they have plenty of other pitching prospects.

SIMON, RICHIE - TR - Age 28

An Eight year farmhand for the Astros and Giants, Richie has had good success at Double-A (20 Saves and 2.18 ERA in 1991).

SIMONS, DOUG - TL - Age 27

Drafted by the Mets under Rule Five, from the Twins in 1990, and kept on the major league roster throughout the 1991 season, though he clearly was overmatched. Then traded to Montreal. He is still a propsect, but fading.

	W	SV	ERA	IP	H	BB	SO	BPI	$
1992 Montreal NL	0	0	23.63	5	15	2	6	3.19	-
1992 Indianapolis AAA	11	0	3.08	120	114	25	66	1.16	
1993 Ottawa AAA	7	0	4.75	116	134	16	75	1.30	

SLOCUMB, HEATHCLIFF - TR - Age 27

One of the greatest names in pro sports. Slocumb has a good fastball, a sharp slider, and so far, these assets haven't done him much good.

	W	SV	ERA	IP	H	BB	SO	BPI	$
1992 Chicago NL	0	1	6.50	36	52	21	27	2.03	-
1993 Chicago NL	1	0	3.38	10	7	4	4	1.08	-
1993 Cleveland AL	3	0	4.28	27	28	16	18	1.62	-
1994 *Projection* >>>	3	0	4.61	40	42	21	25	1.58	-

SLUSARSKI, JOE - TR - Age 27

Only 27 years old, has had some decent minor league seasons, but his major league career has been a disaster thus far and he hasn't exactly been a star at Triple-A. Slusarski has featured a big fastball but not much else. He really needs another pitch.

	W	SV	ERA	IP	H	BB	SO	BPI	$
1992 Oakland AL	5	0	5.45	76	85	27	38	1.47	-
1993 Oakland AL	0	0	5.19	8	9	11	1	2.44	-
1994 *Projection* >>>	2	0	5.36	39	43	18	18	1.57	-

SMALL, AARON - TR - Age 21

Small was converted from starting pitcher to ace reliever at AA Knoxville, after attracting attention in the Arizona fall league, and he responded with 16 saves. He does not have a great fastball nor is he blessed with great control, but his curveball induces more than its fair share of groundballs. He has an outside shot of landing a major league setup job in spring training. Otherwise, he's a year away.

	W	SV	ERA	IP	H	BB	SO	BPI	$
1993 Knoxville AA	4	16	3.39	93	99	40	44	1.49	

SMILEY, JOHN -TL - Age 29

The Reds apparently knew that Smiley had elbow problems when they signed him to a four year deal. Smiley tried to justify the contract by pitching with bone chips in his elbow and the results were predictable. Smiley is an excellent comeback candidate for 1994. Even when he was struggling in 1993, he had a good strikeout/walk ratio.

	W	SV	ERA	IP	H	BB	SO	BPI	$
1992 Minnesota AL	16	0	3.21	241	205	65	163	1.12	20
1993 Cincinnati NL	3	0	5.62	105	117	31	60	1.41	-
1994 *Projection* >>>	9	0	3.91	157	152	43	98	1.24	6

SMITH, BRYN - TR - Age 38

At 38, Smith got released for the last time. He no longer has sharp control of his pitches and was basically throwing batting practice.

	W	SV	ERA	IP	H	BB	SO	BPI	$
1992 Louisville AAA	1	0	1.80	10	6	2	2	0.80	
1992 St. Louis NL	4	0	4.64	21	20	5	9	1.17	0
1993 Colorado NL	2	0	8.49	29	47	11	9	1.99	-

SMITH, DAN -TL - Age 24

Missed almost the entire season due to injury. Has a possible shot at the fifth starter role if healthy, but the Rangers would prefer that he pitch regularly, which likely means Oklahoma City. This former first round pick is a strong candidate for a mid season callup if he doesn't make the opening day roster.

	W	SV	ERA	IP	H	BB	SO	BPI	$
1992 Texas AL	0	0	5.02	14	18	8	5	1.81	-
1992 Tulsa AA	11	0	2.52	146	110	34	122	0.99	
1993 Oklahoma City AAA	0	0	4.70	15	16	5	12	1.53	

SMITH, LEE - TR - Age 36

A proven closer with the all time career save record. Starting to wear down after 14 years in the majors, but has enough for another quality year or two. The forkball lifted his career three years ago when he started to fade. Can he find another new pitch? Doubtful.

	W	SV	ERA	IP	H	BB	SO	BPI	$
1992 St. Louis NL	4	43	3.12	75	62	26	60	1.17	39
1993 St.Louis NL	2	43	4.50	50	49	9	49	1.16	34
1993 New York AL	0	3	0.00	8	4	5	11	1.13	2
1994 *Projection* >>>	3	30	3.94	65	57	21	61	1.21	30

SMITH, PETE - TR - Age 28

Smith couldn't duplicate his remarkable 1992 success last year, getting sent to the bullpen, then losing the last six weeks of the year to shoulder tendinitis. His breaking pitches lost their bite and he had to rely too much on a fastball that isn't overpowering. Smith should be back to full strength for spring training and will be overlooked by many who don't understand that he's good enough to be a number three starter for many teams, like the Mets.

	W	SV	ERA	IP	H	BB	SO	BPI	$
1992 Richmond AAA	7	0	2.14	109	75	24	93	0.91	
1992 Atlanta NL	7	0	2.05	79	63	28	43	1.15	
1993 Atlanta NL	4	0	4.37	90	92	36	53	1.42	-
1994 *Projection* >>>	8	0	3.75	150	141	55	80	1.31	4

SMITH, WILLIE - TR - Age 26

Looks like Lee Smith and pitches like Lee Smith; just hasn't been so successful. The Yankees' attempt to convert Smith into a starter was a failure and set back his career. In 1993 he played in the Texas minor league system and was hurt most of the year.

SMITH, ZANE - TL - Age 33

Smith had a lost year in 1993. Limited to four appearances in the second half of 1992 because of shoulder problems, He underwent rotator cuff surgery in November of 1992 and did not return to the Pirates' rotation until mid-June. Relying on a sinking fastball to induce ground ball outs, Smith showed flashes of his old form but was shut down for good at the beginning of September. The Pirates are optimistic that he will be 100 percent this season; they need his veteran presence in a young rotation.

	W	SV	ERA	IP	H	BB	SO	BPI	$
1992 Pittsburgh NL	8	0	3.06	141	138	19	56	1.11	8
1993 Pittsburgh NL	3	0	4.55	83	97	22	32	1.43	-
1994 *Projection* >>>	6	0	3.73	115	123	23	57	1.27	4

SMITHBERG, ROGER - TR - Age 28

Pitched well at Triple-A, and posted a 2.75 ERA for the A's late in the season, though like so many Oakland pitchers he also walked more than he struck out. Prior to last year his career was going nowhere. He has earned another shot at sticking in the bigs, but is assured of nothing for 1994 except getting that chance.

	W	SV	ERA	IP	H	BB	SO	BPI	$
1993 Tacoma AAA	3	4	1.78	50	50	11	25	1.20	
1993 Oakland AL	1	3	2.75	20	13	7	4	1.04	3
1994 *Projection* >>>	1	2	3.65	24	20	10	10	1.26	2

SMOLTZ, JOHN - TR - Age 26

Smoltz took a small step backward in 1993, yet still helped the Braves. If this is as bad as it gets for Smoltz, he'll be a consistently valuable performer for many years. The Braves deep pitching staff and solid offense make Smoltz even better.

	W	SV	ERA	IP	H	BB	SO	BPI	$
1992 Atlanta NL	15	0	2.85	246	206	80	215	1.16	17
1993 Atlanta NL	15	0	3.62	244	208	100	208	1.27	13
1994 *Projection* >>>	17	0	3.14	241	207	86	211	1.22	16

SODERSTROM, STEVE - TR - Age 22

The sixth player chosen in 1993's June draft (out of Fresno State), Soderstrom started his career in typical Giants fashion, with a sore arm (elbow tendinitis). Between the injury and lengthy contract negotiations (he got a $750,000 signing bonus), he wasn't able to pitch until the Arizona Fall League season.

SOPER, MIKE - TR - Age 27

In 1991, Soper pitched for AA Kinston and led the minors with 41 saves. 1992 was an adjustment year, with Soper pitching well but not dominating. Needs more Triple-A experience.

	W	SV	ERA	IP	H	BB	SO	BPI	$
1992 Canton-Akron AA	3	19	3.02	48	37	17	43	1.13	
1992 Colorado Springs AAA	0	1	6.06	16	26	6	16	1.96	
1993 Canton-Akron AA	1	4	5.63	8	8	4	11	1.50	

SPOLJARIC, PAUL - TL - Age 24

He could be the Jays' counterpart to Montreal's Denis Boucher: a Canadian lefthander. Toronto needs a lefty in its rotation. Last season the Jays considered calling up Spoljaric after just two Triple-A starts, after Spoljaric had shot through their system from A-ball. May need to begin '94 back in Triple-A, but with any success, he wouldn't be there long. He has a blazing fastball and average control. He is durable and keeps his team in the game. Unfortunately, in the minors he has had a tendency for his fastball to fade in the stretch.

	W	SV	ERA	IP	H	BB	SO	BPI	$
1993 Syracuse AAA	8	0	5.29	95	97	52	88	1.56	

SPRADLIN, JERRY - TR - Age 26

A 6'7" righthander, Spradlin demonstrated good control (21 walks in 106 innings in Indianapolis and Cincinnati combined) but he's not really overpowering. He led the Southern League in saves in 1992.

	W	SV	ERA	IP	H	BB	SO	BPI	$
1993 Cincinnati NL	2	2	3.49	49	44	9	24	1.08	4
1994 *Projection* >>>>	1	1	3.69	29	27	8	14	1.22	0

SPRINGER, RUSS - TR - Age 25

When he was with the Yankees, Springer was viewed as a possible closer, and in fact he did well in short relief for a month despite the overall bad numbers. Then California put him back in the starting rotation, and when that didn't work, they made him a reliever again. He suffered periodic bouts of wildness, but didn't do too badly. Good 93 MPH fastball. Could relieve, close or spot start in 1994.

	W	SV	ERA	IP	H	BB	SO	BPI	$
1992 New York AL	0	0	6.19	16	18	10	12	1.75	-
1993 California AL	1	0	7.20	60	73	32	31	1.75	-
1994 *Projection* >>>	1	1	4.71	41	44	20	22	1.55	-

STANTON, MIKE -TL - Age 26

Too many exciting games cost Stanton his closer role early in the second half of last year. He was far too inconsistent in the role of ace reliever, but fared much better once he went back to his accustomed setup job. Stanton can still be a valuable closer or co-closer once he settles into a role. The Braves were in a pennant chase last year and didn't have the luxury of letting Stanton work his way through his problems. Little has changed from 1993, though, so expect him to again see time as a setup man or possibly in a co-closer role with righthander Greg McMichael, or whoever gets chosen by Bobby Cox. Stanton has been a better second half pitcher for most of his career; try to trade for him around the All-Star break.

	W	SV	ERA	IP	H	BB	SO	BPI	$
1992 Atlanta NL	5	8	4.10	63	59	20	44	1.24	6
1993 Atlanta NL	4	27	4.67	52	51	29	43	1.54	19
1994 *Projection* >>>	4	10	3.88	58	54	24	44	1.35	8

ST. CLAIRE, RANDY - TR - Age 33

Had some good years with the Expos in the late 1980's, but now far past his prime.

	W	SV	ERA	IP	H	BB	SO	BPI	$
1992 Atlanta NL	0	0	5.87	15	17	8	7	1.63	-
1993 Syracuse AAA	1	0	2.93	31	34	6	15	1.30	

STEENSTRA, KENNIE - TR - Age 23

Wichita State's ace for the 1992 College World Series championship team has been doing his best to play the same role with five Cubs farm teams since being drafted in the 12th round in 1992. Using a circle change as an out pitch, Steenstra has a pro record of 23-9 with a 2.75 ERA.

STEWART, DAVE - TR - Age 37

Post-season heroics aside, Stewart has become an average major league pitcher. He finished 1993 without a complete game and has been forced to rely more on the forkball than ever as his fastball continues to lose velocity. The problem with his forkball is that he often has trouble throwing it for a strike. He is assured a spot in the rotation, but he's a gamble for any team. The Blue Jays can afford to take this chance.

	W	SV	ERA	IP	H	BB	SO	BPI	$
1992 Oakland AL	12	0	3.66	199	175	79	130	1.27	9
1993 Toronto AL	12	0	4.44	162	146	72	96	1.35	6
1994 *Projection* >>>	12	0	4.27	180	165	78	111	1.35	4

STEVENS, DAVE - TR - Age 24

A righthander climbing up the Cubs minor league ladder, Stevens went 10-1 in a season split between Double-A and Triple-A. A starter at AA Orlando, he was groomed as a reliever at AAA Iowa. His fastball is good enough to earn him a bullpen shot.

	W	SV	ERA	IP	H	BB	SO	BPI	$
1993 Iowa AAA	4	4	4.19	34	24	14	29	1.11	

STIEB, DAVE - TR - Age 36

Continued his downward slide into oblivion in 1993. The Royals needed another starter down the stretch and the decision not to recall Steib says a lot about his future. He posted similarly wretched numbers for the White Sox (before his release) then with AAA Omaha. A steady, solid starting pitcher for several Blue Jays' teams, Stieb has reached the end.

	W	SV	ERA	IP	H	BB	SO	BPI	$
1992 Toronto AL	4	0	5.04	96	98	43	45	1.46	-
1993 Chicago AL	1	0	6.04	22	27	14	11	1.86	-
1994 *Projection* >>>	2	0	5.09	48	51	23	23	1.54	-

STOTTLEMYRE, TODD - TR - Age 28

Stottlemyre can rise to tremendous levels in a one or two game stretch, but usually finds a way to beat himself. Emotionally, he takes losses poorly and shows his frustration on the mound, often throwing fastballs in breaking ball situations. Stottlemyre's fastball is nothing special, but his slider is one of the best in the league. He is known for pitching inside.

	W	SV	ERA	IP	H	BB	SO	BPI	$
1992 Toronto AL	12	0	4.50	174	175	63	98	1.37	2
1993 Toronto AL	11	0	4.84	177	204	69	98	1.55	-
1994 *Projection* >>>	12	0	4.61	180	194	67	100	1.45	2

STURTZE, TANYON - TR - Age 23

On Oakland's protected list for the '92 expansion draft, Sturtze made little progress in 1993. He throws a 90-MPH fastball, but gets into trouble when he's unable to control his curve and slider.

SUTCLIFFE, RICK -TR - Age 37

Sutcliffe has lost his sharpness and couldn't get by with only his guile. Sutcliffe is a horse, always producing lots of innings; the only problem is they have become ugly innings.

	W	SV	ERA	IP	H	BB	SO	BPI	$
1992 Baltimore AL	16	0	4.47	237	251	74	109	1.37	4
1993 Baltimore AL	10	0	5.75	166	212	74	80	1.72	-
1994 *Projection* >>>	11	0	5.16	181	213	71	86	1.57	-

SUTKO, GLENN - TR - Age 25

Once was classified as a good-defense, no-offense type of catcher with a career minor league batting average of .207, Sutko became a pitcher with somewhat more success.

SUZUKI, MAKATO - TR - Age 19

Seattle signed him as a free agent from the California League's independent San Bernardino club, for $750,000. The Japanese fastballer throws at up to 95 MPH.

SWAN, RUSS - TL - Age 30

A classic lefty sinker/slider pitcher, Swan was protected from expansion but apparently lost all ability to pitch in 1993. He was sidelined with a strained elbow. His future is in doubt.

	W	SV	ERA	IP	H	BB	SO	BPI	$
1992 Seattle AL	3	9	4.74	104	104	45	45	1.43	4
1993 Seattle AL	3	0	9.15	20	25	18	10	2.24	-
1994 *Projection* >>>	3	1	5.56	51	55	25	23	1.56	-

SWIFT, BILL - TR - Age 32

The best starting pitcher on a team that won 103 games, Swift has posted sub-3.00 ERAs in each of the last four seasons. If anyone on the Giants staff wins 20 games in 1994, Swift is the most likely candidate. A definite groundball pitcher, Swift's effectiveness depends on good defense.

	W	SV	ERA	IP	H	BB	SO	BPI	$
1992 San Francisco NL	10	1	2.08	164	144	43	77	1.14	15
1993 San Francisco NL	21	0	2.82	233	195	55	157	1.08	26
1994 *Projection* >>>	16	0	2.98	198	171	61	122	1.17	20

SWINDELL, GREG - TL - Age 29

Swindell was hit hard in 1993, particularly in the first half. He was later found to be suffering from a sore shoulder. Swindell was better in the second half, after a rest, but he never did develop any consistency. He finished the season with two strong starts which indicated there is nothing wrong with his arm; he still has excellent control and is committed to be in better physical condition in 1994. Swindell should be able to do much better this year.

	W	SV	ERA	IP	H	BB	SO	BPI	$
1992 Cincinnati NL	12	0	2.70	213	210	41	138	1.17	14
1993 Houston NL	12	0	4.16	190	215	40	124	1.34	5
1994 *Projection* >>>	14	0	3.62	202	213	40	135	1.25	12

SWINGEL, PAUL - TR - Age 27

Hard thrower but wild. Watch the strikeout to walk ratio at Triple-A to see whether he improves.

	W	SV	ERA	IP	H	BB	SO	BPI	$
1993 Vancouver AAA	2	1	6.92	67	85	32	61	1.74	
1993 California AL	0	0	8.38	10	15	6	6	2.28	-
1994 *Projection* >>>	0	0	6	6	9	3	3	2.00	-

TANANA, FRANK - TL - Age 40

A veteran who will make a dependable fourth of fifth starter, Tanana can still finesse his way through about 200 innings a year. Just don't expect them to be nice innings.

	W	SV	ERA	IP	H	BB	SO	BPI	$
1992 Detroit AL	13	0	4.39	186	188	90	91	1.49	0
1993 New York NL	7	0	4.48	183	198	48	104	1.34	1
1993 New York AL	0	0	3.20	20	18	7	12	1.30	-
1994 *Projection* >>>	9	0	4.3	199	208	67	108	1.38	1

TAPANI, KEVIN - TR - Age 30

Sinkerballer Kevin Tapani had a tremendous second half last year: 16 starts, 9-4, 3.12 ERA and a 1.084 ratio. He has a history of slow starts, but one of these years, he may stay sharp all year and what a big year that will be.

	W	SV	ERA	IP	H	BB	SO	BPI	$
1992 Minnesota AL	16	0	3.97	220	226	48	138	1.24	10
1993 Minnesota AL	12	0	4.43	226	243	57	150	1.33	8
1994 *Projection* >>>	14	0	3.95	226	233	52	145	1.26	12

TATAR, KEVIN - TR - Age 25

Once a highly regarded pitching prospect, Tatar missed most of 1993 with injuries.

	W	SV	ERA	IP	H	BB	SO	BPI	$
1993 Chattanooga AAA	0	0	1.93	14	9	5	7	1.00	

TAVAREZ, JULIAN - TR - Age 22

Slender righthander (6'-2", 165) who exploded from Rookie League Burlington in 1992 all the way to the majors in 1993, he was clearly in way over his head. He yielded just 12 walks in 87 innings in Rookie Ball in 1992, and 29 walks in 138 innings in 1993 at Single-A and Double-A, great control for any youngster. Will be among many kids vying for one or two starting spots in the spring; if he's not ready then, look for him by mid-1994 or 1995. He's coming.

	W	SV	ERA	IP	H	BB	SO	BPI	$
1993 Cleveland AL	2	0	6.57	37	53	13	19	1.78	-
1994 *Projection* >>>>	5	0	4.68	80	101	25	40	1.58	-

TAYLOR, BILL - TR - Age 32

You have to admire Taylor's perseverance. He has yet to get to the majors despite throwing over 1300 innings in 14 professional seasons. 1993 may have been Taylor's best year ever, as he got off to a great start at AAA Richmond and set a franchise record with 26 saves. Taylor has steadily increased his strikeout rate in the four years he's been with the Braves organization and does it by throwing a wide assortment of pitches. Despite the big year, the Braves let him become a free agent.

	W	SV	ERA	IP	H	BB	SO	BPI	$
1993 Richmond AAA	2	26	1.98	68	56	26	81	1.20	

TAYLOR, BRIEN - TL - Age 22

Has the ability to be the first 100 MPH thrower since Nolan Ryan, but it's still way too early to translate that velocity into major league success. Showed last season why he was the first player taken in the 1991 draft, why he got such a high bonus and why his baseball cards already are as hot as his fastball.

	W	SV	ERA	IP	H	BB	SO	BPI	$
1992 Ft.Lauderdale A	6	0	2.57	161	121	66	187	1.16	
1993 Albany AA	13	0	3.48	163	127	102	150	1.40	

TAYLOR, KERRY - TR - Age 23

a rule five pick in storage for 1993, Taylor had a good year as a starter of Class A Kenosha in 1992 (10 wins with a 2.75 ERA) but obviously isn't ready for the majors.

	W	SV	ERA	IP	H	BB	SO	BPI	$
1993 San Diego NL	0	0	6.45	68	72	49	45	1.78	-

TAYLOR, SCOTT - TL - Age 26

Taylor's major league numbers make you yawn. But, in six minor league seasons he fanned 544 batters in 616 innings. He has closer stuff, but he's in a very crowded bullpen. May have made a breakthrough in his Triple-A debut, in his fifth pro season with his third organization. He has a better chance with pitching-poor Milwaukee than he might somewhere else.

	W	SV	ERA	IP	H	BB	SO	BPI	$
1992 Boston AL	1	0	4.91	14	13	4	7	1.16	-
1993 Pawtucket AAA	7	1	4.04	122	132	48	88	1.46	
1993 Boston AL	0	0	8.18	11	14	12	8	2.36	-
1994 Projection >>>	0	0	6.42	11	12	6	6	1.66	-

TAYLOR, WADE - TR - Age 28

Something of a flash in 1991, Taylor was set back by a sore arm in 1992, and was still trying to come back in 1993.

TELFORD, ANTHONY - TR - Age 28

Curveballer Telford struggled in Triple-A and was released by the Orioles. He hurt his arm a few years ago, and lost a lot off his fastball. He has tried to make it with a new style emphasizing curveballs, but he hasn't yet succeeded.

TELGHEDER, DAVE - TR - Age 27

Development of a better forkball lifted Telgheder in late 1993. He throws a variety of pitches , but has no solid throw. He could become a starter with a strong spring, but most likely will be seen in relief.

	W	SV	ERA	IP	H	BB	SO	BPI	$
1993 New York NL	6	0	4.76	76	82	21	35	1.36	0
1994 Projection >>>	4	0	4.76	45	48	13	21	1.36	-

TERRELL, WALT - TR - Age 35

The former starter now works as a mop-up guy at AAA Syracuse for part of 1993. He's about done, if not well done.

	W	SV	ERA	IP	H	BB	SO	BPI	$
1992 Detroit AL	7	0	5.20	136	163	48	61	1.54	-
1993 Syracuse AAA	0	0	5.30	36	41	11	20	1.36	

TEWKSBURY, BOB - TR - Age 33

Clearly the best control pitcher in baseball, in terms of results, Tewksbury has had just 20 walks each of the last two years, for a total of 40 walks in his last 446.2 innings. Tewksbury relies on spotting the ball because his stuff is only average.

	W	SV	ERA	IP	H	BB	SO	BPI	$
1992 St. Louis NL	16	0	2.16	233	217	20	91	1.32	26
1993 St. Louis NL	17	0	3.83	214	258	20	97	1.30	10
1994 Projection >>>	15	0	3.24	217	236	22	90	1.19	18

THIGPEN, BOBBY - TR - Age 30

Optimists were ready to waive the mandatory five year waiting period for Hall of Fame eligibility after Thigpen's 57 save season in 1990. He should have had his arm bronzed after that year; he had only that one spectacular season and since then has lost about a yard off of his fastball, making him a pitcher without a future. He has tried an assortment of breaking pitches with unimpressive results.

	W	SV	ERA	IP	H	BB	SO	BPI	$
1992 Chicago AL	1	22	4.75	55	58	33	45	1.65	12
1993 Chicago AL	0	1	5.71	34	51	12	19	1.81	-
1993 Philadelphia NL	3	0	6.05	19	23	9	10	1.68	-
1994 *Projection* >>>	3	2	5.01	56	69	26	30	1.69	-

THOBE, J.J. - TR - Age 21

1992 7th-round draftee who was picked as best right handed starter in South Atlantic League in 1993. Was 11-2, 1.91, with a ratio below 1.00, and a strikeout/walk ratio of over 4-to-1. OK, it's a pitcher's league, but they're still eyepopping numbers. He did OK after moving up to the higher Class A Carolina League, too.

THOMAS, LARRY -TL - Age 24

Finesse pitcher who had some trouble in the high minors last year after a super 1992 season at Single-A. Still developing, he's not overpowering, but good at moving the ball around, pitching inside, and changing speeds.

	W	SV	ERA	IP	H	BB	SO	BPI	$
1992 Sarasota A	5	0	1.62	55	44	7	50	0.92	
1992 Birmingham AA	8	0	1.94	120	102	30	72	1.10	
1993 Nashville AAA	4	0	5.99	101	114	32	67	1.44	

THOMAS, MIKE - TL - Age 24

Had 20 saves in 1991 and 15 in 1993. Moving up slowly but steadily, with plenty of strikeouts along the way.

	W	SV	ERA	IP	H	BB	SO	BPI	$
1992 Rockford A	5	2	3.58	113	98	51	108	1.31	
1993 West Palm Beach A	1	9	3.29	27	19	23	28	1.55	
1993 Harrisburg AA	2	6	4.73	32	34	19	40	1.60	

THOMPSON, JUSTIN - TL - Age 22

Detroit's minor league pitching talent is rather thin, but Thompson is one arm likely to reach the majors. He just needs a couple of years to mature. Thompson has a 3.26 career ERA and almost a strikeout per inning after three minor league seasons.

THOMPSON, MARK - TR - Age 23

Thompson and John Burke are the perfect prospect pair for the pitching-starved Rockies. Drafted second behind Burke in the organization's first amateur draft, Thompson didn't spend much time at Single-A Central Valley, posting a 2.20 ERA in 70 innings (11 starts). Promoted to Triple-A Colorado Springs, Thompson mowed them down there, too, with stamina; he averaged over eight innings per start there (with a 3-0 record in 4 starts). He could make the big club out of spring training in 1994, but Rockies management won't rush him, so the best bet is he'll get a mid-year callup with a definite shot at the starting rotation in 1995.

TIMLIN, MIKE - TR - Age 28

Timlin got so bad at one point last year, he was demoted as low as Class A level. He returned in time to be placed on the post season roster and pitched very well after that point. His sinker can be excellent and his fastball and control are good enough to compete. What he needs is careful pitch selection and a dose of confidence.

	W	SV	ERA	IP	H	BB	SO	BPI	$
1992 Toronto AL	0	1	4.12	43	45	20	35	1.49	-
1993 Toronto AL	4	1	4.69	56	63	27	49	1.63	-
1994 *Projection* >>>	4	1	4.27	57	60	28	44	1.54	-

TOLIVER, FRED - TR - Age 33

This hard throwing righty wound up spending a month with the Pirates last season, his first visit to the major leagues since 1990. He can still throw 95 mph but getting the ball over the plate is another matter. Give him points for perserverance, though, as he has spent most of the past two seasons at either Double-A or Single-A.

	W	SV	ERA	IP	H	BB	SO	BPI	$
1993 Pittsburgh NL	1	0	3.74	22	20	8	14	1.32	-

TOMLIN, RANDY - TL - Age 27

Tomlin injured his elbow late in spring training in 1993 and never regained his steady form of the previous three seasons. A finesse lefty, who relies on mixing his fastball, curveball, slider and changeup, Tomlin often was unable to use his breaking pitches because of his elbow problem. He had a bone spur surgically removed in September; it was considered minor surgery and he's expected to be ready on Opening Day. The Pirates sorely missed the solid six or seven innings he gives in almost every start.

	W	SV	ERA	IP	H	BB	SO	BPI	$
1992 Pittsburgh NL	14	0	3.41	208	226	42	90	1.28	7
1993 Pittsburgh NL	4	0	4.85	98	109	15	44	1.26	0
1994 Projection >>>	7	0	3.97	139	151	26	64	1.27	4

TORRES, SALOMON - TR - Age 22

Torres pitched very well in the minors, and earned the start in fateful Game 162 of the 1993 NL season. He had already delivered some gritty performances for the Giants, but generally had control problems. His minor league performance was fine in this regard. After posting a 16-5 record in 1991 as a 19-year-old in A-ball, and throwing 210 innings, Torres had arm troubles in 1992. The arm seemed fine in 1993, but Torres was only 21, and he led the entire organization in innings pitched. He has the talent; only time will tell if he is being overused at an early age.

	W	SV	ERA	IP	H	BB	SO	BPI	$
1993 Phoenix AAA	7	0	3.50	105	105	27	99	1.25	
1993 San Francisco NL	3	0	4.03	45	37	27	23	1.45	-
1994 Projection >>>	13	0	3.88	188	226	37	98	1.40	4

TRACHSEL, STEVE - TR - Age 23

A righthander without super velocity, Trachsel uses very a nice curve as his out pitch and has an OK forkball. He used them to strike out 135 and lead AAA Iowa with 13 victories; he also made the Triple-A All-Star team. Trachsel showed good poise in limited major league duty. He's not a sure prospect, but is a strong candidate for a major league roster spot in 1994, maybe even on Opening Day, given the state of the Cubs fourth and fifth starters and their bullpen. Trachsel knows how to pitch.

	W	SV	ERA	IP	H	BB	SO	BPI	$
1993 Iowa AAA	13	0	3.96	170	170	45	135	1.25	
1993 Chicago NL	0	0	4.58	20	16	3	14	.95	-
1994 Projection >>>	0	0	4.57	12	12	5	7	1.41	-

TRANBERG, MARK - TR - Age 25

A 35th-round pick from that noted baseball factory Cal. State-Dominguez Hills in 1992, Tranberg put together an impressive season split between the Phils two Single-A teams in 1993, going 15-4 with a 2.23 ERA, a 1.08 ratio, and a 3.64 strikeout/walk ratio. The only problem is the age. The Phils have a knack for drafting players at 23, watching them put up good numbers against kids, and then wondering why they never reach the majors.

TRINIDAD, HECTOR - TR - Age 20

Pitching for the Cubs since age 18, he has a career 2.83 ERA in the low minors with 262 strikeouts and just 60 walks in 340 innings. He'll begin 1994 at Double-A as the Cubs' most developed, real long range pitching prospect. He'll appear in the majors in 1995 at the earliest; the pitching ahead of him is awfully thin.

TRLICEK, RICK - TR - Age 24

Trlicek has average stuff; he won't get hammered but won't dominate, either. He has been and will be used strictly as a middle-innings pitcher to save other pitchers' arms.

	W	SV	ERA	IP	H	BB	SO	BPI	$
1992 Toronto AL	0	0	10.80	1	2	2	1	2.40	-
1993 Los Angeles NL	1	1	4.08	64	59	21	41	1.25	-
1994 Projection >>>	1	1	4.16	39	36	13	22	1.26	0

TROMBLEY, MIKE - TR - Age 26

Many "experts" picked Mike Trombley as their rookie of the year candidate in last year's pre-season. He fell a little short. It was a year for learning, with some erratic ups and downs, but overall, Trombley is now in a good position to move into a starter's role where he can have a good year.

	W	SV	ERA	IP	H	BB	SO	BPI	$
1992 Portland AAA	10	0	3.65	165	149	58	138	1.25	
1992 Minnesota AL	3	0	3.30	46	43	17	38	1.29	1
1993 Minnesota AL	6	2	4.88	114	131	41	85	1.51	1
1994 *Projection* >>>>	8	0	4.61	125	130	45	89	1.40	-

TSAMIS, GEORGE - TL - Age 26

Lefty Tsamis was in the Twins bullpen because of the injury to Mark Guthrie. Although he has had some winning records in Triple-A, he usually gives up a lot of hits. Tsamis is a finesse pitcher whose talent is just throwing strikes to put the ball in play.

	W	SV	ERA	IP	H	BB	SO	BPI	$
1993 Minnesota AL	1	1	6.19	68	86	27	30	1.66	-
1994 *Projection* >>>	1	1	5.40	41	52	16	18	1.65	-

TURNER, MATT -TR - Age 27

A rubber armed righty who pitched 100 innings in relief in the Pacific Coast League in 1992, Turner compiled a solid ratio in 1993, struck out almost a batter per inning, and was especially tough on righties. If the Marlins decide to trade Harvey, Turner's the man in the pen.

	W	SV	ERA	IP	H	BB	SO	BPI	$
1992 Tucson AAA	2	14	3.51	100	93	40	84	1.33	
1993 Florida NL	4	0	2.91	68	55	26	59	1.19	4
1994 *Projection* >>>	2	2	2.91	41	33	16	35	1.19	3

URBANI, TOM - TL - Age 26

Urbani caught the Cardinals' attention with a good spring before he was sent to the minors, then got a major league shot later in the year. He doesn't appear to be a great prospect, but he's young and lefthanded, so there's a chance he'll blossom into a useful setup man. The Cardinals like his versatility and will give him every chance to succeed.

	W	SV	ERA	IP	H	BB	SO	BPI	$
1993 Louisville AAA	9	1	2.47	95	86	23	65	1.14	
1993 St. Louis NL	1	0	4.65	62	73	26	33	1.60	-
1994 *Projection* >>>	1	0	4.65	37	43	16	20	1.6	-

URBINA, UGUETH URTAIN - TR - Age 20

Pronounced "you-get", Urbina has a 90 MPH fastball, a plus slider, a solid changeup and outstanding makeup to go with the best name in baseball. After showing little in A-ball in 1992, Urbina went 10-1 with a 1.99 ERA for Single-A Burlington while fanning 107 in 108 innings and making the All-Star team. He's still young but could be in the Expos' rotation by 1995.

VALDES, MARK - TR - Age 21

A first round draftee in 1993, out of the University of Florida, Valdes established himself as a dominant starter in a tough conference very early in his collegiate career. The Marlins are counting on his rapid ascent through the system, especially with 1992 number two pick John Lynch moonlighting as a safety for the Tampa Bay Buccaneers.

VALDEZ, SERGIO - TR - Age 28

Seemingly, Valdez has bounced around forever, showing flashes of brilliance but never sustaining it. He has a good forkball but his other pitches are average. He'll stay on the fringes of the majors because he has a good arm, but he's running out of chances with the Expos.

	W	SV	ERA	IP	H	BB	SO	BPI	$
1992 Montreal NL	0	0	2.41	37	25	12	32	0.99	1
1993 Ottawa AAA	5	1	3.12	83	77	22	53	1.18	
1993 Montreal NL	0	0	9.00	3	4	1	2	1.67	-
1994 *Projection* >>>	0	0	4.07	15	15	6	9	1.40	-

VALENZUELA, FERNANDO - TL- Age 33

Valenzuela developed a cut fastball to go along with his screwball. After a shaky start, he had an excellent July when he was the American League pitcher of the month. He got hammered later and Manager Johnny Oates said that the hitters caught on to him while Fernando didn't make the necessary adjustments. Lefty pitchers are in short supply, so he may catch on with another team in 1994. Don't expect much.

	W	SV	ERA	IP	H	BB	SO	BPI	$
1993 Baltimore AL	8	0	4.94	179	179	79	78	1.44	
1994 *Projection* >>>	5	0	4.97	108	109	47	47	1.44	4

VALERA, JULIO - TR - Age 25

Very talented, but erratic. Was injured and never found a groove. Valera was tried as a closer, and did pretty well until he broke down. In 1994 he should start, if healthy. Valera has had enough big league experience at a young age (25) to be exceptionally mature.

	W	SV	ERA	IP	H	BB	SO	BPI	$
1992 California AL	8	0	3.73	188	188	64	113	1.34	5
1993 California AL	3	4	6.62	53	77	15	28	1.74	-
1994 *Projection* >>>	4	2	4.76	88	102	29	51	1.49	-

VANLANDINGHAM, BILL - TR - Age 23

He led the Giants organization in strikeouts, fanning 171 in 163 innings at Single-A San Jose. He's at least two years away, but remember his name.

VAN POPPEL, TODD - TR - Age 22

He's still only 22 years old, and he'll get plenty of opportunities to prove himself with Oakland. But he walked 15 more men than he struck out with the A's last year, continuing a four-year pattern of control problems. His minor league record is now 17-25, and in his first real shot at a major league job he did not justifiy the hype.

	W	SV	ERA	IP	H	BB	SO	BPI	$
1992 Tacoma AAA	4	0	3.97	45	44	35	29	1.76	
1993 Oakland AL	6	0	5.04	84	76	62	47	1.64	-
1994 *Projection* >>>	4	0	5.08	51	47	37	29	1.64	-

VANRYN, BEN - TL - Age 22

Rated the nunber one prospect in the Texas League by Baseball America, VanRyn dominated the Texas League with a 14-4 record and a 2.21 ERA in a hitters haven while posting a 3.8 strikeout/walk ratio. VanRyn stumbled in a short stint with AAA Albuquerque, but he's clearly in the express lane to the majors.

VASQUEZ, JULIAN - TR - Age 25

Vasquez was sent to the Angels by the Mets to complete the Dick Schofield trade. He was one of the best Mets relief prospects, and was outstanding at AA Binghamton in 1992. With Bryan Harvey gone, Vasquez could make the Angels bullpen at mid-season and get some saves.

	W	SV	ERA	IP	H	BB	SO	BPI	$
1992 Binghamton AA	2	17	1.35	27	17	7	24	0.89	
1992 Tidewater AAA	1	6	5.56	23	22	8	22	1.30	

VILLONE, RON - TL - Age 24

Seattle's first draft pick in 1992 made his pro debut last season. The former University of Massachusetts tight end (6'3", 230 pounds) throws a fastball in the low 90s, a slider and a curve. Had some control problems. Averaged barely five innings per start, so he may be converted to a closer.

VIOLA, FRANK - TL - Age 33

With that great changeup, he can still pitch. Viola has done as well as any lefty with the Rex Sox in decades.

	W	SV	ERA	IP	H	BB	SO	BPI	$
1992 Boston AL	13	0	3.44	238	214	89	121	1.27	12
1993 Boston AL	11	0	3.14	184	180	72	91	1.38	11
1994 *Projection* >>>	12	0	3.34	205	199	74	104	1.33	12

VITKO, JOSEPH - TR - Age 24

Surfaced with the Mets briefly in 1992, after getting 12 wins with a 2.24 ERA in high A-ball in 1991.

WADE, TERRELL - TL - Age 21

Hiawatha Terrell Wade blazed a trail through the Braves farm system, chopping up batters at three minor league stops. His 208 minor league strikeouts were second best in all of the minors and he had a minor league leading 11.8 strikeouts per nine innings. His great fastball was no match for Single-A hitters as he posted an ERA of 1.73 at Macon, moved quickly through Durham to finish at AA Greenville, where he struck out 18 in one game at the end of the year. Wade was rated as the South Atlantic League's number one prospect by Baseball America. He'll start 1994 at AA Greenville; keep an eye on this one.

WAGNER, BILLY - TL - Age 22

This hard throwing lefty was the Astros' top draft choice in 1993 and number 12 overall. He had unimpressive numbers at short season Auburn but isn't likely to reach the majors in less than three years.

	W	SV	ERA	IP	H	BB	SO	BPI	$
1993 Auburn A	1	0	4.08	28	25	25	31	1.78	

WAGNER, HECTOR - TR - Age 25

Almost made the Kansas City roster out of spring training 1991. Missed all of 1992 with shoulder surgery, then pitched at Single-A and Double-A in 1993.

WAGNER, JOE - TR - Age 22

The fourth of Milwaukee's first-round draft picks in '92, Wagner signed for a $210,000 bonus. He transferred from the University of Wisconsin to Central Florida when the Badgers dropped their baseball program. He's a fastball pitcher, and not afraid to throw inside.

WAGNER, PAUL - TR - Age 26

Wagner has the best arm in the Pirates' organization, consistently clocking in at 95 MPH with his fastball. Wagner still needs to refine his slider and changeup to become a frontline starter but the tools are there. If he doesn't work out in the rotation, the Pirates also feel he could become a first-rate closer. However, the priority is to have him start.

	W	SV	ERA	IP	H	BB	SO	BPI	$
1992 Pittsburgh NL	2	0	0.69	13	9	5	5	1.08	0
1993 Pittsburgh NL	8	2	4.27	141	143	42	114	1.31	5
1994 Projection >>>	5	1	3.81	89	89	27	70	1.30	3

WAINHOUSE, DAVE - TR - Age 26

Another pitcher who was rushed to the majors too quickly by Lou Piniella. Had 21 saves in 1992 and was effective in relief at Calgary. Leaving the Expos system gives him a chance to be a major league closer.

	W	SV	ERA	IP	H	BB	SO	BPI	$
1993 Calgary AAA	0	5	4.02	15	10	7	7	1.08	
1993 Seattle AL	0	0	27.00	2	7	5	2	5.71	-
1994 Projection >>>	0	1	5.20	20	23	7	14	1.50	0

WASDIN, JOHN - TR - Age 21

The first of the two pitchers Oakland drafted in last June's first round. The former Florida State ace signed for a $365,000 bonus. His best pitch is a slider.

WAKEFIELD, TIM - TR - Age 27

Wakefield went from rookie sensation in the final months and the postseason of 1992 to a Double-A pitcher by the middle of the 1993. He completely lost command of his knuckleball. His other pitches, a fastball and a curve, are far below major league standards. Despite pitching poorly in the minors, too, Wakefield ended the season with back-to-back shutouts of the Cubs and Philadelphia. Based on his strong finish, he'll have a good chance to be in the Pirates' rotation again this season. It remains to be seen if his good knuckler will return to stay.

	W	SV	ERA	IP	H	BB	SO	BPI	$
1992 Pittsburgh NL	8	0	2.15	92	76	35	51	1.21	7
1993 Pittsburgh NL	6	0	5.61	128	145	75	59	1.72	-
1994 Projection >>>>	6	0	4.7	105	111	55	51	1.58	-

WALK, BOB - TR - Age 37

After six straight winning seasons, Walk struggled mightily in 1993. He managed to stay off the DL for the first time since 1988, but the crafty veteran had an awful second half. He filed for free agency as the Pirates' only interest was for him to return in a middle relief role.

	W	SV	ERA	IP	H	BB	SO	BPI	$
1992 Pittsburgh NL	10	2	3.20	135	132	43	60	1.30	6
1993 Pittsburgh NL	13	0	5.68	187	214	70	80	1.52	-
1994 *Projection* >>>	12	1	4.92	164	178	58	73	1.44	-

WALKER, MIKE - TR - Age 28

Started three games for the Seattle in 1992, but he's not a prospect. Hasn't had a good year since 1988.

WALKER, PETE - TR - Age 24

A funny thing happened to Walker when he was exiled to the bullpen with a 1-8 record for Binghamton last year; he became their ace closer and continued in the same role in the Arizona Fall League. The road to Shea Stadium is far shorter for a reliever.

WALL, DONNIE - TR - Age 26

Wall has been successful at every level over his five year minor league career, but has not been considered a serious prospect. His career strikeout to walk ratio is 3.5 and he led the Astros minor league organization in strikeouts in 1991 and 1992. Wall may surprise if given a chance.

	W	SV	ERA	IP	H	BB	SO	BPI	$
1992 Osceola A	3	0	2.63	41	37	8	30	1.10	
1992 Jackson AA	9	0	3.54	114	114	26	99	1.23	
1992 Tucson AAA	0	0	1.13	8	11	1	2	1.50	
1993 Tucson AAA	6	0	3.83	132	147	35	89	1.37	

WALLACE, B. J. - TL - Age 23

The Expos' top draft pick in 1992, Wallace had a tired shoulder that limited his work in 1993. He also had some control problems. If healthy, he could move up quickly.

WALLACE, DEREK - TR - Age 22

Wallace followed Jack McDowell, Robin Ventura, Alex Fernandez, and Frank Thomas as Larry Himes' number one draft pick (his first with the Cubs in 1992). So far, it looks like expecting five All-Stars in a row might be stretching it. Wallace is very young, very raw and has a long way to go as a pitcher. He has average major league stuff right now.

WALTON, BRUCE -TR - Age 31

For someone who has appeared in the major leagues both of the last two years, Walton is about as close to a career minor leaguer as you'll ever find. Walton has spent the last five years in Triple-A with just 28.2 major league innings and a career 8.16 ERA to show for it.

	W	SV	ERA	IP	H	BB	SO	BPI	$
1992 Oakland AL	0	0	9.90	10	17	3	7	2.00	-
1993 Ottawa AAA	4	16	1.05	42	32	8	40	0.93	
1993 Montreal NL	0	0	9.53	6	11	3	0	2.69	-
1994 *Projection* >>>	0	0	6.00	8	13	2	3	1.88	-

WARD, DUANE - TR - Age 29

Ward silenced critics who said he wasn't ready to inherit Tom Henke's old role. He responded with a Toronto-record 45 saves last year. Ward's fastball is the best it has ever been. During the World Series, it was clocked at 97 miles per hour . . . and he wasn't really throwing as hard as he can. His control has improved and he's one of the top five closers in baseball. Imagine Rob Dibble in his prime with better control and a stable mental approach. Enter Duane Ward.

	W	SV	ERA	IP	H	BB	SO	BPI	$
1992 Toronto AL	7	12	1.95	101	76	39	103	1.13	19
1993 Toronto AL	2	45	2.13	72	49	25	97	1.04	43
1994 *Projection* >>>	4	40	2.49	84	61	31	95	1.09	42

WARING, JIM - TR - Age 24
An outstanding control pitcher who led all pitchers in the Astros organization with a 1.96 ERA at Single-A in 1992, Waring missed almost all of 1993 with arm problems. He needs a strong recovery in 1994 to regain his status as a prospect.

	W	SV	ERA	IP	H	BB	SO	BPI	$
1992 Burlington A	11	0	2.21	122	100	19	104	0.97	
1993 Osceola A	1	0	2.60	17	16	6	16	1.29	

WASSENAAR, ROB - TR - Age 28
Has produced well at every minor league level, but doesn't figure prominently in anyone's major league plans.

	W	SV	ERA	IP	H	BB	SO	BPI	$
1992 Portland AAA	6	5	3.50	90	96	33	60	1.43	
1993 Phoenix AAA	2	2	6.56	70	117	24	50	2.01	

WATSON, ALLEN - TL - Age 23
Watson came up from Triple-A at midseason and won his first six major league decisions, then finished the year with seven straight losses. His fastball is average, but he has an outstanding slider and changeup. Watson showed great poise and appears to have the talent and mental toughness to become a big winner. He'll probably begin 1994 in the Cardinals rotation.

	W	SV	ERA	IP	H	BB	SO	BPI	$
1992 Louisville AAA	1	0	1.46	12	8	5	9	1.08	
1993 St. Louis NL	6	0	4.60	86	90	28	49	1.37	0
1994 *Projection* >>>	12	0	4.1	156	161	50	87	1.35	3

WATSON, RON - TR - Age 25
Watson is a big hard thrower who has been going along with about a strikeout per inning for four minor league season ... and almost as many walks. If he ever begins to throw strikes consistently, he will move up rapidly. He's a career relief specialist.

WAYNE, GARY - TL - Age 31
A veteran lefty-lefty matchup specialist, Wayne had a team high 65 appearances for the Rockies in 1993. Baylor used him to turn the batters around late in the game.

	W	SV	ERA	IP	H	BB	SO	BPI	$
1992 Minnesota AL	3	0	2.63	48	46	19	29	1.35	1
1993 Colorado NL	5	1	5.05	62	68	26	49	1.51	-
1994 *Projection* >>>	4	1	4.40	53	55	22	39	1.46	-

WEATHERS, DAVE - TR - Age 24
Weathers has the most upside potential of all Marlins' starters. He kept his ERA below 4.00 in the dreaded Pacific Coast League (no easy feat), and had a strikeout/walk ratio of nearly 3 to 1. In his September callup, he was hot and cold, but dominant at times. A lock for the 1994 rotation, he could quickly develop into the Marlins' number one or two starter.

	W	SV	ERA	IP	H	BB	SO	BPI	$
1993 Florida NL	2	0	5.12	46	57	13	34	1.55	-
1994 *Projection* >>>	1	0	5.21	30	37	10	23	1.57	-

WEGLARZ, JOHN - TR - Age 23
Another of Kansas City's hard-throwing young pitching prospects. Had some shoulder trouble in '93.

WEGMAN, BILL - TR - Age 31
One of the most disappointing pitchers of 1993, Wegman has always survived on the strength of fine control. Wegman is never going to be overpowering, but he is likely to be overlooked by many in 1994, and he is not too far away from being as successful as he was at his peak a few years ago.

	W	SV	ERA	IP	H	BB	SO	BPI	$
1992 Milwaukee AL	13	0	3.20	261	251	55	127	1.17	18
1993 Milwaukee AL	4	0	4.48	121	135	34	50	1.41	1
1994 *Projection* >>>	10	0	3.90	170	173	41	77	1.26	8

WEGMANN, TOM - TR - Age 25
A strikeout pitcher who relies on a changeup, Wegmann will most likely start 1994 at AAA Norfolk. Given the current state of the Mets' pitching, it's a small wonder Wegmann didn't reach the majors last season.

WELCH, BOB - TR - Age 37
The American League hit .310 against Welch in 1993. Over the past two seasons he has a strikeout to walk ratio of 110/99, and last year he struck out only 3.4 batters per nine innings. He is 37 years old; since his Cy Young season in 1990 he has averaged fewer than 11 wins a year. He says he is still pitching well, but his performance suggests otherwise.

	W	SV	ERA	IP	H	BB	SO	BPI	$
1992 Oakland AL	11	0	3.27	123	114	43	47	1.27	7
1993 Oakland AL	9	0	5.29	167	208	56	63	1.59	-
1994 *Projection* >>>	10	0	4.72	159	181	54	62	1.48	-

WELLS, BOB - TR - Age 27
Marooned at Single-A for the better part of three seasons, Wells was promoted to AAA Scranton late in 1993. He held his own, fashioning a 2.79 ERA in 19 innings. He's far too old to have just surfaced at Triple-A and has little chance of making it in the majors.

WELLS, DAVID - TL - Age 30
Wells began last season with a sharp 9-1 record, but later came down with some arm problems. He also has a history of slipping late in the season. Even if he stays with the Tigers, Sparky Anderson says Wells may not be in the rotation.

	W	SV	ERA	IP	H	BB	SO	BPI	$
1992 Toronto AL	7	2	5.40	120	138	36	62	1.45	-
1993 Detroit AL	11	0	4.19	187	183	42	139	1.20	11
1994 *Projection* >>>	10	1	4.39	168	171	41	105	1.26	6

WENDELL, TURK - TR - Age 26
Maybe he should try rubbing some licorice or toothpaste on the baseball. The flaky righthander has a good changeup and sinker but little idea of how to pitch, particularly when his stuff is not razor sharp. He's still young enough to develop into a role player for the Cubs and could get a few starts in 1994.

	W	SV	ERA	IP	H	BB	SO	BPI	$
1992 Iowa AAA	2	0	1.44	25	17	15	12	1.28	
1993 Chicago NL	1	0	4.37	23	24	8	15	1.44	-
1994 *Projection* >>>	2	0	4.30	40	45	11	20	1.40	-

WERTZ, BILL - TR - Age 27
A 31st-round pick in 1989, Wertz plodded through the Indians' system, finally striking paydirt in 1993. With good velocity he continued to strike out a batter per inning at the major league level. His upside potential is limited, but he clearly can contribute at the major league level as a middle reliever.

	W	SV	ERA	IP	H	BB	SO	BPI	$
1993 Cleveland AL	2	0	3.62	60	54	32	53	1.45	1
1994 *Projection* >>>	2	0	4.02	72	74	30	42	1.44	0

WEST, DAVID - TL - Age 29
West had a pretty good season in 1993, holding opponents to a .194 average. His performance deteriorated as his body weight went up; West seemed to be on the Shelly Winters diet last year. He trained with Mackie Shilstone in the off season, with fellow Phils John Kruk and Ben Rivera. If he's in shape, he can really help somebody as a setup man, despite control problems.

	W	SV	ERA	IP	H	BB	SO	BPI	$
1992 Portland AAA	7	0	4.44	103	88	65	87	1.48	
1992 Minnesota AL	1	0	6.99	28	32	20	19	1.83	-
1993 Philadelphia NL	6	3	2.92	86	60	51	87	1.29	7
1994 *Projection* >>>	4	2	3.60	67	56	37	56	1.39	2

WESTON, MICKEY - TR - Age 33
Produced ERA's of 2.23, 2.09, and 1.98 in three years of Triple-A competition 1988-1990, but failed in repeated trials with Orioles, Blue Jays, Phils and Mets. Now just a faded prospect.

	W	SV	ERA	IP	H	BB	SO	BPI	$
1992 Philadelphia NL	0	0	12.27	3	7	1	0	2.18	-
1993 New York NL	0	0	7.94	6	11	1	2	2.31	-

WETTELAND, JOHN - TR - Age 27
In just two seasons, Wetteland has established himself as one of the game's premier closers. He has all the ingredients with a mid 90s fastball, aggressive approach and unfailing confidence. Wetteland blew just three saves after the first week of May and was the National League pitcher of the month in September. He fanned 113 in 85 innings and set a club record with 43 saves. Wetteland has come a long way from when he was a struggling young starter with Los Angeles. He figures to be one of the game's star relievers for a long time.

	W	SV	ERA	IP	H	BB	SO	BPI	$
1992 Montreal NL	4	37	2.92	83	64	36	99	1.20	34
1993 Montreal NL	9	43	1.37	85	58	28	113	1.01	47
1994 *Projection* >>>	5	40	2.51	77	54	29	95	1.08	43

WHISENANT, MATT - TL - Age 24
This 24-year-old may be the hardest thrower in the Marlins organization. If his control continues to improve he will move up in the farm system rapidly.

	W	SV	ERA	IP	H	BB	SO	BPI	$
1992 Spartanburg A	11	0	3.23	150	117	85	151	1.34	
1993 Kane County A	2	0	4.69	71	68	56	74	1.74	

WHITE, GABE - TL - Age 22
A hard thrower with great stamina and excellent control, he finished last season at Triple-A and is on the fast track to the majors. White was selected with the compensation pick for losing Mark Langston to free agency. He led the Expos farm system with 187 strikeouts in 1992, then was a Double-A All-Star at Harrisburg last year. The Expos will likely give him a little more polish at Triple-A in 1994 but he could be in Montreal the first time a starter breaks down.

	W	SV	ERA	IP	H	BB	SO	BPI	$
1992 Rockford A	14	0	2.84	187	148	61	176	1.12	
1993 Harrisburg AA	7	0	2.16	100	80	28	80	1.08	

WHITEHURST, WALLY - TR - Age 29
Whitehurst is a direct worker who throws strikes and gets the ball in play. He came to the Padres in the Tony Fernandez trade but was injured until mid season. Starting 19 games, Whitehurst was hit relatively hard, allowing opponents a .276 batting average, but managed a reasonable ERA. Don't look for many victories, but Whitehurst will likely be a Padre starter at the opening of the year. He's a better pitcher in middle relief and has good control.

	W	SV	ERA	IP	H	BB	SO	BPI	$
1992 New York NL	3	0	3.62	97	99	33	70	1.36	-
1993 San Diego NL	4	0	3.83	106	109	30	57	1.32	2
1994 *Projection* >>>	5	0	3.80	117	121	33	70	1.32	3

WHITESIDE, MATT -TR - Age 26
Whiteside had a terrible stretch in the middle of the season, but it was due to overuse, which actually put him on the disabled list. A minor leagur closer, he can be a decent setup man as long as he doesn't pitch more than three times a week. Could split time with Carpenter as the setup guy for Henke.

	W	SV	ERA	IP	H	BB	SO	BPI	$
1992 Texas AL	1	4	1.93	28	26	11	13	1.32	3
1993 Texas AL	2	1	4.32	73	78	23	39	1.38	1
1994 *Projection* >>>	2	2	3.94	52	54	17	27	1.37	2

WICKANDER, KEVIN - TL - Age 29

Wickander was obviously affected by the loss of his friend Steve Olin in the spring training boating tragedy. In 1993 he was used mainly to face one lefty hitter, but was not particularly effective.

	W	SV	ERA	IP	H	BB	SO	BPI	$
1992 Cleveland AL	2	1	3.07	41	39	28	38	1.63	-
1993 Cleveland AL	0	0	4.15	9	15	3	3	2.20	-
1993 Cincinnati NL	1	0	6.75	25	32	19	20	2.03	-
1994 *Projection* >>>	1	0	4.95	33	40	21	22	1.86	-

WICKMAN, BOB - TR - Age 25

Had a good year going from rotation to bullpen. Started out the season 6-0 in his first nine starts. He could start, relieve, or have a utility role. He's still young enough to make the changes and perform well.

	W	SV	ERA	IP	H	BB	SO	BPI	$
1992 New York AL	6	0	4.11	50	51	20	21	1.41	0
1993 New York AL	14	4	4.63	140	156	69	70	1.61	4
1994 *Projection* >>>	8	2	4.52	120	128	52	66	1.50	3

WILKINS, DEAN - TR - Age 27

A second round pick in 1986, Wilkins quickly became a top minor league reliever but failed (7.84 ERA) in three trials with the Cubs and Astros.

WILLIAMS, BRIAN - TR - Age 25

Williams lost out to Darryl Kile in competition for the fifth starter position, making only five starts and spending most of the year in the bullpen with mixed results. He seems to be better suited to starting and will again be a candidate for the number five slot. An excellent athlete with a strong arm, Williams may yet become a quality major league pitcher.

	W	SV	ERA	IP	H	BB	SO	BPI	$
1992 Houston NL	7	0	3.92	96	92	42	54	1.39	-
1993 Houston NL	4	3	4.83	82	76	38	56	1.39	1
1994 *Projection* >>>	4	3	4.93	82	76	38	62	1.39	-

WILLIAMS, MIKE - TR - Age 25

Over the past two seasons he has gone 18-3 and posted a 2.65 ERA at Triple-A with pinpoint control, but as soon as he's called up to the majors he starts nibbling. An offspeed pitcher, he must be very precise to be effective. Phils' need for bullpen help will give him a chance to compete for a bullpen spot.

	W	SV	ERA	IP	H	BB	SO	BPI	$
1992 Philadelphia NL	1	0	5.34	28	29	7	5	1.26	-
1993 Philadelphia NL	1	0	5.29	51	50	22	33	1.41	-
1994 *Projection* >>>	1	0	5.30	39	38	15	21	1.37	-

WILLIAMS, MITCH - TL - Age 29

The clock finally struck midnight for the Phils' erratic closer during the World Series. He has walked an amazing 6.77 batters per nine innings over the course of his career; his ratio climbed to an unsightly 1.61 in 1993. Conventional wisdom might suggest that since he got 43 saves, he must be good. However, a trained seal could have saved 43 games for the Phils, considering the manner in which Williams was used. He was used for more than an inning just once all year, and he inherited only 10 runners all season (five scored), not including the ghastly postseason. His future as a closer is in doubt, though moving to the Astrodome can't hurt.

	W	SV	ERA	IP	H	BB	SO	BPI	$
1992 Philadelphia NL	5	29	3.78	81	69	64	74	1.64	20
1993 Philadelphia NL	3	43	3.34	62	56	44	60	1.61	33
1994 *Projection* >>>	5	33	3.37	70	59	52	67	1.59	27

WILLIAMS, TODD - TR - Age 23

A submarine-style reliever, Williams was voted the Dodgers' minor league pitcher of the year in 1992. One look at his ratio raises concern, however. Williams got a shot to save games at the Triple-A level in 1993 and was successful in that role. Well, successful like Mitch Williams..

	W	SV	ERA	IP	H	BB	SO	BPI	$
1992 San Antonio AA	7	13	3.48	44	47	23	35	1.59	
1993 Albuquerque AAA	5	21	4.99	70	87	31	56	1.68	

WILLIAMS, WOODY - TR - Age 27

Williams made a solid contribution in his first year with a major league club. This right hander appeared in thirty games with the Jays last year, averaging just over per inning an appearance. He is extremely wild, but improving, and might have an outside shot of landing a regular job in the bullpen this year.

	W	SV	ERA	IP	H	BB	SO	BPI	$
1993 Toronto AL	3	0	4.38	37	40	22	24	1.68	-
1994 Projection >>>	2	0	4.38	22	24	13	10	1.68	-

WILLIAMSON, MARK - TR - Age 34

Mark Williamson is an effective long and middle reliever who would benefit from a change to another team. For some reason, Orioles Manager Johnny Oates didn't use him as much as previous managers did. He can be effective if he just throws his fastball and he doesn't.

	W	SV	ERA	IP	H	BB	SO	BPI	$
1992 Baltimore AL	0	1	0.96	19	16	10	14	1.39	0
1993 Baltimore AL	7	0	4.91	88	106	25	45	1.49	0
1994 Projection >>>	5	1	4.52	66	76	22	37	1.49	-

WILLIS, CARL - TR - Age 33

Middle reliever Carl Willis is a good example of traditional stats not telling the whole story. He let a lot of inherited runners score, hurting other pitchers ERA's but not his own, and he had four blown saves.

	W	SV	ERA	IP	H	BB	SO	BPI	$
1992 Minnesota AL	7	1	2.72	79	73	11	45	1.06	8
1993 Minnesota AL	3	5	3.10	58	56	17	44	1.26	7
1994 Projection >>>	5	4	2.9	68	64	15	45	1.16	10

WILLIS, TRAVIS - TR - Age 25

The Cubs' Double-A stopper, Willis finished second in the league in saves and made the All-Star team in midseason. Given his age and overall unimpressive track record, he's not likely to be a part of the Cubs future.

WILSON, STEVE - TL - Age 29

Wilson no longer has the good movement on his fastball that he needs to succeed. Used strictly as a lefty situational reliever, Wilson has only a minor role.

	W	SV	ERA	IP	H	BB	SO	BPI	$
1992 Los Angeles NL	2	0	4.18	66	74	29	54	1.55	-
1993 Los Angeles NL	1	1	4.56	26	30	14	23	1.75	-
1994 Projection >>>	1	1	4.25	38	42	18	25	1.59	-

WILSON, TREVOR - TL - Age 27

1993 was another injury plagued season for Wilson, as he was disabled with sholder tendinitis. He always seems on the verge of greatness, despite never having an ERA lower than 3.56 in the majors. It would be interesting to see what Wilson could do if he stayed healthy. He could win 15 games if he put it all together.

	W	SV	ERA	IP	H	BB	SO	BPI	$
1992 San Francisco NL	8	0	4.21	154	152	64	88	1.40	-
1993 San Francisco NL	7	0	3.60	110	110	40	57	1.36	3
1994 Projection >>>	9	0	3.81	132	129	51	75	1.36	4

WISHNEVSKI, ROB - TR - Age 27

A starter for five seasons in the Toronto organization. The Brewers moved him to the bullpen in '91. After a fast start last season, he tailed off. Milwaukee needs bullpen help, so Wishnevski has a chance to reach the majors in '94.

WITASICK, GERALD- TR - Age 22

The Cardinals' second-round pick in last year's draft from Maryland-Baltimore County, this big righthander has a live fastball and a sharp slider. If he develops a changeup, he could take a quick route to the majors.

	W	SV	ERA	IP	H	BB	SO	BPI	$
1993 Savannah A	4	0	4.12	68	65	19	74	1.23	

WITT, BOBBY - TR - Age 29

Witt's control has improved since his earlier years. Unfortunately, Witt is no longer the same potential star that he seemed in his earlier years. He won 14 games with a last-place team in 1993, and he was clearly the ace of the Oakland staff by the end of '93.

	W	SV	ERA	IP	H	BB	SO	BPI	$
1992 Texas AL	9	0	4.46	161	152	95	100	1.53	-
1992 Oakland AL	1	0	3.41	31	31	19	25	1.60	-
1993 Oakland AL	14	0	4.21	220	226	91	131	1.44	6
1994 Projection >>>	12	0	4.15	199	200	85	124	1.43	1

WITT, MIKE - TR - Age 33

Had elbow surgery in July 1991 to reconstruct a ligament. If the Yankees hadn't given up Dave Winfield to get him, they probably would have given up on Witt by now.

	W	SV	ERA	IP	H	BB	SO	BPI	$
1992 Yankees R	1	0	0.00	12	7	2	13	0.75	
1993 New York AL	3	0	5.27	41	39	22	30	1.49	-
1994 Projection >>>	2	0	5.37	25	24	13	15	1.49	-

WOHLERS, MARK - TR - Age 24

Braves fans have been breathlessly anticipating the full time arrival of Wohlers as a full time reliever in Atlanta. He seems to have finally broken through to the majors, but isn't being used in the closer role as expected. Instead the Braves started him out at AAA Richmond, where he took out his frustration at not making the Opening Day roster on opponent hitters; Wohlers struck out 39 in 29 innings and posted a 1.84 ERA to get back to Atlanta for good. He's probably seen the last of the minor leagues and could be moved into a closer or co-closer role at any time. Wohlers' future is still bright.

	W	SV	ERA	IP	H	BB	SO	BPI	$
1992 Richmond AAA	0	9	3.93	34	32	17	33	1.43	
1992 Atlanta NL	1	4	2.55	35	28	14	17	1.19	3
1993 Atlanta NL	6	0	4.50	48	37	22	45	1.23	1
1994 Projection >>>	4	10	3.94	41	31	19	33	1.23	9

WOODSON, KERRY -TR - Age 24

He missed much of last season due to injuries. Anyone who makes it to the majors at his young age has to be good. In 1990, he was 8-6 with a 3.03 ERA at single-A. The next year he was only 4-6 but kept his ERA at 3.06 while moving up a level. Despite the two quality seasons as a starter, the Mariners moved him to relief last year. He continued to excel and should be a major league pitcher in 1994.

	W	SV	ERA	IP	H	BB	SO	BPI	$
1992 Seattle AL	0	0	3.29	13	12	11	6	1.68	-

WORRELL, TIM - TR - Age 26

Worrell can safely say that he had a better year than his more famous and better paid brother Todd, even if Tim won only 2 of his 16 starts. He's a genuine prospect based upon his two year rise from A-ball to the big leagues. Hard throwing Worrell tossed a no-hitter in Las Vegas in 1992 and figures to be in the Padre rotation with modest success in 1994.

	W	SV	ERA	IP	H	BB	SO	BPI	$
1993 San Diego NL	2	0	4.92	101	104	43	52	1.47	-
1994 Projection >>>	7	0	4.60	120	124	52	62	1.46	1

WORRELL, TODD - TR - Age 34

Worrell's comeback from serious arm problems lasted about a week before he returned to the disabled list for most of the year. He showed flashes of his old form, but is likely to be relegated to a setup role in the future.

	W	SV	ERA	IP	H	BB	SO	BPI	$
1992 St. Louis NL	5	3	2.11	64	45	25	64	1.09	7
1993 Los Angeles NL	1	5	6.05	39	46	11	31	1.49	0
1994 *Projection* >>>	2	4	4.27	42	40	15	36	1.32	2

WRIGHT, JAMEY - TR - Age 19

The Rockies changed their draft strategy somewhat in 1993, moving away from the college pitchers and making this high school pitcher their first choice.Wright throws a high 80's fastball, a slider and a changeup.

WUNSCH, KELLY - TL - Age 21

The 6'5" Wunsch made a bigger impression in the Cape Cod League in '92 than he did at Texas A&M. Based on his summer league play, Milwaukee made him its second of four first-round draft picks last year. He signed for a $400,000 bonus.

YAUGHN, KIP - TR - Age 24

Expansion's 24th overall draft pick, Yaugh was sidelined for much of 1993.

YOCKEY, MARK - TL - Age 25

Yockey cut his ERA in half and struck out three times as many batters as he walked in 1993, but still didn't get promoted to Triple-A. Yockey could only get to the majors in the event of an injury epidemic on the Giants staff (it's happened before).

YORK, CHARLES - TL - Age 23

A big guy (6'4", 240 pounds) who overpowered batters in the Sally League.

YOUNG, ANTHONY - TR - Age 28

Aside from setting the losing streak record, Young had a good season. He uses a sinker/slider to get groundballs and he depends on strong defense, a luxury the Mets didn't have in 1993. Look for Young to pitch in long relief and start a few games if needed. One problem is that his best pitch, a sinker that drops below the knees, is not a strike. Patient hitters can usually get to him.

	W	SV	ERA	IP	H	BB	SO	BPI	$
1992 New York NL	2	15	4.17	121	134	31	64	1.37	9
1993 New York NL	1	3	3.77	100	103	42	62	1.45	1
1994 *Projection* >>>	5	1	3.80	110	112	42	65	1.40	4

YOUNG, CURT - TL - Age 33

Young is 34 years old, injury prone, and hasn't been good for six years.

	W	SV	ERA	IP	H	BB	SO	BPI	$
1992 Kansas City-New York	4	0	3.99	68	80	17	20	1.43	0
1993 Oakland AL	1	0	4.30	15	14	6	4	1.41	-

YOUNG, MATT - TL - Age 35

A promising talent several years ago, Young has been consistently bad since 1991.

	W	SV	ERA	IP	H	BB	SO	BPI	$
1992 Boston AL	0	0	4.58	70	69	42	57	1.57	-
1993 Cleveland AL	1	0	5.21	74	75	57	65	1.78	-
1994 *Projection* >>>	1	0	4.90	50	51	30	36	1.60	-

YOUNG, PETE - TR - Age 26

Young spent most of last season as a middle reliever with AAA Ottawa. He's a mediocre finesse pitcher and is a marginal prospect.

	W	SV	ERA	IP	H	BB	SO	BPI	$
1992 Montreal NL	0	0	3.98	20	18	9	11	1.33	-
1993 Ottawa AAA	4	1	3.73	72	63	33	46	1.33	
1993 Montreal NL	1	0	3.38	5	4	0	3	0.78	-

ZIMMERMAN, MIKE - TR - Age 25

Like many of the Pirates' highly touted pitching prospects, Zimmerman was forced to take a step back last year. After missing out on a chance to win a major league bullpen job in spring training, Zimmerman also bombed at AAA Buffalo and was demoted to Double-A. He eventually worked his way back to Triple-A. He's no longer on the fast track, but the Pirates still believe he could help in middle relief, probably in 1995.

	W	SV	ERA	IP	H	BB	SO	BPI	$
1993 Buffalo AAA	3	1	4.08	46	45	28	32	1.52	

ZOLECKI, MIKE - TR - Age 22

Hard-throwing Zolecki struck out 78 in just 55 innings for short-season Single-A Bend, splitting time between the rotation and the bullpen. He'll need to show more of the same kind of stuff at higher levels to remain a good prospect.

	W	SV	ERA	IP	H	BB	SO	BPI	$
1993 Bend A	4	1	4.42	55	47	30	78	1.40	

THE 1993 DRAFT

In a book about the population of professional baseball players, it is appropriate to give special recognition to each year's new arrivals. To get the most thoughtful evaluation of the latest crop of youngsters who signed pro contracts, we went to the man best-qualified to make those evaluations, Baseball America's Managing Editor, Jim Callis.

Jim selected two "All-Star" teams from the 1993 amateur draft, one for the AL and one for the NL. Players were selected on the basis of likely speed to reach the major leagues and expected impact after arrival. Without further ado (drum roll) ... Our 1993 Major League Draft All-Star teams' selections and analysis by Jim Callis

AMERICAN LEAGUE

Catcher: Todd Greene, Angels

The 411th player drafted overall, from Georgia Southern University, Greene wins our award partly because 1993 wasn't a good year for American League franchises to sign catchers. The first four selected -- Jason Varitek (Twins), Tucker Barr (Athletics), Dennis Twombley (White Sox), and Thad Busby (Blue Jays) -- didn't sign with the teams that drafted them. Greene, the third-leading home run hitter in NCAA history, may be one of the biggest sleepers in the '93 draft. He was named Baseball America's 1993 Short-Season Player of the Year after leading all short-season hitters with 71 RBI. As a converted outfielder, he will need a while to make it to California.

First Base: Ryan McGuire, Red Sox

McGuire led all NCAA Division I players with 26 homers in 1993, and continued to hit for power (.324, 12 doubles, four home runs) while making his pro debut at Winter Haven in the upper-level Class A Florida State League. A slick fielder sometimes compared to former Dodgers Gold Glove first baseman Wes Parker, McGuire shouldn't need too much time in the minors. He was the 79th pick overall, from UCLA.

Second Base: Jason McDonald, Athletics

Drafted 125th, from the University of Houston, McDonald is a former wide receiver at Sacramento City College and Houston. He has speed to burn. He stole 22 bases in 35 games at short-season Southern Oregon, batting .295 in the process. Like McGuire, McDonald also plays good defense, which will help him rise to Oakland quickly.

Third Base: Mike Bell, Rangers

Bell is the son of former major league All-Star and Gold Glove winner Buddy Bell, and has been compared to his father, both offensively and defensively. The latest product of Cincinnati's Moeller High, which also has produced Barry Larkin and Ken Griffey Jr., Bell batted .317 and led the Rookie-level Gulf Coast League with 73 hits and 107 total bases. He was the 30th pick in 1993's draft.

Shortstop: Alex Rodriguez, Mariners

The number one pick overall in 1993, and the recipient of a $1 million signing bonus, Rodriguez is probably the best and most advanced high school prospect since Griffey. Though he has yet to play an inning of professional baseball, Rodriguez could reach the Kingdome as early as 1995. He can hit, hit for power, run, field and throw, a five-tool rarity among shortstops. He projects as a Cal Ripken type with more speed and a better arm, though perhaps a bit less durability.

Outfield: Trot Nixon, Red Sox

Nixon was considered unsignable because of a scholarship to play quarterback for North Carolina State, but Boston landed him for a club-record $890,000 bonus. Noted for his intensity, Nixon was considered the best pure hitter among the high school crop available in the draft, and he has legitimate power potential. Like Rodriguez, he shouldn't require too much time in the minors. Nixon was picked seventh, from Wilmington, NC.

Outfield: Torii Hunter, Twins

Though he batted just .190 and didn't hit a homer in the Gulf Coast League, Hunter is a classic center fielder with a power-speed combination. A bit raw as a player, Hunter will be given plenty of time to develop. He's a product of Pine Bluff (Arkansas) High School, one of the nation's top high school programs. He was the 20th player selected in 1993.

Outfield: Todd Dunn, Brewers

A former linebacker at Georgia Tech, Dunn is another top athlete with power-speed skills. He hit .307 with 11 doubles and 10 home runs in 150 at bats in the Rookie-level Pioneer League. His 450-foot monster blasts were the talk of the league. At age 23 one of the oldest players in the draft, Dunn will be placed on Milwaukee's fast track. He was the 35th pick in '93, from the University of North Florida.

Starting Pitcher: Jeff Granger, Royals

The fifth overall pick, from Texas A&M, Granger already has pitched in the majors as part of his contract, and his current 27.00 big league ERA will shrink dramatically in the future. Also a quarterback while at Texas A&M, Granger has exceptional velocity for a lefthander and already has three major league quality pitches (fastball, slider, changeup). He'll have an outside chance to make the Kansas City roster in spring training.

Relief Pitcher: Jay Powell, Orioles

Powell slumped when he was put in Mississippi State's starting rotation near the end of the 1993 season, but Baltimore was more than happy to take him with the 19th overall selection. Powell had one of the better fastballs available in the draft, and his selection became more important when Orioles closer Gregg Olson went down with elbow problems in August. After striking out 29 in 28 innings at Class A Albany, Powell headed to the Australian Baseball League to accelerate his development.

NATIONAL LEAGUE

Catcher: John Roskos, Marlins

Roskos may not remain a catcher as he moves up the majors, but oh, can he hit. He twice led New Mexico high schools in hitting and never struck out in his prep career. After signing, he hit nine home runs in a batting practice session at Joe Robbie Stadium, including one shot over the clock in left field. Roskos signed late, and went 7-for-40 in a brief Gulf Coast League stint. He was the 69th pick in the draft, from Rio Rancho.

First Base: Derrek Lee, Padres

The son of Leon Lee and the nephew of Leron Lee, sluggers who made their marks in Japan, Derrek won't have to travel across the Pacific to make an impression. Possessor of one of the most powerful high school bats available in the draft, Lee rejected the chance to go out for North Carolina's defending national champion basketball team. And though only 18, he held his own after a late-season promotion to the fast-paced Class A California League, batting .274 with seven extra-base hits in 73 at bats. He was the 14th pick in 1993, from Sacramento.

Second Base: Derek Swafford, Pirates

In 1993, as usual, second base wasn't the best showcase position for prospects. Fact is, most major league second basemen have moved there from other positions such as shortstop. Swafford, a converted outfielder, is a good athlete with above-average, speed but he may need some time to develop after batting .190 in the Gulf Coast League. He appeared on NBC's Today Show after the draft, chronicling how his life had changed dramatically after he left a broken home and was taken in by Dr. Ralph Wilson, who runs a sports-medicine practice. Swafford excelled both academically and athletically under Wilson's guidance, and he was offered a football scholarship by the prestigious Northwestern program. He was the 94th pick, from Ventura, California,

Third Base: Brad Fullmer, Expos

Fullmer was a second-round steal (the 60th pick) because most teams thought he would follow through on his intention to attend Stanford. His $417,500 bonus was a record for a second-rounder, but he earned it with a batting stroke compared to George Brett's. Fullmer has a tremendous makeup. Yet to make his pro debut, he is expected to rush through Montreal's farm system.

Shortstop: Kevin Orie, Cubs

Orie has excellent power for a shortstop, a long-range problem position for Chicago since Shawon Dunston was injured. Orie was undeterred by debuting at Class A Rockford, batting .269 with 17 doubles and seven home runs in 238 at bats. He may eventually move to third base. Orie was the 29th pick overall, from Indiana University.

Outfield: Brooks Kieschnick, Cubs

The 10th overall pick, from the University of Texas, Kieschnick was Baseball America's 1993 College Player of the Year. He was a two-way star at Texas, pitching and hitting, who will now concentrate on batting as a pro. His ideal position is somewhat unclear, but his bat isn't. The best pure college hitter available in the draft, Kieschnick offers plenty of lefthanded power and batted .341 in 91 Double-A at bats. A tremendous competitor, he won't let himself fail.

Outfield: Chris Schwab, Expos

Though he didn't homer in 218 Gulf Coast League at bats or in the instructional league, Schwab was considered the best high school power hitter in the draft. After focusing primarily on football and hockey in high school, Schwab will be given plenty of time to develop. He was the 18th pick overall, from high school in Eagan, Minnesota.

Outfield: Charles Peterson, Pirates

Peterson was South Carolina's 1992 high school football player of the year as a quarterback and an all-state basketball player. He may have been the best all-around athlete in the draft. A solid defensive center fielder, he has plenty of speed and is expected to hit for power. He batted .303 with 15 extra-base hits and eight steals in 188 Gulf Coast League at bats. Peterson was the 22nd player taken in 1993.

Starting Pitcher: Kirk Presley, Mets

A third cousin of Elvis, Presley will constantly be reminded of his connection to The King. But he has enough talent to earn some fame of his own after signing late with New York, getting a $900,000 bonus to forego a baseball/football opportunity at Mississippi State. An outstanding athlete with a live arm and a fluid delivery, Presley already has three solid pitches (fastball, curveball, changeup). He was the eighth player drafted, from Tupelo, Mississippi.

Relief Pitcher: Darren Dreifort, Dodgers

The number two pick overall, from Wichita State University, Dreifort was the winner of the 1993 Golden Spikes Award as the nation's best amateur player. He topped all 1993 signees with a $1.3 million bonus. A power hitter of note last season, Dreifort will stick to pitching for Los Angeles and could become the Dodgers' closer as early as 1994. His fastball and slider are tremendous pitches, and his competitiveness and unselfishness make him even better.

Obviously, ranking players from an amateur draft requires some speculation about how these players will develop as they mature. Many will grow taller and stronger; others won't. Many will learn quickly, while others will keep working on the same lessons for years. The draft is far from an exact science. Consider that Mike Mussina lasted until the 20th pick of the 1990 draft, after such luminaries as Tony Clark and Ron Walden had been selected. Manny Ramirez and Cliff Floyd, two of the brightest prospects in the game, went only as high as the 13th and 14th picks in the 1991 draft. One third of the first round picks never even reach the major leagues, much less become stars.

To keep you up to date on the progress of those drafted before 1993, here is out 1990-1992 First Round Pick Report Card, starting on the next page.

FIRST ROUND REPORT CARD: 1990-92

GRADING SCALE
A--Potential major league star.
B--Potential major league regular.
C--Potential major leaguer.
D--Major disappointment thus far.
F--Failure.

1990 DRAFT

1. Chipper Jones, SS, Braves	A
2. Tony Clark, OF, Tigers	D
3. Mike Lieberthal, C, Phillies	C
4. Alex Fernandez, RHP, White Sox	A
5. Kurt Miller, RHP, Pirates*	B
6. Marc Newfield, 1B-OF, Mariners	A
7. Dan Wilson, C, Reds*	B
8. Tim Costo, 1B, Indians*	B
9. Ron Walden, LHP, Dodgers	F
10. Carl Everett, OF, Yankees*	B
11. Shane Andrews, 3B, Expos	B
12. Todd Ritchie, RHP, Twins	C
13. Donovan Osborne, LHP, Cards	B
14. Todd Van Poppel, RHP, A's	A
15. Adam Hyzdu, OF, Giants	C
16. Dan Smith, LHP, Rangers	C
17. Jeromy Burnitz, OF, Mets	B
18. Aaron Holbert, SS, Cardinals	B
19. Eric Christopherson, C, Giants	C
20. Mike Mussina, RHP, Orioles	A
22. Steve Karsay, RHP, Blue Jays*	A
23. Lance Dickson, LHP, Cubs	C
24. Rondell White, OF, Expos	A
25. Robbie Beckett, LHP, Padres	D
26. Don Peters, RHP, Athletics	F

*NOTE: Miller now with Marlins, Wilson now with Mariners, Costo now with Reds, Everett now with Marlins, Karsay now with Athletics.

1991 DRAFT

1. Brien Taylor, LHP, Yankees	A
2. Mike Kelly, OF, Braves	B
3. David McCarty, 1B-OF, Twins	B
4. Dmitri Young, 3B, Cardinals	B
5. Kenny Henderson, RHP, Brewers	Did Not Sign
6. John Burke, RHP, Astros	Did Not Sign
7. Joe Vitiello, 1B-OF, Royals	B
8. Joey Hamilton, RHP, Padres	C
9. Mark Smith, OF, Orioles	B
10. Tyler Green, RHP, Phillies	B
11. Sean Estes, LHP, Mariners	D
12. Doug Glanville, OF, Cubs	B
13. Manny Ramirez, OF, Indians	A
14. Cliff Floyd, 1B, Expos	A
15. Tyrone Hill, LHP, Brewers	B
16. Shawn Green, OF, Blue Jays	B
17. Eduardo Perez, 1B-3B, Angels	B
18. Al Shirley, OF, Mets	F
19. Benji Gil, SS, Rangers	A
20. Calvin Reese, SS, Reds	B
21. Allen Watson, LHP, Cardinals	A
22. Brian Barber, RHP, Cardinals	B
23. Aaron Sele, RHP, Red Sox	A
24. Jon Farrell, c-OF, Pirates	C
25. Scott Ruffcorn, RHP, White Sox	B
26. Brent Gates, SS-2B, Athletics	B

1992 DRAFT

1. Phil Nevin, 3B, Astros	A
2. Paul Shuey, RHP, Indians	C
3. B.J. Wallace, LHP, Expos	B
4. Jeffrey Hammonds, OF, Orioles	A
5. Chad Mottola, OF, Reds	A
6. Derek Jeter, SS, Yankees	A
7. Calvin Murray, OF, Giants	B
8. Pete Janicki, RHP, Angels	D
9. Preston Wilson, SS-3B, Mets	A
10. Michael Tucker, SS-2B, Royals	A
11. Derek Wallace, RHP, Cubs	B
12. Kenny Felder, OF, Brewers	C
13. Chad McConnell, OF, Phillies	C
14. Ron Villone, LHP, Mariners	B
15. Sean Lowe, RHP, Cardinals	C
16. Rick Greene, RHP, Tigers	C
17. Jim Pittsley, RHP, Royals	B
18. Chris Roberts, LHP, Mets	B
19. Shannon Stewart, OF, Blue Jays	B
20. Benji Grigsby, RHP, Athletics	C
21. Jamie Arnold, RHP, Braves	B
22. Rick Helling, RHP, Rangers	A
23. Jason Kendall, C, Pirates	B
24. Eddie Pearson, 1B, White Sox	C
25. Todd Steverson, OF, Blue Jays	B
26. Dan Serafini, LHP, Twins	B
27. John Burke, RHP, Rockies	B
28. Charles Johnson, C, Marlins	A

WANTED: THE PERFECT DRAFT PICK

AGE 26 OR YOUNGER, WITH EXPERIENCE

1994 marks our fifth year telling you about the "Age 26" phenomenon. The goal is simply to find the perfect draft pick: a player who is going to rise in value in the coming season, exceeding anything he has done in the past, and perform at the star level -- and yet be undervalued on draft day. To find these players, we take advantage of three natural tendencies:

(1) Players who have been around the major leagues for a couple years or more don't attract the same attention as rookies and sophomores. After a player has two or seasons in the record books, there is an appearance that he has an "established" performance level. Fantasy leaguers tend to accept these established levels as good estimates of what will happen in the year to come.

(2) Hitters normally peak around age 27 or 28. At age 25 or 26 they are typically going through their years of biggest improvement. Not by coincidence, age 25 or 26 is also the year when most players first win major league jobs. Many of them thus get caught up in the annual hype about rookies -- but some go through that hype at younger ages.

(3) Players who become full-time major leaguers at younger ages, say 23 or 24, tend to become stars. The best athletes reach that point, earlier than other players, where their talent is good enough for the majors -- but that doesn't mean they must stop improving, just because they have made it in The Show. In fact, star players keep right on improving, just like their less-gifted colleagues, right up to age 27 or 28. The "perfect" draft pick is, therefore, a player who is not yet age 27 (and is thus still in his period of growth and improvement) but also a player who has been in the major leagues long enough to give an impression that he has reached an established level.

In our last three years, the three players who headed this annual list were Jay Bell (1991), Larry Walker (1992), and Jeff Bagwell (1993). In 1990 we gave an alphabetical listing with 16 recommendations; Ron Gant was my favorite pick on that year's list, but since that fact wasn't reflected here in ink, I won't ask you to accept him as part of the following evaluation of my "age 26 with experience" method to identify sleeping stars.

THE YEAR BEFORE AND THE YEAR AFTER

		BAVG	AB	H	HR	RBI	SB
Jay Bell:							
	1990	.254	583	148	7	52	10
	1991	.270	608	164	16	67	10
Larry Walker:							
	1991	.290	487	141	16	64	14
	1992	.301	528	159	23	93	18
Jeff Bagwell:							
	1992	.273	586	160	18	96	10
	1993	.320	535	171	20	88	13
Totals: the year before			1656	449	41	212	34
the year after			1671	494	59	248	41
Average: before		.271	552	150	14	71	11
after		.295	557	165	20	83	14

On average, the top pick from this list got a tiny increase in playing time, just five at bats, but delivered significantly more offense, raising his batting average 24 points, hitting six more home runs, driving in a dozen more than the year before he was selected, and stealing three more bases.

"Is that all?" you may ask. Well, consider that those stats would be enough to make the difference between first place and third place in many tight leagues, and consider also that each player in this study had in fact been around the major leagues playing regularly for a couple years or more, giving an appearance (to many people) of having already reached his peak.

Any fool can look at last year's rookie crop and identify several young players who are bound to do better (Kevin Young, Roberto Mejia, Wil Cordero, Jim Thome, Damion Easley, David McCarty -- you get the idea; it's easy. But it's harder to look at the population of "veterans" and see who's going to reach new high levels in the coming year, unless of course you know this simple method to look for the right combination of age and experience.

Now for 1994. Drum roll ...

1. ERIC ANTHONY, Astros OF: Anthony entered the 1993 season with a .210 career batting average. In parts of four major league seasons, the only stats he was accumulating quickly was strikeouts. With this background, his .249, 15 homer, 66 RBI season looks more encouraging. Anthony was a three-time minor league home run champion in 1987-88-89 and is just now coming into his own. He's still working on his swing; when he begins making more consistent contact, the power stats will roll in. One reason I like Anthony for 1994 is that so many Astros hitters are on this Age 26 With Experience list this year. Batting orders have a tendency to rise and fall together, and Houston's is going up in 1994.

2. DELINO DESHIELDS, Dodgers 2B: Deshields was held back by a thumb injury in 1993, adding to the likelihood that he will be underrated in 1994 drafts. Normally I don't like injury rehab cases for this blue chip list, but Deshields' thumb won't bother his speed any, and that is where his value lies, especially for us stat leaguers.

3. TRAVIS FRYMAN, Tigers 3B: Defensive woes at shortstop distracted Fryman in 1993. In 1994 he is going to play third base exclusively. It may be coincidence, but Fryman hit .331 while playing third last year, and just .275 when was in the lineup as a shortstop. It is a fact that he will benefit from settling down at the less-demanding position in 1994. And for our purposes (good thing) he still qualifies at shortstop in most leagues.

4. REGGIE SANDERS, Reds OF: A budding star whose arrival has been delayed by nagging injuries (back pain last year, arm and leg strains the year before) Sanders has never been 100% through a whole major league season. He may never be 100%, but he's improving anyway. Sanders can do it all: hit for average, hit for power, and steal bases. And will do all these things at bargain prices for those who value him based solely on past accomplishments. Look for a big year in 1994.

5. TINO MARTINEZ, Mariners 1B: OK, I admit it: this year's list is loaded with players who were hurt for part of 1993. Martinez missed September with a strained knee ligament. These guys would all merit attention for up-and-coming careers even if they had just played full healthy seasons. The fact that their most recent stats reflect injuries just raises the likelihood that they will be undervalued. Martinez is a former first round pick and former U.S. Olympian, just coming into his own as a player. He may never reach the same levels as he did in the Triple-A Pacific Coast League (most players don't) but Martinez hit .320 twice in the PCL, and he did it at such a young age that he may be exception to the rule.

6. DEAN PALMER, Rangers 3B: A great power hitter already, Palmer is still trying to master the major league strike zone. When he learns how to lay off bad pitches and make the pitchers come to him, Palmer is going to have a monster season. He has a only .225 career batting average thus far -- a big negative for Rotisserians -- but he is capable of hitting .250 to .290 when he matures, which could well be this year.

7. PHIL PLANTIER, Padres OF: When Plantier first came up to the majors in late 1991, he told me that he had a goal of hitting one home run per week, and expected to add a hot streak or two on top of that every year. That would easily add up to 40 home runs a year, I observed. "Yeah, forty," said Plantier. In 1992 he was held back with a serious arm injury, but in 1993 he got to 34 home runs with 100 RBI, and he had jacks in the second half. Could he hit 40 in 1994? Sure he could. Just one a week, plus an occasional hot streak.

8. MO VAUGHN, Red Sox 1B: Vaughn was on this list last year. If you got him for your 1993 roster, you must have been pleased. Can he improve further? You bet. Vaughn learned a new swing from hitting coach Mike Easler and put it to good use. Meanwhile, he's been accumulating knowledge of the AL's pitchers and will put that to good use in 1994. Look for more home runs.

9. PEDRO MUNOZ, Twins OF: Last September, manager Tom Kelly told me that Munoz will have to win a job in the outfield in 1994; he is assured of nothing. And Munoz told me that he would have to start hitting or give up baseball ... after which he promptly went out and hit three home runs in two games. Look for Munoz to go ahead and win that job in 1994 and have his best year ever. Last year he was slowed by a knee injury.

10. RAY LANKFORD, Cardinals OF: Continuing the injury theme, Lankford's problems in 1993 included wrist and shoulder strains. When he was healthy he tried too hard to make up for missed time, and swung at many bad pitches. He knows better, and will do better in 1994. Lankford was on track to be a big star and will soon be back on that track. He faces a crowded outfield situation in St. Louis but is the best talent in that crowd.

11. DERRICK MAY, Cubs OF: May had a sore shoulder during spring training last year, and started the season as a platooner. He hit well enough to earn a full-time role and should get 500 at bats for the first time in 1994. Look for more home runs and more RBI production.

12. BRET BARBERIE, Marlins 2B: Barberie's problems last year included a torn elbow ligament and then a strained knee ligament, but he played enough to reach a career total of almost 800 at bats. One of the nice aspects of Barberie for fantasy leagues is that he hit .353 in a brief late-season callup two years ago. Everyone who drafted Barberie, with that number in mind, got burned by his .232 performance in 1992 -- and won't ever bid on him again. Removing a bidder or two is a good way to drive the price down, and create a bargain.

13. ANDUJAR CEDENO, Astros SS: Cedeno got to the majors very early. Last year he was still working on his knowledge of the strike zone, and he was succeeding, as he cut his strikeouts and increased his walks significantly. Overall it was a fine season for Cedeno, compared to his early struggles; but he can continue to improve, and will.

14. BERNIE WILLIAMS, Yankees OF: Williams has many dimensions to his developing talent, including speed and power. He already has fine strike zone judgment and can work the count to get a pitch he can drive. Williams was much more comfortable last year after he got dropped down to #6 in the batting order, and responded by hitting .310, including .398 overall in the second half of the season. Look for more power AND more stolen bases in 1994.

15. ROBIN VENTURA, White Sox 3B: Exactly the type of player who belongs on this list, Ventura seems like he's been around forever. It's hard to remember who played third base for the ChiSox before Ventura. But has he reached his peak? Heck, no. He's still just age 26, coming off a down year, and likely to be a bargain for the first time since he came up and hit .249 as a rookie.

16. PAT KELLY, Yankees 2B: Kelly has twice won a full-time in the Yankees infield, only to find himself sidelined with a nagging injury. All he has to do is stay healthy to have a career year in 1994. In addition to hoping for better luck, Kelly has also been improving by studying the league's pitchers to improve his stolen base success.

17. EDDIE TAUBENSEE, Astros C: Remember when Houston traded Kenny Lofton to get Taubensee? That's a comment on how highly regarded this young catcher is. In mid 1993 he changed his stance and was making better contact when the year ended. Taubensee will likely remain in a platoon with Scott Servais, as he has been for two years, but he is going to hit well enough to play more and to post career highs in most offensive categories in 1994.

18. JOSE OFFERMAN, Dodgers SS: Offerman just keeps getting better. Since hitting .155 and .195 in his first two callups to the majors, he has improved his patience at the plate. In 1993 he had almost as many walks as strikeouts, something he hasn't done since he played at Class AA San Antonio in 1989. Look for a higher batting average and more stolen bases in 1994.

19. ROYCE CLAYTON, Giants SS: Clayton has been compared to Barry Larkin, to excess I think. But Clayton is developing nicely and is going to be one of the best shortstops in the National League for many years. He isn't far below the top tier right now, and was a major factor in the Giants' 1993 pennant drive. Look for improved success stealing bases, and a bit more power, in 1994.

20. TODD HUNDLEY, Mets C: Hundley is being eased into the Mets regular catcher job. The switch hitter is still learning the league's pitchers. He came into the 1993 season with an even .200 career batting average and hit just .228 last year, numbers that will scare away many people on draft day. But Hundley is capable of hitting for higher average, and with more power, in 1994.

That's it for the top twenty, but here are more. The "best of the rest" is Mark Lewis, the Indians shortstop -- he was brought to the major league too early and just needed more seasoning. Anyone who values Lewis based on his major league performance up til now is really missing the point of this essay.
Also likely to go up in value in 1994:

Derek Bell, Milt Cuyler, Scott Cooper, Gary Disarcina, Eric Karros, Jeff Kent, Darren Lewis, Pat Listach, Brent Mayne, and Ivan Rodriguez.

Already at or near their peak, or just too famous to be bargains (many of these names were in my "top twenty" last year or the year before, as soon they got in their two years of experience):

Roberto Alomar, Carlos Baerga, Chad Curtis, Juan Gonzalez, Luis Gonzalez, Ken Griffey, Marquis Grissom, Gregg Jefferies, Chuck Knoblauch, Kenny Lofton, John Olerud, Deion Sanders, Gary Sheffield, Sammy Sosa, Frank Thomas, and Omar Vizquel.

About STATS, Inc.

From our humble beginnings less than a decade ago in a bedroom-slash-basement -- okay, maybe it was only for a month --STATS, Inc. has become the unchallenged leader in the field of statistical collection, analysis and publishing.

You want baseball? STATS publishes or co-publishes a number of invaluable baseball books. In addition to the book now in your hands, we do another book with HarperPerennial, STATS 1994 Baseball Scoreboard, which is chock full of baseball questions and answers and should be on the bookstore shelf very near this title sometime in March.

You want more baseball? STATS self-publishes reference books that major league teams and baseball fans everywhere order by the bushelful every fall (that's right, you don't have to wait until spring training). STATS 1994 Major League Handbook is a complete statistical record of every player who saw action in the majors last season, along with platoon splits, ballpark data, Bill James' infamous projections, and assorted other goodies. STATS 1994 Minor League Handbook contains a complete statistical record for everyone who played Double- or Triple-A ball last year but didn't make it to the majors. Also included: Triple-A lefty-righty splits, 1993 stats for those who didn't make it out of A-ball, ballpark effects, and Bill James' infamous MLEs. STATS 1994 Player Profiles is full of various breakdowns and situational stats, in one- and five-season formats, for ever major league player. And new this season: STATS 1994 Batter Versus Pitcher Match-Ups!, in which you can look up any major league pitcher, and see how every batter who's faced him five times or more has done.

You want basketball? Last fall, HarperPerennial published the STATS Basketball Scoreboard 1993-94, "The Thinking Fan's Guide to the NBA." Do you want to know "Which teams can come from (way way) behind?" Or "How did Shaq stack up against the best?" Those are just two of the 60 questions that the Scoreboard asked and answered. Look for the 1994-95 edition in your favorite bookstore this fall, straight from STATS and HarperPerennial.

You want football? No books yet (they're coming, though), but if you have a computer, we have football data coming out the kazoo on STATS On-Line. If the Cowboys and 49ers play at noon Sunday, you can access the game stats by the time 60 Minutes comes on. What about hockey, you ask? As you read this, one of our intrepid STATS employees is busily expanding our hockey data base. Stay tuned.

You want games? We started in 1990 with Bill James Fantasy Baseball, the most realistic fantasy baseball game ever. Then in 1991, STATS Fantasy Football crashed into the end zone. 1993 brought a new baby, Bill James Fantasy Baseball: The Winter Game, in which your roster is composed of your favorite players from the yellowing pages of baseball history. And finally, last fall marked the inaugural tip-off for STATS Fantasy Hoops.

What's that? You have a computer, and you'd like access to most of the information in the various books, along with plenty of other stuff, updated constantly -- In-Progress box scores updated every half-inning by STATS' own press-box scorers, the next three days of probable starting pitchers, injury information, and lots more? Hook up with STATS On-Line, and the world is yours.

Believe it or not, the above barely scratches the surface of what STATS, Inc. can do for the sports fan or professional. For more information, write us at:
STATS, Inc.,7366 N. Lincoln Ave.,Lincolnwood,IL 60646-1708 ... or call us at 1-800-63-STATS (from Illinois or outside the U.S., call 1-708-676-3322). You'll be glad you did.

The Benson Baseball Monthly

When somebody gets hurt, traded, promoted or demoted during the season, you know all about those events from the daily newspapers and TV/radio. But do these media tell you who else is will be affected? And how? Who will fill in while Davis is hurt, and how long will Davis be out? And what does Davis himself have to say about his injury? Why was that rookie brought up? Will he play? Who will sit down to make room for him?

These are the types of questions that are answered by the *BENSON BASEBALL MONTHLY* the first, best, largest publication for serious readers concerned about baseball player performance. Our mission is to give you an informed vision of the future. Scheduled for February to April 1994.

> Exclusive quotes and interviews from front offices and spring training camps.

> Updated forecast stats and values in a Comprehensive Draft Day issue listing every position on every team, with predicted playing time for every player. (Sorry - this issue not offered as a "sample.")

> Final wrap-up of 1993-94 winter ball: who helped themselves and didn't.

> Complete analysis of all players who changed teams during the winter, and the likely effect of the change on the player, his old team, and his new team.

If you like this book, you will love the "newsletter" -- a modest term considering that the monthly is 26 to 40 pages in length and sometimes even more. The BB monthly is published year round. In the winter, we take advantage of the fact that player performance has stopped changing, long enough to do some in-depth analysis and introduce the latest winning methods in Rotisserie Science.

Just like this book and the Roitsserie Baseball Annual are the most current yearly publications for your needs, the BB monthly is the most current monthly publication. You get the same type of information, year round, twelve times a year.

The best statement I can make about the Baseball Monthly is that it has always been sold with a 100% money back guarantee, and for three years in print, NO ONE EVER WANTED THEIR MONEY BACK! That changed when I first boasted about that fact in writing, in one of my books. Within a week after the book reached the public, two long-time subscribers raced to see who could be first to ask for a refund. The guy who came in second was genuinely disappointed. "I want my money back," he said. "OK," I said. "Guess I am the first person ever," he panted. "Nope," I said, "Somebody else just called yesterday; he was the first." "Oooooh;" he sighed. For a second, I thought he was going to drop the idea. The guarantee is still there, with a 30-day return privilege. Now in our fifth year, only three people have taken advantage of this generous offer of assurance.

The Monthly isn't cheap. In a poll of readers, the overwhelming majority said they wanted it to stay expensive! The small audience makes it more valuable. It's not for cheap people, anyway. If you think playing Rotisserie should cost less than going bowling once a month, well, you can't be getting much enjoyment out of the game, and there isn't much that I can do for you. If you don't appreciate the value of CPA/MBA/scout/forecaster analyst/writer working his tail off for a small group of elitist readers, well, then those elitists are glad you don't.

The vital information? A sample issue is $7. If you can't be separated from $7 for a few days (remember the money back guarantee) please don't waste our time. Don't call and ask for "more information about the newsletter." Order a sample, and you will get more information about the newsletter. A six month subscription is $35. One year is $59. Two years is $99. Most people try six months and then renew for two years. Yes we take Mastercard/Visa.

Telephone 800-707-9090 or 203-834-1231 or write:
Diamond Library, 196 Danbury Road, Wilton, CT 06897.

CONVENIENT ORDER FORM ON BACK PAGE

Finally: PERMANENT Rotisserie(r) Books !

After five years of writing "annual" books for Rotisserie competition, John Benson has teamed with Randall Baron (world-famous author and teacher and expert on the subject of bridge, and noted Rotisserie expert) to produce two fantasy-league volumes that will be useful for years and years. This two-volume set covers the whole subject, starting with an elementary explanation of the game, for people who never heard of Rotisserie or fantasy leagues, up to the most advanced strategies and tactics and "state of the art" thinking.

Volume One, ***Rotisserie(r) Baseball - Playing for Fun***, begins with a general introduction of the concept of picking baseball players and tracking their performance in an organized competition. But Volume One is not just for beginners! The book includes a detailed exploration of rules that will offer insights to the most serious competitors, and covers the whole subject of scouting and forecasting in preparation for Draft Day. Publication is available now, and the price is $12.95.

Volume Two, ***Rotisserie(r) Baseball - Playing for Blood***, picks up where Volume One left off: Draft Day. Now that you have finished your scouting and forecasting, how do you value players for an auction, or rank them for a draft? "Blood" explains valuation, auction economics (including inflation and optimal bidding), roster management (including trade methods, dealing with injuries, and synergistic roster concepts). Finally, there is a discussion of advanced scouting techniques such as finding the best minor leaguers for the future. Available now, and the price is $12.95.

Shipping: $3 per book (Canada $5 per book). Use the enclosed order form, or clip and mail the bottom of this sheet to Diamond Library Division of Diamond Analytics, 196 Danbury Road, Wilton, CT 06897. Or call toll free, 24 hours/day **1-800-292-6338** for Mastercard and Visa orders.
>>> For customer service, questions or Canadian orders, call **203-834-0812** <<<

- -

___ copies of Playing for Fun @ $12.95 =   _____
___ copies of Playing for Blood @ 12.95 =   _____
+ Shipping $3 per book (Canada $5/book) =   _____   Total _____

Please print your name _____   Address _____

City _____   State _____   Zip _____   Phone _____

Mastercard/Visa # _____ - _____ - _____ - _____   Exp _____   Signature _____

Please make check or M.O. payable to Diamond Library -- U.S. funds drawn on U.S. banks only.

Rotisserie League Baseball is a registered trademark of R.L.B.A., Inc.

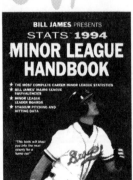

TRY SPORTS FORUM ON COMPUSERVE

For several years I have enjoyed the competition and cameraderie that can be found in the fantasy leagues managed by Sports Forum on CompuServe. They can be accessed by anyone with a computer modem. Just type GO FANS when you log onto CIS, or select Sports Forum from the sports menu choices.

Harry Conover and his staff including especially Bob Hazelwood, Steven Rubio, Adam Stein, Chuck Wright, Tom Naelon, Paul Clements, Owen Mock, Carol Calhoun ... and, hey, this is a really large and highly professional staff who truly know how to make a person feel welcome, and they generate a mighty fine version of the Founding Fathers' field of dreams. You can find just about anything you want in the range of fantasy league competition in Sports Forum. Some of the game's great theorists and fiercest winners play there, and there are many leagues filled with good ol' boys (and gals) just out to enjoy the fun of running a baseball franchise. Send Harry a message at 76701,220 if you'd like to play.

AVAILABLE FROM DIAMOND LIBRARY FOR 1994

Title:	Quantity	Price	Total

The Rotisserie Baseball Annual 1994, by John Benson
The biggest, most serious, most in-depth preview of the coming season
available February 25, 1994 ⎯⎯⎯ $ 22.95 ⎯⎯⎯

Baseball Player Guide A to Z, 1994, by John Benson
Your complete player guide and who's who for 1994 -- over 1400 players
with scouting reports and forecast stats. Avail Jan 25 '94 ⎯⎯⎯ 15.95 ⎯⎯⎯

Rotisserie Baseball - Playing for Fun, by John Benson and Randall Baron
All the essentials of getting organized and playing smart, plus strategies
and tactics useful in all leagues, draft or auction. Avail. NOW ⎯⎯⎯ 12.95 ⎯⎯⎯

Rotisserie Baseball - Playing for Blood, by John Benson and Randall Baron
All the serious stuff: valuation, auction economics, roster management,
with an emphasis on standard leagues. Avail. NOW ⎯⎯⎯ 12.95 ⎯⎯⎯

Back issues of the **Rotisserie Baseball Annual:**
1989 First Edition, just 500 copies printed, limit one per customer (1) 40.00 ⎯⎯⎯

1990, 1991, 1992 or 1993 -- each ⎯⎯⎯ 22.95 ⎯⎯⎯

Benson Draft Software 1994 for IBM and compatibles. Get 1994 forecasts
and three years actual stats. STATE OF THE ART for draft preparation and
draft management. Available Feb 15. Specify disk size ⎯⎯⎯⎯ ⎯⎯⎯ 49.95 ⎯⎯⎯

John Benson's **Baseball Monthly** -- exclusive news, quotes, interviews,
latest developments in player valuation and performance forecasting,
periodic review and update of entire player population. Letters, opinions.
Sample issue $7 -- Six months $35 -- One year $59 -- Two years $99 (Canada add 10%) ⎯⎯⎯

Shipping: $3 per book, $2 per software disk (Canada $5 per book, $4 per disk) ⎯⎯⎯

March 28, 1994 Forecasts Stats and Values Update on paper, $9.95 + $2 S/H = $11.95 ⎯⎯⎯

Order Total ⎯⎯⎯

Call toll free, 24 hours/day **1-800-707-9090** for Mastercard and Visa orders
For customer service, questions or Canadian orders, call **203-834-1231**
Or write: Diamond Library, 196 Danbury Road, Wilton, CT 06897

Please print your name ⎯⎯⎯⎯⎯⎯⎯⎯⎯ Address ⎯⎯⎯⎯⎯⎯⎯⎯⎯

City ⎯⎯⎯⎯⎯⎯⎯ State ⎯⎯⎯ Zip ⎯⎯⎯⎯ Phone ⎯⎯⎯⎯

Mastercard/Visa # ⎯⎯ - ⎯⎯ - ⎯⎯ - ⎯⎯ Exp ⎯⎯⎯ Signature ⎯⎯⎯⎯⎯
Please make check or M.O. payable to Diamond Library -- U.S. funds drawn on U.S. dollar accounts.
Rotisserie League Baseball is a registered trademark of R.L.B.A., Inc.